O9-BRY-352

WITHDRAWAL

RULERS
AND
GOVERNMENTS
OF THE WORLD

RULERS AND GOVERNMENTS OF THE WORLD
General Editor: C. G. Allen

Volume 1
Earliest Times to 1491
Compiled by Martha Ross

Volume 2
1492 to 1929
Compiled by Bertold Spuler

Volume 3
1930 to 1975
Compiled by Bertold Spuler (1930 to 1970)
C. G. Allen & Neil Saunders (1971 to 1975)

RULERS
AND
GOVERNMENTS
OF THE WORLD

Volume 3
1930 to 1975

Compiled by
BERTOLD SPULER (1930 to 1970)
C. G. ALLEN & NEIL SAUNDERS (1971 to 1975)

BOWKER
LONDON & NEW YORK

First published 1977 in Great Britain by Bowker Publishing Company Limited, Epping, Essex and in the United States of America by R. R. Bowker Co., 1180 Avenue of the Americas, New York, NY 10036

© Bowker Publishing Company Limited 1977

All rights reserved. No part of this publication may be reproduced or transmitted in any form or by any means, electronic or mechanical, including photocopy, recording, or any information storage and retrieval system, without permission in writing from the publisher.

Translated from German by John Fletcher
Translation edited by C. G. Allen

This book is a translation of *Regenten und Regierungen der Welt*, compiled by Bertold Spuler, part of volume 4, *Neueste Zeit 1917/18-1964*, 2nd edition, published by A. G. Ploetz Verlag, Würzburg, 1964 (ISBN 3 87640 024 4; copyright A. G. Ploetz Verlag 1964), 1964/65 appendix to volume 4, published by A. G. Ploetz Verlag, Würzburg, 1966 (ISBN 3 87640 025 2; copyright A. G. Ploetz Verlag 1966) and volume 5, *Neueste Zeit 1965-1970*, published by Verlag A. G. Ploetz KG, Würzburg, 1972 (ISBN 3 87640 026 0; copyright © Verlag A. G. Ploetz KG 1972). The translation has been updated. Information for 1970 to 1975 compiled by C. G. Allen and Neil Saunders, first published in this edition, copyright © Bowker Publishing Company Limited 1977.

British Library cataloguing in publication data

Rulers and governments of the world.
   Vol. 3 : 1930 to 1975.
   1. Kings & rulers 2. Heads of state 3. Cabinet officers
   I. Spuler, Bertold II. Allen, Charles Geoffry III. Saunders, Neil
909   JF251

ISBN 0-85935-056-8 for this volume
ISBN 0-85935-051-7 for set of 3 volumes

Library of Congress catalog card number 77-723-39.

Printed in Great Britain by Thomson Litho Ltd., East Kilbride, Scotland.

Reference
D
11
S783x
v. 3

Preface

A generation of reference librarians has found in Bertold Spuler's *Regenten und Regierungen der Welt*, first published in 1953, a handy and comprehensive guide to those in power at various times in various countries and to the basic biographical facts about them. But to make full use of it one did need to be competent in German. Volumes 2 and 3 of this English version are based on the second edition of volumes 3 and 4 of *Regenten und Regierungen der Welt*, covering respectively the periods 1492 to 1918 and 1917/18 to 1964, which appeared in 1964, and on the supplements thereto. Volume 1 of the English version is entirely new, and coverage of volume 3 has been extended to the end of 1975. To have followed the German edition in breaking at 1917/18 would have produced an unduly swollen third volume, and it was decided, with some regrets, to make the break at the end of 1929. This date has no special significance, but as the irregular dating of the German original suggests, it is in fact impossible to find a date when the whole world neatly changes. As in the original, rulers and ministers whose periods of power span the break appear in both volumes.

The characteristics of this edition remain the same as those of the original, of which (volume 1 apart) it is basically a translation, reproducing in English form the abundant materials which Dr Spuler has collected over the years from archival sources, from reliable histories and reference works, from expert informants and from the press. As the introductions make clear, additions and revisions have been made, but what Dr Spuler modestly refers to as 'the arbitrary element' remains. To keep the task and the published volumes within reasonable bounds it has at all times been necessary to restrict the number of states covered and the detail given about each state. It is hoped that the selection reflects the needs of the majority of users of the work. All rulers are given for every state included. For major countries in the modern era, complete lists of cabinets are given; for other states, only the names of prime ministers.

Similarly, though new material is always coming to light and historical judgements are continually being revised, there must inevitably be a limit to the number of sources to which the editors of *Rulers and Governments of the World* can refer. It is believed, however, that the English edition will be of great value to its users just as the German editions have been. The publishers will of course be very grateful for corrections and suggestions for improvement.

The present editor gratefully acknowledges the generous help of the libraries of the Australian and Canadian High Commissions, the South African Embassy, of the School of Slavonic and East European Studies, the School of Oriental and African Studies and the Institute of Historical Research, the British Library of Political and Economic Science, the Scandinavian Library at University College London and The British Library.

C. G. Allen

Introduction to Volume 3

The bulk of the material in this volume derives from volumes 4 to 6 of the German original. Data for the period 1970–75 have been compiled specially for this edition, using news sources and biographical reference books, and the preparation of a specifically English edition has led to revisions and amplifications of the original, in places considerable, as well as to some omissions.

Most national states are included but not the German Länder or the constituent states in other federal regimes. Material relating to newly independent African states is included in this volume, but the exigencies of the publishing schedule have made it necessary to place in volume 1 all the material relating to earlier dynasties, even those that persisted, under colonial suzerainty, into the present period. Cross-references to this material will be found in the present volume.

All states are listed under their currently accepted English names, with references from variants. In a few cases the entry begins with a brief note explaining the origin of the state. The names of successive heads of state follow, the title being given in English, unless there is no recognized equivalent. Changes of dynasty and regime are indicated, but the whole is one sequence. In the case of self-governing colonies and dominions the names of the representatives of the home country (governors, commissioners, etc.) are given. The date of accession, appointment, election or usurpation is given in the left-hand column, and unless otherwise stated the period of rule extends until the date next below. Where it can be done with reasonable consistency, the month and day are given, but even in the twentieth century we have sometimes had to be content with the year alone. Uncertain dates are accompanied by a question mark, and where information is lacking, the day, month, year, or the whole date is replaced by one.

Occasionally, where authorities or the criteria for establishing a date differ, two dates are given. Disputes and civil wars, resulting in gaps in the sequence or the presence of rival claimants, are noted at the appropriate point.

Against the date stands the name of the head of state, with date of birth if known. The date of death of a hereditary ruler is not given unless it differs from the date of accession of his successor, nor usually his place of birth or death. Full information is given where practicable for other heads of state. Where a ruler has a broken reign or a president serves more than once, the biographical information is given the first time only. Names of monarchs are given in their English form where it is still customary to do so; but usage being variable, the form may not always be that to which any particular reader is accustomed.

A dash (——) in a name means that it has not been possible to discover the person's forename.

The lists of members of governments follow. In the simplest cases these consist of a list of prime ministers (or their equivalent in the constitution of the state concerned), with or without a list of foreign ministers. In all these lists the treatment of the entries is the same as for non-hereditary heads of state. For a limited number of countries ministries are given and the layout is different. The dates during which the ministry was in office and the name by which it is known, usually that of the prime minister, are given as a heading. The left-hand column contains the names of the departments, headed by the prime minister and continuing with foreign and home affairs. The order of the remaining posts varies from country to country, even where comparable posts exist, and changes gradually over time within a single country, but is fairly consistent from one cabinet to the next. No attempt is made to indicate the order of precedence within the cabinet, if any. The names of posts are given in English translation, but the posts are not equated with English ones or with each other. Where no date is given ministers can be taken to remain in office for the duration of the ministry; where they change, their period of office is given before the name, and acting office indicated where appropriate. Where there are gaps between ministries, as happens in the Netherlands, this does not preclude the individual ministers remaining at their posts until the formation of a new ministry. Biographical details are given, as for heads of state, on first mention, and on subsequent occasions a reference is made to the name of the ministry in which the minister in question first held office.

Though even today many politicians from Central Europe and the

Balkans are still sometimes referred to in English sources by English (or French) forms of their Christian names, the practice is no longer common except for Greek names. Accordingly all names except Greek ones are given in the vernacular form. (As they have had to be converted from German, it is possible that some have been incorrectly left in German form; but it must also be remembered that Hungarians and Czechs, for instance, may have German names.) In the same pragmatic spirit the transcription of names not in the Latin alphabet has been carried out somewhat loosely, with the result, one hopes, that most readers will find them in the form to which they are accustomed. Thus in Greek both eta and iota are transliterated as i, as they are by most Greeks. The Russian terminations - ий and -ый are both reduced to -y, as in Trotsky; the soft sign has been ignored or represented by y, as in the common sequence -yev-. No diacritical marks are used in the transliteration of the Arabic alphabet, nor are long vowels distinguished. Local variations of pronunciation, inconsistent with the standard transliteration, are taken account of as well as accepted conventional transcriptions. Chinese names are given in Wade-Giles transcription, these being the forms which as yet most users will meet elsewhere; Korean names are frequently given in both of the most commonly used transcriptions.

In the German edition of this work the Christian names of statesmen of a number of European countries are given in their German form, and as it was dangerous to attempt to restore the vernacular form by rule (four different Hungarian names are represented by the German Andreas), recourse was had to vernacular reference books, so that additional biographical information was obtained in the process. This applies to Czechoslovakia, Croatia, Estonia, Finland, Hungary, Lithuania and Poland. More radically, the simple lists of prime ministers and foreign ministers of Australia, Canada, Republic of Ireland and Republic of South Africa have been replaced by full cabinets, and where possible, for these as for other European countries, biographical details have been amplified and brought up to date. The lists for the United Kingdom are now strictly those of the official cabinet, and for this reason the names given may sometimes differ from those in the German edition. With the exception of Mongolia and Tibet, revisions of Asian entries have been slight, consisting mostly of additional biographical information.

C. G. Allen

Index of States

Abbreviations

Afr Dem	African Democratic
Anti-Rev/ARP	Anti-Revolutionaire Partij (Anti-Revolutionary Party)
ARS	Groupe Indépendant d'Action Républicaine et Sociale (Independent Group of Republican and Social Action, also known as 'Dissident Gaullists')
bart	baronet
Bayer VP	Bayrische Volkspartei (Bavarian People's Party)
BHE	Bund der Heimatvertriebenen und Entrechteten (League of Refugees and Disfranchised)
BSP	Belgische Socialistische Partij (Belgian Socialist Party)
Cath	Catholic
CDP	Centre Démocratie et Progrès (Democracy and Progress Centre)
CDU	Christlich-Demokratische Union (Christian Democratic Union)
Chr(ist) Dem	Christian Democratic
Chr(ist) Soc	Christian Socialist
Christ Citizens	Christian Citizens
Christ Nat Workers	Christian National Workers
CHU	Christelijk-Historische Unie (Christian Historical Union)
CNP	National Republican Peasants
Comm	Communist

Cons	Conservative
ČSL	Československá strana lidová (Czechoslovak People's Party)
ČSS	Československá strana socialistická (Czechoslovak Socialist Party)
CSU	Christlich-Soziale Union (Christian Social Union)
CVP	Christelijke Volkspartij (Christian Social Party)
Czech Agrarian	Czechoslovak Agrarian
Czech Pop	Czechoslovak People's Party
Czech Prof	Czechoslovak Professional
Czech Soc	Czechoslovak Socialist

D-66	Democrats-66
DBD	Demokratische Bauernpartei Deutschlands (Democratic Peasants' Party of Germany)
DC	Christian Democratic
Dem	Democratic
Dem Resist	Democratic Resistance
DFP	Demokratische Frauenbund Deutschlands (Democratic Women's League of Germany)
DP	Deutsche Partei (German Party)
DS-70	Democratische Socialisten '70 (Democratic Socialists 1970)
DVP	Demokratische Volkspartei (Democratic People's Party)

Farm	Farmers'
FDP	Freie Demokratische Partei (Free Democratic Party)
Finn Pop	Finnish People's
FVP	Freie Volkspartei (Free People's Party)

Gaull	Gaullist
GDB	Gesamtdeutsche Volkspartei (All German People's Party)
Ger Christ Soc	German Christian Socialist
Ger League	German League
Ger Nat	German Nationalist
Ger Soc	German Socialist

ABBREVIATIONS

Ger State   German State

Ind   Independent

JP/Justice   Justice Party (Adalet Partisi)

KVP   Katholieke Volkspartij (Catholic People's Party)

Lab   Labour
LDP   Liberal-Demokratische   Partei   (Liberal
                   Democratic Party)
Lib   Liberal

Mod Rep   Moderate Republican

NAP   Nationalist Action Party
Nat Comm   National Communist
Nat Dem   National Democratic
Nat Lab   National Labour
Nat Lib   National Liberal
Nat Party of Germ National Party of German Middle Classes
   Middle Classes (Reichspartei des Deutschen Mittelstandes)
Nat Peoples League National People's League
Nat Rel   National Religious
Nat Soc   National Socialist
NDP   National-Demokratische   Partei   (National
                   Democratic Party)
NDPD   National-Demokratische Partei Deutschlands
                   (National Democratic Party of Germany)
NRP   National Reliance Party
NSDAP   Nationalsozialistische Deutsche Arbeiterpartei
                   (German National Socialist Workers' Party)
NSP   National Salvation Party
NTP   New Turkish Party

ÖVP   Österreichische Volkspartei (Austrian People's
                   Party)

PDM	Progrès et Démocratie Moderne (Progress and Modern Democracy)
PLI	Partito Liberale Italiano (Italian Liberal Party)
PLP	Parti de la Liberté et du Progrès (Freedom and Progress Party)
Pol Lab	Polish Labour
Pol Peoples	Polish People's
Pol Utd Lab	Polish United Labour (Polska Zjednoczona Partia Robotnicza, PZPR)
PPR	Politieke Partij Radikalen (Radical Political Party)
PRI	Partito Repubblicano Italiano (Italian Republican Party)
Prog Cons	Progressive Conservative
PSB	Parti Socialiste Belge (Belgian Socialist Party)
PSC	Parti Social-Chrétien (Christian Social Party)
PSDI	Partito Socialista Democratico (Democratic Socialist Party)
PSI	Partito Socialista Italiano (Italian Socialist Party)
PvdA	Partij van de Arbeid (Labour Party)
PVV	Partij voor Vrijheid en Vooruitgang (Freedom and Progress Party)

Rad	Radical
Réform	Réformateur
Rep	Republican
Rep Peoples Mov	Republican People's Movement
Resist Union	Resistance Union
RRP	Republican Reliance Party
RPP	Republican People's Party (Cumhuriyet Halk Partisi)

SED	Sozialistische Einheitspartei Deutschland (German United Socialist Party)
Slov Dem	Slovak Democratic
Slov Farmers	Slovak Farmers'
Slov Freedom	Slovak Freedom
Slov Pop	Slovak People's
Slov Recons	Slovak Reconstruction
Slov Soc	Slovak Socialist

xxi

ABBREVIATIONS

Soc	Socialist
Soc Dem	Social Democratic
SPD	Sozialdemokratische Partei Deutschlands (German Social Democratic Party)
SPÖ	Sozialdemokratische Partei Österreichs (Austrian Social Democratic Party)
Stahlhelm	Steel Helmets
Swed Peoples	Swedish People's
UDR	Union des Démocrates pour la République (Union of Democrats for the Republic), earlier known as Union pour la Défense de la République (Union for the Defence of the Republic)
UDSR	Union Démocratique et Socialiste de la Résistance (Democratic and Socialist Union of the Resistance)
UDT	Union Démocratique du Travail (Democratic Union of Labour)
UNR	Union pour la Nouvelle République (Union for the New Republic)
Utd Farmers	United Farmers'
Utd Peoples	United People's

Afghanistan

HEADS OF STATE

Kings

17 Oct 1929 – 8 Nov 1933	*Nadir Shah*, great-nephew of Dost Mohammad (b. 10 Apr 1880)
8 Nov 1933 – 18 Jul 1973	*(Mohammad) Zahir Shah*, son (b. 15 Oct 1914)

President

from 18 Jul 1973	*Mohammad Daoud* (b. Kabul 18 Jul 1909)

MEMBERS OF GOVERNMENT

Prime Ministers

14 Nov 1929	*Mohammad Hashim Khan* (b. Dehra Dun, India, 1886; d. Kabul 26 Oct 1953)
May 1946 – 6 Sep 1953	*Shah Mahmud Khan Ghazi* (b. 1886/1888; d. Kabul 27 Dec 1959)
20 Sep 1953	*Mohammad Daoud* (for 1st time) (see President)
10 Mar 1963	*Mohammad Yusof* (for 1st time) (b. Kabul 1915)
24 – 29 Oct 1965	*Mohammad Yusof* (for 2nd time)
2 Nov 1965 – 11 Oct 1967	*Mohammad Hashim Maiwandwal* (b. Kandahar 23 Mar/13 May (?) 1921; d. 1 Oct 1973)
1 Nov 1967 – 17 May 1971	*(Mohammad) Nur Ahmad Etemadi* (b. 1920)
8 Jun 1971 – 6 Dec 1972	*Sharifi Abdul Zahir* (b. Laghman 1909)
12 Dec 1972 – 17 July 1973	*Mohammad Musa Shafiq* (b. Kabul 1924)
from 18 Jul 1973	*Mohammad Daoud* (for 2nd time) President and Prime Minister

Albania

HEADS OF STATE

Kings

House of Mat

1 Sep 1928 – 8 Apr 1939	*Achmed Zogu* (b. Burgajet 8 Oct 1895; d. Suresnes, France, 9 Apr 1961) previously President, formally abdicated 2 Jan 1946
7 Apr 1939 – Autumn 1944	Under German and Italian occupation

House of Savoy

12 Apr 1939 – 8 Sep 1943	*Victor Emmanuel III*, King of Italy (b. Naples 11 Nov 1869; d. Alexandria, Egypt, 28 Dec 1947) personal union of the crowns

Italian Governors

23 Apr 1939 – Mar 1943	*Lieutenant General Francesco Jacomoni di San Savino* (b. Reggio 31 Aug 1893)
3 – 6 Sep 1943	*General Alberto Pariani*
from Sep 1943	Council of Regents
from 1 Jan 1946	Republic

Presidents

13 Jan 1946 – 23 Jul 1953	*Omer Nishani*
from 1 Aug 1953	*Haxhi Lleshi* (b. 1913)

MEMBERS OF GOVERNMENT

Prime Ministers

15 Jan 1929 – 3 Mar 1930	*Koço Kota* (for 2nd time) (b. Korça 1889; d. 1949(?))*

*For earlier career see vol. 2

6 Mar 1930	*Pandeli Evangeli* (for 3rd time) (b. Korça 1859)*
12 Apr 1931	*Pandeli Evangeli* (for 4th time)
12 Jan 1933 – 15 Oct 1935	*Pandeli Evangeli* (for 5th time)
22 Oct 1935 – Nov 1936	*Mehdi Frashëri* (for 1st time) (b. Frashëri 15 Feb 1872; d. Rome 25 May 1963)
9 Nov 1936	*Koço Kota* (for 3rd time)
31 May 1938 – 8 Apr 1939	*Koço Kota* (for 4th time)

Under Italian administration

12 Apr 1939	*Shefqet Verlaci* (for 1st time)
4 Dec 1941 – 10 Jan 1943	*Mustafa Merlika-Kruja* (b. 1887(?); d. Niagara Falls 27 Dec 1958)
Jan – Feb 1943	*Eqrem Libohova* (for 1st time) (b. 24 Jan 1882)
22 Feb 1943	*Maliq Bushati*
13 May – mid Sep 1943	*Eqrem Libohova* (for 2nd time)

Under German occupation

11 Sep – 24 Oct 1943	*Ibrahim Biçakçiu* (d. 1945(?)) President of the Provisional Executive Committee
24 Oct 1943	*Mehdi Frashëri* (for 2nd time) head of the Council of Regents
4 Nov 1943	*Rexhep Mitrovica*
21 Jul – Oct 1944	*Fiori Dine*

Communist administration

Nov 1944 – 20 Jul 1954	*Enver Hoxha* † (b. Gjirokastër 16 Oct 1908 or Korça 1911)
23 Jul 1954	*Mehmed Shehu* (for 1st time) (b. 10 Jan 1913)
from 16 Jul 1962	*Mehmed Shehu* (for 2nd time)

*For earlier career see vol. 2
†Hoxha remains Secretary of the Albanian Party of Labour

3

Algeria

HEADS OF STATE

Governors-General

20 Nov 1927	*Pierre Louis Bordes*
3 Oct 1930	*Jules Carde* (b. Batna 3 Jun 1874; d. St. Raphael-du-Var 11 Jul 1949)
21 Sep 1935	*Georges Le Beau*
19 Jul 1940	*Jean Charles Abrial* (b. Réalmont 1879)
16 Jul 1941	*Maxime Weygand* (b. Brussels 18 Jan 1867; d. Paris 28 Jan 1965)
20 Sep 1941	*Yves Chatel*
20 Jan 1943	*Marcel Peyrouton* (b. Paris 2 Jul 1887)
3 Jun 1943 – 1944	*Georges (A. J.) Catroux* (for 1st time) (b. Limoges 29 Jan 1877; d. Paris 21 Dec 1969)
8 Sep 1944	*Yves Chataigneau* (b. Vouille 22 Sep 1891; d. 5 Mar 1969)
Feb 1948	*Marcel Naegelen* (b. Belfort 17 Jan 1892)
Jun 1951	*Roger Léonard* (b. Bordeaux 27 Apr 1898)
31 Jan 1955 – Feb 1956	*Jacques Soustelle* (b. Montpellier 3 Feb 1912)
31 Jan – 6 Feb 1956	*Georges (A. J.) Catroux* (for 2nd time)
10 Feb 1956 – May 1958	*Robert Lacoste* (b. Azerat 5 Jul 1898) Resident General and Resident Minister
15 – 28 May 1958	*André Mutter* (b. Troyes 11 Nov 1901; d. 24 Dec 1973)

Delegates-General

16 Jun – Dec 1958	*Raoul Salan* (b. Rocquecourbe 10 Jun 1899)
19 Dec 1958	*Paul (Albert Louis) Delouvrier* (b. Remiremont 25 Jun 1914)
24 Nov 1960 – Mar 1962	*Jean Morin* (b. Melun 29 Jun 1916)
19 Mar – 3 Jul 1962	*Christian Fouchet* (b. St. Germain-en-Laye 17 Nov 1911; d. 12 Aug 1974)

President

8 Sep 1963	Office created

| 20 Sep 1963 | *Mohammed Ahmed Ben Bella* (b. Marnia/Prov. Oran 25 Dec 1916 (1918, 1919?)) |
| 19 Jun 1965 | Office abolished |

MEMBERS OF GOVERNMENT

Prime Ministers (until 3 Jul 1962 in exile in Cairo and Tripoli)

25 Jun 1958	Formation of cabinet in exile without leader
19 Sep 1958	*Ferhat Abbas* (for 1st time) (b. Tahert 24 Oct 1899)
22 Dec 1959	*(Abdel) Krim Belkassim* (b. 1922; d. Frankfurt am Main 20 Oct 1970)
19 Jan 1960	*Ferhat Abbas* (for 2nd time)
27 Aug 1961 – 24 Jul/7 Aug 1962	*Yusuf ben Khedda* (b. Berrughia 1919 (1922?))
3 Jul – 7 Aug 1962	*Abdur Rahman Farés* (b. Akbu 30 Jan 1911) President of provisional executive council
24 Jul/7 Aug 1962	*Mohammed Ahmed Ben Bella* (see President)
from 19 Jun 1965	*Houari Boumédienne* (b. Guelma 23 Aug 1927) until 10 Jul 1965 leader of the revolutionary council

Foreign Ministers

28 Sep 1962 – 11 Apr 1963	(acting:) *Mohammed Khemisti* (b. Marnia, Oran Province, 1930; d. Algiers 5 May 1963)
11 Apr/5 May 1963	*Mohammed Ahmed Ben Bella* (see President)
from 5 Sep 1963	*Abdul Aziz Boutéflika* (b. Melilla 2 Mar 1937)

Angola

| 11 Nov 1975 | Independence from Portugal |

ANGOLA

HEAD OF STATE

President

from 11 Nov 1975   *Antônio Agostinho Neto* (b. Icola e Bengo 17 Sep 1922)

MEMBER OF GOVERNMENT

Prime Minister

from 14 Nov 1975   *Lopo do Nascimento*

Argentina

HEADS OF STATE

Presidents

1 Apr 1928	*Hipólito Irigoyen* (for 2nd time) (b. 13 Jul 1850; d. 3 Jul 1933)*
7 Sep 1930	*José F. Uriburu*, son of José E. Uriburu (b. 1868; d. 28 Apr 1932)
20 Feb 1932	*Augustín Justo* (b. 26 Feb 1876; d. 10 Jan 1943)
20 Feb 1938 – 22 Jun 1942	*Roberto M. Ortiz* (b. 24 Sep 1886; d. 15 Jul 1942)
27 Jun 1942	*Ramón S. Castillo* (b. 20 Nov 1873; d. 12 Oct 1944) acting President from 12 Aug 1940
6 – 8 Jun 1943	*Arturo Rawson* (b. 4 Jun 1885; d. 1952)
6 Jun 1943 – 24 Feb 1944	*Pedro Pablo Ramírez* (b. 30 Jan 1884; d. 11 Jun 1962)
10 Mar 1944	*Edelmiro (Julian) Farrell* (b. 12 Aug 1887)
4 Jun 1946	*Juan Domingo Perón* (for 1st time) (b. 8 Oct 1895; d. 1 Jul 1974)

*For earlier career see vol. 2

20 – 21 Sep 1955	*Eduardo Lonardi* (b. Buenos Aires 15 Sep 1896; d. 23 Mar 1956) Acting head of Military Junta
13 Nov 1955	*Pedro (Eugenio) Aramburu* (b. Río Cuarto 21 May 1903; d. Timote(?) 1(?) Jun 1970)
1 May 1958	*Arturo Frondizi* (b. Paso de los Libres 28 Oct 1908)
29 Mar 1962	*José María Guido* (b. Buenos Aires 20 Aug 1910; d. 13 Jun 1975)
12 Oct 1963	*Arturo (Umberto) Illía* (b. Pergamino 4 Aug 1901)
28 Jun 1966	*Juan Carlos Onganía* (b. Marcos Paz 17 Mar 1914)
8 Jun 1970	Chiefs of Staff (for 1st time): *Alejandro Agustín Lanusse* (b. Buenos Aires 28 Aug 1918), *Pedro Gnavi* and *Juan Rey*
18 Jun 1970	*Roberto (Marcelo) Levingston* (b. San Luis 1 Jan 1920)
22 Mar 1971	Chiefs of Staff (for 2nd time)
25 Mar 1971	*Alejandro Agustín Lanusse* (see above)
25 May 1973	*Hector J. Cámpora*
14 Jul 1973	(acting:) *Raul Alberto Lastiri*
23 Sep 1973	*Juan Domingo Perón* (for 2nd time)
13 Sep 1975	(acting:) *Italo Argentino Luder* (b. 1916?)
from 16 Oct 1975	*Maria Estela Martínez de Perón*, known as *Isabel Perón*, 2nd wife of Juan Domingo Perón (b. Rioja 1931)

MEMBERS OF GOVERNMENT

Foreign Ministers

12 Oct 1928	*Horacio B. Oyhanarte* (b. Rojas 1885; d. Buenos Aires 7 Nov 1946)
7 Sep 1930	*Ernesto Bosch* (b. Buenos Aires 8 Jan 1863; d. 22 Aug 1951)
10 Oct 1931	*Adolfo Bioy* (b. Buenos Aires Province 27 Jul 1882)
20 Feb 1932	*Carlos Saavedra Lamas* (b. Buenos Aires 1 Nov 1878; d. 5 May 1959)
20 Feb 1938 – 30 Aug 1940	*José María Cantilo* (b. Buenos Aires 28 Aug 1877; d. 29 Jul 1953)
2 Sep 1940 – 24 Jan 1941	*Julio Roca* (b. 1873; d. 1942)
24 Mar 1941 – 5 Jun 1943	*Enrique Ruiz-Guiñazú* (b. Buenos Aires 14 Oct 1882; d. Buenos Aires 13 Nov 1967)
7 Jun – 9 Sep 1943	*Segundo R. Storni* (b. Tucumán 16 Jul 1876)

7

11 Sep 1943 – 15 Feb 1944	*Alberto Gilbert* (b. Ramos Mejfa 1887)
27 Feb 1944	*Diego Nason*
3 May 1944 – 16 Jan 1945	*Osvaldo Peluffo*
18 Jan – 25 Aug 1945	*Cesar Ameghino* (b. Buenos Aires 14 Apr 1871)
28 Aug 1945	*Juan Cooke* (b. Buenos Aires 29 Jul 1895; d. Montevideo 23 Jun 1957)
14 – 20 Oct 1945	*Héctor Vernengo Lima* (b. Goya 2 Sep 1889)
20 Oct 1945	*Juan Cooke* (for 2nd time)
4 Jun 1946	*Juan Atilio Bramuglia* (b. Chascomús 1 Jan 1903; d. 4 Sep 1962)
12 Aug 1949	*Hipólito Jesús Paz* (b. Buenos Aires 9 Jan 1917)
28 Jun 1951	*Jerónimo Remorino* (b. Buenos Aires 15 Nov 1902; d. Buenos Aires 20 Nov 1968)
25 Aug – 19 Sep 1955	*Ildefonso (Felix) Cavagna Martínez* (b. Buenos Aires 14 Mar 1905)
24 Sep 1955	*Luis María de Pablo Pardo* (for 1st time) (b. Buenos Aires 15 Aug 1912)
13 Nov 1955	*Luis A. Podestá Costa* (b. Buenos Aires 6 Oct 1885)
25 Jan 1957 – Apr 1958	*Alfonso de Laferrere* (b. Buenos Aires 24 Nov 1893)
1 May 1958	*Carlos Alberto Florit* (b. Genoa 13 Apr 1929)
16 May 1959	*Diógenes Taboada* (b. Pisco Yacu 1887)
28 Apr – 28 Aug 1961	*Adolfo Mugica* (b. Buenos Aires 14 Nov 1896)
13 Sep 1961 – Oct 1962	*Miguel Ángel Carcano* (b. Buenos Aires 18 Jul 1889)
5 Oct 1962 – 12 May 1963	*Carlos Manuel Muñiz*
25 May 1963	*Juan Carlos Cordini*
12 Oct 1963 – 28 Jun 1966	*Miguel Ángel Zavala Ortiz* (b. San Luis 24 Dec 1906)
5 Jul 1966 – 4 Jun 1969	*Nicanor Costa Méndez* (b. Buenos Aires 30 Oct 1922)
12 Jun 1969	*Juan Bautista Martín* (b. Rosario 7 May 1910)
18 Jun 1970	*Luis María de Pablo Pardo* (for 2nd time)
20 Jun 1972	*Eduardo Francisco McLoughlin* (b. 13 May 1918)
25 May 1973	*Juan Carlos Puig*
14 Jul 1973	*Alberto Vignes*
14 Aug 1975	*Ángel Federico Robledo*
from 1 Oct 1975	*Manuel Guillermo Luis Arauz Castex* (b. 1915?)

8

Australia

HEADS OF STATE

Governors-General

8 Oct 1925 – 2 Oct 1930	*John Lawrence Baird, 1st Baron Stonehaven* (from 1938: *1st Viscount Stonehaven*) (b. 27 Jun 1874; d. 20 Aug 1941)
3 Oct 1930	*Arthur Herbert Tennyson, 6th Baron Somers* (b. Freshwater, Isle of Wight, 20 Mar 1887; d. Eastnor Castle 14 Jul 1944) Administrator
22 Jan 1931	*Sir Isaac Alfred Isaacs* (b. Melbourne 6 Aug 1855; d. 11 Feb 1948)
23 Jan 1936	*Alexander Gore Arkwright Hore-Ruthven, 1st Baron* (from 1945: *1st Earl of*) *Gowrie* (b. Windsor 6 Jul 1872; d. Gloucestershire 2 May 1955)
5 Sep 1944	*Sir Winston Dugan* (from 1949: *1st Baron Dugan of Victoria*) (for 1st time) (b. 8 May 1877; d. 17 Aug 1951) Administrator
30 Jan 1945	*Prince Henry William Frederick Albert, Duke of Gloucester*, son of King George V of Great Britain (b. 31 Mar 1900; d. 9 Jun 1974)
19 Jan 1947	*Sir Winston Dugan* (for 2nd time) Administrator
11 Mar 1947	*Sir William John McKell* (b. Pambula, New South Wales, 26 Sep 1891)
2 Sep 1952	*Sir William Joseph Slim* (from 1960: *1st Viscount Slim*) (b. 6 Aug 1891; d. London 14 Dec 1970)
2 Feb 1960	*William Shepherd Morrison, 1st Viscount Dunrossil* (b. 10 Aug 1893; d. 3 Feb 1961)
4 Feb 1961	*Sir Reginald Alexander Dallas Brooks* (d. 22 Mar 1966) Administrator
3 Aug 1961	*William Philip Sidney, 1st Viscount De L'Isle* (b. 23 May 1909)
7 May 1965	*Sir Kenry Abel Smith*, Administrator
22 Sep 1965	*Richard Gardiner Casey, Baron Casey* (b. Brisbane 29 Aug 1890; d. Melbourne 18 Jun 1976)
1 Apr 1969	*Sir Paul Meernaa Caedwalla Hasluck* (b. Fremantle, 1 Apr 1905)
from 11 Jul 1974	*Sir John Kerr* (b. Sydney 24 Sep 1914)

9

MEMBERS OF GOVERNMENT

22 Oct 1929 – 6 Jan 1932: Scullin

Prime Minister, Foreign Affairs and Industry	*James Henry Scullin* (b. Ballarat 18 Sep 1876; d. Melbourne 28 Jan 1953)
Treasurer	22 Oct 1929 – 9 Jul 1930: *Edward Granville Theodore* (b. Port Adelaide 29 Dec 1884; d. 9 Feb 1950)
	9 Jul 1930 – 29 Jan 1931: *James Henry Scullin* (see above)
	29 Jan 1931 – 6 Jan 1932: *Edward Granville Theodore* (for 2nd time) (see above)
Attorney-General	*Frank Brennan* (b. Sedgewick, Victoria; d. 5 Nov 1950)
Postmaster and Works and Railways	22 Oct 1929 – 4 Feb 1931: *Joseph Aloysius Lyons* (b. 15 Sep 1874; d. 7 Apr 1939)
	4 Feb 1931 – 6 Jan 1932: *Albert Ernest Green* (b. Avoca 21 Dec 1869)
Trade and Customs	22 Oct 1929 – 4 Feb 1931: *James Edward Fenton* (b. Yalloch; d. 2 Dec 1950)
	4 Feb 1931 – 6 Jan 1932: *Francis Michael Forde* (b. Mitchell, Queensland, 18 Jul 1890)
Home Affairs	*Arthur Blakeley*
Health	22 Oct 1929 – 3 Mar 1931: *Frank Anstey* (b. London 18 Aug 1865)
	3 Mar 1931 – 6 Jan 1932: *John McNeill*
Defence	22 Oct 1929 – 4 Feb 1931: *Albert Ernest Green* (see above)
	4 Feb – 3 Mar 1931: *John Joseph Daly* (b. 10 Nov 1891; d. 13 Apr 1942)
	3 Mar 1931 – 6 Jan 1932: *Joseph Benedict Chifley* (b. 22 Sep 1885; d. 13 Jun 1951)

6 Jan 1932 – 7 Nov 1938: Lyons I

Prime Minister	*Joseph Aloysius Lyons* (for 1st time) (see Scullin)
Treasurer	6 Jan 1932 – 3 Oct 1935: *Joseph Aloysius Lyons* (see Scullin)
	3 Oct 1935 – 7 Nov 1938: *Richard Gardiner Casey* (from 1960: *Baron Casey*) (see Governors General)

Foreign Affairs	6 Jan 1932 – 12 Oct 1934: *John Greig Latham* (b. Ascot Vale, Victoria, 25 Aug 1877)* 12 Oct 1934 – 29 Nov 1937: *Sir George Foster Pearce* (b. Mount Barker, South Africa, 14 Jan 1910; d. Melbourne 24 Jun 1952)* 29 Nov 1937 – 7 Nov 1938: *William Morris Hughes* (b. London 25 Sep 1864; d. Sydney 27 Oct 1952)*
Attorney-General	6 Jan 1932 – 12 Oct 1934: *John Greig Latham* (see above) 12 Oct 1934 – 7 Nov 1938: *Robert Gordon Menzies* (from 1963: *Sir*) (b. Jeparit 20 Dec 1894)
Industry	6 Jan 1932 – 12 Oct 1934: *John Greig Latham* (see above) 12 Oct 1934 – 7 Nov 1938: *Robert Gordon Menzies* (see above)
Defence	6 Jan 1932 – 12 Oct 1934: *Sir George Foster Pearce* (see above) 12 Oct 1934 – 20 Nov 1937: *Sir Robert Archdale Parkhill* 20 – 29 Nov 1937: *Joseph Aloysius Lyons* (see Scullin) 29 Nov 1937 – 7 Nov 1938: *Harold Victor Campbell Thorby* (b. Sydney 2 Oct 1888; d. 1 Jan 1973)
Postmaster-General	6 Jan – 13 Oct 1932: *James Edward Fenton* (see Scullin) 13 Oct 1932 – 12 Oct 1934: *Sir Robert Archdale Parkhill* (see above) 12 Oct 1934 – 7 Nov 1938: *Alexander John McLachlan* (b. Naracoorta 2 Nov 1872; d. 28 May 1956)
Development and Scientific Research	6 Jan 1932 – 29 Nov 1937: *Alexander John McLachlan* (see above) 29 Nov 1937 – 7 Nov 1938: *Richard Gardiner Casey* (see Governors General)
Trade and Customs	6 Jan 1932 – 14 Jan 1933: *Sir Henry Somer Gullett* (b. Hanton, Victoria, 26 Mar 1878; d. Canberra 13 Aug 1940)* 14 Jan 1933 – 7 Nov 1938: *Thomas Walter White* (b. Melbourne 26 Apr 1888; d. 28 May 1956)
Home Affairs and Transport (from 12 Apr 1932: Interior)	6 Jan – 13 Oct 1932: *Sir Robert Archdale Parkhill* (see above) 13 Oct 1932 – 12 Oct 1934: *John Arthur Perkins* (b. Tumut 18 May 1878; d. 13 Jul 1954)

*For earlier career see vol. 2

11

12 Oct – 9 Nov 1934: *Eric John Harrison* (from 1954: *Sir*) (b. 1892)

9 Nov 1934 – 29 Nov 1937: *Thomas Paterson* (b. England 20 Nov 1882; d. 21 Jan 1952)

29 Nov 1937 – 7 Nov 1938: *John McEwen* (b. Chiltern, Victoria, 29 Mar 1900)

Markets (from 13 Apr 1932: Commerce)

6 Jan – 23 Sep 1932: *Charles Allan Seymour Hawker* (b. Bungaree 16 May 1894; d. 25 Oct 1938)

3 – 13 Oct 1932: *Joseph Aloysius Lyons* (see Scullin)

13 Oct 1932 – 9 Nov 1934: *Frederick Harold Stewart* (from 1935: *Sir*) (b. Newcastle, New South Wales, 14 Aug 1884; d. 31 Jun 1961)

9 Nov 1934 – 7 Nov 1938: *Sir Earle Christmas Grafton Page* (b. Grafton, New South Wales, 8 Aug 1880)

Health

6 Jan 1932 – 12 Oct 1934: *Charles William Clanan Marr* (b. Petersham 23 Mar 1880; d. 20 Oct 1960)

12 Oct 1934 – 6 Nov 1935: *William Morris Hughes* (see above)

8 Nov 1935 – 26 Feb 1936: *Joseph Aloysius Lyons* (see Scullin)

26 Feb 1936 – 29 Nov 1937: *William Morris Hughes* (see above)

29 Nov 1937 – 7 Nov 1938: *Sir Earle Christmas Grafton Page* (see above)

7 Nov 1938 – 7 Apr 1939: Lyons II

Prime Minister   *Joseph Aloysius Lyons* (for 2nd time) (see Scullin)

Commerce   *Sir Earle Christmas Grafton Page* (see Lyons I)

Foreign Affairs   *William Morris Hughes* (see Lyons I)

Treasurer   *Richard Gardiner Casey* (see Governors General)

Attorney-General

7 Nov 1938 – 20 Mar 1939: *Robert Gordon Menzies* (see Lyons I)

20 Mar – 7 Apr 1939: *William Morris Hughes* (see Lyons I)

Industry

7 Nov 1938 – 20 Mar 1939: *Robert Gordon Menzies* (see Lyons I)

20 Mar – 7 Apr 1939: *William Morris Hughes* (see Lyons I)

Trade and Customs

7 Nov – 8 Nov 1938: *Thomas Walter White* (see Lyons I)

8 Nov 1938 – 7 Apr 1939: *John Arthur Perkins* (see Lyons I)

Works and Civil Aviation (new post)	24 Nov 1938 – 7 Apr 1939: *Harold Victor Campbell Thorby* (see Lyons I)
Home Affairs	*John McEwen* (see Lyons I)
Defence	*Geoffrey Austin Street* (b. Sydney 21 Jan 1894; d. 13 Aug 1940)
Health	*Hattil Spencer Foll* (b. London 31 May 1890)

7 - 26 Apr 1939: Page

Prime Minister and Commerce	*Sir Earle Christmas Grafton Page* (see Lyons I)
Attorney-General, Industry and External Affairs	*William Morris Hughes* (see Lyons I)
Treasurer	*Richard Gardiner Casey* (see Governors General)
Works and Civil Aviation	*Harold Victor Campbell Thorby* (see Lyons I)
Defence	*Geoffrey Austin Street* (see Lyons II)
Home Affairs	*John McEwen* (see Lyons I)
Health	*Hattil Spencer Foll* (see Lyons II)

26 Apr 1939 - 14 Mar 1940: Menzies I

Prime Minister and Treasurer	*Robert Gordon Menzies* (for 1st time) (see Lyons I)
Attorney-General and Industry	*William Morris Hughes* (see Lyons I)
Supply and Development	26 Apr 1939 – 26 Jan 1940: *Richard Gardiner Casey* (see Governors General) 26 Jan – 14 Mar 1940: *Sir Frederick Harold Stewart* (see Lyons I)
Defence	26 Apr – 13 Nov 1939: *Geoffrey Austin Street* (see Lyons II)
Defence Co-ordination (new post)	13 Nov 1939 – 14 Mar 1940: *Robert Gordon Menzies* (see Lyons I)
Army	13 Nov 1939 – 14 Mar 1940: *Geoffrey Austin Street* (see Lyons II)
Foreign Affairs	*Sir Henry Somer Gullett* (see Lyons I)
Commerce	*George McLeay* (b. Port Clinton 6 Aug 1892; d. 14 Sep 1955)
Home Affairs	*Hattil Spencer Foll* (see Lyons II)

13

AUSTRALIA

Trade and Customs	26 Apr 1939 – 23 Feb 1940: *John Norman Lawson* (d. 14 Aug 1956) 23 Feb – 14 Mar 1940: *Robert Gordon Menzies* (see Lyons I)
Health and Social Services	*Sir Frederick Harold Stewart* (see Lyons I)
Information (new post)	12 Sep 1939 – 14 Mar 1940: *Sir Henry Somer Gullett* (see Lyons I)
Navy (new post)	13 Nov 1939 – 14 Mar 1940: *Sir Frederick Harold Stewart* (see Lyons I)
Civil Aviation (from 13 Nov 1939: Air)	*James Valentine Fairbairn* (b. Wadhurst, Surrey, 28 Jul 1897; d. 13 Aug 1940)

14 Mar – 28 Oct 1940: Menzies II

Prime Minister, Defence Co-ordination and Information	*Robert Gordon Menzies* (for 2nd time) (see Lyons I)
Commerce and Navy	*Archie Galbraith Cameron* (b. Happy Valley 22 Mar 1895; d. 9 Aug 1956)
Attorney-General and Industry	*William Morris Hughes* (see Lyons I)
Army	14 Mar – 13 Aug 1940: *Geoffrey Austin Street* (see Lyons II) 14 Aug – 28 Oct 1940: *Philip Albert McBride* (from 1953: *Sir*) (b. 6 Apr 1916)
Scientific Research	14 Mar – 13 Aug 1940: *Sir Henry Somer Gullett* (see Lyons I) 14 Aug – 28 Oct 1940: *Herbert Brayley Collett* (b. St. Peter Port, Guernsey, 12 Aug 1877; d. 17 Aug 1947)
Munitions (new post)	11 Jun – 28 Oct 1940: *Robert Gordon Menzies* (see Lyons I)
Supply	*Sir Frederick Harold Stewart* (see Lyons I)
Health	*Harold Victor Campbell Thorby* (see Lyons I)
Treasurer	*Percy Claude Spender* (b. Sydney 5 Oct 1897)
Trade and Customs	*George McLeay* (see Menzies I)
Foreign Affairs	*John McEwen* (see Lyons I)
Home Affairs	*Hattil Spencer Foll* (see Lyons II)
Air	14 Mar – 13 Aug 1940: *James Valentine Fairbairn* (see Menzies I)

14

14 Aug – 28 Oct 1940: *Arthur William Fadden* (from 1951: *Sir*) (b. 13 Apr 1895; d. 24 Apr 1973)

28 Oct 1940 – 29 Aug 1941: Menzies III

Prime Minister and Defence Co-ordination	*Robert Gordon Menzies* (for 3rd time) (see Lyons I)
Information	28 Oct – 13 Dec 1940: *Robert Gordon Menzies* (see Lyons I) 14 Dec 1940 – 29 Aug 1941: *Hattil Spencer Foll* (see Lyons II)
Treasurer	*Arthur William Fadden* (see Menzies II)
Attorney-General and Navy	*William Morris Hughes* (see Lyons I)
Army	*Percy Claude Spender* (see Menzies II)
Air	*John McEwen* (see Lyons I)
Home Affairs	*Hattil Spencer Foll* (see Lyons II)
Commerce	*Sir Earle Christmas Grafton Page* (see Lyons I)
Foreign Affairs, Health and Social Services	*Sir Frederick Harold Stewart* (see Lyons I)
Munitions	*Philip Albert McBride* (see Menzies II)
Supply	28 Oct 1940 – 26 Jun 1941: *Philip Albert McBride* (see Menzies II) 26 Jun – 29 Aug 1941: *George McLeay* (see Menzies I)
Trade and Customs	*Eric John Harrison* (see Lyons I)
Labour and National Service	*Harold Edward Holt* (b. Sydney 5 Aug 1908; d. off Portsea, south of Melbourne, 19 Dec 1967)
Scientific Research	*Harold Edward Holt* (see above)

29 Aug – 7 Oct 1941: Fadden

Prime Minister and Treasurer	*Arthur William Fadden* (see Menzies II)
Defence Co-ordination	*Robert Gordon Menzies* (see Lyons I) Other ministers continued in same offices as in previous cabinet

7 Oct 1941 – 21 Sep 1943: Curtin I

Prime Minister and Defence Co-ordination	*John Curtin* (for 1st time) (b. 8 Jan 1885; d. 5 Jul 1945)

15

Army	*Francis Michael Forde* (see Scullin)
Treasurer	*Joseph Benedict Chifley* (see Scullin)
Attorney-General and Foreign Affairs	*Herbert Vere Evatt* (b. East Maitland, New South Wales, 30 Apr 1894; d. Canberra 2 Nov 1965)
Supply	*John Albert Beasley* (b. Werribee 9 Nov 1895; d. 2 Sep 1949)
Home Affairs	*Joseph Silver Collings* (b. Brighton, Sussex, 1865(?); d. 20 Jun 1965)
Navy and Munitions	*Norman John Oswald Makin* (b. Petersham, New South Wales, 31 Mar 1889)
Health and Social Services	*Edward James Holloway* (d. 3 Dec 1967)
Trade and Customs	*Richard Valentine Keane* (d. 26 Apr 1946)
Air	*Arthur Samuel Drakeford* (d. 9 Jun 1957)
Commerce and Agriculture	*William James Scully* (b. Bective 1 Feb 1890; d. 19 Mar 1966)
Labour and National Service	*Edward John Ward* (b. Sydney 1889; d. 31 Jul 1963)
Information	*William Patrick Ashley* (b. May 1886; d. 27 Jun 1958)

21 Sep 1943 – 6 Jul 1945: Curtin II

Prime Minister and Defence	*John Curtin* (for 2nd time) (see Curtin I)
Supply	21 Sep 1943 – 2 Feb 1945: *John Albert Beasley* (see Curtin I) 2 Feb – 6 Jul 1945: *William Patrick Ashley* (see Curtin I)
Labour and National Service	*Edward James Holloway* (see Curtin I)
Health and Social Services	*James Mackintosh Fraser* (d. 27 Aug 1961)
Information	*Arthur Augustus Calwell* (b. Melbourne 28 Aug 1896; d. 8 Jul 1973) Other ministers continued in same offices as in previous cabinet

6 Jul – 13 Jul 1945: Forde

Prime Minister and Army	*Francis Michael Forde* (see Scullin)
Defence	*John Albert Beasley* (see Curtin I)

Other ministers continued in same offices as in previous cabinet

13 Jul 1945 – 1 Nov 1946: Chifley I

Prime Minister and Treasury	*Joseph Benedict Chifley* (for 1st time) (see Scullin)
Army	*Francis Michael Forde* (see Scullin)
Defence	13 Jul 1945 – 15 Aug 1946: *John Albert Beasley* (see Curtin I)
	15 Aug – 1 Nov 1946: *Francis Michael Forde* (see Scullin)
Navy	13 Jul 1945 – 15 Aug 1946: *Norman John Oswald Makin* (see Curtin I)
	15 Aug – 1 Nov 1946: *Arthur Samuel Drakeford* (see Curtin I)
Munitions	13 Jul 1945 – 15 Aug 1946: *Norman John Oswald Makin* (see Curtin I)
	15 Aug – 1 Nov 1946: *John Johnstone Dedman* (b. Newton Stewart, Scotland, 2 Jun 1896; d. 23 Nov 1973)
Trade and Customs	13 Jul 1945 – 26 Apr 1946: *Richard Valentine Keane* (see Curtin I)
	29 Apr – 18 Jun 1946: *John Johnstone Dedman* (see above)
	18 Jun – 1 Nov 1946: *James Mackintosh Fraser* (see Curtin II)
Health	13 Jul 1945 – 18 Jun 1946: *James Mackintosh Fraser* (see Curtin II)
	18 Jun – 1 Nov 1946: *Nicholas Edward McKenna* (b. Carlton 9 Sep 1895; d. 22 Apr 1974)
	Other ministers continued in same offices as in previous cabinet

1 Nov 1946 – 19 Dec 1949: Chifley II

Prime Minister and Treasury	*Joseph Benedict Chifley* (for 2nd time) (see Scullin)
Defence and Research	*John Johnstone Dedman* (see Chifley I)
Transport	*Edward John Ward* (see Curtin I)
Home Affairs	*Herbert Victor Johnson* (b. Northampton 25 Oct 1889; d. 10 Jul 1962)

Commerce and Agriculture	*Reginald Thomas Pollard* (b. Castlemaine 31 Oct 1894)
Munitions (from 6 Apr 1948: Supply and Development)	*John Ignatius Armstrong* (b. Sydney 6 Jul 1908; d. 10 Mar 1977)
Army	*Cyril Chambers* (b. Torrensville 28 Feb 1897)
Trade and Customs	*Benjamin Courtice* (b. Bundaberg 28 Mar 1886; d. 9 Jan 1972)
Navy	*William James Frederick Riordan* (b. Chillagoe 8 Feb 1908; d. 15 Jan 1973)
	Other ministers continued in same offices as in previous cabinet

19 Dec 1949 - 11 May 1951: Menzies IV

Prime Minister	*Robert Gordon Menzies* (for 4th time) (see Lyons I)
Treasurer	*Arthur William Fadden* (see Menzies II)
Defence	19 Dec 1949 - 24 Oct 1950: *Eric John Harrison* (see Lyons I)
	24 Oct 1950 - 11 May 1951: *Philip Albert McBride* (see Menzies II)
Labour, National Service and Immigration	*Harold Edward Holt* (see Menzies III)
Commerce and Agriculture	*John McEwen* (see Lyons I)
Foreign Affairs	19 Dec 1949 - 27 Apr 1951: *Percy Claude Spender* (see Menzies II)
	27 Apr - 11 May 1951: *Richard Gardiner Casey* (see Governors General)
Home Affairs	19 Dec 1949 - 24 Oct 1950: *Philip Albert McBride* (see Menzies II)
	24 Oct 1950 - 11 May 1951: *Eric John Harrison* (see Lyons I)
Health	*Sir Earle Christmas Grafton Page* (see Lyons I)
Trade and Customs	*Neil O'Sullivan* (b. Brisbane 2 Aug 1900; d. 4 Jul 1968)
Fuel, Shipping and Transport	*George McLeay* (see Menzies I)
Aviation	*Thomas Walter White* (see Lyons I)
Army and Navy	*Josiah Francis* (b. Ipswich, Queensland, 28 Mar 1898; d. 22 Feb 1964)
Attorney-General	*John Armstrong Spicer* (b. Armadale 5 May 1899)

Social Services	*William Henry Spooner* (from 1963: *Sir*) (b. Sydney 23 Dec 1897; d. 15 Jul 1966)
Information and Supply	*Oliver Howard Beale* (b. Tamworth, New South Wales, 1898)

11 May 1951 – 11 Jan 1956: Menzies V

Prime Minister	*Robert Gordon Menzies* (for 5th time) (see Lyons I)
Navy	11 May – 17 Jul 1951: *Philip Albert McBride* (see Menzies II)
	17 Jul 1951 – 9 Jul 1954: *William McMahon* (from 1977: *Sir*) (b. Sydney 23 Feb 1908)
	9 Jul 1954 – 7 Nov 1955: *Josiah Francis* (see Menzies IV)
	7 Nov 1955 – 11 Jan 1956: *Sir Eric John Harrison* (see Lyons I)
Shipping and Transport	11 May 1951 – 14 Sep 1955: *George McLeay* (see Menzies I)
	15 – 27 Sep 1955: *John Armstrong Spicer* (see Menzies IV)
	27 Sep 1955 – 11 Jan 1956: *Shane Dunne Paltridge* (from 1966: *Sir*) (b. 11 Jan 1910; d. 21 Jan 1966)
Postmaster-General	*Hubert Lawrence Anthony*
Army	11 May 1951 – 7 Nov 1955: *Josiah Francis* (see Menzies IV)
	7 Nov 1955 – 11 Jan 1956: *Sir Eric John Harrison* (see Lyons I)
National Development	*William Henry Spooner* (see Menzies IV)
Supply	*Oliver Howard Beale* (see Menzies IV)
Social Services	11 May 1951 – 9 Jul 1954: *Athol Gordon Townley*
	9 Jul 1954 – 11 Jan 1956: *William McMahon* (see above)
	Other ministers continued in same offices as in previous cabinet

11 Jan 1956 – 10 Dec 1958: Menzies VI

Prime Minister	*Robert Gordon Menzies* (for 6th time) (see Lyons I)
Treasurer	*Sir Arthur William Fadden* (see Menzies II)
Foreign Affairs	*Richard Gardiner Casey* (see Governors General)
Defence	*Sir Philip Albert McBride* (see Menzies II)

19

Shipping and Transport	*Shane Dunne Paltridge* (see Menzies V)
Primary Industry	*William McMahon* (see Menzies V)
Health	*Donald Alastair Cameron* (b. Ipswich, Queensland, 17 Mar 1900; d. 5 Jan 1974)
Home Affairs and Public Works	*Allen Fairhall* (b. Morpeth, New South Wales, 24 Nov 1909)
Labour	*Harold Edward Holt* (see Menzies III)
Army	11 Jan – 28 Feb 1956: *Sir Eric John Harrison* (see Lyons I)
	28 Feb 1956 – 10 Dec 1958: *John Oscar Cramer* (b. Quirindi 18 Feb 1897)
Navy	11 Jan – 24 Oct 1956: *Neil O'Sullivan* (see Menzies IV)
	24 Oct 1956 – 10 Dec 1958: *Charles William Davidson*
Attorney-General	11 Jan – 14 Aug 1956: *John Armstrong Spicer* (see Menzies IV)
	15 Aug 1956 – 10 Dec 1958: *Neil O'Sullivan* (see Menzies IV)
Supply	11 Jan 1956 – 10 Feb 1958: *Oliver Howard Beale* (see Menzies IV)
	11 Feb – 10 Dec 1958: *Athol Gordon Townley* (see Menzies V)
Social Services	11 Jan – 28 Feb 1956: *William McMahon* (see Menzies V)
	28 Feb 1956 – 10 Dec 1958: *Hugh Stevenson Roberton* (b. 18 Dec 1900)
Trade	*John McEwen* (see Lyons I)

10 Dec 1958 – 18 Dec 1963: Menzies VII

Prime Minister	*Robert Gordon Menzies* (from 1963: *Sir*) (for 7th time) (see Lyons I)
Trade	*John McEwen* (see Lyons I)
Treasurer	*Harold Edward Holt* (see Menzies III)
Foreign Affairs	10 Dec 1958 – 4 Feb 1960: *Richard Gardiner Casey* (from 1960: *Baron Casey*) (see Governors General)
	4 Feb 1960 – 22 Dec 1961: *Robert Gordon Menzies* (see Lyons I)
	22 Dec 1961 – 18 Dec 1963: *Sir Garfield Barwick*
National Development	*Sir William Henry Spooner* (see Menzies IV)
Defence	*Athol Gordon Townley* (see Menzies V)
Labour and National Service	*William McMahon* (see Menzies V)

Aviation, Shipping and Transport	10 Dec 1958 – 5 Feb 1960: *Shane Dunne Paltridge* (see Menzies V)
	5 Feb 1960 – 18 Dec 1963: *Hubert Ferdinand Opperman* (b. Rochester, Victoria, 29 May 1904)
Attorney-General	*Sir Garfield Barwick* (see above)
Health	10 Dec 1958 – 22 Dec 1961: *Donald Alastair Cameron* (see Menzies VI)
	22 Dec 1961 – 18 Dec 1963: *Harrie Walter Wade* (b. Clear Lake 10 Jan 1905)
Social Services	*Hugh Stevenson Roberton* (see Menzies VI)
Customs and Excise	*Norman Henry Denham Henty* (b. Longford 13 Oct 1903)
Supply	10 Dec 1958 – 22 Dec 1961: *Alan Shallcross Hulme* (b. Mosman 14 Feb 1907)
	22 Dec 1961 – 18 Dec 1963: *Allen Fairhall* (see Menzies VI)
Home Affairs and Public Works	*Gordon Freeth* (b. Angaston, South Australia, 6 Aug 1914)
Army	*John Oscar Cramer* (see Menzies VI)
Air	10 Dec 1958 – 29 Dec 1960: *Frederick Meares Osborne* (b. Sydney 20 Jan 1909)
	29 Dec 1960 – 22 Dec 1961: *Harrie Walter Wade* (see above)
	22 Dec 1961 – 27 Jul 1962: *Leslie Harry Ernest Bury* (b. London 25 Feb 1913)
	4 Aug 1962 – 18 Dec 1963: *David Eric Fairbairn* (b. Claygate, Surrey, 3 Mar 1917)
Navy	*John Grey Gorton* (from 1977: *Sir*) (b. Melbourne 9 Sep 1911)

18 Dec 1963 – 26 Jan 1966: Menzies VIII

Prime Minister	*Sir Robert Gordon Menzies* (for 8th time) (see Lyons I)
Trade and Industry	*John McEwen* (see Lyons I)
Treasurer	*Harold Edward Holt* (see Menzies III)
National Development	18 Dec 1963 – 10 Jun 1964: *Sir William Henry Spooner* (see Menzies IV)
	10 Jun 1964 – 26 Jan 1966: *David Eric Fairbairn* (see Menzies VII)
Defence	18 Dec 1963 – 24 Apr 1964: *Paul Meernaa Caedwalla Hasluck* (see Governors General)
	24 Apr 1964 – 19 Jan 1966: *Shane Dunne Paltridge* (from 1966: *Sir*) (see Menzies V)

21

Labour and National Service	*William McMahon* (see Menzies V)
Foreign Affairs	18 Dec 1963 – 24 Apr 1964: *Sir Garfield Barwick* (see Menzies VII)
	24 Apr 1964 – 26 Jan 1966: *Paul Meernaa Caedwalla Hasluck* (see Governors General)
Attorney-General	18 Dec 1963 – 4 Mar 1964: *Sir Garfield Barwick* (see Menzies VII)
	4 Mar 1964 – 26 Jan 1966: *Billy Mackie Snedden* (b. Perth 31 Dec 1926)
Primary Industry	*Charles Frederick Adermann* (b. Vernor Siding 3 Aug 1896)
Civil Aviation	18 Dec 1963 – 10 June 1964: *Shane Dunne Paltridge* (see Menzies V)
	10 Jun 1964 – 26 Jan 1966: *Norman Henry Denham Henty* (see Menzies VII)
Health	18 Dec 1963 – 18 Nov 1964: *Harrie Walter Wade* (see Menzies VII)
	21 Nov 1964 – 26 Jan 1966: *Reginald William Swartz* (from 1972: *Sir*) (b. Brisbane 14 Apr 1911)
Supply	*Allen Fairhall* (see Menzies VI)
Customs and Excise	18 Dec 1963 – 10 Jun 1964: *Norman Henry Denham Henty* (see Menzies VII)
	10 Jun 1964 – 26 Jan 1966: *Kenneth McColl Anderson* (from 1970: *Sir*) (b. at sea 11 Oct 1909)
Works	*John Grey Gorton* (see Menzies VII)
Home Affairs	18 Dec 1963 – 4 Mar 1964: *John Grey Gorton* (see Menzies VII)
	4 Mar 1964 – 26 Jan 1966: *John Douglas Anthony* (b. Murwillumbah 31 Dec 1929)
Shipping and Transport	*Gordon Freeth* (see Menzies VII)
Social Services	18 Dec 1963 – 21 Jan 1965: *Hugh Stevenson Roberton* (see Menzies VI)
	21 Jan – 22 Feb 1965: *Reginald William Swartz* (see above)
	22 Feb 1965 – 26 Jan 1966: *Ian McCahon Sinclair* (b. Sydney 10 Jun 1929)
Air	18 Dec 1963 – 10 Jun 1964: *David Eric Fairbairn* (see Menzies VII)
	10 Jun 1964 – 26 Jan 1966: *Peter Howson* (b. London 22 May 1919)
Housing	*Leslie Harry Ernest Bury* (see Menzies VII)

Army	*Alexander James Forbes* (b. 16 Dec 1923)
Navy	18 Dec 1963 – 4 Mar 1964: *Alexander James Forbes* (see above)
	4 Mar 1964 – 26 Jan 1966: *Frederick Charles Chaney* (b. Perth 12 Oct 1914)

27 Jan – 14 Dec 1966: Holt I

Prime Minister	*Harold Edward Holt* (for 1st time) (see Menzies III)
Trade and Industry	*John McEwen* (see Lyons I)
Treasurer	*William McMahon* (see Menzies V)
Foreign Affairs	*Paul Meernaa Caedwalla Hasluck* (see Governors General)
Primary Industry	*Charles Frederick Adermann* (see Menzies VIII)
Defence	*Allen Fairhall* (see Menzies VI)
Supply	*Norman Henry Denham Henty* (see Menzies VII)
National Development	*David Eric Fairbairn* (see Menzies VII)
Works	*John Grey Gorton* (see Menzies VII)
Labour and National Service	*Leslie Harry Ernest Bury* (see Menzies VII)
Shipping and Transport	*Gordon Freeth* (see Menzies VII)
Civil Aviation	*Reginald William Swartz* (see Menzies VIII)
Attorney-General	*Billy Mackie Snedden* (see Menzies VIII)
Health	*Alexander James Forbes* (see Menzies VIII)
Home Affairs	*John Douglas Anthony* (see Menzies VIII)
Navy	*Frederick Charles Chaney* (see Menzies VIII)
Air	*Peter Howson* (see Menzies VIII)
Customs and Excise	*Kenneth McColl Anderson* (see Menzies VIII)
Social Services	*Ian McCahon Sinclair* (see Menzies VIII)
Housing	*Annabelle Jane Mary Rankin* (b. Brisbane)
Army	*John Malcolm Fraser* (b. Melbourne 31 May 1930)

14 Dec 1966 – 19 Dec 1967: Holt II

Prime Minister	*Harold Edward Holt* (for 2nd time) (see Menzies III)
Home Affairs	14 Dec 1966 – 16 Oct 1967: *John Douglas Anthony* (see Menzies VIII)
	16 Oct – 19 Dec 1967: *Peter James Nixon* (b. Orbost 22 Mar 1928)
Primary Industry	14 Dec 1966 – 16 Oct 1967: *Charles Frederick Adermann* (see Menzies VIII)

23

	16 Oct – 19 Dec 1967: *John Douglas Anthony* (see Menzies VIII)
Works	14 Dec 1966 – 21 Feb 1967: *John Grey Gorton* (see Menzies VII)
	21 Feb – 19 Oct 1967: *Charles Robert Kelly* (b. Riverton 22 Jun 1912)
Education	*John Grey Gorton* (see Menzies VII)
Attorney-General	*Nigel Hubert Bowen* (b. Summerland, British Columbia, 26 May 1911)
Immigration	*Billy Mackie Snedden* (see Menzies VIII)
	Other ministers continued in same offices as in previous cabinet

19 Dec 1967 – 10 Jan 1968: McEwen

Prime Minister and Trade and Industry	*John McEwen* (see Lyons I)
	Other ministers continued in same offices as in previous cabinet

10 Jan – 28 Feb 1968: Gorton I

Prime Minister and Education	*John Grey Gorton* (for 1st time) (see Menzies VII)
Deputy Prime Minister and Trade and Industry	*John McEwen* (see Lyons I)
	Other ministers continued in same offices as in previous cabinet

28 Feb 1968 – 12 Nov 1969: Gorton II

Prime Minister	*John Grey Gorton* (for 2nd time) (see Menzies VII)
Deputy Prime Minister and Trade and Industry	*John McEwen* (see Lyons I)
Foreign Affairs	28 Feb 1968 – 11 Feb 1969: *Paul Meernaa Caedwalla Hasluck* (see Governors General)
	11 Feb – 12 Nov 1969: *Gordon Freeth* (see Menzies VII)

Treasurer	*William McMahon* (see Menzies V)
Defence	*Allen Fairhall* (see Menzies VI)
Primary Industry	*John Douglas Anthony* (see Menzies VIII)
Education and Science	*John Malcolm Fraser* (see Holt I)
National Development	*David Eric Fairbairn* (see Menzies VII)
Labour and National Service	*Leslie Harry Ernest Bury* (see Menzies VII)
Shipping and Transport	*Ian McCahon Sinclair* (see Menzies VIII)
Home Affairs	*Peter James Nixon* (see Holt II)
Social Services	*William Charles Wentworth* (b. Sydney 8 Sep 1907)
Attorney-General	*Nigel Hubert Bowen* (see Holt II)
Immigration	*Billy Mackie Snedden* (see Menzies VIII)
Supply	*Kenneth McColl Anderson* (see Menzies VIII)
Air	28 Feb 1968 – 13 Feb 1969: *Gordon Freeth* (see Menzies VII)
Health	*Alexander James Forbes* (see Menzies VIII)
Civil Aviation	*Reginald William Swartz* (see Menzies VIII)
Customs and Excise	*Malcolm Fox Scott* (b. 1911)
Army	*Phillip Reginald Lynch* (b. Melbourne 27 Jul 1933)
Navy	*Charles Robert Kelly* (see Holt II)
Works	*Reginald Charles Wright* (b. Central Castra 10 Jul 1905)
Housing	*Annabelle Jane Mary Rankin* (see Holt I)
Aboriginal Affairs (new post)	*William Charles Wentworth* (see above)

12 Nov 1969 – 10 Mar 1971: Gorton III

Prime Minister	*John Grey Gorton* (for 3rd time) (see Menzies VII)
Deputy Prime Minister and Trade and Industry	12 Nov 1969 – 5 Feb 1971: *John McEwen* (see Lyons I) 5 Feb – 10 Mar 1971: *John Douglas Anthony* (see Menzies VIII)
Treasurer	*Leslie Harry Ernest Bury* (see Menzies VII)
Foreign Affairs	*William McMahon* (see Menzies V)
Defence	*John Malcolm Fraser* (see Holt I)
Primary Industry	12 Nov 1969 – 5 Feb 1971: *John Douglas Anthony* (see Menzies VIII) 5 Feb – 10 Mar 1971: *Ian McCahon Sinclair* (see Menzies VIII)

25

AUSTRALIA

Education and Science	*Nigel Hubert Bowen* (see Holt II)
National Development	*Reginald William Swartz* (see Menzies VIII)
Labour and National Service	*Billy Mackie Snedden* (see Menzies VIII)
Shipping and Transport	12 Nov 1969 – 5 Feb 1971: *Ian McCahon Sinclair* (see Menzies VIII) 5 Feb – 10 Mar 1971: *Peter James Nixon* (see Holt II)
Home Affairs	12 Nov 1969 – 5 Feb 1971: *Peter James Nixon* (see Holt II) 5 Feb – 10 Mar 1971: *Ralph James Dunnet Hunt* (b. Narrabri 31 Mar 1928)
Social Services	*William Charles Wentworth* (see Gorton II)
Attorney-General	*Thomas Eyre Forrest Hughes* (b. 26 Nov 1923)
Immigration	*Phillip Reginald Lynch* (see Gorton II)
Supply	*Kenneth McColl Anderson* (see Menzies VIII)
Air	*Thomas Charles Drake-Brockman* (b. Toodyay 15 May 1919)
Health	*Alexander James Forbes* (see Menzies VIII)
Civil Aviation	*Robert Carrington Cotton* (b. Broken Hill 29 Nov 1915)
Customs and Excise	*Donald Leslie Chipp* (b. Melbourne 21 Aug 1925)
Army	*Andrew Sharp Peacock* (b. Melbourne 13 Feb 1939)
Navy	*Denis James Killen* (b. Dalby 23 Nov 1925)
Works	*Reginald Charles Wright* (see Gorton II)
Housing	*Annabelle Jane Mary Rankin* (see Holt I)
Aboriginal Affairs	*William Charles Wentworth* (see Gorton II)

10 Mar 1971 – 5 Dec 1972: McMahon

Prime Minister	*William McMahon* (see Menzies V)
Deputy Prime Minister and Trade and Industry	*John Douglas Anthony* (see Menzies VIII)
Foreign Affairs	10 – 23 Mar 1971: *William McMahon* (see Menzies V)
Defence	10 Mar – 13 Aug 1971: *John Grey Gorton* (see Menzies VII) 13 Aug 1971 – 5 Dec 1972: *David Eric Fairbairn* (see Menzies VII)
Primary Industry	*Ian McCahon Sinclair* (see Menzies VIII)

Environment, Aborigines and the Arts (new post)	31 May 1971 – 5 Dec 1972: *Peter Howson* (see Menzies VIII)
Supply	10 Mar – 2 Aug 1971: *Sir Kenneth McColl Anderson* (see Menzies VIII) 2 Aug 1971 – 5 Dec 1972: *Ransley Victor Garland* (b. 5 May 1934)
Treasury	10 – 22 Mar 1971: *Leslie Harry Ernest Bury* (see Menzies VII) 22 Mar 1971 – 5 Dec 1972: *Billy Mackie Snedden* (see Menzies VIII)
National Development	*Sir Reginald William Swartz* (see Menzies VIII)
Shipping and Transport	*Peter James Nixon* (see Holt II)
Labour and National Service	10 – 22 Mar 1971: *Billy Mackie Snedden* (see Menzies VIII) 22 Mar 1971 – 5 Dec 1972: *Phillip Reginald Lynch* (see Gorton II)
Education and Science	10 – 22 Mar 1971: *Nigel Hubert Bowen* (see Holt II) 22 Mar – 20 Aug 1971: *David Eric Fairbairn* (see Menzies VII) 20 Aug 1971 – 5 Dec 1972: *John Malcolm Fraser* (see Holt I)
Attorney-General	10 – 22 Mar 1971: *Thomas Eyre Forrest Hughes* (see Gorton III) 22 Mar – 2 Aug 1971: *Nigel Hubert Bowen* (see Holt II) 2 Aug 1971 – 5 Dec 1972: *Ivor John Greenwood* (b. Melbourne 15 Nov 1926; d. Melbourne 13 Oct 1976)
Health	10 – 22 Mar 1971: *Alexander James Forbes* (see Menzies VIII) 22 Mar – 2 Aug 1971: *Ivor John Greenwood* (see above) 2 Aug 1971 – 5 Dec 1972: *Sir Kenneth McColl Anderson* (see Menzies VIII)
Housing	10 – 22 Mar 1971: *Annabelle Jane Mary Rankin* (see Holt I) 22 Mar 1971 – 5 Dec 1972: *Kevin Michael Kiernan Cairns* (b. Sydney 15 May 1929)

Immigration	10 – 22 Mar 1971: *Phillip Reginald Lynch* (see Gorton II)
	22 Mar 1971 – 5 Dec 1972: *Alexander James Forbes* (see Menzies VIII)
Social Services	*William Charles Wentworth* (see Gorton II)
Works	*Reginald Charles Wright* (see Gorton II)
Civil Aviation	*Robert Carrington Cotton* (see Gorton III)
Customs and Excise	*Donald Leslie Chipp* (see Gorton III)
Air	*Thomas Charles Drake-Brockman* (see Gorton III)
Navy	10 – 22 Mar 1971: *Denis James Killen* (see Gorton III)
	22 Mar 1971 – 5 Dec 1972: *Malcolm George McKay* (b. Brighton, South Australia, 29 Dec 1919)
Army	10 Mar 1971 – 2 Feb 1972: *Andrew Sharp Peacock* (see Gorton III)
	2 Feb – 5 Dec 1972: *Robert Cummin Katter* (b. Brisbane 5 Sep 1918)
Home Affairs	*Ralph James Dunnet Hunt* (see Gorton III)

5/19 Dec 1972* – 11 Nov 1975: Whitlam

Prime Minister	*Edward Gough Whitlam* (b. Kew, Victoria, 11 Jul 1916)
Deputy Prime Minister	5 Dec 1972 – 2 Jun 1974: *Lance Herbert Barnard* (b. Launceston 1 May 1919)
	12 Jun 1974 – 2 Jul 1975: *James Ford Cairns* (b. Carlton 4 Oct 1914)
	14 Jul – 11 Nov 1975: *Frank Crean* (b. Hamilton 28 Feb 1912)
Foreign Affairs	19 Dec 1972 – 6 Nov 1973: *Edward Gough Whitlam* (see above)
	6 Nov 1973 – 11 Nov 1975: *Donald Robert Willesee* (b. Derby, Western Australia, 14 Apr 1916)
Defence	19 Dec 1972 – 2 Jun 1975: *Lance Herbert Barnard* (see above)
	2 Jun – 11 Nov 1975: *William Lawrence Morrison* (b. Lithgow 3 Nov 1928)

*From 5 to 19 Dec portfolios were shared between Whitlam and Barnard. The Prime Minister held those of Foreign Affairs, Treasury, Attorney-General, Customs and Excise, Trade and Industry, Shipping and Transport, Education and Science, Civil Aviation, Housing, Works, External, Territories, and Environment. The Deputy Prime Minister was responsible for Defence, Navy, Army, Air, Supply, Postmaster-General, Labour and National Service, Social Services, Immigration, Interior, Primary Industry, Repatriation, Health and National Development. The full cabinet was sworn in on 19 Dec.

Navy, Army and Air	19 Dec 1972 – 30 Nov 1973: *Lance Herbert Barnard* (see above)
	30 Nov 1973: departments merged with Defence (see above)
Supply	19 Dec 1972 – 9 Oct 1973: *Lance Herbert Barnard* (see above)
	9 Oct 1973 – 12 Jun 1974: *Keppel Earl Enderby* (b. Dubbo 25 Jun 1926)
	12 Jun 1974: merged into Manufacturing Industry (see below)
Overseas Trade	19 Dec 1972 – 11 Dec 1974: *James Ford Cairns* (see above)
	11 Dec 1974 – 11 Nov 1975: *Frank Crean* (see above)
Secondary Industry	19 Dec 1972 – 9 Oct 1973: *James Ford Cairns* (see above)
	9 Oct 1973 – 12 Jun 1974: *Keppel Earl Enderby* (see above)
	12 Jun 1974: merged into Manufacturing Industry (see below)
Manufacturing Industry	12 Jun 1974 – 10 Feb 1975: *Keppel Earl Enderby* (see above)
	10 Feb – 14 Jul 1975: *James Robert McClelland* (b. Melbourne 3 Jun 1915)
	14 Jul – 11 Nov 1975: *Lionel Frost Bowen* (b. Sydney 28 Dec 1922)
Social Security	19 Dec 1972 – 14 Jul 1975: *William George Hayden* (b. Brisbane 23 Jan 1933)
	14 Jul – 11 Nov 1975: *John Murray Wheeldon* (b. Subiaco, Western Australia, 9 Aug 1929)
Treasury	19 Dec 1972 – 11 Dec 1974: *Frank Crean* (see above)
	11 Dec 1974 – 14 Jul 1975: *James Ford Cairns* (see above)
	14 Jul – 11 Nov 1975: *William George Hayden* (see above)
Attorney-General	19 Dec 1972 – 10 Feb 1975: *Lionel Keith Murphy* (b. Sydney 31 Aug 1922)
	10 Feb – 14 Jul 1975: *Keppel Earl Enderby* (see above)
	14 Jul – 11 Nov 1975:
Customs and Excise	19 Dec 1972 – 10 Feb 1975: *Lionel Keith Murphy* (see above)
	10 Feb 1975: merged into Police and Customs (see below)
Police and Customs	10 Feb – 14 Jul 1975: *Keppel Earl Enderby* (see above)

29

	14 Jul – 11 Nov 1975: *James Luke Cavanagh* (b. Paddington 21 Jun 1913)
Media	19 Dec 1972 – 14 Jul 1975: *Douglas McClelland* (b. Wentworthville 5 Aug 1926)
	14 Jul – 11 Nov 1975: *Moses Henry Cass* (b. Corrigin 18 Feb 1927)
Northern Development ment	19 Dec 1972 – 14 Jul 1975: *Rex Allan Patterson* (b. Bundaberg 8 Jan 1927)
	14 Jul 1975: merged into Northern Australia Department (see below)
Northern Australia	14 Jul – 21 Oct 1975: *Rex Allan Patterson* (see above)
	21 Oct – 11 Nov 1975: *Paul John Keating* (b. Sydney 18 Jan 1944)
Northern Territory	19 Dec 1972 – 19 Oct 1973: *Keppel Earl Enderby* (see above)
	19 Oct 1973 – 14 Jul 1975: *Rex Allan Patterson* (see above)
	14 Jul 1975: merged into Northern Australia Department (see above)
Services and Property	*Frederick Michael Daly* (b. Corrabubula 13 Jun 1913)
Labour (from 12 Jun 1974: Labour and Immigration)	19 Dec 1972 – 14 Jul 1975: *Clyde Robert Cameron* (b. Murray Bridge 13 Jan 1914)
	14 Jul – 11 Nov 1975: *Douglas McClelland* (see above)
Urban and Regional Development	*Thomas Uren* (b. Balmain 28 May 1921)
Transport	*Charles Keith Jones* (b. Newcastle, New South Wales, 19 Sep 1917)
Civil Aviation	19 Dec 1972 – 30 Nov 1973: *Charles Keith Jones* (see above)
	30 Nov 1973: merged with Transport (see above)
Education	*Kim Edward Beazley* (b. Northam 30 Sep 1917)
Tourism and Recreation	*Francis Eugene Stewart* (b. Belmore 20 Feb 1920)
Works	19 Dec 1972 – 9 Oct 1973: *James Luke Cavanagh* (see above)
	9 Oct – 30 Nov 1973: *Leslie Royston Johnson* (b. Sydney 22 Nov 1924)
	30 Nov 1973: merged into Housing and Construction (see below)

Primary Industry (from 12 Jun 1974: Agriculture)	19 Dec 1972 – 21 Oct 1975: *Kenneth Shaw Wriedt* (b. Melbourne 11 Jul 1927) 21 Oct – 11 Nov 1975: *Rex Allan Patterson* (see above)
Aboriginal Affairs	19 Dec 1972 – 9 Oct 1973: *Gordon Munro Bryant* (b. Lismore 3 Aug 1914) 9 Oct 1973 – 14 Jul 1975: *James Luke Cavanagh* (see above) 14 Jul – 11 Nov 1975: *Leslie Royston Johnson* (see above)
Minerals and Energy	19 Dec 1972 – 21 Oct 1975: *Reginald Francis Xavier Connor* 21 Oct – 11 Nov 1975: *Kenneth Shaw Wriedt* (see above)
Immigration	19 Dec 1972 – 12 Jun 1974: *Albert Jaime Grassby* (b. Brisbane 12 Jul 1926) 12 Jun 1974: merged with Labour
Housing	19 Dec 1972 – 30 Nov 1973: *Leslie Royston Johnson* (see above) 30 Nov 1973: merged into Housing and Construction (see below)
Housing and Construction	30 Nov 1973 – 14 Jul 1975: *Leslie Royston Johnson* (see above) 14 Jul – 11 Nov 1975: *Joseph Martin Riordan* (b. Sydney 27 Feb 1930)
Capital Territory	19 Dec 1972 – 9 Oct 1973: *Keppel Earl Enderby* (see above) 9 Oct 1973 – 11 Nov 1975: *Gordon Munro Bryant* (see above)
Health	*Douglas Nixon Everingham* (b. Wauchope 25 Jun 1923)
Environment (and Conservation)	19 Dec 1972 – 14 Jul 1975: *Moses Henry Cass* (see above) 14 Jul – 11 Nov 1975: *Joseph Max Berinson* (b. Perth 7 Jan 1932)
Science	19 Dec 1972 – 14 Jul 1975: *William Lawrence Morrison* (see above) 14 Jul 1975: merged into Science and Consumer Affairs (see below)
Science and Consumer Affairs	14 Jul – 11 Nov 1975: *Clyde Robert Cameron* (see above)
External Territories	19 Dec 1972 – 30 Nov 1973: *William Lawrence Morrison* (see above)

31

	30 Nov 1973: department abolished
Postmaster-General	19 Dec 1972 - 12 Jun 1974: *Lionel Frost Bowen* (see above)
	12 Jun 1974 - 11 Nov 1975: *Reginald Bishop* (b. Adelaide 4 Feb 1913)
Repatriation	19 Dec 1972 - 12 Jun 1974: *Reginald Bishop* (see above)
	12 Jun 1974: merged into Repatriation and Compensation (see below)
Repatriation and Compensation	12 Jun 1974 - 11 Nov 1975: *John Murray Wheeldon* (see above)
Without Portfolio (Special Minister of State)	19 Dec 1972 - 30 Nov 1973: *Donald Robert Willesee* (see above)
	30 Nov 1973 - 14 Jul 1975: *Lionel Frost Bowen* (see above)
	14 Jul - 11 Nov 1975: *Douglas McClelland* (see above)

11/12 Nov* - 22 Dec 1975: Fraser I (Caretaker Government pending elections)

Prime Minister	*John Malcolm Fraser* (for 1st time) (see Holt I)
Deputy Prime Minister, Overseas Trade, and Minerals and Energy	*John Douglas Anthony* (see Menzies VIII)
Treasury	*Phillip Reginald Lynch* (see Gorton II)
Agriculture and Northern Australia	*Ian McCahon Sinclair* (see Menzies VIII)
Capital Territory, Media, and Tourism and Recreation	*Reginald Grieve Withers* (b. Bunbury 26 Oct 1924) Special Minister of State
Attorney-General and Police and Customs	*Ivor John Greenwood* (see McMahon)
Manufacturing Industry and Science and Consumer Affairs	*Robert Carrington Cotton* (see Gorton III)

*Cabinet sworn in 12 Nov 1975

Transport and Postmaster-General	*Peter James Nixon* (see Holt II)
Foreign Affairs and Environment	*Andrew Sharp Peacock* (see Gorton III)
Social Security, Health, and Repatriation and Compensation	*Donald Leslie Chipp* (see Gorton III)
Defence	*Denis James Killen* (see Gorton III)
Aboriginal Affairs and Administrative Services	*Thomas Charles Drake-Brockman* (see Gorton III)
Housing and Construction and Urban and Regional Development	*John Leslie Carrick* (b. Sydney 4 Sep 1918)
Education	*Margaret Georgina Constance Guilfoyle* (b. Belfast 15 May 1926)

From 22 Dec 1975: Fraser II

Prime Minister	*John Malcolm Fraser* (for 2nd time) (see Holt I)
Natural Resources and Overseas Trade	*John Douglas Anthony* (see Menzies VIII)
Treasury	*Phillip Reginald Lynch* (see Gorton II)
Primary Industry	*Ian McCahon Sinclair* (see Menzies VIII)
Administrative Services	*Reginald Grieve Withers* (see Fraser I)
Environment, Housing and Community Development	*Ivor John Greenwood* (see McMahon)
Industry and Commerce	*Robert Carrington Cotton* (see Gorton III)
Employment and Industrial Relations	*Anthony Austin Street* (b. Melbourne 8 Feb 1926)

Transport	*Peter James Nixon* (see Holt II)
Education and Federal Affairs	*John Leslie Carrick* (see Fraser I)
Foreign Affairs	*Andrew Sharp Peacock* (see Gorton III)
Defence	*Denis James Killen* (see Gorton III)
Social Security	*Margaret Georgina Constance Guilfoyle* (see Fraser I)
Attorney-General	*Robert James Ellicott* (b. Moree 15 Apr 1927)
Business and Consumer Affairs	*John Winston Howard* (b. Earlwood 26 Jul 1939)
Postal and Telecommunications	*Ransley Victor Garland* (see McMahon)
Health	*Ralph James Dunnet Hunt* (see Gorton III)
Immigration and Ethnic Affairs	*Michael John Randal MacKellar* (b. 27 Oct 1938)
Northern Territories	*Albert Evan Adermann* (b. Kingaroy 10 Mar 1927)
Aboriginal Affairs	*Robert Ian Viner* (b. Claremont 21 Jan 1933)
Capital Territory	*Eric Laidlaw Robinson* (b. Brisbane 18 Jan 1929)
Construction	*John Elden McLeay* (b. Adelaide 30 Mar 1922)
Repatriation	*Kevin Eugene Newman*
Science	*James Joseph Webster* (b. Flinders Island 14 Jan 1925)

Austria

HEADS OF STATE

Presidents

10 Dec 1928	*Wilhelm Miklas* (Christ Soc) (b. Krems 15 Oct 1872; d. Vienna 15 Mar 1956)
13 Mar 1938	*Arthur Seyss-Inquart* (b. Stannern bei Iglau 22 Jul 1892; d. Nuremberg 16 Oct 1946) nominated as Chancellor following Miklas's resignation
13 Mar 1938	Merged with Germany
27 Apr 1945	Regained independence

20 Dec 1945 – 31 Dec 1950	*Karl Renner* (SPÖ) (b. Untertannowitz 14 Dec 1870; d. Vienna 31 Dec 1950)*
27 May 1951 – 4 Jan 1957	*Theodor Korner* (SPÖ) (b. Komorn 24 Apr 1873; d. Vienna 4 Jan 1957)
22 May 1957 – 28 Feb 1965	*Adolf Schärf* (SPÖ) (b. Nikolsburg 20 Apr 1890; d. Vienna 28 Feb 1965)
9 Jun 1965 – 23 Apr 1974	*Franz Jonas* (SPÖ) (b. Vienna 4 Oct 1899; d. 23 Apr 1974)
24 Apr – 8 Jul 1974	(acting:) *Bruno Kreisky* (SPÖ) (b. Vienna 22 Jan 1911)
from 8 Jul 1974	*Rudolf Kirchschläger* (SPÖ) (b. Obermuhl 20 Mar 1915)

MEMBERS OF GOVERNMENT

26 Sep 1929 – 25 Sep 1930: Schober III

Chancellor	*Johann Schober* (Schober Group) (for 3rd time) (b. Perg 14 Nov 1874; d. Pottenbrunn 19 Aug 1932)*
Vice Chancellor	26 Sep 1929 – 24 Sep 1930: *Karl Vaugoin* (Christ Soc) (b. Vienna 8 Jul 1873; d. Krems 11 Jun 1949)*
Foreign Affairs	*Johann Schober* (see above)
Home Affairs	*Vinzenz Schumy* (Country Party) (b. Saak bei Arnoldstein 28 Jul 1878)*
Education	26 Sep – 16 Oct 1929: *Johann Schober* (see above) 16 Oct 1929 – 25 Sep 1930: *Heinrich Srbik* (b. Vienna 10 Nov 1878; d. Ehrwald 16 Feb 1951)
Justice	*Franz Slama* (Greater German Party) (b. Brno 19 Jun 1885)*
Finance	26 Sep – 16 Oct 1929: *Johann Schober* (see above) 16 Oct 1929 – 25 Sep 1930: *Otto Juch* (Christ Soc) (b. Kirchbichl 25 Feb 1876)
Commerce and Transport	26 Sep 1929 – 17 Jun 1930: *Michael Hainisch* (Christ Soc) (b. Aue bei Gloggnitz 15 Aug 1858; d. Vienna 26 Feb 1940) 17 Jun – 22 Sep 1930: *Friedrich Schuster* (b. 1863; d. Graz 31 Aug 1932)
Social Administration	*Theodor Innitzer* (from 1933: *Cardinal*) (b. Weipert 25 Dec 1875; d. Vienna 9 Oct 1955)
Army	26 Sep 1929 – 24 Sep 1930: *Karl Vaugoin* (Christ Soc) (see above)

*For earlier career see vol. 2

AUSTRIA

Agriculture and Forestry	26 Sep 1929 – 24 Sep 1930: *Florian Födermayr* (Christ Soc) (b. Kronstorf bei Enns 18 Apr 1877)*

30 Sep – 29 Nov 1930: Vaugoin

Chancellor	*Karl Vaugoin* (Christ Soc) (see Schober III)
Vice Chancellor	*Richard Schmitz* (Christ Soc) (b. Vienna 14 Aug 1885; d. Vienna 27 Apr 1954)*
Foreign Affairs	*Ignaz Seipel* (Christ Soc) (b. Vienna 19 Jul 1876; d. Pernitz 2 Aug 1932)*
Home Affairs	*Ernst Rüdiger Starhemberg* (Home Guard) (b. Linz 10 May 1899; d. Schruns 15 Mar 1956)
Education	*Emmerich Czermak* (Christ Soc) (b. Datschitz 18 Mar 1885)*
Justice	*Franz Hueber* (Home Guard) (b. Grunberg 6 Jan 1894)
Finance	*Otto Juch* (Christ Soc) (see Schober III)
Commerce and Transport	*Eduard Heinl* (Christ Soc) (b. Vienna 9 Apr 1880; d. Vienna 10 Apr 1957)*
Social Administration	*Richard Schmitz* (Christ Soc) (see above)
Army	*Karl Vaugoin* (Christ Soc) (see Schober III)
Agriculture and Forestry	*Andreas Thaler* (Christ Soc) (b. Oberau 10 Sep 1883; d. Dreizehnlinden, Brazil, 1939)

4 Dec 1930 – 16 Jun 1931: Ender

Chancellor	*Otto Ender* (Christ Soc) (b. Altach 24 Dec 1875; d. Bregenz 25 Jun 1960)
Vice Chancellor	*Johann Schober* (Economic Bloc) (see Schober III)
Foreign Affairs	*Johann Schober* (Economic Bloc) (see Schober III)
Home Affairs	*Franz Winkler* (Country Party) (b. Česká Lipa (or Cvikov?) 20 Mar 1890)
Justice	4 Dec 1930 – 30 May 1931: *Hans Schürff* (Economic Bloc) (b. Modling 12 May 1875; d. Vienna 27 Mar 1939)* 30 May – 16 Jun 1931: *Johann Schober* (Economic Bloc) (see Schober III)
Education	*Emmerich Czermak* (Christ Soc) (see Vaugoin)
Finance	*Otto Juch* (see Schober III)
Commerce and Transport	*Eduard Heinl* (Christ Soc) (see Vaugoin)

*For earlier career see vol. 2

Social Administration	4 Dec 1930 – 15 Apr 1931: *Josef Resch* (Christ Soc) (b. Vienna 8 Sep 1880)* 15 Apr – 16 Jun 1931: *Otto Ender* (Christ Soc) (see above)
Army	*Karl Vaugoin* (Christ Soc) (see Schober III)
Agriculture and Forestry	4 Dec 1930 – 18 Mar 1931: *Andreas Thaler* (Christ Soc) (see Vaugoin) 18 Mar – 16 Jun 1931: *Engelbert Dollfuss* (Christ Soc) (b. 4 Oct 1892; d. Vienna 25 Jul 1934)

20 Jun 1931 – 27 Jan 1932: Buresch I

Chancellor	*Karl Buresch* (Christ Soc) (for 1st time) (b. Gross-Enzersdorf 12 Oct 1878; d. Vienna 16 Sep 1936)
Vice Chancellor	*Johann Schober* (Economic Bloc) (see Schober III)
Foreign Affairs	*Johann Schober* (Economic Bloc) (see Schober III)
Home Affairs	*Franz Winkler* (Country Party) (see Ender)
Education	*Emmerich Czermak* (Christ Soc) (see Vaugoin)
Justice	*Hans Schürff* (Economic Bloc) (see Ender)
Finance	20 Jun – 5 Oct 1931: *Joseph Redlich* (b. Goding 18 Jun 1869; d. Vienna 11 Nov 1936) 5 – 16 Oct 1931: *Karl Buresch* (Christ Soc) (see above) 16 Oct 1931 – 27 Jan 1932: *Emanuel Weidenhoffer* (Christ Soc) (b. Napajedl 28 Jan 1874)
Commerce and Transport	*Eduard Heinl* (Christ Soc) (see Vaugoin)
Social Administration	*Josef Resch* (Christ Soc) (see Ender)
Army	*Karl Vaugoin* (Christ Soc) (see Schober III)
Agriculture and Forestry	*Engelbert Dollfuss* (Christ Soc) (see Ender)

29 Jan – 6 May 1932: Buresch II

Chancellor	*Karl Buresch* (Christ Soc) (for 2nd time) (see Buresch I)
Vice Chancellor	*Franz Winkler* (Country Party) (see Ender)
Foreign Affairs	*Karl Buresch* (Christ Soc) (see Buresch I)
Home Affairs	*Franz Winkler* (Country Party) (see Ender)
Education	*Emmerich Czermak* (Christ Soc) (see Vaugoin)
Justice	*Kurt Schuschnigg* (Christ Soc) (b. Riva 14 Dec 1897)
Finance	*Emanuel Weidenhoffer* (Christ Soc) (see Buresch I)

*For earlier career see vol. 2

Commerce and Transport	*Eduard Heinl* (Christ Soc) (see Vaugoin)
Social Administration	*Josef Resch* (Christ Soc) (see Ender)
Army	*Karl Vaugoin* (Christ Soc) (see Schober III)
Agriculture and Forestry	*Engelbert Dollfuss* (Christ Soc) (see Ender)
Without Portfolio (Public Security)	4 Feb – 6 May 1932: *Franz Bachinger* (b. Gaspoltshausen 1892)

20 May 1932 – 21 Sep 1933: Dollfuss I

Chancellor	*Engelbert Dollfuss* (Christ Soc) (for 1st time) (see Ender)
Vice Chancellor	*Franz Winkler* (Country Party) (see Ender) with responsibility for certain aspects of foreign policy
Foreign Affairs	*Engelbert Dollfuss* (see Ender)
Home Affairs	20 May 1932 – 10 May 1933: *Franz Bachinger* (Country Party) (see Buresch II)
	10 May – 21 Sep 1933: *Vinzenz Schumy* (Country Party) (see Schober III)
Education	10 May 1932 – 24 May 1933: *Anton Rintelen* (Christ Soc) (b. Graz 15 Nov 1876; d. Graz 28 Jan 1946)*
	24 May – 21 Sep 1933: *Kurt Schuschnigg* (Christ Soc) (see Buresch II)
Justice	*Kurt Schuschnigg* (Christ Soc) (see Buresch II)
Finance	20 May 1932 – 10 May 1933: *Emanuel Weidenhoffer* (Christ Soc) (see Buresch I)
	10 May – 21 Sep 1933: *Karl Buresch* (Christ Soc) (see Buresch I)
Commerce and Transport	20 May 1932 – 10 May 1933: *Guido Jakoncig* (b. Capodistria 27 Sep 1895)
	10 May – 21 Sep 1933: *Fritz Stockinger* (b. Vienna 22 Sep 1894)
Social Administration	20 May 1932 – 11 Mar 1933: *Josef Resch* (Christ Soc) (see Ender)
	11 Mar – 21 Sep 1933: *Robert Kerber* (Country Party) (b. Stettin 21 May 1884)
Army	*Karl Vaugoin* (Christ Soc) (see Schober III)
Agriculture and Forestry	*Engelbert Dollfuss* (Christ Soc) (see above)

*For earlier career see vol. 2

| Public Security (raised from State Secretariat) | 10 May – 21 Sep 1933: *Emil Fey* (Home Guard) (b. Vienna 23 Mar 1886; d. 16 Mar 1938) |
| Constitutional and Administrative Reform (new post) | 19 Jul – 21 Sep 1933: *Otto Ender* (Christ Soc) (see Ender) |

21 Sep 1933 – 10 Jul 1934: Dollfuss II

Chancellor	*Engelbert Dollfuss* (Christ Soc) (for 2nd time) (see Ender)
Vice Chancellor	21 Sep 1933 – 1 May 1934: *Emil Fey* (Home Defence) (see Dollfuss I)
	1 May – 10 Jul 1934: *Ernst Rüdiger Starhemberg* (Home Guard) (see Vaugoin)
Foreign Affairs	*Engelbert Dollfuss* (Christ Soc) (see Ender)
Home Affairs	*Engelbert Dollfuss* (Christ Soc) (see Ender)
Education	*Kurt Schuschnigg* (Christ Soc) (see Buresch II)
Justice	*Kurt Schuschnigg* (Christ Soc) (see Buresch II)
Finance	*Karl Buresch* (Christ Soc) (see Buresch I)
Commerce and Transport	*Fritz Stockinger* (see Dollfuss I)
Social Administration	21 Sep 1933 – 16 Feb 1934: *Richard Schmitz* (Christ Soc) (see Vaugoin)
	16 Feb – 10 Jul 1934: *Odo Neustädter-Stürmer* (Home Defence) (b. Ljubljana 13 Nov 1885; d. 13(?) Mar 1938)
Army	21 Sep 1933 – 12 Mar 1934: *Engelbert Dollfuss* (Christ Soc) (see Ender)
Defence (new post, previously Secretariat under the Army portfolio)	12 Mar – 10 Jul 1934: *Alois Schönburg-Hartenstein* (b. Karlsruhe 21 Nov 1858; d. Hartenstein 20 Sep 1944)
Agriculture	*Engelbert Dollfuss* (Christ Soc) (see Ender)
Public Security	21 Sep 1933 – 1 May 1934: *Engelbert Dollfuss* (Christ Soc) (see Ender)
	1 May – 10 Jul 1934: *Emil Fey* (Home Defence) (see Dollfuss I)
Constitutional Questions	*Otto Ender* (Christ Soc) (see Ender)

| Without Portfolio | 22 Sep 1933 – 10 Jul 1934: *Robert Kerber* (Country Party) (see Dollfuss I) Head of the newly created Department of Statistics from 1 May 1934 |
| | 16 Feb – 10 Jul 1934: *Richard Schmitz* (Christ Soc) (see Vaugoin) |

11 – 25 Jul 1934: Dollfuss III

Chancellor	*Engelbert Dollfuss* (Christ Soc) (for 3rd time) (see Ender)
Vice Chancellor	*Ernst Rüdiger Starhemberg* (Home Guard) (see Vaugoin)
Foreign Affairs	*Engelbert Dollfuss* (Christ Soc) (see Ender)
Home Affairs	*Engelbert Dollfuss* (Christ Soc) (see Ender)
Home Administration (new post)	No appointment made
Education	*Kurt Schuschnigg* (Christ Soc) (see Buresch II)
Justice	*Egon Berger-Waldenegg* (Home Guard) (b. Vienna 14 Feb 1880)
Finance	*Karl Buresch* (Christ Soc) (see Buresch I)
Commerce and Transport	*Fritz Stockinger* (see Dollfuss I)
Social Administration	*Odo Neustädter-Stürmer* (Home Guard) (see Dollfuss II)
Defence	*Engelbert Dollfuss* (Christ Soc) (see Ender)
Public Security	*Engelbert Dollfuss* (Christ Soc) (see Ender)
Agriculture	*Engelbert Dollfuss* (Christ Soc) (see Ender)
Without Portfolio	*Emil Fey* (Home Defence) (see Dollfuss I)
(Commissioner-General for Public Security)	*Robert Kerber* (Country Party) (see Dollfuss I)

26 – 30 Jul 1934: Starhemberg

| Chancellor | *Ernst Rüdiger Starhemberg* (Home Guard) (see Vaugoin) held office on a caretaker basis |

30 Jul 1934 – 17 Oct 1935: Schuschnigg I

| Chancellor | *Kurt Schuschnigg* (Christ Soc) (for 1st time) (see Buresch II) |
| Vice Chancellor | *Ernst Rüdiger Starhemberg* (Home Guard) (see Vaugoin) |

Foreign Affairs	*Egon Berger-Waldenegg* (Home Guard) (see Dollfuss III)
Home Administration	*Emil Fey* (Home Defence) (see Dollfuss I) also Commissioner-General
Education	*Kurt Schuschnigg* (Christ Soc) (see Buresch II)
Justice	*Egon Berger-Waldenegg* (Home Guard) (see Dollfuss III)
Finance	*Karl Buresch* (Christ Soc) (see Buresch I)
Commerce and Transport	*Fritz Stockinger* (see Dollfuss I)
Social Administration	*Odo Neustädter-Stürmer* (Home Guard) (see Dollfuss I) from 10 Nov 1934 also responsible for corporative reorganization
Defence	*Kurt Schuschnigg* (Christ Soc) (see Buresch II)
Agriculture	31 Jul 1934 – 17 Oct 1935: *Josef Reither* (b. Langenrohr 26 Jul 1880; d. 30 Apr 1950)
Public Security	*Ernst Rüdiger Starhemberg* (Home Guard) (see Vaugoin)

17 Oct 1935 – 14 May 1936: Schuschnigg II

Chancellor	*Kurt Schuschnigg* (Christ Soc) (for 2nd time) (see Buresch II)
Vice Chancellor	*Ernst Rüdiger Starhemberg* (Home Guard) (see Vaugoin)
Foreign Affairs	*Egon Berger-Waldenegg* (Home Guard) (see Dollfuss III)
Home Administration	*Eduard Baar-Baarenfels* (b. Ljubljana 3 Nov 1885)
Education	*Kurt Schuschnigg* (Christ Soc) (see Buresch II)
Justice	*Robert Winterstein* (d. Buchenwald Concentration Camp 1938)
Finance	*Ludwig Draxler* (b. Vienna 18 May 1896)
Commerce and Transport	*Fritz Stockinger* (see Dollfuss I)
Social Administration	*Josef Dobretsberger* (b. Linz 28 Feb 1903)
Defence	*Kurt Schuschnigg* (Christ Soc) (see Buresch II)
Agriculture	*Ludwig Strobl* (b. Mistelbach 22 Jan 1900)
Public Security	*Eduard Baar-Baarenfels* (see above)
Without Portfolio	17 Oct 1935 – 30 Jan 1936: *Karl Buresch* (Christ Soc) (see Buresch I) responsible for administration of overall economic affairs and Chairman of the Ministerial Committee on Economic Affairs

14 May – 3 Nov 1936: Schuschnigg III

Chancellor	*Kurt Schuschnigg* (for 3rd time) (see Buresch II)
Vice Chancellor	*Eduard Baar-Baarenfels* (see Schuschnigg II)
Foreign Affairs	*Kurt Schuschnigg* (see Buresch II)
Home Affairs	*Eduard Baar-Baarenfels* (see Schuschnigg II)
Education	*Hans Pernter* (b. Vienna 3 Oct 1887)
Justice	*Hans Hammerstein-Equord* (b. Sitzental 5 Jan 1888; d. Pernlehn 9 Aug 1947)
Finance	*Ludwig Draxler* (see Schuschnigg II)
Commerce and Transport	*Fritz Stockinger* (see Dollfuss I)
Social Administration	*Josef Resch* (see Ender)
Defence	*Kurt Schuschnigg* (see Buresch II)
Agriculture	(acting:) *Kurt Schuschnigg* (see Buresch II)
	15 May – 3 Nov 1936: *Peter Mandorfer* (b. Waldkirchen 19 Apr 1895)
Public Security	*Eduard Baar-Baarenfels* (see Schuschnigg II)
Without Portfolio	11 Jul – 3 Nov 1936: *Edmund Glaise-Horstenau* (b. Braunau 27 Feb 1882; d. Nuremberg 20 Jul 1946)

3 Nov 1936 – 16 Feb 1938: Schuschnigg IV

Chancellor	*Kurt Schuschnigg* (for 4th time) (see Buresch II)
Vice Chancellor	*Ludwig Hülgerth* (b. Vienna 26 Jan 1875; d. Schloss Rottenstein, Carinthia, 13 Aug 1939)
Foreign Affairs	*Kurt Schuschnigg* (see Buresch II)
Home Affairs	*Edmund Glaise-Horstenau* (see Schuschnigg III)
Education	*Hans Pernter* (see Schuschnigg III)
Justice	*Adolf Pilz* (b. Vienna 1877)
Finance	*Rudolf Neumayer* (b. 1887)
Commerce and Transport	*William Taucher* (b. Fürstenfeld 26 May 1892; d. Graz 18 Apr 1962)
Social Administration	*Josef Resch* (see Ender)
Defence	*Kurt Schuschnigg* (see Buresch II)
Agriculture	*Peter Mandorfer* (see Schuschnigg III)
Public Security	3 Nov 1936 – 20 Mar 1937: *Odo Neustädter-Stürmer* (see Dollfuss II)
	20 Mar 1937 – 16 Feb 1938: *Kurt Schuschnigg* (see Buresch II)

16 Feb – 11 Mar 1938: Schuschnigg V

Chancellor	*Kurt Schuschnigg* (for 5th time) (see Buresch II)
Vice Chancellor	*Ludwig Hülgerth* (see Schuschnigg IV)
Foreign Affairs	*Guido Schmidt* (b. Bludenz 15 Jan 1901; d. Vienna 5 Dec 1957)
Home Affairs	*Arthur Seyss-Inquart* (see Presidents)
Education	*Hans Pernter* (see Schuschnigg III)
Justice	*Ludwig Adamovich* (b. Essegg 30 Apr 1890; d. Vienna 23 Sep 1955)
Finance	*Rudolf Neumayer* (see Schuschnigg IV)
Commerce and Transport	*Julius Raab* (b. St. Polten 29 Nov 1891; d. Vienna 8 Jan 1964)
Social Administration	*Josef Resch* (see Ender)
Defence	*Kurt Schuschnigg* (see Buresch II)
Agriculture	*Peter Mandorfer* (see Schuschnigg III)
Public Security	*Arthur Seyss-Inquart* (see Presidents)
Without Portfolio	*Guido Zernatto* (b. Treffen 21 Jul 1903; d. New York 11 Feb 1943)
	Edmund Glaise-Horstenau (see Schuschnigg III)
	Hans Rott

12 Mar – 24 May 1938: Seyss-Inquart I

Chancellor	*Arthur Seyss-Inquart* (for 1st time) (see Presidents)
Vice Chancellor	*Edmund Glaise-Horstenau* (see Schuschnigg III)
Foreign Affairs	12 – 15 Mar 1938: *William Wolff* (d. St. Polten 27 Jul 1939)
	15 Mar 1938: management of Austrian Foreign Affairs taken over by German Foreign Ministry
Home Affairs	*Arthur Seyss-Inquart* (see Presidents)
Education	*Oswald Menghin* (b. Meran 19 Apr 1888; d. 29 Nov 1974)
Justice	12 Mar – 1 May 1938: *Franz Hueber* (see Vaugoin)
	1 May 1938: ministry dissolved and the administration of its business put under the jurisdiction of the German Department of Justice, Hueber being charged with the job of winding it up
Finance	*Rudolf Neumayer* (see Schuschnigg IV)
Commerce and Transport	*Hans Fischböck* (b. Geras 24 Jan 1895; d. Florida, Buenos Aires Province, Argentina, 3 Jun 1967)
Social Administration	*Hugo Jury* (b. Moravská Radiměř 13 Jul 1887; d. Vienna(?) 24 May 1945)

Defence	*Arthur Seyss-Inquart* (see Presidents)
Agriculture	*Anton Reinthaller* (b. 14 Apr 1895)
Public Security	*Arthur Seyss-Inquart* (see Presidents)
Propaganda	*Hubert Klausner* (b. Raibl 1 Nov 1892; d. Vienna 12 Feb 1939)

24 May 1938 – 30 Apr 1939: Seyss-Inquart II

Prime Minister	*Arthur Seyss-Inquart* (for 2nd time) (see Presidents) as Governor
Home Affairs and Education (combined)	*Arthur Seyss-Inquart* (see Presidents)
Deputy Governor and Minister of the Interior	24 May 1938 – 12 Feb 1939: *Hubert Klausner* (see Seyss-Inquart I)
Justice	24 May 1938 – 8 Apr 1939: *Franz Hueber* (see Vaugoin) engaged in winding up the ministry
Finance	*Hans Fischböck* (see Seyss-Inquart I)
Commerce	*Hans Fischböck* (see Seyss-Inquart I)
Labour	Department wound up
Defence	Department wound up
Agriculture	*Anton Reinthaller* (see Seyss-Inquart I) responsible for forestry development
Public Security	Department wound up
Political Propaganda	Department wound up

From 1 May 1939 the Province of Austria ceased to exist; the districts of Vienna, Lower Danube, Upper Danube, Salzburg, Styria, Carinthia, Tyrol and Vorarlberg were administered directly by their own Reich Governors.

27 Apr – 20 Dec 1945: Renner IV (Government appointed by the occupying powers)

Chancellor	*Karl Renner* (SPÖ) (for 4th time) (see Presidents)
Vice Chancellors	*Leopold Figl* (ÖVP) (b. Rust 2 Oct 1902; d. 1965)
	Adolf Schärf (SPÖ) (see Presidents)
	Johann Koplenig (KPÖ) (b. St. Lorenzen 15 May 1891; d. Vienna 13 Dec 1968)
Foreign Affairs	26 Sep – 20 Dec 1945: *Karl Gruber* (ÖVP) (b. Innsbruck 3 May 1909) Under-Secretary of State in the Chancellery
Home Affairs	*Karl Honner* (KPÖ) (b. Friedberg 10 Sep 1893)

Education and Information	*Ernst Fischer* (KPÖ) (b. Komotau 3 Jul 1899)
Justice	*Josef Gerö* (b. Marien-Theresienstadt 23 Sep 1896; d. Vienna 28 Dec 1954)
Finance	*Georg Zimmermann* (b. Capodistria 18 Nov 1887)
Commerce and Industry	*Eduard Heinl* (ÖVP) (see Vaugoin)
Public Buildings and Reconstruction	*Julius Raab* (ÖVP) (see Schuschnigg V)
Social Administration	*Johann Böhm* (SPÖ) (b. Stogersbach 26 Jan 1886; d. Vienna 13 May 1959)
Agriculture and Forestry	27 Apr – 26 Sep 1945: *Rudolf Buchinger* (ÖVP) (b. Staasdorf 3 Mar 1879; d. Tulln 20 Feb 1950) 26 Sep – 20 Dec 1945: *Josef Kraus* (ÖVP) (b. Kroberg 23 Feb 1890)
Resources and Planning (new post)	26 Sep – 20 Dec 1945: *Vinzenz Schumy* (ÖVP) (see Schober III)
Food	*Andreas Korp* (SPÖ) (b. Graz 15 May 1897)

20 Dec 1945 – 11 Oct 1949: Figl I (Coalition of ÖVP and SPÖ)

Chancellor	*Leopold Figl* (ÖVP) (for 1st time) (see Renner IV)
Vice Chancellor	*Adolf Schärf* (SPÖ) (see Presidents)
Foreign Affairs	*Karl Gruber* (ÖVP) (see Renner IV)
Home Affairs	*Oskar Helmer* (SPÖ) (b. Tattendorf 16 Nov 1887; d. Vienna 13 Feb 1963)
Education	*Felix Hurdes* (ÖVP) (b. Bruneck 9 Aug 1901)
Justice	*Josef Gerö* (see Renner IV)
Finance	*Georg Zimmermann* (see Renner IV)
Commerce (from 18 Feb 1948: amalgamated with Ministry for Reconstruction)	20 Dec 1945 – 31 May 1946: *Eugen Fleischacker* (ÖVP) (b. Vienna 12 Oct 1899; d. Vienna 31 Mar 1953) 31 May 1946 – 18 Feb 1948: *Peter Krauland* (ÖVP) (b. Kraubath 6 Aug 1903) 18 Feb 1948 – 11 Oct 1949: *Ernst Kolb* (ÖVP) (b. Lauterach 9 Jan 1912)
Energy and Supply	20 Dec 1945 – 20 Nov 1947: *Karl Altmann* (KPÖ) (b. Vienna 8 Jan 1904) 24 Nov 1947 – 11 Oct 1949: *Alfred Migsch* (SPÖ) (b. Vienna 5 Nov 1901)
Transport	*Vinzenz Übeleis* (SPÖ) (b. Gramastetten 16 Aug 1889)
Public Works (until 15 May 1948) and Reconstruction	*Julius Raab* (ÖVP) (see Schuschnigg V)

AUSTRIA

Social Administration	*Karl Maisel* (SPÖ) (b. Vienna 3 Nov 1890)
Agriculture and Forestry	*Josef Kraus* (ÖVP) (see Renner IV)
Planning	*Peter Krauland* (ÖVP) (see above)
Food	20 Dec 1945 – 11 Jan 1947: *Hans Frenzel* (SPÖ) (b. Herzogenburg 7 Sep 1895)
	11 Jan 1947 – 11 Oct 1949: *Otto Sagmeister* (SPÖ) (b. Gloggnitz 10 Jan 1906)
Without Portfolio	20 Dec 1945 – 11 Jan 1947: *Alois Weinberger* (ÖVP) (b. Markt-Eisenstein 22 Jun 1902; d. 17 Mar 1961)
	11 Jan 1947 – 11 Oct 1949: *Erwin Altenburger* (ÖVP) (b. Mautern 3 Nov 1903)

7 Nov 1949 – 22 Oct 1952: Figl II (Coalition of ÖVP and SPÖ)

Chancellor	*Leopold Figl* (ÖVP) (for 2nd time) (see Renner IV)
Vice Chancellor	*Adolf Schärf* (SPÖ) (see Presidents)
Foreign Affairs	*Karl Gruber* (ÖVP) (see Renner IV)
Home Affairs	*Oskar Helmer* (SPÖ) (see Figl I)
Education	7 Nov 1949 – 23 Jan 1952: *Felix Hurdes* (ÖVP) (see Figl I)
	23 Jan – 22 Oct 1952: *Ernst Kolb* (ÖVP) (see Figl I)
Justice	7 Nov 1949 – 13 Sep 1952: *Otto Tschadek* (SPÖ) (b. Trautmannsdorf 31 Oct 1904; d. Vienna 4 Feb 1969)
	13 Sep – 22 Oct 1952: *Josef Gerö* (see Renner IV)
Finance	7 Nov 1949 – 23 Jan 1952: *Eugen Margaretha* (ÖVP) (b. Perchtoldsdorf 6 Jul 1885)
	23 Jan – 22 Oct 1952: *Reinhard Kamitz* (ÖVP) (b. Halbstadt 18 Jun 1907)
Commerce and Reconstruction	7 Nov 1949 – 23 Jan 1952: *Ernst Kolb* (see Figl I)
	23 Jan – 22 Oct 1952: *Joseph C. Böck-Greissau* (ÖVP) (b. St. Michael 5 Apr 1893; d. Vienna 21 Apr 1953)
Social Affairs	*Karl Maisel* (SPÖ) (see Figl I)
Transport and Nationalised Undertakings	*Karl Waldbrunner* (SPÖ) (b. Vienna 25 Nov 1906)
Agriculture	7 Nov 1949 – 23 Jan 1952: *Josef Kraus* (ÖVP) (see Renner IV)
	23 Jan – 22 Oct 1952: *Franz Josef Thoma* (ÖVP) (b. Grobming 30 Jul 1886; d. Graz 10 Jul 1966)

28 Oct 1952 – 25 Feb 1953: Figl III (Coalition of ÖVP and SPÖ)

Chancellor *Leopold Figl* (ÖVP) (for 3rd time) (see Renner IV) Ministerial appointments remained unchanged from previous cabinet

1 Apr 1953 – 28 Feb/14 May 1956: Raab I (Coalition of ÖVP and SPÖ)

Chancellor	*Julius Raab* (ÖVP) (for 1st time) (see Schuschnigg V)
Vice Chancellor	*Adolf Schärf* (SPÖ) (see Presidents)
Foreign Affairs	1 Apr – 13 Nov 1953: *Karl Gruber* (ÖVP) (see Renner IV)
	25 Nov 1953 – 14 May 1956: *Leopold Figl* (ÖVP) (see Renner IV)
Home Affairs	*Oskar Helmer* (SPÖ) (see Figl I)
Education	1 Apr 1953 – 21 Oct 1954: *Ernst Kolb* (ÖVP) (see Figl I)
	2 Nov 1954 – 14 May 1956: *Heinrich Drimmel* (ÖVP) (b. Vienna 16 Jan 1912)
Justice	1 Apr 1953 – 28 Dec 1954: *Josef Gerö* (see Renner IV)
	Jan 1955 – 14 May 1956: *Hans Kapfer* (b. Sollenau 5 Sep 1903)
Finance	*Reinhard Kamitz* (ÖVP) (see Figl II)
Commerce and Reconstruction	1 – 21 Apr 1953: *Josef C. Böck-Greissau* (ÖVP) (see Figl II)
	28 Apr 1953 – 14 May 1956: *Udo Illig* (ÖVP) (b. Graz 13 Apr 1897)
Social Affairs	*Karl Maisel* (SPÖ) (see Figl I)
Transport and Public Building	*Karl Waldbrunner* (SPÖ) (see Figl II)
Agriculture	*Franz Josef Thoma* (ÖVP) (see Figl II)

23 Jun 1956 – 11 May 1959: Raab II (Coalition of ÖVP and SPÖ)

Chancellor	*Julius Raab* (ÖVP) (for 2nd time) (see Schuschnigg V)
Vice Chancellor	23 Jun 1956 – 22 May 1957: *Adolf Schärf* (SPÖ) (see Presidents)
	22 May 1957 – 11 May 1959: *Bruno Pittermann* (SPÖ) (b. Vienna 3 Sep 1905)
Foreign Affairs	*Leopold Figl* (ÖVP) (see Renner IV)
Home Affairs	*Oskar Helmer* (SPÖ) (see Figl I)
Education	*Heinrich Drimmel* (ÖVP) (see Raab I)

47

Justice	*Otto Tschadek* (SPÖ) (see Figl II)
Defence	*Ferdinand Graf* (ÖVP) (b. Klagenfurt 15 Jun 1905; d. Vienna 8 Sep 1969)
Finance	*Reinhard Kamitz* (ÖVP) (see Figl II)
Commerce and Reconstruction	23 Jun – 17 Sep 1956: *Udo Illig* (ÖVP) (see Raab I) 19 Sep 1956 – 11 May 1959: *Fritz Bock* (ÖVP) (b. Vienna 26 Feb 1911)
Social Affairs	*Anton Proksch* (SPÖ) (b. Vienna 21 Apr 1897)
Transport and Electricity	*Karl Waldbrunner* (SPÖ) (see Figl II)
Agriculture and Forestry	*Franz Josef Thoma* (ÖVP) (see Figl II)

16 Jul 1959 – 11 Apr 1961: Raab III (Coalition of ÖVP and SPÖ)

Chancellor	*Julius Raab* (ÖVP) (for 3rd time) (see Schuschnigg V)
Vice Chancellor	*Bruno Pittermann* (SPÖ) (see Raab II)
Foreign Affairs	*Bruno Kreisky* (SPÖ) (see Presidents)
Home Affairs	*Josef Afritsch* (SPÖ) (b. Graz 13 Mar 1901; d. Vienna 26 Mar 1964)
Education	*Heinrich Drimmel* (ÖVP) (see Raab I)
Justice	*Otto Tschadek* (SPÖ) (see Figl II)
Defence	*Ferdinand Graf* (ÖVP) (see Raab II)
Finance	16 Jul 1959 – 19 Jun 1960: *Reinhard Kamitz* (ÖVP) (see Figl II) 19 Jun 1960 – 11 Apr 1961: *Eduard Heilingsetzer* (ÖVP) (b. Vienna 12 Jul 1905)
Commerce	*Fritz Bock* (ÖVP) (see Raab II)
Social Affairs	*Anton Proksch* (SPÖ) (see Raab II)
Transport	*Karl Waldbrunner* (SPÖ) (see Figl II)
Nationalised Undertakings	*Bruno Pittermann* (SPÖ) (see Raab II)
Agriculture and Forestry	*Eduard Hartmann* (ÖVP) (b. Vienna 3 Sep 1904; d. Vienna 14 Oct 1966)

11 Apr 1961 – 20 Nov 1962/27 Mar 1963: Gorbach I (Coalition of ÖVP and SPÖ)

Chancellor	*Alfons Gorbach* (ÖVP) (for 1st time) (b. Imst 2 Sep 1898; d. 31 Jul 1972)
Vice Chancellor	*Bruno Pittermann* (SPÖ) (see Raab II)
Foreign Affairs	*Bruno Kreisky* (SPÖ) (see Presidents)
Home Affairs	*Josef Afritsch* (SPÖ) (see Raab III)

Education	*Heinrich Drimmel* (ÖVP) (see Raab I)
Justice	*Hans Christian Broda* (SPÖ) (b. Vienna 12 Mar 1916)
Defence	*Karl Schleinzer* (ÖVP) (b. Kärnten 8 Jan 1924; d. 19 Jul 1975)
Finance	*Josef Klaus* (ÖVP) (b. Mauthen 15 Mar 1910)
Commerce	*Fritz Bock* (ÖVP) (see Raab II)
Social Affairs	*Anton Proksch* (SPÖ) (see Raab II)
Transport	*Karl Waldbrunner* (SPÖ) (see Figl II)
Nationalised Undertakings	(acting:) *Bruno Pittermann* (SPÖ) (see Raab II)
Agriculture and Forestry	*Eduard Hartmann* (ÖVP) (see Raab III)

27 Mar 1963 - 25 Feb/2 Apr 1964: Gorbach II (Coalition of ÖVP and SPÖ)

Chancellor	*Alfons Gorbach* (ÖVP) (for 2nd time) (see Gorbach I)
Vice Chancellor	*Bruno Pittermann* (SPÖ) (see Raab II)
Foreign Affairs	*Bruno Kreisky* (SPÖ) (see Presidents)
Home Affairs	*Franz Olah* (SPÖ) (b. Vienna 13 Mar 1910)
Education	*Heinrich Drimmel* (ÖVP) (see Raab I)
Justice	*Hans Christian Broda* (SPÖ) (see Gorbach I)
Defence	*Karl Schleinzer* (ÖVP) (see Gorbach I)
Finance	*Franz Korinek* (ÖVP) (b. Schlösselhof 20 May 1907)
Commerce	*Fritz Bock* (ÖVP) (see Raab II)
Social Affairs	*Anton Proksch* (SPÖ) (see Raab II)
Transport	*Otto Probst* (SPÖ) (b. Vienna 29 Dec 1911)
Agriculture and Forestry	*Eduard Hartmann* (ÖVP) (see Raab III)

2 Apr 1964 - 23 Oct 1965/19 Apr 1966: Klaus I (Coalition of ÖVP and SPÖ)

Chancellor	*Josef Klaus* (ÖVP) (for 1st time) (see Gorbach I)
Vice Chancellor	*Bruno Pittermann* (SPÖ) (see Raab II)
Foreign Affairs	*Bruno Kreisky* (SPÖ) (see Presidents)
Home Affairs	2 Apr - 17 Sep 1964: *Franz Olah* (SPÖ, later DFP) (see Gorbach II)
	22 Sep 1964 - 23 Oct 1965/19 Apr 1966: *Hans Czettel* (SPÖ) (b. Vienna 20 Apr 1923)
Education	*Theodor Piffl-Perčević* (ÖVP) (b. Meran 17 Sep 1911)
Justice	*Hans Christian Broda* (SPÖ) (see Gorbach I)
Defence	*Georg Prader* (ÖVP) (b. Sankt-Pölten 15 Jun 1917)
Finance	*Wolfgang Schmitz* (ÖVP) (b. Vienna 28 May 1923)
Commerce	*Fritz Bock* (ÖVP) (see Raab II)

49

AUSTRIA

Social Affairs	*Anton Proksch* (SPÖ) (see Raab II)
Transport	*Otto Probst* (SPÖ) (see Gorbach II)
Agriculture and Forestry	*Karl Schleinzer* (ÖVP) (see Gorbach I)

19 Apr 1966 – 19 Jan 1968: Klaus II (ÖVP)

Chancellor	*Josef Klaus* (for 2nd time) (see Gorbach I)
Vice Chancellor	*Fritz Bock* (see Raab II)
Foreign Affairs	*Lujo Tončić-Sorinj* (b. Vienna 12 Apr 1915)
Home Affairs	*Franz Hetzenauer* (b. Kufstein 25 Feb 1911)
Education	*Theodor Piffl-Perčević* (see Klaus I)
Justice	*Hans Klecatsky* (b. Vienna 6 Nov 1920)
Defence	*Georg Prader* (see Klaus I)
Finance	*Wolfgang Schmitz* (see Klaus I)
Commerce and Reconstruction	*Fritz Bock* (see Raab II)
Social Administration	*Grete Rehor* (b. Vienna 30 Jun 1910)
Transport	*Ludwig Weiss* (b. Klagenfurt 25 Aug 1902)
Agriculture and Forestry	*Karl Schleinzer* (see Gorbach I)
Without Portfolio	*Vinzenz Kotzina* (b. Neunkirchen 30 Mar 1908)

19 Jan 1968 – 3 Mar 1970: Klaus III (ÖVP)

Chancellor	*Josef Klaus* (for 3rd time) (see Gorbach I)
Vice Chancellor	*Hermann Withalm* (b. Gaweinstal 21 Apr 1912)
Foreign Affairs	*Kurt Waldheim* (b. St. Andrä 21 Dec 1918)
Home Affairs	*Franz Soronics* (b. Eisenstadt 25 Jul 1920)
Education	19 Jan 1968 – 30 May 1969: *Theodor Piffl-Perčević* (see Klaus I)
	30 May 1969 – 3 Mar 1970: *Alois Mock* (b. Euratsfeld 10 Jun 1934)
Justice	*Hans Klecatsky* (see Klaus II)
Defence	*Georg Prader* (see Klaus I)
Finance	*Stephen Koren* (b. Wiener Neustadt 14 Nov 1919)
Commerce and Industry	*Otto Mitterer* (b. Vienna 22 Oct 1911)
Social Affairs	*Grete Rehor* (see Klaus II)
Transport and Nationalised Undertakings	*Ludwig Weiss* (see Klaus II)
Agriculture and Forestry	*Karl Schleinzer* (see Gorbach I)

| Buildings and Technology | *Vinzenz Kotzina* (see Klaus II) |

from 20 Apr 1970: Kreisky (SPÖ Minority Government)

Chancellor	*Bruno Kreisky* (see Presidents)
Vice Chancellor	*Rudolf Häuser* (b. Vienna 19 Mar 1909)
Foreign Affairs	20 Apr 1970 – 25 Jun 1974: *Rudolf Kirchschläger* (see Presidents)
	from 25 Jun 1974: *Erich Bielka-Karltreu* (b. Vienna 12 May 1908)
Home Affairs	*Otto Rösch* (b. Vienna 24 Mar 1917)
Education	20 Apr 1970 – 21 Oct 1971: *Leopold Gratz* (b. Vienna 4 Nov 1929)
	from 21 Oct 1971: *Alfred Sinowatz* (b. 1929?)
Research (divided from Education)	from Jun 1970: *Hertha Firnberg* (b. Niederrussbach 18 Sep 1909)
Justice	*Hans Christian Broda* (see Gorbach I)
Defence	20 Apr 1970 – 4 Feb 1971: *Johann Freihsler* (b. Vienna 4 Dec 1917)
	from 8 Feb 1971: *Karl Lütgendorf*
Finance	*Hannes Androsch* (b. Vienna 18 Apr 1938)
Commerce	*Josef Staribacher* (b. Vienna 25 Mar 1921)
Social Affairs	*Rudolf Häuser* (see above)
Housing	*Josef Moser* (b. Sankt Lambrecht 2 Jan 1919)
Transport	*Erwin Frühbauer* (b. Knittelfeld 11 Apr 1926)
Agriculture and Forestry	20 Apr – 20 May 1970: *Hans Öllinger* (b. 1917)
	from 21 May 1970: *Oscar Weihs* (b. Vienna 19 Apr 1911)
Health and Environment (new post)	from 21 Oct 1971: *Ingrid Leodolter* (b. 1919?) at first without portfolio
Family Policy (Secretary of State) (new post)	from 21 Oct 1971: *Elfriede Karl* (b. 1933?)

Bahamas

| 7 Jan 1964 | Internal self-government |

9 Jul 1973   Independence (member of Commonwealth)

HEADS OF STATE

Governors

3 Jan 1964   *Sir Ralph Francis Alnwick Grey* (from 17 Sep 1968: *Baron Grey of Naunton*) (b. 15 Apr 1910)
23 Jul 1968   *Sir Francis Edward Hovell-Thurlow-Cumming-Bruce* (from 1971: *8th Baron Thurlow*) (b. 9 Mar 1912)

Governor-General

1 Aug 1973   *Sir Milo (Broughton) Butler* (b. 11 Aug 1906)

MEMBERS OF GOVERNMENT

Prime Ministers

7 Jan 1964   *Sir Roland Theodore Symonette* (b. 16 Dec 1898)
from 16 Jan 1967   *Lynden Oscar Pindling* (b. 22 Mar 1930)

Bangladesh

Until 1971	Part of Pakistan
17 Apr 1971	Declaration of independence followed by fighting between Pakistani forces and secessionists aided by Indian forces
16 Dec 1971	Surrender of Pakistani forces
11 Jan 1972	Adoption of provisional constitution

HEADS OF STATE

Presidents

17 Apr 1971	*Sheikh Mujibur Rahman* (for 1st time) (b. Tungipara, Faridpur district, 17 Mar 1920; d. (assassinated) Dacca 15 Aug 1975)
12 Jan 1972	*Abu Sayeed Chowdhury*
24 Dec 1973	*Mohammadullah* (acting until 24 Jan 1974)
25 Jan 1975	*Sheikh Mujibur Rahman* (for 2nd time)
15 Aug 1975	*Khandaker Moshtaque Ahmed* (b. 1918)
from 6 Nov 1975	*Abusadat Mohammad Sayem* (b. 1 Mar 1916)

MEMBERS OF GOVERNMENT

Prime Ministers

17 Apr 1971	*Tajuddin Ahmed* (d. 3 Nov 1975)
12 Jan 1972	*Sheikh Mujibur Rahman* (see Presidents)
26 Jan 1975	*M. Mansoor Ali*
from 15 Aug 1975	Cabinet led by President

Barbados

30 Nov 1966	Independence (member of the Commonwealth)

HEADS OF STATE

Governors-General

30 Nov 1966	*Sir John Montague Stow* (b. Simla, India, 3 Oct 1911)
from 15 May 1967	*Sir Winston Scott* (b. 27 Mar 1900)

53

BARBADOS

MEMBER OF GOVERNMENT

Prime Minister

from 30 Dec 1966   *Errol Walton Barrow* (b. Barbados 21(12?) Jan 1920)

Belgium

HEADS OF STATE

Kings

17 Dec 1909	*Albert*, nephew of Leopold II (b. 8 Apr 1875)
17 Feb 1934 – 11 Aug 1950	*Leopold III*, son (b. 3 Nov 1901) held prisoner by the Germans at Laeken 1940–1944; in Austria 1944–1945 and Switzerland 1945–1950, returning to Belgium 18 Jul 1950; abdicated
20 Sep 1944 – 17 Jul 1950	*Charles, Count of Flanders*, brother, Regent
from 11 Aug 1950	*Baudouin*, son (b. 7 Sep 1930) Prince Royal, assumed title of King 17 Jul 1951

MEMBERS OF GOVERNMENT

4 Dec 1929 – 21 May 1931: Jaspar III

Prime Minister	*Henri Jaspar* (Cath) (for 3rd time) (b. Schaerbeek 28 Jul 1870; d. Brussels 15 Feb 1939)*
Foreign Affairs	*Paul Hymans* (Lib) (b. Brussels 23 Mar 1865; d. Nice 8 Mar 1941)*
Home Affairs	*Hendrik Baels* (Cath) (b. Ostend 1878; d. Knokke 14 Jun 1951)*
Justice	*Paul Émile Janson* (Lib) (b. 30 May 1872; d. Weimar 4 Jul 1944)*
Finance	*Maurice, Baron Houtart* (Cath)*

*For earlier career see vol. 2

54

Arts and Sciences	*Maurice Vauthier* Lib) (b. 2 Mar 1860; d. Brussels 25 Jun 1931)*
Defence	*Charles, Comte de Broqueville* (Cath) (b. Moll 4 Dec 1860; d. Moll 4 Sep 1940)*
Colonies	4–25 Dec 1929: *Paul Tschoffen* (Cath) (b. Dinant 8 May 1878; d. Liège 11 Jul 1961)*
	25 Dec 1929 – 18 May 1931: *Henri Jaspar* (Cath) (see above)
	18–21 May 1931: *Paul Charles* (Cath) (b. St Josse-ten-Noode 28 Apr 1885; d. St Josse-ten-Noode 6 Apr 1954)

5 Jun 1931 – 18 May 1932: Renkin I

Prime Minister	*Jules Renkin* (Cath) (for 1st time) (b. Elsene 3 Dec 1862; d. Brussels 16 Jul 1934)*
Foreign Affairs	*Paul Hymans* (Lib) (see Jaspar III)
Home Affairs	5 Jun 1931 – 20 Feb 1932: *Jules Renkin* (Cath) (see above)
	20 Feb – 18 May 1932: *Henri, Comte Carton de Wiart* (Cath) (b. Brussels 31 Jan 1869; d. Brussels 6 May 1951)*
Justice	*(Alphonse Lambert Joseph) Fernand Cocq* (Lib) (b. Huy 5 Jul 1861; d. Ixelles 11 Dec 1940)
Finance	5 Jun 1931 – 20 Feb 1932: *Maurice, Baron Houtart* (Cath) (see Jaspar III)
	20 Feb – 18 May 1932: *Jules Renkin* (Cath) (see above)
Arts and Sciences	*Robert (Charles François) Petitjean* (Lib) (b. Ledeberg 25 Oct 1887; d. Brussels 24 Nov 1951)
Defence	*Henri J. C. E. Denis* (b. Marbais 10 Sep 1877; d. Brussels 19 Jan 1957)
Colonies	*Paul (Gustave Corneille) Crokaert* (b. Brussels 1 Dec 1875; d. Brussels 4 Apr 1955)

23 May – 18 Oct 1932: Renkin II

Prime Minister	*Jules Renkin* (Cath) (for 2nd time) (see Renkin I)
Foreign Affairs	*Paul Hymans* (Lib) (see Jaspar III)
Home Affairs	*Henri, Comte Carton de Wiart* (Cath) (see Renkin I)
Justice	*(Alphonse Lambert Joseph) Fernand Cocq* (Lib) (see Renkin I)

*For earlier career see vol. 2

55

Finance	*Jules Renkin* (Cath) (see Renkin I)
Arts and Sciences	*Robert (Charles François) Petitjean* (Lib) (see Renkin I)
Defence	*Paul (Gustave Corneille) Crokaert* (Cath) (see Renkin I)
Colonies	*Paul Tschoffen* (Christ Dem) (see Jaspar III)

22 Oct - 13 Dec 1932: Broqueville II

Prime Minister	*Charles, Comte de Broqueville* (Cath) (for 2nd time) (see Jaspar III)
Foreign Affairs	*Paul Hymans* (Lib) (see Jaspar III)
Home Affairs	*Prosper, Vicomte Poullet* (Christ Dem) (b. Louvain 5 Mar 1868; d. 3 Dec 1937)*
Justice	*Paul Émile Janson* (Lib) (see Jaspar III)
Finance	*Henri Jaspar* (Cath) (see Jaspar III)
Defence	*Georges Theunis* (Cath) (b. Liège 18 Feb 1873; d. Monty-sur-Marchienne 21 Aug 1944)
Colonies	*Paul Tschoffen* (Christ Dem) (see Jaspar III)

18 Dec 1932 - 6 Jun 1934: Broqueville III

Prime Minister	*Charles, Comte de Broqueville* (Cath) (for 3rd time) (see Jaspar III)
Foreign Affairs	*Paul Hymans* (Lib) (see Jaspar III)
Home Affairs	18 Dec 1932 - 11 Jan 1934: *Prosper, Vicomte Poullet* (Christ Dem) (see Broqueville II)
	11 Jan - 6 Jun 1934: *Hubert Pierlot* (Cath) (b. Cugnon 23 Dec 1883; d. Brussels 13 Dec 1963)
Justice	*Paul Émile Janson* (Lib) (see Jaspar III)
Finance	*Henri Jaspar* (Cath) (see Jaspar III)
Arts and Sciences	*Maurice Auguste, Comte Lippens* (Lib) (b. Ghent 21 Aug 1875; d. Brussels 13 Jul 1956)
Defence	*Albert Devèze* (b. Ypres 6 Jun 1881)*
Colonies	*Paul Tschoffen* (Christ Dem) (see Jaspar III)

12 Jun - 13 Nov 1934: Broqueville IV

Prime Minister	*Charles, Comte de Broqueville* (Cath) (for 4th time) (see Jaspar III)

*For earlier career see vol. 2

Foreign Affairs	*Henri Jaspar* (Cath) (see Jaspar III)
Home Affairs	*Hubert Pierlot* (Cath) (see Broqueville III)
Justice	*François (Louis Charles Marie) Bovesse* (Lib) (b. Namur 10 Jun 1890; d. Namur 1 Feb 1944)
Finance	*Gustave Sap* (b. Kortemark 21 Jan 1896; d. Brussels night of 18/19 Mar 1940)
Education	*Victor (Eugene Ange Jules) Maistriau* (Lib) (b. Maurage 5 Oct 1870; d. Mons 21 Jan 1962)
Defence	*Albert Devèze* (see Broqueville III)
Colonies	*Paul Tschoffen* (Christ Dem) (see Jaspar III)

19 Nov 1934 - 19 Mar 1935: Theunis III

Prime Minister	*Georges Theunis* (Cath) (for 3rd time) (see Broqueville II)
Foreign Affairs	*Paul Hymans* (Lib) (see Jaspar III)
Home Affairs	*Hubert Pierlot* (Cath) (see Broqueville III)
Justice	*Georges Theunis* (Cath) (see Broqueville II)
Finance	*Camille Gutt* (no party) (b. Brussels 14 Nov 1884; d. Brussels 7 Jun 1971)
Education	*Jules Hiernaux* (Lib) (b. Berchem 27 Jul 1885; d. Montignies-le-Tilleul 29 Jul 1944)
Defence	*Albert Devèze* (see Broqueville III)
Colonies	*Paul Charles* (no party) (see Jaspar III)
Without Portfolio	*Émile Francqui* (b. Brussels 25 Jun 1863; d. Overyssche 16 Nov 1935)*

26 Mar 1935 - 6 May 1936: Zeeland I

Prime Minister	*Paul van Zeeland* (Cath) (for 1st time) (b. Zinik 11 Nov 1893; d. 22 Sep 1973)
Foreign Affairs	*Paul van Zeeland* (see above)
Home Affairs	*Charles (Paul Marie Léon), Vicomte du Bus de Warnaffe* (Cath) (b. Brussels 16 Sep 1894; d. Brussels 23 Oct 1965)
Justice	*Eugène Soudan* (Soc) (b. 1879?)
Finance	*Max Léo Gérard* (Lib) (b. Liège 24 Apr 1879; d. Brussels 26 Nov 1955)
Education and Fine Arts	*François (Louis Charles Marie) Bovesse* (Lib) (see Broqueville IV)

*For earlier career see vol. 2

57

Defence	*Albert Devèze* (Lib) (see Broqueville III)
Colonies	*Edmond Rubbens* (Cath) (b. Zele 15 Jan 1894; d. 27 Apr 1938)
Without Portfolio	*Emile Vandervelde* (Soc) (b. Elsene 25 Jan 1866; d. Brussels 27 Dec 1938)*
	Prosper, Vicomte Poullet (Christ Dem) (see Broqueville II)
	Paul Hymans (Lib) (see Jaspar III)

13 Jun 1936 – 25 Oct 1937: Zeeland II

Prime Minister	*Paul van Zeeland* (Cath) (for 2nd time) (see Zeeland I)
Foreign Affairs	*Paul Henri Spaak* (Soc) (b. Brussels 25 Jan 1899; d. Brussels 31 Jul 1972)
Home Affairs	*Auguste de Schryver* (Cath) (b. Ghent 16 May 1898)
Justice	13 Jun 1936 – 11 Apr 1937: *François (Louis Charles Marie) Bovesse* (Lib) (see Broqueville IV)
	21 Apr – 13 Jul 1937: *Victor de Laveleye* (Lib) (b. Brussels 5 Nov 1894; d. Ixelles 15 Dec 1945)
	18 Aug – 25 Oct 1937: *Victor (Eugène Ange Jules) Maistriau* (Lib) (see Broqueville IV)
Finance	*Hendrik de Man* (Soc) (b. Antwerp 17 Nov 1885; d. Murten, Switzerland, 20 Jun 1953)
Education	*Jules Hoste* (Lib) (b. Brussels 7 Jun 1884; d. 1 Feb 1953)
Defence	*Henri J. C. E. Denis* (Lib) (see Renkin I)
Colonies	*Edmond Rubbens* (Cath) (see Zeeland I)

24 Nov 1937 – 13 May 1938: Janson

Prime Minister	*Paul Émile Janson* (Lib) (see Jaspar III)
Foreign Affairs	*Paul Henri Spaak* (Soc) (see Zeeland II)
Home Affairs	*Octave Victor Dierckx* (Lib) (b. Antwerp 15 Oct 1882; d. Ukkel 21 Mar 1955)
Justice	*Charles (Paul Marie Léon), Vicomte du Bus de Warnaffe* (Cath) (see Zeeland I)
Finance	24 Nov 1937 – 9 Mar 1938: *Hendrik de Man* (Soc) (see Zeeland II)
	11 Mar – 13 May 1938: *Eugène Soudan* (Soc) (see Zeeland I)
Education	*Jules Hoste* (Lib) (see Zeeland II)
Defence	*Henri J. C. E. Denis* (Lib) (see Renkin I)

*For earlier career see vol. 2

Colonies   24 Nov 1937 – 27 Apr 1938: *Edmond Rubbens* (Cath)
                            (see Zeeland I)

15 May 1938 – 9 Feb 1939: Spaak I

Prime Minister	*Paul Henri Spaak* (Soc) (for 1st time) (see Zeeland II)
Foreign Affairs	15 May 1938 – 15 Jan 1939: *Paul Henri Spaak* (Soc) (see Zeeland II)
	15 Jan – 9 Feb 1939: *Paul Émile Janson* (Lib) (see Jaspar III)
Home Affairs and Public Health	*Joseph Merlot* (b. Liège 14 Sep 1885)
Justice	15 May 1938 – 20 Jan 1939: *(Clovis Louis Marie Emmanuel) Joseph Pholien* (Cath) (b. Liège 28 Dec 1884; d. Brussels 4 Jan 1968)
	20 Jan – 9 Feb 1939: *Josse Emile, Baron van Dievoet* (Christ Dem) (b. St. Katharina Lombeek 10 Jun 1896; d. Louvain 24 Jun 1967)
Finance	15 May – 2 Dec 1938: *Max Léo Gérard* (Lib) (see Zeeland I)
	4 Dec 1938 – 9 Feb 1939: *Albert (Édouard) Janssen* (Cath) (b. Antwerp 1 Apr 1883; d. Hammn-Mille 29 Mar 1966)*
Education and Fine Arts	*Octave Victor Dierckx* (Lib) (see Janson)
Defence	*Henri J. C. E. Denis* (Lib) (see Renkin I)
Colonies	*(Jozef) Albert, Baron de Vleeschauwer* (Cath) (b. Nederbrakel 1 Jan 1897; d. Kortenberg 24 Feb 1971)

20 Feb – 12 Apr 1939: Pierlot I

Prime Minister	*Hubert Pierlot* (Cath) (for 1st time) (see Broqueville III)
Foreign Affairs	*Eugène Soudan* (Soc) (see Zeeland I)
Home Affairs	*Willem Eekelers* (Soc) (b. Mons 2 Sep 1883; d. Brussels 18 May 1954)
Justice	*Auguste de Schryver* (Cath) (see Zeeland II)
Finance	*Camille Gutt* (no party) (see Theunis III)
Education	*Edgard Blancquaert* (no party) (b. Dendermonde 20 Jun 1894; d. Mariakerke 29 Sep 1964)
Defence	*Henri J. C. E. Denis* (Lib) (see Renkin I)

*For earlier career see vol. 2

Colonies   *(Jozef) Albert, Baron de Vleeschauwer* (Cath) (see Spaak I)

18 Apr 1939 – 5 Jan 1940: Pierlot II

Prime Minister	*Hubert Pierlot* (Cath) (for 2nd time) (see Broqueville III)
Foreign Affairs	18 Apr – 4 Sep 1939: *Hubert Pierlot* (Cath) (see Broqueville III)
	4 Sep 1939 – 5 Jan 1940: *Paul Henri Spaak* (Soc) (see Zeeland II)
Home Affairs	*Albert Devèze* (Lib) (see Broqueville III)
Justice	18 Apr – 4 Sep 1939: *Paul Émile Janson* (Lib) (see Jaspar III)
	4 Sep 1939 – 5 Jan 1940: *Eugène Soudan* (Soc) (see Zeeland I)
Finance	*Camille Gutt* (no party) (see Theunis III)
Education	*Jules Duesberg* (Lib) (b. Verviers 29 Sep 1881; d. Louvain 12 Jul 1947)
Defence	*Henri J. C. E. Denis* (Lib) (see Renkin I)
Colonies	*(Jozef) Albert, Baron de Vleeschauwer* (Cath) (see Spaak I)

5 Jan 1940 – 19 Sep 1944: Pierlot III (from 25 May 1940 located at Vichy, terminated on 20 Sep 1940 but reconstituted on same day in London)

Prime Minister	*Hubert Pierlot* (Cath) (for 3rd time) (see Broqueville III) arrived in London on 28 Oct 1940)
Foreign Affairs and Foreign Commerce	*Paul Henri Spaak* (Soc) (see Zeeland II) arrived in London on 28 Oct 1940
Home Affairs	*(Pieter Frans) Arthur Vanderpoorten* (Lib) (b. Puurs 17 Feb 1884; d. Belsen 3 Apr 1945)
Justice	5 Jan – 19 Sep 1940: *Paul Émile Janson* (Lib) (see Jaspar III)
Finance	*Camille Gutt* (no party) (see Theunis III)
Education	*Eugène Soudan* (Soc) (see Zeeland I)
Defence	5 Jan – 19 Sep 1940: *Henri J. C. E. Denis* (no party, later Liberal) (see Renkin I)
	20 Sep 1940 – 3 Oct 1942: *Camille Gutt* (no party) (see Theunis III)
	3 Oct 1942 – 19 Sep 1944: *Hubert Pierlot* (Cath) (see Broqueville III)

Colonies	*(Jozef) Albert, Baron de Vleeschauwer* (Cath) (see Spaak I) During the period of exile there were some changes, the final office-holders being:
Home Affairs	*Auguste de Schryver* (Christ Soc) (see Zeeland II)
Justice	*Antoine (Louis Philippe Ghislain) Delfosse* (b. Opprebais 25 Jun 1895)
Education	*(Jozef) Albert, Baron de Vleeschauwer* (Christ Soc) (see Spaak I)

26 Sep/6 Oct 1944 – 2 Feb 1945: Pierlot IV (All-Party Coalition)

Prime Minister	*Hubert Pierlot* (Cath) (for 4th time) (see Broqueville III)
Foreign Affairs	*Paul Henri Spaak* (Soc) (see Zeeland II)
Home Affairs	*Edmond Ronse* (Christ Soc) (b. Ghent 15 Mar 1889; d. Melsen 3 Jul 1970)
Justice	*Maurice Verbaet* (Christ Soc)
Finance	*Camille Gutt* (Lib) (see Theunis III)
Education	*Victor de Laveleye* (Lib) (see Zeeland II)
Defence	*Fernand Demets* (b. St. Gilles 8 Mar 1884; d. Brussels 29 Sep 1952)
Colonies	*(Jozef) Albert, Baron de Vleeschauwer* (Christ Soc) (see Spaak I)
Labour and Welfare	*Achille van Acker* (Soc) (b. Bruges 8 Apr 1898; d. Bruges 10 Jul 1975)

11 Feb 1945 – 18 Feb 1946: Acker I (All-Party Coalition)

Prime Minister	*Achille van Acker* (Soc) (for 1st time) (see Pierlot IV)
Foreign Affairs	*Paul Henri Spaak* (Soc) (see Zeeland II)
Home Affairs	*Gustave Adolphe van Glabbeke* (Lib) (b. Ostend 8 Aug 1904; d. Zanzibar 5 Jul 1959)
Justice	11 Feb – 31 Jul 1945: *Charles (Paul Marie Léon), Vicomte du Bus de Warnaffe* (Christ Soc) (see Zeeland I) 31 Jul 1945 – 18 Feb 1946: *Marcel Grégoire* (b. Hensy 24 Mar 1907)
Finance	11 Feb – 31 Jul 1945: *Gaston Eyskens* (Christ Soc) (b. Lier 1 Apr 1905) 31 Jul 1945 – 18 Feb 1946: *Franz Joseph de Voghel* (no party) (b. Molenbeek-Saint-Jean 21 Dec 1903)

Education	*Auguste (Dieudonné Eugène) Buisseret* (Lib) (b. Beauraing 16 Aug 1888; d. Liège 15 Apr 1965)
Defence	11 Feb – Sep 1945: *Fernand Demets* (see Pierlot IV) Sep 1945 – 18 Feb 1946: *Léon Henri Mundeleer* (Lib) (b. Ixelles 6 Apr 1885; d. Ixelles 14 Dec 1964)
Colonies	11 Feb – 31 Jul 1945: *Edgar de Bruyne* (Christ Soc) (b. Ypres 18 Apr 1898; d. Brussels 6 May 1959) 31 Jul 1945 – 18 Feb 1946: *Robert (George Constant) Godding* (Lib) (b. Antwerp 8 Nov 1883; d. Léopoldville 6 Dec 1953)

12 – 21 Mar 1946: Spaak II

Prime Minister	*Paul Henri Spaak* (Soc) (for 2nd time) (see Zeeland II)
Home Affairs	*Joseph Merlot* (see Spaak I)

31 Mar – 9 Jul 1946: Acker II (Soc/Lib Coalition)

Prime Minister and Coal Supplies	*Achille van Acker* (Soc) (for 2nd time) (see Pierlot IV)
Foreign Affairs	*Paul Henri Spaak* (Soc) (see Zeeland II)
Home Affairs	*Auguste (Dieudonné Eugène) Buisseret* (Lib) (see Acker I)
Justice	*Gustave Adolphe van Glabbeke* (Lib) (see Acker I)
Finance	*Franz Joseph de Voghel* (no party) (see Acker I)
Education	*Herman Vos* (Soc) (b. Antwerp 30 Mar 1889; d. Berchem 12 May 1952)
Defence	*Raoul Defraiteur* (no party) (b. 1895)
Colonies	*Robert (George Constant) Godding* (Lib) (see Acker I)

2 Aug 1946 – 12 Mar 1947: Huysmans (Soc/Lib Coalition)

Prime Minister	*Camille Huysmans* (Soc) (b. Bilzen 26 May 1871; d. Antwerp 25 Feb 1968)*
Foreign Affairs	*Paul Henri Spaak* (Soc) (see Zeeland II)
Home Affairs	*Auguste (Dieudonné Eugène) Buisseret* (Lib) (see Acker I)
Justice	*Albert Lilar* (Lib) (b. 21 Dec 1900; d. 16 Mar 1976)
Finance	*Jean Vauthier* (no party) (b. 15 Feb 1888)
Education	*Herman Vos* (Soc) (see Acker II)
Defence	*Raoul Defraiteur* (no party) (see Acker II)

*For earlier career see vol. 2

Colonies	Robert (George Constant) Godding (Lib) (see Acker I)

19 Mar 1947 - 19 Nov 1948: Spaak III (Christ Soc/Soc Coalition)

Prime Minister	Paul Henri Spaak (Soc) (for 3rd time) (see Zeeland II)
Foreign Affairs	Paul Henri Spaak (Soc) (see Zeeland II)
Home Affairs	Pierre Vermeylen (Soc) (b. Ukkel 8 Apr 1904)
Justice	Paul Victor Antoine Struye (Christ Soc) (b. Ghent 1 Sep 1896; d. Feb 1974)
Finance	Gaston Eyskens (Christ Soc) (see Acker I)
Education	Camille Huysmans (Soc) (see Huysmans)
Defence	Raoul Defraiteur (no party) (see Acker II)
Colonies	Pierre Wigny (Christ Soc) (b. Liège 18 Apr 1905)

26 Nov 1948 - 28 Jun 1949: Spaak IV (Christ Soc/Soc Coalition)

Prime Minister	Paul Henri Spaak (Soc) (for 4th time) (see Zeeland II)
Foreign Affairs	Paul Henri Spaak (Soc) (see Zeeland II)
Home Affairs	Pierre Vermeylen (Soc) (see Spaak III)
Justice	Henri Moreau de Melen (Christ Soc)
Finance	Gaston Eyskens (Christ Soc) (see Acker I)
Education	Camille Huysmans (Soc) (see Huysmans)
Defence	Raoul Defraiteur (no party) (see Acker II)
Colonies	Pierre Wigny (Christ Soc) (see Spaak III)

10 Aug 1949 - 10 Mar/6 Jun 1950: Eyskens I (Christ Soc/Lib Coalition)

Prime Minister	Gaston Eyskens (Christ Soc) (for 1st time) (see Acker I)
Foreign Affairs and Foreign Trade	Paul van Zeeland (Christ Soc) (see Broqueville IV)
Home Affairs	(Jozef) Albert, Baron de Vleeschauwer (Christ Soc) (see Spaak I)
Justice	Albert Lilar (Lib) (see Huysmans)
Finance	Henry Liebaert (Lib) (b. 29 Nov 1895)
Education	Léon Henri Mundeleer (Lib) (see Acker I)
Defence	Albert Devèze (Lib) (see Broqueville III)
Colonies	Pierre Wigny (Christ Soc) (see Spaak III)

8 Jun - 11 Aug 1950: Duvieusart (Christ Soc)

Prime Minister	Jean Pierre Duvieusart (b. Charleroi 10 Apr 1900)
Foreign Affairs	Paul van Zeeland (see Broqueville IV)

Home Affairs	*(Jozef) Albert, Baron de Vleeschauwer* (see Spaak I)
Justice	*Henri, Comte Carton de Wiart* (see Renkin I)
Finance	*Jean (Marie) van Houtte* (b. Ghent 17 Mar 1907)
Education	*Pierre (Charles José Marie) Harmel* (b. Ukkel 16 Mar 1911)
Defence	*Henri Moreau de Melen* (see Spaak IV)
Colonies	*Pierre Wigny* (see Spaak III)

15 Aug 1950 – 9 Jan 1952: Pholien (Christ Soc)

Prime Minister	*(Clovis Louis Marie Emmanuel) Joseph Pholien* (see Spaak I)
Foreign Affairs	*Paul van Zeeland* (see Zeeland I)
Home Affairs	*Maurice Brasseur* (b. Corbion 15 Jun 1909)
Justice	*Ludovic Moyersoen* (b. Aalst 1 Aug 1904)
Finance	*Jean (Marie) van Houtte* (see Duvieusart)
Education	*Pierre (Charles José Marie) Harmel* (see Duvieusart)
Defence	*Étienne de Greef* (no party) (b. Halle 31 Aug 1900)
Colonies	*André Dequae* (b. Kortrijk 3 Nov 1915)

15 Jan 1952 – 12 Apr 1954: Houtte (Christ Soc)

Prime Minister	*Jean (Marie) van Houtte* (see Duvieusart)
Foreign Affairs	*Paul van Zeeland* (see Zeeland I)
Home Affairs	*Ludovic Moyersoen* (see Pholien)
Justice	15 Jan – 3 Sep 1952: *(Clovis Louis Marie Emmanuel) Joseph Pholien* (see Spaak I)
	5 Sep – 5 Dec 1952: *Léonce (Antoine Aloïs) Lagae* (b. Ghent 4 Sep 1904; d. Ghent 24 Sep 1964)
	5 – 12 Dec 1952 (acting:) *Charles Heger* (b. Brussels 26 May 1904)
	12 Dec 1952 – 12 Apr 1954: *Charles (Paul Marie Léon), Vicomte du Bus de Warnaffe* (see Zeeland I)
Finance	*Albert (Édouard) Janssen* (see Spaak I)
Education	*Pierre (Charles José Marie) Harmel* (see Duvieusart)
Defence	*Étienne de Greef* (no party (see Pholien)
Colonies	*André Dequae* (see Pholien)

22 Apr 1954 – 2 Jun 1958: Acker III (Soc/Lib Coalition)

Prime Minister	*Achille van Acker* (Flemish Soc) (for 3rd time) (see Pierlot IV)

Foreign Affairs	22 Apr 1954 – 11 May 1957: *Paul Henri Spaak* (Soc) (see Zeeland II)
	11 May 1957 – 2 Jun 1958: *Victor Larock* (Soc) (b. Ans 6 Oct 1904; d. Madrid 25 Apr 1977)
Home Affairs	*Pierre Vermeylen* (Soc) (see Spaak III)
Justice	*Albert Lilar* (Lib) (see Huysmans)
Finance	*Henry Liebaert* (Lib) (see Eyskens I)
Education	*Léon Collard* (Soc) (b. Mons 11 Jul 1902)
Defence	*Antoon Octavia Nicolaas Spinoy* (Soc) (b. Mechlin 6 Dec 1906; d. Hasselt 26 May 1967)
Colonies	*Auguste (D. E.) Buisseret* (Lib) (see Acker I)

25 Jun – 4 Nov 1958: Eyskens II (Christ Soc)

Prime Minister	*Gaston Eyskens* (for 2nd time) (see Acker I)
Foreign Affairs	*Pierre Wigny* (see Spaak III)
Home Affairs	*Charles Heger* (see Houtte)
Justice	*Pierre (Charles José Marie) Harmel* (see Duvieusart)
Finance	*Jean (Marie) van Houtte* (see Duvieusart)
Education	*Maurice van Hemelrik* (b. Schaerbeek 20 Apr 1901; d. Brussels 10(?) Oct 1964)
Defence	*Arthur Gilson* (b. Antwerp 27 Feb 1915)
Colonies	25 Jun – 19 Aug 1958: no appointment made
	19 Aug 1958: Ministry abolished
Belgian Congo and Ruanda-Urundi (new post)	19 Aug – 4 Nov 1958: —— *Léo Pétillon* (b. Esneux 22 May 1903)

6 Nov 1958 – 27 Mar 1961: Eyskens III (Christ Soc/Lib Coalition)

Prime Minister	*Gaston Eyskens* (Christ Soc) (for 3rd time) (see Acker I)
Deputy Prime Minister	6 Nov 1958 – 17 Feb 1961: *Théodore Lefèvre* (Christ Soc) (b. Ghent 17 Jan 1914; d. 18 Sep 1973)
Foreign Affairs	*Pierre Wigny* (Christ Soc) (see Spaak III)
Home Affairs	*Théodore Lefèvre* (Christ Soc) (see above)
Justice	6 Nov 1958 – 2 Sep 1960: *Laurent Merchiers* (Lib) (b. Zotteghem 9 Jun 1904)
	2 Sep 1960 – 17 Feb 1961: *Albert Lilar* (Lib) (see Huysmans)
Finance	*Jean (Marie) van Houtte* (Christ Soc) (see Duvieusart)
Education	*Charles Maureaux*

Defence	*Arthur Gilson* (Christ Soc) (see Eyskens II)
Belgian Congo and Ruanda-Urundi	6 Nov 1958 – 3 Sep 1959: *Maurice van Hemelrik* (Christ Soc) (see Eyskens II)
	3 Sep 1959 – 2 Sep 1960: *Auguste de Schryver* (Christ Soc) (see Zeeland II)
	2 Sep 1960: amalgamated with African Affairs (see below)
African Affairs	2 Sep 1960 – 27 Mar 1961: *Harold (René Charles Marie Gobert), Comte d'Aspremont-Lynden* (b. Brussels 17 Jan 1914; d. Natoye 1 Apr 1967)

25 Apr 1961 – 27 Jul 1965: Lefèvre (Christ Soc/Soc Coalition)

Prime Minister and Economic Co-ordination	*Théodore Lefèvre* (Christ Soc) (see Eyskens III)
Deputy Prime Minister, Foreign Affairs and African Affairs	*Paul Henri Spaak* (Soc) (see Zeeland II)
Home Affairs	*Arthur Gilson* (Christ Soc) (see Eyskens II)
Justice	*Pierre Vermeylen* (Soc) (see Spaak III)
Finance	*André Dequae* (Christ Soc) (see Pholien)
Education and Culture (for the Walloons)	25 Apr 1961 – 1 Aug 1963: *Victor Larock* (Soc) (see Acker III)
	1 Aug 1963 – 27 Jul 1965: *Henri Janne* (b. Brussels 20 Feb 1908)
Education and Culture (for the Flemings)	11 Jul 1962 – 27 Jul 1965: *Renaat van Elslande* (Christ Soc) (b. Boekhoute 21 Jan 1916)
Defence	*Paul Willem Segers* (Christ Soc) (b. Antwerp 21 Dec 1900)
Congo and African Affairs	Abolished

27 Jul 1965 – 11 Feb 1966: Harmel (Christ Soc/Soc Coalition)

Prime Minister	*Pierre (Charles José Marie) Harmel* (Christ Soc) (see Duvieusart)
Deputy Prime Minister	*Antoon Octavia Nicolaas Spinoy* (Soc) (see Acker III)
Foreign Affairs	*Paul Henri Spaak* (Soc) (see Zeeland II)
Home Affairs	*Alfons Vranckx* (Soc) (b. Louvain 24 Jan 1907)

Justice	*Pierre Wigny* (Christ Soc) (see Spaak III)
Finance	*Gaston Eyskens* (Christ Soc) (see Acker I)
Education and Public Worship	*Fernand Dehousse* (Soc) (b. Liège 3 Jul 1906)
Secretary of State for Flemish Cultural Affairs	*Albert-Michel de Clerck* (Christ Soc)
Secretary of State for Walloon Cultural Affairs	*Paul de Stexhe* (Christ Soc)
Defence	*Ludovic Moyersoen* (Christ Soc) (see Pholien)

19 Mar 1966 – 7 Feb 1968: Boeynants (Christ Soc/Lib Coalition)

Prime Minister	*Paul Vanden Boeynants* (Christ Soc) (b. Brussels 5 May 1919)
Deputy Prime Minister	*Willy de Clercq* (b. Ghent 8 Jul 1927)
Foreign Affairs	*Pierre (Charles José Marie) Harmel* (Christ Soc) (see Duvieusart)
Home Affairs	*Herman van de Poorten* (Lib)
Justice	*Pierre Wigny* (Christ Soc) (see Spaak III)
Finance	*Robert Henrion* (Lib, resigned) (b. Namur 23 Jul 1915)
Flemish Culture	*Renaat van Elslande* (Christ Soc) (see Lefevre)
Walloon Culture	*Pierre Wigny* (Christ Soc) (see Spaak III)
Defence	*Charles Poswick* (Lib) (b. 6 Oct 1924)

17 Jun 1968 – 8 Nov 1971: Eyskens IV (Christ Soc/Soc Coalition)

Prime Minister	*Gaston Eyskens* (Christ Soc) (for 4th time) (see Acker I)
Deputy Prime Minister	17 Jun 1968 – 21 Jan 1969: *Joseph Jean Merlot* (Soc) (b. Liège 27 Apr 1913; d. night of 21/22 Jan 1969)
	28 Jan 1969 – 8 Nov 1971: *André Cools* (Soc) (b. Flémalle-Grande 1 Aug 1927)
Trade	17 Jun 1968 – 21 Jan 1969: *Joseph Jean Merlot* (see above)
	28 Jan 1969 – 24 Jan 1971: *Edmond Leburton* (Soc) (b. Lantremange 18 Apr 1915)
Foreign Affairs	*Pierre (Charles José Marie) Harmel* (Christ Soc) (see Duvieusart)

67

Home Affairs	*Lucien Harmegnies* (Soc) (b. Flawinne 1916)
Justice	*Alfons Vranckx* (Soc) (see Harmel)
Finance	*Jean-Charles, Baron Snoy et d'Oppuers* (b. Ophain-Bois-Seigneur-Isaac 2 Jul 1907)
Flemish Culture	*Frans van Mechelen* (Christ Soc) (b. Turnhout 1923)
Walloon Culture	*Albert Parisis* (Christ Soc) (b. Verviers 1911)
Defence	*Paul Willem Segers* (Christ Soc) (see Lefevre)

21 Jan – 22 Nov 1972: Eyskens V

Prime Minister	*Gaston Eyskens* (CVP) (for 5th time) (see Acker I)
Deputy Prime Minister and Budget	*André Cools* (PSB) (see Eyskens IV)
Foreign Affairs	*Pierre (Charles Joseph Marie) Harmel* (PSC) (see Duvieusart)
Home Affairs	*Renaat van Elslande* (CVP) (see Lefevre)
Justice	*Alfons Vranckx* (BSP) (see Harmel)
Finance	*Andries Joseph Arthur Vlerick* (CVP) (b. Courtrai 10 Nov 1919)
Flemish Culture	*Frans van Mechelen* (CVP) (see Eyskens IV)
French Culture	*Charles Marie Paul Hanin* (PSC) (b. Wellin 19 Nov 1914)
Defence	*Paul Vanden Boeynants* (PSC) (see Boeynants)
Public Health	*Léon Lambert Servais* (PSC) (b. Liège 7 Nov 1907)
Posts and Telegraphs	*Edouard François Richard Anseele* (BSP) (b. Ghent 21 Mar 1902)
Public Works	*Joszef de Saeger* (CVP) (b. Boom 1911)
Labour and Employment	*Louis Karel Major* (BSP) (b. Ostend 20 Dec 1902)
Economic Affairs	*Henri François Simonet* (PSB) (b. Brussels 10 May 1931)
French Education	*Léon Victorien Paul Hurez* (PSB) (b. St Josse-ten-Noode 31 May 1914)
Flemish Education	*Willy Werner Hubert Claes* (BSP) (b. Brussels 2 Feb 1941)
Social Security	*Louis Hubert Ghislain Namèche* (PSB) (b. Jemeppe sur Sambre 8 Dec 1915)
Agriculture and Middle Classes	*Léo C. Tindemans* (CVP) (b. Zwijndrecht 16 Apr 1922)
Communications	*Fernand Louis Delmotte* (PSB) (b. Jeumont 24 Jul 1920)

26 Jan 1973 – 19 Jan 1974: Leburton

Prime Minister	*Edmond Leburton* (PSB) (see Eyskens IV)
Deputy Prime Minister and Budget	*Léo C. Tindemans* (CVP) (see Eyskens V)
Deputy Prime Minister and Finance	*Willy de Clercq* (PVV) (see Boeynants)
Foreign Affairs	*Renaat van Elslande* (CVP) (see Lefevre)
Home Affairs	*Edouard Nicolas Henri Charles Close* (PSB) (b. Verviers 8 Jul 1929)
Justice	*Herman Frans Gerard Vanderpoorten* (PVV) (b. Lier 25 Aug 1922)
Flemish Culture and Flemish Affairs	*Jozef Philippe Antoon Chabert* (CVP) (b. Etterbeek 16 Mar 1933)
French Culture (from 23 Oct 1973: and Government and Town Planning for Wallonia)	*Pierre Falize* (PSB)
Defence	*Paul Vanden Boeynants* (PSC) (see Boeynants)
Public Health and Environment (from 23 Oct 1973: and Family Affairs)	*Joszef de Saeger* (CVP) (see Eyskens V)
Economic Affairs	*Willy Werner Hubert Claes* (BSP) (see Eyskens V)
Communications (from 23 Oct 1973: and Port Policy)	26 Jan – 23 Oct 1973: *Edouard François Richard Anseele* (BSP) (see Eyskens V) 23 Oct 1973 – 19 Jan 1974: *Jozef M. F. Ramaekers* (BSP) (b. Tienen 5 Jun 1923)
Social Security	*Frank Marie Grégoire van Acker* (BSP) (b. Bruges 10 Jan 1929)
Scientific Policy (from 23 Oct 1973: and Eastern Cantons and Tourism)	*Charles Marie Paul Hanin* (PSC) (see Eyskens V)
Labour and Employment	*Ernest Glinne* (PSB) (b. Forchies-la-Marche 30 Mar 1931)

BELGIUM

Public Works	*Alfred Jean Herman Marie Joseph Califice* (PSC) (b. Melen 2 Oct 1916)
Agriculture	*Albert Lavens* (CVP) (b. Otegem 15 Nov 1920)
Middle Classes (from 23 Oct 1973: and Institutional Reform for Wallonia)	26 Jan – 23 Oct 1973: *Léon Gérard Pierre Mathieu Ghislain Hanotte* (PLP) (b. Dison 21 Mar 1922) 23 Oct 1973 – 19 Jan 1974: *Louis Léon Émile Olivier* (PLP) (b. Bastogne 19 Jul 1923)
Flemish Education	*Willy Gustaaf Jan Calewaert* (BSP) (b. Antwerp 26 Oct 1916)
French Education	*Michel Alfred Edmond Joseph Toussaint* (PLP) (b. Namur 26 Nov 1922)
Walloon Affairs	*Jean-Pierre Grafé* (PSC)
Brussels Affairs (from 23 Oct 1973: and Overseas Development Aid)	*Guy Victor Jean Louis Cudell* (PSB) (b. Woluwe-St Pierre 12 Feb 1917)

from 25 Apr 1974: Tindemans

Prime Minister	*Léo C. Tindemans* (CVP) (see Eyskens V)
Foreign Affairs and Overseas Development Aid	*Renaat van Elslande* (CVP) (see Lefevre)
Home Affairs	25 Apr – 11 Jun 1974: *Charles Marie Paul Hanin* (PSC) (see Eyskens V) from 11 Jun 1974: *Joseph Michel* (PSC) (b. St Mard 25 Oct 1925)
Justice	*Herman Frans Gerard Vanderpoorten* (PVV) (see Leburton)
Finance	*Willy de Clercq* (PVV) (see Boeynants)
Flemish Culture and Flemish Affairs	*Rika de Backer van Ocken* (CVP) (b. Antwerp 1 Feb 1923)
French Culture	25 Apr – 4 Oct 1974: *Jean-Pierre Grafé* (PSC) (see Leburton) from 4 Oct 1974: *Henri-François van Aal* (PSC) (b. Alicante 4 Jan 1933)
Defence and Brussels Affairs	*Paul Vanden Boeynants* (PSC) (see Boeynants)

70

Public Health and Family Affairs	*Joszef de Saeger* (CVP) (see Eyskens V)
Social Security	*Placide Hubert de Paepe* (CVP) (b. Appelterre 2 Nov 1913)
Foreign Trade	*Michel Alfred Edmond Joseph Toussaint* (PLP) (see Leburton)
Agriculture	*Albert Lavens* (CVP) (see Leburton)
Communications and Posts and Telegraphs	*Jozef Philippe Antoon Chabert* (CVP) (see Leburton)
Middle Classes	*Louis Léon Émile Olivier* (PLP) (see Leburton)
Public Works	*Jean Pierre Marie Olivier Germain Defraigne* (PLP) (b. Roosendahl-en-Nispen 19 Apr 1929)
Economic Affairs	25 Apr 1974 – 18 Aug 1975: *André Oleffe* (PSC) (d. 18 Aug 1975)
	from 23 Aug 1975: *Fernand Eugène Paul Hermans* (b. Diest 24 Jul 1911)
Labour and Employment, and Walloon Affairs	*Alfred Jean Herman Marie Joseph Califice* (PSC) (see Leburton)
Flemish Education	*Herman Francies Joseph de Croo* (PVV) (b. Opbrakel 12 Aug 1937)
French Education	*Antoine Joseph André Humblet* (PSC) (b. Serinchamps 28 Dec 1922)
Institutional Reform (Wallonia)	from 11 Jun 1974: *François Louis Eugène Félix Perin* (Rassemblement Wallon) (b. Liège 31 Jan 1921)
Institutional Reform (Flanders)	from 11 Jun 1974: *Robert Vanderckhove* (CVP)

Benin

Formerly Dahomey, name changed on 1 Dec 1975.

4 Dec 1958	Republic within French Community
2 Aug 1960	Left French Community

HEADS OF STATE

Presidents

11 Dec 1960	*Hubert Coutoucou Maga* (for 1st time) (b. Parakou 10 Aug 1916)
28 Oct 1963	*Christophe Soglo* (for 1st time) (b. Abomey 1909)
19 Jan 1964	*Sourou Migan Apithy* (for 1st time) (b. Port Novo 8 Apr 1913)
27 Nov 1965	*Justin Tométin Ahomadegbé* (for 1st time) (b. Abomey 1917)
29 Nov 1965	*Tairou Congacou*
22 Dec 1965 – 17 Dec 1967	*Christophe Soglo* (for 2nd time) Military Dictator
22 Dec 1967	*Alphonse Amadou Alley* (b. 9 Apr 1930)
1 Aug 1968 – 10 Dec 1969	*Émile Derlin Zinsou* (b. Ouidah 23 Mar 1918)
	Presidential Committee (Triumvirate):
10 Dec 1969	*Maurice Kouandete* (b. 1939) President of Committee *Paul Émile De Souza* *Benoit Sinzogan*
16 May 1970	*Hubert Maga* (for 2nd time) *Sourou Migan Apithy* (for 2nd time) *Justin Tométin Ahomadegbé* (for 2nd time)
from 26 Oct 1972	*Mathieu Kerecou* (b. Kouafra, Atakora Province, 1934)

MEMBERS OF GOVERNMENT

Prime Ministers

4 Dec 1958	*Sourou Migan Apithy* (see Presidents)
22 May 1959	*Hubert Coutoucou Maga* (see Presidents)
11 Dec 1960	President also head of government
19 Jan 1964	*Justin Tométin Ahomadegbé* (see Presidents)
27 Nov 1965	President also head of government
18 Dec 1967 – 31 Jul 1968	*Maurice Kouandete* (see Presidents)
from 1 Aug 1968	Head of State also Prime Minister

Bhutan

HEADS OF STATE

Kings

21 Aug 1926 – 30 Mar 1952	*Jigme Wangchuk*, son of King Uggyen Wangchuk
27 Oct 1952	*Jigme Dorji Wangchuk*, son (b. 1929)
21 Jul 1972	*Jigme Singhye Wangchuk*, son (b. 11 Nov 1955)

Biafra

Breakaway eastern region of Nigeria.

30 May 1967	Declaration of separation from Nigeria (recognized by Tanzania, Zambia, Gabon and Ivory Coast)
11 Jan 1970	Re-incorporated into Nigeria after civil war

HEAD OF STATE

President

30 May 1967 – 11 Jan 1970	*General Chukwuemeka Odumegwu Ojukwu* (b. Nnew 4 Nov 1933) fled to Ivory Coast Jan 1970

73

Bolivia

HEADS OF STATE

Presidents

12 Jan 1926	*Hernando Siles* (b. 5 Aug 1883; d. 26 Nov 1942)
27 Jun – 23 Aug 1930	*Roberto Hinojosa*, President of Revolutionaries
25 Jun 1930	*Carlos Blanco Galindo* (b. 12 Mar 1882; d. 2 Oct 1943)
5 Mar 1931	*Daniel Salamanca* (b. 8 Jul 1869; d. 18 Jul 1935)
28 Nov 1934	*José Luis Tejada Sorzano* (b. 1881; d. 1938)
18 May 1936	*(José) David Toro* (b. 1898)
13 Jul 1937	*German Busch Becerra* (b. 23 Mar 1904; d. 23 Aug 1939)
23 Aug 1939	(acting:) *Carlos Quintanilla* (b. Cochabamba 22 Jan 1888; d. 1964)
12 Mar 1940	*Enrique Peñaranda y del Castillo* (b. 1892)
20 Dec 1943	*Gualberto Villaroel* (b. 1908; d. 22 Jul 1946)
23 Jul 1946	(acting:) *Nestor Guillen* (b. 1890)
15 Aug 1946 – 9 Mar 1947	*Tomas Monje Gutiérrez* (b. 1884; d. 1954)
11 Mar 1947 – 23 Oct 1949	*Enrique Hertzog* (b. 1897)
27 Oct 1949	*Mamerto Urriolagoitía* (b. 1895)
16 May 1951	*General Hugo Ballivián* (b. 1901) Chairman of military coup
11 Apr 1952	*Hernán Siles Suazo* (for 1st time) (b. 1914)
17 Apr 1952	*Victor Paz Estenssoro* (for 1st time) (b. 2 Oct 1907)
17 Jun 1956	*Hernán Siles Suazo* (for 2nd time)
6 Aug 1960 – 4 Nov 1964	*Victor Paz Estenssoro* (for 2nd time)
6 Nov 1964	*René Barrientos Ortuño* (b. Tunary 30 May 1919; d. Cochabamba 27 Apr 1969) Leader of Military Junta
26 May 1965	*René Barrientos Ortuño* (for 2nd time) and *Alfredo Ovando Candía* (for 1st time) (b. Cobija 6 Apr 1918)
5 Jan 1966	*Alfredo Ovando Candía* (for 2nd time)
6 Aug 1966	*René Barrientos Ortuño* (for 3rd time)
27 Apr 1969	*Luis Adolfo Siles Salinas* (b. La Paz 21 Jun 1925)
26 Sep 1969	*Alfredo Ovando Candía* (for 3rd time) Military Dictator

6 Oct 1970	*General Rogelio Miranda* (b. c. 1910) Leader of Military Junta
7 Oct 1970	*Juan José Torres Gonzales* (b. Cochabamba 5 Mar 1921) Military Dictator
from 22 Aug 1971	*Hugo Banzer Suárez* (b. Santa Cruz 10 May 1926) Military Dictator

Botswana

Formerly Bechuanaland.

30 Sep 1966	Independence

HEAD OF STATE

President

from 30 Sep 1966	*Sir Seretse Khama* (b. Serowe 1 Jul 1921)

Brazil

HEADS OF STATE

Presidents

15 Nov 1926	*Washington (Luis) Pereira de Souza* (b. Rio de Janeiro 26 Oct 1870 (1869?); d. São Paulo 4 Aug 1957)
24 Oct 1930	*Julio Prestes* (b. 15 Mar 1882; d. 9 Feb 1946)
4 Nov 1930	*Getulio Dornelles Vargas* (for 1st time) (b. São Borja 19 Apr 1882; d. Rio de Janeiro 24 Aug 1954)
30 Oct 1945	*José Linhares* (b. 1886; d. Coxambu 26 Jan 1957)
31 Jan 1946 – 31 Jan 1951	*Enrico Gaspar Dutra* (b. 18 May 1885)

BRAZIL

10 Feb 1951 – 24 Aug 1954	*Getulio Dornelles Vargas* (for 2nd time)
26 Aug 1954	*João Café Filho* (b. Natal, Rio Grande do Norte, 3 Feb 1899; d. Rio de Janeiro 20 Feb 1970)
8 Nov 1955	(acting:) *Carlos Coimbra da Luz* (b. 1894; d. Rio de Janeiro 9 Feb 1961)
11 Nov 1955	(acting:) *Nereu Ramos* (b. 1889; d. Curitiba night of 16/17 Jun 1958)
31 Jan 1956	*Juscelino Kubitschek de Oliveira* (b. Diamantina 12 Sep 1902; d. Rio de Janeiro 22 Aug 1976)
31 Jan – 25 Aug 1961	*Janio (da Silva) Quadros* (b. Campo Grande 25 Jan 1917)
7 Sep 1961	*João (Belchoir Marques) Goulart* (b. São Borja (Rio Grande do Sul) 1 Mar 1918)
2 Apr 1964	(acting:) *Pascoal Ranieri Mazzilli* (b. Caconde 17 Apr 1910; d. Apr 1975)
15 Apr 1964	*Humberto de Alencar Castelo Branco* (b. Mecejana 20 Sep 1900: d. Fortaleza, Ceará Province, 18 Jul 1967)
15 Mar 1967	*Arturo da Costa e Silva* (b. Taquari 3 Oct 1902; d. Rio de Janeiro 17 Dec 1969)
1 Sep 1969	Three-minister Military Junta: *Admiral Augusto Hamann Rademaker Gruenewald*, Leader, Commander of Navy *General Aurelio de Lyra Tavares*, Commander-in-Chief of Army *Air Marshal Marcio de Souza e Mello*, Commander of Air Force
25 Oct 1969	*Emilio Garrastazú Médici* (b. Bagé 4 Dec 1905)
from 22 Aug 1971	*Ernesto Geisel* (b. Rio Grande do Sul 3 Aug 1908)

MEMBERS OF GOVERNMENT

Prime Ministers

Post only existed from 8 Sep 1961 until 24 Jan 1963

8 Sep 1961 – 26 Jun 1962	*Tancredo (de Almeida) Neves* (b. San Joaõ 4 Mar 1910)
3 – 4 Jul 1962	*Auro de Moura Andrada*
10 Jul – 14 Sep 1962	*Francisco Brochado da Rocha* (b. 8 Aug 1910; d. Pôrto Alegre 26 Sep 1962)

76

17 Sep 1962	*Hermes Lima* (b. Livramento 22 Dec 1902)
24 Jan 1963	Post abolished and presidential system reintroduced

Foreign Ministers

15 Nov 1926 – 24 Oct 1930	*João Otavio Mangabeira* (b. Bahia 27 Aug 1886; d. Rio de Janeiro 29 Nov 1960)
3 Nov 1930 – 1933	*Afrânio de Melo Franco* (b. 1870; d. 1943)
23 Jul 1934	*José Carlos de Macedo Soares* (for 1st time) (b. São Paulo 6 Oct 1883)
1937 – 1938	*Mario de Pimentel Brandão* (b. 1889)
1938	*Osvaldo Aranha* (b. Alegrete 15 Feb 1894; d. Rio de Janeiro 27 Jan 1960)
24 Aug 1944	*Pedro Leão Vellozo*
23 Jan – Nov 1946(?)	*João Neves da Fontoura* (for 1st time) (b. Cachoeira 16 Nov 1887; d. Rio de Janeiro 31 Mar 1963)
9 May 1947	*Raul Fernandes* (for 1st time)(b. Vicente 24 Oct 1877)
1 Feb 1951 – 29 Jun 1953	*João Neves da Fontoura* (for 2nd time)
29 Jun/ 12 Sep 1953 – 24 Aug 1954	*Vincente Rao* (b. São Paulo 8 Jun 1892)
25 Aug 1954 – (?)	*Raul Fernandes* (for 2nd time)
11 Nov 1955	*José Carlos de Macedo Soares* (for 2nd time)
3 Jul 1958 – 1 Aug 1959	*Francisco Negrão de Lima* (b. Vila Nepomuceno 24 Aug 1901)
3 Aug 1959	*Horacio Lafer* (b. São Paulo 3 May 1900)
1 Feb – 25 Aug/ 7 Sep 1961	*Affonso Arinos de Melo Franco* (for 1st time) (b. Belo Horizonte 27 Nov 1905)
8 Sep 1961 – 26 Jun 1962	*Francisco Clementino San Tiago Dantas* (b. Prov. Rio de Janeiro 1911; d. 6 Sep 1964)
13 Jul – 13 Sep 1962	*Affonso Arinos de Melo Franco* (for 2nd time)
17 Sep 1962 – 22 Jan 1963	*Hermes Lima* (see Prime Ministers)
24 Jan 1963	*Renato Archer*
20 Jun 1963	*Evandro Lins e Silva*
2 Apr 1964	*Vasco Leitão da Cunha* (b. 2 Sep 1903)
Jan 1966	*Juracy Montenegro Magalhães Kelly* (b. Fortaleza, Ceará Province, 4 Aug 1905)
15 Mar 1967	*José de Magalhães Pinto* (b. 28 Jul 1909)
28 Oct 1969	*Mario Gibson Alves Barbosa* (b. Pernambuco 1918)
from 15 Mar 1974	*Antônio Francisco Azevedo da Silveira*

Buganda

For the kingdom of Buganda, Uganda, from the 13th to the 20th century, see vol. 1.

Bulgaria

HEADS OF STATE

Kings

House of Saxe-Coburg-Gotha

3 Oct 1918	*Boris III*, son of King Ferdinand (b. 30 Jan 1894)
28 Aug 1943 – 8(15) Sep 1946	*Simeon II*, son (b. 16 Jun 1937) during his minority, two Councils of Regents governed on his behalf:
Sep 1943 – 9 Sep 1944	*Prince Cyril*, brother of King Boris III (b. Sofia 17 Nov 1895; d. 1 Feb 1945), *Bogdan Filov* (b. 10 Apr 1883; d. 1 Feb 1945), formerly Prime Minister, and *Nikolai Michov* (b. Tirnova 26 Nov 1891) War Minister
9 Sep 1944 – 8 Sep 1946	*Venelin Ganev* (b. 4 Feb 1880), *Todor Pavlov* (b. 14 Feb 1890) and —— *Boboshevski*
15 Sep 1946	People's Republic

Presidents of the Presidium of the National Council

8 Sep 1946 – 9 Jul 1947	(acting:) *Vasil Kolarov* (b. Shumen 16 Jul 1877; d. Sofia 23 Jan 1950)
9 Dec 1947 – Jan 1950	*Mincho Naichev* (b. Alt-Zagora 23 Mar 1897; d. 11 Aug 1956)
17 Jan/27 May 1950 – 27 Nov 1958	*Georgi Damianov* (b. Lopuschna 23 May 1892; d. Sofia 27 Nov 1958)
30 Nov 1958 – 20 Apr 1964	*Dimitro Ganev* (b. Gradetz 28 Sep 1898; d. Sofia 20 Apr 1964)
23 Apr 1964	*Georgi Traikov (Girovski)* (b. Itia, Florina district, 8 Apr 1898; d. 14 Jan 1975)

from 7 Jul 1971   *Todor Zhivkov* (b. Pravets 7 Sep 1911(?)) †

MEMBERS OF GOVERNMENT

Prime Ministers

13 Sep 1928	*Andrei Lyapchev* (for 2nd time) (b. 30 Nov 1866; d. Nov 1933)*
15 May 1930 – 20 Apr 1931	*Andrei Lyapchev* (for 3rd time)
4 May – 22 Jun 1931	*Andrei Lyapchev* (for 4th time)
29 Jun 1931	*Aleksandŭr Malinov* (for 3rd time) (b. 20 Apr 1867; d. 21 Mar 1938)*
12 Oct 1931 – 28 Dec 1932	*Nikolai Mushanov* (for 1st time) (b. Drenowo 2 Apr 1872; d. Sofia(?) Jul(?) 1951)
31 Dec 1932 – 17 May 1934	*Nikolai Mushanov* (for 2nd time)
19 May 1934	*Kimon Georgiev* (for 1st time) (b. Pazardzhik 11 Aug 1882; d. Sofia 28 Sep 1969)
22 Jan – 18 Apr 1935	*Pencho Zlatev* (b. 2 Nov 1881; d. 24 Jul 1948)
21 Apr 1935	*Andrei Toshev* (b. 20(?) Apr 1867; d. 10 Jan 1944)
23 Nov 1935	*Georgi Kyoseivanov* (for 1st time) (b. 19 Jan 1884; d. 27 Jul 1960)
4 Jul 1936 – 19 Oct 1939	*Georgi Kyoseivanov* (for 2nd time)
23 Oct 1939	*Georgi Kyoseivanov* (for 3rd time)
16 Feb 1940	*Bogdan Filov* (for 1st time) (see Kings)
11 Apr 1942	*Bogdan Filov* (for 2nd time)
14 Sep 1943	*Dobri Bozilov* (b. 30 Oct 1884; d. 1 Feb 1945)
2 Jun 1944	*Ivan Bagrianov* (b. 1892; d. 1 Feb 1945)
2 Sep 1944	*Konstantin Muraviev* (b. Pazardzhik 1893; d. 31 Jan 1965)
9 Sep 1944 – 20 Mar 1946	*Kimon Georgiev* (for 2nd time)
9 Sep 1944 – May 1945	*Asen Zankov* (for 2nd time) (b. 29 Jun 1879; d. Buenos Aires 17 Jul 1959) 'National Government' in in exile in Germany*

† First Secretary of Bulgarian Communist Party since 1953
*For earlier career see vol. 2

31 Mar 1946	*Kimon Georgiev* (for 3rd time)
23 Nov 1946 – 9 Dec 1947	*Georgi Dimitrov* (for 1st time) (b. 17 Jun 1882; d. Moscow 2 Jul 1949)
Dec 1947 – 2 Jul 1949	*Georgi Dimitrov* (for 2nd time)
20 Jul 1949 – 23 Jan 1950	*Vasil Kolarov* (see Presidents of the Presidium of the National Council)
1 Feb 1950 – 16 Apr 1956	*Vŭlko Chervenkov* (b. 6 Sep 1900)
17 Apr 1956 – 5 Nov 1962	*Anton Yugov* (b. Karasuli 5 Aug 1904)
19/27 Nov 1962	*Todor Zhivkov* (for 1st time) (see Presidents of the Presidium of the National Council)
12 Mar 1966	*Todor Zhivkov* (for 2nd time)
from 7 Jul 1971	*Stanko Todorov* (b. Pernik (now Dimitrovo district) 10 Dec 1920)

Foreign Affairs Ministers

4 Jan 1926 – 25 Jun 1931	*Atanas Burov* (b. Orekhovitsa 1875; d. 1954)
29 Jun 1931	*Aleksandŭr Malinov* (see Prime Ministers)
12 Oct 1931 – 19 May 1934	*Nikolai Mushanov* (see Prime Ministers)
24 May 1934 – 18 Apr 1935	*Konstantin Batalov*
21 Apr 1935	*Georgi Kyoseivanov* (see Prime Ministers)
16 Feb 1940	*Ivan Popov* (b. Shvishtov Apr 1890)
12 Apr 1942	*Bogdan Filov* (see Kings)
14 Sep 1943	*Sasha Kirov*
14 Oct 1943	*Dimitŭr Shishmanov* (b. Sofia 19 Nov 1889)
2 – 12 Jun 1944	*Ivan Bagrianov* (see Prime Ministers)
12 Jun – 2 Sep 1944	*Parvan Dragnov* (b. Lom 5 Feb 1890)
4 – 9 Sep 1944	*Konstantin Muraviev* (see Prime Ministers)
9 Sep 1944 – 21 Mar 1946	*Petko Stainov* (b. Kasanlyk 13 May 1899)
9 Sep 1944 – May 1945	*Asen Zankov* (see Prime Ministers) 'National Government' in exile in Germany
1 Apr – 21 Nov 1946	*Georgi Kulichov*

*For earlier career see vol. 2

23 Nov 1946 – 9 Dec 1947	*Kimon Georgiev* (see Prime Ministers)
12 Dec 1947	*Vasil Kolarov* (see Presidents of the Presidium of the National Council)
7 Aug 1949	*Vladimir Poptomov* (b. Belitza 1890; d. 1 May 1952)
27 May 1950 – 11 Aug 1956	*Mincho Naichev* (see Presidents of the Presidium of the National Council)
18 Aug 1956 – 14 Nov 1962	*Karl Lukanov* (b. 1897)
27 Nov 1962 – 13 Dec 1971	*Ivan Basev* (b. Sofia 11 Feb 1916; d. Sofia 13 Dec 1971)
from 16 Dec 1971	*Petŭr Toshev Mladenov* (b. Toshevtsi 22 Aug 1936)

Bulozi (Barotse)

For the Luyana dynasty of Bulozi, Zambia, 17th to 20th centuries, see vol. 1.

Burma

HEADS OF STATE

Governors

1927 – 1932	*Sir Charles Innes* (b. 27 Oct 1874; d. 28 Jun 1959)
1932 – 1936	*Sir Hugh (Lansdown) Stevenson* (b. 8 Apr 1871; d. 6 Sep 1941)
1936 – 1941	*Sir Archibald Douglas Cochrane* (b. 8 Jan 1885; d. 16 Apr 1958)
6 May 1941 – 14 Jul 1946	*Sir Reginald Hugh Dorman-Smith* (b. 1899; d. 20 Mar 1977)

BURMA

31 Aug 1946 – 4 Jan 1948	*Sir Hubert (Elvin) Rance* (b. 17 Jul 1898; d. 24 Jan 1974)

Presidents

1 Aug 1943 – May 1945	*U Ba Maw* (b. 1897; d. Rangoon 29 May 1977) under Japanese rule
Oct 1945 – Jan 1948	British military administration, return of the Governor (see above)
4 Jan 1948	Independence
4 Jan 1948 – Mar 1952	(acting:) *Sao Shwe Thaik (Saopalong Yaung Hwe)* (d. Rangoon 21 Nov 1962)
16 Mar 1952 – 11 Mar 1957	*Agga Maha Thiri Thudhamma Ba U* (b. 26 May 1887; d. Rangoon 9 Nov 1963)
13 Mar 1957	*U Wing Maung* (b. 17 Apr 1916)
16 Feb 1962	*Sama Duwa Sinwa Nawng*
2 Mar 1962	*General Ne Win* (b. 24 May 1911?)

MEMBERS OF GOVERNMENT

Prime Ministers

26 Sep 1946 – 19 Jul 1947	*U Aung San* (b. 1916; d. 19 Jul 1947)
24 Jul 1947	*Thakin Nu* (later *U Nu*) (b. Wakena 25 May 1907)
1 Mar 1948	*Thakin Nu* (for 2nd time)
14 Aug 1948	*Thakin Nu* (for 3rd time)
16 Mar 1952 – 5 Jun 1956	*Thakin Nu* (for 4th time)
12 Jun 1956	*U Ba Swe* (b. 7 Oct 1915)
28 Feb 1957	*U Nu* (for 5th time)
5 Jun – 26 Sep/ 28 Oct 1958	*U Nu* (for 6th time)
28 Oct 1958 – Mar 1960	*General Ne Win* (for 1st time) (see Presidents)
4 Apr 1960	*U Nu* (for 7th time)
2 Mar 1962 – 2 Mar 1974	*General Ne Win* (for 2nd time)
from 4 Mar 1974	*U Sein Win*

Burundi

1 Aug 1962	Separated from Belgian trustee territories, hitherto part of Ruanda-Urundi

HEADS OF STATE

Kings

16 Dec 1915 – 8 Jul 1966	*Mwambutsa IV*, son of Mutagas IV (b. Muramvya 1912) deposed, lives in Switzerland
8 Jul/ 2 Sep 1966	*Ntare V (Charles Ndizeye)*, son (b. Kitega 2 Dec 1947) lives abroad
28 Nov 1966	Establishment of Republic

President

from 29 Nov 1966	*Michel Micombero* (b. 1940) Head of National Committee of Revolution

MEMBERS OF GOVERNMENT

Prime Ministers

Oct 1961/1 Jul 1962 – 10 Jun 1963	*Chief André Muhirwa*
17 Jun 1963	*Pierre Ngendandumwe* (for 1st time) (b. 1937?; d. Bujumbura 15 Jan 1965) of the Bahutu tribe
Apr 1964 – Jan 1965	*Albin Nyamoya* (b. Ngozi Province 1924)
(?) – 15 Jan 1965	*Pierre Ngendandumwe* (for 2nd time)
Mid Jan – Oct 1965	*Joseph Bamina* (d. Oct(?) 1965)
Oct 1965 – 9 Jul 1966	*Léopold Biha*
from 13 Jul 1966	*Michel Micombero* (see President)

Cambodia

11 Aug 1863 – 9 Mar 1945	French protectorate
9 Mar – Aug 1945	Japanese protectorate
Aug 1945 – 9 Nov 1953	French protectorate
16 Dec 1948	Independent within the framework of the French Union
8 Nov 1949	Withdrew from the French Union
25 Sep 1955	Declared itself a sovereign state

HEADS OF STATE

Kings

9 Aug 1927/22 Jul 1928 – 23 Apr 1941	*Sisovath Monivong*, son of King Sisovath (b. 27 Dec 1875; d. 23 Apr 1941)
26 Apr/28 Oct 1941 – 2 Mar 1955	*Norodom Sihanouk II* (from 3 Mar 1955: *Prince Norodom Sihanouk*), grandson (b. 31 Oct 1922) abdicated
3 Mar 1955	*Norodom Suramarit*, father, son-in-law of Sisovath Monivong (b. 6 Mar 1896; d. 3 Apr 1960)
3 Apr 1960 – 18 Mar 1970	Throne unoccupied; duties of King performed by Head of State
1 Nov 1970	Abolition of monarchy and establishment of Khmer Republic

Heads of State

13 Jun 1960	*Prince Norodom Sihanouk* (for 1st time) (see Kings) from 5 May 1970 President of the Government of National Unity, in exile in Peking; returned to Cambodia 10 Sep 1975
18 Mar 1970 – 10 Mar 1972	(acting:) *Cheng Heng* (b. Takéo Province 1916) fled 1975
14 Mar 1972	*Lon Nol* (b. Kompong Neav 13 Nov 1913)
25 Apr 1975	*Prince Norodom Sihanouk* (for 2nd time)

MEMBERS OF GOVERNMENT

French High Commissioners

28 Apr 1953	*Jean Risterucci* (b. Bustanico, Corsica, 11 Apr 1911)
3 Jul 1953 – Jun 1954	*Maurice Dejean* (b. Clichy 30 Sep 1899)

Prime Ministers

Aug – 15 Oct 1945	*Son Ngoc Thanh* (for 1st time) (b. 1907?)
1946 – 1948	*Prince Monireth*
1948 – 1949	*Son Ngoc Thanh* (for 2nd time)
1949 – 1951	*Prince Monipong*
(?) – Oct 1951	*Son Ngoc Thanh* (for 3rd time)
Oct 1951 – 1952	*Huy Kanthoul*
Jun 1952 – May 1953	*Norodom Sihanouk II* (for 1st time) (see Kings)
May – 14 Nov 1953	*Samdech Penn Nouth* (for 1st time) (b. 1 Apr 1906)
16 Nov 1953 – 1954	*Chan Nak* (b. 27 May 1892)
1954 – 1955	*Leng Ngeth*
23 Oct 1955 – Jan 1956	*Prince Norodom Sihanouk* (for 2nd time)
Jan – Feb 1956	*Oum Chheang Sun*
29 Feb – 24 Mar 1956	*Prince Norodom Sihanouk* (for 3rd time)
2 Apr – 29 Jul 1956	*Khim Tit*
15 Sep – 15 Oct 1956	*Prince Norodom Sihanouk* (for 4th time)
25 Oct – Dec 1956	*Sam Yun*
Dec 1956 – 7 Jul 1957	*Prince Norodom Sihanouk* (for 5th time)
26 Jul 1957 – 8 Jan 1958	*Sim Var* (for 1st time)
11 – 16 Jan 1958	*Ek Yi Oun* (b. 1910)
16 Jan – 10 Apr 1958	(acting:) *Samdech Penn Nouth* (for 2nd time)
24 Apr – 22 Jun 1958	*Sim Var* (for 2nd time)
10 Jul 1958 – 12 Apr 1960	*Prince Norodom Sihanouk* (for 6th time)
18 Apr 1960 – Jan 1961	*Pho Proung*
28 Jan – Sep 1961	*Samdech Penn Nouth* (for 3rd time)
Sep 1961 – 29(?) Jul 1962	*Prince Norodom Sihanouk* (for 7th time)
Sep 1962 – 1963	*Prince Norodom Sihanouk* (for 8th time)
1963 – 23 Dec 1964	*Prince Norodom Kantol* (for 1st time) (b. 15 Sep 1920)
24 Dec 1964	*Prince Norodom Kantol* (for 2nd time)

19 Oct 1966 – 30 Apr 1967	*Lon Nol* (for 1st time) (see Presidents)
2 May 1967	*Prince Norodom Sihanouk* (for 9th time)
5 Aug 1967 – 1 Jan 1968	*Prince Norodom Sihanouk* (for 10th time)
29 Jan 1968 – early Aug 1969	*Samdech Penn Nouth* (for 4th time) from 5 May 1970 Prime Minister of the Government of National Unity, in exile in Peking; returned to Cambodia Nov 1973
13 Aug 1969	*Lon Nol* (for 2nd time)
11 – 13 Mar 1972	*Sisovath Sivik Matak* (b. 22 Jan 1914; d. (executed) Apr 1975)
18 Mar – 14 Oct 1972	*Son Ngoc Thanh* (for 4th time)
15 Oct 1972 – 17 Apr 1973	*Hang Thun Hak* (b. 1926?)
16 May – 7 Dec 1973	*In Tam* (b. 22 Sep 1922) fled 19 Apr 1975
26 Dec 1973 – 17 Apr 1975	*Long Boret* (b. 1933; d. (executed) Apr 1975)
from 25 Apr 1975	*Samdech Penn Nouth* (for 5th time)

Cameroon

1916 – 1959	Administered by France under Trusteeship Agreement with League of Nations and United Nations
1 Jan 1960	Independence (named Republic of Cameroon)
1 Oct 1961	United with southern part of former British-administered Trust Territory of Cameroons
May 1972	Name changed to United Republic of Cameroon

HEAD OF STATE

President

from 5 May 1960	*Ahmad Ahidjo* (b. Garoua Aug 1924)

MEMBERS OF GOVERNMENT

Prime Ministers

1 Jan 1960	*Charles Assalé* (b. Ebolowa 4 Nov 1911)
1 Oct 1961 – 29 Jun 1975	President also held office of Prime Minister
from 30 Jun 1975	*Paul Biya* (b. Mvomeoka 13 Feb 1933)

Canada

HEADS OF STATE

Governors and Governors-General

2 Oct 1926	*Freeman Freeman-Thomas, 1st Viscount Willingdon* (from 1931: *1st Earl of Willingdon*; from 1936: *1st Marquess of Willingdon*) (b. Ratton 12 Sep 1866; d. London 12 Aug 1941)
4 Apr 1931	*Vere Brabazon Ponsonby, 9th Earl Bessborough* (b. 27 Oct 1880; d. Rowlands Castle, Hampshire, 10 Mar 1956)
2 Nov 1935 – 11 Feb 1940	*John Buchan, 1st Baron Tweedsmuir* (b. Perth 26 Aug 1875; d. Montreal 11 Feb 1940)
4 Apr/21 Jun 1940	*Alexander Cambridge, 1st Earl of Athlone* (b. London 14 Apr 1874; d. 16 Jan 1957)
12 Apr 1946	*Harold (Rupert Leofric George) Alexander* (from 1952: *1st Earl Alexander of Tunis*) (b. Errigal, Ireland, 10 Dec 1891; d. London 16 Jun 1969)
28 Feb 1952	*(Charles) Vincent Massey* (b. Toronto 20 Feb 1887; d. London 30 Dec 1967)
15 Sep 1959	*George Philias Vanier* (b. Montreal 23 Apr 1888; d. Ottawa 5 Mar 1967)
4 Apr 1967	*(Daniel) Roland Michener* (b. Lacombe, Alberta, 19 Apr 1900)
from Jan 1974	*Jules Léger* (b. Saint Anicet 4 Apr 1913)

MEMBERS OF GOVERNMENT

25 Sep 1926 – 7 Aug 1930: King II (Lib) †

Prime Minister and External Affairs	*William Lyon Mackenzie King* (for 2nd time) (b. Berlin, Ontario, 17 Dec 1874; d. Kingsmere 22 Jul 1950)*
Interior and Indian Affairs	*Charles Stewart* (b. Strabane 26 Aug 1868; d. Ottawa 6 Dec 1946)*
Agriculture	*William Richard Motherwell* (b. Perth, Ontario, 6 Jan 1860; d. Abernethy 24 May 1943)*
Finance and Receiver General	26 Nov 1929 – 7 Aug 1930: *Charles Avery Dunning* (b. Croft, Leicestershire, 31 Jul 1885; d. Montreal 2 Oct 1958)*
Fisheries	17 Jun – 7 Aug 1930: *Cyrus Macmillan* (b. Wood Islands 12 Sep 1882; d. Charlottetown 29 Jun 1953)
Immigration and Colonization	30 Dec 1929 – 26 Jun 1930 (acting:) *Charles Stewart* (see above)
	27 Jun – 7 Aug 1930: *Ian Alistair Mackenzie* (b. Assynt, Scotland, 27 Jul 1890; d. Banff 2 Sep 1949)
Justice and Attorney General	*Ernest Lapointe* (b. St-Éloi 6 Oct 1876; d. Montreal 26 Nov 1941)*
Labour	*Peter Heenan* (b. Tullaree, Ireland, 19 Feb 1875; d. 12 May 1948)
Marine	14 Jun – 7 Aug 1930: *Pierre Joseph Arthur Cardin* (b. Sorel 28 Jun 1879; d. Sorel 20 Oct 1946)*
Marine and Fisheries	25 Sep 1926 – 13 Jun 1930: *Pierre Joseph Arthur Cardin* (see above)
	14 Jun 1930: ministry divided
Mines	*Charles Stewart* (see above)
National Defence	8 Oct 1926 – 7 Aug 1930: *James Layton Ralston* (b. Amherst 27 Sep 1881; d. Montreal 22 May 1948)
National Revenue	31 Mar 1927 – 7 Aug 1930: *William Daum Euler* (b. Conostego 10 Jul 1875; d. Kitchener 15 Jul 1961)*
Pensions and National Health	11 Jun 1928 – 18 Jun 1930: *James Horace King* (b. Chipman 18 Jan 1873; d. Ottawa 14 Jul 1955)*
	19 Jun – 7 Aug 1930 (acting:) *James Layton Ralston* (see above)
Postmaster General	*Peter John Veniot* (b. Richibucto 4 Oct 1863; d. Bathurst 6 Jul 1936)

† For ministers no longer in office in 1930 see vol. 2
*For earlier career see vol. 2

President of the Privy Council	*William Lyon Mckenzie King* (see above)
Public Works	*John Campbell Elliott* (b. Ekfrid Township 25 Jul 1872; d. London, Ontario, 20 Dec 1941)*
Railways and Canals	30 Dec 1929 – 7 Aug 1930: *Thomas Alexander Crerar* (b. Molesworth 17 Jun 1876)*
Secretary of State of Canada	*Fernand Rinfret* (b. Montreal 28 Feb 1883; d. Los Angeles 12 Jul 1939)
Solicitor General	*Lucien Cannon* (b. Arthabaska 16 Jan 1887; d. Quebec 14 Feb 1950)
Trade and Commerce	*James Malcolm* (b. Kincardine 14 Jul 1880; d. Kincardine 6 Dec 1935)
Without Portfolio	*Raoul Dandurand* (b. Montreal 4 Nov 1861; d. Montreal 11 Mar 1942)*

7 Aug 1930 – 23 Oct 1935: Bennett (Cons)

Prime Minister and External Affairs	*Richard Bedford Bennett* (from 1941: *1st Viscount Bennett*) (b. Hopewell 3 Jul 1870; d. Mickleham, Surrey, 27 Jun 1947)*
Interior and Indian Affairs	*Thomas Gerow Murphy* (b. Northumberland County, Ontario, 29 Oct 1883)
Agriculture	8 Aug 1930 – 23 Oct 1935: *Robert Weir* (b. Wingham 5 Dec 1882; d. Weldon 7 Mar 1939)
Finance and Receiver General	7 Aug 1930 – 2 Feb 1932: *Richard Bedford Bennett* (see above)
	3 Feb 1932 – 23 Oct 1935: *Edgar Nelson Rhodes* (b. Amherst 5 Jan 1876; d. Ottawa 15 Mar 1942)
Immigration and Colonization	(acting from 3 Feb 1932:) *Wesley Ashton Gordon* (b. Owen Sound 11 Feb 1884; d. Toronto 9 Feb 1943)
Justice and Attorney General	7 Aug 1930 – 11 Aug 1935: *Hugh Guthrie* (b. Guelph 13 Aug 1866; d. Ottawa 3 Nov 1939)*
	14 Aug – 23 Oct 1935: *George Reginald Geary* (b. Strathroy 12 Aug 1873; d. 30 Apr 1954)
Labour	7 Aug 1930 – 2 Feb 1932: *Gideon Decker Robertson* (b. Welland County 26 Aug 1874; d. Ottawa 25 Aug 1933)*
	3 Feb 1932 – 23 Oct 1935: *Wesley Ashton Gordon* (see above)
Marine	7 Aug 1930 – 19 Jul 1935: *Alfred Duranleau* (b. West Farnham 1 Nov 1871; d. 11 Mar 1951)

*For earlier career see vol. 2

	30 Aug – 23 Oct 1935: *Lucien Henri Gendron* (b. St-Hyacinthe 28 Aug 1890; d. 5 Apr 1959)
Mines	*Wesley Ashton Gordon* (see above)
National Defence	7 Aug 1930 – 16 Nov 1934: *Donald Matheson Sutherland* (b. Norwich, Ontario, 3 Dec 1879)
	17 Nov 1934 – 23 Oct 1935: *Grote Stirling* (b. Tunbridge Wells 31 Jul 1875; d. Kelowna 18 Jan 1953)
National Revenue	7 Aug 1930 – 1 Dec 1933: *Edmund Baird Ryckman* (b. Huntingdon 15 Apr 1866; d. Toronto 11 Jan 1934)*
	6 Dec 1933 – 13 Aug 1935: *Robert Charles Matthews* (b. Lindsay 14 Jun 1871; d. 19 Sep 1952)
	14 Aug – 23 Oct 1935: *James Earl Lawson* (b. Hamilton 21 Oct 1891; d. 13 May 1950)
Pensions and National Health	7 Aug 1930 – 16 Nov 1934: *Murray MacLaren* (b. Richibucto 30 Apr 1861; d. Saint John 24 Dec 1942)
	17 Nov 1934 – 23 Oct 1935: *Donald Matheson Sutherland* (see above)
Postmaster General	7 Aug 1930 – 13 Aug 1925: *Arthur Sauvé* (b. St-Hermas 1 Oct 1875; d. Montreal 6 Feb 1944)
	16 Aug – 23 Oct 1935: *Samuel Gobeil* (b. La Patrie 17 Aug 1875; d. Quebec 1 Jan 1961)
President of the Privy Council	*Richard Bedford Bennett* (see above)
Public Works	*Hugh Alexander Stewart* (b. Elizabethtown 29 Sep 1871; d. Brockville 4 Sep 1956)
Railways and Canals	*Robert James Manion* (b. Pembroke 19 Nov 1881; d. Ottawa 2 Jul 1943)*
Secretary of State of Canada	*Charles Hazlitt Cahan* (b. Hebron 31 Oct 1861; d. Montreal 15 Aug 1944)
Solicitor General	*Maurice Dupré* (b. Lévis 20 Mar 1888; d. Trois Rivières 3 Oct 1941)
Trade and Commerce	7 Aug 1930 – 26 Oct 1934: *Henry Herbert Stevens* (b. Bristol 8 Dec 1878)*
	17 Nov 1934 – 23 Oct 1935: *Richard Burpee Hanson* (b. Bocabec 20 Mar 1879; d. Fredericton 14 Jul 1948)
Without Portfolio	7 Aug 1930 – 13 Aug 1935: *John Alexander Macdonald* (b. Tracadie 12 Apr 1874; d. Cardigan 15 Nov 1948)*
	Sir George Halsey Perley (b. Lebanon, New Hampshire, 12 Sep 1857; d. Ottawa 4 Jan 1938)*

*For earlier career see vol. 2

3 Feb 1932 – 23 Oct 1935: *Arthur Meighen* (b. Anderson 16 Jun 1874; d. Toronto 5 Aug 1960)*
30 Aug – 23 Oct 1935: *Onésime Gagnon* (b. Standon 23 Oct 1888; d. Quebec 30 Sep 1961)
30 Aug – 23 Oct 1935: *William Earl Rowe* (b. Hull, Iowa, 13 May 1894)

23 Oct 1935 – 15 Nov 1948: King III (Lib)

Prime Minister	*William Lyon Mackenzie King* (for 3rd time) (see King II)
External Affairs	23 Oct 1935 – 3 Sep 1946: *William Lyon Mackenzie King* (see King II)
	4 Sep 1946 – 9 Sep 1948: *Louis Stephen St-Laurent* (b. Compton 1 Feb 1882; d. 25 Jul 1973)
	10 Sep – 15 Nov 1948: *Lester Bowles Pearson* (b. Newtonbrook 23 Apr 1897; d. 27 Dec 1972)
Interior and Indian Affairs	23 Oct 1935 – 30 Nov 1936: *Thomas Alexander Crerar* (see King II)
	1 Dec 1936: office abolished
Agriculture	25 Oct – 3 Nov 1935 (acting:) *Thomas Alexander Crerar* (see King II)
	4 Nov 1935 – 15 Nov 1948: *James Garfield Gardiner* (b. Farquhar 30 Nov 1883; d. Balcanes 12 Jan 1962)
Finance and Receiver General	23 Oct 1935 – 5 Sep 1939: *Charles Avery Dunning* (see King II)
	6 Sep 1939 – 4 Jul 1940: *James Layton Ralston* (see King II)
	8 Jul 1940 – 95 Dec 1946: *James Lorimer Ilsley* (b. Somerset, Nova Scotia, 3 Jan 1894; d. Halifax 14 Jan 1967)
	10 Dec 1946 – 15 Nov 1948: *Douglas Charles Abbott* (b. Lennoxville 29 May 1899)
Fisheries	23 Oct 1935 – 5 Oct 1942: *Joseph Enoil Michaud* (b. St-Antonin 26 Sep 1888; d. Edmundston 23 May 1967)
	7 Oct 1942 – 28 Aug 1945: *Ernest Bertrand* (b. Somerset, Quebec, 14 Dec 1888; d. Montreal 11 Oct 1958)
	30 Aug 1945 – 10 Aug 1947: *Hedley Francis Gregory Bridges* (b. Fredericton 7 Apr 1902; d. 10 Aug 1947)

*For earlier career see vol. 2

	14 Aug – 1 Sep 1947 (acting:) *Ernest Bertrand* (see above)
	2 Sep 1947 – 18 Jan 1948: *Milton Fowler Gregg* (b. Mountain Dale 10 Apr 1892)
	19 Jan – 10 Jun 1948: *James Angus MacKinnon* (b. Port Elgin 4 Oct 1881; d. Ottawa 18 Apr 1958)
	11 Jun – 15 Nov 1948: *Robert Wellington Mayhew* (b. Cobden 13 Oct 1880; d. 28 Jul 1971)
Immigration and Colonization	23 Oct 1935 – 30 Nov 1936: *Thomas Alexander Crerar* (see King II)
	1 Dec 1936: office abolished
Justice and Attorney General	23 Oct 1935 – 26 Nov 1941: *Ernest Lapointe* (see King II)
	27 Nov – 9 Dec 1941 (acting:) *Joseph Enoil Michaud* (see above)
	10 Dec 1941 – 9 Dec 1946: *Louis Stephen St-Laurent* (see above)
	10 Dec 1946 – 30 Jun 1948: *James Lorimer Ilsley* (see above)
	1 Jul – 15 Nov 1948 (acting until 9 Sep 1948:) *Louis Stephen St-Laurent* (see above)
Labour	23 Oct 1935 – 18 Sep 1939: *Norman McLeod Rogers* (b. Amherst 25 Jul 1894; d. Newtonville 10 Jun 1940)
	19 Sep 1939 – 14 Dec 1941: *Norman Alexander McLarty* (b. St Thomas 18 Feb 1889; d. Ottawa 6 Sep 1945)
	15 Dec 1941 – 15 Nov 1948: *Humphrey Mitchell* (b. Old Shoreham, Sussex, 9 Sep 1894; d. Ottawa 8 Oct 1961)
Marine	23 Oct 1935 – 1 Nov 1936: *Clarence Decatur Howe* (b. Waltham, Massachusetts, 15 Jan 1886; d. Montreal 31 Dec 1960)
	2 Nov 1936: amalgamated with Railways and Canals to form Ministry of Transport (see below)
Mines	23 Oct 1935 – 30 Nov 1936: *Thomas Alexander Crerar* (see King II)
	1 Dec 1936: superseded by Ministry of Mines and Resources (see below)
Mines and Resources (new post)	1 Dec 1936 – 17 Apr 1945: *Thomas Alexander Crerar* (see King II)
	18 Apr 1945 – 10 Jun 1948: *James Allison Glen* (b. Renton, Scotland, 18 Dec 1877; d. Ottawa 28 Jun 1950)

11 Jun – 15 Nov 1948: *James Angus MacKinnon* (see above)

Munitions and Supply 9 Apr 1940 – 31 Dec 1945: *Clarence Decatur Howe* (see above)
1 Jan 1946: superseded by Ministry of Reconstruction and Supply (see below)

National Defence 23 Oct 1935 – 18 Sep 1939: *Ian Alistair Mackenzie* (see King II)
19 Sep 1939 – 10 Jun 1940: *Norman McLeod Rogers* (see above)
11 Jun – 4 Jul 1940 (acting:) *Charles Gavan Power* (b. Sillery 18 Jan 1888; d. 30 May 1968)
5 Jul 1940 – 1 Nov 1944: *James Layton Ralston* (see King II)
2 Nov 1944 – 20 Aug 1945: *Andrew George Latta McNaughton* (b. Moosoomin 25 Feb 1887; d. 11 Jul 1966)
21 Aug 1945 – 11 Dec 1946: *Douglas Charles Abbott* (see above)
12 Dec 1946 – 15 Nov 1948: *Brooke Claxton* (b. Montreal 23 Aug 1898; d. Ottawa 13 Jun 1960)

National Defence (Associate Minister) 12 Jul 1940 – 26 Nov 1946: *Charles Gavan Power* (see above)
27 Nov 1946 – 15 Nov 1948: office temporarily suspended

National Defence (Air) 23 May 1940 – 26 Nov 1944: *Charles Gavan Power* (see above)
30 Nov 1944 – 10 Jan 1945 (acting:) *Angus Lewis Macdonald* (b. Dunvegan 10 Aug 1890; d. Halifax 13 Apr 1954)
11 Jan 1945 – Dec 1946 (acting until 7 Mar 1945:) *Colin William George Gibson* (b. Hamilton 16 Feb 1891)
12 Dec 1946: office abolished

National Defence (Naval Services) 12 Jul 1940 – 17 Apr 1945: *Angus Lewis Macdonald* (see above)
18 Apr 1945 – 11 Dec 1946: *Douglas Charles Abbott* (see above)
12 Dec 1946: office abolished

National Health and Welfare (new post) 18 Oct 1944 – 11 Dec 1946: *Brooke Claxton* (see above)
12 Dec 1946 – 15 Nov 1948: *Paul Joseph James Martin* (b. Ottawa 23 Jun 1903)

93

National Revenue	23 Oct 1935 – 7 Jul 1940: *James Lorimer Ilsley* (see above) 8 Jul 1940 – 7 Mar 1945: *Colin William George Gibson* (see above) 8 Mar – 18 Apr 1945 (acting:) *James Angus MacKinnon* (see above) 19 Apr – 29 Jul 1945: *David Laurence MacLaren* (b. Saint John 27 Oct 1893; d. 11 Apr 1961) 30 Jul – 28 Aug 1945 (acting:) *James Angus MacKinnon* (see above) 29 Aug 1945 – 15 Nov 1948: *Paul Joseph James Martin* (see above)
Pensions and National Health	23 Oct 1935 – 18 Sep 1939: *Charles Gavan Power* (see above) 19 Sep 1939 – 17 Oct 1944: *Ian Alistair Mackenzie* (see King II) 18 Oct 1944: superseded by Ministry of National Health and Welfare (see above)
Postmaster General	23 Oct 1935 – 22 Jan 1939: *John Campbell Elliott* (see King II) 23 Jan – 18 Sep 1939: *Norman Alexander McLarty* (see above) 19 Sep 1939 – 22 May 1940: *Charles Gavan Power* (see above) 23 May – 7 Jul 1940 (acting:) *James Lorimer Ilsley* (see above) 8 Jul 1940 – 8 Jun 1945: *William Pate Mulock* (b. Toronto 8 Jul 1897; d. Toronto 25 Aug 1954) 29 Aug 1945 – 15 Nov 1948: *Ernest Bertrand* (see above)
President of the Privy Council	*William Lyon Mackenzie King* (see King II)
Public Works	23 Oct 1935 – 12 May 1942: *Pierre Joseph Arthur Cardin* (see King II) 13 May – 6 Oct 1942 (acting:) *Joseph Enoil Michaud* (see above) 7 Oct 1942 – 15 Nov 1948: *Alphonse Fournier* (b. Methuen, Massachusetts, 24 Mar 1893; d. Hull 8 Oct 1961)
Railways and Canals	23 Oct 1935 – 1 Nov 1936: *Clarence Decatur Howe* (see above) 2 Nov 1936: amalgamated with Marine to form Ministry of Transport (see below)

Reconstruction	13 Oct 1944 – 31 Dec 1945: *Clarence Decatur Howe* (see above) 1 Jan 1946: superseded by Ministry of Reconstruction and Supply (see below)
Reconstruction and Supply (new post)	1 Jan 1946 – 15 Nov 1948: *Clarence Decatur Howe* (see above)
Secretary of State of Canada	23 Oct 1935 – 12 Jul 1939: *Fernand Rinfret* (see King II) 26 Jul 1939 – 8 May 1940 (acting:) *Ernest Lapointe* (see King II) 9 May 1940 – 14 Dec 1941: *Pierre François Casgrain* (b. Montreal 4 Aug 1886; d. Westmount 2 Aug 1950) 15 Dec 1941 – 17 Apr 1945: *Norman Alexander McLarty* (see above) 18 Apr 1945 – 11 Dec 1946: *Paul Joseph James Martin* (see above) 12 Dec 1946 – 15 Nov 1948: *Colin William George Gibson* (see above)
Solicitor General	23 Oct 1935 – 18 Apr 1945: office vacant 18 Apr 1945 – 15 Nov 1948: *Joseph Jean* (b. St-Philippe de Néri 7 Feb 1890; d. 18 Jul 1973)
Trade and Commerce	23 Oct 1935 – 8 May 1940: *William Daum Euler* (see King II) 9 May 1940 – 18 Jan 1948: *James Angus MacKinnon* (see above) 19 Jan – 15 Nov 1948: *Clarence Decatur Howe* (see above)
Transport (new post)	2 Nov 1936 – 7 Jul 1940: *Clarence Decatur Howe* (see above) 8 Jul 1940 – 12 May 1942: *Pierre Joseph Arthur Cardin* (see King II) 13 May – 5 Oct 1942 (acting:) *Clarence Decatur Howe* (see above) 6 Oct 1942 – 17 Apr 1945: *Joseph Enoil Michaud* (see above) 18 Apr 1945 – 15 Nov 1948: *Lionel Chevrier* (b. Cornwall 2 Apr 1903)
Veterans Affairs (new post)	18 Oct 1944 – 18 Jan 1948: *Ian Alistair Mackenzie* (see King II) 19 Jan – 15 Nov 1948: *Milton Fowler Gregg* (see above)
Without Portfolio	23 Oct 1935 – 11 Mar 1942: *Raoul Dandurand* (see

95

King II)
23 Jan 1939 – 8 May 1940: *James Angus MacKinnon*
(see above)
26 May 1942 – 23 Aug 1945: *James Horace King* (see
King II)
4 Sep 1945 – 15 Nov 1948: *Wishart McLea Robertson*
(b. Barrington Passage 15 Feb 1891; d. 16 Aug 1967)

15 Nov 1948 – 21 Jun 1957: St-Laurent (Lib)

Prime Minister	*Louis Stephen St-Laurent* (see King III)
External Affairs	*Lester Bowles Pearson* (see King III)
Agriculture	*James Garfield Gardiner* (see King III)
Citizenship and Immigration	18 Jan 1950 – 30 Jun 1954: *Walter Edward Harris* (b. Kimberley, Ontario, 14 Jan 1904)
	1 Jul 1954 – 21 Jun 1957: *John Whitney Pickersgill* (b. Wyecombe 23 Jun 1905)
Defence Production	1 Apr 1951 – 21 Jun 1957: *Clarence Decatur Howe* (see King III)
Finance and Receiver General	15 Nov 1948 – 30 Jun 1954: *Douglas Charles Abbott* (see King III)
	1 Jul 1954 – 21 Jun 1957: *Walter Edward Harris* (see above)
Fisheries	15 Nov 1948 – 14 Oct 1952: *Robert Wellington Mayhew* (see King III)
	15 Oct 1952 – 21 Jun 1957: *James Sinclair* (b. Banff, Scotland, 26 May 1908)
Justice and Attorney General	*Stuart Sinclair Garson* (b. St Catherines 1 Dec 1898)
Labour	15 Nov 1948 – 2 Aug 1950: *Humphrey Mitchell* (see King III)
	3 – 6 Aug 1950 (acting:) *Paul Joseph James Martin* (see King III)
	7 Aug 1950 – 21 Jun 1957: *Milton Fowler Gregg* (see King III)
Mines and Resources	15 Nov 1948 – 31 Mar 1949: *James Angus MacKinnon* (see King III)
	1 Apr 1949 – 17 Jan 1950: *Colin William George Gibson* (see King III)
	18 Jan 1950: superseded by Ministry of Mines and Technical Surveys and Ministry of Resources and Development

Mines and Technical Surveys (new post)	18 Jan – 12 Dec 1950: *James Joseph McCann* 13 Dec 1950 – 21 Jun 1957: *George Prudham* (b. Kilbride 27 Feb 1904)
National Defence	15 Nov 1948 – 30 Jun 1954: *Brooke Claxton* (see King III) 1 Jul 1954 – 21 Jun 1957: *Ralph Osborne Campney* (b. Picton 6 Jun 1894; d. 6 Oct 1967)
National Defence (Associate Minister)	12 Feb 1953 – 30 Jun 1954: *Ralph Osborne Campney* (see above) 26 Apr – 21 Jun 1957: *Paul Theodore Hellyer* (b. Waterford 6 Aug 1923)
National Health and Welfare	*Paul Joseph James Martin* (see King III)
National Revenue	*James Joseph McCann* (see above)
Northern Affairs and National Resources (new post)	16 Dec 1953 – 21 Jun 1957: *Jean Lesage* (b. Montreal 10 Jun 1912)
Postmaster General	15 Nov 1948 – 23 Aug 1949: *Ernest Bertrand* (see King III) 25 Aug 1949 – 12 Feb 1952: *Gabriel Édouard Rinfret* (b. St-Jérôme 12 May 1905) 13 Feb 1952 – 7 Aug 1955: *Alcide Côté* (b. St-Jean 19 May 1903; d. St-Jean 7 Aug 1955) 16 Aug – 2 Nov 1955 (acting:) *Roch Pinard* (b. Nicolet 26 Jul 1910) 3 Nov 1955 – 21 Jun 1957: *Hugues Lapointe* (b. Rivière-du-Loup 3 Mar 1911)
President of the Privy Council	15 Nov 1948 – 24 Apr 1957: *Louis Stephen St-Laurent* (see King III) 25 Apr – 21 Jun 1957: *Lionel Chevrier* (see King III)
Public Works	15 Nov 1948 – 11 Jun 1953: *Alphonse Fournier* (see King III) 12 Jun – 16 Sep 1953 (acting:) *Walter Edward Harris* (see above) 17 Sep 1953 – 21 Jun 1957: *Robert Henry Winters* (b. Lunenburg 18 Aug 1910; d. 10 Oct 1969)
Reconstruction and Supply	15 Nov 1948 – 17 Jan 1950: *Robert Henry Winters* (see above) 18 Jan 1950: office superseded by Ministry of Resources and Development (see below)
Resources and Development (new post)	18 Jan 1950 – 16 Sep 1953: *Robert Henry Winters* (see above)

	17 Sep – 15 Dec 1953: *Jean Lesage* (see above)
	16 Dec 1953: functions taken over by Ministry of Mines and Technical Surveys and Ministry of Northern Affairs and National Resources (see above)
Secretary of State of Canada	15 Nov 1948 – 31 Mar 1949: *Colin William George Gibson* (see King III)
	1 Apr 1949 – 11 Jun 1953: *Frederick Gordon Bradley* (b. St John's 21 Mar 1888; d. Bonavista 30 Mar 1960)
	12 Jun 1953 – 30 Jun 1954: *John Whitney Pickersgill* (see above)
	1 Jul 1954 – 21 Jun 1957: *Roch Pinard* (see above)
Solicitor General	15 Nov 1948 – 23 Aug 1949: *Joseph Jean* (see King III)
	25 Aug 1949 – 6 Aug 1950: *Hugues Lapointe* (see above)
	7 Aug 1950 – 14 Oct 1952: *Stuart Sinclair Garson* (see above)
	15 Oct 1952 – 11 Jan 1954: *Ralph Osborne Campney* (see above)
	12 Jan 1954 – 21 Jun 1957: *William Ross Macdonald* (b. Toronto 25 Dec 1891)
Trade and Commerce	*Clarence Decatur Howe* (see King III)
Transport	15 Nov 1948 – 30 Jun 1954: *Lionel Chevrier* (see King III)
	1 Jul 1954 – 21 Jun 1957: *George Carlyle Marler* (b. Montreal 14 Sep 1901)
Veterans Affairs	15 Nov 1948 – 6 Aug 1950: *Milton Fowler Gregg* (see King III)
	7 Aug 1950 – 21 Jun 1957: *Hugues Lapointe* (see above)
Without Portfolio	15 Nov 1948 – 13 Oct 1953: *Wishart McLea Robertson* (see King III)
	1 Apr 1949 – 13 Dec 1950: *James Angus MacKinnon* (see King III)
	14 Oct 1954 – 11 Jan 1954: *William Ross Macdonald* (see above)

21 Jun 1957 – 22 Apr 1963: Diefenbaker (Prog Cons)

Prime Minister	*John George Diefenbaker* (b. Neustadt 18 Sep 1895)
External Affairs	21 Jun – 12 Sep 1957: *John George Diefenbaker* (see above)
	13 Sep 1957 – 17 Mar 1959: *Sidney Earle Smith* (b. Port Hood 9 Mar 1897; d. Ottawa 17 Mar 1959)

19 Mar – 3 Jun 1959 (acting:) *John George Diefenbaker* (see above)
4 Jun 1959 – 22 Apr 1963: *Howard Charles Green* (b. Kaslo 5 Nov 1895)

Agriculture
21 Jun 1957 – 10 Oct 1950 (acting until 6 Aug 1957:) *Douglas Scott Harkness* (b. Toronto 29 Mar 1903)
11 Oct 1960 – 22 Apr 1963: *Francis Alvin George Hamilton* (b. Kenora 30 Mar 1912)

Citizenship and Immigration
21 Jun 1957 – 11 May 1958: *Edmund Davie Fulton* (b. Kamloops 10 Mar 1916)
12 May 1958 – 8 Aug 1962: *Ellen Louks Fairclough* (b. Hamilton 28 Jan 1905)
9 Aug 1962 – 22 Apr 1963: *Richard Albert Bell* (b. Britannia Bay 4 Sep 1913)

Finance and Receiver General
21 Jun 1957 – 8 Aug 1962: *Donald Methuen Fleming* (b. Exeter, Ontario, 23 May 1905)
9 Aug 1962 – 22 Apr 1963: *George Clyde Nowlan* (b. Havelock 14 Aug 1898; d. Ontario 31 May 1965)

Fisheries
John Angus MacLean (b. Lewis 15 May 1914)

Forestry
11 Oct 1960 – 17 Mar 1963: *Hugh John Flemming* (b. Peel 5 Jan 1899)
18 Mar – 22 Apr 1963: *Martial Asselin* (b. La Malbaie 3 Feb 1924)

Justice and Attorney General
21 Jun 1957 – 8 Aug 1962: *Edmund Davie Fulton* (see above)
9 Aug 1962 – 22 Apr 1963: *Donald Methuen Fleming* (see above)

Labour
Michael Starr (b. Copper Cliff 14 Nov 1910)

Mines and Technical Surveys
21 Jun – 6 Aug 1957 (acting:) *Léon Balcer* (b. Trois Rivières 13 Oct 1917)
7 Aug 1957 – 6 Oct 1961: *Paul Comtois* (b. Pierreville 22 Aug 1895; d. Ottawa 21 Feb 1966)
10 Oct – 27 Dec 1961 (acting:) *Walter Gilbert Dinsdale* (b. Brandon 3 Apr 1916)
28 Dec 1961 – 12 Jul 1962: *Jacques Flynn* (b. St-Hyacinthe 22 Aug 1915)
18 Jul – 8 Aug 1962 (acting:) *Hugh John Flemming* (see above)
9 Aug 1962 – 22 Apr 1963: *Paul Martineau* (b. Bryson 10 Apr 1921)

National Defence
21 Jun 1957 – 10 Oct 1960: *George Randolph Pearkes* (b. Watford, Hertfordshire, 26 Feb 1888)
11 Oct 1960 – 3 Feb 1963: *Douglas Scott Harkness* (see above)

99

12 Feb – 22 Apr 1963: *Gordon Churchill* (b. Coldwater 8 Nov 1898)

National Defence (Associate Minister)
20 Aug 1959 – 8 Feb 1963: *Joseph Pierre Albert Sévigny* (b. Quebec 17 Sep 1917)

National Health and Welfare
21 Jun – 21 Aug 1957 (acting:) *Alfred Johnson Brooks* (b. Gagetown 14 Nov 1890; d. 7 Dec 1967)

22 Aug 1957 – 22 Apr 1963: *Jay Waldo Monteith* (b. Stratford 24 Jun 1903)

National Revenue
21 Jun 1957 – 8 Aug 1962: *George Clyde Nowlan* (see above)

9 Aug 1962 – 22 Apr 1963: *Hugh John Flemming* (see above)

Northern Affairs and National Resources
21 Jun – 18 Aug 1957: *Douglas Scott Harkness* (see above)

22 Aug 1957 – 10 Oct 1960: *Francis Alvin George Hamilton* (see above)

11 Oct 1960 – 22 Apr 1963: *Walter Gilbert Dinsdale* (see above)

Postmaster General
21 Jun 1957 – 12 Jul 1962: *William McLean Hamilton* (b. Montreal 23 Feb 1919)

18 Jul – 8 Aug 1962 (acting:) *John Angus MacLean* (see above)

9 Aug 1962 – 2b Apr 1963: *Ellen Louks Fairclough* (see above)

President of the Privy Council
28 Dec 1961 – 5 Jul 1962: *Noël Dorion* (b. Charlesbourg 24 Jul 1904)

21 Dec 1962 – 22 Apr 1963: *John George Diefenbaker* (see above)

Public Works
21 Jun 1957 – 19 Aug 1959: *Howard Charles Green* (see above)

20 Aug 1959 – 12 Jul 1962: *David James Walker* (b. Toronto 10 May 1905)

18 Jul – 8 Aug 1962 (acting:) *Howard Charles Green* (see above)

9 Aug 1962 – 22 Apr 1963: *Edmund Davie Fulton* (see above)

Secretary of State of Canada
21 Jun 1957 – 11 May 1958: *Ellen Louks Fairclough* (see above)

12 May 1958 – 19 Jan 1960: *Henri Courtemanche* (b. Mont-Laurier 7 Aug 1916)

21 Jan – 10 Oct 1960 (acting:) *Léon Balcer* (see above)

11 Oct 1960 – 5 Jul 1962: *Noël Dorion* (see above)

	11 Jul – 8 Aug 1962 (acting:) *Léon Balcer* (see above) 9 Aug 1962 – 22 Apr 1963: *George Ernest Halpenny* (b. Plantagenet 14 Jun 1903)
Solicitor General	21 Jun 1957 – 10 Oct 1960: *Léon Balcer* (see above) 11 Oct 1960 – 9 Aug 1962: *William Joseph Browne* (b. St John's 3 May 1897)
Trade and Commerce	21 Jun 1957 – 10 Oct 1960: *Gordon Churchill* (see above) 11 Oct 1960 – 8 Feb 1963: *George Harris Hees* (b. Toronto 17 Jan 1910) 12 Feb – 22 Apr 1963: *Malcolm Wallace McCutcheon* (b. London, Ontario, 18 May 1906; d. 23 Jan 1969)
Transport	21 Jun 1957 – 10 Oct 1960: *George Harris Hees* (see above) 11 Oct 1960 – 22 Apr 1963: *Léon Balcer* (see above)
Veterans Affairs	21 Jun 1957 – 10 Oct 1960: *Alfred Johnson Brooks* (see above) 11 Oct 1960 – 11 Feb 1963: *Gordon Churchill* (see above) 12 Feb – 22 Apr 1963: *Marcel Joseph Aimé Lambert* (b. Edmonton 21 Aug 1919)
Without Portfolio	21 Jun 1957 – 10 Oct 1960: *William Joseph Browne* (see above) 21 Jun 1957 – 19 Aug 1959: *James McKerras Macdonnell* (b. Kingston 15 Dec 1884) 9 Oct 1957 – 11 May 1958: *John Thomas Haig* (b. Colborne 15 Dec 1877; d. Winnipeg 22 Oct 1962) 11 Oct 1960 – 8 Aug 1962: *George Ernest Halpenny* (see above) 9 Aug 1962 – 11 Feb 1963: *Malcolm Wallace McCutcheon* (see above) 18 Mar – 22 Apr 1963: *Frank Charles McGee* (b. Ottawa 3 Mar 1926) 18 Mar – 22 Apr 1963: *Théogène Ricard* (b. St-Guillaume 30 Apr 1909)

22 Apr 1963 – 20 Apr 1968: Pearson (Lib)

Prime Minister	*Lester Bowles Pearson* (see King III)
External Affairs	*Paul Joseph James Martin* (see King III)
Agriculture	22 Apr 1963 – 17 Dec 1965: *Harry William Hays* (b. Carstairs 25 Dec 1909) 18 Dec 1965 – 20 Apr 1968: *John James Greene* (b.

	Toronto 24 Jun 1920)
Citizenship and Immigration	22 Apr 1963 – 2 Feb 1964: *Guy Favreau* (b. Montreal 20 May 1917)
	3 Feb 1964 – 14 Feb 1965: *René Tremblay* (b. Luceville 12 Nov 1922)
	15 Feb – 17 Dec 1965: *John Robert Nicholson* (b. Newcastle, New Brunswick, 1 Dec 1901)
	18 Dec 1965 – 30 Sep 1966: *Jean Marchand* (b. Champlain 20 Dec 1918)
	1 Oct 1966: superseded by Ministry of Manpower and Immigration (see below)
Consumer and Corporate Affairs (new post)	21 Dec 1967 – 20 Apr 1968: *John Napier Turner* (b. Richmond, Surrey, 7 Jun 1929)
Defence Production	*Charles Mills Drury* (b. Westmount 7 May 1912)
Energy, Mines and Resources (new post)	1 Oct 1966 – 20 Apr 1968: *Jean Luc Pepin* (b. Drummondville 1 Nov 1924)
Finance and Receiver General	22 Apr 1963 – 10 Nov 1965: *Walter Lockhart Gordon* (b. Toronto 27 Jan 1906)
	11 Nov 1965 – 20 Apr 1968 (acting until 17 Dec 1965:) *Mitchell William Sharp* (b. Winnipeg 11 May 1911)
Fisheries	*Hédard Robichaud* (b. Shippegan 2 Nov 1911)
Forestry	22 Apr 1963 – 2 Feb 1964: *John Robert Nicholson* (see above)
	3 Feb 1964 – 30 Sep 1966: *Maurice Sauvé* (b. Montreal 20 Sep 1923)
	1 Oct 1966: superseded by Ministry of Forestry and Rural Development (see below)
Forestry and Rural Development (new post)	1 Oct 1966 – 20 Apr 1968: *Maurice Sauvé* (see above)
Indian Affairs and Northern Development (new post)	1 Oct 1966 – 20 Apr 1968: *Arthur Laing* (b. Eburne 9 Sep 1904)
Industry	*Charles Mills Drury* (see above)
Justice and Attorney General	22 Apr 1963 – 2 Feb 1964: *Lionel Chevrier* (see King III)
	3 Feb 1964 – 29 Jun 1965: *Guy Favreau* (see above)
	30 Jun – 6 Jul 1965 (acting:) *George James McIlwraith* (b. Lanark 29 Jul 1908)

7 Jul 1965 – 3 Apr 1967: *Louis Joseph Lucien Cardin* (b. Providence, Rhode Island, 1 Mar 1919)

4 Apr 1967 – 20 Apr 1968: *Pierre Elliott Trudeau* (b. Montreal 18 Oct 1919)

Labour

22 Apr 1963 – 17 Dec 1965: *Allan Joseph MacEachen* (b. Inverness, Nova Scotia, 6 Jul 1921)

18 Dec 1965 – 20 Apr 1968: *John Robert Nicholson* (see above)

Manpower and Immigration (new post)

1 Oct 1966 – 20 Apr 1968: *Jean Marchand* (see above)

Mines and Technical Surveys

22 Apr 1963 – 6 Jul 1965: *William Moore Benidickson* (b. Dauphin 8 Apr 1911)

7 Jul – 17 Dec 1965: *John Watson MacNaught* (b. Coleman 19 Jun 1904)

18 Dec 1965 – 30 Sep 1966: *Jean Luc Pepin* (see above)

1 Oct 1966: superseded by Ministry of Energy, Mines and Resources (see above)

National Defence

22 Apr 1963 – 18 Sep 1967: *Paul Theodore Hellyer* (see St-Laurent)

19 Sep 1967 – 20 Apr 1968: *Léo Alphonse Joseph Cadieux* (b. St-Jérôme 28 May 1908)

National Defence (Associate Minister)

22 Apr 1963 – 14 Feb 1965: *Louis Joseph Lucien Cardin* (see above)

15 Feb 1965 – 18 Sep 1967: *Léo Alphonse Joseph Cadieux* (see above)

National Health and Welfare

22 Apr 1963 – 17 Dec 1965: *Julia Verlyn LaMarsh* (b. Chatham, Ontario, 20 Dec 1924)

18 Dec 1965 – 20 Apr 1968: *Allan Joseph MacEachen* (see above)

National Revenue

22 Apr 1963 – 14 Mar 1964: *John Richard Garland* (b. Smiths Falls 1 Jan 1918; d. Ottawa 14 Mar 1964)

19 – 28 Mar 1964 (acting:) *George James McIlwraith* (see above)

29 Mar 1964 – 17 Jan 1968: *Edgar John Benson* (b. Cobourg 28 May 1923)

18 Jan – 20 Apr 1968: *Joseph Jacques Jean Chrétien* (b. Shawinigan 11 Jan 1934)

Northern Affairs and National Resources

23 Apr 1963 – 30 Sep 1966: *Arthur Laing* (see above)

1 Oct 1966: functions taken over by Ministry of Indian Affairs and Northern Development and Ministry of Energy, Mines and Resources

Postmaster General

22 Apr 1963 – 2 Feb 1964: *Azellus Denis* (b. St-Norbert 26 Mar 1907)
3 Feb 1964 – 14 Feb 1965: *John Robert Nicholson* (see above)
15 Feb – 17 Dec 1965: *René Tremblay* (see above)
18 Dec 1965 – 20 Apr 1968: *Joseph Julien Jean Pierre Côté* (b. Montreal 9 Jan 1926)

President of the Privy Council

22 Apr 1963 – 2 Feb 1964: *Maurice Lamontagne* (b. Mont-Joli 7 Sep 1917)
3 Feb 1964 – 6 Jul 1965: *George James McIlwraith* (see above)
7 Jul 1965 – 3 Apr 1967: *Guy Favreau* (see above)
4 Apr 1967 – 10 Mar 1968: *Walter Lockhart Gordon* (see above)
11 Mar – 20 Apr 1968 (acting:) *Pierre Elliott Trudeau* (see above)

President of the Treasury Board (exercised hitherto by Minister of Finance)

1 Oct 1966 – 20 Apr 1968: *Edgar John Benson* (see above)

Public Works

22 Apr 1963 – 11 Feb 1965: *Jean Paul Deschatelets* (b. Montreal 9 Oct 1912)
15 Feb – 6 Jul 1965: *Louis Joseph Lucien Cardin* (see above)
7 Jul 1965 – 20 Apr 1968: *George James McIlwraith* (see above)

Registrar General (exercised hitherto by Secretary of State of Canada)

1 Oct 1966 – 3 Apr 1967: *Guy Favreau* (see above)
4 Apr – 20 Dec 1967: *John Napier Turner* (see above)
21 Dec 1967: functions taken over by Minister of Consumer and Corporate Affairs (see above)

Secretary of State of Canada

22 Apr 1963 – 2 Feb 1964: *John Whitney Pickersgill* (see St-Laurent)
3 Feb 1964 – 17 Dec 1965: *Maurice Lamontagne* (see above)
18 Dec 1965 – 9 Apr 1968: *Julia Verlyn LaMarsh* (see above)
10 – 20 Apr 1968: *John Joseph Connolly* (b. Ottawa 31 Oct 1906)

Solicitor General	22 Apr 1963 – 6 Jul 1965: *John Watson MacNaught* (see above) 7 Jul 1965 – 19 Apr 1968: *Lawrence Pennell* (b. Brantford 11 Mar 1915)
Trade and Commerce	22 Apr 1963 – 3 Jan 1966: *Mitchell William Sharp* (see above) 4 Jan 1966 – 29 Mar 1968: *Robert Henry Winters* (see St-Laurent) 30 Mar – 20 Apr 1968 (acting:) *Jean Luc Pepin* (see above)
Transport	23 Apr 1963 – 2 Feb 1964: *George James McIlwraith* (see above) 3 Feb 1964 – 18 Sep 1967: *John Whitney Pickersgill* (see St-Laurent) 19 Sep 1967 – 20 Apr 1968: *Paul Theodore Hellyer* (see St-Laurent)
Veterans Affairs	*Roger Joseph Teillet* (b. St-Vital 21 Aug 1912)
Without Portfolio	22 Apr 1963 – 2 Feb 1964: *William Ross Macdonald* (see St-Laurent) 22 Apr 1963 – 6 Jul 1965: *John Watson MacNaught* (see above) 22 Apr 1963 – 2 Feb 1964: *René Tremblay* (see above) 3 Feb 1964 – 20 Apr 1968: *John Joseph Connolly* (see above) 3 Feb 1964 – 21 Jan 1965: *Yvon Dupuis* (b. Montreal 11 Oct 1926) 7 Jul 1965 – 30 Sep 1966: *Lawrence Pennell* (see above) 7 Jul – 17 Dec 1965: *Jean Luc Pepin* (see above) 18 Dec 1965 – 3 Apr 1967: *John Napier Turner* (see above) 9 Jan – 3 Apr 1967: *Walter Lockhart Gordon* (see above) 4 Apr 1967 – 17 Jan 1968: *Joseph Jacques Jean Chrétien* (see above) 25 Sep 1967 – 20 Apr 1968: *Charles Ronald McKay Granger* (b. Catalina 12 Aug 1912) 9 Feb – 20 Apr 1968: *Bryce Stuart Mackasey* (b. Quebec 25 Aug 1921)

from 20 Apr 1968: Trudeau (Lib)

Prime Minister	*Pierre Elliott Trudeau* (see Pearson)

CANADA

External Affairs	20 Apr 1968 – 7 Aug 1974: *Mitchell William Sharp* (see Pearson) from 8 Aug 1974: *Allan Joseph MacEachen* (see Pearson)
Agriculture	20 Apr – 5 Jul 1968: *John James Greene* (see Pearson) 6 Jul 1968 – 26 Nov 1972: *Horace Andrew Olson* (b. Iddesleigh 6 Oct 1925) from 27 Nov 1972: *Eugene Francis Whelan* (b. Amherstburg 11 Jul 1924)
Communications (new post)	1 Apr 1969 – 28 Apr 1971: *Eric William Kierans* (b. Montreal 24 Feb 1914) 29 Apr – 10 May 1971 (acting:) *Joseph Julien Jean Pierre Côté* (see Pearson) 11 May – 11 Aug 1971 (acting:) *Gérard Pelletier* (b. Victoriaville 21 Jun 1919) 12 Aug 1971 – 26 Nov 1972: *Robert Douglas George Stanbury* (b. Exeter, Ontario, 26 Jun 1929) 27 Nov 1972 – 29 Aug 1975: *Gérard Pelletier* (see above) 29 Aug – 5 Dec 1975: *Pierre Juneau* from 5 Dec 1975: *Jeanne Sauvé*
Consumer and Corporate Affairs	20 Apr – 5 Jul 1968: *John Napier Turner* (see Pearson) 6 Jul 1968 – 27 Jan 1972: *(Stanley) Ronald Basford* (b. Winnipeg 22 Apr 1932) 28 Jan – 26 Nov 1972: *Robert Knight Andras* (b. Lachine 20 Feb 1921) 27 Nov 1972 – 7 Aug 1974: *Herbert Eser Gray* (b. Windsor, Ontario, 25 May 1931) from 8 Aug 1974: *André Ouellet* (b. St-Pascal 6 Apr 1939)
Defence Production	20 Apr – 5 Jul 1968: *Charles Mills Drury* (see Pearson) 6 Jul 1968 – 31 Mar 1969: *Donald Campbell Jamieson* (b. St John's 30 Apr 1921) 1 Apr 1969: superseded by Ministry of Supply and Services (see below)
Energy, Mines and Resources	20 Apr – 5 Jul 1968: *Jean Luc Pepin* (see Pearson) 6 Jul 1968 – 27 Jan 1972: *John James Greene* (see Pearson) 28 Jan 1972 – 10 Sep 1975: *Donald Stovel Macdonald* (b. Ottawa 1 Mar 1932) from 10 Sep 1975: *Alastair William Gillespie* (b.

	Victoria 1 May 1922)
Environment	11 Jun 1971 – 7 Aug 1974: *Jack Davis*
(new post)	(b. Kamloops 31 Jul 1916)
	8 Aug 1974 – 5 Dec 1975: *Jeanne Sauvé* (b.
	Prud'homme 26 Apr 1922)
	from 5 Dec 1975 (acting:) *Romeo A. LeBlanc* (b.
	L'Anse-aux-Cormier 18 Dec 1927)
Finance (and until	20 Apr 1968 – 27 Jan 1972: *Edgar John Benson*
31 Mar 1969:	(see Pearson)
Receiver	28 Jan 1972 – 10 Sep 1975: *John Napier Turner*
General)	(see Pearson)
	from 10 Sep 1975: *Donald Stovel Macdonald* (see
	above)
Fisheries	20 Apr – 5 Jul 1968: *Hédard Robichaud* (see Pearson)
	6 Jul 1968 – 31 Mar 1969: *Jack Davis* (see above)
	1 Apr 1969 – 7 Aug 1974: superseded by Ministry of
	Fisheries and Forestry (see below)
	from 8 Aug 1974 (office re-established:) *Romeo A.*
	LeBlanc (see above)
Fisheries and	1 Apr 1969 – 10 Jun 1971: *Jack Davis* (see
Forestry	above)
	11 Jun 1971: superseded by Ministry of the
	Environment (see above)
Forestry and Rural	20 Apr – 5 Jul 1968: *Maurice Sauvé* (see
Development	Pearson)
	6 Jul 1968 – 31 Mar 1969: *Jean Marchand* (see
	Pearson)
	1 Apr 1969: superseded by Ministry of Fisheries and
	Forestry (see above)
Indian Affairs and	20 Apr – 5 Jul 1968: *Arthur Laing* (see
Northern	Pearson)
Development	6 Jul 1968 – 7 Aug 1974: *Joseph Jacques Jean Chrétien*
	(see Pearson)
	from 8 Aug 1974: *J. Judd Buchanan* (b. Edmonton 25
	Jul 1929)
Industry	20 Apr – 5 Jul 1968: *Charles Mills Drury* (see Pearson)
	6 Jul 1968 – 31 Mar 1969: *Jean Luc Pepin* (see
	Pearson)
	1 Apr 1969: superseded by Ministry of Industry, Trade
	and Commerce (see below)
Industry, Trade and	1 Apr 1969 – 26 Nov 1972: *Jean Luc Pepin* (see
Commerce	Pearson)
(new post)	27 Nov 1972 – 10 Sep 1975: *Alastair William Gillespie*
	(see above)

	from 10 Sep 1975: *Donald Campbell Jamieson* (see above)
Justice and Attorney General	20 Apr – 5 Jul 1968: *Pierre Elliott Trudeau* (see Pearson)
	6 Jul 1968 – 27 Jan 1972: *John Napier Turner* (see Pearson)
	28 Jan 1972 – 10 Sep 1975: *Otto Emil Lang* (b. Handel 14 May 1932)
	from 10 Sep 1975: *(Stanley) Ronald Basford* (see above)
Labour	20 Apr – 5 Jul 1968: *Jean Luc Pepin* (see Pearson)
	6 Jul 1968 – 27 Jan 1972: *Bryce Stuart Mackasey* (see Pearson)
	28 Jan – 26 Nov 1972: *Martin Patrick O'Connell* (b. Victoria 1 Aug 1916)
	from 27 Nov 1972: *John Carr Munro* (b. Hamilton 6 Mar 1931)
Leader of the Government in the Senate	1 Apr 1969 – 7 Aug 1974: *Paul Joseph James Martin* (see King III)
Manpower and Immigration	20 Apr – 5 Jul 1968: *Jean Marchand* (see Pearson)
	6 Jul 1968 – 23 Sep 1970: *Allan Joseph MacEachen* (see Pearson)
	24 Sep 1970 – 27 Jan 1972: *Otto Emil Lang* (see above)
	28 Jan – 26 Nov 1972: *Bryce Stuart Mackasey* (see Pearson)
	from 27 Nov 1972: *Robert Knight Andras* (see above)
National Defence	20 Apr 1968 – 16 Sep 1970: *Léo Alphonse Joseph Cadieux* (see Pearson)
	17 – 23 Sep 1970 (acting:) *Charles Mills Drury* (see Pearson)
	24 Sep 1970 – 27 Jan 1972: *Donald Stovel Macdonald* (see above)
	28 Jan – 21 Aug 1972: *Edgar John Benson* (see Pearson)
	1 – 6 Sep 1972 (acting:) *Jean Eudes Dubé* (b. Matapédia 6 Nov 1926)
	7 Sep – 26 Nov 1972: *Charles Mills Drury* (see Pearson)
	from 27 Nov 1972: *James Armstrong Richardson* (b. Winnipeg 28 Mar 1922)

National Health and Welfare	20 Apr – 5 Jul 1968: *Allan Joseph MacEachen* (see Pearson) 6 Jul 1968 – 26 Nov 1972: *John Carr Munro* (see above) from 27 Nov 1972: *Marc Lalonde* (b. Ile Perrot 26 Jul 1929)
National Revenue	20 Apr – 5 Jul 1968: *Joseph Jacques Jean Chrétien* (see Pearson) 6 Jul 1968 – 23 Sep 1970: *Joseph Julien Jean Pierre Côté* (see Pearson) 24 Sep 1970 – 26 Nov 1972: *Herbert Eser Gray* (see above) 27 Nov 1972 – 7 Aug 1974: *Robert Douglas George Stanbury* (see above) 8 Aug 1974 – 10 Sep 1975: *(Stanley) Ronald Basford* (see above) from 10 Sep 1975: *Jack Cullen*
Postmaster General	20 Apr – 5 Jul 1968: *Joseph Julien Jean Pierre Côté* (see Pearson) 6 Jul 1968 – 28 Apr 1971: *Eric William Kierans* (see above) 29 Apr 1971 – 26 Nov 1972 (acting until 10 Jun 1971:) *Joseph Julien Jean Pierre Côté* (see Pearson) 27 Nov 1972 – 7 Aug 1974: *André Ouellet* (see above) from 8 Aug 1974: *Bryce Stuart Mackasey* (see Pearson)
President of the Privy Council	20 Apr – 1 May 1968 (acting:) *Pierre Elliott Trudeau* (see Pearson) 2 May – 5 Jul 1968 (acting:) *Allan Joseph MacEachen* (see Pearson) 6 Jul 1968 – 23 Sep 1970: *Donald Stovel Macdonald* (see above) 24 Sep 1970 – 7 Aug 1974: *Allan Joseph MacEachen* (see Pearson) from 8 Aug 1974: *Mitchell William Sharp* (see Pearson)
President of the Treasury Board	20 Apr – 5 Jul 1968: *Edgar John Benson* (see Pearson) 6 Jul 1968 – 7 Aug 1974: *Charles Mills Drury* (see Pearson) from 8 Aug 1974: *Joseph Jacques Jean Chrétien* (see Pearson)

109

Public Works · · · · · 20 Apr – 5 Jul 1968: *George James McIlwraith* (see Pearson)
6 Jul 1968 – 27 Jan 1972: *Arthur Laing* (see Pearson)
28 Jan 1972 – 7 Aug 1974: *Jean Eudes Dubé* (see above)
from 8 Aug 1974: *Charles Mills Drury* (see Pearson)

Regional Economic Expansion (new post) · · · · · 1 Apr 1969 – 26 Nov 1972: *Jean Marchand* (see Pearson)
27 Nov 1972 – 10 Sep 1975: *Donald Campbell Jamieson* (see above)
from 10 Sep 1975: *Marcel Lessard*

Science and Technology (Minister of State) · · · · · 12 Aug 1971 – 26 Nov 1972: *Alastair William Gillespie* (see above)
27 Nov 1972 – 7 Aug 1974: *Jeanne Sauvé* (see above)
from 8 Aug 1974: *Charles Mills Drury* (see Pearson)

Secretary of State of Canada · · · · · 20 Apr – 5 Jul 1968: *Jean Marchand* (see Pearson)
6 Jul 1968 – 26 Nov 1972: *Gérard Pelletier* (see above)
from 27 Nov 1972: *James Hugh Faulkner* (b. Montreal 9 Mar 1933)

Solicitor General · · · · · 20 Apr – 5 Jul 1968: *John Napier Turner* (see Pearson)
6 Jul 1968 – 21 Dec 1970: *George James McIlwraith* (see Pearson)
22 Dec 1970 – 26 Nov 1972: *Jean Pierre Goyer* (b. St-Laurent 17 Jan 1932)
from 27 Nov 1972: *William Warren Allmand* (b. Montreal 19 Sep 1932)

Supply and Services (new post) · · · · · 1 Apr – 4 May 1969: *Donald Campbell Jamieson* (see above)
5 May 1969 – 26 Nov 1972: *James Armstrong Richardson* (see above)
from 27 Nov 1972: *Jean Pierre Goyer* (see above)

Trade and Commerce · · · · · 20 Apr – 5 Jul 1968: *Charles Mills Drury* (see Pearson)
6 Jul 1968 – 31 Mar 1969: *Jean Luc Pepin* (see Pearson)
1 Apr 1969: superseded by Ministry of Industry, Trade and Commerce (see above)

Transport · · · · · 20 Apr 1968 – 29 Apr 1969: *Paul Theodore Hellyer* (see St-Laurent)
30 Apr – 4 May 1969 (acting:) *James Armstrong Richardson* (see above)
5 May 1969 – 26 Nov 1972: *Donald Campbell*

Jamieson (see above)
27 Nov 1972 – 10 Sep 1975: *Jean Marchand* (see Pearson)
from 10 Sep 1975: *Otto Emil Lang* (see above)

Urban Affairs (Minister of State) 30 Jun 1971 – 27 Jan 1972: *Robert Knight Andras* (see above)
28 Jan 1972 – 7 Aug 1974: *(Stanley) Ronald Basford* (see above)
from 8 Aug 1974: *Barnett J. Danson* (b. Toronto 8 Feb 1921)

Veterans Affairs 20 Apr – 5 Jul 1968: *Roger Joseph Teillet* (see Pearson)
6 Jul 1968 – 27 Jan 1972: *Jean Eudes Dubé* (see above)
28 Jan – 26 Nov 1972: *Arthur Laing* (see Pearson)
from 27 Nov 1972: *Daniel Joseph MacDonald* (b. Bothwell 23 Jul 1918)

Without Portfolio 20 Apr – 5 Jul 1968: *Charles Ronald McKay Granger* (see Pearson)
20 Apr 1968 – 31 Mar 1969: *Paul Joseph James Martin* (see King III)
20 Apr – 5 Jul 1968: *Donald Stovel Macdonald* (see above)
20 Apr – 5 Jul 1968: *Bryce Stuart Mackasey* (see Pearson)
20 Apr – 5 Jul 1968: *John Carr Munro* (see above)
20 Apr – 5 Jul 1968: *Gérard Pelletier* (see above)
26 Apr – 5 Jul 1968: *Jack Davis* (see above)
6 Jul 1968 – 29 Jun 1971: *Robert Knight Andras* (see above)
6 Jul 1968 – 23 Sep 1970: *Otto Emil Lang* (see above)
6 Jul 1968 – 4 May 1969: *James Armstrong Richardson* (see above)
20 Oct 1969 – 23 Sep 1970: *Herbert Eser Gray* (see above)
20 Oct 1969 – 11 Aug 1971: *Robert Douglas George Stanbury*
24 Sep 1970 – 10 Jun 1971: *Joseph Julien Jean Pierre Côté* (see Pearson)
from 10 Sep 1975: *Jean Marchand* (see above)

Minister of State 12 Aug 1971 – 27 Jan 1972: *Martin Patrick O'Connell* (see above)
28 Jan – 26 Nov 1972: *Patrick Morgan Mahoney* (b. Winnipeg 20 Jan 1929)

111

27 Nov 1972 – 7 Aug 1974: *Stanley Haidasz* (b. Toronto 4 Mar 1923)

Cape Verde

5 Jul 1975   Independence from Portugal

HEAD OF STATE

President

from 5 Jul 1975   *Aristides Maria Pereira* (b. Boa Vista 17 Nov 1924)

MEMBER OF GOVERNMENT

Prime Minister

from 15 Jul 1975   *Pedro Pires*

Carpatho-Ukraine

8 Oct 1938   Autonomous state
14 Mar 1939   Declaration of independence
15 Mar 1939   Annexed by Hungary

HEAD OF STATE

President

14 – 15 Mar 1939   *Augustin Voloshyn* (b. 1874; d. Galicia Dec 1945)

MEMBERS OF GOVERNMENT

9(19) - 26 Oct 1938: Brody

Prime Minister	*András Brody*
Home Affairs	*Edmund Batsynsky*
Transport	*Gyula Révay*
Commerce	*Stefan Fenchyk*
Social Affairs and Health	*Augustin Voloshyn* (see President)
Justice	*Ivan Pyeshchak*

28 Oct - 1 Dec 1938: Voloshyn I

Prime Minister	*Augustin Voloshyn* (for 1st time) (see President)
Home Affairs	*Edmund Batsynsky* (see Brody)

1 Dec 1938 - 15 Mar 1939: Voloshyn II

Prime Minister	*Augustin Voloshyn* (for 2nd time) (see President)
Home Affairs	1 Dec 1938 - 6 Mar 1939: *Gyula Révay* (see Brody) removed from office 11 Mar 1939 by Czech government, removal not recognized by Carpatho-Ukraine 16 - 18 Jan 1939: *Leo Prchala* (b. 1892(?); d. Feldbach 11 Jun 1963) not recognized by Carpatho-Ukraine 6 - 15 Mar 1939: *Leo Prchala* (see above) not recognized
Education	*Augustin Voloshyn* (see President)
Commerce	*Augustin Voloshyn* (see President)
Transport	1 Dec 1938 - 6 Mar 1939: *Gyula Révay* (see Brody) 6 - 15 Mar 1939: *Stefan Klochurak*, not recognized, arrested by the Russians in Prague 1945

15 - 16 Mar 1939: Révay

Prime Minister	*Gyula Révay* (see Brody)
Ministers	*Yuly Brashchaiko*, arrested by the Russians in 1944 *Stefan Klochurak* (see Volosin II) *Nikolai Dolinai*, arrested by the Russians in Prague 1945 *Yury Perevuznik*, arrested by the Russians in Prague 1945

113

29 Jun 1945   Annexed by the Soviet Union
22 Jan 1946   Incorporated in the Ukrainian Soviet Socialist
                    Republic

Catalonia

25 Sep 1932   Autonomous state

HEADS OF STATE

Presidents

Apr 1931 – 25 Dec   *Francesc Maciá i Llussá* (b. Villanueva y
1933   Geltrú 21 Oct 1859; d. 25 Dec 1933)
1 Jan – 7 Oct   *Lluis Companys i Jover* (for 1st time) (b.
1934   Tarros 1883; d. Barcelona 16 Oct 1940)
8 Oct 1934 – Feb   *Antonio Jiménez Arenas*
1936
Feb 1936   *Lluis Companys i Jover* (for 2nd time)
5 Feb 1939   Administration exiled to France; autonomy rescinded

Central African Federation

The Federation, comprising Southern Rhodesia (later Rhodesia, see page 441),
Northern Rhodesia (later Zambia, see page 606) and Nyasaland (later Malawi,
see page 370) was in existence from 27 Jul 1953 until 31 Dec 1963.

HEADS OF STATE

Governors-General

4 Sep 1953 – 24 Jan 1957	*John Jestyn Llewellin, 1st Baron Llewellin* (b. Chevening 6 Feb 1893; d. Salisbury, Rhodesia, 24 Jan 1957)
1957 – 31 Dec 1963	*Simon Ramsay, 16th Earl of Dalhousie* (b. 17 Oct 1914)

MEMBERS OF GOVERNMENT

Prime Ministers

7 Sep 1953 – Nov 1956	*Sir Godfrey Huggins* (from 1955: *1st Viscount Malvern*) (b. Bexley 6 Jul 1883; d. Salisbury, Rhodesia, 8 May 1971)
Nov 1956	*Sir Roy Welensky* (for 1st time) (b. Salisbury, Rhodesia, 20 Jan 1907)
8 Dec 1958 – 31 Dec 1963	*Sir Roy Welensky* (for 2nd time)

Central African Republic

Until 1 Dec 1958	French colony of Ubangi-Shari
1 Dec 1958	Name changed to Central African Republic, member of the French Community
17 Aug 1960	Left French Community (From 4 Dec 1976, name changed to Central African Empire)

HEADS OF STATE

Presidents

17 Aug 1960	*David Dacko* (b. Bouchia 1930)
from 1 Jan 1966	*Jean Bedel Bokassa* (b. Bobangui 22 Feb 1921)

Chad

28 Nov 1958	Member of French Community
11 Aug 1960	Left French Community

HEADS OF STATE

Presidents and Prime Ministers

12 Aug 1960 – 13 Apr 1975	*François Tombalbaye* (from 1973: *N'Garta Tombalbaye*) (b. Bodaya 15 Jun 1918; d. 13 Apr 1975)
from 15 Apr 1975	*Félix Malloum* (b. Fort Archambault (later Sahr) 10 Sep 1932) President of the Supreme Military Council and of the Council of Ministers

Chile

HEADS OF STATE

Presidents

9 Apr 1927	*Carlos Ibáñez del Campo* (for 1st time) (b. 2 Nov 1877; d. Santiago 28 Apr 1960)
27 Jul 1931	*Pedro Opazo Letelier* (b. 12 Jun 1876)
28 Jul 1931	*José Esteban Montero Rodríguez* (for 1st time) (b. 1879; d. 25 Feb 1948)
17 Aug – 3 Sep 1931	*Manuel Trucco Franzani* (b. 1874)
4 Oct 1931	*José Esteban Montero Rodríguez* (for 2nd time)
5 Jun 1932	*Carlos (Guillermo) Dávila* (for 1st time) (b. 15 Sep 1884; d. Washington 19 Oct 1955)
13 Jun 1932	*Marmaduke Grove*, Head of "Social Junta"
17 Jun 1932	*Carlos (Guillermo) Dávila* (for 2nd time)
13 Sep 1932	*Bartolomé Blanche Espejo* (b. 6 Jul 1879)

2 Oct 1932	*Abraham Oyanedel Urrutia* (b. 25 May 1874)
25 Dec 1932	*Arturo Alessandri y Palma* (for 2nd time) (b. 20 Dec 1868; d. 24 Aug 1950)*
24 Dec 1938	*Pedro Aguirre Cerda* (b. 29 Jun 1879; d. 25 Nov 1941)
25 Nov 1941	*Gerónimo Méndez Arancibia* (b. 1884; d. 1959)
1 Apr 1942	*Juan Antonio Rios Morales* (b. 10 Nov 1888; d. 27 Jun 1946)
27 Jun 1946	*Alfredo Duhalde Vázquez* (b. 1894)
3 Aug 1946	*Vicente Mariño Bielech*
24 Oct 1946	*Gabriel González Vileda* (b. 23 Nov 1898)
3 Nov 1952	*Carlos Ibáñez del Campo* (for 2nd time)
3 Nov 1958	*Jorge Alessandri Rodríguez,* son of Arturo Alessandri y Palma (b. 19 May 1896)
4 Nov 1964	*Eduardo Frei Montalva* (b. Santiago 16 Jan 1911)
4 Nov 1970	*Salvador Allende Gossens* (b. Valparaiso 26 Jul 1908; d. 11 Sep 1973)
from 11 Sep 1973	*General Augusto Pinochet Ugarte* (b. Valparaiso 25 Nov 1915) Chairman of Military Junta

China

HEADS OF STATE

Presidents

10 Oct 1928	*Chiang Kai-shek (Chiang Chung-cheng)* (for 1st time) (b. Fenghua 31 Oct 1887; d. Taipei 5 Apr 1975)*
15 Dec 1931	(acting:) *Ch'eng Ming-hsu*
1 Jan 1932 – 1943	*Lin Sen* (b. 11 Feb 1867; d. 1 Aug 1943)
30 Mar 1940 – 10 Nov 1944	*Wang Ching-wei* (b. Canton 4 May 1883; d. Nanking 10 Nov 1944) in Japanese occupied territory
30 May 1943	*Chiang Kai-shek (Chiang Chung-cheng)* (for 2nd time)
21 Jan 1949	*Li Tsung-jen* (b. 1890) from 4 Dec 1949 in Taiwan

*For earlier career see vol. 2

CHINA

MEMBERS OF GOVERNMENT

Presidents of Executive Council (Nationalist)

25 Oct 1928 – 22 Sep 1930	*T'an Yen-k'ai* (for 2nd time) (b. Hangchow 1879; d. Nanking 22 Sep 1930)*
Sep – Nov 1930	(acting:) *Sung Tzu-wen (T.V. Soong)* (for 1st time) (b. Shanghai 1891; d. San Francisco 25 Apr 1971)
	Peking Administration:
13 Jul – 10 Oct 1930	*Wang Ching-wei* (for 1st time) (see Presidents)
22 Dec 1930 – 15 Dec 1931	*Chiang Kai-shek (Chiang Chung-cheng)* (for 2nd time) (see Presidents)
28 Dec 1931 – 28 Jan 1932	*Sun Fo*, son of Sun Yat-sen (for 1st time) (b. 1895)
Dec 1931 – Jan 1932	(acting:) *Chong Ming-shu* (b. 1891)
28 Jan 1932 – 1935	*Wang Ching-wei* (for 2nd time)
12 Dec 1935 – 31 Dec 1937	*Chiang Kai-shek (Chiang Chung-cheng)* (for 3rd time)
Apr 1937 – Jan 1938	(acting:) *Wang Ch'ung-hui* (b. 1881; d. 15 Mar 1958)
1 Jan 1938 – Nov 1939	*K'ung Hsiang-hsi (H. H. K'ung)* (b. 1891; d. New York 15 Aug 1967)
12 Nov 1939 – Dec 1944	*Chiang Kai-shek (Chiang Chung-cheng)* (for 4th time)
4 Dec 1944	*Sung Tzu-wen (T.V. Soong)* (for 2nd time)
1 Mar – Apr 1947	(acting:) *Chiang Kai-shek (Chiang Chung-cheng)* (for 5th time)
18 Apr 1947 – 5 May 1948	*Chang Ch'ün* (b. 1889)
May – Nov 1948	*Wong Wen-hao* (b. Ningpo 1889)
26 Nov 1948 – 8 Mar 1949	*Sun Fo* (for 2nd time)
21 Mar – 30 Apr 1949	*Ho Ying-ch'in* (b. 1890)
3 Jun 1949 – Mar 1950	*Yen Hsi-shan* (b. 1883; d. Taipei 23 May 1960) from 4 Dec 1949 in Taiwan
1945 – 1949	Civil war between Communist and Nationalist forces culminated in proclamation of People's Republic of China (see p.119) on 1 Oct 1949 and withdrawal of Nationalist government to Taiwan (see Republic of China, p.120)

*For earlier career see vol. 2

China, People's Republic of

HEADS OF STATE

Chairmen

1 Oct 1949	*Mao Tse-tung* (b. Shao Shan, Hunan Province, 26 Dec 1893; d. Peking 9 Sep 1976)
27 Apr 1959 – 15 Oct 1968	*Liu Shao-ch'i* (b. Yinshan, Hunan Province, 1898; d. Nov 1972)
from 1969	*Sung Ching-ling,* widow of Sun Yat-sen (b. Shanghai 1890) Deputy Chairman Apr 1959 – 1972 *Tung Pi-wu* (b. Hupei 1886) Deputy Chairman from 1959

MEMBERS OF GOVERNMENT

Prime Minister

from 21 Sep 1949	*Chou En-lai* (b. Shaohing, Chekiang Province, 1898; d. Peking 8 Jan 1976)

Foreign Ministers

1 Oct 1949	*Chou En-lai* (see Prime Minister) post combined with Prime Minister
11 Feb 1958 – 6 Jan 1972	*Ch'en-yi* (b. Loshan, Szechwan Province, 1901(?); d. Peking(?) 6 Jan 1972)
20 Jan 1972	*Chi Peng-fei* (b. 1911)
from 15 Nov 1974	*Chiao Khuan-hua* (b. 1914)

119

China, Republic of (Taiwan)

HEADS OF STATE

Presidents

1 Mar 1950 – 5 Apr 1975	*Chiang Kai-shek (Chiang Chung-cheng)* (b. Fenghua 31 Oct 1887; d. Taipei 5 Apr 1975)
from 6 Apr 1975	*Yen Chia-kan* (b. Kiangsu 23 Oct 1905)

MEMBERS OF GOVERNMENT

Presidents of Executive Council

7 Mar 1950 – May 1954	*Ch'en Ch'eng* (for 1st time) (b. Kaoshih 4 Jan 1897; d. Taipei 5 Mar 1965)
25 May 1954 – 30 Jun 1958	*O. K. Yui (Yü Hung-chün)* (b. Shanghai 1897; d. Taipei 1 Jun 1960)
30 Jun/ 15 Jul 1958	*Ch'en Ch'eng* (for 2nd time)
4 Dec 1963 – 11 May 1972	*Yen Chia-kan* (see Presidents)
from 26 May 1972	*Chiang Ching-kuo*, son of Chiang Kai-shek (b. Chikuo 1910)

Colombia

HEADS OF STATE

Presidents

7 Aug 1926	*Miguel Abadía Méndez* (b. 5 Jun 1867; d. 15 May 1947)
7 Aug 1930	*Enrique Olaya Herrera* (b. 12 Nov 1881; d. 20 Feb 1937)
7 Aug 1934	*Alfonso López Pumarejo* (for 1st time) (b. 31 Jan 1886; d. London 20 Nov 1959)

7 Aug 1938	*Eduardo Santos Montejo* (b. 1888)
7 Aug 1942 – Jul 1945	*Alfonso López Pumarejo* (for 2nd time)
7 Aug 1945	*Alberto Lleras Camargo* (for 1st time) (b. 1906)
7 Aug 1946	*Mariano Ospina Pérez* (b. 24 Nov 1891; d. Bogotá 14 Apr 1976)
7 Aug 1950 – 13 Jun 1953	*Laureano Gómez Castro* (b. 20 Feb 1889; d. Bogotá 13 Jul 1965)
5 Nov 1951 – 15 Jun 1953	*Roberto Urdaneta Arbeláez* (b. 1890) Deputy
13 Jun 1953	*Gustavo Rojas Pinilla* (b. 12 Mar 1900; d. 17 Jan 1975) Dictator
10 May 1957	*Gabriel Paris*, Head of Military Junta
7 Aug 1958	*Alberto Lleras Camargo* (for 2nd time)
7 Aug 1962	*Guillermo León Valencia* (b. Popayán 27 Apr 1909; d. New York night of 4/5 Nov 1971)
7 Aug 1966	*Carlos Lleras Restrepo* (b. Bogotá 12 Apr 1908)
7 Aug 1970	*Misael Pastraña Borrero* (b. Neiva 14 Nov 1923)
from 7 Aug 1974	*Alfonso López Michelsen* (b. Bogotá 1914 or 1917)

Comoro Islands

6 Jul 1975	Declaration of independence from France
10 Dec 1975	Recognition of independence by France

HEADS OF STATE

6 Jul – 3 Aug 1975	*Ahmed Abdallah*
from 5 Aug 1975	*Prince Said Mohamed Jaffar* (b. Mutsamudu 14 Apr 1918) (President of National Executive Council)

Congo, People's Republic of

Formerly Middle Congo, part of French Equatorial Africa; capital at Brazzaville.

15 Aug 1960	Independence from France (named Republic of Congo)
1 Jan 1970	Name changed to People's Republic of Congo

121

CONGO, PEOPLE'S REPUBLIC OF

HEADS OF STATE

Presidents

15 Aug 1960 – 15 Aug 1963	*Abbé Fulbert Youlou* (b. Brazzaville 9 Jun 1917; d. 5 May 1972) also Prime Minister
16 Aug 1963	(acting until 24 Dec 1963:) *Alphonse Massemba-Debat* (for 1st time) (b. Nkolo 1921; d. (executed) 25 Mar 1977)
2 Aug 1968	*Marien Ngouabi* (for 1st time) (b. Ambele 1938; d. (assassinated) Brazzaville 18 Mar 1977) Head of National Revolutionary Council
4 Aug 1968	*Alphonse Massemba-Debat* (for 2nd time)
4 Sep 1968	*Alfred Raoul* (b. Pointe-Noire 1930)
from 1 Jan 1969	*Marien Ngouabi* (for 2nd time)

MEMBERS OF GOVERNMENT

Prime Ministers

24 Dec 1963 – 15 Apr 1966	*Pascal Lissouba* (b. Tsinguidi 10 Nov 1931)
6 May 1966	*Ambroise Noumazalay* (b. Brazzaville 23 Sep 1933)
12 Jan 1968	President also Prime Minister
25 Aug 1973	*Henri Lopes* (b. Kinshasa Sep 1937)
from 13 Dec 1975	*Louis Sylvain Goba*

Costa Rica

HEADS OF STATE

Presidents

8 May 1928	*Cleto González Víquez* (for 3rd time) (b. 1858; d. 1937)*

*For earlier career see vol. 2

8 May 1932	*Ricardo Jiménez Oreamuno* (for 3rd time) (b. 1859; d. 1945)*
8 May 1936	*León Cortés Castro* (b. 1882)
8 May 1940	*Rafael Ángel Calderón Guardia* (b. 10 Mar 1900; d. San José 9 Jun 1970)
8 May 1944	*Teodoro Picado Michalski* (b. 1901; d. Managua, Nicaragua, 1 Jun 1960)
24 Apr 1948	*Santos León Herrera* (b. 1874?)
3 May 1948	*José Figueres Ferrer* (for 1st time) (b. San Ramón 25 Sep 1906)
16 Jan 1949	*Otilio Ulate Blanco* (b. 1895)
26 Sep 1952	*Alberto Oreamuno Flores*
Jun 1953 – 8 Feb 1958	*José Figueres Ferrer* (for 2nd time)
8 May 1958	*Mario Echandi Jiménez* (b. San José 17 Jun 1915)
8 May 1962	*Francisco José Orlich Bolmarcich* (b. San Ramón de Alajuela 10 Mar 1907; d. San José 29 Oct 1969)
8 May 1966	*José Joaquín Trejos Fernández* (b. 18 Apr 1916)
8 May 1970	*José Figueres Ferrer* (for 3rd time)
from 8 May 1974	*Daniel Oduber Quiros* (b. San José 25 Aug 1921)

Croatia

HEADS OF STATE

| 18 May 1941 – 12 Sep 1943 | *Tomislav II (Haimon, Duke of Spoleto)*, grandson of King Amadeus of Spain (b. 9 Mar 1900; d. 30 Jan 1948) nominated King |
| Apr 1941 – May 1945 | *Ante Pavelić* (b. Bradina, Herzegovina, 14 Jul 1889; d. Madrid 28 Dec 1959) in addition to the King |

*For earlier career see vol. 2

CROATIA

MEMBERS OF GOVERNMENT

Prime Ministers

Apr 1941	*Ante Pavelić* (see Heads of State)
2 Sep 1943 – May 1945	*Nikola Mandić* (b. Travnik 1869)

Foreign Ministers

16 Apr 1941	*Ante Pavelić* (see Heads of State)
11 Jun 1941	*Mladen Lorković*
23 Apr 1943	*Mile Budak* (b. Sveti Rok 30 Aug 1889; d. 1945)
5 Nov 1943 – 2 May 1944	*Stijepo Perić*
5 May 1944 – 9 May 1945	*Mehmed Alajbegović* (d. 20(?) Jun 1947)

Cuba

HEADS OF STATE

Presidents

20 May 1925	*Gerardo Machado de Morales* (b. 29 Nov 1871; d. 28 Mar 1939)
12 Aug – 5 Sep 1933	*Carlos Manuel de Céspedes y Quesada* (b. New York 12 Aug 1871; d. 1939)
10 Sep 1933	*Ramón Grau San Martin* (for 1st time) (b. 1889; d. Havana 28 Jul 1969)
15 – 17 Jan 1934	*Carlos Hevia* (b. 1900)
18 Jan 1934	*Carlos Mendieta Montefur* (b. 1873; d. 27 Sep 1960)
12 Dec 1935	*José A. Barnet y Vinagres* (b. 1864; d. 1945)
20 May 1936	*Miguel Mariano Gómez y Arias* (b. 6 Oct 1890; d. 26 Oct 1950)
28 Dec 1936	*Frederico Laredo Brú* (b. 23 Apr 1875; d. 1946)
10 Oct 1940	*Fulgencio E. Batista y Zaldívar* (b. 16 Jan 1901; d. Marbella 6 Aug 1973) Dictator

10 Oct 1944	*Ramón Grau San Martín* (for 2nd time)
10 Oct 1948	*Carlos Prío Socarrás* (b. 14 Jul 1903; d. Miami Beach Apr 1977)
10 Mar 1952	*Fulgencio E. Batista y Zaldívar* (for 2nd time) Dictator
1 Jan 1959	(acting:) *Manuel Urratía Lleo* (b. 8 Dec 1901)
from 17 Jul 1959	*Osvaldo Dórticos Torrado* (b. Cienfuegos 17 Apr or 27 Apr or 17 Jun 1919)

MEMBERS OF GOVERNMENT

Prime Ministers

5 Jan – 13 Feb 1959	*José Miró Cardona* (b. 1901; d. 10 Aug 1974)
16 Feb – 17 Jul 1959	*Fidel Castro* (for 1st time) (b. Mayari 13 Aug 1927)
from 27 Jul 1959	*Fidel Castro* (for 2nd time)

Cyprus

16 Aug 1960	Independence from Great Britain

HEADS OF STATE

Presidents

16 Aug 1960	*Archbishop Makarios III* (for 1st time) (b. Ano Panaya 13 Aug 1913; d. Nicosia 3 Aug 1977) escaped following coup Jul 1974
15 Jul 1974	*Nikos Sampson* (b. 1935?) usurper
23 Jul 1974	(acting:) *Glafkos John Clerides (Kliridis)* (b. 1919)
from 14 Jan 1975	*Archbishop Makarios III* (for 2nd time) returned 7 Dec 1974

Vice-Presidents

16 Aug 1960	*Fazil Küchük* (b. Nicosia 14 Mar 1906)

| 28 Feb 1973 | *Rauf Denktash* (b. 27 Jan 1924) |
| 13 Feb 1975 | Turkish Cypriot Federated State proclaimed, with Rauf Denktash as President |

Czechoslovakia

HEADS OF STATE

Presidents

28 Oct 1918 – 14 Dec 1935	*Tomáš Garrigue Masaryk* (b. Hodonin 7 Mar 1850; d. Lány Castle 14 Sep 1937)
18 Dec 1935	*Edvard Beneš* (for 1st time) (b. Kozlan, Bohemia, 28 May 1884; d. Lány Castle 3 Sep 1948)*
5 Oct 1938	(acting:) *Jan Syrový* (b. Třebíč 24 Jan 1888; d. Jun 1971)*
30 Nov 1938	*Emil Hacha* (b. Trhové Sviny 12 Jul 1872; d. Prague 1(?)/27 Jun 1945)
4 May 1945 – 7 Jun 1948	*Edvard Beneš* (for 2nd time)
14 Jun 1948 – 14 Mar 1953	*Klemens Gottwald* (b. Dědice 23 Nov 1896; d. Prague 14 Mar 1953)
21 Mar 1953 – 13 Nov 1957	*Antonín Zápotocký* (b. Zakolany 19 Dec 1884; d. Prague 13 Nov 1957)
19 Nov 1957 – 22 Mar 1968	*Antonín Novotný* (b. Prague 10 Dec 1904; d. 28 Jan 1975)
30 Mar 1968	*General Ludvík Svoboda* (b. Hroznatin 25 Nov 1895)
from 29 May 1975	*Gustáv Husák* (b. Dúbravka 10 Jan 1913)

MEMBERS OF GOVERNMENT

7 Dec 1929 – 21 Oct 1932: Udržal II

Prime Minister	*František Udržal* (Czech Agrarian) (for 2nd time) (b. Dolní Roveň 3 Jan 1866; d. Prague 25 Sep 1938)*
Foreign Affairs	*Edvard Beneš* (Nat Soc) (see Presidents)*

*For earlier career see vol. 2

126

Home Affairs	*Juraj Slávik* (b. Dobrovina 28 Jan 1890)*
Justice	*Alfréd Meissner* (Czech Soc) (b. Mladá Boleslav 10 Apr 1871; d. 1950)*
Defence	*Karel Viškovský* (Czech Agrarian) (b. Šušice 8 Jul 1868; d. Prague 20 Nov 1932)*
Posts and Telegraphs	*Emil Franke* (Czech Soc) (b. Březno Velké 3 Apr 1880)*
Finance	7 Dec 1929 – 16 Apr 1931: *Karel Engliš* (Nat Dem) (b. Hrabyně 17 Aug 1880; d. 1961)* 16 Apr 1931 – 21 Oct 1932: *Karl Trapl* (Nat Soc) (b. Chrudim 31 Aug 1881; d. Prague 7 Apr 1940)
Commerce	*Josef Matoušek* (Nat Dem) (b. Železný Brod 25 May 1876)
Agriculture	*Bohumir Bradáč* (Czech Agrarian) (b. Židovice 31 May 1881; d. Oct 1935)
Food	*Rudolf Bechyně* (Czech Soc) (b. Nymburk 6 Apr 1881; d. Prague 3 Jan 1948)*
Railways	7 Dec 1929 – 8 Apr 1932: *Rudolf Mlčoch* (Czech Prof) (b. Třebčín 17 Apr 1880)* 9 Apr – 21 Oct 1932: *Josef Hůla* (b. 5 Jun 1873)
Social Welfare	*Ludwig Czech* (Ger Soc) (b. Lvov 14 Feb 1870; d. Theresienstadt May(?)1945)
Education	*Ivan Dérer* (Slov Soc) (b. Malacký 2 Feb 1884)*
Public Works	*Jan Dostálek* (Czech Pop) (b. Šedivec 28 Apr 1883)
Health	*Franz Spina* (Ger League) (b. Trnávka 5 Oct 1868; d. Prague 7 Sep 1938)*
Unification	*Jan Šrámek* (Czech Pop) (b. Grygova 11 Aug 1870; d. 21(?) Aug 1955)*

31 Oct 1932 – 14 Feb 1934: Malypetr I

Prime Minister	*Jan Malypetr* (Czech Pop) (for 1st time) (b. Klobúky 20 Dec 1873; d. 21 Sep 1947)*
Foreign Affairs	*Edvard Beneš* (Nat Soc) (see Presidents)
Home Affairs	*Jan Černý* (b. Uherský Ostroh 4 Mar 1874; d. Uherský Ostroh 10 Apr 1957)*
Justice	*Alfréd Meissner* (Czech Soc) (see Udržal II)
Defence	*Bohumir Bradáč* (Czech Agrarian) (see Udržal II)
Posts and Telegraphs	*Emil Franke* (Czech Soc) (see Udržal II)
Finance	*Karl Trapl* (Nat Soc) (see Udržal II)
Commerce	*Josef Matoušek* (Nat Dem) (see Udržal II)

*For earlier career see vol. 2

127

Agriculture and Food	*Milan Hodža* (Czech Agrarian) (b. Sučany 1 Feb 1878; d. Clearwater, Florida, 27 Jun 1944)*
Railways	*Rudolf Bechyně* (Czech Soc) (see Udržal II)
Social Welfare	*Ludwig Czech* (Ger Soc) (see Udržal II)
Education	*Ivan Dérer* (Slov Soc) (see Udržal II)
Public Works	*Jan Dostálek* (Czech Pop) (see Udržal II)
Health	*Franz Spina* (Ger League) (see Udržal II)
Unification	*Jan Šrámek* (Czech Pop) (see Udržal II)

14 Feb 1934 – 29 May 1935: Malypetr II

Prime Minister	*Jan Malypetr* (Czech Pop) (for 2nd time) (see Malypetr I)
Foreign Affairs	*Edvard Beneš* (Nat Soc) (see Presidents)
Home Affairs	*Josef Černý* (Czech Agrarian) (b. 1885; d. 1971)
Justice	*Ivan Dérer* (Slov Soc) (see Udržal II)
Defence	*Bohumir Bradáč* (Czech Agrarian) (see Udržal II)
Posts and Telegraphs	*Emil Franke* (Czech Soc) (see Udržal II)
Finance	*Karl Trapl* (see Udržal II)
Commerce	*Jan Dostálek* (Czech Pop) (see Udržal II)
Agriculture	*Milan Hodža* (Czech Agrarian) (see Malypetr I)
Railways	*Rudolf Bechyně* (Czech Soc) (see Udržal II)
Social Welfare	*Alfréd Meissner* (Czech Soc) (see Udržal II)
Education	*Jan Krčmář* (b. Prague 27 Jul 1877; d. 1950)*
Public Works	*Ludwig Czech* (Ger Soc) (see Udržal II)
Health	*Franz Spina* (Ger League) (see Udržal II)
Unification	*Jan Šrámek* (Czech Pop) (see Udržal II)

14 Jun – 6 Nov 1935: Malypetr III

Prime Minister	*Jan Malypetr* (Czech Pop) (for 3rd time) (see Malypetr I)
Foreign Affairs	*Edvard Beneš* (Nat Soc) (see Presidents)
Home Affairs	*Josef Černý* (Czech Agrarian) (see Malypetr II)
Justice	*Ivan Dérer* (Slov Soc) (see Udržal II)
Defence	*František Machník* (Czech Agrarian) (b. Nebřevice 1886)
Posts and Telegraphs	*Emil Franke* (Czech Soc) (see Udržal II)
Finance	*Karl Trapl* (see Udržal II)
Commerce	*Josef V. Najman* (Czech Prof) (b. Bohdanecká Skála 20 Apr 1882; d. Prague 4 Dec 1937)*

*For earlier career see vol. 2

Agriculture	*Milan Hodža* (Czech Agrarian) (see Malypetr I)
Railways	*Rudolf Bechyně* (Czech Soc) (see Udržal II)
Social Welfare	*Jaromír Nečas* (Czech Soc) (b. Nové Město na Moravě 17 Nov 1888; d. 1945)
Education	*Jan Krčmář* (see Malypetr II)
Public Works	*Jan Dostálek* (Czech Pop) (see Udržal II)
Health	*Ludwig Czech* (Ger Soc) (see Udržal II)
Unification	*Jan Šrámek* (Czech Pop) (see Udržal II)
Without Portfolio	*Franz Spina* (Ger League) (see Udržal II)

9 Nov – 18 Dec 1935: Hodža I

Prime Minister	*Milan Hodža* (Czech Agrarian) (for 1st time) (see Malypetr I)
Foreign Affairs	*Edvard Beneš* (Nat Soc) (see Presidents)
Home Affairs	*Josef Černý* (Czech Agrarian) (see Malypetr II)
Justice	*Ivan Dérer* (Slov Soc) (see Udržal II)
Defence	*František Machník* (Czech Agrarian) (see Malypetr III)
Posts and Telegraphs	*Emil Franke* (Czech Soc) (see Udržal II)
Finance	*Karl Trapl* (see Udržal II)
Commerce	*Josef V. Najman* (Czech Prof) (see Malypetr III)
Agriculture	*Josef Zadina* (Czech Agrarian) (b. Vlkanova 16 Jun 1887)
Railways	*Rudolf Bechyně* (Czech Soc) (see Udržal II)
Social Welfare	*Jaromír Nečas* (Czech Soc) (see Malypetr III)
Education	*Jan Krčmář* (see Malypetr II)
Public Works	*Jan Dostálek* (Czech Pop) (see Udržal II)
Health	*Ludwig Czech* (Ger Soc) (see Udržal II)
Unification	*Jan Šrámek* (Czech Pop) (see Udržal II)
Without Portfolio	*Franz Spina* (Ger League) (see Udržal II)

18 Dec 1935 – 16 Jul 1937: Hodža II

Prime Minister	*Milan Hodža* (Czech Agrarian) (for 2nd time) (see Malypetr I)
Foreign Affairs	18 Dec 1935 – 29 Feb 1936 (acting:) *Milan Hodža* (see Malypetr I)
	29 Feb 1936 – 16 Jul 1937: *Kamil Krofta* (b. Plzen 17 Jul 1876; d. Ejpovice 16 Aug 1945)
Home Affairs	*Josef Černý* (Czech Agrarian) (see Malypetr II)
Justice	*Ivan Dérer* (Slov Soc) (see Udržal II)
Defence	*František Machník* (Czech Agrarian) (see Malypetr III)

129

Posts and Telegraphs	18 Dec 1935 – 23 Jan 1936: *Emil Franke* (Czech Soc) (see Udržal II)
	23 Jan 1936 – 16 Jul 1937: *Alois Tučný* (Nat Soc) (b. Frenštát 4 Jun 1881)*
Finance	18 Dec 1935 – 18 Mar 1936: *Karl Trapl* (see Udržal II)
	29 Mar 1936 – 16 Jul 1937: *Josef Kalfus* (b. Železny Brod 25 Jan 1880)
Commerce	*Josef V. Najman* (Czech Prof) (see Malypetr III)
Agriculture	*Josef Zadina* (Czech Agrarian) (see Hodža I)
Railways	*Rudolf Bechyně* (Czech Soc) (see Udržal II)
Social Welfare	*Jaromír Nečas* (Czech Soc) (see Malypetr III)
Education	18 Dec 1935 – 23 Jan 1936: *Jan Krčmář* (see Malypetr II)
	23 Jan 1936 – 16 Jul 1937: *Emil Franke* (Czech Soc) (see Udržal II)
Public Works	*Jan Dostálek* (Czech Pop) (see Udržal II)
Health	*Ludwig Czech* (Ger Soc) (see Udržal II)
Unification	*Jan Šrámek* (Czech Pop) (see Udržal II)
Without Portfolio	*Franz Spina* (Ger League) (see Udržal II)
	3 Jul 1936 – 16 Jul 1937: *Erwin Zajiček* (Germ Christ Soc) (b. 22 Nov 1890)

21 Jul 1937 – 22 Sep 1938: Hodža III

Prime Minister	*Milan Hodža* (Czech Agrarian) (for 3rd time) (see Malypetr I)
Foreign Affairs	*Kamil Krofta* (see Hodža II)
Home Affairs	*Josef Černý* (Czech Agrarian) (see Malypetr II)
Justice	*Ivan Dérer* (Slov Soc) (see Udržal II)
Defence	*František Machník* (Czech Agrarian) (see Malypetr III)
Posts and Telegraphs	*Alois Tučný* (Nat Soc) (see Hodža II)
Finance	21 Jul – 2 Oct 1937 (acting:) *Emil Franke* (Czech Soc) (see Udržal II)
	2 Oct 1937 – 22 Sep 1938: *Josef Kalfus* (see Hodža II)
Commerce	21 Jul – 4 Dec 1937: *Josef V. Najman* (Czech Prof) (see Malypetr III)
	5 – 13 Dec 1937 (acting:) *Josef Černý* (Czech Agrarian) (see Malypetr II)
	13 Dec 1937 – 22 Sep 1938: *Rudolf Mlčoch* (Czech Prof) (see Udržal II)

*For earlier career see vol. 2

Agriculture	*Josef Zadina* (Czech Agrarian) (see Hodža I)
Railways	*Rudolf Bechyně* (Czech Soc) (see Udržal II)
Social Welfare	*Jaromír Nečas* (Czech Soc) (see Malypetr III)
Education	*Emil Franke* (Czech Soc) (see Udržal II)
Public Works	*Jan Dostálek* (Czech Pop) (see Udržal II)
Health	21 Jul 1937 – 11 Apr 1938: *Ludwig Czech* (Czech Pop) (see Udržal II)
	11 Apr – 10 May 1938 (acting:) *Ivan Dérer* (Slov Soc) (see Udržal II)
	10 May – 22 Sep 1938: *František Ježek* (Nat Peoples League) (b. Chrudim 6 Sep 1890)
Unification	*Jan Šrámek* (Czech Pop) (see Udržal II)
Propaganda (new post)	16 – 22 Sep 1938: *Hugo Varečka*
Without Portfolio	22 Jul 1937 – 23 Mar 1938: *Franz Spina* (Ger League) (see Udržal II)
	22 Jul 1937 – 23 Mar 1938: *Erwin Zajiček* (Ger Christ Soc) (see Hodža II)
	19 Mar – 12 May 1938: *František Ježek* (Nat Peoples League) (see above)

22 Sep – 4 Oct 1938: Syrový I

Prime Minister	*Jan Syrový* (for 1st time) (see Presidents)
Foreign Affairs	*Kamil Krofta* (see Hodža II)
Home Affairs	*Josef Černý* (Czech Agrarian) (see Malypetr II)
Justice	*Vladimír Fajnor* (b. Senice na Hané 23 Oct 1875)*
Defence	*Jan Syrový* (see Presidents)
Posts and Telegraphs	*Karel Dunovský*
Finance	*Josef Kalfus* (see Hodža II)
Commerce	*Jan Janáček* (b. 25 Sep 1877?)
Agriculture	*Edvard Reich* (b. Velká Bystřice 17 Mar 1885)
Railways	*Jindřich Kamenický*
Social Welfare	*Bedřich Horák*
Education	*Engelbert Šubert*
Public Works	*Karel Husárek*
Health	*Stanislav Mentl*
Unification	*Josef Fritz Nosal*
Propaganda	*Hugo Varečka* (see Hodža III)
Without Portfolio	*Peter Zenkl* (Nat Soc) (b. Tabor 13 Jun 1884; d. Raleigh, Virginia, Nov 1975)
	Stanislav Bukovský

*For earlier career see vol. 2

131

24 Sep – 4 Oct 1938: *Matúš Černák* (Slov Pop) (b. 23 Aug 1903; d. Munich 5 Jul 1955)
24 Sep – 4 Oct 1938: *Imrich Karvaš*

4 Oct – 1 Dec 1938: Syrový II

Prime Minister	*Jan Syrový* (for 2nd time) (see Presidents)
Foreign Affairs	*František Chvalkovský* (b. Jílova 30 Jul 1875; d. 1945)
Home Affairs	*Josef Černý* (see Malypetr II)
Justice	4 – 14 Oct 1938: *Vladimír Fajnor* (see Syrový I)
	14 Oct – 29 Nov 1938: *Ladislav Feierabend* (b. Kostelec nad Orlicí 14 Jun 1891; d. 1969)
Defence	*Jan Syrový* (see Presidents)
Posts and Telegraphs	(temporary:) *Vladimír Kajdoš*
Finance	*Josef Kalfus* (see Hodža II)
Commerce and Industry	*Imrich Karvaš* (see Syrový I)
Agriculture	*Ladislav Feierabend* (see above)
Railways	*Vladimír Kajdoš* (see above)
Education	(acting:) *Stanislav Bukovský* (see Syrový I)
Public Works	*Karel Husárek* (see Syrový I)
Health	*Peter Zenkl* (Nat Soc) (see Syrový I)
Unification	4 – 14 Oct 1938 (acting:) *Vladimír Fajnor* (see Syrový I)
	14 Oct – 29 Nov 1938 (acting:) *Ladislav Feierabend* (see above)
Slovakian Affairs	6 Oct – 28 Nov 1938: *Jozef Tiso* (b. Velká Bytča 13 Oct 1887; d. Bratislava 18 Apr 1947)*
Without Portfolio	4 Oct – 14 Oct 1938: *Ivan Parkányi*
	Hugo Varečka (see Hodža III)

1 Dec 1938 – 13 Mar 1939: Beran

Prime Minister	*Rudolf Beran* (b. 28 Dec 1887; d. Leopoldstadt Prison 3 or 23 Apr 1954 or 1957)
Deputy Prime Minister and Slovakian Affairs	*Karol Sidor* (Slov Pop) (b. Ružomberok 16 Jul 1901; d. Montreal Oct 1953)
Foreign Affairs	*František Chvalkovský* (see Syrový II)

*For earlier career see vol. 2

132

Defence	*Jan Syrový* (see Presidents)
Finance	*Josef Kalfus* (see Hodža II)
Transport, Posts and Telegraphs	*Alois Eliáš* (b. Prague 29 Sep 1890; d. 19 Jun 1942)
Minister of State	*Jiří Havelka* (b. Orel, Russia, 25 Jul 1892)
	Ministers for Bohemia and Moravia:
Home Affairs	*Otakar Fischer* (b. Kollin 20 May 1883; d. Prague 12 Mar 1939)
Justice	*Jaroslav Krejčí* (b. 27 Jun 1892)
Education	*Jan Kapras*
Agriculture	*Ladislav Feierabend* (see Syrový II)
Commerce	*Vlastimil Šádek* (b. Vicemerice 17 Dec 1893)
Public Works	*Dominik Čipera* (b. Prague 1893)
Health	*Ladislav Klumpár* (b. Prague 9 Aug 1893?)

Until 1 Mar 1939, the members of the autonomous Slovakian government (see Slovakia) were also members of the Cabinet

Slovakia declared itself independent 14 Mar 1939 (see page 451)
Bohemia and Moravia were declared German protectorates 14/15 Mar 1939

Reich Protectorate of Bohemia-Moravia

Reich Protectors

18 Mar/15 Apr 1939	*Konstantin, Baron Neurath* (b. Klein-Glattbach, Wurtemberg, 2 Feb 1873; d. Teinfelder Hof, Wurtemberg, 14 Aug 1956)
27 Sep 1941	*Reinhard Heydrich* (b. Halle 7 Mar 1904; d. Prague 4 Jun 1942)
28 May 1942	*Kurt Daluege* (b. Kreuzburg, Upper Silesia, 15 Sep 1897; d. Prague 23 Oct 1946)
2 Sep 1943 – 8 May 1945	*Wilhelm Frick* (b. Alsenz 12 Mar 1877; d. Nuremberg 16 Oct 1946)

27 Apr 1939 – 28 Sep 1941: Eliáš

Prime Minister	*Alois Eliáš* (see Beran)
Deputy Prime Minister	27 Apr 1939 – 3 Feb 1940: *Jiří Havelka* (see Beran)
	3 Feb 1940 – 28 Sep 1941: *Jaroslav Krejčí* (see Beran)
Home Affairs	27 Apr – 4 Jul 1939: *Alois Eliáš* (see Beran)
	4 Jul 1939 – 28 Sep 1941: *Josef Ežek*
Transport (incorporating Railways)	*Jiří Havelka* (see Beran)

133

CZECHOSLOVAKIA

Finance	*Josef Kalfus* (see Hodža II)
Commerce	27 Apr 1939 – 3 Feb 1940: *Vlastimil Šádek* (see Beran) 3 Feb 1940 – 28 Sep 1941: *Jaroslav Kratochvíl* (b. 1900?)
Agriculture	27 Apr 1939 – 3 Feb 1940: *Ladislav Feierabend* (see Syrový II) 3 Feb 1940 – 28 Sep 1941: *Nicholas, Count Bubna- Littitz* (b. Daudleb 14 Jun 1897; d. Graz 17 Aug 1954)
Social Welfare and Health	*Ladislav Klumpár* (see Beran)
Education	*Jan Kapras* (see Beran)
Public Works	*Dominik Čipera* (see Beran)

19 Jan 1942 – 4 May 1945: Krejčí

Prime Minister	*Jaroslav Krejčí* (see Beran)
Home Affairs	*Richard Bienert*
Justice	*Jaroslav Krejčí* (see Beran)
Finance	*Josef Kalfus* (see Hodža II)
Agriculture and Forestry	*Adolf Hrubý* (b. Mlaky 21 May 1893)
Transport	*Jindřich Kamenický* (see Syrový I)
Schools and Education	*Emanuel Moravec* (d. Prague 5 May 1945)
Labour and Economic Affairs	*Walter Bertsch* (b. Oppenweiler 4 Jan 1900; d. Brno 5 Jan 1952)

18 Jul 1940 – May 1945: Šrámek (Government in exile in London)

Prime Minister	*Jan Šrámek* (Czech Pop) (see Udržal II)
Foreign Affairs	*Jan Masaryk* (b. Prague 14 Sep 1886; d. 10 Mar 1948)
Justice	*Jaroslav Stránský* (Nat Soc) (b. 1884)
Minister of State	*Hubert Ripka* (Nat Soc) (b. 1895; d. London 7 Jan 1958)

May 1945	Czechoslovakia regained independence

5 Apr 1945 (in Košice)/early May 1945 (in Prague) – 19 Jun 1946: Fierlinger

Prime Minister	*Zdeněk Fierlinger* (Soc) (b. Olomouc 11 Jul 1891; d. 2 May 1976)
Deputy Prime Ministers	*Jan Šrámek* (Czech Pop) (see Udržal II) 5 Apr – 7 Nov 1945: *Jozef David* (Nat Soc) (b. 1894)

	7 Nov 1945 – 19 Jun 1946: *Jaroslav Stránský* (Nat Soc) (see Šrámek)
	Klement Gottwald (Comm) (see Presidents)
	Jan Ursiný (Slov Dem) (b. 1896)
	Viliam Široký (Comm) (b. Bratislava 31 May 1902; d. Prague 6 Oct 1971)
Foreign Affairs	*Jan Masaryk* (see Šrámek)
Home Affairs	*Vlado Clementis* (Comm) (b. Slovakia 1900; d. Prague 3 Dec 1952) Under Secretary of State
	Václav Nosek (Comm) (b. Kladno 1893; d. Prague 22 Jul 1955)
Justice	7 Apr – 7 Nov 1945: *Jaroslav Stránský* (Nat Soc) (see Šrámek)
	7 Nov 1945 – Jun 1946: *Prokop Drtina* (Nat Soc) (b. 1900)
Defence	*Ludvík Svoboda* (see Presidents)
Post Office	*František Hála* (Czech Pop) (b. 1893)
Finance	*Vavro Jan Šrobár* (b. Lisková 9 Aug 1867; d. Olomouc 6 Dec 1950)*
Overseas Trade	*Hubert Ripka* (Nat Soc) (see Šrámek)
Domestic Trade	*Ivan Pietor* (Slov Dem)
Agriculture	*Július D'úriš* (Comm) (b. Rovňany 9 Mar 1904)
Transport	*Anton Hasal-Nizborský* (b. 1893(?); d. Fort Meyer, Virginia, 22 Apr 1960)
Information	*Václav Kopecký* (Comm) (b. Prague 27 Aug 1897; d. Prague 5 Aug 1961)
Labour and Social Welfare	*Jozef Šoltész* (Comm)
Education	*Zdeněk Nejedlý* (Comm) (b. 10 Feb 1878; d. Prague 9 Mar 1962)
Industry	*Bohumil Laušman* (Soc) (b. 1903; d. Prague late Jun 1958)
Health	*Adolf Procházka* (Czech Pop) (b. 1900)
Food	*Václav Majer* (Soc)

3 Jul 1946 – 25 Feb 1948: Gottwald I

Prime Minister	*Klement Gottwald* (Comm) (for 1st time) (see Presidents)
Deputy Prime Ministers	3 Jul 1946 – 23 Nov 1947: *Zdeněk Fierlinger* (Soc) (see Fierlinger)

*For earlier career see vol. 2

135

CZECHOSLOVAKIA

	Viliam Široký (Comm) (see Fierlinger) *Jan Šrámek* (Czech Pop) (see Udržal II) *Peter Zenkl* (see Syrový I) 3 Jul 1946 – 3 Oct 1947: *Jan Ursiný* (Slov Dem) (see Fierlinger) 24 Nov 1947 – 25 Feb 1948: *František Tymeš* (Soc) (b. Leipnik 14 Oct 1895) 7 Nov 1947 – 25 Feb 1948: *Stefan Kocvara* (b. 1896?)
Foreign Affairs	*Jan Masaryk* (see Šrámek)
Home Affairs	*Václav Nosek* (Comm) (see Fierlinger)
Justice	*Prokop Drtina* (Nat Soc) (see Fierlinger)
Defence	*Ludvík Svoboda* (see Presidents)
Post Office	*František Hála* (Czech Pop) (see Fierlinger)
Finance	*Jaromír Dolanský* (Comm) (b. Prague 25 Feb 1895; d. 16 Jul 1973)
Overseas Trade	*Hubert Ripka* (Nat Soc) (see Šrámek)
Domestic Trade	3 Jul 1946 – 2 Dec 1947: *Anton Smrhal* 2 Dec 1947 – 25 Feb 1948: *Alexej Čepička* (Comm) (b. Kremsier 18 Aug 1910)
Agriculture	*Július D'úriš* (Comm) (see Fierlinger)
Transport	*Ivan Pietor* (Slov Dem) (see Fierlinger)
Information	*Václav Kopecký* (Comm) (see Fierlinger)
Labour and National Insurance	*Zdeněk Nejedlý* (Comm) (see Fierlinger)
Education	*Jaroslav Stranský* (Nat Soc) (see Šrámek)
Industry	3 Jul 1946 – 24 Dec 1947: *Bohumil Laušman* (Soc) (see Fierlinger) 24 Dec 1947 – 25 Feb 1948: *Ludmilla Jankovcová* (Soc) (b. Kutná Hora 8 Aug 1897)
Health	*Adolf Procházka* (Czech Pop) (see Fierlinger)
Food	*Václav Majer* (Soc) (see Fierlinger)
Public Works	*Jaromír Vosahlík* (Czech Pop) (b. 1899?; d. Moscow 29 Nov 1958)
Unification	*Nikolaus Franck* (Dem)

25 Feb – 14 Jun 1948: Gottwald II

Prime Minister	*Klement Gottwald* (Comm) (for 2nd time) (see Presidents)
Deputy Prime Ministers	*Eugen Erban* (Soc) (b. Vsetín 8 Jun 1912) *Antonín Zápotocký* (Comm) (see Presidents) 25 Feb – 3 May 1948: *Bohumil Laušman* (Soc) (see Fierlinger)

	Zdeněk Fierlinger (Soc) (see Fierlinger)
	Viliam Široký (Comm) (see Fierlinger)
Foreign Affairs	25 Feb – 10 Mar 1948: *Jan Masaryk* (see Šrámek)
	19 Mar – 14 Jun 1948: *Vlado Clementis* (Comm) (see Fierlinger)
Home Affairs	*Václav Nosek* (Comm) (see Fierlinger)
Justice	*Alexej Čepička* (Comm) (see Gottwald I)
Defence	*Ludvík Svoboda* (see Presidents)
Post	*Alois Neuman* (Nat Soc) (b. Smidar 12 Mar 1901)
Finance	*Jaromír Dolanský* (Comm) (see Gottwald I)
Overseas Trade	*Antonín Gregor* (Comm) (b. Staré Město 9 Sep 1908)
Domestic Trade	*František Krajčír* (Comm) (b. Vienna 12 Jun 1913)
Agriculture	*Július D'úriš* (Comm) (see Fierlinger)
Transport	*Alois Petr* (Czech Pop) (b. 1889?; d. Prague 14 Dec 1951)
Information	*Václav Kopecký* (Comm) (see Fierlinger)
Technical Planning	*Emanuel Šlechta* (Nat Soc) (b. 1885?; d. Vienna 17 Mar 1960)
Welfare and Labour	*Eugen Erban* (Soc) (see above)
Education	*Zdeněk Nejedlý* (Comm) (see Fierlinger)
Industry	*Zdeněk Fierlinger* (Soc) (see Fierlinger)
Health	*Josef Plojhar* (Czech Pop) (b. České Budějovice 2 Mar 1902)
Food	*Ludmilla Jankovcová* (Soc) (see Gottwald I)
Unification	*Vavro Jan Šrobár* (Slov Freedom) (see Fierlinger)

15 Jun 1948 – 21 Mar 1953: Zápotocký

Prime Minister	*Antonín Zápotocký* (see Presidents)
Deputy Prime	*Zdeněk Fierlinger* (Soc) (see Fierlinger)
Ministers	15 Jun 1948 – 14 Mar 1950 and 3 Feb – 21 Mar 1953: *Viliam Široký* (Comm) (see Fierlinger)
	15 Jun 1948 – 30 May 1952: *Ján Ševčík* (Slov Recon) (b. Bacolupy 13 Feb 1896)
	25 Apr 1950 – 7 Sep 1951: *Ludvík Svoboda* (see Presidents)
	7 Sep – 27 Nov 1951: *Rudolf Slánský* (b. Nezvěstice 31 Jul 1901; d. Prague 3 Dec 1952)
	22 Dec 1951 – 21 Mar 1953: *Jaromír Dolanský* (Comm) (see Gottwald I)
	7 Jun 1952 – 3 Feb 1953: *Jozef Kyselý* (Slov Dem) (b. Prešav 20 Mar 1912)

3 Feb – 21 Mar 1953: *Karel Jozef Bacílek* (Comm) (b. Chot'ánky 2 Oct 1896)

3 Feb – 21 Mar 1953: *Alexej Čepička* (Comm) (see Gottwald I)

3 Feb – 21 Mar 1953: *Václav Kopecký* (Comm) (see Fierlinger)

3 Feb – 21 Mar 1953: *Zdeněk Nejedlý* (Comm) (see Fierlinger)

3 Feb – 21 Mar 1953: *Jindřich Uher* (Comm) (b. Předměřice 18 Jun 1911)

3 Feb – 21 Mar 1953: *Antonín Novotný* (Comm) (see Presidents)

Foreign Affairs
15 Jun 1948 – 14 Mar 1950: *Vlado Clementis* (Comm) (see Fierlinger)

14 Mar 1950 – 3 Feb 1953: *Viliam Široký* (Comm) (see Fierlinger)

3 Feb – 21 Mar 1953: *Václav David* (Comm) (b. Studené 23 Sep 1910)

Home Affairs
Václav Nosek (Comm) (see Fierlinger)

Justice
15 Jun 1948 – 25 Apr 1950: *Alexej Čepička* (Comm) (see Gottwald I)

25 Apr 1950 – 21 Mar 1953: *Štefan Rais* (Comm) (b. Zliechov-Gapel 8 Aug 1909)

Ecclesiastical Affairs (new post)
25 Oct 1949 – 25 Apr 1950: *Alexej Čepička* (Comm) (see Gottwald I)

25 Apr 1950 – 3 Feb 1953: *Zdeněk Fierlinger* (Soc) (see Fierlinger)

Defence
15 Jun 1948 – 25 Apr 1950: *Ludvík Svoboda* (see Presidents)

25 Apr 1950 – 21 Mar 1953: *Alexej Čepička* (Comm) (see Gottwald I)

Post (from Apr 1952: Communications)
Alois Neuman (Nat Soc) (see Gottwald II)

Finance
15 Jun 1948 – 5 Apr 1949: *Jaromír Dolanský* (Comm) (see Gottwald I)

5 Apr 1949 – 21 Mar 1953: *Jaroslav Kabeš* (b. Tabor 18 Jun 1896)

President of State Planning Board (new post)
5 Apr 1949 – 21 Dec 1951: *Jaromír Dolanský* (Comm) (see Gottwald I)

21 Dec 1951 – 21 Mar 1953: *Jozef Púčik* (b. Hronec 9 Mar 1912)

Overseas Trade
15 Jun 1948 – 2 Dec 1952: *Antonín Gregor* (Comm) (see Gottwald II)

2 Dec 1952 – 21 Mar 1953: *Richard Dvořák* (Comm)
(b. Křešice 28 Dec 1913)

Domestic Trade	*František Krajčír* (Comm) (see Gottwald II)
Agriculture	15 Jun 1948 – 10 Sep 1951: *Július D'úriš* (Comm) (see Fierlinger)
	10 Sep 1951 – 21 Mar 1953: *Jozef Nepomucký* (Comm) (b. Prague 12 Oct 1897)
Transport	15 Jun 1948 – 14 Dec 1951: *Alois Petr* (Czech Pop) (see Gottwald II)
	24 Dec 1951 – 21 Mar 1953: *Antonín Pospíšil* (b. Mourinov 10 Jun 1903)
Information	15 Jun 1948 – 3 Feb 1953: *Václav Kopecký* (Comm) (see Fierlinger)
	3 Feb 1953: post abolished
Technical Planning	15 Jun 1948 – 20 Dec 1950: *Emanuel Šlechta* (Nat Soc) (see Gottwald II)
	20 Dec 1950: post abolished
Welfare (and Labour)	15 Jun 1948 – 7 Sep 1951: *Eugen Erban* (Soc) (see Gottwald II)
	7 Sep 1951 – 21 Mar 1953: *Jaroslav Havelka* (Comm) (b. Prague 19 Feb 1917)
Education	15 Jun 1948 – 3 Feb 1953: *Zdeněk Nejedlý* (Comm) (see Fierlinger)
	3 Feb 1953: divided into Schools and National Culture and Higher Education (see below)
Schools and National Culture	3 Feb – 21 Mar 1953: *Arnošt Sýkora* (b. Báňská Bystřice 2 Aug 1914)
Higher Education	3 Feb – 21 Mar 1953: *Ladislav Štoll* (b. Gablonz 26 Jun 1902)
Industry	15 Jun 1948 – 19 Dec 1950: *Augustin Kliment* (Comm) (b. Bohemia 1889?; d. 22 Oct 1953)
	19 Dec 1950: divided into a number of ministries
Health	*Josef Plojhar* (Czech Pop) (see Gottwald II)
Food	15 Jun 1948 – 19 Dec 1950: *Ludmilla Jankovcová* (Soc) (see Gottwald I)
	19 Dec 1950: post abolished
Unification	15 Jun 1948 – 16 Dec 1950: *Vavro Jan Šrobár* (Slov Freedom) (see Fierlinger)
	19 Dec 1950: post abolished
State Security (new post)	23 May 1950 – 24 Jan 1952: *Ladislav Kopřiva* (Comm) (b. Ivanovice 28 Jun 1897)
	24 Jan 1952 – 21 Mar 1953: *Karel Jozef Bacílek* (Comm) (see above)

139

21 Mar – 11 Sep 1953: Široký I

Prime Minister	*Viliam Široký* (Comm) (for 1st time) (see Fierlinger)
Deputy Prime	*Zdeněk Fierlinger* (Soc) (see Fierlinger)
Ministers	*Jaromír Dolanský* (Comm) (see Gottwald I)
	Karel Jozef Bacílek (Comm) (see Zápotocký)
	Alexej Čepička (Comm) (see Gottwald I)
	Zdeněk Nejedlý (Comm) (see Fierlinger)
	Jindřich Uher (Comm) (see Zápotocký)
	Antonín Novotný (Comm) (see Zápotocký)
	25 Mar – 11 Sep 1953: *Oldřich Beran* (Comm) (b. 22 Feb 1905)
	25 Mar – 11 Sep 1953: *Rudolf Barák* (Comm) (b. 1913; d. Prague Dec 1967?)
	2 Jun – 11 Sep 1953: *Václav Kopecký* (Comm) (see Fierlinger)
Foreign Affairs	*Václav David* (Comm) (see Zápotocký)
Home Affairs	*Václav Nosek* (Comm) (see Fierlinger)
Justice	*Štefan Rais* (Comm) (see Zápotocký)
Defence	*Alexej Čepička* (Comm) (see Gottwald I)
Communications	*Alois Neuman* (Nat Soc) (see Gottwald II)
Finance	*Jaroslav Kabeš* (see Zápotocký)
President of State Planning Board	*Jozef Púčik* (see Zápotocký)
Overseas Trade	*Richard Dvořak* (Comm) (see Zápotocký)
Domestic Trade	*František Krajčír* (Comm) (see Gottwald II)
Agriculture	*Jozef Nepomucký* (Comm) (see Zápotocký)
Transport	*Antonín Pospíšil* (see Zápotocký)
Welfare and Labour	*Jaroslav Havelka* (Comm) (see Zápotocký)
Schools and National Culture	*Arnošt Sýkora* (see Zápotocký)
Higher Education	*Ladislav Štoll* (see Zápotocký)
Health	*Josef Plojhar* (Czech Pop) (see Gottwald II)
State Security	*Karel Jozef Bacílek* (see Zápotocký)

15 Sep 1953 – 12 Dec 1954: Široký II

Prime Minister	*Viliam Široký* (Comm) (for 2nd time) (see Fierlinger)
First Deputy Prime Minister	*Jaromír Dolanský* (Comm) (see Gottwald I)
	Alexej Čepička (Comm) (see Gottwald I)
Deputy Prime Ministers	*Václav Kopecký* (Comm) (see Fierlinger)
	Jindřich Uher (Comm) (see Zápotocký)
Foreign Affairs	*Václav David* (Comm) (see Zápotocký)

Home Affairs (incorporating State Security)	Rudolf Barák (Comm) (see Široký I)
Justice	Václav Škoda (b. 1913)
Ecclesiastical Affairs	Jaroslav Havelka (Comm) (see Zápotocký)
Defence	Alexej Čepička (Comm) (see Gottwald I)
Transport and Communications	Alois Neuman (Nat Soc) (see Gottwald II)
Finance	Július D'úriš (Comm) (see Fierlinger)
Chairman of State Planning Board	15 Sep 1953 – Jun 1954: Jozef Púčik (see Zápotocký)
Audit	Oldřich Beran (Comm) (see Široký I)
Overseas Trade	Richard Dvořák (Comm) (see Zápotocký)
Domestic Trade	František Krajčír (Comm) (see Gottwald II)
Agriculture	Jindřich Uher (Comm) (see Zápotocký)
Transport	Antonín Pospíšil (see Zápotocký)
Welfare and Labour	Václav Nosek (Comm) (see Fierlinger)
Cultural Affairs	Václav Kopecký (Comm) (see Fierlinger)
Schools (including Higher Education)	Ladislav Štoll (see Zápotocký)
Health	Josef Plojhar (Czech Pop) (see Gottwald II)

12 Dec 1954 – 21 Sep 1963: Široký III

Prime Minister	Viliam Široký (Comm) (for 3rd time) (see Fierlinger)
First Deputy Prime Minister	Jaromír Dolanský (Comm) (see Gottwald I)
Second Deputy Prime Minister	12 Dec 1954 – 25 Apr 1956: Alexej Čepička (Comm) (see Gottwald I)
Deputy Prime Ministers	Ludmilla Jankovcová (Soc) (see Gottwald I) 12 Dec 1954 – 25 Apr 1956: Václav Kopecký (Comm) (see Fierlinger) 12 Dec 1954 – 25 Jun 1956: Václav Škoda (see Široký II) 14 Oct 1955 – 1958: Karel Poláček (b. Starý Plzenec 7 Jul 1913) 1958 – 8 Feb 1962: Rudolf Barák (Comm) (see Široký I) 1958/59 – 28 Jul 1962: Rudolf Strechaj (Comm) (b. Čachovice 25 Jul 1914; d. Prague 28 Jul 1962) 1958(?) – 21 Sep 1963: Otakar Šimůnek (Comm) (b. Nachod 23 Oct 1908)

141

	9 Feb 1962 – 21 Sep 1963: *Jan Piller* (Comm)
	7 Jan – 21 Sep 1963: *František Krajčír* (Comm) (see Gottwald II)
Foreign Affairs	*Václav David* (Comm) (see Zápotocký)
Home Affairs	12 Dec 1954 – 24 Jun 1961: *Rudolf Barák* (Comm) (see Široký I)
	24 Jun 1961 – 21 Sep 1963: *Lubomír Štrougal* (Comm) (b. Veselí 24 Oct 1924)
Justice	12 Dec 1954 – 25 Jun 1956: *Jan Bartuška*
	25 Jun 1956 – 7 Jun 1960: *Václav Škoda* (see Široký II)
	7 Jun 1960 – 21 Sep 1963: *Alois Neuman* (Nat Soc) (see Gottwald II)
Ecclesiastical Affairs	*Jaroslav Havelka* (Comm) (see Zápotocký)
Defence	12 Dec 1954 – 25 Apr 1956: *Alexej Čepička* (Comm) (see Gottwald I)
	25 Apr 1956 – 21 Sep 1963: *Bohumír Lomský* (Comm) (b. České Budějovice 22 Apr 1914)
Transport and Communications	12 Dec 1954 – Jul 1960: *Alois Neuman* (see Gottwald II)
Finance	*Július D'úriš* (Comm) (see Fierlinger)
President of State Planning Board	12 Dec 1954 – 11 Jul 1962: *Otakar Šimůnek* (Comm) (see above)
	12 Jul 1962 – 21 Sep 1963: *Alois Indra* (Comm) (b. Medzev 17 Mar 1921)
Audit	12 Dec 1954 – 14 Oct 1955: *Oldřich Beran* (Comm) (see Široký I)
	14 Oct 1955 – 25 Jun 1956: *Michal Bakul'a* (b. Malinec 23 Aug 1911)
	25 Jun 1956 – 21 Sep 1963: *Jozef Krosnár*
Overseas Trade	12 Dec 1954 – 17 Jan 1959: *Richard Dvořak* (Comm) (see Zápotocký)
	17 Jan 1959 – 7 Jan 1963: *František Krajčír* (Comm) (see Gottwald II)
	7 Jan – 21 Sep 1963: *František Hamouz* (Comm) (b. Chrašťány 15 Aug 1919)
Domestic Trade	12 Dec 1954 – 17 Jan 1959: *František Krajčír* (Comm) (see Gottwald II)
	17 Jan 1959 – 24 Jun 1961: *Ladislav Brabec*
	24 Jun 1961 – 21 Sep 1963: *Jindřich Uher* (Comm) (see Zápotocký)

Agriculture (from 25 Jun 1956: Agriculture, Forestry and Waterways)	12 Dec 1954 – 14 Oct 1955: *Markus Smida* 14 Oct 1955 – 25 Jun 1956: *Vratislav Krutina* (b. 1913) 25 Jun 1956 – Mar 1959: *Michal Bakuľa* (see above) Mar 1959 – 24 Jun 1961: *Lubomír Štrougal* (Comm) (see above) 24 Jun 1961 – 21 Sep 1963: *Vratislav Krutina* (see above)
Transport	12 Dec 1954 – Jan 1958: *Antonín Pospíšil* (see Zápotocký) Jan 1958 – 7 Jan 1963: *František Vlasák* (Comm) (b. Libusín 30 Aug 1912) 7 Jan – 21 Sep 1963: *František Vokáč*
Welfare and Labour	12 Dec 1954 – 22 Jul 1955: *Václav Nosek* (Comm) (see Fierlinger) Oct 1955 – Aug 1957: *Jozef Tesla* (b. Ostrava 22 Feb 1905) Aug 1957: post abolished
Culture	12 Dec 1954 – 15 Jun 1956: *Ladislav Štoll* (see Zápotocký) 15 Jun 1956: merged with Schools (see below)
Schools	*František Kahuda* (b. Nový Drůr 3 Jan 1911)
Health	*Josef Plojhar* (Czech Pop) (see Gottwald II)

21 Sep 1963 – 6 Apr 1968: Lenárt

Prime Minister	*Jozef Lenárt* (Comm) (b. Liptovská Porubka 3 Apr 1923)
Deputy Prime Minister and Chairman of State Planning Committee	*Oldřich Černík* (Comm) (b. Moravská Ostrava 27 Oct 1921)
Deputy Prime Ministers	*František Krajčír* (Comm) (see Gottwald II) 21 Sep 1963 – 11 Nov 1965: *Jan Piller* (Comm) (see Široký III) 11 Nov 1965 – 6 Apr 1968: *Josef Krejčí* (Comm) (b. Pochvalov 29 Jan 1912) 21 Sep 1963 – 3 Mar 1968: *Otakar Šimůnek* (Comm) (see Široký III)
Foreign Affairs	*Václav David* (Comm) (see Zápotocký)

143

Home Affairs	21 Sep 1963 – 24 Apr 1965: *Lubomír Štrougal* (Comm) (see Široký III) 24 Apr 1965 – 14 Mar 1968: *Josef Kudrna* (b. Ostředek 1 Sep 1920)
Justice	*Alois Neuman* (ČSS) (see Gottwald II)
Defence	21 Sep 1963 – 3 Mar 1968: *Bohumír Lomský* (Comm) (see Široký III)
Transport	*Alois Indra* (Comm) (see Široký III)
Finance	21 Sep 1963 – 23 Jan 1967: *Richard Dvořák* (Comm) (see Zápotocký) 23 Jan 1967 – 6 Apr 1968: *Bohumil Sucharda* (Comm) (b. Tuhaň 20 Apr 1914)
President of the State Planning Commission for Development and Co-ordination of Science and Technology	21 Sep 1963 – (?) Nov 1965: *František Vlasák* (Comm) (see Široký III)
Central Audit and Statistics Office	21 Sep 1963 – 23 Jan 1967: *Pavel Majling* (Comm) (b. 13 Jun 1911) 23 Jan 1967 – 6 Apr 1968: *Jan Kazimour* (Comm) (b. Prague 16 Feb 1914)
Overseas Trade	*František Hamouz* (Comm) (see Široký III)
Domestic Trade	*Jindřich Uher* (Comm) (see Zápotocký)
Agriculture (including Forestry)	21 Sep 1963 – 23 Jan 1967: *Jiří Burian* (Comm) (b. Rošovice 3 Jan 1921) 23 Jan 1967: divided into Agriculture and Forestry and Waterways (see below)
Agriculture	23 Jan – 12 Apr 1967: *Jiří Burian* (Comm) (see above) 12 Apr 1967 – 6 Apr 1968: *Karel Mestek* (Comm) (b. Slapy 1 Oct 1907)
Forestry and Waterways	23 Jan 1967 – 6 Apr 1968: *Josef Smrkovský* (Comm) (b. Velenka 26 Feb 1911; d. 15 Jan 1974)
Culture and Education	21 Sep 1963 – 5 Nov 1965: *Čestmír Císař* (Comm) (b. Hostomice 2 Jan 1920) 5 Nov 1965 – 23 Jan 1967: *Jiří Hájek* (Comm) (b. Krhanice 6 Jun 1913) 23 Jan 1967: divided into Schools and Culture and Information (see below)
Schools	23 Jan 1967 – 6 Apr 1968: *Jiří Hájek* (Comm) (see above)

Culture and Information	23 Jan 1967 – 6 Apr 1968: *Karel Hoffmann* (Comm) (b. Stod 15 Jun 1924)
Health	*Josef Plojhar* (ČSL) (see Gottwald II)
Without Portfolio	21 Sep 1963 – 11 Nov 1965: *Michal Chudík* (Comm) (b. Polomka 29 Sep 1914) Prime Minister of Slovakia
	11 Nov 1965 – 6 Apr 1968: *Jan Marko* (Comm) (b. Točnica 6 Sep 1920)
	Vincenc Krahulec (b. 1925?)

8 Apr – 27 Dec 1968: Černík I

Prime Minister	*Oldřich Černík* (Comm) (for 1st time) (see Lenárt)
Deputy Prime Ministers	*Peter Colotka* (Comm) (b. Sedliacká Dubová 10 Jan 1925)
	František Hamouz (Comm) (see Široký III)
	Gustav Husák (Comm) (see Presidents)
	10 Apr – 1 Sep 1968: *Ota Šik* (Comm) (b. Pilsen 11 Sep 1919)
	Lubomír Štrougal (Comm) (see Široký III)
Foreign Affairs	18 Apr – 19 Sep 1968: *Jiří Hájek* (Comm) (see Lenárt)
	19 Sep – Oct 1968 (acting:) *Oldřich Černík* (Comm) (see Lenárt)
	Oct – 27 Dec 1968 (acting:) *Václav Pleskot* (Comm) (b. Melostin 1 Jan 1921)
Home Affairs	8 Apr – 1 Sep 1968: *Josef Pavel* (Comm) (b. Novosedly 1908)
	1 Sep – 27 Dec 1968: *Jan Pelnář* (Comm) (b. Mrakov 24 Apr 1911)
Justice	*Bohuslav Kučera* (ČSS) (b. Lomnice 26 Mar 1923)
Defence	*Martin Dzúr* (Comm) (b. Ploštín 12 Jul 1919)
Transport	*František Řehák* (Comm) (b. Řibin 5 Oct 1924)
Finance	*Bohumil Sucharda* (Comm) (see Lenárt)
President of State Planning Commission	*František Vlasák* (Comm) (see Široký III)
Overseas Trade	*Václav Valeš* (Comm) (b. Smecno 7 Apr 1922)
Domestic Trade	*Oldřich Pavlovský* (Comm) (b. Hodonín 31 May 1920)
Agriculture and Food	*Josef Borůvka* (Comm) (b. Čáslavek 18 Dec 1911)
Forestry and Waterways	*Július Hanus* (Comm) (b. Turicka 12 Feb 1923)
Schools	*Vladimír Kadlec* (Comm) (b. Prague 4 Oct 1912)

145

CZECHOSLOVAKIA

Culture and Information	*Miroslav Galuška* (Comm) (b. Prague 9 Oct 1922)
Health	*Vladislav Vlček* (ČSL) (b. Prague 30 Jul 1912)
Without Portfolio	*Václav Hůla* (Comm) (b. Skryje 21 Sep 1925)
	Michal Štancel (Comm) (b. Malý Čepčin 20 Oct 1921)

1 Jan – 27 Sep 1969: Černík II

Prime Minister	*Oldřich Černík* (Comm) (for 2nd time) (see Lenárt)
Deputy Prime Ministers	1 – 30 Jan 1969: *Peter Colotka* (Comm) (see Černík I)
	30 Jan – 27 Sep 1969: *Samuel Falt'aň* (Comm) (b. Hradiště 22 Feb 1920)
	Karol Laco (Comm) (b. Sobotište 28 Oct 1921)
	František Hamouz (Comm) (see Široký III)
	Václav Valeš (Comm) (see Černík I)
Foreign Affairs	*Jan Marko* (Comm) (see Lenárt)
Home Affairs	*Jan Pelnář* (Comm) (see Černík I)
Defence	*Martin Dzúr* (Comm) (see Černík I)
Finance	*Bohumil Sucharda* (Comm) (see Lenárt)
Planning	*František Vlasák* (Comm) (see Široký III)
Overseas Trade	*Jan Tabáček* (Comm) (b. Bytča 14 Feb 1927)
Labour and Social Affairs	*Michal Štancel* (Comm) (see Černík I)
Without Portfolio	*Bohuslav Kučera* (ČSS) (see Černík I)

27 Sep 1969 – 28 Jan 1970: Černík III

Prime Minister	*Oldřich Černík* (Comm) (for 3rd time) (see Lenárt)
Deputy Prime Ministers	*Josef Kempný* (Comm) (b. Orlova-Lazy 19 Jul 1920)
	Peter Colotka (Comm) (see Černík I)
	František Hamouz (Comm) (see Široký III)
	Václav Hůla (Comm) (see Černík I)
	Miroslav Hruškovič (Comm) (b. Pukanec 25 Jan 1925) also Chairman of Committee for Technical and Investment Development
	Karol Laco (Comm) (see Černík II)
Foreign Affairs	*Jan Marko* (Comm) (see Lenárt)
Home Affairs	*Jan Pelnář* (Comm) (see Černík I)
Defence	*Martin Dzúr* (Comm) (see Černík I)

Finance	*Rudolf Rohlíček* (Comm) (b. Malacky 14 Jul 1929)
Planning	*Václav Hůla* (Comm) (see Černík I)
Overseas Trade	*František Hamouz* (Comm) (see Široký III)
Labour and Social Affairs	*Michal Štancel* (Comm) (see Černík I)
Without Portfolio	*Bohuslav Kučera* (ČSS) (see Černík I) *Jan Pauly* (ČSL) (b. Prague 22 Aug 1910)

from 28 Jan 1970: Štrougal

Prime Minister	*Lubomír Štrougal* (Comm) (see Široký III)
Deputy Prime Ministers	28 Jan 1970 – 3 Jan 1971: *František Hamouz* (Comm) (see Široký III)
	28 Jan 1970 – 3 Jan 1971: *Miroslav Hruškovič* (Comm) (see Černík III)
	Josef Korčák (Comm) (b. Holštejn 17 Dec 1921)
	Peter Colotka (Comm) (see Černík I)
	Karol Laco (Comm) (see Černík II)
	Václav Hůla (Comm) (see Černík I)
	from 3 Jan 1971: *Matej Lucan*
	from 3 Jan 1971: *Jindřich Zahradník*
	from 3 Jan 1971: *Jan Gregor*
	from 14 Dec 1973: *Rudolf Rohlíček* (Comm) (see Černík III)
	14 Dec 1973 – 2 Dec 1974: *Vlastimil Ehrenberger*
	from 2 Dec 1974: *Josef Šimon*
Foreign Affairs	28 Jan 1970 – 9 Dec 1971: *Jan Marko* (Comm) (see Lénart)
	from 9 Dec 1971: *Bohuslav Chňoupek*
Home Affairs	28 Jan 1970 – 28 Feb 1973: *Radko Kaska* (b. Josefov 23 Feb 1928; d. (aircraft crash) near Szczecin 28 Feb 1973)
	from 30 Mar 1973: *Jaromír Obzina*
Defence	*Martin Dzúr* (Comm) (see Černík I)
Finance	28 Jan 1970 – 14 Dec 1973: *Rudolf Rohlíček* (Comm) (see Černík III)
	from 14 Dec 1973: *Leopold Lér*
Planning (from 3 Jan 1971: State Planning Commission)	*Václav Hůla* (Comm) (see Černík I)
Overseas Trade	*Andrej Barčák* (b. Mlynky 19 Jan 1920)

147

Labour and Social Affairs	*Michal Štancel* (Comm) (see Černík I)
Fuel and Energy	28 Jan 1970 – Sep 1974: *Jaromir Matoušek* (d. Sep 1974) from 2 Dec 1974: *Vlastimil Ehrenberger* (see above)
Metallurgy and Engineering (from 14 Dec 1973: Metallurgy and Heavy Engineering)	28 Jan 1970 – 2 Dec 1974: *Josef Simon* (see above) from 2 Dec 1974: *Zdeněk Půček*
Agriculture and Food Supply	*Bohuslav Vecara*
Technology and Investments	28 Jan – 23 Jun 1970: *Oldřich Černík* (Comm) (see Lenárt) 23 Jun 1970 – 3 Jan 1971: *Ladislav Šupka* from 3 Jan 1971: *Ignac Rendek*
Posts and Telecommunications	28 Jan 1970 – 4 May 1971: *Karel Hoffman* (Comm) (see Lenárt) from 4 May 1971: *Vlastimil Chalupa*
Transport	28 Jan 1970 – 21 Nov 1975: *Stefan Sutka* from 21 Nov 1975: *Vladimír Blažek*
Control Commission	28 Jan 1970 – 20 Aug 1972: *Drahomir Kolder* (d. 20 Aug 1972) from 20 Aug 1972: *František Ondřich*
General Engineering (new post)	from 14 Dec 1973: *Pavol Bahyl*
Deputy Chairman of State Planning Commission (of ministerial rank)	from 14 Dec 1973: *Vladimir Janza*
Without Portfolio	28 Jan 1970 – 3 Jan 1971: *Jan Pauly* (ČSL) (see Černík III) 28 Jan 1970 – 9 Dec 1971: *Bohuslav Kučera* (ČSS) (see Černík I) *Karol Martinka* (Comm) (b. Púchov 5 Jul 1923)

First Secretary of the Central Committee of Czechoslovak Communist Party

1953 – 5 Jan 1968	*Antonín Novotný* (see Presidents)
5 Jan 1968 – 1969	*Alexander Dubček* (b. Uhrovec 27 Nov 1921)
from 17 Apr 1969	*Gustáv Husák* (see Presidents)

Denmark

HEADS OF STATE

Kings and Queens

14 May 1912	*Christian X*, son of Frederick VIII (b. 29 Sep 1870)
20 Apr 1947	*Frederick IX*, son (b. 11 Mar 1899)
14 Jan 1972	*Margrethe II*, daughter (b. 16 Apr 1940)

MEMBERS OF GOVERNMENT

Prime Ministers or Chief Ministers

20 Apr 1929 – 4 Nov 1935	*Thorvald August Marinus Stauning* (for 2nd time) (b. Copenhagen 26 Oct 1873; d. Copenhagen 3 May 1942)*
7 Nov 1935	*Thorvald August Marinus Stauning* (for 3rd time)
5 Jul 1940	*Thorvald August Marinus Stauning* (for 4th time)
3 May 1942	*Wilhelm Buhl* (for 1st time) (b. 16 Oct 1881; d. Copenhagen 18 Dec 1954)
10 Nov 1942	*(Harald R.) Erik Scavenius* (b. 13 Jun 1877; d. 22 Nov 1962)*
29 Aug 1943	The government refused to continue in office, but its resignation was not formally accepted by the King until 5 May 1945
5 May – 7 Nov 1945	*Wilhelm Buhl* (for 2nd time)
8 Nov 1945 – 4 Oct/ 13 Nov 1947	*Knud Kristensen* (b. 13 Jul 1895; d. 28 Sep 1962)
12/13 Nov 1947 – 9 Aug 1950	*Hans Hedtoft* (for 1st time) (b. Aarhus 21 Apr 1903; d. Stockholm 29 Jan 1955)
13 Sep – 25 Oct 1950	*Hans Hedtoft* (for 2nd time)
28 Oct 1950	*Erik Eriksen* (b. 10 Nov 1902; d. 7 Oct 1972)
30 Sep 1953 – 29 Jan 1955	*Hans Hedtoft* (for 3rd time)
1 Feb 1955 – 15 May 1957	*Hans Christian Hansen* (Soc) (for 1st time) (b. Aarhus 8 Nov 1906; d. Copenhagen 19 Feb 1960)
27 May 1957 – 19 Feb 1960	*Hans Christian Hansen* (Soc) (for 2nd time)

*For earlier career see vol. 2

DENMARK

25 Dec 1959 – 19 Feb 1960	*Viggo Kampmann* (Soc) (for 1st time) (b. Copenhagen 21 Jul 1910; d. Copenhagen 3 Jun 1976) Caretaker during Hansen's final illness
21 Feb 1960	*Viggo Kampmann* (Soc) (for 2nd time)
18 Nov 1960 – 31 Aug 1962	*Viggo Kampmann* (Soc) (for 3rd time)
3 Sep 1962	*Jens Otto Krag* (Soc) (for 1st time) (b. Randers 15 Sep 1914)
24 Sep 1964 – 2 Nov 1966	*Jens Otto Krag* (Soc) (for 2nd time)
28 Nov 1966 – 16 Dec 1967/24 Jan 1968	*Jens Otto Krag* (Soc) (for 3rd time)
1 Feb 1968 – 6 Oct 1971	*Hilmar (Tormod Ingolf) Baunsgaard* (b. Slagelse 26 Feb 1920)
11 Oct 1971 – 3 Oct 1972	*Jens Otto Krag* (Soc) (for 4th time)
5 Oct 1972	*Anker Jørgensen* (Soc) (for 1st time) (b. Copenhagen 13 Jul 1922)
19 Dec 1973 – 29 Jun 1975	*Poul Hartling* (Cons) (b. Copenhagen 14 Aug 1914)
from 13 Feb 1975	*Anker Jørgensen* (Soc) (for 2nd time)

Foreign Ministers

30 Apr 1929	*Peter R. Munch* (b. Redsted 25 Jul 1870; d. Copenhagen 12 Jan 1948)
5 Jul 1940	*(Harald R.) Erik Scavenius* (for 2nd time) (see Prime Ministers)
29 Aug 1943	No appointment made
5 May 1945	*J. Christmas Møller* (b. Copenhagen 3 Apr 1894; d. 13 Apr 1948)
8 Nov 1945 – 26 Oct 1950	*Gustav Rasmussen* (b. 1895; d. Copenhagen 13 Sep 1953)
28 Oct 1950 – 29 Sep 1953	*Ole Biorn Kraft* (b. Copenhagen 17 Dec 1893)
1 Oct 1953	*Hans Christian Hansen* (Soc) (see Prime Ministers)
7 Oct 1958	*Jens Otto Krag* (Soc) (for 1st time) (see Prime Ministers)
3 Sep 1962	*Per Haekkerup* (Soc) (b. Ringsted 25 Dec 1915)
28 Nov 1966	*Jens Otto Krag* (Soc) (for 2nd time)
1 Oct 1967 – 24 Jan 1968	*Hans (Rasmussen) Tabor* (Soc) (b. Copenhagen 25 Apr 1922)

1 Feb 1968 – 6 Oct 1971	*Poul Hartling* (Cons) (see Prime Ministers)
11 Oct 1971 – 3 Oct 1972	*Knud Borge Andersen* (for 1st time) (b. Copenhagen 1 Dec 1914)
5 Oct 1972	*Knud Borge Andersen* (for 2nd time)
Dec 1973 – 29 Jan 1975	*Ove Guldberg* (b. Nysted 2 Dec 1918)
from 13 Feb 1975	*Knud Borge Andersen* (for 3rd time)

Dominican Republic

HEADS OF STATE

Presidents

12 Jul 1924 – 18 Feb 1930	*Horacio Vásquez* (for 3rd time) (b. 1855; d. 1936)*
2 Mar – 16 Aug 1930	*Rafael Estrella Urena*
18 Aug 1930	*Rafael Leónida Trujillo y Molina* (for 1st time) (b. San Cristóbal 24 Oct 1891; d. 30 May 1961)
18 Jun 1938 – 1940	*Jacinto Bienvenudo Peynado* (b. 1878; d. 1940)
12 Mar 1940	*Manuel de Jesús Troncoso de la Concha* (b. 1878; d. 1955)
May 1942	*Rafael Leónida Trujillo y Molina* (for 2nd time)
16 May 1952	*Hector Bienvenido Trujillo*, brother|(b. San Cristóbal 6 Apr 1909)
3 Aug 1960	*Joaquín Videla Balaguer* (for 1st time) (b. Santiago 1 Sep 1907)
1 Jan 1962	*Rafael (Filiberto) Bonnelly* (for 1st time) (b. Santiago 22 Aug 1904) Head of seven-man administration
17 Jan 1962	*Huberto Bogaert*, Head of Junta
19 Jan 1962	*Rafael (Filiberto) Bonnelly* (for 2nd time)
27 Feb 1963	*Juan Bosch Gavino* (b. La Vega 30 Jun 1909)
26 Sep 1963	*Emilio de los Santos*, Head of Junta
22 Dec 1963	*Donald Reid Cabral*
25 Apr – 3 Sep 1965	Disturbances, civil war

*For earlier career see vol. 2

28 Apr – 11(?) May 1965	*Elías Wessin y Wessin*, Leader of Loyalists
7 May – 30 Aug 1965	*Antonio Imbert Barreras* (b. 3 Dec 1920) Leader of Loyalists
25 Apr – 3 Sep 1965	*Francisco Caamaño Deñó* (b. 1933?) Leader of Rebel Government (Constitutionalists)
3 Sep 1965	*Héctor García Godoy Cáceres* (b. Mocca 11 Jul 1921; d. Santa Domingo 20 Apr 1970)
from 1 Jul 1966	*Joaquín Videla Balaguer* (for 2nd time)

Ecuador

HEADS OF STATE

Presidents

1 Apr 1926	*Isidro Ayora* (b. 31 Aug 1879)
24 Aug 1931	*Luis Larrea Alba* (b. 1895)
15 Oct 1931	*Alfredo Baquerizo Moreno* (for 2nd time) (b. 1859; d. New York 19 Mar 1951)*
2 Sep 1932	*Alberto Guerrero Martínez* (b. Guayaquil 1878; d. Guayaquil 21 May 1941)
6 Dec 1932 – 18 Oct 1933	*Juan de Dios Martínez Mera* (b. 1875(?); d. 27 Oct 1955)
20 Oct 1933 – 31 Aug 1934	*Abelardo Montalvo* (b. Quito 1 Jun 1876; d. Quito 26 Dec 1950)
1 Sep 1934	*José María Velasco Ibarra* (for 1st time) (b. 19 Mar 1893)
21 Aug 1935	*Antonio Pons* (b. 10 Nov 1897)
26 Sep 1935	*Frederico Páez* (b. Quito 6 Jun 1876)
23 Oct 1937	*Alberto Enríquez* (b. 1896(?); d. Quito 13 Jul 1962)
10 Aug 1938	*Manuel María Borrero* (b. Cuenca 1883)
3 Dec 1938 – 19 Nov 1939	*Aurelio Mosquera Narváez* (b. 1884; d. 19 Nov 1939)
16/19 Nov 1939	(acting:) *Carlos Alberto Arroyo del Río* (for 1st time) (b. Guayaquil 17 Nov 1893; d. Guayaquil 31 Oct 1969)

*For earlier career see vol. 2

11 Dec 1939	(acting:) *Andrés F. Córdova*
10 – 31 Aug 1940	(acting:) *Julio E. Moreno*
1 Sep 1940 – 29 May 1944	*Carlos Alberto Arroyo del Río* (for 2nd time)
31 May 1944	*José María Velasco Ibarra* (for 2nd time)
24 Aug 1947	*Carlos Mancheno Cajas*
3 – 15 Sep 1947	(acting:) *Mariano Suárez Veintimilla*
17 Sep 1947	*Carlos Julio Arosemena Tola* (b. 1894; d. 1952)
1 Sep 1948	*Galo Plaza Lasso* (b. 1906)
1 Sep 1952	*José María Velasco Ibarra* (for 3rd time)
1 Sep 1956	*Camilo Ponce Enríquez* (b. 1912)
1 Sep 1960	*José María Velasco Ibarra* (for 4th time)
7 Nov 1961	*Carlos Julio Arosemena Monroy* (b. Guayaquil 1919)
11 Jul 1963	*Rear-Admiral Ramón Castro Jijón* (b. Esmeraldas Nov 1915) Head of Junta
29 Mar 1966	*Clemente Yerovi Indaburú* (b. Guayaquil Aug 1904)
16 Nov 1966	(acting:) *Otto Arosemena Gómez* (b. Guayaquil 19 Jul 1925(1922?))
1 Sep 1968	*José María Velasco Ibarra* (for 5th time)
from 15 Feb 1972	*Guillermo Rodríguez Lara* (b. 4 Nov 1923) Head of Military Government

Egypt

See also United Arab Republic.

HEADS OF STATE

Kings

7 Oct 1917	*Ahmed Fuad I*, brother of Hussein Kamil (b. 26 Mar 1868) Sultan 1917–1922, from 1922 King
28 Apr 1936	*Farouk*, son (b. 11 Feb 1920; d. Rome 18 Mar 1965)
26 Jul 1952 – 18 Jun 1953	*Ahmed Fuad II*, son (b. 16 Jan 1952) nominal King

EGYPT

Presidents

18 Jun 1953 – 14 Nov 1954	*Mohammed Neguib* (b. Khartoum 20 Feb 1901)
17 Nov 1954 – 28 Sep 1970	*Gamal Abdul Nasser* (b. Beni Mor 15 Jan 1918; d. Heliopolis 28 Sep 1970)
from 29 Sep 1970	*Anwar Sadat* (b. Talah 25 Dec 1918)

British High Commissioners

1929	*Sir Percy Lyham Loraine, bart* (b. 5 Nov 1880; d. 23 May 1961)
1933 – 1936	*Sir Miles Wedderburn Lampson* (from 1943: *1st Baron Killearn*) (b. 24 Aug 1880; d. 18 Sep 1964)

MEMBERS OF GOVERNMENT

Prime Ministers

1 Jan – 19 Jun 1930	*Mustafa an-Nahas Pasha* (for 2nd time) (b. 15 Jun 1879)*
20 Jun 1930 – 4 Jan 1933	*Ismail Sidqi Pasha* (for 1st time) (b. 1975(?); d. Paris 9 Jul 1950)
5 Jan – 22 Sep 1933	*Ismail Sidqi Pasha* (for 2nd time)
27 Sep 1933 – 6 Nov 1934	*Abdul Fatah Yahya Ibrahim Pasha* (for 2nd time) (b. 1876; d. 27 Sep 1951)*
15 Nov 1934 – 10 Dec 1935	*Mohammed Tawfiq Nasim Pasha* (for 3rd time) (d. Cairo 6 Mar 1938)*
12 Dec 1935 – 22 Jan 1936	*Mohammed Tawfiq Nasim Pasha* (for 4th time)
30 Jan – 9 May 1936	*Ali Mahir Pasha* (b. 1884; d. Geneva 24 Aug 1960)
11 May 1936 – 3 Aug 1937	*Mustafa an-Nahas Pasha* (for 3rd time)
3 Aug 1937	*Mustafa an-Nahas Pasha* (for 4th time)
30 Dec 1937	*Mohammed Mahmud Pasha* (for 2nd time) (d. Cairo 2 Feb 1941)*
27 Apr 1938 – 12 Aug 1939	*Mohammed Mahmud Pasha* (for 3rd time)

*For earlier career see vol. 2

154

18 Aug 1939 – 23 Jun 1940	*Ali Mahir Pasha* (for 2nd time)
29 Jun – 14 Nov 1940	*Hassan Sabri Pasha* (d. Cairo 14 Nov 1940)
15 Nov 1940 – 4 Jun 1941	*Hussein Siri Pasha* (for 1st time) (b. 1892(?); d. Cairo 15 Dec 1960)
6 Jun 1941 – 2 Feb 1942	*Hussein Siri Pasha* (for 2nd time)
6 Feb – 26 May 1942	*Mustafa an-Nahas Pasha* (for 5th time)
27 May 1942 – 9 Oct 1944	*Mustafa an-Nahas Pasha* (for 6th time)
10 Oct 1944	*Ahmad Mahir Pasha* (for 1st time) (b. 1888; d. Cairo 24 Feb 1945)
3 Jan – 24 Feb 1945	*Ahmad Mahir Pasha* (for 2nd time)
26 Feb 1945 – 16 Feb 1946	*Mahmud Fahmi an-Noqrashi Pasha* (for 1st time) (b. 1888?; d. 28 Dec 1948)
17 Feb – 5 Sep 1946	*Ismail Sidqi Pasha* (for 3rd time)
12 Sep – 1 Oct 1946	*Ismail Sidqi Pasha* (for 4th time)
2 Oct – 7 Dec 1946	*Ismail Sidqi Pasha* (for 5th time)
9 Dec 1946 – 28 Dec 1948	*Mahmud Fahmi an-Noqrashi Pasha* (for 2nd time)
29 Dec 1948 – 25 Jul 1949	*Ibrahim Abdul Hadi*
26 Jul 1949	*Hussein Siri Pasha* (for 3rd time)
3 Nov 1949 – 12 Jan 1950	*Hussein Siri Pasha* (for 4th time)
14 Jan 1950	*Mustafa an-Nahas Pasha* (for 7th time)
27 Jan – 1 Mar 1952	*Ali Mahir Pasha* (for 3rd time)
2 Mar – 28 Jun 1952	*Ahmad Naguib Hilali Pasha* (for 1st time) (b. 1891; d. Cairo 11 Dec 1958)
2 – 20 Jul 1952	*Hussein Siri Pasha* (for 5th time)
22 – 23 Jul 1952	*Ahmad Naguib Hilali Pasha* (for 2nd time)
24 Jul 1952	*Ali Mahir Pasha* (for 4th time)
7 Sep 1952 – 25 Feb 1954	*Mohammed Neguib* (for 1st time) (see Presidents)
27 Feb 1954	*Gamal Abdul Nasser* (for 1st time) (see Presidents)
8 Mar – 17 Apr 1954	*Mohammed Neguib* (for 2nd time)
18 Apr 1954	*Gamal Abdul Nasser* (for 2nd time)
29 Jun 1956	President also Head of Government and from 6 Mar 1958 until 28 Sep 1961 Head of the Cabinet of the United Arab Republic
25 Sep 1962 – 29 Sep 1965	*Ali Sabri* (b. 30 Aug 1920)

3 Oct 1965 – 9 Sep 1966	*Zakaria Muji ad-Din* (b. May 1918)
10 Sep 1966	*Mohammed Sidqi Suleiman* (b. 1919)
19 Jun 1967 – 28 Sep 1970	*Gamal Abdul Nasser* (for 3rd time)
21 Oct – 15 Nov 1970	*Mahmud Fawzi* (for 1st time) (b. Shubra Bihom 19 Sep 1900)
18 Nov 1970 – Oct 1971	*Mahmud Fawzi* (for 2nd time)
16 Jan 1972	*Aziz Sidky* (b. Cairo Jul 1930)
from 26 Mar 1973	*Anwar Sadat* (see Presidents)

Foreign Ministers

9 Dec 1952	*Mahmud Fawzi* (see Prime Ministers) 25 Mar 1964 – 19 Jun 1967: Deputy Prime Minister for Foreign Affairs; 19 Jun 1967 – 21 Oct 1970: Presidential Adviser on Foreign Affairs
25 Mar 1964	*Mahmud Riad* (b. Cairo 8 Jan 1917)
17 Jan 1972	*Mohammed Murad Ghaleb* (b. Cairo 1 Apr 1922)
8 Sep 1972	*Mohammed Hassan al-Zaiyat* (b. Damietta 14 Feb 1915)
from Oct 1973	*Ismail Fahmi* (b. Cairo 2 Oct 1922)

El Salvador

HEADS OF STATE

Presidents

1 Mar 1927 – 28 Feb 1931	*Pio Rómeo Bosque*
1 Mar 1931	*Arturo Araujo*
1 Mar 1932	*Maximiliano Hernández Martínez* (b. 29 Oct 1882; d. Honduras 17 May 1966)
9 May 1944	*Andrés Ignacio Menéndez* (b. 1879)
21 Oct 1944	*Osmin Aguirre Salinas* (b. 1889)

8 Mar 1945	*Salvador Castañeda Castro* (b. Cojutepeque 1888; d. San Salvador 5 Mar 1965)
15 Dec 1948	*Manuel de Jesús Córdoba,* Head of Military Junta
19 Feb 1949	*Óscar Osorio* (for 1st time) (b. 1910; d. Houston 6 Mar 1969) Chairman of Junta
14 Sep 1950	*Óscar Osorio* (for 2nd time)
4 Mar/5 Sep 1956	*José María Lemus* (b. La Union 22 Jul 1911)
26 Oct 1960	*Colonel Miguel Ángel Castillo,* Head of Military Junta
25 Jan 1961	*Aníbal Portillo,* Leader of Military Junta
25 Jan 1962	(acting:) *Eusebio Rodolfo Cordón Cera* (b. 1899?)
1 Jul 1962	*Julio Adalberto Rivera Carballo* (b. 1921; d. 29 Jul 1973)
1 Jul 1967	*Fidel Sánchez Hernández* (b. El Divisadero 1917)
from 1 Jul 1972	*Arturo Armando Molina*

Equatorial Guinea

Formerly Río Muni and Fernando Po.

12 Oct 1968	Independence from Spain

HEAD OF STATE

President and Prime Minister

from 12 Oct 1968	*Francisco Macías Nguema* (b. Nsegayong, Río Muni, 1 Jan 1924) President for life from 14 Jul 1972

Eritrea

Until 1941	Part of Italian East Africa
1941	Administered by UK
1952	Federated with Ethiopia as an autonomous unit

Prime Ministers

29 Aug 1952 – 29 Jul 1955	*Prince Ato Tedla Bairu*
8 Aug 1955 – 20 May 1960	*Fitaurari Asfaha Woldemikael* (b. 1914?)
20 May 1960	Became an Ethiopian province

Estonia

HEADS OF STATE

Presidents

19 May 1919 – 24 Apr 1938	Prime Minister also President (see below)
24 Apr 1938 – Jun 1940	*Konstantin Päts* (b. 23 Feb 1874; d. Ufa 18 Jan 1956) deported 1941
1940	Incorporated in Union of Soviet Socialist Republics

MEMBERS OF GOVERNMENT

Prime Ministers (and Presidents until 24 Apr 1938)

10 Jul 1929 – 3 Feb 1931	*Otto Strandman* (for 2nd time) (b. 30 Nov 1875; d. 1941)*
12 Feb 1931 – 29 Jan 1932	*Konstantin Päts* (for 2nd time) (see Presidents)
18 Feb – 20 Jun 1932	*Jaan Teemant* (for 3rd time) (b. Vigala 24 Sep 1872)*
19 Jul – 3 Oct 1932	*Kaarel August Einbund*, later *Eenpalu* (for 1st time) (b. 1888; d. 1942)
1 Nov 1932 – 26 Apr 1933	*Konstantin Päts* (for 3rd time)
17 May – 17 Oct 1933	*Jaan Tõnisson* (for 4th time) (b. 22 Dec 1868)*

*For earlier career see vol. 2

Ethiopia

HEADS OF STATE

Emperors

7 Oct 1928	*Haile Selassie* (for 1st time) (b. Egersa Goro, Harar Province, 23 Jul 1892; d. 27 Aug 1975)
9 May 1936 – 5 May 1941	*Victor Emmanuel III* (b. 11 Nov 1869; d. 28 Dec 1947) King of Italy, assumed title of Emperor after Italian annexation of Ethiopia

Viceroys

9 May 1936	*Pietro Badoglio* (b. Grazzano 28 Sep 1871; d. 31 Oct 1956) Duke of Addis Ababa 1936 – 1943
11 Jun 1936	*Rodolfo Graziani* (b. Filettino 11 Aug 1882; d. Rome 11 Jan 1955)
20 Nov 1937 – 18 Nov 1940	*Amadeo, Duke of Aosta* (b. 21 Oct 1898; d. 3 Mar 1942)

Heads of State

5 May 1941 – 12 Sep 1974	*Haile Selassie* (for 2nd time) Emperor, deposed after coup
12 Sep 1974	*Merid Azmatch Asfa Wossen* (b. near Harar 27 Jul 1917) King Designate
12 Sep 1974 – 23 Nov 1974	*Aman Mikhail Andom* (b. 1924; d. (executed) 23 Nov 1974) President of Provisional Military Government
from 28 Nov 1974	*Teferi Benti* (b. 1921; d. 4 Feb 1977) Chairman of Military Council

MEMBERS OF GOVERNMENT

Chief Ministers

1944 – 1 Nov 1957	*Makonnen Endelkatchew* (b. 1891; d. Addis Ababa 27 Feb 1963)
21 Nov 1957 – 31 Mar 1961	*Akliku Habte Wold* (b. Addis Ababa 12 Mar 1912; d. (executed) 23 Nov 1974) Deputy Prime Minister

159

Prime Ministers

31 Mar 1961	*Akliku Habte Wold* (see Chief Ministers)
28 Feb 1974	*Lij Endelkatchew Makonnen* (d. (executed) 23 Nov 1974)
from 22 Jul 1974	*Lij Mikhail Imru Haile Selassie* (b. 1930)

Fiji

20 Sep 1966	Internal self-government
10 Oct 1970	Independence from Great Britain

HEADS OF STATE

Governors

20 Sep 1966	*Sir (Francis) Derek Jakeway* (b. 6 Jun 1915)
1968	*Sir Robert (Sidney) Foster* (b. 11 Aug 1913)

Governors-General

10 Oct 1970	*Sir Robert (Sidney) Foster* (previously Governor)
from Jul 1973	*Ratu Sir George Kadavulevu Cakobau* (b. Suva 6 Nov 1912)

MEMBER OF GOVERNMENT

Prime Minister

from 20 Sep 1966	*Ratu Sir Kamisese Kapaiwai Tuimacilai Mara* (b. 13 May 1920) (Chief Minister until 10 Oct 1970)

Finland

HEADS OF STATE

Presidents

1 Mar 1925 – 28 Feb 1931	*Lauri Kristian Relander* (b. Kurkijoki 31 May 1883; d. Helsinki 9 Feb 1942)
1 Mar 1931 – 28 Feb 1937	*Pehr Evind Svinhufvud* (b. Sääksmäki 15 Dec 1861; d. Luumäki 29 Feb 1944)*
1 Mar 1937 – 28 Nov 1940	*Kyösti Kallio* (b. Ylivieskä 10 Apr 1873; d. Helsinki 19 Dec 1940)*
19 Dec 1940 – 1 Aug 1944	*Risto (Heikki) Ryti* (b. 3 Feb 1889; d. Helsinki 25 Oct 1956)
4 Aug 1944 – 4 Mar 1946	*Karl Gustaf Emil, Baron Mannerheim* (b. Louhisaari 4 Jun 1867; d. Lausanne 27 Jan 1951)*
5 Mar 1945	*Juho Kusti Paasikivi* (b. Tampere 27 Nov 1870; d. Helsinki 14 Dec 1956) Deputy President*
9 Mar 1946 – 29 Feb 1956	*Juho Kusti Paasikivi* (see above)
from 1 Mar 1956	*Urho Kaleva Kekkonen* (b. 3 Sep 1900)

MEMBERS OF GOVERNMENT

Prime Ministers

16 Aug 1929 – 2 Jul 1930	*Kyösti Kallio* (for 3rd time) (see Presidents)
4 Jul 1930	*Pehr Evind Svinhufvud* (for 2nd time) (see Presidents)
16 Feb – 4 Mar 1931	*Juho (Heikki) Vennola* (for 3rd time) (b. Oulu 19 Jun 1872; d. Helsinki 3 Dec 1938)*
21 Mar 1931 – 7 Dec 1932	*Juho Emil Sunila* (for 2nd time) (b. Liminka 16 Aug 1875; d. Helsinki 2 Oct 1936)*
15 Dec 1932 – 26 Sep 1936	*Toivo Kivimäki* (b. 5 Jun 1886; d. Helsinki 7(?) May 1968)
7 Oct 1936 – 1 Mar 1937	*Kyösti Kallio* (for 4th time)

*For earlier career see vol. 2

161

FINLAND

12 Mar 1937	*Aimo Kaarlo Cajander* (for 3rd time) (b. Uusikaupunki 4 Mar 1879; d. Helsinki 21 Jan 1943)*
1 Dec 1939	*Risto (Heikki) Ryti* (for 1st time) (see Presidents)
27 Mar – 19 Dec 1940	*Risto (Heikki) Ryti* (for 2nd time)
3 Jan 1941 – 1 Mar 1943	*Johann Wilhelm Rangell* (b. 25 Oct 1894)
5 Mar 1943 – 4 Aug 1944	*Edwin Linkomies* (b. 22 Dec 1894; d. night of 7/8 Sep 1963)
8 Aug – 22 Sep 1944	*Andreas Hackzell* (b. 20 Sep 1881; d. 14 Jan 1946)
21 Sep – 11 Nov 1944	*Urho Jonas Castrén* (b. 30 Dec 1886; d. Helsinki 8 Mar 1965)
17 Nov 1944 – 4 Mar 1946	*Juho Kusti Paasikivi* (for 2nd time) (see Presidents)
4/26 Mar 1946 – 11 Apr 1947	*Mauno Pekkala* (for 1st time) (b. 17 Jan 1890; d. 1 Jul 1952)
21 May 1947 – 23 Jul 1948	*Mauno Pekkala* (for 2nd time)
29 Jul 1948 – 1 Mar 1950	*Karl August Fagerholm* (for 1st time) (b. Turku 31 Dec 1901)
17 Mar 1950	*Urho Kaleva Kekkonen* (for 1st time) (see Presidents)
17 Jan 1951	*Urho Kaleva Kekkonen* (for 2nd time)
20 Sep 1951 – 20 Jun 1953	*Urho Kaleva Kekkonen* (for 3rd time)
9 Jul – 4 Nov 1953	*Urho Kaleva Kekkonen* (for 4th time)
15 Nov 1953 – 25 Mar/1 Apr 1954	*Sakari Tuomioja* (b. Tampere 29 Aug 1911; d. Helsinki 9 Sep 1964)
5 May – 14 Oct 1954	*Ralf Törngren* (b. Oulu 1 Mar 1899; d. Turku 15 May 1961)
17 Oct 1954 – 27 Jan 1956	*Urho Kaleva Kekkonen* (for 5th time)
3 Mar 1956 – 22 May 1957	*Karl August Fagerholm* (for 2nd time)
27 May – 18 Oct 1957	*Väinö Johannes Sukselainen* (for 1st time) (b. 12 Oct 1906)
29 Nov 1957 – 18 Apr 1958	*(Berndt) Rainer von Fieandt* (b. Turku 26 Dec 1890; d. 28 Apr 1972)
26 Apr 1958	*Reino Iisakki Kuuskoski* (b. Loimijoki 18 Jan 1907; d. Helsinki 27 Jan 1965)

*For earlier career see vol. 2

29 Aug – 4 Dec 1958	*Karl August Fagerholm* (for 3rd time)
13 Jan 1959 – 29 Jun/3 Jul 1961	*Väinö Johannes Sukselainen* (for 2nd time)
14 Jul 1961 – 1 Mar 1962	*Martti Johannes Miettunen* (b. Simo 17 Apr 1907)
13 Apr 1962 – 30 Aug 1963	*Ahti Karjalainen* (for 1st time) (b. Hirvensalmi 10 Feb 1923)
17 Oct – 17 Dec 1963	*Ahti Karjalainen* (for 2nd time)
18 Dec 1963	*Reino Ragnar Lehto* (b. Turku 2 May 1898; d. Helsinki 13 Jul 1966)
12 Sep 1964	*Johannes Virolainen* (b. Viipuri 31 Jan 1914)
27 May 1966 – 1 Mar 1968	*(Kustaa) Rafael Paasio* (for 1st time) (b. Uskela 6 Jun 1903)
22 Mar 1968	*Mauno Koivisto* (b. Turku 25 Nov 1923)
15 May 1970	*Teuvo Ensio Aura* (for 1st time) (b. Ruskeala 28 Dec 1912)
15 Jul 1970 – 14 Mar 1971	*Ahti Karjalainen* (for 3rd time)
29 Oct 1971	*Teuvo Ensio Aura* (for 2nd time) Caretaker
23 Feb 1972	*(Kustaa) Rafael Paasio* (for 2nd time)
4 Sep 1972	*(Taisto) Kalevi Sorsa* (b. Keuruu 21 Dec 1930)
13 Jun 1975	*Keijo Antero Liinamaa* (b. Mänttä 6 Apr 1929) Caretaker
from 30 Nov 1975	*Martti Emil Miettunen* (b. Viipuri 31 Aug 1922)

Foreign Ministers

22 Dec 1927 – 16 Feb 1931	*Hjalmar Procopé* (Swed Pop) (for 2nd time) (b. Helsinki 8 Aug 1889; d. 8/9 Mar 1954)
21 Mar 1931 – 7 Dec 1932	*Aarno Armas Sakari, Baron Yrjö-Koskinen* (United) (b. Helsinki 9 Dec 1885; d. 1951)
15 Dec 1932 – 26 Sep 1936	*Andreas Hackzell* (Cons) (see Prime Ministers)
7 Oct 1936 – 17 Nov 1938	*Rudolf Holsti* (Progress) (for 2nd time) (b. Jyväskylä 8 Oct 1881; d. 1945)
12 Dec 1938	*(Juho) Eljas Erkko* (b. Helsinki 1 Jun 1895; d. Helsinki 20 Feb 1965)
1 Dec 1939	*Väinö Alfred Tanner* (Soc) (b. Helsinki 12 Mar 1881;

FINLAND

	d. Helsinki 19 Apr 1966)*
27 Mar 1940 – 1 Mar 1943	*R(ud)olf Witting* (Cons) (b. Viipuri 30 Sep 1879; d. 11(?) Oct 1944)
5 Mar 1943	*Henrik Ramsay* (b. Helsinki 31 Mar 1886; d. 1951)
9 Aug 1944 – 1 Mar 1950	*Carl Johan Alexis Enckell* (for 4th time) (b. St. Petersburg 7 Jun 1876; d. Helsinki 28 Mar 1959)
17 Mar 1950 – 13 Sep 1951	*Åke Henrik Gartz* (Swed Pop) (b. Helsinki 9 Jun 1888)
19 Sep 1951	*Sakari Tuomioja* (see Prime Ministers)
19 Sep 1952 – 28 Jun 1953	*Urho Kaleva Kekkonen* (for 1st time) (see Presidents)
9 Jul 1953 – May 1954	*Ralf Törngren* (Swed Pop) (for 1st time) (see Prime Ministers)
5 May – 14 Oct 1954	*Urho Kekkonen* (for 2nd time)
20 Oct 1954 – 1 Mar 1956	*Johannes Virolainen* (for 1st time) (see Prime Ministers)
3 Mar 1956 – 22 May 1957	*Ralf Törngren* (Swed Pop) (for 2nd time)
27 May – 18 Oct 1957	*Johannes Virolainen* (for 2nd time)
29 Nov 1957 – Aug 1958	*Paavo Juho Hynninen* (b. Joroinen 31 May 1883)
29 Aug – 27 Nov 1958	*Johannes Virolainen* (for 3rd time)
13 Jan 1959 – 15 May 1961	*Ralf Törngren* (Swed Pop) (for 3rd time)
19 Jun 1961 – 1 Mar 1962	*Ahti Karjalainen* (Farm) (for 1st time) (see Prime Ministers)
14 Mar 1962 – 17 Dec 1963	*Veli Merikoski* (Finn Pop) (b. Pyhtää 2 Jan 1905)
18 Dec 1963	*Jaakko Hallamaa* (b. Kuopio 28 Mar 1917)
12 Sep 1964	*Ahti Karjalainen* (Farm) (for 2nd time)
15 May 1970	*Väinö Leskinen* (b. 1917; d. Helsinki 9(?) Mar 1972)
29 Oct 1971	*Olavi Johannes Mattila* (for 1st time) (b. Hyvinkää 24 Oct 1918)
23 Feb 1972	*(Taisto) Kalevi Sorsa* (see Prime Ministers)
4 Sep 1972	*Ahti Karjalainen* (Farm) (for 3rd time)
13 Jun 1975	*Olavi Johannes Mattila* (for 2nd time)
from 30 Nov 1975	*(Taisto) Kalevi Sorsa* (for 2nd time)

*For earlier career see vol. 2

164

France

HEADS OF STATE

Presidents

13 Jun 1924	*Gaston Doumergue* (b. Aigues-Vives 1 Aug 1863; d. Aigues-Vives 18 Jun 1937)*
13 Jun 1931 – 7 May 1932	*Paul Doumer* (b. Aurillac 22 Mar 1857; d. Paris 7 May 1932)*
10 May 1932	*Albert Lebrun* (b. Mercy-le-Haut 29 Aug 1871; d. Paris 6 Mar 1950)*
11 Jul 1940 – 24 Apr 1945	*Henri Philippe Pétain* (b. Cauchy-à-la-Tour 24 Apr 1856; d. Isle d'Yeu 23 Jul 1951) Head of semi-fascist French government during German occupation
28 Aug 1944	(acting:) *Charles de Gaulle* (for 1st time) (b. Lille 22 Nov 1890; d. Colombey-les-deux-Églises 9 Nov 1970) Paris liberated by Allies 25 Aug 1944
16 Jan 1947	*Vincent Auriol* (b. Revel 27 Aug 1884; d. Paris 1 Jan 1966)
16 Jan 1954	*René Coty* (b. Le Havre 20 Mar 1882; d. 22 Nov 1962)
8 Jan 1959	*Charles de Gaulle* (for 2nd time)
28 Apr 1969	(acting:) *Alain Poher* (for 1st time) (b. Ablon-sur-Seine 17 Apr 1909)
20 Jun 1969	*Georges (Jean Raymond) Pompidou* (b. Montboudif 5 Jul 1911; d. Paris 2 Apr 1974)
3 Apr – 18 May 1974	(acting:) *Alain Poher* (for 2nd time)
from 27 May 1974	*Valéry Giscard d'Estaing* (b. Coblenz 2 Feb 1926)

MEMBERS OF GOVERNMENT

2 Nov 1929 – 17 Feb 1930: Tardieu I

Prime Minister	*André Tardieu* (for 1st time) (b. Paris 22 Sep 1876; d. Menton 15 Sep 1945)*
Foreign Affairs	*Aristide Briand* (b. Nantes 28 Mar 1862; d. Paris 7 Mar 1932)*
Home Affairs	*André Tardieu* (see above)

*For earlier career see vol. 2

Justice	*Lucien Hubert* (b. Chesne-Populeux 27 Aug 1868; d. Charleville 18 May 1938)
Finance	*Henri Chéron* (b. Lisieux 11 May 1867; d. Lisieux 14 Apr 1936)*
War	*André Maginot* (b. Paris 17 Feb 1877; d. Paris 8 Jan 1932)*
Navy	*Georges Leygues* (b. Villeneuve-sur-Lot 28 Nov 1858; d. St-Cloud 2 Nov 1933)*
Education	*Alexandre Marraud* (b. Port-Sainte-Marie 8 Jan 1861)*
Public Works	*Georges Pernot* (b. Besançon 6 Nov 1879)
Labour	*Louis Loucheur* (b. Roubaix 12 Aug 1872; d. Paris 22 Nov 1931)*
Commerce	*Pierre Étienne Flandin* (b. Paris 12 Apr 1889; d. St Jean Cap Ferrat 13 Jun 1958)*
Mercantile Marine (new post)	*Louis Rollin* (b. Uzerche 17 Mar 1879; d. 3 Nov 1952)
Aviation	*André Victor Laurent-Eynac* (b. Monestier 4 Oct 1886; d. Paris 16 Dec 1970)*
Colonies	*François Piétri* (b. La Bastia, Corsica, 8 Aug 1882; d. Ajaccio 18 Aug 1966)
Agriculture	*Jean Hennessy* (b. Richemont 26 Apr 1874)*
Pensions	*C. Gallet*
Posts	*Germain Martin* (b. Le Puy 1872; d. Paris 1948)

21 - 25 Feb 1930: Chautemps I

Prime Minister	*Camille Chautemps* (for 1st time) (b. Paris 1 Feb 1885; d. Washington 1 Jul 1963)*
Foreign Affairs	*Aristide Briand* (see Tardieu I)
Home Affairs	*Camille Chautemps* (see above)
Justice	*Théodore Steeg* (b. Libourne 19 Dec 1868; d. Paris 10 Dec 1950)*
Finance	*Charles Dumont* (b. Bramans 1867; d. Meulan 23 Apr 1939)*
War	*René Besnard* (b. Artannes 12 Apr 1879; d. 12 Mar 1952)*
Navy	*Albert Sarraut* (b. Bordeaux 28 Jul 1872)*
Education	*Jean Durand* (b. Castelnaudary 1865)*
Public Works	*Édouard Daladier* (b. Carpentras 18 Jun 1884; d. Paris 10 Oct 1970)*

*For earlier career see vol. 2

Labour	*Louis Loucheur* (see Tardieu I)
Commerce	*Georges Bonnet* (b. Bassillac 23 Jul 1889; d. 18 Jun 1973)*
Mercantile Marine	*Charles Daniélou* (b. Douarneyez 13 Jul 1887; d. Neuilly-sur-Seine 30 Dec 1953)
Treasury	*Maurice Palmade*
Aviation	*André Victor Laurent-Eynac* (see Tardieu I)
Colonies	*Lucien Lamoureux* (b. Viplaix 16 Sep 1888; d. Vichy 5 Aug 1970)*
Agriculture	*Henri Queuille* (b. Neuvic d'Ussel 31 Mar 1884; d. Paris 15 Jun 1970)*
Pensions	*C. Gallet* (see Tardieu I)
Posts and Telegraph	*Julien Durand*

2 Mar – 5 Dec 1930: Tardieu II

Prime Minister	*André Tardieu* (for 2nd time) (see Tardieu I)
Foreign Affairs	*Aristide Briand* (see Tardieu I)
Home Affairs	*André Tardieu* (see Tardieu I)
Justice	2 Mar – 18 Nov 1930: *Raoul Péret* (b. Châtellerault 29 Nov 1870; d. Paris 22(?) Jul 1942)*
	18 Nov – 5 Dec 1930: *Henri Chéron* (see Tardieu I)
Finance	*Paul Reynaud* (b. Barcelonette 15 Oct 1878; d. Neuilly-sur-Seine 21 Sep 1966)
War	*André Maginot* (see Tardieu I)
Navy	*Jacques Louis Dumesnil* (b. Larchant 4 Dec 1882; d. Paris 15 Jun 1956)*
Education	*Alexandre Marraud* (see Tardieu I)
Public Works	*Georges Pernot* (see Tardieu I)
Labour	*Pierre Laval* (b. Châteldun 28 Jun 1883; d. Paris 15 Oct 1945)*
Health	*Désiré Ferry* (b. Metz 26 Oct 1886)*
Commerce	*Pierre Étienne Flandin* (see Tardieu I)
Mercantile Marine	*Louis Rollin* (see Tardieu I)
Budget	*Germain Martin* (see Tardieu I)
Aviation	*André Victor Laurent-Eynac* (see Tardieu I)
Colonies	*François Piétri* (see Tardieu I)
Agriculture	*Ferdinand David* (b. Annemasse 15 Oct 1869; d. Paris 17 Jan 1935)*
Pensions	*Alexandre Champetier de Ribes* (b. Anthony 30 Jul 1882; d. Paris 6 Mar 1947)

*For earlier career see vol. 2

Posts and Telegraph   *André Mallarmé*

13 Dec 1930 – 24 Jan 1931: Steeg

Prime Minister	*Théodore Steeg* (see Chautemps I)
Foreign Affairs	*Aristide Briand* (see Tardieu I)
Home Affairs	*Georges Leygues* (see Tardieu I)
Justice	*Henri Chéron* (see Tardieu I)
Finance	*Germain Martin* (see Tardieu I)
Budget	*Maurice Palmade* (see Chautemps I)
War	*Louis Barthou* (b. Oloron-Ste-Marie 25 Aug 1862; d. Marseille 9 Oct 1934)*
Navy	*Albert Sarraut* (see Chautemps I)
Aviation	*Paul Painlevé* (b. Paris 5 Dec 1863; d. 29 Oct 1933)*
Education	*Camille Chautemps* (see Chautemps I)
Public Works	*Édouard Daladier* (see Chautemps I)
Labour	*Édouard Grinda* (b. 25 Dec 1866)
Health	*Henri Queuille* (see Chautemps I)
Commerce	*Louis Loucheur* (see Tardieu I)
Mercantile Marine	*Charles Daniélou* (see Chautemps I)
Colonies	*Théodore Steeg* (see Chautemps I)
Agriculture	*Victor Boret* (b. Saumur 18 Aug 1872; d. Saumur 23 Mar 1952)*
Pensions	*Robert Thoumyre* (b. Dieppe 16 Feb 1883)
Posts and Telegraph	*Georges Bonnet* (see Chautemps I)

27 Jan 1931 – 12 Jan 1932: Laval I

Prime Minister	*Pierre Laval* (for 1st time) (see Tardieu II)
Foreign Affairs	*Aristide Briand* (see Tardieu I)
Home Affairs	*Pierre Laval* (see Tardieu II)
Justice	*Léon Bérard* (b. Sauveterre-de-Béarn 6 Jan 1876; d. Paris night of 24/25 Feb 1960)*
Finance	*Pierre Étienne Flandin* (see Tardieu I)
Budget	*François Piétri* (see Tardieu I)
War	27 Jan 1931–8 Jan 1932: *André Maginot* (see Tardieu I) 8 – 12 Jan 1932: no appointment made
Navy	*Charles Dumont* (see Chautemps I)
Aviation	*Jacques Louis Dumesnil* (see Tardieu II)
Education	*Marius Roustan* (b. Sète 20 Feb 1860; d. Montpellier 3 Feb 1942)

*For earlier career see vol. 2

Public Works	*M. Deligne*
Labour	*Adolphe Landry* (b. Ajaccio 29 Nov 1874; d. Paris 1956)*
Health	*Camille Blaisot* (b. Valognes 19 Jan 18881; d. Dachau Concentration Camp late Feb 1945)
Commerce	*Louis Rollin* (see Tardieu I)
Mercantile Marine	*Louis, Vicomte de Chappedelaine* (b. Saint-Just 21 Jun 1876; d. Ville d'Avray 9 Dec 1939)
Colonies	*Paul Reynaud* (see Tardieu II)
Agriculture	*André Tardieu* (see Tardieu I)
Pensions	*Alexandre Champetier de Ribes* (see Tardieu II)
Posts and Telegraph	*Charles Guernier* (b. Saint-Malo 26 Apr 1870)

13 Jan – 16 Feb 1932: Laval II

Prime Minister and Foreign Affairs	*Pierre Laval* (for 2nd time) (see Tardieu II)
Home Affairs	*Pierre Cathala* (b. Montfort-sur-Mell 22 Sep 1888; d. Paris 27 Jul 1947)
Justice	*Léon Bérard* (see Laval I)
Finance	*Pierre Étienne Flandin* (see Tardieu I)
Budget	*François Piétri* (see Tardieu I)
War	*André Tardieu* (see Tardieu I)
Navy	*Achille Fould* (b. Condé-sur-Sarthe 19 Sep 1890)
Aviation	*Jacques Louis Dumesnil* (see Tardieu II)
Education	*Marius Roustan* (see Laval I)
Public Works	*M. Deligne* (see Laval I)
Labour	*Adolphe Landry* (see Laval I)
Health	*Camille Blaisot* (see Laval I)
Commerce	*Louis Rollin* (see Tardieu I)
Mercantile Marine	*Louis, Vicomte de Chappedelaine* (see Laval I)
Colonies	*Paul Reynaud* (see Tardieu II)
Agriculture	*André Tardieu* (see Tardieu I)
Pensions	*Alexandre Champetier de Ribes* (see Tardieu II)
Posts and Telegraph	*Charles Guernier* (see Laval I)

20 Feb – 10 May 1932: Tardieu III

Prime Minister and Foreign Affairs	*André Tardieu* (for 3rd time) (see Tardieu I)
Home Affairs	*Albert Mathieu*

*For earlier career see vol. 2

Justice	*Paul Reynaud* (see Tardieu II)
Finance (incorporating Budget)	*Pierre Étienne Flandin* (see Tardieu I)
National Defence (incorporating War, Navy and Aviation)	*François Piétri* (see Tardieu I)
Education	*Marius Roustan* (see Laval I)
Public Works	*Charles Guernier* (see Laval I)
Transport	*Charles Guernier* (see Laval I)
Labour	*Pierre Laval* (see Tardieu II)
Health	*Camille Blaisot* (see Laval I)
Commerce	*Louis Rollin* (see Tardieu I)
Mercantile Marine	*Charles Guernier* (see Laval I)
Colonies	*Louis, Vicomte de Chappedelaine* (see Laval I)
Agriculture	*Claude Chauveau* (b. Pouilly-en-Auxois 22 Aug 1861; d. 27 Feb 1940)
Pensions and Liberated Territories	*Alexandre Champetier de Ribes* (see Tardieu II)
Posts and Telegraph	*Louis Rollin* (see Tardieu I)

4 Jun – 14 Dec 1932: Herriot III

Prime Minister and Foreign Affairs	*Édouard Herriot* (for 3rd time) (b. Troyes 5 Jul 1872; d. Ste Eugénie, Lyon, 26 Mar 1957)*
Home Affairs	*Camille Chautemps* (see Chautemps I)
Justice	*René Renoult* (b. Paris 29 Aug 1867)*
Finance	*Germain Martin* (see Tardieu I)
Budget	*Maurice Palmade* (see Chautemps I)
War	*Joseph Paul-Boncour* (b. St Aignan 4 Aug 1873; d. 28 Mar 1972)*
Navy	*Georges Leygues* (see Tardieu I)
Aviation	*Paul Painlevé* (see Steeg)
Education	*Anatole de Monzie* (b. Bazas 22 Nov 1876; d. Paris 11 Jan 1947)*
Public Works	*Édouard Daladier* (see Chautemps I)
Labour	*Albert Dalimier* (b. Bordeaux 20 Feb 1875; d. Neuilly-sur-Seine 6 May 1936)
Health	*Justin Godart* (b. Lyon 1871; d. Paris 13 Dec 1956)
Commerce	*Julien Durand* (see Chautemps I)

*For earlier career see vol. 2

Mercantile Marine	*Léon Meyer* (b. Le Havre 11 Sep 1868; d. Paris 22 Jan 1948)
Colonies	*Albert Sarraut* (see Chautemps I)
Agriculture	*Abel Gardey*
Pensions	*Aimé Berthod* (b. Champagnole 9 Aug 1878; d. Normandy 16 Jun 1944)
Posts and Telegraph	*Henri Queuille* (see Chautemps I)

14 Dec 1932 – 29 Jan 1933: Paul-Boncour

Prime Minister and Foreign Affairs	*Joseph Paul-Boncour* (see Herriot III)
Home Affairs	*Camille Chautemps* (see Chautemps I)
Justice	*Abel Gardey* (see Herriot III)
Finance	*Henri Chéron* (see Tardieu I)
Budget	14 Dec 1932: abolished
War	*Édouard Daladier* (see Chautemps I)
Navy	*Georges Leygues* (see Tardieu I)
Aviation	*Paul Painlevé* (see Steeg)
Education	*Anatole de Monzie* (see Herriot III)
Public Works	*Georges Bonnet* (see Chautemps I)
Labour	*Albert Dalimier* (see Herriot III)
Health	*Charles Daniélou* (see Chautemps I)
Commerce	*Julien Durand* (see Chautemps I)
Mercantile Marine	*Léon Meyer* (see Herriot III)
Colonies	*Albert Sarraut* (see Chautemps I)
Agriculture	*Henri Queuille* (see Chautemps I)
Pensions	*Édouard Miellet* (b. Montbouton 1 Nov 1880)
Post Office	*André Victor Laurent-Eynac* (see Tardieu I)

31 Jan – 23 Oct 1933: Daladier I

Prime Minister	*Édouard Daladier* (for 1st time) (see Chautemps I)
Foreign Affairs	*Joseph Paul-Boncour* (see Herriot III)
Home Affairs	*Camille Chautemps* (see Chautemps I)
Justice	*Eugène Penancier*
Finance	*Georges Bonnet* (see Chautemps I)
Budget (re-instated)	*Lucien Lamoureux* (see Chautemps I)
War	*Édouard Daladier* (see Chautemps I)
Navy	31 Jan – 2 Sep 1933: *Georges Leygues* (see Tardieu I)
	8 Sep – 23 Oct 1933: *Albert Sarraut* (see Chautemps I)
Aviation	*Pierre Cot* (b. Grenoble 20 Nov 1895)
Education	*Anatole de Monzie* (see Herriot III)

Public Works	*Joseph Paganon* (b. Vourey 19 Mar 1880; d. Paris night of 1/2 Nov 1937)
Labour	—— *François-Albert* (b. 1877(?); d. Paris 22 Nov 1933)*
Health	*Charles Daniélou* (see Chautemps I)
Commerce	*Louis Serre* (b. Lagnes 17 Aug 1873)
Mercantile Marine	*Eugène Frot* (b. Montargis 2 Oct 1893)
Colonies	31 Jan – 8 Sep 1933: *Albert Sarraut* (see Chautemps I)
	8 Sep – 23 Oct 1933: *Albert Dalimier* (see Herriot III)
Pensions	*Édouard Miellet* (see Paul-Boncour)
Agriculture	*Henri Queuille* (see Chautemps I)
Posts and Telegraph	*André Victor Laurent-Eynac* (see Tardieu I)

26 Oct – 24 Nov 1933: Sarraut I

Prime Minister	*Albert Sarraut* (for 1st time) (see Chautemps I)
Foreign Affairs	*Joseph Paul-Boncour* (see Herriot III)
Home Affairs	*Camille Chautemps* (see Chautemps I)
Justice	*Albert Dalimier* (see Herriot III)
Finance	*Georges Bonnet* (see Chautemps I)
Budget	*Abel Gardey* (see Herriot III)
War	*Édouard Daladier* (see Chautemps I)
Navy	*Albert Sarraut* (see Chautemps I)
Aviation	*Pierre Cot* (see Daladier I)
Education	*Anatole de Monzie* (see Herriot III)
Public Works	*Joseph Paganon* (see Daladier I)
Labour	*Eugène Frot* (see Daladier I)
Health	*(Joseph) Émile Lisbon* (b. Nyons 20 Jun 1876; d. Paris 21 Dec 1947)
Commerce	*André Victor Laurent-Eynac* (see Tardieu I)
Mercantile Marine	*Jacques Stern* (b. 1882; d. New York 21 Dec 1949)
Colonies	*François Piétri* (see Tardieu I)
Agriculture	*Henri Queuille* (see Chautemps I)
Pensions	*Hippolyte Ducos* (b. Saint-André 3 Oct 1881; d. 14 Nov 1970)
Posts and Telegraph	*Jean Mistler* (b. Sorèze 1 Sep 1897)

27 Nov 1933 – 27 Jan 1934: Chautemps II

Prime Minister	*Camille Chautemps* (for 2nd time) (see Chautemps I)
Foreign Affairs	*Joseph Paul-Boncour* (see Herriot III)

*For earlier career see vol. 2

Home Affairs	*Camille Chautemps* (see Chautemps I)
Justice	*E. Raynaldy* (b. Rodez 23 Dec 1869)*
Finance	*Georges Bonnet* (see Chautemps I)
Budget	*Paul Marchandeau* (b. Gaillax 10 Aug 1882; d. Paris 30 May 1968)
War	*Édouard Daladier* (see Chautemps I)
Navy	*Albert Sarraut* (see Chautemps I)
Aviation	*Pierre Cot* (see Daladier I)
Education	*Anatole de Monzie* (see Herriot III)
Public Works	*Joseph Paganon* (see Daladier I)
Labour	27 Nov 1933 – 9 Jan 1934: *Lucien Lamoureux* (see Chautemps I)
	9 – 27 Jan 1934: *Eugène Frot* (see Daladier I)
War	*Alexandre Israel* (b. Algiers 25 Nov 1868; d. Paris 23 Aug 1937)
Commerce	*André Victor Laurent-Eynac* (see Tardieu I)
Mercantile Marine	27 Nov 1933 – 9 Jan 1934: *Eugène Frot* (see Daladier I)
	9 – 27 Jan 1934: *William Bertrand* (b. Morennes 9 Nov 1881)
Colonies	27 Nov 1933 – 9 Jan 1934: *Albert Dalimier* (see Herriot III)
	9 – 27 Jan 1934: *Lucien Lamoureux* (see Chautemps I)
Agriculture	*Henri Queuille* (see Chautemps I)
Pensions	*Hippolyte Ducos* (see Sarraut I)
Posts and Telegraph	*Jean Mistler* (see Sarraut I)

30 Jan – 7 Feb 1934: Daladier II

Prime Minister and Foreign Affairs	*Édouard Daladier* (for 2nd time) (see Chautemps I)
Home Affairs	*Eugène Frot* (see Daladier I)
Justice	*Eugène Penancier* (see Daladier I)
Finance	30 Jan – 3 Feb 1934: *François Piétri* (see Tardieu I)
	4 – 7 Feb 1934: *Paul Marchandeau* (see Chautemps II)
War	30 Jan – 3 Feb 1934: *Jean Fabry* (b. Villefranche-de-Rouergue 6 Jun 1876; d. 1 Jun 1968)*
	4 – 7 Feb 1934: *Joseph Paul-Boncour* (see Herriot III)
Navy	*Louis, Vicomte de Chappedelaine* (see Laval I)
Aviation	*Pierre Cot* (see Daladier I)
Education	*Aimé Berthod* (see Herriot III)
Public Works	*Joseph Paganon* (see Daladier I)

*For earlier career see vol. 2

173

Labour	*Édouard Valadier* (b. Alès 7 Sep 1878)
Health	*(Joseph) Émile Lisbon* (see Sarraut I)
Commerce	*Jean Mistler* (see Sarraut I)
Mercantile Marine	*Guy La Chambre* (b. Paris 5 Jun 1898)
Colonies	*Henry de Jouvenel* (b. Paris 15 Apr 1876; d. Paris 4 Oct 1935)*
Agriculture	*Henri Queuille* (see Chautemps I)
Pensions	*Hippolyte Ducos* (see Sarraut I)
Posts and Telegraph	*Paul Marie Bernier* (b. Ligueil 10 Jul 1866; d. Mouzay 20 Aug 1957)

9 Feb – 8 Nov 1934: Doumergue II

Prime Minister	*Gaston Doumergue* (for 2nd time) (see Presidents)
Foreign Affairs	9 Feb – 9 Oct 1934: *Louis Barthou* (see Steeg)
	10 – 13 Oct 1934 (acting:) *Gaston Doumergue* (see Presidents)
	13 Oct – 8 Nov 1934: *Pierre Laval* (see Tardieu II)
Home Affairs	9 Feb – 11 Oct 1934: *Albert Sarraut* (see Chautemps I)
	13 Oct – 8 Nov 1934: *Paul Marchandeau* (see Chautemps II)
Justice	9 Feb – 13 Oct 1934: *Henri Chéron* (see Tardieu I)
	15 Oct – 8 Nov 1934: *Henri Lémery* (b. Saint-Pierre, Martinique, 9 Dec 1874; d. 27 Apr 1972)
Finance	*Germain Martin* (see Tardieu I)
Budget	*Paul Maurice Jacquier* (b. Bordeaux 26 Mar 1879; d. Paris 3 Mar 1961)
War	*Henri Philippe Pétain* (see Presidents)
Navy	*François Piétri* (see Tardieu I)
Aviation	*Victor Léon Ernest Denain* (b. Dax 6 Nov 1880; d. Nice 31 Dec 1952)
Education	*Aimé Berthod* (see Herriot III)
Public Works	*Pierre Étienne Flandin* (see Tardieu I)
Labour	*Adrien Marquet* (b. 1885(?); d. Bordeaux 3 Apr 1955)
Health	*Louis Marin* (b. Faulx 7 Feb 1871; d. Paris 23 May 1960)*
Commerce	*Lucien Lamoureux* (see Chautemps I)
Mercantile Marine	*William Bertrand* (see Chautemps II)
Colonies	9 Feb – 13 Oct 1934: *Pierre Laval* (see Tardieu II)
	13 Oct – 8 Nov 1934: *Louis Rollin* (see Tardieu I)
Agriculture	*Henri Queuille* (see Chautemps I)

*For earlier career see vol. 2

174

| Pensions | *Georges Rivollet* (b. Paris 3 Nov 1888) |

9 Nov 1934 - 30 May 1935: Flandin

Prime Minister	*Pierre Étienne Flandin* (see Tardieu I)
Foreign Affairs	*Pierre Laval* (see Tardieu II)
Home Affairs	*Marcel Régnier* (b. Billy 16 Feb 1867; d. 28 Jul 1958)
Justice	*Georges Pernot* (see Tardieu I)
Finance	*Germain Martin* (see Tardieu I)
War	*Louis Félix Thomas Maurin* (b. Cherbourg 5 Jan 1869; d. Paris 6 Jun 1956)
Navy	*François Piétri* (see Tardieu I)
Aviation	*Victor Léon Ernest Denain* (see Doumergue II)
Education	*André Mallarmé* (see Tardieu II)
Public Works	*Henry Roy* (b. Bouchard 17 Feb 1873)
Labour	*Paul Maurice Jacquier* (see Doumergue II)
Health	*Henri Queuille* (see Chautemps I)
Commerce	*Paul Marchandeau* (see Chautemps II)
Mercantile Marine	*William Bertrand* (see Chautemps II)
Colonies	*Louis Rollin* (see Tardieu I)
Agriculture	*Émile Cassez* (b. Bournonville 23 Jul 1871; d. Sep 1948)
Pensions	*Georges Rivollet* (see Doumergue II)
Posts and Telegraph	*Georges Mandel* (b. Châtou 5 Jun 1885; d. 15 Jul 1944)
Without Portfolio	*Édouard Herriot* (see Herriot III)
	Louis Marin (see Doumergue II)

1 - 4 Jun 1935: Bouisson

Prime Minister	*Fernand Bouisson* (b. Constantine 16 Jun 1874; d. Antibes 28 Dec 1959)
Foreign Affairs	*Pierre Laval* (see Tardieu II)
Home Affairs	*Fernand Bouisson* (see above)
Justice	*Georges Pernot* (see Tardieu I)
Finance	*Joseph Caillaux* (b. Le Mans 30 Mar 1863; d. Mamers night of 21/22 Nov 1944)*
War	*Louis Félix Thomas Maurin* (see Flandin)
Navy	*François Piétri* (see Tardieu I)
Aviation	*Victor Léon Ernest Denain* (see Doumergue II)
Education	*Marius Roustan* (see Laval I)

*For earlier career see vol. 2

175

Public Works	*Joseph Paganon* (see Daladier I)
Labour	*Ludovic Oscar Frossard* (b. Foussemagne 5 Mar 1889; d. Paris 1946)
Health	*Louis Ernest Lafont* (b. Lyons 26 Jul 1879; d. 7 May 1946)
Commerce	*André Victor Laurent-Eynac* (see Tardieu I)
Mercantile Marine	*William Bertrand* (see Chautemps II)
Colonies	*Louis Rollin* (see Tardieu I)
Agriculture	*Paul Maurice Jacquier* (see Doumergue II)
Pensions	*Camille Perfetti* (b. Ciudad Bolivar, Venezuela, 21 Oct 1875)
Posts and Telegraph	*Georges Mandel* (see Flandin)
Without Portfolio	*Henri Philippe Pétain* (see Presidents)
	Édouard Herriot (see Herriot III)
	Louis Marin (see Doumergue II)

7 Jun 1935 – 22 Jan 1936: Laval III

Prime Minister and Foreign Affairs	*Pierre Laval* (for 3rd time) (see Tardieu II)
Home Affairs	*Joseph Paganon* (see Daladier I)
Justice	*Léon Bérard* (see Laval I)
Finance	*Marcel Régnier* (see Flandin)
War	*Jean Fabry* (see Daladier II)
Navy	*François Piétri* (see Tardieu I)
Aviation	*Victor Léon Ernest Denain* (see Doumergue II)
Education	7 – 13 Jun 1935: *Philippe Marcombes* (b. Murat 5 Dec 1877; d. Paris 13 Jun 1935)
	17 Jun 1935 – 22 Jan 1936: *Marius Roustan* (see Laval I)
Public Works	*André Victor Laurent-Eynac* (see Tardieu I)
Labour	*Ludovic Oscar Frossard* (see Bouisson)
Health	*Louis Ernest Lafont* (see Bouisson)
Commerce	*Georges Bonnet* (see Chautemps I)
Mercantile Marine	7 – 17 Jun 1935: *Marius Roustan* (see Laval I)
	17 Jun 1935 – 22 Jan 1936: *William Bertrand* (see Chautemps II)
Colonies	*Louis Rollin* (see Tardieu I)
Agriculture	*Pierre Cathala* (see Laval II)
Pensions	*Henri Maupoil* (b. Dezize-les-Maranges 11 Jul 1891; d. 31 Nov 1971)
Posts and Telegraph	*Georges Mandel* (see Flandin)
Without Portfolio	*Pierre Étienne Flandin* (see Tardieu I)

Édouard Herriot (see Herriot III)
Louis Marin (see Doumergue II)

24 Jan – 4 Jun 1936: Sarraut II

Prime Minister	*Albert Sarraut* (for 2nd time) (see Chautemps I)
Foreign Affairs	*Pierre Étienne Flandin* (see Tardieu I)
Home Affairs	*Albert Sarraut* (see Chautemps I)
Justice	*Yvon Delbos* (b. Thonac 7 May 1885; d. Paris 15 Nov 1956)*
Finance	*Marcel Régnier* (see Flandin)
War	*Louis Félix Thomas Maurin* (see Flandin)
Navy	*François Piétri* (see Tardieu I)
Aviation	*Marcel Déat* (b. Guérigny 7 Mar 1894; d. Turin 5 Jan 1955)
Education	*Henri Guernut* (b. Lavaqueresse 2 Nov 1876)
Public Works	*Camille Chautemps* (see Chautemps I)
Labour	*Ludovic Oscar Frossard* (see Bouisson)
Health	*Louis Nicolle* (b. Lille 16 Jun 1871)
Commerce	*Georges Bonnet* (see Chautemps I)
Mercantile Marine	*Louis, Vicomte de Chappedelaine* (see Laval I)
Colonies	*Jacques Stern* (see Sarraut I)
Agriculture	*Paul Thellier* (b. Tangry 20 Dec 1899)
Pensions	*René (Amadée Marcel Joseph) Besse* (b. Toulon 20 Feb 1891; d. Paris 13 Feb 1947)
Posts and Telegraph	*Georges Mandel* (see Flandin)
Without Portfolio	*Joseph Paul-Boncour* (see Herriot III)

4 Jun 1936 – 21 Jun 1937: Blum I (Popular Front)

Prime Minister	*Léon Blum* (for 1st time) (b. Paris 9 Apr 1872; d. 30 Mar 1950)
Foreign Affairs	*Yvon Delbos* (see Sarraut II)
Home Affairs	4 Jun – 17 Nov 1936: *Roger Salengro* (b. Lille 30 May 1890; d. 17 Nov 1936)
	24 Nov 1936 – 21 Jun 1937: *Marx Dormoy* (b. Montluçon 1889; d. Nice 1941)
Justice	*Marc Émile Rucart* (b. Coulommiers 24 Jul 1893)
Finance	*Vincent Auriol* (see Presidents)
National Defence	*Édouard Daladier* (see Chautemps I)
Navy	*A. Gasnier-Duparc*

*For earlier career see vol. 2

Aviation	*Pierre Cot* (see Daladier I)
National Education	*Jean Zay* (b. Orléans 6 Aug 1904; d. Algiers 21 Jun 1944)
Public Works	*Albert Bedouce* (b. Toulouse 8 Jan 1869; d. Paris 2 Aug 1947)
Labour	*Jean Baptiste Lebas* (b. Roubaix 24 Oct 1878; d. Sonneberg, Thuringia, 1944)
Health	*Henri Sellier* (b. Bourges 22 Dec 1883; d. Suresnes 24 Nov 1943)
National Economy (formerly Commerce)	*Charles Spinasse* (b. Egletons 22 Oct 1893)
Mercantile Marine	*Paul Bastid* (b. Paris 17 May 1892; d. 30 Oct 1974)
Colonies	*Marius Moutet* (b. Nîmes 19 Apr 1876; d. Paris 29 Oct 1968)
Agriculture	*Georges Monnet* (b. Aurillac 12 Aug 1898)
Pensions	*Albert Rivière*
Posts and Telegraph	*Robert (Louis Antoine) Jardillier* (b. Caen 31 Mar 1890; d. Marseille 19 May 1945)
Without Portfolio	*Paul Faure* (b. Périgueux 1878; d. Paris 18 Nov 1960)
	Camille Chautemps (see Chautemps I)
	Maurice Viollette (b. Janville 3 Nov 1870; d. Paris 9 Sep 1960)*

22 Jun 1937 – 14 Jan 1938: Chautemps III

Prime Minister	*Camille Chautemps* (for 3rd time) (see Chautemps I)
Deputy Prime Minister	*Léon Blum* (see Blum I)
Foreign Affairs	*Yvon Delbos* (see Sarraut II)
Home Affairs	*Marx Dormoy* (see Blum I)
Justice	*Vincent Auriol* (see Presidents)
Finance	*Georges Bonnet* (see Chautemps I)
National Defence	*Édouard Daladier* (see Chautemps I)
Navy	*César Campinchi* (b. Calcatoggio, Corsica, 4 May 1882; d. Marseille 23 Feb 1941)
Aviation	*Pierre Cot* (see Daladier I)
National Education	*Jean Zay* (see Blum I)
Public Works	*Henri Queuille* (see Chautemps I)
Labour	*André Louis Février* (b. Le Vigan 30 Nov 1885)
Health	*Marc Émile Rucart* (see Blum I)

*For earlier career see vol. 2

Commerce	*Fernand Chapsal* (b. Limoges 10 Mar 1862; d. Paris 10 Feb 1939)*
Mercantile Marine	*César Campinchi* (see above)
Colonies	*Marius Moutet* (see Blum I)
Agriculture	*Georges Monnet* (see Blum I)
Pensions	*Albert Rivière* (see Blum I)
Posts and Telegraph	*Jean Baptiste Lebas* (see Blum I)
Without Portfolio	*Albert Sarraut* (see Chautemps I)
	Paul Faure (see Blum I)
	Maurice Viollette (see Blum I)

18 Jan – 10 Mar 1938: Chautemps IV

Prime Minister	*Camille Chautemps* (for 4th time) (see Chautemps I)
Deputy Prime Minister	*Édouard Daladier* (see Chautemps I)
Foreign Affairs	*Yvon Delbos* (see Sarraut II)
Home Affairs	*Albert Sarraut* (see Chautemps I)
Justice	*César Campinchi* (see Chautemps III)
Finance	*Paul Marchandeau* (see Chautemps II)
National Defence	*Édouard Daladier* (se Chautemps I)
Navy	*William Bertrand* (see Chautemps II)
Aviation	*Guy La Chambre* (see Daladier II)
National Education	*Jean Zay* (see Blum I)
Public Works	*Henri Queuille* (see Chautemps I)
Labour	*Paul Ramadier* (b. La Rochelle 17 Mar 1888; d. Rodez 14 Oct 1961)
Health	*Marc Émile Rucart* (see Blum I)
Commerce	*Pierre Cot* (see Daladier I)
Mercantile Marine	*Paul Elbel* (b. 6 Mar 1875)
Colonies	*Théodore Steeg* (see Chautemps I)
Agriculture	*Fernand Chapsal* (see Chautemps III)
Pensions	*Robert Lasalle* (b. 1882)
Posts and Telegraph	*Fernand Gentin* (b. 1876/77)
Minister of State (Economic and Financial Co-ordination)	*Georges Bonnet* (see Chautemps I)
Minister of State (Prime Minister's Office)	*Ludovic Oscar Frossard* (see Bouisson)

*For earlier career see vol. 2

FRANCE

13 Mar – 8 Apr 1938: Blum II

Prime Minister	*Léon Blum* (for 2nd time) (see Blum I)
Prime Minister's Office	*Vincent Auriol* (see Presidents)
Foreign Affairs	*Joseph Paul-Boncour* (see Herriot III)
Home Affairs	*Marx Dormoy* (see Blum I)
Justice	*Marc Émile Rucart* (see Blum I)
Finance	*Léon Blum* (see Blum I)
Budget	*Charles Spinasse* (see Blum I)
National Defence	*Édouard Daladier* (see Chautemps I)
Navy	*César Campinchi* (see Chautemps III)
Aviation	*Guy La Chambre* (see Daladier II)
National Education	*Jean Zay* (see Blum I)
Public Works	*Jules Moch* (b. Paris 15 Mar 1893)
Labour	*Albert Sérol* (b. Roanne 21 Jul 1877)
Health	*Fernand Gentin* (see Chautemps IV)
Commerce	*Pierre Cot* (see Daladier I)
Colonies	*Marius Moutet* (see Blum I)
Agriculture	*Georges Monnet* (see Blum I)
Pensions	*Albert Rivière* (see Blum I)
Posts and Telegraph	*Jean Baptiste Lebas* (see Blum I)
Propaganda	*Ludovic Oscar Frossard* (see Bouisson)
Minister of State for North Africa	*Albert Sarraut* (see Chautemps I)
Ministers of State	*Paul Faure* (see Blum I)
	Maurice Viollette (see Blum I)
	Théodore Steeg (see Chautemps I)

10 Apr 1938 – 20 Mar 1940: Daladier III

Prime Minister	*Édouard Daladier* (for 3rd time) (see Chautemps I)
Prime Minister's Office	*Camille Chautemps* (see Chautemps I)
Minister of State	13 Sep 1939 – 20 Mar 1940: *Albert Sarraut* (see Chautemps I)
Foreign Affairs	10 Apr 1938 – 13 Sep 1939: *Georges Bonnet* (see Chautemps I)
	13 Sep 1939 – 20 Mar 1940: *Édouard Daladier* (see Chautemps I)
Home Affairs	*Albert Sarraut* (see Chautemps I)

Justice	10 Apr – 2 Nov 1938: *Paul Reynaud* (see Tardieu II) 2 Nov 1938 – 13 Sep 1939: *Paul Marchandeau* (see Chautemps II) 13 Sep 1939 – 20 Mar 1940: *Georges Bonnet* (see Chautemps I)
Finance	10 Apr – 2 Nov 1938: *Paul Marchandeau* (see Chautemps II) 2 Nov 1938 – 20 Mar 1940: *Paul Reynaud* (see Tardieu II)
Economic Affairs	10 Apr 1938 – 13 Sep 1939: *Raymond Patenôtre* (b. Washington 1900; d. Paris 19 Jun 1951) 13 Sep 1939: abolished
Defence	*Édouard Daladier* (see Chautemps I)
Navy	*César Campinchi* (see Chautemps III)
Aviation	*Guy La Chambre* (see Daladier II)
Blockade (new post)	13 Sep 1939 – 20 Mar 1940: *Georges Pernot* (see Tardieu I)
Armaments (new post)	13 Sep 1939 – 20 Mar 1940: *Raoul Dautry* (b. Montluçon 13 Sep 1880; d. Lourmarin 21 Aug 1951)
National Education	13 Sep 1939 – 20 Mar 1940: *Jean Zay* (see Blum I)
Public Works	10 Apr – 22 Aug 1938: *Ludovic Oscar Frossard* (see Bouisson) 22 Aug 1938 – 20 Mar 1940: *Anatole de Monzie* (see Herriot III)
Labour	10 Apr – 22 Aug 1938: *Paul Ramadier* (see Chautemps IV) 22 Aug 1938 – 20 Mar 1940: *Charles Pomaret* (b. Montpellier 16 Aug 1897)
Health	*Marc Émile Rucart* (see Blum I)
Commerce	*Fernand Gentin* (see Chautemps IV)
Mercantile Marine	10 Apr 1938 – 13 Sep 1939: *Louis, Vicomte de Chappedelaine* (see Laval I) 13 Sep 1939 – 20 Mar 1940: *Alphonse Rio* (b. Carnac 28 Oct 1873)
Colonies	*Georges Mandel* (see Flandin)
Agriculture	*Henri Queuille* (see Chautemps I)
Military Welfare and Pensions	10 Apr 1938 – 13 Sep 1939: *Alexandre Champetier de Ribes* (see Tardieu II) 13 Sep 1939 – 20 Mar 1940: *René (Amadée Marcel Joseph) Besse* (see Sarraut II)
Posts and Telegraph	*Jules Julien* (b. Avignon 29 Sep 1881; d. 16 Apr 1968)

181

FRANCE

21 Mar – 17 Jun 1940: Reynaud

Prime Minister	*Paul Reynaud* (see Tardieu II)
Deputy Prime Minister	21 Mar – 19 May 1940: *Camille Chautemps* (see Chautemps I)
	19 May – 17 Jun 1940: *Henri Philippe Pétain* (see Presidents)
Foreign Affairs	*Paul Reynaud* (see Tardieu II)
Home Affairs	21 Mar – 19 May 1940: *Henry Roy* (see Flandin)
	19 May – 17 Jun 1940: *Georges Mandel* (see Flandin)
Information	21 Mar – 5 Jun 1940: *Ludovic Oscar Frossard* (see Bouisson)
	5 – 17 Jun 1940: *Jean Prouvost* (b. Roubaix 24 Apr 1885)
Justice	*Albert Sérol* (see Blum II)
Finance	21 Mar – 5 Jun 1940: *Lucien Lamoureux* (see Chautemps I)
	5 – 17 Jun 1940: *Yves Bouthillier* (b. 1901?)
French Family (new post)	5 – 17 Jun 1940: *Georges Pernot* (see Tardieu I)
Social Affairs	21 Mar – 5 Jun 1940: *Marcel Héraud* (b. Cerilly 8 May 1883)
	5 Jun 1940: amalgamated with Ministry for French Family (see above)
Defence	21 Mar – 19 May 1940: *Édouard Daladier* (see Chautemps I)
	19 May – 17 Jun 1940: *Paul Reynaud* (see Tardieu II)
Navy	*César Campinchi* (see Chautemps III)
Aviation	*André Victor Laurent-Eynac* (see Tardieu I)
Armaments	*Raoul Dautry* (see Daladier III)
Blockade	*Georges Monnet* (see Blum I)
National Education	21 Mar – 5 Jun 1940: *Albert Sarraut* (see Chautemps I)
	5 – 17 Jun 1940: *Yvon Delbos* (see Sarraut II)
Public Works	21 Mar – 5 Jun 1940: *Anatole de Monzie* (see Herriot III)
	5 – 17 Jun 1940: *Ludovic Oscar Frossard* (see Bouisson)
Labour	*Charles Pomaret* (see Daladier III)
Health	21 Mar – 5 Jun 1940: *Georges Pernot* (see Tardieu I)
	5 Jun 1940: amalgamated with Ministry for French Family (see above)
Commerce	21 Mar – 19 May 1940: *Louis Rollin* (see Tardieu I)
	19 May – 5 Jun 1940: *Léon Barety* (b. Nice 18 Oct

1883; d. Paris 10 Feb 1971)
5 - 17 Jun 1940: *Albert Chichery* (b. Blanc 12 Oct 1888; d. Blanc 15 Aug 1944)

Mercantile Marine	*Alphonse Rio* (see Daladier III)
Colonies	21 Mar - 19 May 1940: *Georges Mandel* (see Flandin)
	19 May - 17 Jun 1940: *Louis Rollin* (see Tardieu I)
Agriculture	*Paul Thellier* (see Sarraut II)
Pensions	*Albert Rivière* (see Blum I)
Without Portfolio	10 May - 17 Jun 1940: *Louis Marin* (see Doumergue II)
	10 May - 17 Jun 1940: *Jean Ybarnegaray* (b. Uhart-Cize 16 Oct 1883; d. Paris 25 Apr 1956)

17 Jun - 12 Jul 1940: Pétain I

Prime Minister	*Henri Philippe Pétain* (for 1st time) (see Presidents)
Minister of State and Deputy Prime Minister	17 - 22 Jun 1940: *Camille Chautemps* (see Chautemps I)
	22 Jun - 12 Jul 1940: *Pierre Laval* (see Tardieu II)
Foreign Affairs	*Paul Baudouin* (b. Paris 19 Dec 1894; d. 11 Feb 1964)
Home Affairs	17 - 29 Jun 1940: *Charles Pomaret* (see Daladier III)
	29 Jun - 12 Jul 1940: *Adrien Marquet* (see Doumergue II)
Information	*Jean Prouvost* (see Reynaud)
Justice	*C. Frémecourt*
Finance	*Yves Bouthillier* (see Reynaud)
Defence	*Maxime Weygand* (b. Brussels 18 Jan 1867; d. Paris 28 Jan 1965)
War	*Louis-Antoine Colson* (b. Toulouse 27 Oct 1875; d. Paris 7 Mar 1951
Navy and Shipping	*François Darlan* (b. Nérac 7 Aug 1881; d. Algiers 24 Dec 1942)
Aviation	*General Pujo*
Education	*Albert Rivaud*
Public Works	29 Jun - 12 Jul 1940: *Ludovic Oscar Frossard* (see Bouisson)
Labour	17 - 29 Jun 1940: *André L. Février* (see Chautemps III)
	29 Jun - 12 Jul 1940: *Charles Pomaret* (see Daladier III)
Transport	17 - 29 Jun 1940: *Ludovic Oscar Frossard* (see Bouisson)
	29 Jun - 12 Jul 1940: *André Louis Février* (see Chautemps III)

Commerce	*Yves Bouthillier* (see Reynaud)
Colonies	*Albert Rivière* (see Blum I)
Agriculture	*Albert Chichery* (see Reynaud)
Pensions	*Jean Ybarnegaray* (see Reynaud)
Without Portfolio	22 Jun – 12 Jul 1940: *Adrien Marquet* (see Doumergue II)

13 Jul – 6 Sep 1940: Pétain II

Prime Minister	*Henri Philippe Pétain* (for 2nd time) (see Presidents)
Deputy Prime Minister	*Pierre Laval* (see Tardieu II)
Foreign Affairs	*Paul Baudouin* (see Pétain I)
Home Affairs	*Adrien Marquet* (see Doumergue II)
Justice	*Raphaël Alibert* (b. Montcuq 1886; d. Paris 6(?) Jun 1963)
Finance	*Yves Bouthillier* (see Reynaud)
Youth and Family	*Jean Ybarnegaray* (see Reynaud)
National Defence	*Maxime Weygand* (see Pétain I)
Communications	*François Piétri* (see Tardieu I)
Colonies	*Henri Lémery* (see Doumergue II)
Agriculture and Food	*Pierre Caziot* (b. Vailly-sur-Sauldre 24 Sep 1876; d. Paris 4 Jan 1953)

6 Sep 1940 – 25 Feb 1941: Pétain III

Prime Minister	*Henri Philippe Pétain* (for 3rd time) (see Presidents)
Secretary of State	28 Oct 1940 – 4 Jan 1941: *Paul Baudouin* (see Pétain I)
Deputy Prime Minister	6 Sep – 13 Dec 1940: *Pierre Laval* (see Tardieu II)
	13 Dec 1940 – 25 Jan 1941: *François Darlan* (see Pétain I)
Foreign Affairs	6 Sep – 28 Oct 1940: *Paul Baudouin* (see Pétain I)
	28 Oct – 13 Dec 1940: *Pierre Laval* (see Tardieu II)
	13 Dec 1940 – 24 Feb 1941: *Pierre Étienne Flandin* (see Tardieu I)
Home Affairs	*Marcel Peyrouton* (b. Paris 2 Jul 1887)
Justice	6 Sep 1940 – 27 Jan 1941: *Raphaël Alibert* (see Pétain II)
	27 Jan – 25 Feb 1941: *Joseph Barthélemy* (b. Toulouse 9 Jul 1874; d. early May 1945)
Finance	*Yves Bouthillier* (see Reynaud)
National Defence	*Charles Huntziger* (b. Lesneven 25 Jun 1880; d. Le Vigan 12 Nov 1941)

Education and   *René Belin* (d. Jan 1977)
    Labour
Agriculture   *Pierre Caziot* (see Pétain II)

25 Feb – 11 Aug 1941: Pétain IV

Prime Minister ,	*Henri Philippe Pétain* (for 4th time) (see Presidents)
Deputy Prime	*François Darlan* (see Pétain I)
Minister	
Foreign Affairs	*François Darlan* (see Pétain I)
Home Affairs	25 Feb – 18 Jul 1941: *François Darlan* (see Pétain I)
	18 Jul – 11 Aug 1941: *Pierre Pucheu* (b. 1899; d.
	Algiers 20 Mar 1944)
Justice	*Joseph Barthélemy* (see Pétain III)
Finance and	*Yves Bouthillier* (see Reynaud)
National	
Economy	
National Defence	*Charles Huntziger* (see Pétain III)
Navy	*François Darlan* (see Pétain I)
Agriculture	25 Feb – (?) 1941: *Pierre Caziot* (see Pétain II)
Information	*François Darlan* (see Pétain I)
Director-General	*Paul Marion* (b. Asnières 1899; d. night of
for Information	1/2 Mar 1954)
Director-General	—— *Barnaud*
for German-	
French Economic	
co-operation	
Director-General	*François Lehideux* (b. Paris 30 Jan 1904)
for Employment	

11 Aug 1941 – 17 Apr 1942: Pétain V

Prime Minister	*Henri Philippe Pétain* (for 5th time) (see Presidents)
Deputy Prime	*François Darlan* (see Pétain I)
Minister	
Foreign Affairs	*François Darlan* (see Pétain I)
Home Affairs	*Pierre Pucheu* (see Pétain IV)
Justice	*Joseph Barthélemy* (see Pétain III)
Finance and	*Yves Bouthillier* (see Reynaud)
Economy	
National Defence	*François Darlan* (see Pétain I)
War	11 Aug – 12 Nov 1941: *Charles Huntziger* (see Pétain
	III)

Navy	*François Darlan* (see Pétain I)
Agriculture	*Pierre Caziot* (see Pétain II)
Supply	*Paul Charbin* (b. Lyon 1877; d. 22 Oct 1956)
Ministers of State	*Henri Mousset* (b. 1875)
	Lucien Romier (b. Noire 1885; d. Paris 7 Jan 1944)
Information and Propaganda	*Paul Marion* (see Pétain IV)

18 Apr 1942 – 29 Sep 1944 (from early Aug 1944 in Belfort): Laval IV

Prime Minister, Foreign and Home Affairs	*Pierre Laval* (for 4th time) (see Tardieu II)
Justice	18 Apr 1942 – 27 Mar 1943: *Joseph Barthélemy* (see Pétain III)
	27 Mar 1943 – 29 Sep 1944: *Maurice Gabolde*
Finance	*Pierre Cathala* (see Laval II)
Education	*Abel Bonnard* (b. 17 Dec 1883; d. 1 Jun 1968)
Labour	27 Mar 1943 – 17 Mar 1944: *Hubert Lagardelle*
	17 Mar – 29 Sep 1944: *Marcel Déat* (see Sarraut II)
Agriculture and Supply	18 Apr – 11 Sep 1942: *Jacques Leroy-Ladurie*
	11 Sep 1942 – (?): *Max Bonnafous*
	(?) – Dec 1943: *Lucien Romier* (see Pétain V)
	Dec 1943 – 29 Sep 1944: *Pierre Cathala* (see Laval II)
Minister of State (10-Year Plan of Economic Mobilization)	18 Apr – 28 Dec 1942: *Lucien Romier* (see Pétain V)
	28 Dec 1942 – 29 Sep 1944: *Pierre Cathala* (see Laval II)

10 Sep 1944 – 16 Nov 1945: de Gaulle I

Prime Minister	*Charles de Gaulle* (for 1st time) (see Presidents)
Ministers of State	*Jules Jeanneney* (Rad) (b. Besançon 6 Jul 1864; d. Paris 27 Apr 1957)
	André Le Troquer (Soc) (b. Paris 24 Oct 1884; d. 11 Nov 1963)
	André Philip (Soc) (b. Pont-Saint-Esprit 28 Jun 1902; d. Paris 7 Jul 1970)
Foreign Affairs	*Georges Bidault* (Rep Peoples Mov) (b. Moulins 5 Oct 1899)
Home Affairs	*Adrien Tixier* (Soc) (b. 1897(?); d. 18 Feb 1946)
Justice	10 Sep 1944 – 31 May 1945: *François de Menthon* (b. Montmirey 8 Jan 1900)

	31 May – 16 Nov 1945: *Pierre Henri Teitgen* (b. Rennes 29 May 1908)
Finance	10 Sep – 10 Nov 1944: *Aimé Lepercq* (b. 1889(?); d. Paris 10 Nov 1944)
	15 Nov 1944 – 16 Nov 1945: *René Pleven* (Dem Resist) (b. Rennes 13 Apr 1901)
Commerce	10 Sep 1944 – 4 Jun 1945: *Pierre Mendès-France* (Rad) (b. Paris 11 Jan 1907)
	4 Jun – 16 Nov 1945: *René Pleven* (Dem Resist) (see above)
Production	*Robert Lacoste* (Soc) (b. Azérat 5 Jul 1898)
War	*André Diethelm* (b. Bourg 3 Jul 1896; d. Paris 11 Jan 1954)
Navy	*Louis Jacquinot* (Mod Rep) (b. Goudrecourt-le-Chateau 16 Sep 1898)
Aviation	*Charles Tillon* (Comm) (b. Rennes 3 Jul 1897)
Agriculture	*François Tanguy-Prigent* (Soc) (b. Saint-Jean-du-Doigt 11 Oct 1909; d. 20 Jan 1970)
Colonies	10 Sep – 15 Nov 1944: *René Pleven* (Dem Resist) (see above)
	15 Nov 1944 – 16 Nov 1945: *Paul Giacobbi* (Rad Soc) (b. Venaco, Corsica, 1896; d. Neuilly-sur-Seine 5 Apr 1951)
Education	*René Capitant* (Dem Resist) (b. La Tronde 19 Aug 1901; d. near Paris 23 May 1970)
Transport and Public Works	*René Mayer* (b. Paris 4 May 1895; d. 13 Dec 1972)
Labour	*Alexandre Parodi* (Dem Resist) (b. Paris 1 Jun 1901)
Posts and Telegraph	10 Sep 1944 – 26 Jun 1945: *Augustin Laurent* (Soc) (b. Wahagnies 1896)
	26 Jun – 16 Nov 1945: *Eugène Thomas* (Soc) (b. Vieux-Condé 23 Jul 1903; d. 28 Jan 1969)
Health	*François Billoux* (Comm) (b. St Romain-la-Motte 21 May 1903)
North Africa	*Georges (Albert Julien) Catroux* (b. Limoges 29 Jan 1877; d. Paris 21 Dec 1969)
Prisoners of War and Pensions	*Henri Frenay* (Dem Resist) (b. Lyon 18 Nov 1905)
Food	10 Sep – 15 Nov 1944: *Paul Giacobbi* (Rad Soc) (see above)
	15 Sep 1944 – 31 May 1945: *Paul Ramadier* (Soc) (see Chautemps IV)
	31 May – 16 Nov 1945: *Christian Pineau* (Soc) (b.

Reconstruction and Planning	Chaumont-en-Bassigny 14 Oct 1904) 24 Nov 1944 – 16 Nov 1945: *Raoul Dautry* (see Daladier III)
Information	31 May – 20 Oct 1945: *Jacques Soustelle* (Gaull) (b. Montpellier 3 Feb 1912) 20 Oct – 16 Nov 1945: *André Malraux* (b. Paris 3 Nov 1901; d. Paris 23 Nov 1976)

21 Nov 1945 – 20 Jan 1946: de Gaulle II

Prime Minister	*Charles de Gaulle* (for 2nd time) (see Presidents)
Foreign Affairs	*Georges Bidault* (Rep Peoples Mov) (see de Gaulle I)
Home Affairs	*Adrien Tixier* (Soc) (see de Gaulle I)
Justice	*Pierre Henri Teitgen* (see de Gaulle I)
Finance	*René Pleven* (Dem Resist) (see de Gaulle I)
Commerce	*François Billoux* (Comm) (see de Gaulle I)
Defence	*Charles de Gaulle* (see Presidents)
War	*Edmond Michelet* (b. Paris 8 Oct 1899; d. 9 Oct 1970)
Armaments	*Charles Tillon* (Comm) (see de Gaulle I)
Industrial Production	*Marcel Paul* (b. Paris 12 Jul 1900)
Public Works	*Jules Moch* (see Blum II)
Labour	*Ambroise Croizat* (b. Notre-Dame-de-Briançon 28 Jan 1901; d. Suresnes 11 Feb 1951)
Education	*Paul Giacobbi* (Rad Soc) (see de Gaulle I)
Colonies	*Jacques Soustelle* (Gaull) (see de Gaulle I)
Posts	*Eugène Thomas* (Soc) (see de Gaulle I)
Health	*Robert Prigent* (b. Saint-Pol-sur-Mer 24 Nov 1910)
Reconstruction	*Raoul Dautry* (see Daladier III)
Information	*André Malraux* (see de Gaulle I)
Agriculture	*François Tanguy-Prigent* (Soc) (see de Gaulle I)
Without Portfolio	*Maurice Thorez* (Comm) (b. Noyelle-Godault 28 Apr 1900; d. 11 Jul 1964) *Vincent Auriol* (see Presidents) *Francisque Gay* (Rep Peoples Mov) (b. Roanne 8 May 1885) *Louis Jacquinot* (Ind Rep) (see de Gaulle I)

26 Jan – 12 Jun 1946: Gouin

Prime Minister	*Félix Gouin* (b. Peypin 4 Aug 1884)
Deputy Prime Ministers	*Maurice Thorez* (Comm) (see de Gaulle II) *Francisque Gay* (Rep Peoples Mov) (see de Gaulle II)

Alexandre Varennes

Foreign Affairs	*Georges Bidault* (Rep Peoples Mov) (see de Gaulle I)
Home Affairs	*André Le Troquer* (Soc) (see de Gaulle I)
Justice	*Pierre Henri Teitgen* (see de Gaulle I)
Finance and National Economy	*André Philip* (Soc) (see de Gaulle I)
Industrial Production	*Marcel Paul* (Comm) (see de Gaulle II)
Reconstruction	*François Billoux* (Comm) (see de Gaulle I)
Army	*Edmond Michelet* (see de Gaulle II)
Armaments	*Charles Tillon* (Comm) (see de Gaulle I)
Education	*Marcel Naegelen* (b. Belfort 17 Jan 1892)
Public Works	*Jules Moch* (see Blum II)
Labour	*Ambroise Croizat* (Comm) (see de Gaulle II)
Health	*Robert Prigent* (Rep Peoples Mov) (see de Gaulle II)
Food	*Henri Longchambon* (b. Clermont-Ferrand 27 Jul 1896; d. 20 Mar 1969)
Colonies	*Marius Moutet* (see Blum I)
Agriculture	*François Tanguy-Prigent* (Soc) (see de Gaulle I)
Posts	*Jean Letourneau* (b. Lure 18 Sep 1907)
Transport	*Jules Moch* (see Blum II)
Ex-Servicemen	*Laurent Casanova* (Comm) (b. Arras 1906)

24 Jun – 28 Nov 1946: Bidault I

Prime Minister	*Georges Bidault* (for 1st time) (Rep Peoples Mov) (see de Gaulle I)
Minister of State and Deputy Prime Minister	*Félix Gouin* (Soc) (see Gouin)
Foreign Affairs	*Georges Bidault* (Rep Peoples Mov) (see de Gaulle I)
Home Affairs	*Édouard Depreux* (Soc) (b. Viesly 31 Oct 1898)
Justice	*Pierre Henri Teitgen* (see de Gaulle I)
Finance	*Robert Schuman* (Rep Peoples Mov) (b. Luxembourg 29 Jun 1886; d. Metz 4 Sep 1963)
Commerce	*François de Menthon* (Rep Peoples Mov) (see de Gaulle I)
Industrial Production	*Marcel Paul* (Comm) (see de Gaulle II)
Reconstruction	*François Billoux* (Comm) (see de Gaulle I)
Army	*Edmond Michelet* (Rep Peoples Mov) (see de Gaulle II)

Armaments	*Charles Tillon* (Comm) (see de Gaulle I)
Education	*Marcel Naegelen* (Soc) (see Gouin)
Public Works	*Jules Moch* (Soc) (see Blum II)
Labour	*Ambroise Croizat* (Comm) (see de Gaulle II)
Health	*René Arthaud* (Comm) (b. Marseille 20 Sep 1915)
Food	(?) Jun – 28 Nov 1946: *Yves Farge* (b. Salon-de-Provence 1899; d. Gori, Georgia, 30 Mar 1953)
Agriculture	*François Tanguy-Prigent* (Soc) (see de Gaulle I)
Colonies	*Marius Moutet* (Soc) (see Blum I)
Population	*Robert Prigent* (Rep Peoples Mov) (see de Gaulle II)
Ex-Servicemen	*Laurent Casanova* (Comm) (see Gouin)
Posts and Telegraph	*Jean Letourneau* (Rep Peoples Mov) (see Gouin)
Information	*Georges Bidault* (Rep Peoples Mov) (see de Gaulle I)

16 Dec 1946 – 16 Jan 1947: Blum III (Soc)

Prime Minister	*Léon Blum* (for 3rd time) (see Blum I)
Ministers of State	*Augustin Laurent* (see de Gaulle I)
	Guy Mollet (b. Flers 31 Dec 1905; d. 3 Oct 1975)
Foreign Affairs	*Léon Blum* (see Blum I)
Home Affairs	*Édouard Depreux* (see Bidault I)
Justice	*Paul Ramadier* (see Chautemps IV)
Finance	*André Philip* (see de Gaulle I)
Planning	*Félix Gouin* (see Gouin)
National Defence	*André Le Troquer* (see de Gaulle I)
Education	*Marcel Naegelen* (see Gouin)
Public Works, Transport and Reconstruction	*Jules Moch* (see Blum II)
Labour and Social Security	*Daniel Mayer* (b. Paris 29 Apr 1909)
Industrial Production	*Robert Lacoste* (see de Gaulle I)
Agriculture	*François Tanguy-Prigent* (see de Gaulle I)
Health	*Pierre Segelle* (b. Médéa, Algeria, 11 Sep 1899)
Ex-Servicemen	*Max Lejeune* (b. Flessilly 19 Feb 1909)
Overseas Territories	*Marius Moutet* (see Blum I)
Posts and Telegraph	*Eugène Thomas* (see de Gaulle I)

22 Jan – 22 Oct 1947: Ramadier I

Prime Minister	*Paul Ramadier* (Soc) (for 1st time) (see Chautemps IV)

Deputy Prime Ministers	22 Jan – 5 May 1947: *Maurice Thorez* (Comm) (see de Gaulle II)
	Pierre Henri Teitgen (Rep Peoples Mov) (see de Gaulle I)
Ministers of State	*Félix Gouin* (Soc) (see Gouin)
	22 Jan – 5 May 1947: *Yvon Delbos* (Left Rep Union) (see Sarraut II)
	Marcel Roclore (Ind Rep)
Foreign Affairs	*Georges Bidault* (Rep Peoples Mov) (see de Gaulle I)
Home Affairs	*Édouard Depreux* (Soc) (see Bidault I)
Justice	*André Marie* (Left Rep Union) (b. Honfleur 3 Dec 1897; d. 12 Jun 1974)
Finance	*Robert Schuman* (Rep Peoples Mov) (see Bidault I)
National Economy	*André Philip* (Soc) (see de Gaulle I)
Defence	22 Jan – 5 May 1947: *François Billoux* (Comm) (see de Gaulle I)
	9 May – 22 Oct 1947: *Paul Béchard* (Soc) (b. Alès 25 Dec 1899)
War	*Paul Coste-Floret* (Rep Peoples Mov) (b. Montpellier 9 Apr 1911)
Navy	*Louis Jacquinot* (Ind Rep) (see de Gaulle I)
Aviation	*André Maroselli* (Rad Soc) (b. Rutali, Corsica, 22 Feb 1893; d. 7 Apr 1970)
Education	*Marcel Naegelen* (Soc) (see Gouin)
Public Works and Transport	*Jules Moch* (Soc) (see Blum II)
Labour	21 Jan – 5 May 1947: *Ambroise Croizat* (Comm) (see de Gaulle II)
	5 – 9 May 1947: *Robert Lacoste* (Soc) (see de Gaulle I)
	9 May – 22 Oct 1947: *Daniel Mayer* (Soc) (see Blum III)
Health	22 Jan – 5 May 1947: *Georges Marrane* (Comm) (b. Louviens 20 Jan 1888)
	9 May – 22 Oct 1947: *Robert Prigent* (Rep Peoples Mov) (see de Gaulle II)
Agriculture	*François Tanguy-Prigent* (Soc) (see de Gaulle I)
Industrial Production	*Robert Lacoste* (Soc) (see de Gaulle I)
Reconstruction	22 Jan – 5 May 1947: *Charles Tillon* (Comm) (see de Gaulle I)
	5 – 9 May 1947: *Jules Moch* (Soc) (see Blum II)
	9 May – 22 Oct 1947: *Jean Letourneau* (Rep Peoples Mov) (see Gouin)

Commerce	*Jean Letourneau* (Rep Peoples Mov) (see Gouin)
Colonies	*Marius Moutet* (Soc) (see Blum I)
Youth, Arts and Sciences	*Pierre Bourdan* (Left Rep Union) (b. Perpignan 13 May 1909; d. Lavedan early Jul 1948)
Ex-Servicemen	*François Mitterand* (Left Rep Union) (b. Sarnes 26 Oct 1916)
Food Supply	*Georges Rastel* (b. Montgeron 29 Oct 1910)
Posts and Telegraph	9 May – 22 Oct 1947: *Eugène Thomas* (Soc) (see de Gaulle I)

24 Oct – 19 Nov 1947: Ramadier II

Prime Minister	*Paul Ramadier* (Soc) (for 2nd time) (see Chautemps IV)
Minister of State	*Yvon Delbos* (Rad Soc) (see Sarraut II)
Foreign Affairs	*Georges Bidault* (Rep Peoples Mov) (see de Gaulle I)
Home Affairs	*Édouard Depreux* (Soc) (see Bidault I)
Justice	*André Marie* (Rad Soc) (see Ramadier I)
Finance	*Robert Schuman* (Rep Peoples Mov) (see Bidault I)
Armed Forces	*Pierre Henri Teitgen* (Rep Peoples Mov) (see de Gaulle I)
Defence	*Paul Béchard* (Soc) (see Ramadier I)
Education	*Marcel Naegelen* (Soc) (see Gouin)
National Economy, Public Works, Reconstruction, Transport and Planning	*Jules Moch* (Soc) (see Blum II)
Social Affairs	*Daniel Mayer* (Soc) (see Blum III)
Agriculture	*Marcel Roclore* (Ind Rep) (see Ramadier I)
Industry	*Robert Lacoste* (Soc) (see de Gaulle I)
Colonies	*Paul Béchard* (Soc) (see Ramadier I)

24 Nov 1947 – 19 Jul 1948: Schuman I

Prime Minister	*Robert Schuman* (Rep Peoples Mov) (for 1st time) (see Bidault I)
Foreign Affairs	*Georges Bidault* (Rep Peoples Mov) (see de Gaulle I)
Home Affairs	*Jules Moch* (Soc) (see Blum II)
Justice	*André Marie* (Rad Soc) (see Ramadier I)
Finance and National Economy	*René Mayer* (Rad Soc) (see de Gaulle I)

Reconstruction	*René Coty* (Ind Rep) (see Presidents)
Defence	24 Nov 1947 – 12 Feb 1948: *Paul Béchard* (Soc) (see Ramadier I)
	12 Feb – 19 Jul 1948: *Max Lejeune* (Soc) (see Blum III)
Education	24 Nov 1947 – 12 Feb 1948: *Marcel Naegelen* (Soc) (see Gouin)
	12 Feb – 19 Jul 1948: *Édouard Depreux* (Soc) (see Bidault I)
Labour	*Daniel Mayer* (Soc) (see Blum III)
Health	*Germaine Poinso-Chapuis* (b. Marseille 6 Mar 1901)
Agriculture	*Pierre Pflimlin* (Rep Peoples Mov) (b. Roubaix 5 Feb 1907)
Pensions and Ex-Servicemen	*François Mitterand* (Left Rep Union) (see Ramadier I)
Industry and Commerce	*Robert Lacoste* (Soc) (see de Gaulle I)
Colonies	*Paul Coste-Floret* (Rep Peoples Mov) (see Ramadier I)

27 Jul – 27 Aug 1948: Marie

Prime Minister	*André Marie* (Rad Soc) (see Ramadier I)
Ministers of State	*Paul Ramadier* (Soc) (see Chautemps IV)
	Henri Queuille (Rad Soc) (see Chautemps I)
Deputy Prime Ministers	*Léon Blum* (Soc) (see Blum I)
	Pierre Henri Teitgen (Rep Peoples Mov) (see de Gaulle I)
Foreign Affairs	*Robert Schuman* (Rep Peoples Mov) (see Bidault I)
Home Affairs	*Jules Moch* (Soc) (see Blum II)
Justice	*Robert Lecourt* (Rep Peoples Mov) (b. Pavilly 19 Sep 1908)
Finance	*Paul Reynaud* (Ind Rep) (see Tardieu II)
Reconstruction	*René Coty* (Ind Rep) (see Presidents)
Commerce and Industry	*Robert Lacoste* (Soc) (see de Gaulle I)
Defence	*René Mayer* (Rad Soc) (see de Gaulle I)
Education	*Yvon Delbos* (Rad Soc) (see Sarraut II)
Labour	*Daniel Mayer* (Soc) (see Blum III)
Health	*Pierre Schneiter* (Rep Peoples Mov) (b. Reims 13 May 1905)
Ex-Servicemen	*André Maroselli* (Rad Soc) (see Ramadier I)
Agriculture	*Pierre Pflimlin* (Rep Peoples Mov) (see Schuman I)

| Transport | *Christian Pineau* (Soc) (see de Gaulle I) |
| Colonies | *Paul Coste-Floret* (Rep Peoples Mov) (see Ramadier I) |

31 Aug/5 Sep – 8 Sep 1948: Schuman II

Prime Minister and Foreign Affairs	*Robert Schuman* (Rep Peoples Mov) (for 2nd time) (see Bidault I)
Deputy Prime Minister	*André Marie* (Rad Soc) (see Ramadier I)
Finance	*Christian Pineau* (Soc) (see de Gaulle I)
Education	*Tony Revillon* (Rad Soc) (b. Paris 24 Aug 1891)
Ex-Servicemen	*Jules Catoire* (Rep Peoples Mov) (b. Arras 31 Jan 1892)
	Other ministers continued in same offices as in previous cabinet

13 Sep 1948 – 6 Oct 1949: Queuille I

Prime Minister	*Henri Queuille* (Rad Soc) (for 1st time) (see Chautemps I)
Deputy Prime Minister	13 Sep 1948 – 13 Feb 1949: *André Marie* (Rad Soc) (see Ramadier I)
Foreign Affairs	*Robert Schuman* (Rep Peoples Mov) (see Bidault I)
Home Affairs	*Jules Moch* (Soc) (see Blum II)
Justice	13 Sep 1948 – 13 Feb 1949: *André Marie* (Rad Soc) (see Ramadier I)
	13 Feb – 6 Oct 1949: *Robert Lecourt* (Rep Peoples Mov) (see Marie)
Finance	13 Sep 1948 – 13 Jan 1949: *Henri Queuille* (Rad Soc) (see Chautemps I)
	13 Jan – 6 Oct 1949: *Maurice Petsche* (b. Paris 1 Dec 1895; d. 16 Sep 1951)
Reconstruction	*Eugène Claudius-Petit* (Dem Resist) (b. Angers 22 May 1907)
Defence	*Paul Ramadier* (Soc) (see Chautemps IV)
Education	*Yvon Delbos* (Rad Soc) (see Sarraut II)
Labour	*Daniel Mayer* (Soc) (see Blum III)
Public Works and Transport	*Christian Pineau* (Soc) (see de Gaulle I)
Commerce and Industry	*Robert Lacoste* (Soc) (see de Gaulle I)
Mercantile Marine	*André Colin* (Rep Peoples Mov) (b. Brest 19 Jan 1910)

Health	*Pierre Schneiter* (Rep Peoples Mov) (see Marie)
Ex-Servicemen	*Robert Betolaud* (Rep Freedom) (b. Paris Feb 1901)
Agriculture	*Pierre Pflimlin* (Rep Peoples Mov) (see Schuman I)
Overseas Territories	*Paul Coste-Floret* (Rep Peoples Mov) (see Ramadier I)

28 Oct 1949 – 24 Jun 1950: Bidault II

Prime Minister	*Georges Bidault* (Rep Peoples Mov) (for 2nd time) (see de Gaulle I)
Deputy Prime Ministers	*Henri Queuille* (Rad Soc) (see Chautemps I) 28 Oct 1949 – 3 Feb 1950: *Jules Moch* (Soc) (see Blum II)
Foreign Affairs	*Robert Schuman* (Rep Peoples Mov) (see Bidault I)
Home Affairs	28 Oct 1949 – 3 Feb 1950: *Jules Moch* (Soc) (see Blum II) 7 Feb – 24 Jun 1950: *Henri Queuille* (Rad Soc) (see Chautemps I)
Justice	*René Mayer* (Rad Soc) (see de Gaulle I)
Finance	*Maurice Petsche* (see Queuille I)
Reconstruction	*Eugène Claudius-Petit* (Dem Resist) (see Queuille I)
Defence	*René Pleven* (Dem Resist) (see de Gaulle I)
Education	*Yvon Delbos* (Rad Soc) (see Sarraut II)
Information	*Pierre Henri Teitgen* (Rep Peoples Mov) (see de Gaulle I)
Labour	28 Oct 1949 – 3 Feb 1950: *Pierre Segelle* (Soc) (see Blum III) 7 Feb – 24 Jun 1950: *Paul Bacon* (Rep Peoples Mov) (b. Paris 1 Nov 1907)
Public Works	28 Oct 1949 – 3 Feb 1950: *Christian Pineau* (Soc) (see de Gaulle I) 7 Feb – 24 Jun 1950: *Jacques Chastellain* (b. Rouen 7 Jun 1885)
Commerce and Industry	28 Oct 1949 – 3 Feb 1950: *Robert Lacoste* (Soc) (see de Gaulle I) 7 Feb – 24 Jun 1950: *Jean-Marie Louvel* (Rep Peoples Mov) (b. La Ferté-Macé 1 Jul 1900; d. 13 Jun 1970)
Transport	28 Oct 1949 – 3 Feb 1950: *Eugène Thomas* (Soc) (see de Gaulle I) 7 Feb – 24 Jun 1950: *Charles Brune* (Rad Soc) (b. Arbois 31 Jul 1891; d. 13 Jan 1956)
Health	*Pierre Schneiter* (Rep Peoples Mov) (see Marie)
Ex-Servicemen	*Louis Jacquinot* (see de Gaulle I)

Agriculture	28 Oct – 2 Dec 1949: *Pierre Pflimlin* (Rep Peoples Mov) (see Schuman I) 2 Dec 1949 – 24 Jun 1950: *Gabriel Valay* (Rep Peoples Mov) (b. Salon-de-Provence 17 Sep 1905)
Overseas Territories	*Jean Letourneau* (Rep Peoples Mov) (see Gouin)

30 Jun/2 Jul – 4 Jul 1950: Queuille II

Prime Minister	*Henri Queuille* (Rad Soc) (for 2nd time) (see Chautemps I)
Deputy Prime Minister	*Georges Bidault* (Rep Peoples Mov) (see de Gaulle I)
Foreign Affairs	*Robert Schuman* (Rep Peoples Mov) (see Bidault I)
Home Affairs	*Henri Queuille* (Rad Soc) (see Chautemps I)
Justice	*René Mayer* (Rad Soc) (see de Gaulle I)
Finance	*Maurice Petsche* (see Queuille I)
Budget	*Edgar Faure* (Rad Soc) (b. Béziers 18 Aug 1908)
Civil Service	*Paul Giacobbi* (Rad Soc) (see de Gaulle I)
Defence	*René Pleven* (Dem Resist) (see de Gaulle I)
Indo China and Far East	*Paul Reynaud* (Ind Rep) (see Tardieu II)

11/12 Jul 1950 – 28 Feb 1951: Pleven I

Prime Minister	*René Pleven* (Dem Resist) (for 1st time) (see de Gaulle I)
Foreign Affairs	*Robert Schuman* (Rep Peoples Mov) (see Bidault I)
Council of Europe	*Guy Mollet* (Soc) (see Blum III)
Home Affairs	*Henri Queuille* (Rad Soc) (see Chautemps I)
Justice	*René Mayer* (Rad Soc) (see de Gaulle I)
Finance	*Maurice Petsche* (see Queuille I)
Reconstruction	*Eugène Claudius-Petit* (Dem Resist) (see Queuille I)
Budget	*Edgar Faure* (Rad Soc) (see Queuille II)
Defence	*Jules Moch* (Soc) (see Blum II)
Information	*Albert Gazier* (Soc) (b. Valenciennes 16 May 1908)
Education	*Pierre-Olivier Lapie* (Soc) (b. Rennes 2 Apr 1901)
Labour	*Paul Bacon* (Rep Peoples Mov) (see Bidault II)
Public Works	*Antoine Pinay* (Farm) (b. St. Symphorien 30 Dec 1891)
Commerce and Industry	*Jean-Marie Louvel* (Rep Peoples Mov) (see Bidault II)
Mercantile Marine	*Gaston Defferre* (Soc) (b. Marsillagues 14 Sep 1909)

Posts and Telegraph	*Charles Brune* (Rad Soc) (see Bidault II)
Health	*Pierre Schneiter* (Rep Peoples Mov) (see Marie)
Ex-Servicemen	*Louis Jacquinot* (see de Gaulle I)
Agriculture	*Pierre Pflimlin* (Rep Peoples Mov) (see Schuman I)
Overseas Territories	*François Mitterand* (Dem Resist) (see Ramadier I)
Associated Territories	*Jean Letourneau* (Rep Peoples Mov) (see Gouin)
Without Portfolio	*Paul Giacobbi* (Rad Soc) (see de Gaulle I)

9/10 Mar - 10 Jul 1951: Queuille III

Prime Minister	*Henri Queuille* (Rad Soc) (for 3rd time) (see Chautemps I)
Deputy Prime Ministers	*Georges Bidault* (Rep Peoples Mov) (see de Gaulle I)
	René Pleven (Dem Resist) (see de Gaulle I)
	Guy Mollet (Soc) (see Blum III)
Overseas Territories	9/10 Mar – 4 Apr 1951: *François Mitterand* (Dem Resist) (see Ramadier I)
	Remaining ministers continued in same offices as in previous cabinet, with exception of Paul Giacobbi who was not re-appointed Minister without Portfolio

8/11 Aug 1951 - 8 Jan 1952: Pleven II

Prime Minister	*René Pleven* (Dem Resist) (for 2nd time) (see de Gaulle I)
Deputy Prime Minister	*Georges Bidault* (Rep Peoples Mov) (see de Gaulle I)
Foreign Affairs	*Robert Schuman* (Rep Peoples Mov) (see Bidault I)
Home Affairs	*Charles Brune* (Rad Soc) (see Bidault II)
Justice	*Edgar Faure* (Rad Soc) (see Queuille II)
Finance and National Economy	*René Mayer* (Rad Soc) (see de Gaulle I)
Reconstruction	*Eugène Claudius-Petit* (Dem Resist) (see Queuille I)
Budget	*Pierre Courant* (b. Le Havre 12 Sep 1897)
Defence	*René Pleven* (Dem Resist) (see de Gaulle I)
Information	*Robert Buron* (Rep Peoples Mov) (b. Paris 27 Feb 1910; d. 30 Apr 1973)
Education	*André Marie* (Rad Soc) (see Ramadier I)
Labour and Social Affairs	*Paul Bacon* (Rep Peoples Mov) (see Bidault II)
Public Works and Transport	*Antoine Pinay* (Farm) (see Pleven I)

197

Foreign and Domestic Trade	*Pierre Pflimlin* (Rep Peoples Mov) (see Schuman I)
Production	*Jean-Marie Louvel* (Rep Peoples Mov) (see Bidault II)
Mercantile Marine	*André Morice* (Rad Soc) (b. Nantes 11 Oct 1900)
Posts and Telegraph	11 Aug – 6 Oct 1951: *Joseph Laniel* (b. Vimoutiers 12 Oct 1889)
	6 Oct 1951 – 8 Jan 1952: *Roger Duchet* (Ind Rep) (b. Lyons 4 Jul 1906)
Health	*Paul Ribeyre* (Farm) (b. Aubagne 1906)
Ex-Servicemen	*Emmanuel Temple* (b. Montpellier 21 Sep 1895)
Agriculture	11 Aug – 22 Nov 1951: *Paul Antier* (Farm) (b. Puy 20 May 1905)
	22 Nov 1951 – 8 Jan 1952: *Camille Laurens* (Farm) (b. 12 Aug 1906)
Overseas Territories	*Louis Jacquinot* (see de Gaulle I)
Ministers of State	*Henry Queuille* (Rad Soc) (see Chautemps I)
	11 Aug – 16 Sep 1951: *Maurice Petsche* (see Queuille I)
	6 Oct 1951 – 8 Jan 1952: *Joseph Laniel* (see above)
	Jean Letourneau (Rep Peoples Mov) (see Gouin)

18/20 Jan – 29 Feb 1952: Faure I

Prime Minister	*Edgar Faure* (Rad Soc) (for 1st time) (see Queuille II)
Ministers of State	*Henri Queuille* (Rad Soc) (see Chautemps I)
	Joseph Laniel (see Pleven II)
Foreign Affairs	*Robert Schuman* (Rep Peoples Mov) (see Bidault I)
Council of Europe	*Pierre Pflimlin* (Rep Peoples Mov) (see Schuman I)
Home Affairs	*Charles Brune* (Rad Soc) (see Bidault II)
Justice	*Léon Martinaud-Déplat* (b. Lyons 9 Aug 1899; d. 5 Oct 1969)
Finance	*Edgar Faure* (Rad Soc) (see Queuille II)
Reconstruction	*Eugène Claudius-Petit* (Dem Resist) (see Queuille I)
Budget	*Pierre Courant* (see Pleven II)
Defence	*Georges Bidault* (Rep Peoples Mov) (see de Gaulle I)
Armaments	*Maurice Bourgès-Maunoury* (Rad Soc) (b. Luisant 19 Aug 1914)
National Economy	*Robert Buron* (Rep Peoples Mov) (see Pleven II)
Information	*Paul Coste-Floret* (Rep Peoples Mov) (see Ramadier I)
Education	*André Marie* (Rad Soc) (see Ramadier I)

Labour	*Paul Bacon* (Rep Peoples Mov) (see Bidault II)
Public Works	*Antoine Pinay* (Farm) (see Pleven I)
Commerce	*Édouard Bonnefous* (UDSR) (b. Paris 24 Aug 1907)
Industry	*Jean-Marie Louvel* (Rep Peoples Mov) (see Bidault II)
Mercantile Marine	*André Morice* (Rad Soc) (see Pleven II)
Posts and Telegraph	*Roger Duchet* (Ind Rep) (see Pleven II)
Health	*Paul Ribeyre* (Farm) (see Pleven II)
Ex-Servicemen	*Emmanuel Temple* (see Pleven II)
Agriculture	*Camille Laurens* (Farm) (see Pleven II)
Overseas Territories	*Jean Letourneau* (Rep Peoples Mov) (see Gouin)
Without Portfolio	*François Mitterand* (Dem Resist) (see Ramadier I)
	Louis Jacquinot (see de Gaulle I)

8 Mar – 23 Dec 1952: Pinay

Prime Minister	*Antoine Pinay* (Farm) (see Pleven I)
Deputy Prime Minister	*Henri Queuille* (Rad Soc) (see Chautemps I)
Foreign Affairs	*Robert Schuman* (Rep Peoples Mov) (see Bidault I)
Home Affairs	*Charles Brune* (Rad Soc) (see Bidault II)
Justice	*Léon Martinaud-Déplat* (see Faure I)
Finance (incorporating National Economy)	*Antoine Pinay* (Farm) (see Pleven I)
Reconstruction	*Eugène Claudius-Petit* (Dem Resist) (see Queuille I)
Defence	*René Pleven* (Dem Resist) (see de Gaulle I)
Education	*André Marie* (Rad Soc) (see Ramadier I)
Labour	*Pierre Garet* (Farm) (b. Montdidier 7 Sep 1905; d. 10 Dec 1972)
Public Works and Transport	*André Morice* (Rad Soc) (see Pleven II)
Industry	*Jean-Marie Louvel* (Rep Peoples Mov) (see Bidault II)
Posts and Telegraph	*Roger Duchet* (Ind Rep) (see Pleven II)
Health	*Paul Ribeyre* (Farm) (see Pleven II)
Ex-Servicemen	*Emmanuel Temple* (see Pleven II)
Agriculture	*Camille Laurens* (Farm) (see Pleven II)
Overseas Territories	*Pierre Pflimlin* (Rep Peoples Mov) (see Schuman I)
Indo China	*Jean Letourneau* (Rep Peoples Mov) (see Gouin)

7/9 Jan – 21 May 1953: Mayer

Prime Minister	*René Mayer* (Rad Soc) (see de Gaulle I)
Foreign Affairs	*Georges Bidault* (Rep Peoples Mov) (see de Gaulle I)
Home Affairs	*Charles Brune* (Rad Soc) (see Bidault II)
Justice	*Léon Martinaud-Déplat* (see Faure I)
Finance	*Maurice Bourgès-Maunoury* (Rad Soc) (see Faure I)
Reconstruction	*Pierre Courant* (Ind Rep) (see Pleven II)
Budget	*Jean Moreau* (Ind Rep) (b. Paris 31 Jul 1888)
National Economy	*Robert Buron* (Rep Peoples Mov) (see Pleven II)
Defence	*René Pleven* (Dem Resist) (see de Gaulle I)
Education	*André Marie* (Rad Soc) (see Ramadier I)
Labour and Social Affairs	*Paul Bacon* (Rep Peoples Mov) (see Bidault II)
Public Works and Transport	*André Morice* (Rad Soc) (see Pleven II)
Commerce	9 Jan – 11 Feb 1953: *Paul Ribeyre* (Farm) (see Pleven II)
	11 Feb – 21 May 1953: *Guy Petit* (b. Biarritz 23 Nov 1905)
Industry	*Jean-Marie Louvel* (Rep Peoples Mov) (see Bidault II)
Posts and Telegraph	*Roger Duchet* (Ind Rep) (see Pleven II)
Health	9 Jan – 11 Feb 1953: *André Boutémy* (Ind Farm) (b. Bécherel 21 Dec 1905)
	11 Feb – 21 May 1953: *Paul Ribeyre* (Farm) (see Pleven II)
Ex-Servicemen	*Henri Bergasse* (Rep Soc Action) (b. Marseille 26 Sep 1894)
Agriculture	*Camille Laurens* (Farm, from 2 Apr 1953 no party) (see Pleven II)
Overseas Territories	*Louis Jacquinot* (see de Gaulle I)
Associated Territories	*Jean Letourneau* (Rep Peoples Mov) (see Gouin)
Without Portfolio	*Paul Coste-Floret* (Rep Peoples Mov) (see Ramadier I)
	Édouard Bonnefous (UDSR) (see Faure I)

26/28 Jun 1953 – 12/14 Jun 1954: Laniel

Prime Minister	*Joseph Laniel* (see Pleven II)

Deputy Prime Minister	*Paul Reynaud* (Ind Rep) (see Tardieu II)
	Henri Queuille (Rad Soc) (see Chautemps I)
	Pierre Henri Teitgen (Rep Peoples Mov) (see de Gaulle I)
European Affairs	28 Jun – 3 Sep 1953: *François Mitterand* (Resist Union) (see Ramadier I)
Foreign Affairs	*Georges Bidault* (Rep Peoples Mov) (see de Gaulle I)
Home Affairs	*Léon Martinaud-Déplat* (Rad Soc) (see Faure I)
Justice	*Paul Ribeyre* (Farm) (see Pleven II)
Finance	*Edgar Faure* (Rad Soc) (see Queuille II)
Reconstruction	*Maurice Lemaire* (Rep Peoples Mov) (b. Gerbépal 25 May 1895)
Constitutional Reform	*Edmond Barrachin* (b. Paris 12 Jan 1900)
Defence	*René Pleven* (Dem Resist) (see de Gaulle I)
Education	*André Marie* (Rad Soc) (see Ramadier I)
Labour and Social Affairs	*Paul Bacon* (Rep Peoples Mov) (see Bidault II)
Public Works and Transport	*Jacques Chastellain* (see Bidault II)
Aviation	*Louis Christiaens* (b. Boulogne-sur-Mer 20 Dec 1890; d. 17 Jan 1975)
Commerce and Industry	*Jean-Marie Louvel* (Rep Peoples Mov) (see Bidault II)
Posts and Telegraph	*Pierre Ferri* (Gaull)
Health	*Paul Coste-Floret* (Rep Peoples Mov) (see Ramadier I)
Ex-Servicemen	*André Mutter* (Farm) (b. Troyes 11 Nov 1901; d. 24 Dec 1973)
Agriculture	*Roger Houdet* (b. Angers 14 Jun 1899)
Overseas Territories	*Louis Jacquinot* (see de Gaulle I)
Associated Territories	2 Jul 1953 – 30 May 1954: *Marc Jacquet* (b. Mercy-le-Bas 17 Feb 1913)
	3 – 14 Jun 1954: *Édouard Frédéric-Dupont* (b. Paris 10 Jul 1902)
Without Portfolio	*Edward Corniglion-Molinier* (Gaull) (b. Nice 23 Jan 1899; d. Paris 9 May 1963)

18/19 Jun 1954 – 5 Feb 1955: Mendès-France

Prime Minister	*Pierre Mendès-France* (Rad Soc) (see de Gaulle I)

Foreign Affairs	19 Jun 1954 – 20 Jan 1955: *Pierre Mendès-France* (Rad Soc) (see de Gaulle I)
	20 Jan – 5 Feb 1955: *Edgar Faure* (Rad Soc) (see Queuille II)
Home Affairs	*François Mitterand* (Resist Union) (see Ramadier I)
Justice	19 Jun – 2 Sep 1954: *Émile Hugues* (Rad Soc) (b. Nice 7 Apr 1901)
	3 Sep 1954 – 5 Feb 1955: *Jean Guerin de Bosq de Beaumont* (b. 29 Aug 1896; d. Nice 13 Oct 1955)
Finance	19 Jun 1954 – 20 Jan 1955: *Edgar Faure* (Rad Soc) (see Queuille II)
	20 Jan – 5 Feb 1955: *Robert Buron* (Rep Peoples Mov) (see Pleven II)
Reconstruction and Housing	19 Jun – 13 Aug 1954: *Maurice Lemaire* (Rep Peoples Mov) (see Laniel)
	3 Sep – 13 Nov 1954 (acting:) *Jacques Chaban-Delmas* (Gaull) (b. Paris 7 Feb 1915)
	13 Nov 1954 – 5 Feb 1955: *Maurice Lemaire* (Rep Peoples Mov) (see Laniel)
Defence	19 Jun – 13 Aug 1954: *Pierre Koenig* (Gaull) (b. Caen 10 Oct 1898; d. Paris 2 Sep 1970)
	3 Sep 1954 – 5 Feb 1955: *Emmanuel Temple* (Ind Rep) (see Pleven II)
Education	*Jean Bertholin* (Soc) (b. Enghien-les-Bains 12 Jan 1895)
Labour and Social Affairs	19 Jun – 2 Sep 1954: *Eugène Claudius-Petit* (Dem Resist) (see Queuille I)
	3 Sep 1954 – 5 Feb 1955: *Louis Aujoulat* (Ind Rep) (b. Said, Algeria, 28 Aug 1910)
Public Works and Transport	19 Jun – 13 Aug 1954: *Jacques Chaban-Delmas* (Gaull) (see above)
	3 Sep 1954 – 5 Feb 1955: *Jacques Chaban-Delmas* (Gaull) (see above)
Commerce and Industry	19 Jun – 2 Sep 1954: *Maurice Bourgès-Maunoury* (Rad Soc) (see Faure I)
	3 Sep 1954 – 5 Feb 1955: *Henri Ulver* (Gaull) (b. Paris 24 Mar 1901)
Health	19 Jun – 3 Sep 1954: *Louis Aujoulat* (Ind Rep) (see above)
	3 Sep 1954 – 5 Feb 1955: *André Monteil* (Rep Peoples Mov) (b. Juillac 15 Aug 1915)
Ex-Servicemen	19 Jun – 3 Sep 1954: *Emmanuel Temple* (Ind Rep) (see Pleven II)

	3 Sep 1954 – 5 Feb 1955: *Jean Masson* (Rad Soc) (b. Bayon 8 Sep 1907)
Agriculture	*Roger Houdet* (see Laniel)
Overseas Territories (from 3 Sep 1954: Development of Relations with Overseas Territories)	*Guy La Chambre* (see Daladier II)
Moroccan and Tunisian Affairs	*Christian Fouchet* (Gaull) (b. St Germain-en-Laye 17 Nov 1911; d. 12 Aug 1974)

23 Feb 1955 – 19 Jan 1956: Faure II

Prime Minister	*Edgar Faure* (Rad Soc) (for 2nd time) (see Queuille II)
Minister of State	23 Feb – 6 Oct 1955: *Gaston Palewski* (Gaull) (b. Paris 20 Mar 1901)
Foreign Affairs	*Antoine Pinay* (Ind Right/Farm) (see Pleven I)
Home Affairs	*Maurice Bourgès-Maunoury* (Rad Soc) (see Faure I)
Justice	*Robert Schuman* (Rep Peoples Mov) (see Bidault I)
Finance	*Pierre Pflimlin* (Rep Peoples Mov) (see Schuman I)
Reconstruction	*Roger Duchet* (Ind Rep) (see Pleven II)
Defence	23 Feb – 6 Oct 1955: *Pierre Koenig* (Gaull) (see Mendès-France)
	7 Oct 1955 – 19 Jan 1956: *Pierre Billotte* (Dissident Gaull) (b. Paris 8 Mar 1906)
Education	*Jean Bertholin* (Soc) (see Mendès-France)
Labour and Social Affairs	*Paul Bacon* (Rep Peoples Mov) (see Bidault II)
Public Works	*Edward Corniglion-Molinier* (Gaull) (see Laniel)
Commerce and Industry	*André Morice* (Rad Soc) (see Pleven II)
Mercantile Marine	*Paul Antier* (Farm) (see Pleven II)
Health and Population	*Bernard Lafay* (Rad Soc) (b. Malakoff 8 Sep 1905; d. Paris 13 Feb 1977)
Ex-Servicemen	23 Feb – 6 Oct 1955: *Raymond Triboulet* (Gaull) (b. Paris 3 Oct 1906)
	(?) Oct 1955 – 19 Jan 1956: *Vincent Badie* (b. Béziers 16 Jul 1902)
Agriculture	*Jean Sourbet* (Ind Right/Farm) (b. Morizès 1 Nov 1900)

Posts	*Édouard Bonnefous* (Dem Resist) (see Faure I)
Overseas	*Pierre Henri Teitgen* (Rep Peoples Mov) (see
Territories	de Gaulle I)
North Africa	*Pierre July* (ARS) (b. Vitry-le-François 9 Sep 1906)

31 Jan/2 Feb 1956 - 21 May/10 Jun 1957: Mollet

Prime Minister	*Guy Mollet* (Soc) (see Blum III)
Delegate Minister	*Félix Houphouet-Boigny* (Afr Dem) (b. Yamoussoukro, Ivory Coast, 10 May 1905)
Minister of State and Deputy Prime Minister	*Pierre Mendès-France* (Rad Soc) (see de Gaulle I)
Foreign Affairs	*Christian Pineau* (Soc) (see de Gaulle I)
Home Affairs	*Jean Gilbert-Jules* (Rad Soc) (b. Chaulnes 1 Sep 1903)
Justice	*François Mitterand* (Dem Resist) (see Ramadier I)
Finance and National Economy	2 - 9 Feb 1956: *Robert Lacoste* (Soc) (see de Gaulle I) 14 Feb 1956 - 10 Jun 1957: *Paul Ramadier* (Soc) (see Chautemps IV)
Defence	*Maurice Bourgès-Maunoury* (Rad Soc) (see Faure I)
Education	*René Billères* (Rad Soc) (b. Ger-près-Lourdes 29 Aug 1910)
Social Affairs	*Albert Gazier* (Soc) (see Pleven I)
Ex-Servicemen	*François Tanguy-Prigent* (Soc) (see de Gaulle I)
Overseas Territories	*Gaston Defferre* (Soc) (see Pleven I)
Algeria	2 - 9 Feb 1956: *Georges (Albert Julien) Catroux* (see de Gaulle I) 9 Feb 1956 - 10 Jun 1957: *Robert Lacoste* (Soc) (see de Gaulle I)
Without Portfolio	20 Feb 1956 - 10 Jun 1957: *Jacques Chaban-Delmas* (Gaull) (see Mendès-France)

11/13 Jun - 30 Sep 1957: Bourgès-Maunoury

Prime Minister	*Maurice Bourgès-Maunoury* (Rad Soc) (see Faure I)
Minister of State	*Félix Houphouet-Boigny* (Afr Dem) (see Mollet)
Foreign Affairs	*Christian Pineau* (Soc) (see de Gaulle I)
Home Affairs	*Jean Gilbert-Jules* (Rad Soc) (see Mollet)
Justice	*Edward Corniglion-Molinier* (Centre) (see Laniel)

Finance	*Félix Gaillard* (Rad Soc) (b. Paris 5 Nov 1919; d. off Jersey probably 9 Jul 1970)
Defence	*André Morice* (Rad Soc) (see Pleven II)
Education	*René Billères* (Rad Soc) (see Mollet)
Labour and Social Affairs	*Albert Gazier* (Soc) (see Pleven I)
Public Works	*Édouard Bonnefous* (Dem Resist) (see Faure I)
Overseas Territories	*Pierre-Olivier Lapie* (Soc) (see Pleven I)
Algeria and North Africa	*Robert Lacoste* (Soc) (see de Gaulle I)
Sahara (new post)	*Max Lejeune* (Soc) (see Blum III)

6 Nov 1957 – 15 Apr 1958: Gaillard

Prime Minister	*Félix Gaillard* (Rad Soc) (see Bourgès-Maunoury)
Foreign Affairs	*Christian Pineau* (Soc) (see de Gaulle I)
Home Affairs	*Maurice Bourgès-Maunoury* (Rad Soc) (see Faure I)
Justice and Constitutional and Electoral Reform	*Robert Lecourt* (Rep Peoples Mov) (see Marie)
Finance and National Economy	*Pierre Pflimlin* (Rep Peoples Mov) (see Schuman I)
Reconstruction	*Pierre Garet* (Ind) (see Pinay)
Defence	*Jacques Chaban-Delmas* (Gaull) (see Mendès-France)
Education	*René Billères* (Rad Soc) (see Mollet)
Labour and Social Affairs	*Paul Bacon* (Rep Peoples Mov) (see Bidault II)
Public Works	*Édouard Bonnefous* (Dem Resist) (see Faure I)
Agriculture	*Roland Boscary-Monsservin* (Ind) (b. Rodez 12 May 1904)
Industry and Commerce	*Paul Ribeyre* (Ind) (see Pleven II)
Overseas Territories	*Gérard Jaquet* (Soc) (b. Malakoff 12 Jan 1916)
Algeria	*Robert Lacoste* (Soc) (see de Gaulle I)
Sahara	*Max Lejeune* (Soc) (see Blum III)
Ex-Servicemen	*Antoine Quinson* (Left) (b. Béziers 12 Jun 1904)
Health	*Félix Houphouet-Boigny* (Afr Dem) (see Mollet)

205

14 - 28 May 1958: Pflimlin

Prime Minister	*Pierre Pflimlin* (Rep Peoples Mov) (see Schuman I)
Deputy Prime Minister	15 - 28 May 1958: *Guy Mollet* (Soc) (see Blum III)
Minister of State	*Félix Houphouet-Boigny* (Afr Dem) (see Mollet)
Foreign Affairs	*René Pleven* (Dem Resist) (see de Gaulle I)
Home Affairs	14 - 16 May 1958: *Maurice Faure* (Rad Soc) (b. Azeret 2 Jan 1922)
	16 - 28 May 1958: *Jules Moch* (Soc) (see Blum II)
Justice	*Robert Lecourt* (Rep Peoples Mov) (see Marie)
Finance	*Edgar Faure* (Rad Soc Splinter Group) (see Queuille II)
Reconstruction and Housing	14 - 27 May 1958: *Pierre Garet* (Ind) (see Pinay)
Defence	*Pierre, Comte de Chevigné* (Rep Peoples Mov) (b. Toulon 16 Jun 1909)
Education	*Jacques Bordeneuve* (Rad Soc) (b. Sainte-Livrade-sur-Lot 28 Aug 1908)
Labour and Social Affairs	*Paul Bacon* (Rep Peoples Mov) (see Bidault II)
Public Works	*Édouard Bonnefous* (Dem Resist) (see Faure I)
Agriculture	14 - 27 May 1958: *Roland Boscary-Monsservin* (Ind) (see Gaillard)
Industry and Commerce	14 - 27 May 1958: *Paul Ribeyre* (Ind) (see Pleven II)
Information	16 - 28 May 1958: *Albert Gazier* (Soc) (see Pleven I)
Overseas Territories	*André Colin* (Rep Peoples Mov) (see Queuille I)
Algeria	*André Mutter* (Ind) (see Laniel)
Sahara	*Edward Corniglion-Molinier* (Rad Soc Splinter Group) (see Laniel)
Ex-Servicemen	*Vincent Badie* (Dissident Rad Soc) (see Faure II)
Health	*André Maroselli* (Rad Soc) (see Ramadier I)
Without Portfolio	16 - 28 May 1958: *Max Lejeune* (Soc) (see Blum III)

1 Jun 1958 - 8 Jan 1959: de Gaulle III

Prime Minister	*Charles de Gaulle* (for 3rd time) (see Presidents)
Ministers of State	*Félix Houphouet-Boigny* (Afr Dem) (see Mollet)
	1 Jun 1958 - 6 Jan 1959: *Guy Mollet* (Soc) (see Blum III)
	Pierre Pflimlin (Rep Peoples Mov) (see Schuman I)
	Louis Jacquinot (Ind) (see de Gaulle I)

	7 Jul 1958 – 8 Jan 1959: *André Malraux* (see de Gaulle I)
Foreign Affairs	*Maurice Couve de Murville* (b. Reims 24 Jan 1907)
Home Affairs	*Emile Pelletier* (b. Saint-Brieuc 11 Feb 1898)
Justice	*Michel Debré* (Gaull) (b. Paris 15 Jan 1912)
Finance	*Antoine Pinay* (Farm) (see Pleven I)
Housing	4 – 9 Jun 1958 (acting:) *Michel Debré* (see above)
	9 Jun 1958 – 8 Jan 1959: *Pierre Sudreau* (b. Paris 13 May 1919)
Defence	2 Jun 1958 – 8 Jan 1959: *Charles de Gaulle* (see Presidents)
Army	*Pierre Guillaumat* (b. La Flèche 5 Aug 1909)
Education	*Jean Bertholin* (Rad Soc) (see Mendès-France)
Labour	2 Jun 1958 – 8 Jan 1959: *Paul Bacon* (Rep Peoples Mov) (see Bidault II)
Public Works	9 Jun 1958 – 8 Jan 1959: *Robert Buron* (Rep Peoples Mov) (see Pleven II)
National Economy	*Antoine Pinay* (Farm) (see Pleven I)
Agriculture	9 Jun 1958 – 8 Jan 1959: *Roger Houdet* (Ind) (see Laniel)
Industry and Commerce	2/9 Jun 1958 – 8 Jan 1959: *Édouard Ramonet* (Rad Soc) (b. Cerbère 14 Jun 1909)
Information	4 Jun – 7 Jul 1958: *André Malraux* (see de Gaulle I)
	7 Jul 1958 – 8 Jan 1959: *Jacques Soustelle* (Gaull) (see de Gaulle I)
Overseas Territories	4 Jun 1958 – 8 Jan 1959: *Bernard Cornut-Gentille* (UNR) (b. Brest 26 Jul 1909)
Algeria	5 Jun 1958 – 8 Jan 1959: *Charles de Gaulle* (see Presidents)
Ex-Servicemen	*Edmond Michelet* (Gaull) (see de Gaulle II)
Health	7 Jul 1958 – 8 Jan 1959: *Bernard Chenot* (b. Paris 20 May 1909)
Posts and Transport	9 Jun 1958 – 6 Jan 1959: *Eugène Thomas* (Soc) (see de Gaulle I)
Special Affairs	7 Jul 1958 – 8 Jan 1959: *André Boulloche* (b. Paris 7 Sep 1915)

8 Jan 1959 – 14 Apr 1962: Debré

Prime Minister	*Michel Debré* (UNR) (see de Gaulle III)
Minister Delegate (for Saharan Affairs and Atomic Energy)	8 Jan 1959 – 5 Feb 1960: *Jacques Soustelle* (UNR, Apr 1960 expelled) (see de Gaulle I)

Administration	24 Aug 1961 – 14 Apr 1962: *Louis Terrenoire* (UNR) (b. Lyons 10 Nov 1908)
Ministers of State	8 Jan – 30 Apr 1959: *Félix Houphouet-Boigny* (Afr Dem) (see Mollet)
	Louis Jacquinot (Ind) (see de Gaulle I)
	5 Feb 1960 – May 1961: *Roger Frey* (UNR) (b. Nouméa, New Caledonia, 11 Jun 1913)
	André Malraux (see de Gaulle I)
Minister of State (for Franco-African Community)	8 Jan 1959 – 5 Feb 1960: *Robert Lecourt* (Rep Peoples Mov) (see Marie)
Foreign Affairs	*Maurice Couve de Murville* (see de Gaulle III)
Home Affairs	8 Jan – 28 May 1959: *Jean Bertholin* (Rad Soc) (see Mendès-France)
	28 May 1959 – May 1961: *Pierre Chatenet* (b. Paris 6 Mar 1917)
	May 1961 – 14 Apr 1962: *Roger Frey* (UNR) (see above)
Justice	8 Jan 1959 – 24 Aug 1961: *Edmond Michelet* (UNR) (see de Gaulle II)
	24 Aug 1961 – 14 Apr 1962: *Bernard Chenot* (see de Gaulle III)
Finance and National Economy	8 Jan 1959 – 13 Jan 1960: *Antoine Pinay* (Farm) (see Pleven I)
	14 Jan 1960 – 18 Jan 1962: *Wilfrid Baumgartner* (b. Paris 21 May 1902)
Finance	18 Jan – 14 Apr 1962: *Valéry Giscard d'Estaing* (Ind) (see Presidents)
National Economy	18 Jan – 14 Apr 1962: *Michel Debré* (UNR) (see de Gaulle III)
Housing	*Pierre Sudreau* (see de Gaulle III)
Defence and Armed Forces	8 Jan 1959 – 8 Feb 1960: *Pierre Guillaumat* (see de Gaulle III)
	8 Feb 1960 – 14 Apr 1962: *Pierre Messmer* (b. Vincennes 20 Mar 1916)
Education	8 Jan – 23 Dec 1959: *André Boulloche* (see de Gaulle III)
	15 Jan – 22 Nov 1960: *Louis Joxe* (b. Bourg-la-Reine 15 Dec 1901)
	20 Feb 1961 – 14 Apr 1962: *Lucien Paye* (b. Vernoil-le-Fourrier 28 Jun 1907; d. 24 Apr 1972)
Labour	*Paul Bacon* (Rep Peoples Mov) (see Bidault II)

Public Works, Transport and Tourism	*Robert Buron* (Rep Peoples Mov) (see Pleven II)
Agriculture	8 Jan – 28 May 1959: *Roger Houdet* (Ind) (see Laniel)
	28 May 1959 – 24 Aug 1961: *Henri Rochereau* (b. Chantonnay 25 Mar 1908)
	24 Aug 1961 – 14 Apr 1962: *Edgar Pisani* (Dem Left) (b. Tunis 9 Oct 1918)
Information	8 Jan 1959 – 5 Feb 1960: *Roger Frey* (see above)
	5 Feb 1960 – 24 Aug 1961: *Louis Terrenoire* (UNR) (see above)
	24 Aug 1961 – 14 Apr 1962: State Secretariat under chairmanship of *Christian Lunet de la Malène* (UNR) (b. Nîmes 5 Dec 1920)
Overseas Territories and Sahara	8 Jan 1959 – 5 Feb 1960: *Jacques Soustelle* (UNR) (see de Gaulle I)
	5 Feb 1960 – 24 Aug 1961: *Robert Lecourt* (Rep Peoples Mov) (see Marie)
	24 Aug 1961: State Secretariat under chairmanship of *Jean, Prince de Broglie* (Ind Right) (b. Paris 21 Jun 1921; d. (murdered) 24 Dec 1976)
Algeria	22 Nov 1960 – 14 Apr 1962: *Louis Joxe* (see above)
Relations within French Union	5 Feb 1960 – 19 May 1961: *Jean Foyer* (UNR) (b. Coutigné 27 Apr 1921)
Co-operation with African States (new post)	19 May 1961 – 14 Apr 1962: *Jean Foyer* (UNR) (see above)
Ex-Servicemen	*Raymond Triboulet* (UNR) (see Faure II)
Industry and Commerce	*Jean-Marcel Jeanneney* (b. Paris 13 Nov 1910)
Health	8 Jan 1959 – 24 Aug 1961: *Bernard Chenot* (UNR) (see de Gaulle III)
	24 Aug 1961 – 14 Apr 1962: *Joseph Fontanet* (Rep Peoples Mov) (b. Frontenex 9 Feb 1921)
Posts and Transport	8 Jan 1959 – 5 Feb 1960: *Bernard Cornut-Gentille* (UNR) (see de Gaulle III)
	5 Feb 1960 – 14 Apr 1962: *Michel Maurice-Bokanowski* (UNR) (b. Paris 6 Nov 1912)

15/27 Apr – 5 Oct 1962: Pompidou I

Prime Minister	*Georges Pompidou* (UNR) (for 1st time) (see Presidents)

Minister of State (for Co-operation with African States)	27 Apr – 16 May 1962: *Pierre Pflimlin* (Rep Peoples Mov) (see Schuman I) 16 May – 5 Oct 1962: *Georges Gorse*
Minister of State (for Algeria)	*Louis Joxe* (see Debré)
Minister of State (for Culture)	*André Malraux* (see de Gaulle I)
Minister of State (for Research)	*Gaston Palewski* (UNR) (see Faure II)
Regional Planning	27 Apr – 16 May 1962: *Maurice Schumann* (UNR) (b. Paris 10 Apr 1911)
Foreign Affairs	*Maurice Couve de Murville* (see de Gaulle III)
Home Affairs	*Roger Frey* (UNR) (see Debré)
Justice	*Jean Foyer* (UNR) (see Debré)
Finance and National Economy	*Valéry Giscard d'Estaing* (Ind) (see Presidents)
Housing	*Jacques Maziol* (UNR) (b. Aurillac 13 Jan 1918)
Defence	*Pierre Messmer* (see Debré)
Education	27 Apr – Oct 1962: *Pierre Sudreau* (see de Gaulle III) 16 Oct – 14 Dec 1962 (acting:) *Louis Joxe* (see Debré)
Labour	27 Apr – 16 May 1962: *Paul Bacon* (Rep Peoples Mov) (see Bidault II) 16 May – 5 Oct 1962: *Gilbert Grandval* (Gaull) (b. Paris 12 Feb 1904)
Public Works	27 Apr – 16 May 1962: *Robert Buron* (Rep Peoples Mov) (see Pleven II) 16 May – 5 Oct 1962: *Roger Dusseaulx* (UNR) (b. Paris 18 Jul 1913)
Agriculture	*Edgar Pisani* (Dem Left) (see Debré)
Information	27 Apr – 10 Sep 1962: *Alain Peyrefitte* (UNR) (b. Paris 26 Aug 1925) 10 Sep – 5 Oct 1962: *Christian Fouchet* (see Mendès-France)
Overseas Territories	*Louis Jacquinot* (see de Gaulle I)
Overseas Refugees (new post)	10 Sep – 5 Oct 1962: *Alain Peyrefitte* (UNR) (see above)
Ex-Servicemen	*Raymond Triboulet* (UNR) (see Faure II)
Commerce and Industry	*Michel Maurice-Bokanowski* (UNR) (see Debré)
Health	27 Apr – 16 May 1962: *Joseph Fontanet* (Rep Peoples

Mov) (see Debré)
16 May – 5 Oct 1962: *Raymond Marcellin* (Ind) (b.
Sézanne 19 Aug 1914)
Posts and Transport   *Jacques Marette* (UNR)

14 Dec 1962 – 9 Jan 1966: Pompidou II

Prime Minister	*Georges Pompidou* (for 2nd time) (see Presidents)
Minister of State (for Overseas)	*Louis Jacquinot* (see de Gaulle I)
Minister of State (for Cultural Affairs)	*André Malraux* (see de Gaulle I)
Minister of State (for Science)	*Gaston Palewski* (UNR) (see Faure II)
Minister of State (for Administrative Reform)	*Louis Joxe* (see Debré)
Foreign Affairs	*Maurice Couve de Murville* (see de Gaulle III)
Home Affairs	*Roger Frey* (UNR) (see Debré)
Justice	*Jean Foyer* (UNR) (see Debré)
Finance and National Economy	*Valéry Giscard d'Estaing* (Ind) (see Presidents)
Housing	*Jacques Maziol* (UNR) (see Pompidou I)
Defence	*Pierre Messmer* (see Debré)
Education	*Christian Fouchet* (see Mendès-France)
Labour	*Gilbert Grandval* (Gaull) (see Pompidou I)
Public Works	*Marc Jacquet* (see Laniel)
Agriculture	*Edgar Pisani* (Dem Left) (see Debré)
Information	*Alain Peyrefitte* (UNR) (see Pompidou I)
Co-operation with African States	*Raymond Triboulet* (UNR) (see Faure II)
Overseas Refugees	14 Dec 1962 – 22 Jul 1964: *François Missoffe* (UNR) (b. Toulon 13 Oct 1919) 22 Jul 1964: ministry abolished
Ex-Servicemen	*Jean Sainteny* (b. Paris 29 May 1907)
Industry	*Michel Maurice-Bokanowski* (UNR) (see Debré)
Health	*Raymond Marcellin* (Ind) (see Pompidou I)
Posts and Transport	*Jacques Marette* (UNR) (see Pompidou I)

9 Jan 1966 – 1 Apr 1967: Pompidou III

Prime Minister	*Georges Pompidou* (for 3rd time) (see Presidents)
Minister Delegate (for Economic Research, Atomic and Space Affairs)	*Alain Peyrefitte* (see Pompidou I)
Minister of State (for Overseas Territories)	*Pierre Billotte* (see Faure II)
Minister of State (for Cultural Affairs)	*André Malraux* (see de Gaulle I)
Minister of State (for Administrative Reform)	*Louis Joxe* (see Debré)
Foreign Affairs	*Maurice Couve de Murville* (see de Gaulle III)
Home Affairs	*Roger Frey* (UNR) (see Debré)
Justice	*Jean Foyer* (UNR) (see Debré)
Finance and National Economy	*Michel Debré* (UNR) (see de Gaulle III)
Defence	*Pierre Messmer* (see Debré)
Education	*Christian Fouchet* (see Mendès-France)
Supply, Public Works and Transport	*Edgar Pisani* (Dem Left) (see Debré)
Labour, Health and Social Affairs	*Jean-Marcel Jeanneney* (see Debré)
Agriculture	*Edgar Faure* (Rad Soc) (see Queuille II)
Information	*Yvon Bourges* (b. Paris 29 Jun 1921)
Ex-Servicemen	*Alexandre Sanguinetti* (b. Cairo 27 Mar 1913)
Industry	*Raymond Marcellin* (Ind) (see Pompidou I)
Youth and Sport	*François Missoffe* (UNR) (see Pompidou II)
Posts and Telecommunications	*Jacques Marette* (UNR) (see Pompidou I)

6/8 Apr 1967 – 1 Jun 1968: Pompidou IV

Prime Minister	*Georges Pompidou* (UDR : UNR) (for 4th time) (see Presidents)

Minister Delegate (for Regional Planning)	*Raymond Marcellin* (UDR : Ind Rep) (see Pompidou I)
Minister of State (for Cultural Affairs)	*André Malraux* (see de Gaulle I)
Minister of State (for Public Administration)	*Edmond Michelet* (UDR : UNR) (see de Gaulle II)
Minister of State (for Overseas Affairs)	*Pierre Billotte* (UDR : UNR) (see Faure II)
Minister of State (for Scientific Research)	*Maurice Schumann* (UDR) (see Pompidou I)
Minister of State (for Parliamentary Affairs)	*Roger Frey* (UDR : UNR) (see Debré)
Foreign Affairs	*Maurice Couve de Murville* (see de Gaulle III)
Home Affairs	*Christian Fouchet* (UDR : UNR) (see Mendès-France)
Justice	*Louis Joxe* (UDR) (see Debré)
Finance and National Economy	*Michel Debré* (UDR : UNR) (see de Gaulle III)
Supply, Housing and Public Works	*Edgar Pisani* (Dem Left) (see Debré)
Transport	*Jean Chamant* (UDR : Ind Rep) (b. Chagny 23 Nov 1913)
Defence	*Pierre Messmer* (see Debré)
Education	*Alain Peyrefitte* (UDR : UNR) (see Pompidou I)
Social Affairs	*Jean-Marcel Jeanneney* (see Debré)
Industry	*Olivier, Baron Guichard* (UDR : UNR) (b. Néac 27 Jul 1920)
Agriculture	*Edgar Faure* (Rad Soc) (see Queuille iI)
Information	*Georges Gorse* (UDR) (b. Cahors 15 Feb 1915)
Ex-Servicemen	*Henri Duvillard* (UDR : UNR) (b. Luxeuil-les-Bains 3 Nov 1910)
Youth and Sport	*François Missoffe* (UDR : UNR) (see Pompidou II)
Posts and Tele-communications	*Yves Guéna* (UDR : UNR) (b. Brest 6 Jul 1922)

213

1 Jun – 10 Jul 1968: Pompidou V

Prime Minister	*Georges Pompidou* (UDR : UNR) (for 5th time) (see Presidents)
Minister Delegate (for Regional Planning)	*Olivier, Baron, Guichard* (UDR : UNR) (see Pompidou IV)
Ministers of State	*Edmond Michelet* (UDR : UNR) (see de Gaulle II) *Henri Rey* (UDR : UNR) (b. Pont-Aven 2 Nov 1903)
Minister of State (for Cultural Affairs)	*André Malraux* (see de Gaulle I)
Minister of State (for Social Questions)	*Maurice Schumann* (UDR : UNR) (see Pompidou I)
Foreign Affairs	*Michel Debré* (UDR : UNR) (see de Gaulle III)
Home Affairs	*Raymond Marcellin* (UDR : Ind Rep) (see Pompidou I)
Justice	*René Capitant* (UDR : UDT) (see de Gaulle I)
Finance and National Economy	*Maurice Couve de Murville* (see de Gaulle III)
Supply and Housing	*Robert Galley* (b. Paris 11 Jan 1921)
Transport	*Jean Chamant* (UDR : Ind Rep) (see Pompidou IV)
Defence	*Pierre Messmer* (UDR : UNR) (see Debré)
Education	*François-Xavier Ortoli* (UDR : UNR) (b. Ajaccio 16 Feb 1925)
Public Administration	*Robert Boulin* (UDR : UNR) (b. Villandraut 20 Jul 1920)
Agriculture	*Edgar Faure* (Rad Soc) (see Queuille II)
Information	*Yves Guéna* (UDR : UNR) (see Pompidou IV)
Ex-Servicemen	*Henri Duvillard* (UDR : UNR) (see Pompidou IV)
Overseas Departments and Territories	*Joël le Theule* (UDR : UNR) (b. Sablé-sur-Sarthe 22 Mar 1930)
Industry	*Albin Chalandon* (UDR : UNR) (b. Reyrieux 11 Jun 1920)
Science, Atomic and Space Affairs	*Christian Lunet de la Malène* (UDR : UNR) (see Debré)
Youth and Sport	*Roland Nungesser* (UNR) (b. Nogent-sur-Marne 9 Oct 1925)
Posts and Telecommunications	*André Bettencourt* (Ind Rep) (b. Saint-Maurice d'Ételan 21 Apr 1919)

13 Jul 1968 – 20 Jun 1969: Couve de Murville

Prime Minister	*Maurice Couve de Murville* (UDR) (see de Gaulle III)
Minister Delegate (for Planning)	*Olivier, Baron Guichard* (UDR) (see Pompidou IV)
Minister Delegate (for Scientific Research, Atomic and Space Affairs)	*Robert Galley* (UDR) (see Pompidou V)
Minister of State	*Jean-Marcel Jeanneney* (UDR) (see Debré)
Minister of State (for Cultural Affairs)	*André Malraux* (see de Gaulle I)
Minister of State (for Social Questions)	*Maurice Schumann* (UDR) (see Pompidou I)
Minister of State (for Parliamentary Relations)	*Roger Frey* (UDR) (see Debré)
Foreign Affairs	*Michel Debré* (UDR) (see de Gaulle III)
Home Affairs	*Raymond Marcellin* (Ind Rep) (see Pompidou I)
Justice	13 Jul 1968 – 28 Apr 1969: *René Capitant* (UDR) (see de Gaulle I)
	28 Apr – 20 Jun 1969: *Jean-Marcel Jeanneney* (UDR) (see Debré)
Finance and National Economy	*François-Xavier Ortoli* (UDR) (see Pompidou V)
Industry	*Albin Chalandon* (UDR) (see Pompidou V)
Transport	*Jean Chamant* (Ind Rep) (see Pompidou IV)
Defence	*Pierre Messmer* (UDR) (see Debré)
Education	*Edgar Faure* (Ind Rep) (see Queuille II)
Public Administration	*Philippe Malaud* (Ind Rep) (b. Paris 1925)
Agriculture	*Robert Boulin* (UDR) (see Pompidou V)
Information	*Joël le Theule* (UDR) (see Pompidou V)
Ex-Servicemen	*Henri Duvillard* (UDR) (see Pompidou IV)
Overseas Departments and Territories	*Michel Inchauspé* (UDR)
Industry	*André Bettencourt* (UDR) (see Pompidou V)
Youth and Sport	*Joseph Comiti* (UDR) (b. Sotta, Corsica, 1920)

Posts and Tele- communications	*Yves Guéna* (UDR) (see Pompidou IV)

24 Jun 1969 – 5 Jul 1972: Chaban-Delmas

Prime Minister	*Jacques Chaban-Delmas* (UDR) (see Mendès-France)
Minister Delegate (for Planning)	*André Bettencourt* (Ind Rep) (see Pompidou V)
Minister Delegate (for Overseas Departments and Territories	24 Jun 1969 – 25 Feb 1971: *Henri Rey* (UDR) (see Pompidou V) 25 Feb 1971 – 5 Jul 1972: *Pierre Messmer* (UDR) (see Debré)
Minister of State (for Defence)	*Michel Debré* (UDR) (see de Gaulle III)
Minister of State (for Cultural Affairs)	24 Jun 1969 – 9 Oct 1970: *Edmond Michelet* (UDR) (see de Gaulle II) 7 Jan 1971 – 5 Jul 1972: *Jacques Duhamel* (PDM) (b. Paris 24 Sep 1924; d. Jul 1977)
Minister of State (for Parlia- mentary Affairs)	24 Jun 1969 – 7 Jan 1971: *Roger Frey* (UDR) (see Debré) 7 Jan 1971 – 5 Jul 1972: *Jacques René Chirac* (b. Paris 29 Nov 1932)
Minister of State (for Administr- ative Reform)	7 Jan 1971 – 5 Jul 1972: *Roger Frey* (UDR) (see Debré)
Minister Delegate (for Protection of Nature and Environment)	7 Jan 1971 – 5 Jul 1972: *Robert Poujade* (UDR) (b. Moulins 6 May 1928)
Foreign Affairs	*Maurice Schumann* (UDR) (see Pompidou I)
Home Affairs	*Raymond Marcellin* (Ind Rep) (see Pompidou I)
Justice	*René Pleven* (PDM) (see de Gaulle I)
Finance and National Economy	*Valéry Giscard d'Estaing* (Ind Rep) (see Debré)
Housing and Capital Investment	*Albin Chalandon* (UDR) (see Pompidou V)
Labour, Employment and Population	*Joseph Fontanet* (PDM) (see Debré)
Transport	24 Jun 1969 – 31 Dec 1970: *Raymond Mondon* (Ind Rep) (b. Ancy 8 Mar 1914; d. Metz 31 Dec 1970) 7 Jan 1971 – 5 Jul 1972: *Jean Chamant* (Ind Rep) (see Pompidou IV)

Education	*Olivier, Baron Guichard* (UDR) (see Pompidou IV)
Technical Development	*Francois-Xavier Ortoli* (UDR) (see Pompidou V)
Health and Social Insurance	*Robert Boulin* (UDR) (see Pompidou V)
Agriculture	24 Jun 1969 – 7 Jan 1971: *Jacques Duhamel* (PDM) (see above) 7 Jan 1971 – 5 Jul 1972: *Michel Cointat* (UDR) (b. Paris 13 Apr 1921)
Ex-Servicemen	*Henri Duvillard* (UDR) (see Pompidou IV)
Posts and Telecommunications	*Robert Galley* (UDR) (see Pompidou V)

6 Jul 1972 – 28 Mar 1973: Messmer I

Prime Minister	*Pierre Messmer* (UDR) (for 1st time) (see Debré)
Minister of State (for National Defence)	*Michel Debré* (UDR) (see de Gaulle III)
Minister of State (for Foreign Affairs)	*Edgar Faure* (UDR) (see Queuille II)
Minister Delegate (for Relations with Parliament)	*Robert Boulin* (UDR) (see Pompidou V)
Minister Delegate (for Protection of Nature and Environment)	*Robert Poujade* (UDR) (see Chaban-Delmas)
Minister Delegate (for Foreign Affairs)	*André Bettencourt* (Ind Rep) (see Pompidou V)
Foreign Affairs	*Maurice Schumann* (UDR) (see Pompidou I)
Home Affairs (Interior)	*Raymond Marcellin* (Ind Rep) (see Pompidou I)
Justice	*René Pleven* (CDP) (see de Gaulle I)
Finance and National Economy	*Valéry Giscard d'Estaing* (Ind Rep) (see Presidents)
Equipment, Housing and Aménagement du Territoire	*Olivier, Baron Guichard* (UDR) (see Pompidou IV)
Transport	*Robert Galley* (UDR) (see Pompidou V)

217

Education	*Joseph Fontanet* (CDP) (see Debré)
Industrial and Scientific Development	*Jean Charbonnel* (UDR) (b. La Fère 22 Apr 1927)
Agriculture and Rural Development	*Jacques René Chirac* (UDR) (see Chaban-Delmas)
Cultural Affairs	*Jacques Duhamel* (CDP) (see Chaban-Delmas)
Public Health	*Jean Foyer* (UDR) (see Debré)
Ex-Servicemen	*André Bord* (UDR) (b. Saint-Marien 31 Dec 1914)
Posts and Tele-communications	*Hubert Jean Louis Germain* (UDR) (b. Paris 6 Aug 1920)
Trade, Craftsmen and Small Businesses	*Yvon Bourges* (UDR) (see Pompidou III)

2 Apr 1973 – 27 Feb 1974: Messmer II

Prime Minister	*Pierre Messmer* (UDR) (for 2nd time) (see Debré)
Foreign Affairs	*Michel Jobert* (b. Meknès 11 Sep 1921)
Interior	*Raymond Marcellin* (Ind Rep) (see Pompidou I)
Justice	*Jean Taittinger* (UDR) (see Messmer I)
Finance and National Economy	*Valéry Giscard d'Estaing* (Ind Rep) (see Debré)
Armed Forces	*Robert Galley* (UDR) (see Pompidou V)
Equipment, Housing, Tourism and Aménagement du Territoire	*Olivier, Baron Guichard* (UDR) (see Pompidou IV)
Transport	*Yves Guéna* (UDR) (see Pompidou IV)
Education	*Joseph Fontanet* (CDP) (see Debré)
Industrial and Scientific Development	*Jean Charbonnel* (UDR) (see Messmer I)
Agriculture and Rural Development	*Jacques René Chirac* (UDR) (see Chaban-Delmas)
Cultural Affairs	*Maurice Samuel Roger Charles Druon* (no party) (b. Paris 23 Apr 1918)
Public Health and Social Security	*Prince Michel Casimir Poniatowski* (Ind Rep) (b. Paris 16 May 1922)
Administrative Reform	*Alain Peyrefitte* (UDR) (see Pompidou I)
Ex-Servicemen	*André Bord* (UDR) (see Messmer I)

Posts and Tele- communications	*Hubert Jean Louis Germain* (UDR) (see Messmer I)
Commerce, Handi- crafts and Small Businesses	*Jean Royer* (see Debré)
Information	2 Apr – 23 Oct 1973: *Philippe Malaud* (Ind Rep) (see Couve de Murville) 23 Oct 1973 – 27 Feb 1974: *Jean-Philippe Lecat* (UDR) (b. Dijon 29 Jul 1935)
Relations with Parliament	*Joseph Comiti* (UDR) (see Couve de Murville)
Labour, Employment and Population	*Georges Gorse* (UDR) (see Pompidou IV)
Protection of Nature and Environment	*Robert Poujade* (UDR) (see Chaban-Delmas)
Overseas Depart- ments and Territories	*Bernard Paul Raymond Stasi* (CDP) (b. Reims 4 Jul 1930)

1 Mar – 28 May 1974: Messmer III

Prime Minister	*Pierre Messmer* (UDR) (for 3rd time) (see Debré)
Foreign Affairs	*Michel Jobert* (no party) (see Messmer II)
Interior	*Jacques René Chirac* (UDR) (see Chaban-Delmas)
Justice	*Jean Taittinger* (UDR) (b. Paris 25 Jan 1923)
Finance and National Economy	*Valéry Giscard d'Estaing* (Ind Rep) (see Presidents)
Armed Forces	*Robert Galley* (UDR) (see Pompidou V)
Regional Develop- ment, Equipment and Transport	*Olivier, Baron Guichard* (UDR) (see Pompidou IV)
Education	*Joseph Fontanet* (CDP) (see Debré)
Agriculture and Rural Develop- ment	*Raymond Marcellin* (Ind Rep) (see Pompidou I)
Cultural Affairs and Environment	*Alain Peyrefitte* (UDR) (see Pompidou I)
Industry, Commerce, and Handicrafts and Small Businesses	*Yves Guéna* (UDR) (see Pompidou IV)

219

Relations with Parliament	*Hubert Jean Louis Germain* (UDR) (see Messmer I)
Labour, Employment and Population	*Georges Gorse* (UDR) (see Pompidou IV)
Public Health and Social Security	*Prince Michel Casimir Poniatowski* (Ind Rep) (see Messmer II)
Posts and Tele- communications	1 Mar – 12 Apr 1974: *Jean Royer* (see Debré) 12 Apr – 28 May 1974 (acting:) *Hubert Jean Louis Germain* (UDR) (see Messmer I)
Information	*Jean-Philippe Lecat* (UDR) (see Messmer II)

from 28 May 1974: Chirac

Prime Minister	*Jacques René Chirac* (UDR) (see Chaban-Delmas)
Foreign Affairs	*Jean Victor Sauvagnargues* (no party) (b. Paris 2 Apr 1915)
Interior	*Prince Michel Casimir Poniatowski* (Ind Rep) (see Messmer II)
Justice	*Jean Adrien François Lecanuet* (Centre Dem) (b. Rouen 4 Mar 1920)
Finance and National Economy	*Jean Pierre Fourcade* (Ind Rep) (b. Marmande 18 Oct 1929)
Defence	28 May 1974 – 31 Jan 1975: *Jacques Lucien Soufflet* (UDR) (b. Lesboeuf 4 Oct 1912) from 31 Jan 1975: *Yvon Bourges* (UDR) (see Pompidou III)
Reforms (new post)	28 May – 9 Jun 1974: *Jean Jacques Servan-Schreiber* (Rad) (b. Paris 13 Feb 1924) from 9 Jun 1974: no appointment made
Education	*René Jean Haby* (no party) (b. Dombasle 9 Oct 1919)
Co-operation	*Pierre Abelin* (Centre Dem) (b. Poitiers 16 May 1909)
Supply	*Robert Galley* (UDR) (see Pompidou V)
Agriculture	*Christian Bonnet* (Ind Rep) (b. Paris 14 Jun 1921)
Quality of Life (new post)	*André Jarrot* (UDR) (b. Lux 13 Dec 1909)
Labour	*Michel André François Durafour* (Réform) (b. Saint-Étienne 11 Apr 1920)
Health	*Simone Annie Veil* (no party) (b. Nice 13 Jul 1927)
Industry (from 5 Jun 1974: and Research)	*Michel, Comte d'Ornano* (Ind Rep) (b. Paris 12 Jul 1924)

| Commerce, Handicrafts and Small Businesses | *Vincent Ansquer* (UDR) (b. Treize-Septiers 11 Jan 1925) |

Fulani Emirates

For the emirates of Gwandu and Sokoto see vol. 1.

Gabon

| 28 Nov 1958 | Member of French Community |
| 17 Aug 1960 | Left French Community |

HEADS OF STATE

Presidents

17 Aug 1960	*Léon M'ba* (for 1st time) (b. Libreville 9 Feb 1902; d. Paris 28 Nov 1967)
18 Feb 1964	*Jean-Hilaire Aubame* (b. 10 Nov 1912)
20 Feb 1964 – 28 Nov 1967	*Léon M'ba* (for 2nd time) (see above)
from 3 Dec 1967	*Albert Bernard Bongo* (from Oct 1973: *Omar Bongo*) (b. Lewai, Franceville, 30 Dec 1935)

HEADS OF GOVERNMENT

Prime Ministers

| 27 Feb 1959 | *Léon M'ba* (see Presidents) |
| from 17 Aug 1960 | President also Head of Cabinet |

Gambia

3 Oct 1963	Internal self-government
18 Feb 1965	Independence from Great Britain
24 Apr 1970	Republic

HEADS OF STATE

Governor

1962	*Sir John (Warburton) Paul* (b. 29 Mar 1916)

Governors-General

18 Feb 1965	*Sir John (Warburton) Paul* (previously Governor)
9 Feb 1966 – 24 Apr 1970	*Al-Haji Sir Farimang (Mohamadu) Singateh* (b. 30 Nov 1912)

President

from 24 Apr 1970	*Sir Dauda Kairaba Jawara* (b. Barajally, MacCarthey Island, 11 May 1924)

HEAD OF GOVERNMENT

Prime Minister

from 3 Oct 1963	*Sir Dauda Kairaba Jawara* (see President)

German Democratic Republic

HEADS OF STATE

Presidents

11 Oct 1949	*Wilhelm Pieck* (b. Guben 3 Jan 1876; d. Berlin 7 Sep 1960)
12 Sep 1960 – 1 Aug 1973	*Walter Ernst Karl Ulbricht* (b. Leipzig 30 Jun 1893; d. 1 Aug 1973)
from 3 Oct 1973	*Willi Stoph* (b. Berlin 8 Jul 1914)

MEMBERS OF GOVERNMENT

11 Oct 1949 – 8 Nov 1950: Grotewohl I (National Front)

Prime Minister	*Otto Grotewohl* (SED) (for 1st time) (b. Brunswick 11 Mar 1894; d. Berlin 21 Sep 1964)
Deputy Prime Ministers	*Walter Ernst Karl Ulbricht* (SED) (see Presidents)
	Hermann Kastner (LDP) (b. Berlin 25 Oct 1886; d. Munich 6 Sep 1957)
	Otto Nuschke (CDU) (b. Frohburg 23 Sep 1883; d. Berlin 27 Dec 1957)
Foreign Affairs	*Georg Dertinger* (CDU) (b. Berlin 25 Dec 1902; d. Leipzig 21 Jan 1968)
Home Affairs	*Karl Steinhoff* (SED) (b. Herford 24 Nov 1892)
Finance	*Hans Loch* (LDP) (b. Cologne 2 Nov 1898; d. Berlin 13 Jul 1960)
Education	*Paul Wandel* (SED) (b. Mannheim 6 Feb 1905)
Industry	*Fritz Selbmann* (SED) (b. Lauterbach 29 Sep 1899)
Planning	*Heinrich Rau* (SED) (b. Stuttgart 2 Apr 1899; d. Berlin 23 Mar 1961)
Trade and Materials	*Georg Handke* (SED) (b. Hanau 22 Apr 1894; d. Berlin 7 Sep 1962)
Supply	*Karl Hamann* (LPD) (b. Hildesheim 4 Mar 1903)
Reconstruction	*Lothar Bolz* (NDP) (b. Gleiwitz 3 Sep 1903)
Labour and Health	*Luitpold Steidle* (CDU) (b. Ulm 12 Mar 1898)
Justice	*Max Fechner* (SED) (b. Berlin 27 Jul 1892)

223

Post and Tele-communications	*Friedrich Burmeister* (CDU) (b. Wittenberge 24 Mar 1888; d. Berlin 25 Jul 1968)
Transport	*Hans Reingruber* (b. Wuppertal 30 Apr 1888; d. Dresden 14 Jan 1964)
Land and Forestry	*Ernst Goldenbaum* (Dem Peasants) (b. Parchim 15 Dec 1898)
Public Security (new post)	17 Feb – 8 Nov 1950: *Wilhelm Zaisser* (SED) (b. Rotthausen 20 Jun 1893; d. Berlin night of 2/3 Mar 1958)
Information (new post)	19 Sep 1949 – 8 Nov 1950: *Gerhard Eisler* (SED) (b. Leipzig 20 Feb 1887; d. Armenia 21 Mar 1968)

15 Nov 1950 – 3 Dec 1958: Grotewohl II

Prime Minister	*Otto Grotewohl* (SED) (for 2nd time) (see Grotewohl I)
Deputy Prime Ministers	*Walter Ernst Karl Ulbricht* (SED) (see Presidents) from 3 Dec 1955 First Deputy Prime Minister
	Heinrich Rau (SED) (see Grotewohl I)
	15 Nov 1950 – 27 Dec 1957: *Otto Nuschke* (CDU) (see Grotewohl I)
	10 Feb – 3 Dec 1958: *Max Sefrin* (CDU) (b. Stambach 21 Nov 1913)
	Hans Loch (LDP) (see Grotewohl I)
	Lothar Bolz (NDP) (see Grotewohl I)
	Paul Scholz (Dem Peasants) (b. Braunau 2 Oct 1902)
	19 Nov 1954 – 3 Dec 1958: *Willi Stoph* (SED) (see Presidents)
	26 Nov 1955 – 15 Feb 1958: *Fred Oelssner* (SED) (b. Weissenfels 27 Feb 1903)
	26 Nov 1955 – 24 Sep 1958: *Fritz Selbmann* (SED) (see Grotewohl I)
	3 Dec 1955 – 3 Dec 1958: *Bruno Leuschner* (SED) (b. Berlin 12 Aug 1913; d. East Berlin 10 Feb 1965)
Administrative Co-ordination	23 May – 20 Jul 1952: *Herbert Stampfer* (SED)
	20 Jul 1952 – 18 Feb 1954: *Werner Eggerath* (SED) (b. Elberfeld 16 Mar 1900)
Cultural Co-ordination	3 Jul 1952 – 29 Jan 1954: *Paul Wandel* (SED) (see Grotewohl I)
Co-ordination of Internal Trade	*Herbert Stampfer* (SED) (see above)
Head of Planning Commission	23 May 1952 – 3 Dec 1958: *Bruno Leuschner* (SED) (see above) from Apr 1957 Chairman of

Council of Ministers

Central Commission for Audit	15 Nov 1950 – 19 Nov 1954: *Fritz Lange* (SED) (b. Berlin 23 Nov 1898)
Foreign Affairs	15 Nov 1950 – 15 Jan 1953: *Georg Dertinger* (CDU) (see Grotewohl I)
	23 Jan – 1 Oct 1953 (acting:) *Anton Ackermann* (SED) (b. Thalheim 25 Dec 1905)
	1 Oct 1953 – 3 Dec 1958: *Lothar Bolz* (NDP) (see Grotewohl I)
Home Affairs	15 Nov 1950 – 6 May 1952: *Karl Steinhoff* (SED) (see Grotewohl I)
	6/10 May 1952 – 1 Jul 1955: *Willi Stoph* (SED) (see Presidents)
	1 Jul 1955 – 3 Dec 1958: *Karl Maron* (SED) (b. Berlin 27 Apr 1903)
Public Security	15 Nov 1950 – 24 Jul 1953: *Wilhelm Zaisser* (SED) (see Grotewohl I)
	24 Jul 1953 – 26 Nov 1955: State Secretariat in Home Affairs Ministry
	26 Nov 1955 – 31 Oct 1957: *Ernst (Friedrich) Wollweber* (SED) (b. Hannoversch-Münden 28 Oct 1898; d. Berlin 3 May 1967)
	31 Oct 1957 – 3 Dec 1958: *Erich Mielke* (SED) (b. Berlin 28 Dec 1907)
Defence (new post created 18 Jan 1956)	21 Jan 1956 – 3 Dec 1958: *Willi Stoph* (SED) (see Presidents)
Finance	15 Nov 1950 – 26 Nov 1955: *Hans Loch* (LDP) (see Grotewohl I)
	26 Nov 1955 – 3 Dec 1958: *Willy Rumpf* (SED) (b. Berlin 4 Apr 1903)
Education	15 Nov 1950 – 3 Jul 1952: *Paul Wandel* (SED) (see Grotewohl I)
	3 Jul 1952 – 5 Nov 1953: *Else Zaisser* (SED) (b. Essen 1904)
	5 Nov 1953 – 19 Nov 1954: *Hans Joachim Laabs* (SED) (b. Kolberg 1922)
	19 Nov 1954 – 3 Dec 1958: *Fritz Lange* (SED) (see above)
Culture (new post)	8 Jan 1954 – 11 Oct 1958: *Johannes Robert Becher* (SED) (b. Munich 22 May 1891; d. Berlin 11 Oct 1958)
Pan-German Affairs	26 Nov 1955 – 3 Dec 1958: *Hans Loch* (LDP) (see Grotewohl I)

Heavy Industry	15 Nov 1950 – 26 Nov 1955: *Fritz Selbmann* (SED) (see Grotewohl I)
	26 Nov 1955: Ministry divided into Mining and Metallurgy, Chemical Industry, and Coal and Energy (see below)
Mining and Metal-lurgy (new post)	26 Nov 1955 – 31 Jul 1958: *Rudolf Steinwand* (SED)
	31 Jul 1958: post abolished
Chemical Industry (new post created 26 Nov 1955)	14 Jun 1956 – 31 Jul 1958: *Werner Winkler* (b. 27 Dec 1913)
	31 Jul 1958: post abolished
Coal and Energy (new post)	26 Nov 1955 – 31 Jul 1958: *Richard Goschutz* (SED) (b. Königshütte 12 Oct 1912)
	31 Jul 1958: post abolished
Nuclear Research	10 Nov 1955 – 3 Dec 1958: *Willi Stoph* (SED) (see Presidents)
Mechanical Engineer-ing	15 Nov 1950 – 19 Dec 1952: *Gerhard Ziller* (SED) (b. Dresden 19 Apr 1912; d. 14 Dec 1957)
	19 Dec 1952 – Nov 1953: Ministry divided into Heavy Machinery, Farm Machinery and Means of Transport, and General Machinery (see below)
	Nov 1953 – 3 Dec 1958: *Heinrich Rau* (SED) (see Grotewohl I)
Heavy Machinery	2 Feb 1953 – 30 Jan 1954: *Gerhard Ziller* (SED) (see above)
	16 Apr 1955 – 8 Feb 1958: *Erich Apel* (SED) (b. Judenbach 3 Oct 1917; d. Berlin 3 Dec 1965)
	31 Jul 1958: post abolished
Farm Machinery and Means of Trans-port (new post created 19 Dec 1952)	2 Feb – 30 Jul 1953: *Bernd Weinberger* (SED)
	30 Jul 1953: no further appointments made (?)
General Machinery	3 Feb 1953/16 Apr 1955 – 31 Jul 1958: *Helmut Wunderlich* (SED)
	31 Jul 1958: post abolished
Food Industry	26 Jun/30 Jul 1953 – 31 Jul 1958: *Kurt Westphal* (SED) (b. 31 Dec 1913)
	31 Jul 1958: post abolished
Light Industry	15 Nov 1950 – 31 Jul 1958: *Wilhelm Feldmann* (NDP) (b. Koln-Deutz 10 Feb 1910)
	31 Jul 1958: post abolished
Building	15 Nov 1950 – 1 Oct 1953: *Lothar Bolz* (NDP) (see

Grotewohl I)
Nov 1953 – 25 Jun 1958: *Heinz Winkler* (CDU) (b. Chemnitz 7 May 1910; d. Berlin 25 Jun 1958)

Commerce and Supply	15 Nov 1950 – 6 Dec 1952: *Karl Hamann* (LPD) (see Grotewohl I) 2 Feb 1953 – 3 Dec 1958: *Curt Wach* (SED) (b. 5 Feb 1906)
Prime Minister's Commission for Commerce and Supply	2 Feb – 12 Sep 1953: *Elli Schmidt* (SED) (b. Berlin 9 Aug 1908)
Foreign and Intra-German Trade	15 Nov 1950 – 12 Sep 1952: *Georg Handke* (SED) (see Grotewohl I) 12 Sep 1952 – 19 Nov 1954: *Kurt Gregor* (SED) (b. 21 Aug 1907) 16 Apr 1955 – 3 Dec 1958: *Heinrich Rau* (SED) (see Grotewohl I)
Co-ordination and Audit	23 May – 12 Sep 1952: *Georg Handke* (SED) (see Grotewohl I)
Labour and Vocational Education	15 Nov 1950 – 23 Apr 1953: *Roman Chwalek* (SED) (b. Weihendorf 24 Jul 1898) Apr 1953 – 31 Jul 1958: *Fritz Macher* (SED) (b. 1922) 31 Jul 1958: post abolished
Health	*Luitpold Steidle* (CDU) (see Grotewohl I)
Justice	15 Nov 1950 – 15 Jul 1953: *Max Fechner* (SED) (see Grotewohl I) 15 Jul 1953 – 3 Dec 1958: *Hilde Benjamin* (SED) (b. Bernburg 5 Feb 1902)
Attorney-General	23 May 1952 – 3 Dec 1958: *Ernst Melsheimer* (SED) (b. Neunkirchen 8 Apr 1897; d. Berlin 25 Mar 1960)
Post	*Friedrich Burmeister* (CDU) (see Grotewohl I)
Transport (15 Apr 1953 – 19 Nov 1954: and Railways)	15 Nov 1950 – 10 Apr 1953: *Hans Reingruber* (see Grotewohl I) 23 Apr 1953 – 19 Nov 1954: *Roman Chwalek* (SED) (see above) 19 Nov 1954 – 3 Dec 1958: *Erwin Kramer* (SED) (b. Schneidemuhl 22 Aug 1902)
Land and Forestry	15 Nov 1950 – May 1952: *Paul Scholz* (Dem Peasants) (see above) May 1952 – 16 May 1953 (acting:) *Wilhelm Schröder* (SED) 16 May/26 Jun – Nov 1953 (acting:) *Hans Reichelt* (Dem Peasants) (b. Proskau 30 Mar 1925)

Nov 1953 – Mar 1955: *Paul Scholz* (Dem Peasants) (see above)

19 Mar 1955 – 3 Dec 1958: *Hans Reichelt* (Dem Peasants) (see above)

Information | 15 Nov 1950 – 31 Dec 1952: *Gerhard Eisler* (SED) (see Grotewohl I)

1 Jan 1953: post abolished

8 Dec 1958 – 14 Nov 1963: Grotewohl III

Prime Minister	*Otto Grotewohl* (SED) (for 3rd time) (see Grotewohl I)
First Deputy Prime Ministers	8 Dec 1958 – 13 Sep 1960: *Walter Ernst Karl Ulbricht* (SED) (see Presidents)
	28 Aug 1961 – 14 Nov 1963: *Willi Stoph* (SED) (see Presidents) from 4 Jul 1962 Standing Deputy, the Prime Minister being ill
Deputy Prime Ministers	8 Dec 1958 – 28 Aug 1961: *Willi Stoph* (SED) (see Presidents)
	8 Dec 1958 – 23 Mar 1961: *Heinrich Rau* (SED) (see Grotewohl I)
	8 Dec 1958 – 13 Jul 1960: *Hans Loch* (LDP) (see Grotewohl I)
	Max Sefrin (CDU) (see Grotewohl II)
	Lothar Bolz (NDP) (see Grotewohl I)
	Paul Scholz (Dem Peasants) (see Grotewohl II)
	Bruno Leuschner (SED) (see Grotewohl II)
	9 Feb 1961 – 14 Nov 1963: *Grete Wittkowski* (SED) (b. Poznan 18 Aug 1910; d. 1973)
	Jun 1961 – 14 Nov 1963: *Max Suhrbier* (LDP) (b. Rostock 12 Oct 1902; d. 16 Jan 1971)
Industrial Production	4 Jul 1962/13 Jan 1963 – 14 Nov 1963: *Erich Apel* (SED) (see Grotewohl II)
	4 Jul 1962 – 6 Feb 1963: *Gerhard Grüneberg* (SED)
	4 Jul 1962 – 12 Jan 1963: *Karl Mewis* (SED) (b. Kassel 22 Nov 1907)
	4 Jul 1962 – 14 Nov 1963: *Alfred Neumann* (SED) (b. Berlin 15 Dec 1909)
Co-ordination and Control of Policies of SED Central Committee and the Ministries (new post)	4 Jul 1960 – 14 Nov 1963: *Willi Stoph* (SED) (see Presidents)

Head of Planning Commission (Co-ordination of Fundamental Economic Questions)	8 Dec 1958 – 6 Jul 1961: *Bruno Leuschner* (SED) (see Grotewohl II) 7 Jul 1961: reorganized into New Planning Commission (see below)
First Deputy Chairmen	*Kurt Gregor* (SED) (see Grotewohl II) 14 Jul 1960 – 7 Jul 1961: *Walter Hieke* (SED) 14 Jul 1960 – 7 Jul 1961: *Hugo Meiser* (SED)
Head of New Planning Commission	7 Jul 1961 – 14 Nov 1963: *Bruno Leuschner* (SED) (see Grotewohl II) 7 Jul 1961 – 12 Jan 1963: *Karl Mewis* (SED) (see above) Deputy Head 4 Jul 1962 – Mar 1963: *Rudolf Müller* (SED)
First Deputy Chairman (for Long-term Planning)	8 Feb (20 Apr) – 14 Nov 1963: *Gerhard Schürer* (SED) (b. Zwickau 14 Apr 1921)
First Deputy Chairman (for Annual Plan)	8 Feb (20 Apr) – 14 Nov 1963: *Karl Grünheld* (SED)
Co-ordination of Fundamental Economic Questions (from 8 Jan 1963: Committee for Integration of GDR Economy within Eastern Bloc)	6 Jul 1961 – 14 Nov 1963: *Bruno Leuschner* (SED) (see Grotewohl II)
Central Commission for Audit (Economic Council) (new post)	8 Dec 1958 – 7 Jul 1961: *Ernst Wabra* 7 Jul 1961 – 14 Nov 1963: *Alfred Neumann* (SED) (see above)
Deputy Chairman Central Bureau of Statistics	4 Jul 1962 – 14 Nov 1963: *Erich Markowitsch* (SED) 4 Jul – 19 Dec 1962: *Heinz Rauch* (SED) (b. 1914(?); d. Warsaw 19 Dec 1962)
Foreign Affairs	*Lothar Bolz* (NDP) (see Grotewohl I)
Home Affairs	*Karl Maron* (SED) (see Grotewohl II)
Public Security	*Erich Mielke* (SED) (see Grotewohl II)

229

Defence	8 Dec 1958 – 14 Jul 1960: *Willi Stoph* (SED) (see Presidents)
	14 Jul 1960 – 14 Nov 1963: *Karl Heinz Hoffmann* (SED) (b. Mannheim 28 Nov 1910)
Finance	*Willy Rumpf* (SED) (see Grotewohl II)
President of Bank of Issue	4 Jul 1962 – 14 Nov 1963: *Rudolf Wetzel* (SED)
Education	*Alfred Lemnitz* (SED) (b. 1905)
Culture	8 Dec 1958 – 23 Feb 1961: *Alexander Abusch* (SED) (b. Krakow 14 Feb 1902)
	23 Feb 1961 – 14 Nov 1963: *Hans Bentzien* (SED) (b. Greifswald 4 Jan 1927)
Building	8 Dec 1958 – 6 Feb 1963: *Ernst Scholz* (SED)
	6 Feb – 14 Nov 1963: *Wolfgang Junker* (SED)
Commerce and Supply	8 Dec 1958 – 10 Jul 1959: *Curt Wach* (SED) (see Grotewohl II)
	10 Jul 1959 – 19(?) Sep 1963: *Curt-Heinz Merkel* (SED) (b. Hamburg 1920)
Foreign and Intra-German Trade	8 Dec 1958 – 23 Mar 1961: *Heinrich Rau* (SED) (see Grotewohl I)
	7 Jul 1961 – 14 Nov 1963: *Julius Balkow* (SED) (b. Berlin 26 Aug 1909)
Health	*Max Sefrin* (CDU) (see Grotewohl II)
Justice	*Hilde Benjamin* (SED) (see Grotewohl II)
Post	*Friedrich Burmeister* (CDU) (see Grotewohl I)
Transport	*Erwin Kramer* (SED) (see Grotewohl II)
Agriculture and Forestry	8 Dec 1958 – 6 Feb 1963: *Hans Reichelt* (Dem Peasants) (see Grotewohl II)
	8 – 9 Feb 1963: *Karl-Heinz Bartsch* (SED) (b. Lobau 25 Nov 1923)
	14 Feb – 14 Nov 1963: *Georg Ewald* (SED) (b. Buchholz 30 Oct 1926; d. 14 Sep 1973)
Chairman of State Committee for Requisitioning and Buying up of Agricultural Produce	8 Feb – 14 Nov 1963: *Helmut Koch* (SED)

14 Nov 1963 – 24 Sep 1964: Grotewohl IV

Prime Minister	14 Nov 1963 – 21 Sep 1964: *Otto Grotewohl* (SED) (for 4th time) (see Grotewohl I)

Acting Prime Minister	*Willi Stoph* (SED) (see Presidents) during Grotewohl's final illness
Deputy Prime Ministers	*Bruno Leuschner* (SED) (see Grotewohl II) Chairman of Planning Commission *Alfred Neumann* (SED) (see Grotewohl III) Chairman of Department of Commerce *Erich Apel* (SED) (see Grotewohl II) Industrial Production *Grete Wittkowski* (SED) (see Grotewohl III) *Alexander Abusch* (SED) (see Grotewohl III) *Max Sefrin* (CDU) (see Grotewohl II) *Lothar Bolz* (NDP) (see Grotewohl I) *Paul Scholz* (Dem Peasants) (see Grotewohl II) 4 Jun – 24 Sep 1964: *Kurt Seibt* (SED) (b. 1908)
Head of the Central Commission for Audit	*Ernst Wabra* (see Grotewohl III)
Chairman of Agricultural Produce Committee	*Helmut Koch* (SED) (see Grotewohl III)
President of Bank of Issue	21 Nov 1963 – 29 Jun 1964: *Rudolf Wetzel* (SED) (see Grotewohl III) 29 Jun – 24 Sep 1964: *Helmut Dietrich* (SED)
First Deputy Chairman (for Annual Plan)	*Karl Grünheld* (SED) (see Grotewohl III)
Deputy Chairman of Economic Council	*Erich Markowitsch* (SED) (see Grotewohl III)
Head of Local Government Board (new post)	4 Jun – 24 Sep 1964: *Kurt Seibt* (SED) (see above)
Foreign Affairs	*Lothar Bolz* (NDP) (see Grotewohl I)
Home Affairs	*Friedrich Dickel* (SED) (b. Wuppertal 8 Dec 1913)
Public Security	*Erich Mielke* (SED) (see Grotewohl II)
Defence	*Karl Heinz Hoffmann* (SED) (see Grotewohl III)
Finance	*Willy Rumpf* (SED) (see Grotewohl II)
Education	*Margot Honecker* (SED) (b. Halle 17 Apr 1927)
Culture	*Hans Bentzien* (SED) (see Grotewohl III)
Building	*Wolfgang Junker* (SED) (see Grotewohl III)
Commerce and Supply	*Gerhardt Lucht* (SED) (b. Berlin 10 Jun 1913)
Foreign and Intra-German Trade	*Julius Balkow* (SED) (see Grotewohl III)

231

Health	*Max Sefrin* (CDU) (see Grotewohl II)
Justice	*Hilde Benjamin* (SED) (see Grotewohl II)
Post	*Rudolph Schulze* (CDU) (b. Chemnitz 18 Nov 1918)
Transport	*Erwin Kramer* (SED) (see Grotewohl II)
Agriculture and Forestry	*Georg Ewald* (SED) (see Grotewohl III)

24 Sep 1964 – 13 Jul 1967: Stoph I

Prime Minister	*Willi Stoph* (SED) (for 1st time) (see Presidents)
Deputy Prime Minister (Chairman of Planning Commission)	24 Sep 1964 – 10 Feb 1965: *Bruno Leuschner* (SED) (see Grotewohl II)
Deputy Prime Minister (Chairman of Economic Council)	24 Sep 1964 – 23 Dec 1965: *Alfred Neumann* (SED) (see Grotewohl III) 23 Dec 1965: Economic Council abolished
Deputy Prime Minister (Industrial Production)	14 Nov 1963 – 3 Dec 1965: *Erich Apel* (SED) (see Grotewohl II) 23 Dec 1965 – 13 Jul 1967: *Gerhard Schürer* (SED) (see Grotewohl III)
Deputy Prime Ministers (without special duties)	*Grete Wittkowski* (SED) (see Grotewohl III) *Alexander Abusch* (SED) (see Grotewohl III) *Max Sefrin* (CDU) (see Grotewohl II) 24 Sep 1964 – 24 Jun 1965: *Lothar Bolz* (NDPD) (see Grotewohl I) *Paul Scholz* (DBD) (see Grotewohl II) 24 Sep 1964 – 23 Dec 1965: *Kurt Seibt* (SED) (see Grotewohl IV) (?) – 23 Dec 1965: *Max Suhrbier* (LDP) (see Grotewohl III) 25 Mar 1965 – 13 Jul 1967: *Julius Balkow* (SED) (see Grotewohl III) 25 Mar 1965 – 13 Jul 1967: *Gerhard Weiss* (SED) (b. Erfurt 30 Jul 1919) (?) – 13 Jul 1967: *Siegfried Böhm* (SED) (b. Plauen 20 Aug 1928)
Remaining Members of Presidium of the Council of Ministers	23 Dec 1965 – 13 Jul 1967: *Georg Ewald* (SED) (see Grotewohl III) *Willy Rumpf* (SED) (see Grotewohl II) *Gerhard Zimmermann* (SED) (b. Ahlbeck 31 May 1927)

23 Dec 1965 – 5 May 1966: *Siegbert Löschau* (b.
Freital 1929)
Kurt Wünsche (LDP) (b. Trebnitz 14 Dec 1929)
Wolfgang Rauchfuss (b. Chemnitz 27 Nov 1931)

Head of Central Commission for Audit	*Ernst Wabra* (see Grotewohl III)
Chairman of Agricultural Produce Committee	*Helmut Koch* (SED) (see Grotewohl III)
President of Bank of Issue	*Helmut Dietrich* (SED) (see Grotewohl IV)
Head of State Board for Work and Wages (new post)	23 Dec 1965 – 13 Jul 1967: *Helmut Geyer* (SED)
Head of Board for Vocational Education (new post)	23 Dec 1965 – 13 Jul 1967: *Erich Markowitsch* (SED) (see Grotewohl III)
First Deputy Chairman of Planning Commission for Annual Plan	*Karl Grünheld* (SED) (see Grotewohl III)
Deputy Chairman of Economic Council	24 Sep 1964 – 23 Dec 1965: *Erich Markowitsch* (SED) (see Grotewohl III)
Head of Local Government Board	24 Sep 1964 – 23 Dec 1965: *Kurt Seibt* (SED) (see Grotewohl IV) 23 Dec 1965 – 13 Jul 1967: *Fritz Scharfenstein* (SED) (b. Aue 14 Jun 1925)
Foreign Affairs	24 Sep 1964 – 24 Jun 1965: *Lothar Bolz* (NDPD) (see Grotewohl I) 24 Jun 1965 – 13 Jul 1967: *Otto Winzer* (SED) (b. Berlin-Reinickendorf 3 Apr 1902)
Home Affairs	*Friedrich Dickel* (SED) (see Grotewohl IV)
Public Security	*Erich Mielke* (SED) (see Grotewohl II)
Defence	*Karl Heinz Hoffmann* (SED) (see Grotewohl III)
Finance	24 Sep 1964 – 12 Dec 1966: *Willy Rumpf* (SED) (see Grotewohl II) 12 Feb – 13 Jul 1967: *Siegfried Böhm* (SED) (see above)
Education	*Margot Honecker* (SED) (see Grotewohl IV)

233

Culture	24 Sep 1964 – 12 Jan 1966: *Hans Bentzien* (SED) (see Grotewohl III) 12 Jan 1966 – 13 Jul 1967: *Klaus Gysi* (b. Berlin 3 Mar 1912)
Building	*Wolfgang Junker* (SED) (see Grotewohl III)
Commerce and Supply	24 Sep 1964 – 25 Mar 1965: *Gerhard Lucht* (SED) (see Grotewohl IV) 25 Mar 1965 – 13 Jul 1967: *Günter Sieber* (b. Ilmenau 11 Mar 1930)
Foreign and Intra-German Trade	24 Sep 1964 – 25 Mar 1965: *Julius Balkow* (SED) (see Grotewohl III) 25 Mar 1965 – 13 Jul 1967: *Horst Sölle* (SED) (b. Leipzig 3 Jun 1924)
Health	*Max Sefrin* (CDU) (see Grotewohl II)
Justice	*Hilde Benjamin* (SED) (see Grotewohl II)
Post	*Rudolph Schulze* (CDU) (see Grotewohl IV)
Transport	*Erwin Kramer* (SED) (see Grotewohl II)
Agriculture and Forestry	*Georg Ewald* (SED) (see Grotewohl III)
Raw Materials (new post)	23 Dec 1965 – 13 Jul 1967: *Klaus Siebold* (SED) (b. Laubusch 12 Sep 1930)
Mining and Metallurgy (new post)	23 Dec 1965 – 13 Jul 1967: *Kurt Fichtner* (SED) (b. 16 Aug 1916)
Chemical Industry (new post)	23 Dec 1965 – 5 May 1966: *Siegbert Löschau* (see above) 5 May 1966 – 13 Jul 1967: *Günther Wyschofsky* (SED) (b. Bischofswerda 8 May 1929)
Electrical Engineering and Electronics (new post)	23 Dec 1965 – 13 Jul 1967: *Otfried Steger* (SED) (b. Wechselburg 25 Sep 1926)
Heavy Machinery and Industrial Plants (new post)	23 Dec 1965 – 13 Jul 1967: *Gerhard Zimmermann* (SED) (see above)
Processing Machinery and Vehicles (new post)	23 Dec 1965 – 13 Jul 1967: *Rudi Georgi* (SED) (b. Bockau 25 Dec 1927)
Light Industry (new post)	23 Dec 1965 – 13 Jul 1967: *Johann Wittik* (SED) (b. Reichenberg 9 Aug 1923)
Regionally Administered Industry and Food Industry (new post)	23 Dec 1965 – 13 Jul 1967: *Erhard Krack* (SED) (b. 1930)

| Management of Materials | *Alfred Neumann* (SED) (see Grotewohl III) |

14 Jul 1967 – 26 Nov 1971: Stoph II

Prime Minister	*Willi Stoph* (SED) (for 2nd time) (see Presidents)
First Deputy Prime Minister	*Alfred Neumann* (SED) (see Grotewohl III)
Deputy Prime Ministers	*Alexander Abusch* (SED) (see Grotewohl III)
	Max Sefrin (CDU) (see Grotewohl II)
	14 Jul – 22 Nov 1967: *Julius Balkow* (SED) (see Grotewohl III)
	Gerhard Weiss (SED) (see Stoph I)
	Kurt Fichtner (SED) (see Stoph I)
	Manfred Flegel (NDPD) (b. Magdeburg 3 Jun 1927)
	Wolfgang Rauchfuss (SED) (see Stoph I)
	Gerhard Schürer (SED) (see Grotewohl III)
	Werner Titel (DBD) (b. Arnswalde 2 May 1931; d. 25 Dec 1971)
	Herbert Weiz (SED) (b. Cumbach 27 Jun 1924)
	Kurt Wünsche (LDP) (see Stoph I)
Chairman of Agricultural Council	*Georg Ewald* (SED) (see Grotewohl III)
Head of Local Government Board	*Fritz Scharfenstein* (SED) (see Stoph I)
Head of Central Statistical Administration	*Arno Donda* (SED) (b. Berlin 1930)
Head of Board for Higher and Technical Education	14 Jul 1967 – 16 Sep 1970: *Ernst Joachim Giessmann* (SED) (b. Berlin 12 Feb 1919) 16 Sep 1970 – 26 Nov 1971: *Hans-Joachim Böhme* (SED)
Head of Price Board	*Walter Halbritter* (SED) (b. Hoym 17 Nov 1927)
First Deputy Chairman of Agricultural Council	*Heinz Kuhrig* (SED) (b. 1929)
Chairman of Planning Commission	*Gerhard Schürer* (SED) (see Grotewohl III)

Chairman of Committee for Supervision of Workers and Peasants	*Heinz Matthes* (SED) (b. 1927)
Foreign Affairs	*Otto Winzer* (SED) (see Stoph I)
Home Affairs	*Friedrich Dickel* (SED) (see Grotewohl IV)
Public Security	*Erich Mielke* (SED) (see Grotewohl II)
Defence	*Karl Heinz Hoffmann* (SED) (see Grotewohl III)
Finance	*Siegfried Böhm* (SED) (see Stoph I)
Education	*Margot Honecker* (SED) (see Grotewohl IV)
Culture	*Klaus Gysi* (SED) (see Stoph I)
Building	*Wolfgang Junker* (SED) (see Grotewohl III)
Commerce and Supply	*Günter Sieber* (SED) (see Stoph I)
Foreign Trade	*Horst Sölle* (SED) (see Stoph I)
Health	*Max Sefrin* (CDU) (see Grotewohl II)
Justice	*Kurt Wünsche* (LDP) (see Stoph I)
Post and Telecommunications	*Rudolph Schulze* (CDU) (see Grotewohl IV)
Transport	14 Jul 1967 – 15 Dec 1970: *Erwin Kramer* (SED) (see Grotewohl II)
	15 Dec 1970 – 26 Nov 1971: *Otto Arndt*
Agriculture and Forestry	*Georg Ewald* (SED) (see Grotewohl III)
Raw Materials	*Klaus Siebold* (SED) (see Stoph I)
Mining, Metallurgy and Potash	*Kurt Singhuber* (SED) (b. Vienna 20 Apr 1932)
Chemical Industry	*Günther Wyschofsky* (SED) (see Stoph I)
Electronics and Electrical Engineering	*Otfried Steger* (SED) (see Stoph I)
Heavy Machinery and Industrial Plants	*Gerhard Zimmermann* (SED) (see Stoph I)
Manufacturing Machinery and Vehicles	*Rudi Georgi* (SED) (see Stoph I)
Light Industry	*Johann Wittik* (SED) (see Stoph I)
Local Industry and Food Industry	*Erhard Krack* (SED) (see Stoph I)
Management of Materials	*Erich Haase* (SED) (b. 1928)
Economics and Technology	*Günter Prey* (SED) (b. 1930)

from 29 Nov 1971: Stoph III/Sindermann

Prime Minister	29 Nov 1971 – 3 Oct 1973: *Willi Stoph* (SED) (for 3rd time) (see Presidents) from 3 Oct 1973: *Horst Sindermann*
First Deputy Prime Ministers	*Alfred Neumann* (SED) (see Grotewohl III) 29 Nov 1971 – 3 Oct 1973: *Horst Sindermann* (see above) from 2 Oct 1973: *Gunter Mittag*
Deputy Prime Ministers	*Kurt Fichtner* (SED) (see Stoph I) *Manfred Flegel* (NDPD) (see Stoph II) *Wolfgang Rauchfuss* (SED) (see Stoph I) *Gerhard Schürer* (SED) (see Grotewohl III) *Gerhard Weiss* (SED) (see Stoph I) *Hubert Weiz* (SED) (see Stoph II) *Kurt Wünsche* (LDP) (see Stoph I) 29 Nov – 25 Dec 1971: *Werner Titel* (DBD) (see Stoph II) *Rudolph Schulze* (CDU) (see Grotewohl IV) *Günther Kleiber* from 9 Mar 1972: *Hans Reichelt* (see Grotewohl II)
Foreign Affairs	29 Nov 1971 – 20 Jan 1975: *Otto Winzer* (SED) (see Stoph I) from 20 Jan 1975: *Oskar Fischer* (SED)
Home Affairs and Chief of People's Police	*Friedrich Dickel* (SED) (see Grotewohl IV)
State Security	*Erich Mielke* (SED) (see Grotewohl II)
Defence	*Karl Heinz Hoffmann* (SED) (see Grotewohl III)
Finance	*Siegfried Böhm* (SED) (see Stoph I)
Education	*Margot Honecker* (SED) (see Grotewohl IV)
Culture	29 Nov 1971 – 31 Jan 1973: *Klaus Gysi* (SED) (see Stoph I) from 31 Jan 1973: *Hans-Joachim Hoffmann*
Housing	*Wolfgang Junker* (SED) (see Grotewohl III)
Commerce and Supply	29 Nov 1971 – 22 Nov 1972: *Günter Sieber* (SED) (see Stoph I) from 22 Nov 1972: *Gerhard Briksa*
Foreign Trade	*Horst Sölle* (SED) (see Stoph I)
Health	*Ludwig Mecklinger*
Justice	29 Nov 1971 – 16 Oct 1972: *Kurt Wünsche* (LDP) (see Stoph I) from 16 Oct 1972: *Hans-Joachim Heusinger*

237

Post and Tele-communications	*Rudolph Schulze* (CDU) (see Grotewohl IV)
Transport	*Otto Arndt* (see Stoph II)
Agriculture, Forestry and Food Economy	29 Nov 1971 – 14 Sep 1973: *Georg Ewald* (SED) (see Grotewohl III) from 3 Oct 1973: *Heinz Kuhrig* (SED) (see Stoph II)
University and Technical Training	*Hans-Joachim Böhme* (SED) (see Stoph II)
Supply of Materials	29 Nov 1971 – 14 Feb 1974: *Manfred Flegel* (NDPD) (see Stoph II) from 14 Feb 1974: *Wolfgang Rauchfuss* (SED) (see Stoph I)
Chairman of Planning Commission	*Gerhard Schürer* (SED) (see Grotewohl III)
Environment and Water Affairs	29 Nov – 25 Dec 1971: *Werner Titel* (DBD) (see Stoph II) from 9 Mar 1972: *Hans Reichelt* (see Grotewohl II)
Light Industry	29 Nov 1971 – 22 Nov 1972: *Johann Wittik* (SED) (see Stoph I) from 22 Nov 1972: *Karl Bettin*
Science and Technology	29 Nov 1971 – 14 Feb 1974: *Günter Prey* (SED) (see Stoph II) from 14 Feb 1974: *Hubert Weiz* (SED) (see Stoph I)
Local Industry and Foodstuffs Industry	29 Nov 1971 – 14 Feb 1974: *Erhard Krack* (SED) (see Stoph I) from 14 Feb 1974: *Udo-Dieter Wange*
Geology (new post)	from 1 Jul 1974: *Manfred Bochmann*

Germany

HEADS OF STATE

Presidents

12 May 1925 – 2 Aug 1934	*Paul (Anton Hans Ludwig) von Beneckendorf und Hindenburg* (b. Poznan 2 Oct 1847; d. Gut Neudeck 2 Aug 1934)

2/19 Aug 1934 – 30 Apr 1945	*Adolf Hitler* (b. Braunau am Inn 20 Apr 1889; d. Berlin 30 Apr 1945)
1 – 8/23 May 1945	*Karl Dönitz* (b. Berlin-Grünau 16 Sep 1891)

British, French, American and Russian occupation, followed by division of country into two states: German Democratic Republic (see p. 223) and the Federal Republic of Germany (see p. 248)

MEMBERS OF GOVERNMENT

28 Jun 1928 – 27 Mar 1930: Müller II

Chancellor	*Hermann Müller* (SPD) (for 2nd time) (b. Mannheim 18 May 1876; d. Berlin 20 Mar 1931)*
Vice Chancellor	No appointment made
Foreign Affairs	28 Jun 1928 – 3 Oct 1929: *Gustav Stresemann* (DVP) (b. Berlin 10 May 1878; d. Berlin 3 Oct 1929)*
	4 Oct 1929 – 27 Mar 1930 (acting until 11 Nov 1929:) *Julius Curtius* (DVP) (b. Duisburg 7 Feb 1877; d. Heidelberg 10 Nov 1948)*
Home Affairs	*Karl Severing* (SPD) (b. Herford 1 Jun 1875; d. Bielefeld 23 Jul 1952)
Finance	28 Jun 1928 – 21 Dec 1929: *Rudolf Hilferding* (SPD) (b. Vienna 10 Aug 1877; d. Buchenwald Concentration Camp 1943 or La Santé Prison, Paris, Feb 1941?)*
	23 Dec 1929 – 27 Mar 1930: *Paul Moldenhauer* (DVP) (b. Cologne 2 Dec 1876; d. Cologne 1 Feb 1947)
Economic Affairs	28 Jun 1928 – 11 Nov 1929: *Julius Curtius* (DVP) (see above)
	11 Nov – 23 Dec 1929: *Paul Moldenhauer* (DVP) (see above)
	23 Dec 1929 – 27 Mar 1930: *Robert Schmidt* (SPD) (b. Berlin 15 May 1864; d. Berlin 16 Sep 1943)*
Labour	*Rudolf Wissell* (SPD) (b. Göttingen 8 Mar 1869; d. Berlin 13 Dec 1962)
Justice	28 Jun 1928 – 13 Apr 1929: *Erich (Friedrich Ludwig) Koch* (Dem) (b. Bremerhaven 26 Feb 1875; d. Paraná, Brazil, Oct 1944)*

*For earlier career see vol. 2

239

	13 Apr 1929 – 27 Mar 1930: *Theodor von Guérard* (Centre) (b. Koblenz 29 Dec 1863; d. Ahaus 21 Jul 1943)
Defence	*Wilhelm Groener* (no party) (b. Ludwigsburg 22 Nov 1867; d. Berlin 4 May 1939)
Post Office	*Georg Schätzel* (Bayer VP) (b. Neustadt an der Aisch 13 Jul 1874; d. Berlin 27 Nov 1934)*
Transport	28 Jun 1928 – 6 Feb 1929: *Theodor von Guérard* (Centre) (see above)
	7 Feb – 13 Apr 1929 (acting:) *Georg Schätzel* (Bayer VP) (see above)
	13 Apr 1929 – 27 Mar 1930: *Adam Stegerwald* (Centre) (b. Greussenheim 14 Dec 1874; d. Würzburg 3 Dec 1945)
Food	*Hermann (Robert) Dietrich* (Dem) (b. Oberprechtal 14 Dec 1879; d. Stuttgart 6 Mar 1954)
Occupied Territories	28 Jun 1928 – 6 Feb 1929: *Theodor von Guérard* (Centre) (see above)
	7 Feb – 13 Apr 1929 (acting:) *Karl Severing* (SPD) (see above)
	13 Apr 1929 – 27 Mar 1930: *Josef (Karl) Wirth* (Centre) (b. Freiburg 6 Sep 1879; d. Freiburg 3 Jan 1956)*

30 Mar 1930 – 7 Oct 1931: Brüning I

Chancellor	*Heinrich Brüning* (Centre) (for 1st time) (b. Munster 26 Nov 1885; d. Norwich, Vermont, 30 Mar 1970)
Vice Chancellor	*Hermann (Robert) Dietrich* (Dem, from 30 Jul 1930 Ger State) (see Müller II)
Foreign Affairs	*Julius Curtius* (DVP) (see Müller II)
Home Affairs	*Josef (Karl) Wirth* (Centre) (see Müller I)
Finance	30 Mar – 20 Jun 1930: *Paul Moldenhauer* (DVP) (see Müller II)
	20 – 26 Jun 1930 (acting:) *Heinrich Brüning* (Centre) (see above)
	26 Jun 1930 – 7 Oct 1931: *Hermann (Robert) Dietrich* (Dem, from 30 Jul 1930 Ger State) (see Müller II)
Economic Affairs	30 Mar – 26 Jun 1930: *Hermann (Robert) Dietrich* (Dem) (see Müller II)

*For earlier career see vol. 2

240

	26 Jun 1930 – 7 Oct 1931 (acting:) *Ernst Trendelenburg* (b. 13 Feb 1882)
Labour	*Adam Stegerwald* (Centre) (see Müller II)
Justice	30 Mar – 5 Dec 1930: *Johann Viktor Bredt* (Nat Party of Ger Middle Classes) (b. Barmen 2 Mar 1879; d. Marburg 6 Dec 1940)
	5 Dec 1930 – 7 Oct 1931 (acting:) *Kurt (Walter) Joël* (no party) (b. 18 Jan 1865; d. Berlin 15 Apr 1945)*
Defence	*Wilhelm Groener* (no party) (see Müller II)
Post Office	*Georg Schätzel* (Bayer VP) (see Müller II)
Transport	*Theodor von Guérard* (Centre) (see Müller II)
Food	*Martin Schiele* (Ger Nat, from 22 Jul 1930 Christ Citizens) (b. Gross-Schwarzlosen 17 Jan 1870; d. Suckow 16 Feb 1939)*
Occupied Territories	30 Mar – 30 Sep 1930: *Gottfried Reinhold Treviranus* (Christ Nat Workers, from 23 Jul 1930 Cons) (b. Schieder 20 Mar 1891; d. 7 Jun 1971) from 1 Oct 1930: post abolished
Without Portfolio	1 Oct 1930 – 7 Oct 1931: *Gottfried Reinhold Treviranus* (Cons) (see above)

9 Oct 1931 – 30 May 1932: Brüning II

Chancellor	*Heinrich Brüning* (Centre) (for 2nd time) (see Brüning I)
Vice Chancellor	*Hermann (Robert) Dietrich* (Ger State) (see Müller II)
Foreign Affairs	(acting:) *Heinrich Brüning* (Centre) (see Brüning I)
Home Affairs	(acting:) *Wilhelm Groener* (no party) (see Müller II)
Finance	*Hermann (Robert) Dietrich* (Centre) (see Müller II)
Economic Affairs	9 Oct 1931 – 6 May 1932: *Hermann Warmbold* (no party) (b. Hildesheim 21 Apr 1876) 6 – 30 May 1932 (acting:) *Ernst Trendelenburg* (no party) (see Brüning I)
Labour	*Adam Stegerwald* (Centre) (see Müller II)
Justice	*Kurt (Walter) Joël* (no party) (see Brüning I)
Defence	*Wilhelm Groener* (no party) (see Müller II)
Post Office	*Georg Schätzel* (Bayer VP) (see Müller II)
Transport	*Gottfried Reinhold Treviranus* (Cons) (see Brüning I)
Food	*Martin Schiele* (Christ Citizens) (see Brüning I)

*For earlier career see vol. 2

Commissioner for	5 Nov 1931 – 30 May 1932: *Hans Schlange-*
Settlement of	*Schöningen* (Christ Citizens) (b. Schöningen 17 Nov
Eastern Districts	1886; d. Bad Godesberg 20 Jul 1960)
(new post)	

1 Jun – 17 Nov 1932: Papen

Chancellor	*Franz von Papen* (Centre, from 3 Jun 1932 no party) (b. Werl 29 Oct 1879; d. Obersasbach 2 May 1969)
Vice Chancellor	No appointment made
Foreign Affairs	2 Jun – 17 Nov 1932: *Konstantin, Baron Neurath* (no party) (b. Klein-Glattbach 2 Feb 1873; d. Teinfelder Hof 14 Aug 1956)
Home Affairs	*Wilhelm, Baron Gayl* (Ger Nat) (b. Königsberg 4 Feb 1879; d. Potsdam 7 Nov 1945)
Finance	2 Jun – 17 Nov 1932: *Johann Ludwig, Count Schwerin von Krosigk* (no party) (b. Rathmannsdorf 22 Aug 1887; d. 4 Mar 1977)
Economic Affairs	*Hermann Warmbold* (no party) (see Brüning II)
Labour	2 – 6 Jun 1932 (acting:) *Hermann Warmbold* (no party) (see Brüning II) 6 Jun – 17 Nov 1932: *Hugo Schäffer* (no party) (b. Edelfingen 13 Jun 1875)
Justice	2 Jun – 17 Nov 1932: *Franz Gürtner* (Ger Nat) (b. Regensburg 26 Aug 1881; d. Berlin 29 Jan 1941)
Defence	*Kurt von Schleicher* (no party) (b. Brandenburg 7 Apr 1882; d. Berlin 30 Jun 1934)
Post Office	*Paul, Baron Eltz von Rübenach* (no party) (b. Cologne 9 Feb 1875; d. Linz 25 Aug 1943)
Transport	*Paul, Baron Eltz von Rübenach* (no party) (see above)
Food	*Magnus, Baron Braun* (Ger Nat) (b. Neukken 7 Feb 1878; d. Oberaufdorf 29 Aug 1972)
Eastern Settlements	*Magnus, Baron Braun* (Ger Nat) (see above)
Without Portfolio	29/31 Oct – 17 Nov 1932: *Franz Bracht* (no party, associated with right wing of Centre) (b. Berlin 23 Nov 1877; d. Berlin 26 Sep 1933) 29/31 Oct – 17 Nov 1932: *Johannes Popitz* (no party) (b. Leipzig 2 Dec 1884; d. Berlin 2 Feb 1945)

3 Dec 1932 – 28 Jan 1933: Schleicher

Chancellor	*Kurt von Schleicher* (no party) (see Papen)
Vice Chancellor	No appointment made

242

Foreign Affairs	*Konstantin, Baron Neurath* (no party) (see Papen)
Home Affairs	*Franz Bracht* (no party) (see Papen)
Finance	*Johann Ludwig, Count Schwerin von Krosigk* (no party) (see Papen)
Economic Affairs	4 Dec 1932 – 28 Jan 1933: *Hermann Warmbold* (no party) (see Brüning II)
Labour	*Friedrich Syrup* (no party) (b. Lüchow 9 Oct 1881; d. 1945)
Justice	*Franz Gürtner* (Ger Nat) (see Papen)
Defence	(acting:) *Kurt von Schleicher* (no party) (see Papen)
Post Office	*Paul, Baron Eltz von Rübenach* (no party) (see Papen)
Transport	*Paul, Baron Eltz von Rübenach* (no party) (see Papen)
Food	4 Dec 1932 – 28 Jan 1933: *Magnus, Baron Braun* (Ger Nat) (see Papen)
Eastern Settlements	Dec 1932 – 28 Jan 1933: *Günter Gereke* (Peoples) (b. Gruhna 6 Oct 1893; d. Berlin(?) 4 May 1970)
Without Portfolio	*Johannes Popitz* (no party) (see Papen)

30 Jan 1933 – 30 Apr 1945: Hitler

Chancellor	*Adolf Hitler* (NSDAP) (see Presidents)
Vice Chancellor	30 Jan 1933 – 7 Aug 1934: *Franz von Papen* (Ger Nat) (see Papen I)
	from 7 Aug 1934: no appointment made
Foreign Affairs	30 Jan 1933 – 5 Feb 1938: *Konstantin, Baron Neurath* (no party) (see Papen)
	5 Feb 1938 – 30 Apr 1945: *Joachim von Ribbentrop* (NSDAP) (b. Wesel 30 Apr 1893; d. Nuremberg 16 Oct 1946)
Home Affairs	30 Jan 1933 – 24 Aug 1943: *Wilhelm Frick* (NSDAP) (b. Alsenz 12 Mar 1877; d. Nuremberg 16 Oct 1946)
	24 Aug 1943 – 30 Apr 1945: *Heinrich Himmler* (NSDAP) (b. Munich 7 Oct 1900; d. Lüneburg 23 May 1945)
Finance	*Johann Ludwig, Count Schwerin von Krosigk* (no party) (see Papen)
Economic Affairs	30 Jan – 29 Jun 1933: *Alfred Hugenberg* (Ger Nat) (b. Hannover 19 Jun 1865; d. Rinteln 12 Mar 1951)
	29 Jun 1933 – 3 Aug 1934: *Kurt Schmitt* (no party) (b. Heidelberg 7 Oct 1886; d. 22 Nov 1950)
	3 Aug 1934 – 26 Nov 1937: *Hjalmar (Horace Greeley)*

Schacht (no party) (b. Tingleff 22 Jan 1877; d. Munich 3 Jun 1970)

26 Nov 1937 – 15 Jan 1938: *Hermann Göring* (NSDAP) (b. Rosenheim 12 Jan 1893; d. Nuremberg 15 Oct 1946)

5 Feb 1938 – 30 Apr 1945: *Walter Funk* (NSDAP) (b. Ebenrode 18 Aug 1890; d. Düsseldorf night of 31 May/1 Jun 1960)

Labour — *Franz Seldte* (Stahlhelm, from 27 Apr 1933 NSDAP) (b. Magdeburg 29 Jun 1882; d. Fürth 1 Apr 1947)

Justice — 7 Feb 1933 – 29 Jan 1941: *Franz Gürtner* (from late Jun 1933 Ger Nat) (see Papen)

Feb 1941 – 24 Aug 1942 (acting:) *Franz Schlegelberger* (no party) (b. Königsberg 23 Oct 1876; d. Flensburg 14 Dec 1970)

24 Aug 1942 – 30 Apr 1945: *Otto Georg Thierack* (NSDAP) (b. Wurzen 19 Apr 1889; d. Eselheide Camp 22 Nov 1946)

Defence (from 21 May 1935: War) — 30 Jan 1933 – 5 Feb 1938: *Werner von Blomberg* (no party) (b. Stargard 2 Sep 1878; d. Nuremberg 13 Mar 1946)

from 5 Feb 1938: post abolished

Chief of Staff — 5 Feb 1938 – 30 Apr 1945: *Wilhelm Keitel* (b. Helmscherode 22 Sep 1882; d. Nuremberg 16 Oct 1946)

Post Office — 30 Jan 1933 – 2 Feb 1937: *Paul, Baron Eltz von Rübenach* (no party) (see Papen)

2 Feb 1937 – 30 Apr 1945: *Wilhelm Ohnesorge* (NSDAP) (b. Grafenhainichen 8 Jun 1872; d. Munich 1 Feb 1962)

Transport — 30 Jan 1933 – 2 Feb 1937: *Paul, Baron Eltz von Rübenach* (see Papen)

2 Feb 1937 – 30 Apr 1945: *Julius Dorpmüller* (NSDAP) (b. Elberfeld 24 Jul 1869; d. Malente-Gremsmühlen 5 Jul 1945)

Food — 30 Jan – 29 Jun 1933: *Alfred Hugenberg* (Ger Nat) (see above)

29 Jun 1933 – 23 May 1942: *(Richard) Walter Darré* (NSDAP) (b. Buenos Aires 1 Jul 1895; d. Munich 5 Sep 1953)

23 May 1942 – 30 Apr 1945 (acting until 6 Apr 1944:) *Herbert Backe* (NSDAP) (b. Tiflis 1 May 1896; d. Nuremberg night of 5/6 Apr 1947)

Propaganda (new post)	13 Mar 1933 – 30 Apr 1945: *(Paul) Josef Goebbels* (NSDAP) (b. Rheydt 29 Oct 1897; d. Berlin 1 May 1945)
Aviation (new post)	28 Apr 1933 – 24 Apr 1945: *Hermann Göring* (NSDAP) (see above)
Science and Education (new post)	1 May 1934 – 30 Apr 1945: *Bernhard Rust* (NSDAP) (b. Hannover 30 Sep 1883; d. between Berend and Nübel 8 May 1945)
Forestry	3 Jul 1934 – 24 Apr 1945: *Hermann Göring* (NSDAP) (see above)
Ecclesiastical Affairs (new post)	18 Jul 1935 – 13 Dec 1941: *Hanns Kerrl* (NSDAP) (b. Fallersleben 11 Dec 1887; d. Berlin night of 13/14 Dec 1941)
	14 Dec 1941 – 30 Apr 1945: no appointment made
Commander-in-Chief of Armed Forces	20 Apr 1936 – 4 Feb 1938: *Werner, Baron Fritsch* (b. Benrath 4 Aug 1880; d. before Warsaw 22 Sep 1939)
	5 Feb 1938 – 9 Dec 1941: *Walter von Brauchitsch* (b. Berlin 4 Nov 1881; d. Hamburg 18 Oct 1948)
	9 Dec 1941 – 30 Apr 1945: *Adolf Hitler* (NSDAP) (see Presidents)
Commander-in-Chief of Navy	20 Apr 1936 – 30 Jan 1943: *Erich Raeder* (b. Wandsbek 24 Apr 1876; d. Kiel 6 Nov 1960)
	30 Jan 1943 – 30 Apr 1945: *Karl Dönitz* (no party) (b. Berlin-Grunau 16 Sep 1891)
Commander-in-Chief of Air Force	7 Mar 1935 – 24 Apr 1945: *Hermann Göring* (NSDAP) (see above)
Without Portfolio (description discontinued after 5 Feb 1938)	30 Jan – 28 Apr 1933: *Hermann Göring* (NSDAP) (see above)
	1 Dec 1933 – 30 Jun 1934: *Ernst Röhm* (NSDAP) (b. Munich 28 Nov 1887; d. 1 Jul 1934)
	1 Dec 1933 – 10 May 1941: *Rudolf Hess* (NSDAP) (b. Alexandria, Egypt, 26 Apr 1894)
	16 Jun 1934 – 18 Jul 1935: *Hanns Kerrl* (NSDAP) (see above)
	19 Dec 1934 – 30 Apr 1945: *Hans Frank* (NSDAP) (b. Karlsruhe 23 May 1900; d. Nuremberg 16 Oct 1946)
	26 Nov 1937 – 23 Jul 1944 (temporarily suspended 22 Jan 1943:) *Hjalmar (Horace Greeley) Schacht* (no party) (see above)
	1 Dec 1937 – 30 Apr 1945: *Otto Meissner* (NSDAP) (b. Bischweiler 13 Mar 1880; d. Munich 27 May 1953) Minister of State and Head of Chancellery
	5 Feb 1938 – 30 Apr 1934: *Konstantin, Baron Neurath*

245

(see Papen) Cabinet Secretary
1 May 1939 – 30 Apr 1945: *Arthur Seyss-Inquart*
(NSDAP) (b. Stannern bei Iglau 22 Jul 1892; d.
Nuremberg 16 Oct 1946)*

30 Apr – 1 May 1945: Goebbels (Cabinet named in Hitler's will)

Chancellor	*(Paul) Josef Goebbels* (NSDAP) (see Hitler)
Party Affairs	*Martin Bormann* (NSDAP) (b. Halberstadt 17 Jun 1900; d. Berlin 2 May 1945)
Foreign Affairs	*Arthur Seyss-Inquart* (NSDAP) (see Hitler)
Home Affairs	*Paul Giesler* (NSDAP) (b. 15 Jun 1895; d. Berchtesgaden May 1945)
Finance	*Johann Ludwig, Count Schwerin von Krosigk* (no party) (see Papen)
Commerce	*Walter Funk* (NSDAP) (see Hitler)
Labour	*Theo Hupfauer* (NSDAP) (b. 17 Jul 1906)
Justice	*Otto Georg Thierack* (NSDAP) (see Hitler)
Defence	*Karl Dönitz* (no party) (see Hitler)
Commander-in-Chief of Army	*Ferdinand Schörner* (b. Munich 1892)
Commander-in-Chief of Navy	*Karl Dönitz* (no party) (see Hitler)
Armaments	—— *Saur*
Commander-in-Chief of Air Force	*Robert von Greim* (b. Bayreuth 22 Jun 1892; d. Salzburg 24 May 1945)
Head of SS and Chief of Police	*Karl Hanke* (NSDAP) (b. Lauban 24 Aug 1903; d. Jun 1945(?))
Food	*Herbert Backe* (NSDAP) (see Hitler)
Education	*Gustav Adolf Scheel* (NSDAP) (b. Rosenberg 22 Oct 1907)
Propaganda	*Werner Naumann* (NSDAP) (b. Guhrau 16 Sep 1909)
Leader of German Labour Front	*Robert Ley* (b. Niederbreidenbach 15 Feb 1890; d. Nuremberg 25 Oct 1945)

3/5 – 23 May 1945: Schwerin von Krosigk (Caretaker Government)

Leader, Foreign Affairs and Finance	*Johann Ludwig, Count Schwerin von Krosigk* (no party) (see Papen)
Home Affairs and Culture	*Wilhelm Stuckart* (b. Wiesbaden 16 Nov 1902; d. near Hannover 16 Nov 1953)

*For earlier career see vol. 2

Labour and Social Affairs	*Franz Seldte* (see Hitler)
Food, Agriculture and Forestry	*Herbert Backe* (see Hitler)
Industry	*Albert Speer* (b. Mannheim 19 Mar 1905)
Transport and Post Office	*Julius Dorpmüller* (see Hitler)

ALLIED ZONES OF OCCUPATION

American and British (1946 – 1949)

24 Jul 1947 – 20 Sep 1949: Administrative Council

Overall Director (post created 2 Mar 1948)	2 Mar 1948 – 20 Sep 1949: *Hermann Pünder* (CDU) (b. Trier 1 Apr 1888)
Director for Food	*Hans Schlange-Schöningen* (CDU) (see Brüning II)
Finance	9 Aug 1947 – 20 Sep 1949: *Alfred Hartmann* (b. Duisburg 12 Sep 1894; d. Bad Godesberg 27 Aug 1967)
Law	*Walter Strauss* (CDU) (b. Berlin 15 Jun 1900)
Transport	9 Aug 1947 – 20 Sep 1949: *Edmund Frohne* (b. Leipzig 22 Jun 1891; d. 8 Aug 1971)
Posts and Tele-communications	*Hans Schuberth* (CSU) (b. Schwabach 5 Apr 1897)
Economic Affairs	24 Jul 1947 – 27 Jan 1948: *Johannes Semler* (b. Hamburg 16 Dec 1888) 2 Mar 1948 – 20 Sep 1949: *Ludwig Erhard* (from Feb 1949 CDU) (b. Fürth 4 Feb 1897)
Labour (new post)	20 Aug 1948 – 20 Sep 1949: *Anton Storch* (CDU) (b. Fulda 1 Apr 1892)

Russian (1945 – 1949)

15 Jun 1947/10 Mar 1948 – 11 Oct 1949: German Economic Commission

Chairman	*Heinrich Rau* (SED) (b. Stuttgart 2 Apr 1899; d. Berlin 23 Mar 1961)
Deputy Chairman	*Bruno Leuschner* (SED) (b. 12 Aug 1913; d. 10 Feb 1965)
Finance and Mining	*Hermann Kastner* (LPD) (b. Berlin 25 Oct 1886; d. Munich 6 Sep 1957)

247

Industry   *Fritz Selbmann* (SED) (b. Lauterbach 29 Sep 1899)
Agriculture and   *Luitpold Steidle* (CDU) (b. Ulm 12 Mar 1898)
Labour

Germany, Federal Republic of

HEADS OF STATE

Presidents

12 Sep 1949   *Theodor Heuss* (b. Brackenheim 31 Jan 1884; d. Stuttgart 12 Dec 1963)
13 Sep 1959   *Heinrich Lübke* (CDU) (b. Enkhausen 14 Oct 1894; d. Bonn 6 Apr 1972)
1 Jul 1969 – 30 Jun 1974   *Gustav W. Heinemann* (SPD) (b. Schwelm 23 Jul 1899; d. Essen 7 Jul 1976)
from 15 May 1974   *Walter Scheel* (FDP) (b. Solingen 8 Jul 1919)

MEMBERS OF GOVERNMENT

15/20 Sep 1949 – 6 Oct 1953: Adenauer I (CDU/CSU, FDP and DP Coalition)

Chancellor   *Konrad Adenauer* (CDU) (for 1st time) (b. Cologne 5 Jan 1876; d. Rhöndorf 19 Apr 1967)
Vice Chancellor   *Franz Blücher* (FDP) (b. Essen 24 Mar 1896; d. Bad Godesberg 26 Mar 1959)
Foreign Affairs   13 Mar – 6 Oct 1951: *Konrad Adenauer* (CDU) (see above)
Home Affairs   20 Sep 1949 – 9 Oct 1950: *Gustav Heinemann* (CDU) (see Presidents)
11 Oct 1950 – 6 Oct 1953: *Robert Lehr* (CDU) (b. Celle 20 Aug 1883; d. Düsseldorf 13 Oct 1956)
Finance   *Fritz Schäffer* (CSU) (b. Munich 12 May 1888; d. Berchtesgaden 29 Mar 1967)
Economic Affairs   *Ludwig Erhard* (CDU) (b. Fürth 4 Feb 1897; d. 5 May 1977)

Labour	*Anton Storch* (CDU) (b. Fulda 1 Apr 1892)
Justice	*Thomas Dehler* (FDP) (b. Lichtenfels 14 Dec 1897; d. Streitberg 21 Jul 1967)
Posts	*Hans Schuberth* (CSU) (b. Schwabach 5 Apr 1897)
Transport	*Hans Christof Seebohm* (DP) (b. Emmanuelssegen 4 Aug 1903; d. Bad Godesberg 17 Sep 1967)
Agriculture and Food	*Wilhelm Niklas* (CSU) (b. Traunstein 23 Sep 1887; d. Munich 12 Apr 1957)
European Affairs	*Franz Blücher* (FDP) (see above)
Pan-German Affairs	*Jakob Kaiser* (CDU) (b. Hammelburg 8 Feb 1888; d. Berlin 7 May 1961)
Refugees	*Hans Lukaschek* (CDU) (b. Breslau 22 May 1885; d. Freiburg 26 Jan 1960)
Reconstruction	20 Sep 1949 – 9 Mar 1952: *Eberhard Wildermuth* (FDP) (b. Stuttgart 23 Oct 1890; d. Tubingen 9 Mar 1952)
	16 Jul 1952 – 6 Oct 1953: *Fritz Neumayer* (FDP) (b. Kaiserslautern 29 Jul 1884)
Federal Council Affairs	*Heinrich Hellwege* (DP) (b. Neuenkirchen 18 Aug 1908)

9/20 Oct 1953 – 22 Oct 1957: Adenauer II (CDU/CSU, FDP and DP Coalition)

Chancellor	*Konrad Adenauer* (CDU) (for 2nd time) (see Adenauer I)
Vice Chancellor	21 Oct 1953 – 22 Oct 1957: *Franz Blücher* (FDP, from Feb 1956 FVP) (see Adenauer I)
Foreign Affairs	20 Oct 1953 – 6 Jun 1955: *Konrad Adenauer* (CDU) (see above)
	6 Jun 1955 – 22 Oct 1957: *Heinrich von Brentano di Tremezzo* (CDU) (b. Offenbach 20 Jun 1904; d. Darmstadt 14 Nov 1964)
Home Affairs	*Gerhard Schröder* (CDU) (b. Saarbrucken 11 Sep 1910)
Finance	*Fritz Schäffer* (CSU) (see Adenauer I)
Defence (new post)	6/8 Jun 1955 – 16 Oct 1956: *Theodor Blank* (CDU) (b. Elz an der Lahn 19 Sep 1905; d. 14 May 1972)
	16 Oct 1956 – 22 Oct 1957: *Franz Josef Strauss* (CSU) (b. Munich 6 Sep 1915)
Atomic Energy (new post)	12 Oct 1955 – 16 Oct 1956: *Franz Josef Strauss* (CSU) (see above)
	16 Oct 1956 – 22 Oct 1957: *Siegfried Balke* (CSU) (b. Bochum 1 Aug 1902)

249

Economic Affairs	*Ludwig Erhard* (CDU) (see Adenauer I)
Labour	*Anton Storch* (CDU) (see Adenauer I)
Justice	20 Oct 1953 – 16 Oct 1956: *Fritz Neumayer* (FDP, from Feb 1956 FVP) (see Adenauer I) 16 Oct 1956 – 22 Oct 1957 (acting:) *Hans Joachim von Merkatz* (DP) (b. Stargard 7 Jul 1905)
Posts	9 Dec 1953 – 16 Oct 1956: *Siegfried Balke* (from 16 Jan 1954 CSU) (see above) 14 Nov 1956 – 22 Oct 1957: *Ernst Lemmer* (CDU) (b. Remscheid 28 Apr 1898; d. Berlin night of 17/18 Aug 1970)
Transport	*Hans Christof Seebohm* (DP) (see Adenauer I)
Food and Agriculture	*Heinrich Lübke* (CDU) (see Presidents)
European Affairs	*Franz Blücher* (FDP, from Feb 1956 FVP) (see Adenauer I)
Pan-German Affairs	*Jakob Kaiser* (CDU) (see Adenauer I)
Refugees	*Theodor Oberländer* (BHE, from 20 Mar 1956 CDU) (b. Meiningen 1 May 1905)
Housing	*Viktor Emanuel Preusker* (FDP, from Feb 1956 FVP, from Sep 1957 DP) (b. Berlin 25 Feb 1913)
Federal Council Affairs	20 Oct 1953 – 26 May 1955: *Heinrich Hellwege* (DP) (see Adenauer I) 6 Jun 1955 – 22 Oct 1957: *Hans Joachim von Merkatz* (DP) (see above)
Special Tasks (from 12 Aug 1954: examining problems of dependent middle class and its advancement)	20 Oct 1953 – 16 Oct 1956: *Herman Schäfer* (FDP) (b. Remscheid 6 Apr 1892; d. Bad Godesberg 26 May 1966) 20 Oct 1953 – 16 Oct 1956: *Waldemar Kraft* (GDB/BHE, from 11 Jul 1955 CDU) (b. Posnan 19 Feb 1898) 20 Oct 1953 – 12 Oct 1955: *Franz Josef Strauss* (CSU) (see above) 20 Oct 1953 – 12 Nov 1955: *Robert Tillmanns* (CDU) (b. Wuppertal 5 Apr 1896; d. Berlin 12 Nov 1955)
Special Tasks (Family Affairs)	*Franz Josef Wuermeling* (CDU) (b. Berlin-Charlottenburg 8 Nov 1900)

22/28 Oct 1957 – 7 Nov 1961: Adenauer III (CDU/CSU and DP Coalition)

Chancellor	*Konrad Adenauer* (CDU) (for 3rd time) (see Adenauer I)
Vice Chancellor	30 Oct 1957 – 7 Nov 1961: *Ludwig Erhard* (CDU) (see Adenauer I)

Foreign Affairs	28 Oct 1957 – 30 Oct 1961: *Heinrich von Brentano di Tremezzo* (CDU) (see Adenauer II)
Home Affairs	*Gerhard Schröder* (CDU) (see Adenauer II)
Finance	*Franz Etzel* (CDU) (b. Wesel 12 Aug 1902; d. Wittlaer 9 May 1970)
Treasury	28 Oct 1957 – 27 Feb 1960: *Hermann Lindrath* (CDU) (b. Eisleben 29 Jun 1896; d. Mannheim 27 Feb 1960) 8 Apr 1960 – 7 Nov 1961: *Hans Wilhelmi* (CDU) (b. Mainz 27 Aug 1899; d. Frankfurt am Main 5 Jun 1970)
Defence	*Franz Josef Strauss* (CSU) (see Adenauer II)
Atomic Energy and Hydro-Electric Power	*Siegfried Balke* (CSU) (see Adenauer II)
Economic Affairs	*Ludwig Erhard* (CDU) (see Adenauer I)
Labour and Social Affairs	*Theodor Blank* (CDU) (see Adenauer II)
Justice	*Fritz Schäffer* (CSU) (see Adenauer I)
Posts	*Richard Stücklen* (CSU) (b. Heideck 20 Aug 1916)
Transport	*Hans Christof Seebohm* (DP, from 1960 CDU) (see Adenauer I)
Food and Agriculture	28 Oct 1957 – 12 Sep 1959: *Heinrich Lübke* (CDU) (see Presidents) 30 Sep 1959 – 7 Nov 1961: *Werner Schwarz* (CDU) (b. Hamburg 21 Jan 1900)
European Affairs	Post abolished
Pan-German Affairs	*Ernst Lemmer* (CDU) (see Adenauer II)
Refugees	28 Oct 1957 – 4 May 1960: *Theodor Oberländer* (CDU) (see Adenauer II) 27 Oct 1960 – 7 Nov 1961: *Hans Joachim von Merkatz* (DP, from 1 Jul 1960 CDU) (see Adenauer II)
Housing	*Paul Lücke* (CDU) (b. Schonborn 13 Nov 1914)
Federal Council Affairs	*Hans Joachim von Merkatz* (DP, from 1 Jul 1960 CDU) (see Adenauer II)
Families and Youth	*Franz Josef Wuermeling* (CDU) (see Adenauer II)

14 Nov 1961 – 20 Nov/13 Dec 1962: Adenauer IV (CDU/CSU and FDP Coalition)

Chancellor	*Konrad Adenauer* (CDU) (for 4th time) (see Adenauer I)
Vice Chancellor	*Ludwig Erhard* (CDU) (see Adenauer I)
Foreign Affairs	*Gerhard Schröder* (CDU) (see Adenauer II)

Home Affairs	*Hermann Höcherl* (CSU) (b. Brennberg 31 Mar 1912)
Finance	14 Nov 1961 – 19 Nov 1962: *Heinz Starke* (FDP) (b. Schweidnitz 27 Feb 1911)
Treasury	14 Nov 1961 – 19 Nov 1962: *Hans Lenz* (FDP) (b. Trossingen 12 Jul 1907; d. Trossingen 28 Aug 1968)
Defence	*Franz Josef Strauss* (CSU) (see Adenauer II)
Atomic Energy	*Siegfried Balke* (CSU) (see Adenauer II)
Economic Affairs	*Ludwig Erhard* (see Adenauer I)
Labour and Social Affairs	*Theodor Blank* (CDU) (see Adenauer II)
Justice	14 Nov 1961 – 19 Nov 1962: *Wolfgang Stammberger* (FDP) (b. Coburg 14 Jul 1920)
Posts and Tele-communications	*Richard Stücklen* (CSU) (see Adenauer III)
Transport	*Hans Christof Seebohm* (CDU) (see Adenauer I)
Food, Agriculture and Forestry	*Werner Schwarz* (CDU) (see Adenauer III)
Health	*Elisabeth Schwarzhaupt* (CDU) (b. Frankfurt 7 Jan 1901)
Economic Co-operation	14 Nov 1961 – 19 Nov 1962: *Walter Scheel* (FDP) (see Presidents)
Pan-German Affairs	*Ernst Lemmer* (CDU) (see Adenauer II)
Refugees and War Wounded	14 Nov 1961 – 19 Nov 1962: *Wolfgang Mischnick* (FDP) (b. Dresden 29 Sep 1921)
Town and Regional Planning	*Paul Lücke* (CDU) (see Adenauer III)
Federal Council and Länder	*Hans Joachim von Merkatz* (CDU) (see Adenauer II)
Families and Youth	*Franz Josef Wuermeling* (CDU) (see Adenauer II)
Special Tasks	*Heinrich Krone* (CDU) (b. Hessisch-Oldendorf 1 Dec 1895)

13 Dec 1962 – 15 Oct 1963: Adenauer V (CDU/CSU and FDP Coalition)

Chancellor	*Konrad Adenauer* (CDU) (for 5th time) (see Adenauer I)
Vice Chancellor	*Ludwig Erhard* (CDU) (see Adenauer I)
Foreign Affairs	*Gerhard Schröder* (CDU) (see Adenauer II)
Home Affairs	*Hermann Höcherl* (CSU) (see Adenauer IV)
Finance	*Rolf Dahlgrün* (FDP) (b. Hannover 19 May 1908; d. Dec 1969)
Treasury	*Werner Dollinger* (CSU) (b. Neustadt 10 Oct 1918)

Defence	13 Dec 1962 – 9 Jan 1963 (acting:) *Franz Josef Strauss* (CSU) (see Adenauer II) 9 Jan – 15 Oct 1963: *Kai-Uwe von Hassel* (CDU) (b. Neu-Köln, German East Africa (now Gare, Tanzania), 21 Apr 1913)
Science and Research (from 7 Dec 1962: under control of Atomic Energy)	*Hans Lenz* (FDP) (see Adenauer IV)
Economic Affairs	*Ludwig Erhard* (CDU) (see Adenauer I)
Labour	*Theodor Blank* (CDU) (see Adenauer II)
Justice	*Ewald Bucher* (FDP) (b. Rottenburg 19 Aug 1914)
Posts	*Richard Stücklen* (CSU) (see Adenauer III)
Transport	*Hans Christof Seebohm* (CDU) (see Adenauer I)
Food and Agriculture	*Werner Schwarz* (CDU) (see Adenauer III)
Health	*Elisabeth Schwarzhaupt* (CDU) (see Adenauer IV)
Economic Co- operation	*Walter Scheel* (FDP) (see Presidents)
Pan-German Affairs	*Rainer Barzel* (CDU) (b. Braunsberg 20 Jun 1924)
Refugees	*Wolfgang Mischnick* (FDP) (see Adenauer IV)
Housing	*Paul Lücke* (CDU) (see Adenauer III)
Federal Council and Länder	*Alois Niederalt* (CSU) (b. Niedermurach 10 Apr 1911)
Families and Youth	*Bruno Heck* (CDU) (b. Aalen 20 Jan 1917)
Special Tasks	*Heinrich Krone* (CDU) (see Adenauer IV)

16/17 Oct 1963 – 25 Oct 1965: Erhard I (CDU/CSU and FDP Coalition)

Chancellor	*Ludwig Erhard* (for 1st time) (CDU) (see Adenauer I)
Vice Chancellor	*Erich Mende* (FDP) (b. Gross-Strehlitz 28 Oct 1916)
Foreign Affairs	*Gerhard Schröder* (CDU) (see Adenauer II)
Home Affairs	*Hermann Höcherl* (CSU) (see Adenauer IV)
Finance	*Rolf Dahlgrün* (FDP) (see Adenauer V)
Treasury	*Werner Dollinger* (CDU) (see Adenauer V)
Defence	*Kai-Uwe von Hassel* (CDU) (see Adenauer V)
Scientific Research	*Hans Lenz* (FDP) (see Adenauer IV)
Economic Affairs	*Kurt Schmücker* (CDU) (b. Loningen 10 Nov 1919)
Labour	*Theodor Blank* (CDU) (see Adenauer II)
Justice	17 Oct 1963 – 27 Mar 1965: *Ewald Bucher* (FDP) (see Adenauer V) 27 Mar – 25 Oct 1965: *Karl Weber* (CDU) (b. Arenberg 8 Mar 1898)

Posts	*Richard Stücklen* (CSU) (see Adenauer III)
Transport	*Hans Christof Seebohm* (CDU) (see Adenauer I)
Food and Agriculture	*Werner Schwarz* (CDU) (see Adenauer III)
Health	*Elisabeth Schwarzhaupt* (CDU) (see Adenauer IV)
Economic Co-operation	*Walter Scheel* (FDP) (see Presidents)
Pan-German Affairs	*Erich Mende* (FDP) (see above)
Refugees	17 Oct 1963 – 22 Jan/7 Feb 1964: *Hans Krüger* (CDU) (b. Neustettin 6 Jul 1902; d. Röttgen 3 Nov 1971) 17 Feb 1964 – 25 Oct 1965: *Ernst Lemmer* (CDU) (see Adenauer II)
Housing	*Paul Lücke* (CDU) (see Adenauer III)
Federal Council and Länder	*Alois Niederalt* (CSU) (see Adenauer V)
Families and Youth	*Bruno Heck* (CDU) (see Adenauer V)
Special Tasks	*Heinrich Krone* (CDU) (see Adenauer IV)

26 Oct 1965 – 1 Dec 1966: Erhard II (CDU/CSU and FDP Coalition)

Chancellor	*Ludwig Erhard* (for 2nd time) (CDU) (see Adenauer I)
Vice Chancellor	26 Oct 1965 – 27 Oct 1966: *Erich Mende* (FDP) (see Erhard I)
Foreign Affairs	*Gerhard Schröder* (CDU) (see Adenauer II)
Home Affairs	*Paul Lücke* (CDU) (see Adenauer III)
Finance	26 Oct 1965 – 27 Oct 1966: *Rolf Dahlgrün* (FDP) (see Adenauer V) 28 Oct – 1 Dec 1966: *Kurt Schmücker* (CDU) (see Erhard I)
Treasury	*Werner Dollinger* (CSU) (see Adenauer V)
Defence	*Kai-Uwe von Hassel* (CDU) (see Adenauer V)
Scientific Research	*Gerhard Stoltenberg* (CDU) (b. Kiel 29 Sep 1928)
Economic Affairs	*Kurt Schmücker* (CDU) (see Erhard I)
Labour and Social Affairs	*Hans Katzer* (CDU) (b. Cologne 31 Jan 1919)
Justice	*Richard Jaeger* (CSU) (b. Berlin 16 Feb 1913)
Posts and Tele-communications	*Richard Stücklen* (CSU) (see Adenauer III)
Transport	*Hans Christof Seebohm* (CDU) (see Adenauer I)
Food, Agriculture and Forestry	*Hermann Höcherl* (CSU) (see Adenauer IV)
Health	*Elisabeth Schwarzhaupt* (CDU) (see Adenauer IV)

Economic Co-operation	26 Oct 1965 – 27 Oct 1966: *Walter Scheel* (FDP) (see Presidents) 28 Oct – 1 Dec 1966: *Werner Dollinger* (CSU) (see Adenauer V)
Pan-German Affairs	26 Oct 1965 – 27 Oct 1966: *Erich Mende* (FDP) (see Erhard I) 28 Oct – 1 Dec 1966: *Johann Baptist Gradl* (CDU) (b. Berlin 25 Mar 1904)
Refugees and War Wounded	*Johann Baptist Gradl* (see above)
Housing and Town Planning	26 Oct 1965 – 27 Oct 1966: *Ewald Bucher* (FDP) (see Adenauer V) 28 Oct – 1 Dec 1966: *Bruno Heck* (CDU) (see Adenauer V)
Federal Council and Länder	*Alois Niederalt* (CSU) (see Adenauer V)
Families and Youth	*Bruno Heck* (CDU) (see Adenauer V)
Defence Council Affairs	*Heinrich Krone* (CDU) (see Adenauer IV)
Special Tasks	26 Oct 1965 – 5 Oct 1966: *Ludger Westrick* (CDU) (b. Münster 23 Oct 1894)

1 Dec 1966 – 21 Oct 1969: Kiesinger (CDU/CSU and SPD Coalition)

Chancellor	*Kurt Georg Kiesinger* (CDU) (b. Ebingen 6 Apr 1904)
Vice Chancellor	*Willy Brandt* (SPD) (b. Lübeck 18 Dec 1913)
Foreign Affairs	*Willy Brandt* (SPD) (see above)
Home Affairs	1 Dec 1966 – 2 Apr 1968: *Paul Lücke* (CDU) (see Adenauer III) 2 Apr 1968 – 21 Oct 1969: *Ernst Benda* (CDU) (b. Berlin 15 Jan 1925)
Finance	*Franz Josef Strauss* (CSU) (see Adenauer II)
Treasury	*Kurt Schmücker* (CDU) (see Erhard I)
Defence	*Gerhard Schröder* (CDU) (see Adenauer II)
Scientific Affairs	*Gerhard Stoltenberg* (CDU) (see Erhard II)
Economic Affairs	*Karl Schiller* (SPD) (b. Breslau 24 Apr 1911)
Labour and Social Affairs	*Hans Katzer* (CDU) (see Erhard II)
Justice	1 Dec 1966 – 26 Mar 1969: *Gustav W. Heinemann* (see Presidents) 26 Mar – 21 Oct 1969: *Horst Ehmke* (SPD) (b. Danzig 4 Feb 1927)

Posts and Tele-communications	*Werner Dollinger* (CSU) (see Adenauer V)
Transport	*Georg Leber* (SPD) (b. Obertiefenbach 7 Oct 1920)
Food, Agriculture and Forestry	*Hermann Höcherl* (CSU) (see Adenauer IV)
Health	*Käte Strobel* (SPD) (b. Nuremberg 23 Jul 1907)
Economic Co-operation	1 Dec 1966 – 2 Oct 1968: *Hans-Jürgen Wischnewski* (SPD) (b. Allenstein 24 Jul 1922) 2 Oct 1968 – 21 Oct 1969: *Erhard Eppler* (SPD) (b. Ulm 9 Dec 1926)
Pan-German Affairs	*Herbert Wehner* (SPD) (b. Dresden 11 Jul 1906)
Displaced Persons, Refugees and War Wounded	1 Dec 1966 – 5 Feb 1969: *Kai-Uwe von Hassel* (CDU) (see Adenauer V) 7 Feb – 21 Oct 1969: *Heinrich Windelen* (CDU) (b. Bolkenhain 25 Jun 1921)
Housing and Town Planning	*Lauritz Lauritzen* (SPD) (b. Kiel 20 Jan 1910)
Federal Council and Länder	*Carlo Schmid* (SPD) (b. Perpignan, France, 3 Dec 1896)
Families and Youth	1 Dec 1966 – 2 Oct 1968: *Bruno Heck* (CDU) (see Adenauer V) 2 Oct 1968 – 21 Oct 1969: *Aenne Brauksiepe* (CDU) (b. Duisburg 23 Feb 1912)

22 Oct 1969 – 15 Dec 1972: Brandt I (SPD and FDP Coalition)

Chancellor	*Willy Brandt* (SPD) (for 1st time) (see Kiesinger)
Vice Chancellor and Foreign Affairs	*Walter Scheel* (FDP) (see Presidents)
Home Affairs	*Hans-Dietrich Genscher* (FDP) (b. Reideburg 21 Mar 1927)
Finance	22 Oct 1969 – 13 May 1971: *Alex Möller* (SPD) (b. Dortmund 28 Apr 1903) from 13 May 1971: amalgamated with Economic Affairs (see below)
Defence	22 Oct 1969 – 7 Jul 1972: *Helmut Schmidt* (SPD) (b. Hamburg 23 Sep 1918) 7 Jul – 15 Dec 1972: *Georg Leber* (SPD) (see Kiesinger)
Education and Research	22 Oct 1969 – 27 Jan 1972: *Hans Leussink* (b. Schüttorf 2 Feb 1912) 27 Jan – 15 Dec 1972: *Klaus von Dohnanyi* (SPD) (b. Hamburg 23 Jun 1928)

Economic Affairs (from 13 May 1971: incorporating Finance)	22 Oct 1969 – 2 Jul 1972: *Karl Schiller* (SPD) (see Kiesinger)
	7 Jul – 15 Dec 1972: *Helmut Schmidt* (SPD) (see above)
Labour	*Walter Arendt* (SPD) (b. Heessen 17 Jan 1925)
Justice	*Gerhard Jahn* (SPD) (b. Kassel 10 Sep 1927)
Transport (incorporating Posts and Telecommunications)	22 Oct 1969 – 7 Jul 1972: *Georg Leber* (SPD) (see Kiesinger)
	7 Jul – 15 Dec 1972: *Lauritz Lauritzen* (SPD) (see Kiesinger)
Food and Agriculture	*Josef Ertl* (FDP) (b. Munich 7 Mar 1925)
Health (incorporating Family and Youth Affairs)	*Käte Strobel* (SPD) (see Kiesinger)
Economic Cooperation	*Erhard Eppler* (SPD) (see Kiesinger)
German Internal Relations	*Egon Franke* (SPD) (b. Hannover 11 Apr 1913)
Special Tasks (in Chancellor's Office)	*Horst Ehmke* (SPD) (see Kiesinger)

15 Dec 1972 – 6 May 1974: Brandt II (SPD and FDP Coalition)

Chancellor	*Willy Brandt* (SPD) (for 2nd time) (see Kiesinger)
Vice Chancellor and Foreign Affairs	*Walter Scheel* (FDP) (see Presidents)
Home Affairs	*Hans-Dietrich Genscher* (FDP) (see Brandt I)
Finance	*Helmut Schmidt* (SPD) (see Brandt I)
Economic Affairs	*Hans Friderichs* (FDP) (b. Wittlich 16 Oct 1931)
Defence	*Georg Leber* (SPD) (see Kiesinger)
Education and Science	*Klaus von Dohnanyi* (SPD) (see Brandt I)
Labour and Social Affairs	*Walter Arendt* (SPD) (see Brandt I)
Justice	*Gerhard Jahn* (SPD) (see Brandt I)
Transport	*Lauritz Lauritzen* (SPD) (see Kiesinger)
Food, Agriculture and Forestry	*Josef Ertl* (FDP) (see Brandt I)
Health and Family and Youth Affairs	*Katherina Focke* (SPD) (b. Bonn 8 Oct 1922)
Economic Cooperation	*Erhard Eppler* (SPD) (see Kiesinger)

German Internal Relations	*Egon Franke* (SPD) (see Brandt I)
Housing and Town Planning	*Hans-Jochen Vogel* (SPD)
Research and Technology (new post)	*Horst Ehmke* (SPD) (see Kiesinger)
Special Tasks	*Egon Bahr* (SPD) (b. Treffurt 18 Mar 1922)
	Werner Maihofer (FDP) (b. Konstanz 20 Oct 1918)

from 16 May 1974: Schmidt (SPD and FDP Coalition)

Chancellor	*Helmut Schmidt* (SPD) (see Brandt I)
Vice Chancellor and Foreign Affairs	*Hans-Dietrich Genscher* (FDP) (see Brandt I)
Home Affairs	*Werner Maihofer* (FDP) (see Brandt II)
Finance	*Hans Eberhard Apel* (SPD) (b. Hamburg 25 Feb 1932)
Economic Affairs	*Hans Friderichs* (FDP) (see Brandt II)
Defence	*Georg Leber* (SPD) (see Kiesinger)
Education and Science	*Helmut Rohde* (SPD) (b. Hannover 9 Nov 1925)
Labour and Social Affairs	*Walter Arendt* (SPD) (see Brandt I)
Justice	*Hans-Jochen Vogel* (SPD) (see Brandt II)
Transport, Posts and Telecommunications	*Kurt Gscheidle* (SPD) (b. Stuttgart 16 Dec 1924)
Food, Agriculture and Forestry	*Josef Ertl* (FDP) (see Brandt I)
Health and Family and Youth Affairs	*Katherina Focke* (SPD) (see Brandt II)
Economic Cooperation	16 May – 4 Jul 1974: *Erhard Eppler* (SPD) (see Kiesinger)
	from 8 Jul 1974: *Egon Bahr* (SPD) (see Brandt II)
German Internal Relations	*Egon Franke* (SPD) (see Brandt I)
Housing and Town Planning	*Karl Friedrich Ravens* (SPD) (b. Achim 29 Jun 1927)
Research and Technology	*Hans Matthöfer* (SPD) (b. Bochum 25 Sep 1925)

Ghana

6 Mar 1957	Formed by amalgamation of Gold Coast colony and mandated territory of West Togoland, and became a member of British Commonwealth
1 Jul 1960	Republic

HEADS OF STATE

Presidents

1 Jul 1960	*Kwame Nkrumah* (b. Nkroful 21 Sep 1909; d. Romania 27 Apr 1972)
25 Feb 1966	*Joseph Arthur Ankrah* (b. Accra 18 Aug 1915) Chairman of National Liberation Council
2 Apr 1969	*Akwasi Amankwa Afrifa* (for 1st time) (b. Mampong 24 Apr 1936) Chairman of National Liberation Council
1 Oct 1969	Presidential Committee (Triumvirate): *Akwasi Amankwa Afrifa* (for 2nd time) *John Willie Kofi Harlley* (b. Akagla 9 May 1919) *A. K. Okran* (b. Brakwa 21 Jul 1929)
31 Aug 1970 – 12 Jan 1972	*Edward Akufo-Addo* (b. Akropong 26 Jun 1906)
from 13 Jan 1972	*Ignatius Kuti Acheampong* (b. Kumasi, Ashanti, 23 Sep 1931) Leader of National Redemption Council

MEMBERS OF GOVERNMENT

Prime Ministers

1 Jul 1960 – 31 Aug 1969	President also Prime Minister
3 Sep 1969 – 13 Jan 1972	*Kofi Abrefa Busia* (b. Brong Ahafo region 1913)
from 13 Jan 1972	President also Prime Minister

Greece

HEADS OF STATE

President

15 Dec 1929 – Oct 1935	*Alexander T. Zaïmis* (b. Athens 9 Nov 1855; d. 15 Sep 1936)*
Oct 1935	Restoration of monarchy

Kings

Oct – 3 Nov 1935	*George Kondylis* (b. 1879; d. 31 Jan 1936) Regent*
3 Nov 1935 – 1 Apr 1947	*George II*, son of Constantine I (for 2nd time) (b. 19 Jul 1890) Apr 1941 – 27 Sep 1946 in exile*
Jan 1945 – 5 Sep 1946	*Damaskinos, Archbishop of Athens* (b. Dobitza 1891; d. Athens 20 May 1949) Regent
1 Apr 1947	*Paul*, brother of George II (b. 14 Dec 1901)
6 Mar 1964 – 13 Dec 1967	*Constantine II*, son (b. 2 Jun 1940) ousted in military coup and forced into exile
13 Aug 1973	Republic accepted by referendum
8 Dec 1974	Monarchy formally abolished

Viceroys

13 Dec 1967	*George Zoitakis* (b. Naupactus 1910)
21 Mar 1972 – 1 Jun 1973	*George Papadopoulos* (b. Eleochorion 1919)

Presidents

1 Jun 1973	*George Papadopoulos* (see Viceroys) Republic accepted by referendum 29 Jul/ 13 Aug 1973
25 Nov 1973	*Phaedon Gizikis* (b. Volos 16 Jun 1917)
from 18 Dec 1974	*Michael Stasinopoulos* (b. Kalamata 27 Jul 1905)

*For earlier career see vol. 2

MEMBERS OF GOVERNMENT

Prime Ministers

16 Dec 1929 – 21 Dec 1930	*Eleftherios K. Venizelos* (for 7th time) (b. Mournies 23 Aug 1864; d. Paris 18 Mar 1936)*
23 Dec 1930 – 21 May 1932	*Eleftherios K. Venizelos* (for 8th time)
26 May – 3 Jun 1932	*Alexander Papanastasiou* (for 2nd time) (b. Tripolis 1876; d. Ekali 17 Nov 1936)*
6 Jun – 31 Oct 1932	*Eleftherios K. Venizelos* (for 9th time)
4 Nov 1932 – 13 Jan 1933	*Panagiotis Tsaldaris* (for 1st time) (b. 1868; d. 17 May 1936)
17 Jan – 6 Mar 1933	*Eleftherios K. Venizelos* (for 10th time)
6 Mar 1933	*Nicholas Plastiras* (for 1st time) (b. 1884; d. 26 Jul 1953) Military Dictator
6 – 8 Mar 1933	*Alexander Othonaos* (b. 1879(?); d. Athens 20 Sep 1970)
10 Mar 1933	*Panagiotis Tsaldaris* (for 2nd time)
20 Mar 1935	*Panagiotis Tsaldaris* (for 3rd time)
20 Jul 1935	*Panagiotis Tsaldaris* (for 4th time)
10 Oct – 25 Nov 1935	*George Kondylis* (for 2nd time) (see Kings)
30 Nov 1935	*Constantine Demertis* (for 1st time) (b. 7 Nov 1876; d. 12 Apr 1936)
14 Mar 1936	*Constantine Demertzis* (for 2nd time)
13 Apr 1936	*John Metaxas* (for 1st time) (b. 1871; d. 29 Jan 1941)
4 Aug 1936	*John Metaxas* (for 2nd time)
29 Jan 1941	*Alexander Koryzis* (b. 1885/86; d. Athens 18 Apr 1941)
19 – 21 Apr 1941	*George II* (see Kings) Chairman of ministers
21 Apr 1941	*Emmanuel Tsouderos* (b. 1882; d. Genoa 10 Feb 1956) German occupation:
1 May 1941	*George Tsolakoglou* (b. 1887(?); d. 22 May 1948)
2 Dec 1942	*Constantine Logothetopoulos* (d. 3 Jan 1951)
7 Apr 1943 – 12 Oct 1944	*John Rallis* (b. Athens 1878; d. 26 Oct 1946)
	Government in exile:
29 Jun 1941	*Emmanuel Tsouderos* (for 2nd time)
27 Mar 1943 – 3 Apr 1944	*Emmanuel Tsouderos* (for 3rd time)
15 – 27 Apr 1944	*Sophocles Venizelos* (for 1st time) (b. 17 Nov 1894; d.

*For earlier career see vol. 2

	between Crete and Athens night of 6/7 Feb 1964)
26 May – 31 Dec 1944	*George Papandreou* (for 1st time) (b. Kalentizi Jan 1888; d. Athens 1 Nov 1968) returned to Athens 20 Oct 1944 after Greek liberation
3 Jan 1945	*Nicholas Plastiras* (for 2nd time)
9 Apr – 9 Oct 1945	*Peter Voulgaris* (b. Hydra 1884; d. Athens 26 Nov 1957)
17 Oct 1945	*Damaskinos, Archbishop of Athens* (see Kings)
1 – 20 Nov 1945	*Panagiotis Kanellopoulos* (for 1st time) (b. Patras 13 Dec 1902)
21 Nov 1945 – 1 Apr 1946	*Themistocles Sophoulis* (for 2nd time) (b. Vathy 20 Nov 1860; d. Athens 24 Jun 1949)*
7 Apr 1946	*Panagiotis Politzas*
21 Apr – 28 Sep 1946	*Constantine Tsaldaris* (for 1st time) (b. Alexandria 1884; d. Athens 15 Nov 1970)
3 Oct – 3 Nov 1946	*Constantine Tsaldaris* (for 2nd time)
4 Nov 1946 – 22 Jan 1947	*Constantine Tsaldaris* (for 3rd time)
25 Jan – 1 Apr 1947	*Demetrius Maximos* (for 1st time) (b. Patras 6 Jul 1873; d. Athens 15 Oct 1955)
2 Apr – 25 Aug 1947	*Demetrius Maximos* (for 2nd time)
30 Aug – 5 Sep 1947	*Constantine Tsaldaris* (for 4th time)
8 Sep 1947 – 12 Nov 1948**	*Themistocles Sophoulis* (for 3rd time)
17 Nov 1948	*Themistocles Sophoulis* (for 4th time)
19 Jan – 12 Apr 1949	*Themistocles Sophoulis* (for 5th time)
14 Apr – 24 Jun 1949	*Themistocles Sophoulis* (for 6th time)
30 Jun 1949 – 5 Jan 1950	*Alexander Diomedes* (b. 1875(?); d. Athens 11(?) Nov 1950)00
7 Jan – 5 Mar 1950	*John Theotokis* (b. Corfu 1880)
23 Mar – 14 Apr 1950	*Sophocles Venizelos* (for 2nd time)
15 Apr – 18 Aug 1950	*Nicholas Plastiras* (for 3rd time)
21 Aug – 9 Sep 1950	*Sophocles Venizelos* (for 3rd time)
13 Sep – 2 Nov 1950	*Sophocles Venizelos* (for 4th time)
9 Nov 1950 – 28 Jul 1951	*Sophocles Venizelos* (for 5th time)

*For earlier career see vol. 2
**Communist Administration in Northern Greece (abroad from 1948)

24 Dec 1947 – 7 Feb 1949	*General Markos*
7 Feb – Apr 1949	*Nikos Zachariadis* (b. Asia Minor 1900(?))
Apr 1949 – Feb 1956	*Demetrius Partsalidis* (b. 1903?)
Feb 1956	*Apostolos Grozos* (b. 1891?)

30 Jul – 27 Oct 1951	*Sophocles Venizelos* (for 6th time)
1 Nov 1951	*Nicholas Plastiras* (for 4th time)
11 Oct 1952	*Demetrius Kiusopoulos* (b. Andritsaina 1892)
19 Nov 1952	*Alexander Papagos* (b. 9 Oct 1883; d. Athens 4 Oct 1955)
4 Oct 1955	*Stephen C. Stefanopoulos* (for 1st time) (b. Prygos 1898)
6 Oct 1955	*Constantine (Kostas) Karamanlis* (for 1st time) (b. Athens 6 Jan 1907)
3 Mar 1958	*Constantine Georgakopoulos* (b. Tripolis 1890)
17 May 1958	*Constantine (Kostas) Karamanlis* (for 2nd time)
20 Sep 1961	*Constantine Dovas* (b. Conitsa 1898(?))
4 Nov 1961 – 11 Jun 1963	*Constantine (Kostas) Karamanlis* (for 3rd time)
19 Jun – 26 Sep 1963	*Panagiotis Pipinellis* (b. Piraeus 21 Mar 1899; d. Athens 19 Jul 1970)
28 Sep 1963	*Stylianos Mavromichalis*
7 Nov – 24 Dec	*George Papandreou* (for 2nd time)
30 Dec 1963	*John Paraskevopoulos* (for 1st time) (b. Olympia 25 Dec 1900)
19 Feb 1964	*George Papandreou* (for 3rd time)
15 Jul – 5 Aug 1965	*George Athanasiadis-Novas* (b. Naupactus Feb 1893)
19 – 29 Aug 1965	*Elias Tsirimokos* (b. Lamia 2 Aug 1907; d. Athens 13 Jul 1968)
17 Nov 1965	*Stephen C. Stefanopoulos* (for 2nd time)
22 Dec 1966 – 30 Mar 1967	*John Paraskevopoulos* (for 2nd time)
3 Apr 1967	*Panagiotis Kanellopoulos* (for 2nd time)
21 Apr 1967	*Constantine Kollias* (b. Stylia 1901)
13 Dec 1967	*George Papadopoulos* (see Viceroys)
1 Oct 1973	*Spyridon Markezinis*
25 Nov 1973	*Adamantios Androutsopoulos* (b. Psari 1919)
from 24 Jul 1974	*Constantine (Kostas) Karamanlis* (for 4th time) returned from self-imposed exile in Paris following resignation of Military Junta

Foreign Ministers

6 Jul 1929 – 21 May 1932	*Andrew Michalakopoulos* (for 3rd time) (b. 1876; d. 27 Mar 1938)*
27 May – 2 Jun 1932	*Alexander Papanastasiou* (for 2nd time) (see Prime Ministers)

*For earlier career see vol. 2

263

6 Jun – 31 Oct 1932	*Andrew Michalakopoulos* (for 4th time)
5 Nov 1932	*John Rallis* (see Prime Ministers)
17 Jan – 5 Mar 1933	*Andrew Michalakopoulos* (for 5th time)
10 Mar 1933	*Demetrius Maximos* (for 1st time) (see Prime Ministers)
3 – 20 Mar 1935	*Panagiotis Tsaldaris* (for 1st time) (see Prime Ministers)
27 Mar – Jun 1935	*Demetrius Maximos* (for 2nd time)
Jun 1935	*Panagiotis Tsaldaris* (for 2nd time)
13 Jul 1935	*Demetrius Maximos* (for 3rd time)
10 Oct – 25 Nov 1935	*John Theotokis* (see Prime Ministers)
30 Nov 1935	*Constantine Demertzis* (see Prime Ministers)
13 Apr 1936	*John Metaxas* (see Prime Ministers)
29 Jan 1941	*Alexander Koryzis* (see Prime Ministers)
19 Apr – Jun 1941	*Emmanuel Tsouderos* (for 1st time) (see Prime Ministers)
29 Jun 1941 – Oct 1944	No Foreign Minister appointed during German occupation Government in exile:
29 Jun 1941 – 3 Apr 1944	*Emmanuel Tsouderos* (for 2nd time)
26 May – 31 Dec 1944	*George Papandreou* (see Prime Ministers) returned to Athens 20 Oct 1944 after Greek liberation
3 Jan – 24 Jul 1945	*John Sophianopoulos* (for 1st time) (b. Sopoton 1887; d. Jul 1951)
11 Aug 1945	*Peter Voulgaris* (see Prime Ministers)
19 Aug – Oct 1945	*John Politis* (for 1st time) (b. 1890(?); d. Athens 3 Jun 1959)
21 Nov 1945 – 29 Jan 1946	*John Sophianopoulos* (for 2nd time)
30 Jan – 1 Apr 1946	*Constantine Rendis* (for 4th time) (b. 1884; d. 1958)*
4 Apr 1946 – 5 Jan 1950**	*Constantine Tsaldaris* (see Prime Ministers)
7 Jan 1950	*Panagiotis Pipinellis* (for 1st time) (see Prime Ministers)

*For earlier career see vol. 2

**Communist Administration in Northern Greece (abroad from 1948)

31 Aug 1947	—— *Porphyrogennis*
24 Dec 1947 – Aug 1948	*Peter Rousos*

23 Mar – 7 Apr 1950	*Sophocles Venizelos* (for 1st time) (see Prime Ministers)
16 Apr – 17 Aug 1950	(acting:) *Nicholas Plastiras* (see Prime Ministers)
21 Aug 1950	*Sophocles Venizelos* (for 2nd time)
10 Aug – 27 Oct 1951	*John Politis* (for 2nd time)
29 Oct 1951	*Sophocles Venizelos* (for 3rd time)
11 Oct 1952	*Philip Dragoumis* (b. Athens 14 Jan 1890)
20 Nov 1952	*Stephen C. Stefanopoulos* (for 1st time) (see Prime Ministers)
6 Oct 1955 – 23 Apr 1956	*Spyrios Theotokis* (b. 1908)
28 May 1956	*Evangelos Averof* (for 1st time) (b. Trikkala 1910)
20 Sep 1961	*Michael Pesmazoglou*
4 Nov 1961 – 13 Jun 1963	*Evangelos Averof* (for 2nd time)
19 Jun – 26 Sep 1963	*Panagiotis Pipinellis* (for 2nd time)
28 Sep 1963	*Paul Oikonomou-Gouras* (for 1st time) (b. Corinth 1897 or 1898)
7 Nov – 24 Dec 1963	*Sophocles Venizelos* (for 4th time)
30 Dec 1963	*Christos Xanthopoulos-Palamas* (b. Missolonghi 1902; d. Jan 1977)
19 Feb 1964	*Stavros Kostopoulos* (b. 14 Sep 1900; d. 23 Jun 1968)
20 Jul – 5 Aug 1965	*George Melas*
20 Aug 1965	*Elias Tsirimokos* (see Prime Ministers)
12 Apr 1966	*Stephen C. Stefanopoulos* (for 2nd time)
11 May 1966	*John Toumbas* (b. 24 Feb 1901)
22 Dec 1966 – 30 Mar 1967	*Paul Oikonomou-Gouras* (for 2nd time)
3 – 21 Apr 1967	*Panagiotis Kanellopoulos* (see Ministers)
24 Apr 1967	*Paul Oikonomou-Gouras* (for 3rd time)
2 Nov 1967	(acting:) *Constantine Kollias* (see Prime Ministers)
20 Nov 1967 – 20 Jul 1970	*Panagiotis Pipinellis* (for 3rd time)
21 Jul 1970	(acting:) *George Papadopoulos* (see Viceroys) with *Christos Xanthopoulos-Palamas* (for 2nd time) as acting Secretary of State
8 Oct 1973	*Christos Xanthopoulos-Palamas* (for 3rd time)
25 Nov 1973	*Spyridon Tetenes* (b. 1908?)
26 Jul 1974	*George Mavros* (b. Kastellorizon 1909) Deputy Prime Minister
from 15 Oct 1974	(acting until 21 Nov 1974:) *Demetrius S. Bitsios* (b. 1915)

265

Grenada

3 Mar 1967	Internal self-government (state in association with the UK)
7 Feb 1974	Independence (member of the Commonwealth)

HEADS OF STATE

Governors

1968 – 14 Jan 1974	*Dame Hilda Louisa Bynoe* (b. Grenada 18 Nov 1921)
24 Jan 1974	*Sir Leo (Victor) de Gale* (b. 28 Dec 1921) (acting)

Governor-General

From 7 Feb 1974	*Sir Leo (Victor) de Gale*, previously acting Governor

MEMBERS OF GOVERNMENT

Prime Minister

from 7 Feb 1974	*Eric Matthew Gairy* (from 1977: *Sir*) (b. 1922) (Chief Minister from 7 Mar 1972)

Guatemala

HEADS OF STATE

Presidents

27 Sep 1926	*Lázaro Chacón* (b. 27 Jun 1873; d. 1931)
13 Dec 1930	*Baudillo Palma* (b. 1884; d. San Salvador 1946)

17 – 31 Dec 1930	*Manuel María Orellana*
2 Jan 1931	*José María Reyna Andrade* (b. 1860; d. 1947)
15 Feb 1931	*Jorge Ubico Castañeda* (b. 10 Nov 1878; d. New Orleans 17 May 1946)
1 Jul – 21 Oct 1944	*Federico Ponce Vaidez* (b. 1889; d. 1956)
19 Dec 1944 – 1 Mar 1945	*Jacobo Arbenz Guzmán* (for 1st time) (b. Quezaltenango 14 Sep 1913; d. Mexico City 27 Jan 1971)
11 Mar 1945	*Juán José Arévalo* (b. 10 Sep 1904)
1 Mar 1951	*Jacobo Arbenz Guzmán* (for 2nd time)
27 Jun 1954	*Carlos Díaz*, President of Military Junta
29 Jun 1954	*Elfego J. Monzón*
8 Jul 1954	*Carlos Castillo Armas* (b. 1914; d. 26 Jul 1957)
20 Jul 1957	*Oscar Mendoza Azurdia*, Head of Military Junta
27 Jul – 20 Oct 1957	*Luis Arturo González López* (b. Zacapa 21 Dec 1900; d. Guatemala City 11 Dec 1965)
28 Oct 1957	(acting:) *Guillermo Flores Avendaño* (b. 1898) Head of Military Junta
2 Mar 1958	*Miguel Ydígoras Fuentes* (b. 17 Oct 1895)
31 Mar 1963	*Enrique Peralta Azurdia* (b. Guatemala la Nueva 17 Jun 1908) Head of Military Junta
1 Jul 1966	*Julio César Méndez Montenegro* (b. Guatemala la Nueva 23 Nov 1915)
1 Jul 1970	*Carlos Araña Osorio* (b. Barbarena 17 Jul 1918)
from 1 Jul 1974	*Kjell Eugenio Laugerua García* (b. 24 Jan 1930)

Guinea

Named French Guinea until 2 Oct 1958.

2 Oct 1958	Independence from France

HEAD OF STATE

President

from 15 Jan 1961	*Ahmed Sekou Touré* (b. Faranah, Guinea, 9 Jan 1922) 1922)

MEMBER OF GOVERNMENT

Prime Minister

2 Oct 1958	*Ahmed Sekou Touré* (see President)
from 26 Apr 1972	*Louis Lansana Beavogui* (b. Macenta 1923)

Guinea-Bissau

Named Portuguese Guinea until 24 Sep 1973.

24 Sep 1973	Independence from Portugal

HEAD OF STATE

President

from 24 Sep 1973	*Luis de Almeida Cabral* (b. Bissau 1931)

MEMBER OF GOVERNMENT

Chief State Commissioner

from 24 Sep 1973	*Francisco Mendes* (b. Enxudé 1930)

Guyana

Named British Guiana until 26 May 1966.

26 May 1966	Independence from Great Britain
23 Feb 1970	Co-operative Republic

HEADS OF STATE

Governors-General

26 May 1966	*Sir Richard Luyt* (b. 8 Nov 1915)
16 Dec 1966 – 10 Nov 1969	*Sir David Rose* (b. 10 Apr 1923; d. London 10 Nov 1969)
(?) Nov 1969 – 23 Feb 1970	(acting:) *Sir Edward A. Luckhoo*

Presidents

23 Feb 1970	(acting:) *Sir Edward A. Luckhoo* (see Governors-General)
from 17 Mar 1970	*Arthur Chung* (b. Demerara 10 Jan 1918)

MEMBER OF GOVERNMENT

Prime Minister

from 26 May 1966	*Linden Forbes Sampson Burnham* (b. Georgetown 20 Feb 1923)

Haiti

HEADS OF STATE

Presidents

15 May 1922 – 23 Apr 1930	*Joseph Louis Bornó* (b. 20 Sep 1865; d. 29 Jul 1942)
15 May – Nov 1930	*Étienne Roy*
18 Nov 1930 – Apr 1941	*Stenio Vincent* (b. c. 1874; d. Port-au-Prince 3 Sep 1959)
Apr 1941	*Élie Lescot* (b. 1883; d. 22 Oct 1974)
12 Jan 1946	*Frank Lavaud* (for 1st time) leader of junta

15 Aug 1946	*Dumarsais Estimé* (b. Verelles 21 Apr 1900; d. New York 20 Jul 1953)
10 May – 6 Dec 1950	*Frank Lavaud* (for 2nd time) leader of junta
8 Oct/6 Dec 1950	*Paul (Eugène) Magloire* (b. 1907)
12 Dec 1956	*Joseph Nemours Pierre-Louis*
7 Feb – 2 Apr 1957	*François Sylvain*
6 Apr 1957	Executive Committee of 13 Ministers under the protection of the Army
20 May 1957	*General Léon Cantave* (b. Mirebalais 4 Jul 1910)
26 May 1957	*Daniel Fignolé* (b. Pestel 12 Nov 1914)
14 Jun – 15 Oct 1957	*Antoine Kebreau* (b. Port-au-Prince 11 Nov 1909; d. Port-au-Prince 13 Jan 1963)
15/22 Oct 1957	*François Duvalier* (b. Port-au-Prince 14 Apr 1909; d. 21 Apr 1971)
from 22 Apr 1971	*Jean-Claude Duvalier*, son (b. Port-au-Prince 3 Jul 1951)

Hatay

1938	Separated from Syria

HEAD OF STATE

President

2 Sep 1938 – 21 Jul 1939	*Tayfur Sökmen* (b. Kırıkhan 1889/90)
21 Jul 1939	Incorporated into Turkey

Hausa States

For the Kingdom of Daura and the Emirates of Kano, Katsina and Nupe see volume 2.

Honduras

HEADS OF STATE

Presidents

1 Feb 1929	*Vincente Mejía Colindres* (b. 1878; d. Tegucigalpa 24 Aug 1966)
1 Feb 1933	*Tiburcio Carías Andino* (b. 15 Mar 1876; d. Tegucigalpa 23 Dec 1969)
1 Jan 1949	*Juan Manuel Gálvez* (b. 1887)
Dec 1954	*Julio Lozano Díaz* (b. 1895(?); d. Miami 20 Aug 1957)
21 Oct 1956	*Roque I. Rodríguez*, Head of Military Triumvirate
21 Dec 1957	*José Ramón Villeda Morales* (b. Ocotepeque 26 Nov 1908; d. New York 8 Oct 1971)
4 Oct 1963	*Oswaldo López Arellano* (for 1st time) (b. Danlí 30 Jun 1921) Head of Military Junta, from 6 Jun 1965 President
5 Jun 1971	*Ramón Ernesto Cruz Uclés* (b. 4 Jan 1903)
4 Dec 1972	*Oswaldo López Arellano* (for 2nd time) Head of State
from 22 Apr 1975	*Juan Alberto Melgar Castro* (b. 1930?)

Hungary

HEADS OF STATE

Presidents

1 Mar 1920	*Miklós Horthy* (b. Kenderes 18 Jun 1868; d. Estoril near Lisbon 9 Feb 1957)
15 Oct 1944 – Apr 1945	*Ferenc Szálasi* (b. Kassa 6 Jan 1897; d. Budapest 12 Mar 1946)
2 Feb 1946 – 30 Jul 1948	*Zoltán Tildy* (b. 1889; d. Budapest 2(?) Aug 1961)
2 Aug 1948	*Árpád Szakasits* (b. Budapest 8 Dec 1888; d. Budapest 3 May 1965)

271

24 Apr 1950	*Sándor Rónai* (b. 6 Oct 1892; d. 27(?) Sep 1965)
14 Aug 1952	*István Dobi* (b. Szöny 31 Dec 1898; d. Budapest 24 Nov 1968)
from 14 Apr 1967	*Pál Losonczi* (b. Bolhó 18 Sep 1919)

MEMBERS OF GOVERNMENT

3 Dec 1921 – 19 Aug 1931: Bethlen II †

Prime Minister	*István, Count Bethlen* (for 2nd time) (b. Gernyeszég 3 Oct 1874; d. in prison camp in USSR 1947)*
Foreign Affairs	17 Mar 1925 – 10 Dec 1930: *Lajos Walko* (b. Budapest 30 Oct 1880; d. Visegrád 10 Jan 1954)
	10 Dec 1930 – 19 Aug 1931: *Gyula, Count Károlyi* (b. Nyirbakta 7 May 1871; d. Budapest 23 Apr 1947)
Home Affairs	15 Oct 1926 – 19 Aug 1931: *Tibor Scitovszky* (b. Nötincs 21 Jun 1875; d. Los Angeles 12 Apr 1959)*
Justice	4 Jan 1929 – 19 Aug 1931: *Tibor Zsitvay* (b. Bratislava 10 Nov 1884)
Finance	1928 – 19 Aug 1931: *Sándor Wekerle* (b. Budapest 26 Jun 1878; d. Budapest 23 Dec 1963)
Education	16 Jun 1922 – 19 Aug 1931: *Kunó, Count Klebelsberg* (b. Magyarpécska 13 Nov 1875; d. Budapest 11 Oct 1932)*
Defence	10 Oct 1929 – 19 Aug 1931: *Gyula Gömbös* (b. Murga 26 Dec 1886; d. Munich 6 Oct 1936)

22 Aug 1931 – 21 Sep 1932: Gyula Károlyi

Prime Minister	*Gyula, Count Károlyi* (see Bethlen II)
Foreign Affairs	*Lajos Walko* (see Bethlen II)
Home Affairs	*Ferenc Keresztes-Fischer* (b. 1881; d. 1948)
Justice	*Tibor Zsitvay* (see Bethlen II)
Finance	22 Aug – 19 Dec 1931 (acting:) *Gyula, Count Károlyi* (see Bethlen II)
	19 Dec 1931 – 21 Sep 1932: *Frigyes, Baron Korányi* (b. Pest 21 Jun 1869; d. Budapest 27 Dec 1935)*
Education	22 Aug – 12 Dec 1931: *Sándor Ernszt* (b. Freistadtl 21 Apr 1870; d. 1944)

† For ministers no longer in office in 1930 see vol. 2
*For earlier career see vol. 2

War	19 Dec 1931 – 21 Sep 1932: *Jenő Karafioth*
	Gyula Gömbös (see Bethlen II)

30 Sep 1932 – 6 Oct 1936: Gömbös

Prime Minister	*Gyula Gömbös* (see Bethlen II)
Foreign Affairs	30 Sep 1932 – 5 Jan 1933: *Endre Puky*
	18 Jan 1933 – 6 Oct 1936: *Kalmán Kania* (b. Sopron 7 Nov 1869; d. Almady 1944)
Home Affairs	30 Sep 1932 – 2 Mar 1935: *Ferenc Keresztes-Fischer* (see Gyula Károlyi)
	4 Mar 1935 – 6 Oct 1936: *Miklós Kozma* (b. Nagyvárad 5 Sep 1869; d. Ungvár 8 Dec 1941)
Justice	*András Lázár* (b. Papa 8 Mar 1882)
Finance	30 Sep 1932 – 8 Jan 1935: *Aladár Imrédy*
	4 Mar 1935 – 6 Oct 1936: *Tihamér Fabinyi* (b. 1890)
Education	*Bálint Hóman* (b. Budapest 29 Dec 1885; d. 1951)
Defence	*Gyula Gömbös* (see Bethlen II)

11 Oct 1936 – 9 Mar 1938: Darányi I

Prime Minister	*Kalmán Darányi* (for 1st time) (b. Budapest 22 Mar 1886; d. Budapest 1 Nov 1939)
Foreign Affairs	*Kalmán Kania* (see Gömbös)
Home Affairs	11 Oct 1936 – 1 Feb 1937: *Miklós Kozma* (see Gömbös)
	9 Apr 1937 – 9 Mar 1938: *József Széll* (b. Szombathely 14 Oct 1880; d. Budapest 27 Aug 1956)
Justice	*András Lázár* (see Gömbös)
Finance	*Tihamér Fabinyi* (see Gömbös)
Education	*Bálint Hóman* (see Gömbös)
Defence	*Vilmos Röder* (b. 1881)

9 Mar – 13 May 1938: Darányi II

Prime Minister	*Kalmán Darányi* (for 2nd time) (see Darányi I)
Foreign Affairs	*Kalmán Kania* (see Gömbös)
Home Affairs	*József Széll* (see Darányi I)
Justice	*Ödön Mikécz* (b. Nyiregyháza 1894; d. Budapest 21 Jan 1965)
Finance	*Lajos Reményi-Schneller* (b. 1892; d. 24 Aug 1946)
Education	*Bálint Hóman* (see Gömbös)
Defence	*Vilmos Röder* (see Darányi I)

273

13 May 1938 - 15 Feb 1939: Imrédy

Prime Minister	*Béla Imrédy* (b. Budapest 29 Dec 1891; d. 28 Feb 1946)
Foreign Affairs	13 May - 28 Nov 1938: *Kalmán Kania* (see Gömbös)
	10 Dec 1938 - 15 Feb 1939: *István, Count Csáky* (b. Uncsukfalva 18 Jul 1894; d. Budapest 27 Jan 1941)
Home Affairs	*Ferenc Keresztes-Fischer* (see Gyula Károlyi)
Justice	13 May - 16 Nov 1938: *Ödön Mikécz* (see Darányi II)
	16 Nov 1938 - 15 Feb 1939: —— *Tasnady-Nagy*
Finance	*Lajos Reményi-Schneller* (see Darányi II)
Education	*Pál, Count Teleki* (b. Budapest 1 Nov 1879; d. Budapest night of 2/3 Apr 1941)*
Defence	13 May - 16 Nov 1938: *Jenő Rácz* (b. 1880)
	16 Nov 1938 - 15 Feb 1939: *Károly Bartha* (b. 1884)
Without Portfolio (for Upper Hungary)	16 Nov 1938 - 15 Feb 1939: *Andor Jaross* (b. Komáromcsehi 1896; d. 11 Apr 1946)

16 Feb 1939 - 2/3 Apr 1941: Teleki III

Prime Minister	*Pál, Count Teleki* (for 3rd time) (see Imrédy)
Foreign Affairs	16 Feb 1939 - 27 Jan 1941: *István, Count Csaky* (see Imrédy)
	5 Feb - 2/3 Apr 1941: *László Bardossy* (b. Szombathely 10 Dec 1890; d. Budapest 10 Jan 1946)
Home Affairs	*Ferenc Keresztes-Fischer* (see Gyula Károlyi)
Justice	—— *Tasnady-Nagy* (see Imrédy)
Finance	*Lajos Reményi-Schneller* (see Darányi II)
Education	*Bálint Hóman* (see Gömbös)
Defence	*Károly Bartha* (see Imrédy)

3 Apr 1941 - 9 Mar 1942: Bardossy

Prime Minister	*László Bardossy* (see Teleki III) Other ministers continued in same offices as previous cabinet

10 Mar 1942 - 22 Mar 1944: Kállay

Prime Minister	*Miklós Kállay* (b. Kallosemjen 1887; d. New York 14 Jan 1967)

*For earlier career see vol. 2

HUNGARY

Foreign Affairs	10 Mar 1942 – 26 Jul 1943 (acting:) *Miklós Kállay* (see above)
	26 Jul 1943 – 22 Mar 1944: *Jenő Ghyczy* (b. 1893?)
Home Affairs	*Ferenc Keresztes-Fischer* (see Gyula Károlyi)
Justice	10 Mar 1942 – 1943: —— *Tasnady-Nagy* (see Imrédy)
	1943 – 22 Mar 1944: *László Radocsay* (b. Istvánfölde 1878)
Finance	*Lajos Reményi-Schneller* (see Darányi II)
Education	10 Mar – 4 Jul 1942: *Bálint Hóman* (see Gömbös)
	4 Jul 1942 – 22 Mar 1944: *Jenő Szinnyei-Merse* (b. 1890)
Defence	10 Mar – 25 Sep 1942: *Károly Bartha* (see Imrédy)
	25 Sep 1942 – 12 Jun 1943: *Vilmos Nagybaczoni Nagy* (b. 1884)
	12 Jun 1943 – 22 Mar 1944: *Lajos Csatay* (b. 1886)

22 Mar – 30 Aug 1944: Sztójay

Prime Minister	*Döme Sztójay* (b. Budapest 5 Jan 1883; d. 22 Aug 1946)
Deputy Prime Minister	*Jenő Rácz* (see Imrédy)
Foreign Affairs	*Döme Sztójay* (see above)
Home Affairs	22 Mar – 7 Aug 1944: *Andor Jaross* (see Imrédy)
	7 – 30 Aug 1944: *Miklós Bonczos*
Justice	*István Antal* (b. 1896)
Finance	*Lajos Reményi-Schneller* (see Darányi II)
Education	(acting:) *István Antal* (see above)
War	*Lajos Csatay* (see Kállay)

30 Aug – 15 Oct 1944: Lakatos

Prime Minister	*Géza Lakatos* (b. 30 Apr 1890; d. Adelaide Jan 1967)
Foreign Affairs	*Gusztáv Hennyey*
Home Affairs	30 Aug – 13 Oct 1944: *Miklós Bonczos* (see Sztójay)
	15 Oct 1944: *Péter, Baron Schell* (b. Nagyida 5 Sep 1898)
Justice	—— *Vladar*
Finance	*Lajos Reményi-Schneller* (see Darányi II)
Education	*Ivan Rakovszky* (b. Budapest 5 May 1885; d. Jászapáti 9 Sep 1960)*

*For earlier career see vol. 2

275

Defence   *Lajos Csatay* (see Kállay)

16 Oct 1944 – Apr 1945: Szálasi

Prime Minister	*Ferenc Szálasi* (see Presidents)
Deputy Prime Minister	*Jenő Szőllősi* (b. 1894; d. 12 Mar 1946)
Foreign Affairs	*Gábor, Baron Kemény* (b. 1883; d. 1948)
Home Affairs	*Gábor Vajna* (b. Kézdivásárhely 1871; d. Budapest 12 Mar 1946)
Education	*Ferenc Rajniss* (b. 1883; d. 12 Mar 1946)
Defence	*Károly Beregfy* (b. 1878; d. 12 Mar 1946)

3 Dec 1944 – 15 Nov 1945: Dálnoki-Miklós (Provisional Government established under Soviet auspices)

Prime Minister	*Béla Dálnoki-Miklós* (b. 1890; d. 1948)
Foreign Affairs	*János Gyöngyössi* (Smallholders) (d. 1(?) Nov 1952)
Home Affairs	*Ferenc Erdei* (Peasants) (b. 1910; d. 13 Apr 1971)
Justice	*Ágoston Valentiny* (Soc) (b. Kalossa 6 Oct 1888; d. Budapest 21 Aug 1958)
Finance	*István Vásáry* (Smallholders) (b. 1874(?); d. New York 17 Mar 1951)
Education	*Count Géza Pál Teleki* (b. Budapest 27 Nov 1911)
Defence	*János Vörös* (no party) (b. 1891)

15 Nov 1945 – 1 Feb 1946: Tildy

Prime Minister	*Zoltán Tildy* (Smallholders) (see Presidents)
Deputy Prime Ministers	*Matyás Rákosi* (Comm) (b. Ada 14 Mar 1892; d. Gorky 5 Feb 1971)
	Árpád Szakasits (Soc) (see Presidents)
	István Dobi (Smallholders) (see Presidents)
Foreign Affairs	*János Gyöngyössi* (Smallholders) (see Dálnoki-Miklós)
Home Affairs	*Imre Nagy* (Comm) (b. Kaposvár 1896; d. 16 Jun 1958)
Justice	*István Riesz* (Soc) (b. 1885; d. in prison 1955(?))
Finance	*Ferenc Gordon* (Smallholders) (b. 1893)
Education	*Dezső Keresztury* (Peasants) (b. Zalaegerszeg 6 Sep 1904)
Defence	*Jenő Tombor* (Smallholders) (b. Nyitra 3 Mar 1880; d. Budapest 25 Jul 1946)

4 Feb - Jun 1946: Ferenc Nagy I

Prime Minister	*Ferenc Nagy* (Smallholders) (for 1st time) (b. Bisse 8 Oct 1903)
Deputy Prime Ministers	*Matyás Rákosi* (Comm) (see Tildy)
	Árpád Szakasits (Soc) (see Presidents)
	István Dobi (Smallholders) (see Presidents)
Foreign Affairs	*János Gyöngyössi* (Smallholders) (see Dálnoki-Miklós)
Home Affairs	*Imre Nagy* (Comm) (see Tildy)
Justice	*István Riesz* (Soc) (see Tildy)
Finance	*Ferenc Gordon* (Smallholders) (see Tildy)
Education	*Dezső Keresztury* (Peasants) (see Tildy)
Defence	*Jenő Tombor* (Smallholders) (see Tildy)

Jul 1946 - 30 May 1947: Ferenc Nagy II

Prime Minister	*Ferenc Nagy* (Smallholders) (for 2nd time) (see Nagy I)
Deputy Prime Ministers	*Árpád Szakasits* (Soc) (see Presidents)
	Matyás Rákosi (Comm) (see Tildy)
Foreign Affairs	*János Gyöngyössi* (Smallholders) (see Dálnoki-Miklós)
Home Affairs	*László Rajk* (Comm) (b. 1909; d. Budapest 15 Oct 1949)
Justice	*István Riesz* (Soc) (see Tildy)
Finance	Jul 1946 - 13 Mar 1947: *Jenő Rast* (Smallholders)
	13 Mar - 30 May 1947: *Miklós Nyárády* (Smallholders) (b. 1905)
Defence	20 Aug 1946 - 13 Mar 1947: *Albert Bartha* (Smallholders) (b. Cluj 12 Aug 1877; d. New York 2 Dec 1960)
	13 Mar - 30 May 1947: *Lajos Dinnyés* (Smallholders) (b. 1900; d. Budapest 4 May 1961)
Information	Jul 1946 - 13 Mar 1947: *József Bognár* (Smallholders) (b. 1917)
	13 Mar - 30 May 1947: *Ernő Mihályfi* (Smallholders) (b. 1898; d. 20 Nov 1972)

31 May - 4 Sep 1947: Dinnyés I

Prime Minister	*Lajos Dinnyés* (Smallholders) (for 1st time) (see Ferenc Nagy II)

Foreign Affairs	*István Kertész* (b. Putnok 8 Apr 1904)
Justice	31 May – 30 Aug 1947: *István Riesz* (Soc) (see Tildy) Other ministers continued in same offices as previous cabinet

24 Sep 1947 – 9 Dec 1948: Dinnyés II

Prime Minister	*Lajos Dinnyés* (Smallholders) (for 2nd time) (see Ferenc Nagy II)
Deputy Prime Ministers	*Matyás Rákosi* (Comm) (see Tildy) *István Dobi* (Smallholders) (see Presidents) 24 Sep 1947 – 3 Aug 1948: *Árpád Szakasits* (Soc) (see Presidents) 3 Aug – 9 Dec 1948: *Ferenc Erdei* (Peasants) (see Dálnoki-Miklós)
Foreign Affairs	24 Sep 1947 – 11 Aug 1948: *Erik Molnár* (Comm) (b. Újvidék 16 Dec 1894; d. Budapest 8 Aug 1966) 11 Aug – 9 Dec 1948: *László Rajk* (Comm) (see Ferenc Nagy II)
Home Affairs	24 Sep 1947 – 11 Aug 1948: *László Rajk* (Comm) (see Ferenc Nagy II) 11 Aug – 9 Dec 1948: *János Kádár* (Comm) (b. Kapoly 26 May 1912)
Justice	*István Riesz* (Soc) (see Tildy)
Finance	24 Sep 1947 – 4 Dec 1948: *Miklós Nyárády* (Smallholders) (see Ferenc Nagy II)
Education	*Gyula Ortutay* (Smallholders) (b. 1910)
Defence	*Péter Vérés* (Peasants) (b. 1897; d. Apr 1970)

9 Dec 1948 – 8 Jun 1949: Dobi I

Prime Minister	*István Dobi* (Smallholders) (for 1st time) (see Presidents)
Deputy Prime Minister	*Matyás Rákosi* (Comm) (see Tildy)
Foreign Affairs	*László Rajk* (Comm) (see Ferenc Nagy II)
Home Affairs	*János Kádár* (Comm) (see Dinnyés II)
Justice	*István Riesz* (Soc) (see Tildy)
Finance	*Ernő Gerő* (Comm) (b. 1898)
Education	*Gyula Ortutay* (Smallholders) (see Dinnyés II)
Defence	9 Dec 1948 – mid Mar 1949: *Péter Vérés* (Peasants) (see Dinnyés II) mid Mar – 10 Jun 1949: *Mihály Farkas* (Comm)

8 Jun 1949 - 14 Aug 1952: Dobi II

Prime Minister	*István Dobi* (Smallholders) (for 2nd time) (see Presidents)
Deputy Prime Minister	*Matyás Rákosi* (Comm) (see Tildy)
Foreign Affairs	10 Jun 1949 – 12 May 1951: *Gyula Kállai* (Comm) (b. 1 Jun 1910)
	12 May 1951 – 14 Aug 1952: *Károly Kiss* (Comm) (b. 1903)
Home Affairs	10 Jun 1949 – 23 Jun 1950: *János Kádár* (Comm) (see Dinnyés II)
	23 Jun 1950 – 21 Apr 1951: *Sándor Zöld* (Comm) (b. Nagyvárad 19 May 1913; d. Budapest 30 Apr 1951)
	21 Apr 1951 – 14 Aug 1952: *Árpád Házi* (Comm) (b. 1907?)
Justice	10 Jun 1949 – 18 Jul 1950: *István Riesz* (Soc) (see Tildy)
	18 Jul 1950 – 14 Aug 1952: *Erik Molnár* (Comm) (see Dinnyés II)
Finance	10 Jun 1949 – 26 Feb 1950: *István Kossa* (Comm) (b. 1904; d. Budapest 8(?) Apr 1965)
	26 Feb 1950 – 14 Aug 1952: *Károly Olt* (Comm) (b. 1904)
Education	10 Jun 1949 – 26 Feb 1950: *Gyula Ortutay* (Smallholders) (see Dinnyés II)
	26 Feb 1950 – 14 Aug 1952: *József Darvas* (Peasants) (b. 1912; d. 3 Dec 1973)
Adult Education	*József Révai* (Comm) (b. 1898; d. Budapest 4 Aug 1959)
Defence	*Mihály Farkas* (Comm) (see Dobi I)

14 Aug 1952 - 2 Jul 1953: Rákosi

Prime Minister	*Matyás Rákosi* (Comm) (see Tildy)
Deputy Prime Ministers (all from 15 Nov 1952)	*Károly Kiss* (Comm) (see Dobi II)
	Árpád Házi (Comm) (see Dobi II)
	Imre Nagy (Comm) (see Tildy)
	Ernő Gerő (Comm) (see Dobi I)
	István Hidas (b. 1918)
Foreign Affairs	14 Aug – 15 Nov 1952: *Károly Kiss* (Comm) (see Dobi II)
	15 Nov 1952 – Feb 1953(?): *Erik Molnár* (Comm) (see Dinnyés II)

279

HUNGARY

Home Affairs	14 Aug – 15 Nov 1952: *Árpád Házi* (Comm) (see Dobi II)
	15 Nov 1952 – 2 Jul 1953: *József Györe*
Justice	14 Aug – 15 Nov 1952: *Erik Molnár* (Comm) (see Dinnyés II)
	15 Nov 1952 – 8 Feb 1953: *Gyula Décsi* (Comm) (b. 1916?)
	8 Feb – 2 Jul 1953: *Béla Kovács* (Smallholders) (b. Mecsekalja-Patacs 20 Apr 1908; d. Pécs 21 Jun 1959)
Finance	*Károly Olt* (Comm) (see Dobi II)
Education	*József Darvas* (Peasants) (see Dobi II)
Adult Education	*József Révai* (Comm) (see Dobi II)
Defence	*Mihály Farkas* (Comm) (see Dobi I)

4 Jul 1953 – 14 Apr 1955: Imre Nagy I

Prime Minister	*Imre Nagy* (Comm) (for 1st time) (see Tildy)
Deputy Prime	*Ernő Gerő* (Comm) (see Dobi I)
Ministers	*András Hegedüs* (Comm) (b. 1922)
Foreign Affairs	*János Boldoczki* (Comm)
Home Affairs	4 Jul 1953 – 6 Jul 1954: *Ernő Gerő* (Comm) (see Dobi I)
	6 Jul 1954 – 14 Apr 1955: *László Piros*
Justice	*Ferenc Erdei* (Peasants) (see Dálnoki-Miklós)
Finance	*Károly Olt* (Comm) (see Dobi II)
Education	*Tibor Erdey-Grúz* (b. 1902)
Adult Education	*József Darvas* (Peasants) (see Dobi II)
Defence	*István Bata* (Comm) (b. 1910)
Food	*Iván Altomare* (Comm) (b. 1893)

18 Apr 1955 – 23 Oct 1956: Hegedüs

Prime Minister	*András Hegedüs* (Comm) (see Imre Nagy I)
First Deputy Prime Minister	30 Jul – 23 Oct 1956: *István Hidas* (see Rákosi)
Deputy Prime Ministers	18 Apr 1955 – 30 Jul 1956: *Ernő Gerő* (Comm) (see Dobi I)
	30 Jul – 23 Oct 1956: *György Marosán* (b. May 1908) *Antal Apró* (Comm)
	Ferenc Erdei (Peasants) (see Dálnoki-Miklós) *József Mekis*
Foreign Affairs	18 Apr 1955 – 30 Jul 1956: *János Boldoczki* (Comm) (see Imre Nagy I)

	30 Jul – 23 Oct 1956: *Imre Horváth* (Comm) (b. 1901; d. Budapest 2 Feb 1958)
Home Affairs	*László Piros* (see Imre Nagy I)
Justice	*Erik Molnár* (Comm) (see Dinnyés II)
Finance	*Károly Olt* (Comm) (see Dobi II)
Education	18 Apr 1955 – 30 Jul 1956: *Tibor Erdey-Grúz* (see Imre Nagy I)
	30 Jul – 23 Oct 1956: *Albert Kónya* (Comm) (b. 1917)
Adult Education	*József Darvas* (Peasants) (see Dobi II)
Defence	*István Bata* (Comm) (see Imre Nagy I)
Food	18 Apr 1955 – 30 Jul 1956: *Iván Altomare* (Comm) (see Imre Nagy I)
	30 Jul – 23 Oct 1956: *Rezső Nyers* (Comm, formerly Soc) (b. Budapest 1923)
Foreign Trade	18 Apr 1955 – 16 Apr 1956: *László Hay*
	16 Apr – 23 Oct 1956: *József Bognár* (formerly Smallholders) (see Ferenc Nagy II)

24 Oct – 4 Nov 1956: Imre Nagy II (Revolutionary Government)

Prime Minister	*Imre Nagy* (Nat Comm) (for 2nd time) (see Tildy)
Deputy Prime Minister	*Antal Apró* (Comm) (see Hegedüs)
Ministers of State	*Zoltán Tildy* (Smallholders) (see Presidents)
	30 Oct – 4 Nov 1956: *János Kádár* (Comm) (see Dinnyés II)
	30 Oct – 4 Nov 1956: *Géza Losonczy* (Comm)
	30 Oct – 4 Nov 1956: *Béla Kovács* (Smallholders) (see Rákosi)
	30 Oct – 4 Nov 1956: *Ferenc Erdei* (Peasants) (see Dálnoki-Miklós)
	3 – 4 Nov 1956: *István B. Szabó* (Smallholders)
	3 – 4 Nov 1956: *Anna Kethly* (Soc) worked in Austria for the new government, then moved abroad
	3 – 4 Nov 1956: *Gyula Kelemén* (Soc)
	3 – 4 Nov 1956: *József Fischer* (Soc)
	3 – 4 Nov 1956: *István Bibó* (Peasants)
	3 – 4 Nov 1956: *Ferenc Farkas* (Peasants)
Foreign Affairs	27 – 30 Oct 1956: *Imre Horváth* (Comm) (see Hegedüs)
	1 – 4 Nov 1956: *Imre Nagy* (Comm) (see Tildy)
Home Affairs	27 Oct – (?) 1956: *Ferenc Münnich* (Comm) (b. Seregélyes 1886; d. Budapest 29 Nov 1967)

	(?) – 4 Nov 1956: *György Adam*
Justice	*Erik Molnár* (Comm) (see Dinnyés II)
Finance	*István Kossa* (Comm) (see Dobi II)
Education	*Albert Kónya* (Comm) (see Hegedüs)
Adult Education	*György Lukács* (Comm) (b. Budapest 13 Apr 1885; d. Budapest 4 Jun 1971)*
Defence	27 Oct – 3 Nov 1956: *Károly Janza* (Comm) 3 – 4 Nov 1956: *Pál Maléter* (d. 16 Jun 1958)
Food	*Rezső Nyers* (Comm) (see Hegedüs)
Foreign Trade	*József Bognár* (Smallholders) (see Ferenc Nagy II)

4 Nov 1956 – 9 May 1957: Kádár I (Ministry imposed by Soviet invasion forces)

Prime Minister	*János Kádár* (Comm) (for 1st time) (see Dinnyés II)
Deputy Prime Minister (from 28 Feb 1957: First Deputy Prime Minister)	*Ferenc Münnich* (Comm) (see Imre Nagy II)
Minister of State	*György Marosán* (see Hegedüs)
Foreign Affairs	*Imre Horváth* (Comm) (see Hegedüs)
Home Affairs and Security	4 Nov 1956 – 28 Feb 1957: *Ferenc Münnich* (Comm) (see Imre Nagy II) 28 Feb – 9 May 1957: *Béla Biszkú* (Comm) (b. 13 Sep 1921)
Justice	No appointment made
Finance	*István Kossa* (Comm) (see Dobi II)
Education	4 Nov 1956 – 28 Feb 1957: no appointment made 28 Feb – 9 May 1957: *Gyula Kállai* (Comm) (see Dobi II)
Defence	(?) 1956 – 28 Feb 1957: *Ferenc Münnich* (Comm) (see Imre Nagy II) 28 Feb – 9 May 1957: *Géza Révész* (b. Sátoraljaújhely 1902)
Food	No appointment made
Foreign Trade	*Sándor Rónai* (see Presidents)

9 May 1957 – 27 Jan 1958: Kádár II

Prime Minister	*János Kádár* (Comm) (for 2nd time) (see Dinnyés II)

*For earlier career see vol. 2

282

First Deputy Prime Minister	*Ferenc Münnich* (Comm) (see Imre Nagy II)
Deputy Prime Minister	*Antal Apró* (Comm) (see Hegedüs)
Minister of State	*György Marosán* (see Hegedüs)
Foreign Affairs	*Imre Horváth* (Comm) (see Hegedüs)
Home Affairs	*Béla Biszkú* (Comm) (see Kádár I)
Justice	*Ferenc Nezvál* (b. Győr 7 Feb 1909)
Finance	*István Antos* (b. 1907(?); d. Budapest 5 Jan 1960)
Education	*Gyula Kállai* (see Dobi II)
Defence	*Géza Révész* (see Kádár I)
Food	*Imre Kovács* (b. 1913)
Foreign Trade	*Jenő Incze* (b. Transylvania 6 Apr 1901; d. 4 May 1969)

27 Jan – 26 Nov 1958: Münnich I

Prime Minister	*Ferenc Münnich* (Comm) (for 1st time) (see Imre Nagy II)
First Deputy Prime Minister	*Antal Apró* (Comm) (see Hegedüs)
Foreign Affairs	27 Jan – 2 Feb 1958: *Imre Horváth* (Comm) (see Hegedüs)
	14 Feb – 26 Nov 1958: *Endre Sik* (b. Budapest 1891)
Home Affairs	*Béla Biszkú* (Comm) (see Kádár I)
Finance	*István Antos* (see Kádár II)
Education	*Valeria Benke* (b. 1920)
Defence	*Géza Révész* (see Kádár I)
Agriculture	*Imre Kovács* (see Kádár II)
Foreign Trade	*Jenő Incze* (see Kádár II)

26 Nov 1958 – 13 Sep 1961: Münnich II

Prime Minister	*Ferenc Münnich* (Comm) (for 2nd time) (see Imre Nagy II)
First Deputy Prime Ministers	*Antal Apró* (Comm) (see Hegedüs)
	16 Jan 1960 – 13 Sep 1961: *Gyula Kállai* (Comm) (see Dobi II)
Minister of State	26 Nov 1958 – 16 Jan 1960: *György Marosán* (see Hegedüs)
Foreign Affairs	*Endre Sik* (Comm) (see Münnich I)
Home Affairs	*Béla Biszkú* (Comm) (see Kádár I)
Justice	*Ferenc Nezvál* (see Kádár II)

Finance	26 Nov 1958 – 5 Jan 1960: *István Antos* (see Kádár II)
	16 Jan 1960 – 13 Sep 1961: *Rezső Nyers* (Comm) (see Hegedüs)
Education	*Valeria Benke* (Comm) (see Münnich I)
Defence	26 Nov 1958 – 17 May 1960: *Géza Révész* (see Kádár I)
	17 May 1960 – 13 Sep 1961: *Lajos Czinege* (Comm) (b. Karcag 24 Mar 1924)
Agriculture	26 Nov 1958 – 16 Jan 1960: *Imre Dögei* (Comm) (b. Törökszentmiklós 23 Jun 1912; d. Budapest 12 Jan 1964)
	16 Jan 1960 – 13 Sep 1961: *Pál Losonczi* (Comm) (see Presidents)
Foreign Trade	*Jenő Incze* (see Kádár II)

13 Sep 1961 – 14 Apr 1967: Kádár III/ Kállai

Prime Minister	13 Sep 1961 – 28 Jun 1965: *János Kádár* (Comm) (for 3rd time) (see Dinnyés II)
	28 Jun 1965 – 14 Apr 1967: *Gyula Kállai* (Comm) (see Dobi II)
Deputy Prime Ministers	*Antal Apró* (Comm) (see Hegedüs)
	Jenő Fock (Comm) (b. Budapest 17 May 1916)
	13 Sep 1961 – 27 Nov 1962: *Béla Biszkú* (Comm) (see Kádár I)
	7 Dec 1963 – 28 Jun 1965: *János Pap* (b. Kaposvár 23 Dec 1925)
	13 Sep 1961 – 28 Jun 1965: *Gyula Kállai* (Comm) (see Dobi II)
	27 Nov 1962 – 14 Apr 1967: *Lajos Fehér* (b. 1917)
Ministers of State	13 Sep 1961 – 13 Oct 1962: *György Marosán* (Comm) (see Hegedüs)
	13 Sep 1961 – 28 Jun 1965: *Ferenc Münnich* (Comm) (see Imre Nagy II)
Foreign Affairs	*János Péter* (b. 1910) until 1946 Protestant bishop
Home Affairs	13 Sep 1961 – 7 Dec 1963: *János Pap* (see above)
	7 Dec 1963 – 14 Apr 1967: *András Benkei* (b. Nyíregyháza 11 Sep 1923)
Ecclesiastical Affairs (new post)	*József Prantner* (b. 1911)
Justice	13 Sep 1961 – 7 Dec 1966: *Ferenc Nezvál* (see Kádár II)
	7 Dec 1966 – 14 Apr 1967: *Mihály Korom* (b. Mindszent 9 Oct 1927)

Finance	13 Sep 1961 – 27 Nov 1962: *Rezső Nyers* (Comm) (see Hegedüs) 27 Nov 1962 – 14 Apr 1967: *Mátyás Timár* (b. Mohács 1923)
Education	*Pál Ilkú* (b. 8 Oct 1912; d. 13 Jul 1973)
Defence	*Lajos Czinege* (Comm) (see Münnich II)
Agriculture	*Pál Losonczi* (Comm) (see Presidents)
Foreign Trade	13 Sep 1961 – 7 Dec 1963: *Jenő Incze* (see Kádár II) 7 Dec 1963 – 14 Apr 1967: *József Biró* (b. 13 Feb 1921)

14 Apr 1967 – 13 May 1971: Fock I

Prime Minister	*Jenő Fock* (Comm) (for 1st time) (see Kádár III)
Deputy Prime	*Antal Apró* (Comm) (see Hegedüs)
Ministers	*Lajos Fehér* (see Kádár III)
	Mátyás Timár (see Kádár III)
	Miklós Ajtai (b. Rákosliget 19 May 1914)
Foreign Affairs	*János Péter* (see Kádár III)
Home Affairs	*András Benkei* (see Kádár III)
Ecclesiastical Affairs	*József Prantner* (see Kádár III)
(State Secretary)	
Justice	*Mihály Korom* (see Kádár III)
Finance	*Péter Vályi* (b. Szombathely 1919; d. 18 Sep 1973)
Education	*Pál Ilkú* (see Kádár III)
Defence	*Lajos Czinege* (see Münnich II)
Agriculture	*Imre Dimény* (b. Komolló 3 Aug 1922)
Foreign Trade	*József Biró* (see Kádár III)

13 May 1971 – 15 May 1975: Fock II

Prime Minister	*Jenő Fock* (Comm) (for 2nd time) (see Kádár III)
Deputy Prime	*Antal Apró* (Comm) (see Hegedüs)
Ministers	*Mátyás Timár* (see Kádár III)
	13 May 1971 – 20/21 Mar 1974: *Lajos Fehér* (see Kádár II)
	13 May 1971 – 20/21 Mar 1974: *Miklós Ajtai* (see Fock I)
	13 May 1971 – 18 Sep 1973: *Péter Vályi* (see Fock I)
	29 Jun 1973 – 15 May 1975: *György Lázár* (b. Isaszeg, near Budapest, 1924)
	21 Mar 1974 – 15 May 1975: *György Aczél* (b. Budapest 1917)
	21 Mar 1974 – 15 May 1975: *János Borbándi* (b. 1923)

285

	1 Nov 1973 – 15 May 1975: *István Huszar* (b. Hernádek 1927) First Deputy President of State Planning Office
Foreign Affairs	13 May 1971 – 14 Dec 1973: *János Péter* (see Kádár III)
	14 Dec 1973 – 15 May 1975: *Frigyes Puja* (b. 1921)
Home Affairs	*András Benkei* (see Kádár III)
Health	13 May 1971 – 15 Feb 1974: *Zoltán Szabó* (b. 1964)
	15 Feb – 15 May 1975: *Emil Schultheisz* (b. Budapest 1923)
Justice	*Mihály Korom* (see Kádár III)
Finance	*Lajos Faluvégi*
Education and Culture	13 May 1971 – 13 Jul 1973: *Pál Ilkú* (see Kádár III)
	13 Jul 1973 – 29 Apr 1974: *Miklós Nagy* (b. Kaba 1932; d. 29 Apr 1974)
	29 Apr – 21 Jun 1974: *Károly Polinszky* (b. Budapest 1922)
	21 Jun 1974: divided into separate ministries of Education and Culture (see below)
Education	21 Jun 1974 – 15 May 1975: *Károly Polinszky* (see above)
Culture	21 Jun 1974 – 15 May 1975: *László Orbán* (b. Nógrádverőce (now Verőce) 1912)
Transport and Post	13 May 1971 – 27 Apr 1974: *György Csanádi* (b. 1905; d. 27 Apr 1974)
	27 Apr 1974 – 15 May 1975: *Károly Rödönyi* (b. Budapest 1911)
Defence	*Lajos Czinege* (see Münnich II)
Agriculture	*Imre Dimény* (see Foch I)
Foreign Trade	*József Biró* (see Kádár III)

from 15 May 1975: Lázár

Prime Minister	*György Lázár* (see Fock II)
Deputy Prime Ministers	*György Aczél* (see Fock II)
	János Borbándi (see Fock II)
	from 4 Jul 1975: *Ferenc Havasi* (b. Piszke 1929)
	István Huszár (see Fock II)
	15 May – 4 Jul 1975: *Mátyás Timár* (see Kádár III)
	Gyula Szekér
Foreign Affairs	*Frigyes Puja* (see Fock II)
Home Affairs	*András Benkei* (see Kádár III)
Justice	*Mihály Korom* (see Kádár III)

Finance	*Lajos Faluvégi* (see Fock II)
Education	*Károly Polinszky* (see Fock II)
Defence	*Lajos Czinege* (see Münnich II)
Agriculture and Food	15 May – 4 Jul 1975: *Imre Dimény* (see Fock I)
	from 4 Jul 1975: *Pál Romány* (b. Szajol 1929)
Foreign Trade	*József Biró* (see Kádár III)
Health	*Emil Schultheisz* (see Fock II)
Culture	*László Orbán* (see Fock II)
Building and City Planning	*József Bondor* (b. 1917)
Metallurgy and Machine Engineering	*Tivadar Nemeslaki* (b. Tatabánya 1923)
Light Industry	*János Keserü*
Post and Communications	*Károly Rödönyi*
Labour	*László Karakas*
Heavy Industry	*Pál Simon* (b. Miskolc 1929)
President of National Planning Office	*István Huszar* (see Fock II)

Iceland

30 Nov 1918 – 17 Jun 1944	Self-governing state in union with Denmark
17 Jun 1944	Independent Republic

HEADS OF STATE

Presidents

17 Jun 1944 – 24 Jan 1952	*Sveinn Björnsson* (b. Reykjavík 27 Feb 1881; d. 24 Jan 1952)
29 Jun 1952 – 30 Jun 1968	*Ásgeir Ásgeirsson* (b. Koranesi 13 May 1894; d. 15 Sep 1972)
from 30 Jun 1968	*Kristian Eldjarn* (b. Tjorn 6 Dec 1916)

MEMBERS OF GOVERNMENT

Prime Ministers

28 Aug 1927 – Aug 1931	*Trygvi Thorhallson* (for 1st time) (b. 9 Feb 1889; d. 31 Jul 1935)
22 Aug 1931 – 26 May 1932	*Trygvi Thorhallson* (for 2nd time)
2 Jun 1932 – 15 Nov 1933	*Ásgeir Ásgeirsson* (see Presidents)
29 Mar/Jun 1934 – 10 Nov 1941	*Hermann Jónasson* (for 1st time) (b. 25 Dec 1896)
Nov 1941 – 5 May 1942	*Hermann Jónasson* (for 2nd time)
18 May – Dec 1942	*Olafur Tryggvason Thors* (for 1st time) (b. Borgarnes 19 Jan 1892; d. Reykjavík 31 Dec 1964)
18 Dec 1942 – 16 Sep 1944	*Björn Thordarson* (b. 1879)
21 Oct 1944 – 10 Oct 1946	*Ólafur Tryggvason Thors* (for 2nd time)
4 Feb 1947 – 2 Nov 1949	*Stefán Jóhann Stefánsson* (b. 20 Jul 1894)
6 Dec 1949 – 2 Mar 1950	*Ólafur Tryggvason Thors* (for 3rd time)
13 Mar 1950 – Sep 1953	*Steingrímur Steinthórsson* (b. Álftagardur 12 Feb 1893; d. 14 Nov 1966)
12(?) Sep 1953 – 27 Mar 1956	*Ólafur Tryggvason Thors* (for 4th time)
21 Jul 1956 – 4 Dec 1958	*Hermann Jónasson* (for 3rd time)
24 Dec 1958 – 18 Nov 1949	*(Gudmundur) Emil Jónsson* (b. Hafnarfjördur 27 Oct 1902)
20 Nov 1959 – 12 Nov 1963	*Ólafur Tryggvason Thors* (for 5th time)
10 Nov 1963 – 10 Jul 1970	*Bjarni Benediktsson* (b. Reykjavík 30 Apr 1909; d. Thingvallavatn 10 Jul 1970)
11 Jul 1970 – 14 Jun 1971	*Johann Hafstein* (b. 19 Sep 1915)
14 Jul 1971	*Ólafur Jóhannesson* (b. Skagafjördur 1 Mar 1913)
from 29 Aug 1974	*Geir Hallgrímsson* (b. Reykjavík 16 Dec 1925)

Foreign Ministers

16 May 1942 – 21 Oct 1944	*Vilhjalmur Thor* (d. Jul 1972)
4 Feb 1947	*Johann Josefsson*
14 Mar 1950	*Bjarni Benediktsson* (see Prime Ministers)
1956	*Gudmundur Gudmundsson* (b. 1909?)
30 Aug 1965 – 14 Jun 1971	*(Gudmundur) Emil Jónsson* (see Prime Ministers)
from 14 Jul 1971	*Einar Águstsson* (b. Rangárvallasysla 23 Sep 1922)

India

HEADS OF STATE

Viceroys

Jun 1929 – Apr 1931	(acting:) *George Joachim Goschen, 2nd Viscount Goschen* (b. 15 Oct 1866; d. 24 Jul 1952)
17 Apr 1931	*Freeman Freeman-Thomas, 1st Earl* (from 1936: *1st Marquess*) *of Willingdon* (b. Ratton 12 Sep 1866; d. London 12 Aug 1941)
18 Apr 1936	*Victor Alexander John Hope, 2nd Marquess of Linlithgow* (b. 24 Sep 1887; d. Scotland 5 Jan 1952)
1 Oct 1943	*Sir Archibald Percival Wavell, Viscount* (from 1947: *Earl*) *Wavell* (b. Colchester May 1883; d. London 24 May 1950)
21 Feb – 15 Aug 1947	*Louis (Francis Albert Victor Nicholas) Mountbatten, 1st Viscount* (from 28 Oct 1947: *1st Earl*) *Mountbatten of Burma* (b. Windsor 25 Jun 1900)

Governors-General

15 Aug 1947	*Louis (Francis Albert Victor Nicholas) Mountbatten, 1st Viscount* (from 28 Oct 1947: *1st Earl*) *Mountbatten of Burma* (see Viceroys)
21 Jun 1948 – 26 Jan 1950	*Chakravarti Rajagopalacharia* (b. Hosur 1879; d. 25 Dec 1972)

INDIA

Presidents

26 Jan 1950	*Rajendra Prasad* (b. Zeeradai 3 Dec 1884; d. Patna 26 Feb 1963)
13 May 1962	*Sarvepalli Radhakrishnan* (b. Madras 5 Sep 1888; d. 17 Apr 1975)
13 May 1967	*Zakir Husain* (b. Hyderabad 8 Feb 1897; d. New Delhi 3 May 1969)
3 May 1969	(acting:) *Varahagiri Venkata Giri* (for 1st time) (b. Berhampore 10 Aug 1894)
20 Jul 1969	(acting:) *Mohammad Hidayatullah* (b. Betul 17 Dec 1905)
24 Aug 1969	*Varahagiri Venkata Giri* (for 2nd time)
from 20 Aug 1974	*Fakhruddin Ali Ahmed* (b. 13 May 1905; d. New Delhi 11 Feb 1977)

MEMBERS OF GOVERNMENT

16 Aug 1947 – 10 May 1952: Nehru I

Prime Minister and Foreign Affairs	*(Pandit) Jawaharlal Nehru* (Congress) (for 1st time) (b. Allahabad 14 Nov 1889; d. New Delhi 27 May 1964)
Home Affairs	16 Aug 1947 – 15 Dec 1950: *Sardar Vallabhai Patel* (b. 1875(?); d. Bombay 15 Dec 1950)
	26 Dec 1950 – 10 May 1952: *Chakravarti Rajagopalacharia* (see Governors General)
Finance	16 Aug 1947 – 16 Aug 1948: *Shanmugam Chetty* (b. 17 Oct 1892; d. May 1953)
	25 Sep 1948 – 26 May 1950: *John Matthaei* (b. 1886; d. Bombay 2 Nov 1959)
	26 May 1950 – 10 May 1952: *Chintaman Desmukh* (b. 14 Jan 1896)
Education	*Maulana Abu'l-Kalam Azad* (Muslim) (b. Mecca 1888; d. New Delhi 21 Feb 1958)
Defence	*Sardar Baldey Singh* (Sikh) (b. 1909(?); d. New Delhi 29 Jun 1961)

13 May 1952 – 16 Apr 1957: Nehru II

Prime Minister and Foreign Affairs	*(Pandit) Jawaharlal Nehru* (Congress) (for 2nd time) (see Nehru I)

290

Home Affairs	13 May 1952 – 23 Nov 1954: *Kailash Nath Katju* (b. Jaora 17 Jun 1887; d. Feb 1968) 23 Nov 1954 – 16 Apr 1957: *Pandit Govind Ballabh Pant* (b. Khunt, United Provinces, 10 Sep 1887; d. New Delhi 7 Mar 1961)
Finance	13 May 1952 – 18 Jun/24 Jul 1956: *Chintaman Desmukh* (see Nehru I) 30 Aug 1956 – 16 Apr 1967: *Tiruvallur Thattai Krishnamachari* (b. 26 Nov 1889)
Education	*Maulana Abu'l-Kalam Azad* (Muslim) (see Nehru I)
Defence	13 May 1952 – 9 Feb 1953: *Sir Gopalaswami Ayyangar* (b. 1881(?); d. 9 Feb 1953) 16 Mar 1953 – 23 Nov 1954: *Mahavir Tyagi* (b. 1907) 23 Nov 1954 – 30 Jan 1957: *Kailash Nath Katju* (see above) 30 Jan – 16 Apr 1957 (acting:) *(Pandit) Jawaharlal Nehru* (Congress) (see Nehru I)

17 Apr 1957 – 9 Apr 1962: Nehru III

Prime Minister, Foreign and Atomic Affairs	*Jawaharlal Nehru* (Congress) (for 3rd time) (see Nehru I)
Home Affairs	17 Apr 1957 – 7 Mar 1961: *Pandit Govind Ballabh Pant* (see Nehru II) 5 Apr 1961 – 9 Apr 1962: *Lal Bahadur Shastri* (b. Benares 2 Oct 1904; d. Tashkhent, USSR, 11 Jan 1966)
Finance	17 Apr 1957 – 13 Feb 1958: *Tiruvallur Thattai Krishnamachari* (see Nehru II) 13 Mar 1958 – 9 Apr 1962: *Morarji Ranchhodji Desai* (b. Bhadeli 29 Feb 1896)
Education and Scientific Research	17 Apr 1957 – 21 Feb 1958: *Maulana Abu'l-Kalam Azad* (see Nehru I) 21 Feb 1958: divided into separate ministries of Education and Scientific Research (see below)
Education	Feb 1958 – 9 Apr 1962: *Kalu Lal Shrimali* (b. 1900)
Scientific Research	Feb 1958 – 9 Apr 1962: *Humayun Kabir* (Muslim) (b. 22 Feb 1906; d. 18 Aug 1969)
Defence	*(Vengalil Krishnan) Krishna Menon* (b. 3 May 1897; d. 15 Oct 1974)

9/10 Apr 1962 – 27 May 1964: Nehru IV

Prime Minister, Foreign and Atomic Affairs	*Jawaharlal Nehru* (Congress) (for 4th time) (see Nehru I)
Home Affairs	10 Apr 1962 – 24 Aug 1963: *Lal Bahadur Shastri* (see Nehru III) 29 Aug 1963 – 27 May 1964: *Gulzari Lal Nanda* (b. Sialkot 4 Jul 1898)
Finance	10 Apr 1962 – 24 Aug 1963: *Morarji Ranchhodji Desai* (see Nehru III) 29 Aug 1963 – 27 May 1964: *Tiruvallur Thattai Krishnamachari* (see Nehru II)
Education	10 Apr 1962 – 24 Aug 1963: *Kalu Lal Shrimali* (see Nehru III) Aug 1963 – 27 May 1964: *Mohammed Currim Chagla* (b. Bombay 30 Sep 1900)
Scientific Research and Cultural Affairs	*Humayun Kabir* (Muslim) (see Nehru III)
Defence	10 Apr – 7 Nov 1962: *(Vengalil Krishnan) Krishna Menon* (see Nehru III) 14 Nov 1962 – 27 May 1964: *Yashwantrao Balwantrao Chavan* (b. Devrashire 14 Mar 1914)

2/9 Jun 1964 – 11 Jan 1966: Shastri

Prime Minister	*Lal Bahadur Shastri* (see Nehru III)
Foreign Affairs	9 Jun – 18 Jul 1964: *Lal Bahadur Shastri* (see Nehru III) 18 Jul 1964 – 11 Jan 1966: *Sardar Swaram Singh* (Sikh) (b. Jullundar 19 Aug 1907)
Atomic Affairs	*Lal Bahadur Shastri* (see Nehru III)
Home Affairs	*Gulzari Lal Nanda* (see Nehru IV)
Finance	9 Jun 1964 – 31 Dec 1965: *Tiruvallur Thattai Krishnamachari* (see Nehru II) 31 Dec 1965 – 11 Jan 1966: *Sachindra Chaudhury* (b. 24 Feb 1903)
Education and Schools	*Mohammed Currim Chagla* (see Nehru IV)
Research	*Humayun Kabir* (Muslim) (see Nehru III)
Defence	*Yashwantrao Balwantrao Chavan* (see Nehru IV)

24 Jan 1966 – 12 Mar 1967: Gandhi I

Prime Minister	*Indira Gandhi*, daughter of Jawaharlal Nehru (for 1st time) (b. Allahabad 19 Nov 1917)
Foreign Affairs	24 Jan – 13 Nov 1966: *Sardar Swaram Singh* (Sikh) (see Shastri)
	13 Nov 1966 – 12 Mar 1967: *Mohammed Currim Chagla* (see Nehru IV)
Atomic Affairs	*Indira Gandhi* (see above)
Home Affairs	24 Jan – 8 Nov 1966: *Gulzari Lal Nanda* (see Nehru IV)
	13 Nov 1966 – 12 Mar 1967: *Yashwantrao Balwantrao Chavan* (see Nehru IV)
Finance	*Sachindra Chaudhury* (see Shastri)
Education	24 Jan – 13 Nov 1966: *Mohammed Currim Chagla* (see Nehru IV)
	13 Nov 1966 – 12 Mar 1967: *Fakhruddin Ali Ahmed* (see Presidents)
Scientific Research and Cultural Affairs	*Humayun Kabir* (Muslim) (see Nehru III)
Defence	24 Jan – 13 Nov 1966: *Yashwantrao Balwantrao Chavan* (see Nehru IV)
	13 Nov 1966 – 12 Mar 1967: *Sardar Swaram Singh* (Sikh) (see Shastri)

13 Mar 1967 – 18 Mar 1971: Gandhi II

Prime Minister	*Indira Gandhi* (for 2nd time) (see Gandhi I)
Deputy Prime Minister	13 Mar 1967 – 19 Jul 1969: *Morarji Ranchhodji Desai* (see Nehru III)
Foreign Affairs	13 Mar – 5 Sep 1967: *Mohammed Currim Chagla* (see Nehru IV)
	5 Sep 1967 – 14 Feb 1969 (acting:) *Indira Gandhi* (see Gandhi I)
	14 Feb 1969 – 26 Jun 1970: *Dinesh Singh, Rajah of Kalakankar* (b. Kalakankar 19 Jul 1925)
	26 Jun 1970 – 18 Mar 1971: *Sardar Swaram Singh* (Sikh) (see Shastri)
Atomic Affairs	*Indira Gandhi* (see Gandhi I)
Home Affairs	13 Mar 1967 – 26 Jun 1970: *Yashwantrao Chavan* (see Nehru IV)

293

	26 Jun 1970 – 18 Mar 1971: *Indira Gandhi* (see Gandhi I)
Education	13 Mar 1967 – 14 Feb 1969: *Triguna Sen* (b. 24 Dec 1905)
	14 Feb 1969 – 18 Mar 1961: *Vijendra Kasturi Ranga Varadaraja Rao* (b. 8 Jul 1908)
Defence	13 Mar 1967 – 26 Jun 1970: *Sardar Swaram Singh* (Sikh) (see Shastri)
	26 Jun 1970 – 18 Mar 1971: *Jagjivan Ram* (b. 5 Apr 1908)

from 18 Mar 1971: Gandhi III

Prime Minister and Atomic Affairs (and from 2 Jun 1972: Space)	*Indira Gandhi* (for 3rd time) (see Gandhi I)
Foreign Affairs	18 Mar 1971 – 10 Oct 1974: *Sardar Swaram Singh* (Sikh) (see Shastri)
	from 10 Oct 1974: *Yashwantrao Balwantrao Chavan* (see Nehru IV)
Home Affairs	18 Mar 1971 – 4 Feb 1973: *Indira Gandhi* (see Gandhi I)
	4 Feb 1973 – 10 Oct 1974: *Uma Shankar Dikshit* (b. 12 Jan 1901)
	from 10 Oct 1974: *Kasu Brahmananda Reddy* (b. 28 Jul 1909)
Education and Social Welfare	*Siddhartha Shankar Ray* (b. 20 Oct 1920)
Finance	18 Mar 1971 – 10 Oct 1974: *Yashwantrao Balwantrao Chavan* (see Nehru IV)
	from 10 Oct 1974: *Chidambaram Subramaniam* (b. Pollachi, Coimbatore District, 30 Jan 1910)
Science and Technology	2 May 1971 – 10 Oct 1974: *Chidambaram Subramaniam* (see above)
	from 10 Oct 1974 (acting:) *Tonse Ananth Pai* (b. 17 Jan 1922)
Defence	18 Mar 1971 – 10 Oct 1974: *Jagjivan Ram* (see Gandhi II)
	10 Oct 1974 – 30 Nov 1975: *Sardar Swaram Singh* (Sikh) (see Shastri)

	30 Nov – 20 Dec 1975 (acting:) *Indira Gandhi* (see Gandhi I)
	from 20 Dec 1975: *Bansi Lal* (b. Golagarh, Punjab, 10 Oct 1927)
Food and Agriculture (from 2 May 1971: Agriculture; from 10 Oct 1974: Agriculture and Irrigation)	18 Mar 1971 – 1 Jul 1974: *Fakhruddin Ali Ahmed* (see Presidents)
	3 Jul – 10 Oct 1974: *Chidambaram Subramaniam* · (see above)
	from 10 Oct 1974: *Jagjivan Ram* (see Gandhi II)
Railways	18 Mar 1971 – 22 Jul 1972: *Kengal Hanumanthaiya* (b. 1908)
	22 Jul 1972 – 4 Feb 1973: *Tonse Ananth Pai* (see above)
	4 Feb 1973 – 2 Jan 1975: *Lalit Narayan Mishra* (d. (assassinated) 2 Jan 1975)
	from 10 Feb 1975: *Kamlapati Tripathi*
Tourism and Civil Aviation	18 Mar 1971 – 8/9 Nov 1973: *Karan Singh* (b. Cannes 9 Mar 1931)
	from 8/9 Nov 1973 (acting until 11/12 Jan 1974:) *Raj Bahadur* (b. 21 Aug 1912)
Shipping and Transport	18 Mar 1971 – 8/9 Nov 1973: *Raj Bahadur* (see above)
	8/9 Nov 1973 – 10 Feb 1975: *Kamlapati Tripathi* (see above)
	10 Feb – 30 Nov 1975: *Uma Shankar Dikshit* (see above)
	from 30 Nov 1975: *Gurdial Singh Dhillon* (b. 1915)
Parliamentary Affairs	18 Mar 1971 – 4 Feb 1973: *Raj Bahadur* (see above)
	from 4 Feb 1973: *Kotha Raghu Ramaiah* (b. 6 Aug 1912)
Industrial Development	18 Mar 1971 – 22 Jul 1972: *Moinul Huq Chaudhury*
	from 22 Jul 1972: *Chidambaram Subramaniam* (see above)
Supply (from 10 Oct 1974: Industries and Civil Supplies; from 30 Nov 1975: Supply and Rehabilitation)	18 Mar 1971 – 10 Oct 1974: *Moinul Huq Chaudhury* (see above)
	10 Oct 1974 – 30 Nov 1975: *Tonse Ananth Pai* (see above)
	from 30 Nov 1975: *Kotha Raghu Ramaiah* (see above)

Culture	(acting until 2 May 1971:) *Siddhartha Shankar Ray* (see above)
Law and Justice	*Hari Ramchandra Gokhale* (b. 5 Oct 1915)
Steel and Heavy Engineering (from 2 May 1971: Steel and Mines)	18 Mar 1971 – 31 May 1973: *Surendra Mohan Kumaramangalam* (b. 1 Nov 1916; d. 31 May 1973) 23 Jul 1973 – 11/12 Jan 1974: *Tonse Ananth Pai* (see below) from 11/12 Jan 1974: *Keshav Deva Malaviya* (b. 11 Jun 1904)
Health and Family Planning	18 Mar 1971 – 8/9 Nov 1973: *K. K. Shah* (b. Goregaon, Kolaba District, 27 Oct 1908) from 8/9 Nov 1973: *Karan Singh* (see above)
Planning	18 Mar – 26 Apr 1971: *Indira Gandhi* (see Gandhi I) 26 Apr 1971 – 22 Jul 1972: *Chidambaram Subramaniam* (see above) 22 Jul 1972 – 31 Dec 1974: *Durga Prasad Dhar* from 2 Jan 1975: *Indira Gandhi* (see Gandhi I)
Works and Housing	2 May 1971 – 4 Feb 1973: *Uma Shankar Dikshit* (see above) 4 Feb 1973 – 10 Oct 1974: *Bhola Paswan Shastri* from 10 Oct 1974: *Kotha Raghu Ramaiah* (see above)
Heavy Industry (new post)	from 4 Feb 1973: *Tonse Ananth Pai* (see above)
Petroleum and Chemicals	4 Feb 1973 – 10 Oct 1974: *Deva Kant Barooah* 10 Oct 1974 – 20 Dec 1975: *Keshav Deva Malaviya* (see above) 20 Dec 1975: divided into separate ministries of Petroleum and Chemicals and Fertilizers (see below)
Petroleum	from 20 Dec 1975: *Keshav Deva Malaviya* (see above)
Chemicals and Fertilizers	from 20 Dec 1975: *Prakash Chandra Sethi* (b. 19 Oct 1920)
Communications	18 Mar 1971 – 8/9 Nov 1973: *H. N. Bahaguna* (b. Bughani, Garhwal, 1921) 8/9 Nov 1973 – 11/12 Jan 1974: *Raj Bahadur* (see above) 11/12 Jan – 10 Oct 1974: *Kasu Brahmananda Reddy* (see above) from 10 Oct 1974: *Shanker Dayal Sharma* (b. 19 Aug 1918)
Irrigation and Power	18 Mar 1971 – 8/9 Nov 1973: *Kannru Lakshman Rao* (b. 15 Jul 1902) 8/9 Nov 1973 – 10 Oct 1974: *Krishna Chandra Pant* (b. Bhowali, Nainital District, 10 Aug 1931)

Information and Broadcasting	10 Oct 1974: merged with Agriculture (see above) 18 Mar 1971 – 8/9 Nov 1973: *Indira Gandhi* (see Gandhi I) from 8/9 Nov 1973: *Inder Kumar Gujral* (b. Jhelum 4 Dec 1919)
Banking and Revenue (new post)	from 20 Dec 1975: *Pranab Kumar Mukherjee* (b. 11 Dec 1935)
Without Portfolio	10 Oct 1974 – 10 Feb 1975: *Uma Shankar Dikshit* (see above) from 30 Nov 1975: *Bansi Lal* (see above)

Indo-China

See also Cambodia, Laos and Vietnam.

HEADS OF STATE

Governors-General

Aug 1928 – Feb 1934	*Pierre Pasquier*
27 Feb 1934 – Sep 1936	*René Robin*
Sep 1936 – Aug 1939	*Jules Brevié*
20 Aug 1939 – Jun 1940	(acting:) *Georges (Albert Julien) Catroux* (b. Limoges 29 Jan 1877; d. Paris 21 Dec 1969)
25 Jun 1940 – 9 Mar 1945	*Jean Decoux* (b. Bordeaux 5 May 1884; d. Paris 22 Nov 1963)
9 Mar – Sep 1945	Japanese occupation

High Commissioners

6 Sep 1945 – Mar 1947	*Georges Thierry d'Argenlieu* (b. Brest 1889; d. 7 Sep 1964)
27 Mar 1947 – 11 Oct 1948	*Émile Bollaert* (b. Dunkirk 13 Nov 1890)

20 Oct 1948 – Dec 1950	*Léon Pignon* (b. Angoulême 19 Apr 1908)
7 Dec 1950 – 11 Jan 1952	*Jean de Lattre de Tassigny* (b. Mouilleron 2 Feb 1889; d. Paris 11 Jan 1952)
1 Apr 1952 – 1953	*Jean Letourneau* (b. Lure 18 Sep 1907)
28 Jul 1953 – 1954	*Maurice Dejean* (b. Clichy 30 Sep 1899)
10 Apr 1954 – 1955	*Paul Ely* (b. Salonica 17 Dec 1897; d. 16 Jan 1975)
Spring 1955 – 1956	*Henri Hoppenot* (b. Paris 25 Oct 1891)

Indonesia

30 Dec 1949	Republic of United States of Indonesia as an independent and sovereign state under Dutch throne
13 Feb 1956	Dutch-Indonesian Union abolished

HEADS OF STATE

Presidents

17 Aug 1945 / 16 Dec 1949	*Ahmed Sukarno* (b. Blitar 6 Jun 1901; d. Djakarta 21 Jun 1970)
from 12 Mar 1966	*T. N. J. Suharto* (b. Jogjakarta 28 Feb (8 Jun?) 1921) 11 Mar 1966 de facto ruler; 21 Jun 1966 confirmed by National Congress; 12 Mar 1967 acting President; since 27 Mar 1967 definitively

High Commissioners (representing Dutch throne)

1948 – 1949	*Z. Beel*
14 Dec 1949 – 1 Sep 1950	*Hans Max Hirschfeld* (b. Bremen 1899; d. The Hague 4 Nov 1961)
1 / 26 Sep 1950 – early Oct 1952	*Arnold Theodor Lamping* (d. 1 Jan 1970)

298

Prime Ministers

19 Aug 1945	*R. A. A. Wiranatakusumah* (b. Bandung 1888)
14 Nov 1945	*Sutan Sjahrir* (for 1st time) (b. 5 Mar 1909; d. Zurich 9 Apr 1966)
29 Jun – Aug 1946	*Sutan Sjahrir* (for 2nd time)
2 Oct 1946 – 26 Jun 1947	*Sutan Sjahrir* (for 3rd time)
3 Jul 1947 – 21 Jan 1948	*Amir Sjarifuddin* (b. Medan 1903; d. 17 Oct 1948)
29 Jan – Dec 1948	*Mohammed Hatta* (for 1st time) (b. Menang, West Sumatra, 12 Aug 1902) interned by Dutch 19 Dec 1948 – 7 Jul 1949
19 Dec 1948 – May 1949	*Sjarifuddin Prawiraranegara*
16 May 1949	*Susanto Tirtoprodjo* (b. Solo 1900)
7 Jul 1949	*Mohammed Hatta* (for 2nd time)
16 Jan – 15 Aug 1950	*Dr. Halim*
6 Sep 1950 – 21 Mar 1951	*Mohammed Natsir* (b. Alahan Pandjang 17 Jul 1908)
26 Apr 1951 – 23 Feb 1952	*Sukiman Wirjosandjojo* (b. 1896)
1 Apr 1952 – 2 Jun 1953	*Dr. Wilopo*
30 Jul 1953 – 23 Jun 1955	*Ali Sastroamidjojo* (for 1st time) (b. Grabag Merbabu 21 May 1903; d. Jakarta 13 Mar 1975)
11 Aug 1955 – 17 Mar 1956	*Burhanuddin Harahap*
17/20 Mar 1956 – 14 Mar 1957	*Ali Sastroamidjojo* (for 2nd time)
8 Apr 1957	*Raden Haji Djuanda Kurtawidjaja* (b. Tjiannis 14 Jan 1911; d. Djakarta 6 Nov 1963)
9 Jul 1959 – 6 Nov 1963	*Ahmed Sukarno* (see Presidents) introduced a 'guided democracy' and took over leadership of cabinet; inner cabinet established under *Raden Haji Djuanda Kurtawidjaja* (see above)
11 Nov 1963 – 11 Mar 1966	*S. E. Subandrio* (b. Kapandjen 15 Sep 1914) from 8 Apr 1957 Foreign Minister
from 25 Jul 1966	*T. N. J. Suharto* (see Presidents) Chief of Cabinet, Prime Minister's powers abolished

Iran

Named Persia until 1935.

HEADS OF STATE

Shahs

Pehlevi

12 Dec 1925	*(Mohammad) Reza Khan*, son of Abbas Ali Khan (b. 16 Mar 1878; d. Johannesburg 26 Jul 1944)
from 16 Sep 1941	*Mohammad Reza* (b. 26 Oct 1919)

MEMBERS OF GOVERNMENT

Prime Ministers

2 Jun 1927 – 18 Jan 1931	*Mahdi Qoli Khan Hedayat* (for 1st time)
20 Jan 1931 – 13 Sep 1933	*Mahdi Qoli Khan Hedayat* (for 2nd time)
18 Sep 1933	*Mohammad Ali Khan Forughi* (for 2nd time) (d. Teheran 21 Dec 1942)*
3 Dec 1935	*Mahmud Jam*
26 Oct 1939	*Matin Daftari*
2 Jul 1940	*Ali Mansur* (for 1st time) (b. 1895)
27 Aug – 26 Nov 1941	*Mohammad Ali Khan Forughi* (for 3rd time)
8 Dec 1941 – 27 Feb 1942	*Mohammad Ali Khan Forughi* (for 4th time)
9 Mar – 30 Jul 1942	*Ali Soheili* (for 1st time) (b. 1897; d. London 1 May 1958)
9 Aug 1942	*Ahmad Qawam os-Saltaneh* (for 4th time) (b. Manzandaran 1876; d. Teheran 23 Jul 1955)*
22 Jan – 12 Feb 1943	*Ahmad Qawam os-Saltaneh* (for 5th time)
15 Feb 1943 – 6/16 Mar 1944	*Ali Soheili* (for 2nd time)
6 Apr – 26 Aug 1944	*Mohammad Maragha os-Said* (for 1st time) (b. 1881)
31 Aug – 9 Nov 1944	*Mohammad Maragha os-Said* (for 2nd time)
25 Nov 1944 – 19 Apr 1945	*Murteza Qoli Khan Bayat*

*For earlier career see vol. 2

11 May – 4 Jun 1945	*Ebrahim Hakimi* (for 1st time) (b. 1869(?); d. 21 Oct 1959)
Jun – 22 Oct 1945	*Mohammad Sadr*
4 Nov 1945 – 21 Jan 1946	*Ebrahim Hakimi* (for 2nd time)
26 Jan – 17 Oct 1946	*Ahmad Qawam os-Saltaneh* (for 6th time)
19 Oct 1946 – 20 Jun 1947	*Ahmad Qawam os-Saltaneh* (for 7th time)
25 Jun – 27 Aug 1947	*Ahmad Qawam os-Saltaneh* (for 8th time)
12 Sep – 10 Dec 1947	*Ahmad Qawam os-Saltaneh* (for 9th time)
18 – 19 Dec 1947	*Fakher Hekmat*
29 Dec 1947 – 8 Jun 1948	*Ebrahim Hakimi* (for 3rd time)
13 Jun – 6 Nov 1948	*Abdol Hosein Hajir*
9 Nov 1948 – 11 Jan 1950	*Mohammad Maragha os-Said* (for 3rd time)
23 Feb – 19 Mar 1950	*Mohammad Maragha os-Said* (for 4th time)
3 Apr 1950	*Ali Mansur* (for 2nd time)
26 Jun 1950 – 7 Mar 1951	*Ali Razmara* (b. 1899 or 1901; d. 7 Mar 1951)
9/20 Mar – 3 Apr 1951	*Hosain Ala* (for 1st time) (b. 1883(?); d. Teheran 13 Jul 1964)
30 Apr 1951 – 5 Jul 1952	*Mohammad Mosaddeq* (for 1st time) (b. 1881 or 1883; d. Teheran night of 4/5 Mar 1967)
10 – 16 Jul 1952	*Mohammad Mosaddeq* (for 2nd time)
17 – 21 Jul 1952	*Ahmad Qawam os-Saltaneh* (for 10th time)
22 Jul 1952	*Mohammad Mosaddeq* (for 3rd time)
19 Aug 1953	*Fazlo'llah Zahedi* (for 1st time) (b. 1897; d. 2 Sep 1963)
22 Apr 1954	*Fazlo'llah Zahedi* (for 2nd time)
6 Apr 1955	*Hosain Ala* (for 2nd time)
15 Jun 1956	*Hosain Ala* (for 3rd time)
3 Apr 1957 – 29 Aug 1960	*Manuchehr Eqbal* (b. Mashhad Sep 1909)
31 Aug 1960	*Jaafar Sharif Emami* (for 1st time) (b. Teheran 1910)
12 Mar 1961	*Jaafar Sharif Emami* (for 2nd time)
5 May 1961	*Ali Amini* (b. Teheran 1905)
19 Jul 1962	*Asad Ollah Alam* (for 1st time) (b. 1918)
19 Feb 1963	*Asad Ollah Alam* (for 2nd time)
20 Oct 1963	*Asad Ollah Alam* (for 3rd time)
8 Mar 1964	*Hasan Ali Mansur* (b. 1923; d. 26 Jan 1965)
from 26 Jan 1965	*Amir Abbas Hoveyda* (b. Feb 1919)

Iraq

HEADS OF STATE

Kings

23 Aug 1921	*Faisal I*, son of King Husain ibn Ali of Hejaz (b. 20 May 1883)
8 Sep 1933	*Ghazi I*, son (b. 21 Mar 1912)
4 Apr 1939 – 14 Jul 1958	*Faisal II*, son (b. 2 May 1935; d. 14 Jul 1958)
4 Apr 1939 – 2 May 1953	*Abdul Illah*, cousin of Ghazi I (b. 1913; d. 14 Jul 1958) Regent

Head of Council of State (functioning as President)

14 Jul 1958 – 8 Feb 1963	*Mohammed Najib ar-Rubai* (b. Baghdad 1904)

Presidents

8 Feb 1963 – 13 Apr 1966	*Abdul Salim Muhammad Arif* (b. Baghdad 21 Mar 1921; d. Basra 13 Apr 1966)
16 Apr 1966	*Abdur Rahman Muhammad Arif*, brother (b. 1916)
from 17 Jul 1968	*Said Ahmad Hasan al-Bakr* (b. Takrit 1912 or Baghdad 1914)

MEMBERS OF GOVERNMENT

Prime Ministers

18 Nov 1929 – 9 Mar 1930	*Naji Bey as-Suwaidi* (d. 21(?) Sep 1942)
23 Mar 1930	*Nuri Pasha Al Said* (for 1st time) (b. 1888; d. Baghdad 15 Jul 1958)
19 Oct 1930 – 27 Oct 1932	*Nuri Pasha Al Said* (for 2nd time)
3 Nov 1932 – 18 Mar 1933	*Naji Shaukat*
20 Mar – 29 Oct 1933	*Rashid Ali al-Gilani* (for 1st time) (b. 1893(?); d. Beirut 28 Aug 1965)

302

9 Nov 1933 – 10 Feb 1934	*Jamil Bey Midfai* (for 1st time)
21 Feb – 25 Aug 1934	*Jamil Bey Midfai* (for 2nd time)
27 Aug 1934 – 23 Feb 1935	*Ali Jaudat al-Aiyubi* (for 1st time) (b. 1893?)
4 – 16 Mar 1935	*Jamil Bey Midfai* (for 3rd time)
17 Mar 1935	*Yasin Pasha al-Hashimi* (for 2nd time) (d. 21 Jan 1937)*
17 Sep 1935	*Yasin Pasha al-Hashimi* (for 3rd time)
29 Oct 1936	*Hikmet Suleiman*
17 Aug 1937	*Jamil Bey Midfai* (for 4th time)
25 Dec 1938	*Nuri Pasha Al Said* (for 3rd time)
6 Apr 1939	*Nuri Pasha Al Said* (for 4th time)
18 Feb 1940	*Nuri Pasha Al Said* (for 5th time)
31 Mar 1940	*Rashid Ali al-Gilani* (for 2nd time)
1 Feb – 1 Apr 1941	*Taha al-Hashimi* (b. Baghdad 1888; d. London 11 Jun 1961)
4 Apr – 29 May 1941	*Rashid Ali al-Gilani* (for 3rd time)
2 Jun – 21 Sep 1941	*Jamil Bey Midfai* (for 5th time)
19 Oct 1941 – 3 Oct 1942	*Nuri Pasha Al Said* (for 6th time)
8 Oct 1942 – 11 Dec 1943	*Nuri Pasha Al Said* (for 7th time)
25 Dec 1943	*Nuri Pasha Al Said* (for 8th time)
4 Jun – 28 Aug 1944	*Hamdi al-Pachachi* (for 1st time) (b. 1891; d. 27 Mar 1948)
29 Aug 1944 – 31 Jan 1946	*Hamdi al-Pachachi* (for 2nd time)
23 Feb – 30 May 1946	*Taufiq Bey as-Suwaidi* (for 2nd time) (b. 1891; d. 1968)*
1 Jun – 14 Nov 1946	*Arshad al-Umari* (for 1st time)
21 Nov 1946 – 11 Mar 1947	*Nuri Pasha Al Said* (for 9th time)
29 Mar 1947 – 27 Jan 1948	*Said Salih Jabr* (b. 1892(?); d. Baghdad 6 Jun 1957)
29 Jan 1948	*Said Muhammad as-Sadir* (b. Kazimija 1882)
26 Jun 1948	*Muzahim al-Pachachi*
6 Jan – 6 Dec 1949	*Nuri Pasha Al Said* (for 10th time)
10 Dec 1949 – 1 Feb 1950	*Ali Jaudat al-Aiyubi* (for 2nd time)
5 Feb – 12 Sep 1950	*Taufiq Bey as-Suwaidi* (for 3rd time)
25 Sep 1950 – 10 Jul 1952	*Nuri Pasha Al Said* (for 11th time)

*For earlier career see vol. 2

303

12 Jul 1952	*Mustafa Mahmud al-Umari* (b. 1894)
22 Nov – 22 Dec 1952	*Nur ad-Din Mahmud* (b. Mossul 1889)
29 Jan – 5 May 1953	*Jamil Bey Midfai* (for 6th time)
7 May – 31 Aug 1953	*Jamil Bey Midfai* (for 7th time)
17 Sep 1953 – 27 Feb 1954	*Muhammad Fadel al-Jamali* (for 1st time)
8 Mar 1954	*Muhammad Fadel al-Jamali* (for 2nd time)
29 Apr 1954	*Arshad al-Umari* (for 2nd time)
3 Aug 1954	*Nuri Pasha Al Said* (for 12th time)
17 Dec 1955 – 7 Jun 1957	*Nuri Pasha Al Said* (for 13th time)
19 Jun – 11 Dec 1957	*Ali Jaudat al-Aiyubi* (for 3rd time)
15 Dec 1957	*Abdul Wahab Marjan* (d. 16 Mar 1964)
3 Mar – 13 May 1958	*Nuri Pasha Al Said* (for 14th time)
19 May – 14 Jul 1958	*Nuri Pasha Al Said*, Prime Minister of Arabian Federation jointly founded 14 Feb 1958 by Iraq and Jordan
19 May 1958	*Ahmed Mukhtar Baban*
14 Jul 1958	*Abdul Karim Qassim* (b. Baghdad 1914; d. 9 Feb 1963) Military Dictator
8 Feb – 11 May 1963	*Said Ahmad Hasan al-Bakr* (for 1st time) (see Presidents)
13 May – 18 Nov 1963	*Said Ahmad Hasan al-Bakr* (for 2nd time)
21 Nov 1963	*Tahir Yahya* (for 1st time) (b. 1913)
17 Jun 1964	*Tahir Yahya* (for 2nd time)
6 – 16 Sep/1965	*Arif Abdur Razzak*
22 Sep 1965 – 16 Apr 1966	*Abdur Rahman al-Bazzaz* (for 1st time) (b. Baghdad 20 Feb 1913; d. 28 Jun 1973)
18 Apr – 6 Aug 1966	*Abdur Rahman al-Bazzaz* (for 2nd time)
10 Aug 1966 – 7 May 1967	*Naji Talib* (b. Nasiriya 1917)
10 May 1967	*Abdur Rahman Muhammad Arif* (see Presidents)
10 Jul 1967 – 17 Jul 1968	*Tahir Yahya* (for 3rd time)
18 – 30 Jul 1968	*Abdur Razzak an-Naif*
from 31 Jul 1968	President also Prime Minister

Foreign Ministers

18 Nov 1929 – 9 Mar 1930	*Naji Bey as-Suwaidi* (see Prime Ministers)
23 Mar 1930	*Nuri Pasha Al Said* (for 1st time) (see Prime Ministers)

19 Oct 1931 – 27 Oct 1932	*Jaffar Pasha al-Askari* (for 2nd time)*
3 Nov 1932 – 18 Mar 1933	*Abdul Kadir Rashid*
20 Mar 1933 – 10 Feb 1934	*Nuri Pasha Al Said* (for 2nd time)
21 Feb – 18 Jul 1934	*Abd Allah ad-Damluji* (for 1st time)
25 Aug 1934	*Nuri Pasha Al Said* (for 3rd time)
29 Oct 1936	*Naji al-Asil* (d. Baghdad 16 Feb 1963)
17 Aug 1937	*Abbas Mahdi*
25 Dec 1938	*Nuri Pasha Al Said* (for 4th time)
25 Apr 1939	*Ali Jaudat al-Aiyubi* (for 1st time) (see Prime Ministers)
18 Feb 1940	*Nuri Pasha Al Said* (for 5th time)
1 Feb 1941	*Taha al-Hashimi* (see Prime Ministers)
1 Apr – 29 May 1941	*Musa Shabandari* (for 1st time)
2 Jun 1941	*Ali Jaudat al-Aiyubi* (for 2nd time)
19 Oct 1941	*Nuri Pasha Al Said* (for 6th time)
9 Feb 1942	*Abd Allah ad-Damluji* (for 2nd time)
31 May – 3 Oct 1942	(acting:) *Nuri Pasha Al Said* (for 7th time)
7 Oct 1942	*Abdul Ilah Hafiz* (for 1st time)
23 Jun 1943	*Nusret al-Farisi* (for 1st time)
27 Sep – 19 Dec 1943	(acting:) *Abdul Ilah Hafiz* (for 2nd time)
25 Dec 1943	*Mahmud Subhi ad-Daftari*
4 Jun 1944	*Arshad al-Umari* (see Prime Ministers)
25 Aug 1945 – 29 Jan 1946	(acting:) *Hamdi al-Pachachi* (for 1st time) (see Prime Ministers)
23 Feb 1946	(acting:) *Taufiq Bey as-Suwaidi* (for 1st time) (see Prime Ministers)
21 May 1946	*Ali Mumtaz* (for 1st time)
1 Jun 1946 – 27 Jan 1948	*Muhammad Fadel al-Jamali* (for 1st time) (see Prime Ministers)
29 Jan 1948	*Hamdi al-Pachachi* (for 2nd time)
27 Mar – 16 Jun 1948	*Nusret al-Farisi* (for 2nd time)
26 Jun 1948	(acting:) *Muzahim al-Pachachi* (see Prime Ministers)
20 Nov 1948	*Ali Jaudat al-Aiyubi* (for 3rd time)
6 Jan 1949	*Abdul Ilah Hafiz* (for 3rd time)
17 Sep – 6 Dec 1949	*Shakir al-Wadi* (for 1st time)
10 Dec 1949 – 1 Feb 1950	No appointment made
5 Feb – 12 Sep 1950	*Taufiq Bey as-Suwaidi* (for 2nd time)

*For earlier career see vol. 2

25 Sep 1950	*Shakir al-Wadi* (for 2nd time)
5 Feb 1951	(acting:) *Taufiq Bey as-Suwaidi* (for 3rd time)
15 Jul 1951 – 10 Jul 1952	*Shakir al-Wadi* (for 3rd time)
15 Jul – 22 Dec 1952	*Muhammad Fadel al-Jamali* (for 2nd time)
29 Dec 1952 – 31 Aug 1953	*Taufiq Bey as-Suwaidi* (for 4th time)
17 Sep 1953 – 27 Feb 1954	*Abd Allah Ibrahim Bakr* (b. 1907)
8 Mar 1954	*Musa Shabandari* (for 2nd time)
29 Apr 1954	*Muhammad Fadel al-Jamali* (for 3rd time)
3 Aug 1954 – 12 Dec 1955	*Musa Shabandari* (for 3rd time)
17 Dec 1955 – 8 Jun 1957	*Burhaneddin Bashayan* (for 1st time) (b. Basra)
20 Jun 1957	(acting:) *Ali Mumtaz* (for 2nd time)
15 Dec 1957	*Burhaneddin Bashayan* (for 2nd time)
3 May 1958	*Muhammad Fadel al-Jamali* (for 4th time)
14 May 1958	No appointment made by Arabian Federation
14 Jul 1958	*Taufiq Abdul Jabbar*
Feb 1959 – 8 Feb 1963	*Hashim Jawad* (b. 1911)
13 May – 14 Nov 1963	*Talib Husain ash-Shabib*
17 Nov 1963	(acting:) *Salih Mahdi Ammash*
21 Nov 1963	*Subhi Abdul Hamid* (b. 31 Jan 1924)
14 Nov 1964	*Naji Talib* (see Prime Ministers)
6 Sep 1965	*Abdur Rahman al-Bazzaz* (see Prime Ministers)
9 Aug 1966	*Adnan al-Pachachi* (b. 14 May 1923)
10 Jul 1967	*Ismail Khair Allah*
18 Jul 1968	*Nasir alKhani* (b. 1920; d. Baghdad 11 Nov 1968)
31 Jul 1968 – 28 Sep 1971	*Abdul Karim ash-Shaikhli*
30 Oct 1971	*Murtada al Hadithi* (b. 1939)
23 Jun – 20 Oct 1974	*Chazel Taka* (d. 20 Oct 1974)
from 11 Nov 1974	*Saadun Hammadi* (b. Karbala 22 Jun 1930)

Ireland, Republic of

8 Jan 1922	Free State within British Empire
18 Apr 1949	Left British Commonwealth

HEADS OF STATE

Governors-General

15 Dec 1927/1 Feb 1928 – Nov 1932	*James McNeill* (b. Glenarm, Country Antrim, 27 Mar 1869; d. 12 Dec 1938)
26 Nov 1932 – 11 Dec 1936	*Donald Buckley*

Presidents

3 May 1938	*Douglas Hyde* (b. Roscommon 17 Jan 1860; d. Dublin 12 Jul 1949)
25 Jun 1945	*Sean Thomas O'Kelly* (b. Dublin 25 Aug 1882; d. Dublin 23 Nov 1966)
25 Jun 1959	*Eamon de Valera* (b. New York 14 Oct 1882; d. Dublin 29 Aug 1975)*
24 Jun 1973 – 17 Nov 1974	*Erskine H. Childers* (b. Ireland 11 Dec 1905; d. Dublin 17 Nov 1974)
from 3 Dec 1974	*Carroll Daly (Cearbhall Ó Dálaigh)* (b. Bri Chualann, County Wicklow, 12 Feb 1911)

MEMBERS OF GOVERNMENT

Oct 1927 – Mar 1932: William Cosgrave (Cumann na nGaedheal)

President of Executive Council	*William T. Cosgrave* (b. Dublin 6 Jun 1880; d. Dublin 16 Nov 1965)
Justice	*J. Fitzgerald Kenny*
Defence	*Desmond Fitzgerald* (d. 9 April 1947)
External Affairs	*Patrick McGilligan* (b. Coleraine 12 Apr 1889)
Finance and Vice-President	*Ernest Blythe* (b. Magheragall Lisburn, County Antrim, 13 Apr 1889)
Industry and Commerce	*Patrick McGilligan* (see above)
Posts and Telegraphs	*Ernest Blythe* (see above)
Agriculture	*Patrick Hogan* (b. Kilrickle, Co Galway, June 1891; d. 14 Jul 1936)
Lands and Fisheries	*Finian Lynch* (b. 17 Mar 1889; d. 3 Jun 1966)
Education	*John M. O'Sullivan* (b. Killarney 18 Feb 1881; d. 9 Feb 1948)

*For earlier career see vol. 2

Local Government and Public Health	*Richard Mulcahy* (b. Waterford 10 May 1886; d. 16 Dec 1971)
Attorney-General	*John Aloysius Costello* (b. Dublin 20 Jun 1891; d. 5 Jan 1976)

Mar 1932 – Feb 1933: De Valera II (Fianna Fáil)

President of Executive Council	*Eamon de Valera* (for 2nd time) (see Presidents)
Justice	*James Geoghegan* (d. 27 Mar 1951)
Defence	*Frank Aiken* (b. Camlough 13 Feb 1898)
External Affairs	*Eamon de Valera* (see Presidents)
Finance	*John Francis (Sean) MacEntee* (b. Belfast 22 Aug 1889)
Industry and Commerce	*Seán Lemass* (b. Dublin 15 Jul 1899; d. 11 May 1971)
Posts and Telegraphs	*James Connolly* (b. 6 Dec 1892; d. 25 Sep 1970)
Agriculture	*Joseph Ryan* (b. Belfast 19 Jan 1885; d. 1971(?))
Lands and Fisheries	*P. J. Ruttledge*
Education	*Tomás Ó Deirg (Thomas Derrig)* (b. 26 Nov 1897; d. 19 Nov 1956)
Local Government and Public Health and Vice-President	*Sean Thomas O'Kelly* (see Presidents)
Attorney-General	*Conor A. Maguire* (b. 16 Dec 1889)

Feb 1933 – Jul 1937: De Valera III (Fianna Fáil)

President of Executive Council	*Eamon de Valera* (for 3rd time) (see Presidents)
Justice	*P. J. Ruttledge* (see De Valera II)
Defence	*Frank Aiken* (see De Valera II)
External Affairs	*Eamon de Valera* (see Presidents)
Finance	*John Francis (Sean) MacEntee* (see De Valera II)
Industry and Commerce	*Seán Lemass* (see De Valera II)
Posts and Telegraphs	Feb 1933 – 11 Nov 1936: *G. Boland* 11 Nov 1936 – Jul 1937: *O. Traynor*
Agriculture	*James Ryan* (see De Valera II)
Lands and Fisheries (from 1934: Lands)	Feb 1933 – 29 May 1936: *Joseph Connolly* (see De Valera II) 29 May – 11 Nov 1936: *Frank Aiken* (see De Valera II) 11 Nov 1936 – Jul 1937: *G. Boland* (see above)

Education	*Tomás Ó Deirg* (see De Valera II)
Local Government and Public Health and Vice-President	*Sean Thomas O'Kelly* (see De Valera II)
Attorney-General	Feb 1933 – 2 Nov 1936: *Conor A. Maguire* (see De Valera II) 2 Nov – 22 Dec 1936: *James Geoghegan* (see De Valera II) 22 Dec 1936 – Jul 1937: *Patrick Lynch* (d. 9 Dec 1947)

Jul 1937 – Jun 1938: De Valera IV (Fianna Fáil)

President of Executive Council (from Dec 1937: Prime Minister)	*Eamon de Valera* (for 4th time) (see Presidents)
Justice	*P. J. Ruttledge* (see De Valera II)
Defence	*Frank Aiken* (see De Valera II)
External Affairs	*Eamon de Valera* (see Presidents)
Finance	*John Francis (Sean) MacEntee* (see De Valera II)
Industry and Commerce	*Seán Lemass* (see De Valera II)
Posts and Telegraphs	*O. Traynor* (see De Valera III)
Agriculture	*James Ryan* (see De Valera II)
Lands	*G. Boland* (see De Valera III)
Education	*Tomás Ó Deirg* (see De Valera II)
Local Government and Public Health and Vice-President (from Dec 1937: Deputy Prime Minister)	*Sean Thomas O'Kelly* (see De Valera II)
Attorney-General	*Patrick Lynch* (see De Valera III)

Jun 1938 – Jul 1943: De Valera V (Fianna Fáil)

Prime Minister	*Eamon de Valera* (for 5th time) (see Presidents)
Deputy Prime Minister	*Sean Thomas O'Kelly* (see De Valera II)
Justice	Jun 1938 – 8 Sep 1939: *P. J. Ruttledge* (see De Valera II) 8 Sep 1939 – Jul 1943: *G. Boland* (see De Valera III)

309

Defence	Jun 1938 – 8 Sep 1939: *Frank Aiken* (see De Valera II) 8 Sep 1939 – Jul 1943: *O. Traynor* (see De Valera III)
Co-ordination of Defensive Measures (new post)	8 Sep 1939 – Jul 1943: *Frank Aiken* (see De Valera II)
External Affairs	*Eamon de Valera* (see Presidents)
Finance	Jun 1938 – 16 Sep 1939: *John Francis (Sean) MacEntee* (see De Valera II) 16 Sep 1939 – Jul 1943: *Sean Thomas O'Kelly* (see De Valera II)
Industry and Commerce	Jun 1938 – 16 Sep 1939: *Seán Lemass* (see De Valera II) 16 Sep 1939 – 18 Aug 1941: *John Francis (Sean) MacEntee* (see De Valera II) 18 Aug 1941 – Jul 1943: *Seán Lemass* (see De Valera II)
Supplies (new post)	16 Sep 1939 – Jul 1943: *Seán Lemass* (see De Valera II)
Posts and Telegraphs	Jun 1938 – 8 Sep 1939: *O. Traynor* (see De Valera III) 8 – 27 Sep 1939: *Tomás Ó Deirg* (see De Valera II) 27 Sep 1939 – Jul 1943: *P. J. Little*
Agriculture	*J. Ryan* (see De Valera II)
Lands	Jun 1938 – 8 Sep 1939: *G. Boland* (see De Valera III) 8 Sep 1939 – Jul 1943: *Tomás Ó Deirg* (see De Valera II)
Education	Jun 1938 – 8 Sep 1939: *Tomás Ó Deirg* (see De Valera II) 8 – 27 Sep 1939: *Sean Thomas O'Kelly* (see De Valera II) 27 Sep – 18 Jun 1940: *Eamon de Valera* (see Presidents) 18 Jun 1940 – Jul 1943: *Tomás Ó Deirg* (see De Valera II)
Local Government and Public Health	Jun 1938 – 8 Sep 1939: *Sean Thomas O'Kelly* (see De Valera II) 8 Sep 1939 – 14 Aug 1941: *P. J. Ruttledge* (see De Valera II) 14 Aug 1941 – Jul 1943: *John Francis (Sean) MacEntee* (see De Valera II)
Attorney-General	Jun 1938 – 1 Mar 1940: *P. Lynch* (see De Valera III) 1 Mar 1940 – 10 Oct 1942: *Kevin O'Hanrahan Haugh*

(b. 17 Nov 1901; d. 5 Apr 1969)
10 Oct 1942 – Jul 1943: *Kevin Dixon* (b. 22 Jun 1902;
d. Oct 1959

Jul 1943 – May 1944: De Valera VI (Fianna Fáil)

Prime Minister	*Eamon de Valera* (for 6th time) (see Presidents)
Deputy Prime Minister	*Sean Thomas O'Kelly* (see De Valera II)
Justice	*G. Boland* (see De Valera III)
Defence	*O. Traynor* (see De Valera III)
Co-ordination of Defensive Measures	*Frank Aiken* (see De Valera II)
External Affairs	*Eamon de Valera* (see Presidents)
Finance	*Sean Thomas O'Kelly* (see De Valera II)
Industry and Commerce	*Seán Lemass* (see De Valera II)
Supplies	*Seán Lemass* (see De Valera II)
Posts and Telegraphs	*P. J. Little* (see De Valera V)
Agriculture	*James Ryan* (see De Valera II)
Lands	*S. Moylan*
Education	*Tomás Ó Deirg* (see De Valera II)
Local Government and Public Health	*John Francis (Sean) MacEntee* (see De Valera II)
Attorney-General	*Kevin Dixon* (see De Valera V)

May 1944 – Feb 1948: De Valera VII (Fianna Fáil)

Prime Minister	*Eamon de Valera* (for 6th time) (see Presidents)
Deputy Prime Minister	May 1944 – 14 Jun 1945: *Sean Thomas O'Kelly* (see De Valera II) 14 Jun 1945 – Feb 1948: *Seán Lemass* (see De Valera II)
Justice	*G. Boland* (see De Valera III)
Defence	*O. Traynor* (see De Valera III)
Co-ordination of Defensive Measures	May 1944 – 19 Jun 1945: *Frank Aiken* (see De Valera II) 19 Jun 1945: post abolished
External Affairs	*Eamon de Valera* (see Presidents)
Finance	May 1944 – 14 Jun 1945: *Sean Thomas O'Kelly* (see De Valera II) 14 Jun 1945 – Feb 1948: *Frank Aiken* (see De Valera II)

311

Industry and Commerce	*Seán Lemass* (see De Valera II)
Supplies	May 1944 – 31 Jul 1945: *Seán Lemass* (see De Valera II)
Posts and Telegraphs	*P. J. Little* (see De Valera V)
Agriculture	May 1944 – 21 Jan 1947: *James Ryan* (see De Valera II)
	21 Jan 1947 – Feb 1948: *Patrick Smith* (b. Tunnyduff Bailieborogh, County Cavan, 17 Jul 1901)
Lands	*S. Moylan* (see De Valera VI)
Education	*Thomás Ó Deirg* (see De Valera II)
Local Government and Public Health (from 1947: Local Government)	*John Francis (Sean) MacEntee* (see De Valera II)
Health (new post)	21 Jan 1947 – Feb 1948: *James Ryan* (see De Valera II)
Social Welfare (new post)	21 Jan 1947 – Feb 1948: *James Ryan* (see De Valera II)
Attorney-General	May 1944 – 30 Apr 1946: *Kevin Dixon* (see De Valera V)
	30 Apr 1946 – Feb 1948: *Carroll Daly (Cearbhall Ó Dálaigh)* (see Presidents)

Feb 1948 – Jun 1951: Costello I (Inter-Party)

Prime Minister	*John Aloysius Costello* (for 1st time) (see William Cosgrave)
Deputy Prime Minister	*William Norton* (d. 4 Dec 1963)
Justice	Feb 1948 – 7 Mar 1951: *Seán MacEoin* (b. County Longford 30 Sep 1893; d. 7 Jul 1973)
	7 Mar – Jun 1951: *D. Morrissey*
Defence	Feb 1948 – 7 Mar 1951: *T. F. O'Higgins*
	7 Mar – Jun 1951: *Seán MacEoin* (see above)
External Affairs	*Sean MacBride* (b. 26 Jan 1904)
Finance	*Patrick McGilligan* (see William Cosgrave)
Industry and Commerce	Feb 1948 – 7 Mar 1951: *D. Morrissey* (see above)
	7 Mar – Jun 1951: *T. F. O'Higgins* (see above)
Posts and Telegraphs	*J. Everett*
Agriculture	*J. Dillon*
Lands	*J. Blowick*
Education	*Richard Mulcahy* (see William Cosgrave)

Local Government	Feb 1948 – 29 Apr 1949: *T. J. Murphy*
	29 Apr 1949 – Jun 1951: *M. Keyes*
Health	Feb 1948 – 11 Apr 1951: *N. C. Browne*
	11 Apr – Jun 1951: *John Aloysius Costello* (see William Cosgrave)
Social Welfare	*William Norton* (see above)
Attorney-General	Feb 1948 – 21 Apr 1951: *Cecil Lavery* (b. 6 Oct 1894; d. 16 Dec 1967)
	21 Apr – Jun 1951: *C. F. Casey*

Jun 1951 – Jun 1954: De Valera VIII (Fianna Fáil)

Prime Minister	*Eamon de Valera* (for 8th time) (see Presidents)
Deputy Prime Minister	*Seán Lemass* (see De Valera II)
Justice	*G. Boland* (see De Valera III)
Defence	*O. Traynor* (see De Valera III)
External Affairs	*Frank Aiken* (see De Valera II)
Finance	*John Francis (Sean) MacEntee* (see De Valera II)
Industry and Commerce	*Seán Lemass* (see De Valera II)
Posts and Telegraphs	*Erskine H. Childers* (see Presidents)
Agriculture	*T. Walsh*
Lands	*Tomás Ó Deirg* (see De Valera II)
Education	*S. Moylan* (see De Valera VI)
Local Government	*Patrick Smith* (see De Valera VII)
Health	*James Ryan* (see De Valera II)
Social Welfare	*James Ryan* (see De Valera II)
Attorney-General	Jun 1951 – 11 Jul 1953: *Carroll Daly (Cearbhall Ó Dálaigh)* (see Presidents)
	11 Jul 1953 – Jun 1954: *Tomas Leslie Teevan* (b. Jul 1927; d. 11 Oct 1954)

Jun 1954 – Mar 1957: Costello II (Inter-Party)

Prime Minister	*John Aloysius Costello* (for 2nd time) (see William Cosgrave)
Deputy Prime Minister	*William Norton* (see Costello I)
Justice	*J. Everett* (see Costello I)
Defence	*Seán MacEoin* (see Costello I)
External Affairs	*Liam Cosgrave* (b. Templeogne 30 Apr 1920)
Finance	*G. Sweetman*

313

Industry and Commerce	*William Norton* (see Costello I)
Posts and Telegraphs	*M. Keyes* (see Costello I)
Agriculture	*J. Dillon* (see Costello I)
Lands	*J. Blowick* (see Costello I)
Irish-speaking Regions (new post)	2 Jul – 24 Oct 1956: *Richard Mulcahy* (see William Cosgrave) 24 Oct 1956 – Mar 1957: *Patrick James Lindsay* (b. Dublin 18 Jan 1914)
Education	*Richard Mulcahy* (see William Cosgrave)
Local Government	*P. O'Donnell*
Health	*T. F. O'Higgins* (see Costello I)
Social Welfare	*Brendan Corish* (b. Wexford 19 Nov 1918)
Attorney-General	*Patrick McGilligan* (see William Cosgrave)

Mar 1957 – Jun 1959: De Valera IX (Fianna Fáil)

Prime Minister	*Eamon de Valera* (for 9th time) (see Presidents)
Deputy Prime Minister	*Seán Lemass* (see De Valera II)
Justice	*O. Traynor* (see De Valera III)
Defence	*Kevin Boland*
External Affairs	*Frank Aiken* (see De Valera II)
Finance	*J. Ryan* (see De Valera II)
Industry and Commerce	*Seán Lemass* (see De Valera II)
Posts and Telegraphs	Mar – 4 Dec 1957: *Neil T. Blaney* 4 Dec 1957 – Jun 1959: *J. Ormonde*
Agriculture	Mar – 16 May 1957: *Frank Aiken* (see De Valera II) 16 May – 16 Nov 1957: *S. Moylan* (see De Valera VI) 16 Nov 1957 – Jun 1959: *Patrick Smith* (see De Valera VII)
Lands	*Erskine H. Childers* (see Presidents)
Irish-speaking Regions	Mar – 26 Jun 1957: *John Lynch* (b. Cork 15 Aug 1917) 26 Jun 1957 – Jun 1959: *Micheál Ó Moráin*
Education	*John Lynch* (see above)
Local Government	Mar – 27 Nov 1957: *Patrick Smith* (see De Valera VII) 27 Nov 1957 – Jun 1959: *Neil T. Blaney* (see above)
Health	*John Francis (Sean) MacEntee* (see De Valera II)
Social Welfare	Mar – 27 Nov 1975: *Patrick Smith* (see De Valera VII) 27 Nov 1975 – Jun 1959: *John Francis (Sean) MacEntee* (see De Valera II)
Attorney-General	*A. Ó Caoimh*

Jun 1959 – Oct 1961: Lemass I (Fianna Fáil)

Prime Minister	*Seán Lemass* (for 1st time) (see De Valera II)
Deputy Prime Minister	*John Francis (Sean) MacEntee* (see De Valera II)
Justice	*O. Traynor* (see De Valera III)
Defence	*Kevin Boland* (see De Valera IX)
External Affairs	*Frank Aiken* (see De Valera II)
Finance	*James Ryan* (see De Valera II)
Industry and Commerce	*John Lynch* (see De Valera IX)
Transport and Power (new post)	27 Jul 1959 – Oct 1961: *Erskine H. Childers* (see Presidents)
Posts and Telegraphs	*Michael Hilliard* (b. Navan, County Meath, Mar 1903)
Agriculture	*Patrick Smith* (see De Valera VII)
Lands	Mar – 23 Jul 1959: *Erskine H. Childers* (see Presidents)
	23 Jul 1959 – Oct 1961: *Micheál Ó Moráin* (see De Valera IX)
Irish-speaking Regions	Mar – 23 Jul 1959: *Micheál Ó Moráin* (see De Valera IX)
	23 Jul 1959 – Oct 1961: *G. Bartley*
Education	*Patrick John Hillery* (b. County Clare 2 May 1923)
Local Government	*Neil T. Blaney* (see De Valera IX)
Health	*John Francis (Sean) MacEntee* (see De Valera II)
Social Welfare	*John Francis (Sean) MacEntee* (see De Valera II)
Attorney-General	*A. Ó Caoimh* (see De Valera IX)

Oct 1961 – Apr 1965: Lemass II (Fianna Fáil)

Prime Minister	*Seán Lemass* (for 2nd time) (see De Valera II)
Deputy Prime Minister	*John Francis (Sean) MacEntee* (see De Valera II)
Justice	Oct 1961 – 8 Oct 1964: *Charles J. Haughey* (b. Castlebar, County Mayo, 16 Sep 1925)
	8 Oct – 3 Nov 1964: *Seán Lemass* (see De Valera II)
	3 Nov 1964 – Apr 1965: *Brian Joseph Lenihan* (b. Dundalk 17 Nov 1930)
Defence	*G. Bartley* (see Lemass I)
External Affairs	*Frank Aiken* (see De Valera II)
Finance	*James Ryan* (see De Valera II)
Industry and Commerce	*John Lynch* (see De Valera IX)

Transport and Power	*Erskine H. Childers* (see Presidents)
Posts and Telegraphs	*Michael Hilliard* (see Lemass I)
Agriculture	Oct 1961 – 8 Oct 1964: *Patrick Smith* (see De Valera VII)
	8 Oct 1964 – Apr 1965: *Charles J. Haughey* (see above)
Lands	*Micheál Ó Moráin* (see De Valera IX)
Irish-speaking Regions	*Micheál Ó Moráin* (see De Valera IX)
Education	*Patrick John Hillery* (see Lemass I)
Local Government	*Neil T. Blaney* (see De Valera IX)
Health	*John Francis (Sean) MacEntee* (see De Valera II)
Social Welfare	*Kevin Boland* (see De Valera IX)
Attorney-General	Oct 1961 – 16 Mar 1965: *A. Ó Caoimh* (see De Valera IX)
	16 Mar – Apr 1965: *Colm Condon* (b. Ashbourne, County Meath, 16 Jul 1921)

Apr 1965 – Nov 1966: Lemass III (Fianna Fáil)

Prime Minister	*Sean Lemass* (for 3rd time) (see De Valera II)
Deputy Prime Minister	*Frank Aiken* (see De Valera II)
Justice	*Brian Joseph Lenihan* (see Lemass II)
Defence	*Michael Hilliard* (see Lemass I)
External Affairs	*Frank Aiken* (see De Valera II)
Finance	*John Lynch* (see De Valera IX)
Industry and Commerce	Apr – 13 Jul 1966: *Patrick John Hillery* (see Lemass I)
	13 Jul – Nov 1966: *George J. Colley* (b. Dublin 18 Oct 1925)
Transport and Power	*Erskine H. Childers* (see Presidents)
Posts and Telegraphs	*Joseph Brennan* (b. Donegal 14 Feb 1913; d. 3 Mar 1976)
Agriculture (from Jul 1965: and Fisheries)	*Charles J. Haughey* (see Lemass II)
Lands	*Micheál O Moráin* (see De Valera IX)
Irish-speaking Regions	*Micheál O Moráin* (see De Valera IX)
Education	Apr 1965 – 13 Jul 1966: *George J. Colley* (see above)
	13 Jul – Nov 1966: *D. B. O'Malley*
Local Government	*Neil T. Blaney* (see De Valera IX)
Health	Apr 1965 – 13 Jul 1966: *D. B. O'Malley* (see above)
	13 Jul – Nov 1966: *Sean M. Flanagan* (b. Mayo 26 Jan 1922)

Social Welfare	*Kevin Boland* (see De Valera IX)
Labour (new post)	13 Jul – Nov 1966: *Patrick John Hillery* (see Lemass I)
Attorney-General	*Colm Condon* (see Lemass II)

Nov 1966 – 2 Jul 1969: Lynch I (Fianna Fáil)

Prime Minister	*John Lynch* (for 1st time) (see De Valera IX)
Deputy Prime Minister	*Frank Aiken* (see De Valera II)
Justice	Nov 1966 – 26 Mar 1968: *Brian Joseph Lenihan* (see Lemass II)
	26 Mar 1968 – 2 Jul 1969: *Micheál Ó Moráin* (see De Valera IX)
Defence	*Michael Hilliard* (see Lemass I)
External Affairs	*Frank Aiken* (see De Valera II)
Finance	*Charles J. Haughey* (see Lemass II)
Industry and Commerce	*George J. Colley* (see Lemass III)
Transport and Power	*Erskine H. Childers* (see Presidents)
Posts and Telegraphs	*Erskine H. Childers* (see Presidents)
Agriculture and Fisheries	*Neil T. Blaney* (see De Valera IX)
Lands	Nov 1966 – 26 Mar 1968: *Micheál Ó Moráin* (see De Valera IX)
	26 Mar 1968 – 2 Jul 1969: *Pádraig Faulkner* (b. Dunleer, County Louth, 12 Mar 1918)
Irish-speaking Regions	Nov 1966 – 26 Mar 1968: *Micheál Ó Moráin* (see De Valera IX)
	26 Mar 1968 – 2 Jul 1969: *Pádraig Faulkner* (see above)
Education	Nov 1966 – 10 Mar 1968: *D. B. O'Malley* (see Lemass III)
	10 – 26 Mar 1968: *John Lynch* (see De Valera IX)
	26 Mar 1968 – 2 Jul 1969: *Brian Joseph Lenihan* (see Lemass II)
Local Government	*Kevin Boland* (see De Valera IX)
Health	*Sean M. Flanagan* (see Lemass III)
Social Welfare	*Joseph Brennan* (see Lemass III)
Labour	*Patrick John Hillery* (see Lemass I)
Attorney-General	*Colm Condon* (see Lemass II)

2 Jul 1969 – 14 Mar 1973: Lynch II (Fianna Fáil)

| Prime Minister | *John Lynch* (for 2nd time) (see De Valera IX) |

Deputy Prime Minister	*Erskine H. Childers* (see Presidents)
Justice	*Micheál Ó Moráin* (see De Valera IX)
Defence	2 Jul 1969 – 8 May 1970: *James Gibbons*
	8 May 1970 – 14 Mar 1973: *Jeremiah Cronin* (b. Currabeha Fermoy 15 Sep 1929)
External Affairs (from 3 Mar 1971: Foreign Affairs)	2 Jul 1969 – 29 Dec 1972: *Patrick John Hillery* (see Lemass I)
	29 Dec 1972 – 14 Mar 1973: *Brian Joseph Lenihan* (see Lemass II)
Finance	2 Jul 1969 – 6 May 1970: *Charles J. Haughey* (see Lemass II)
	8 May 1970 – 14 Mar 1973: *George J. Colley* (see Lemass III)
Industry and Commerce	2 Jul 1969 – 8 May 1970: *George J. Colley* (see Lemass III)
	8 May 1970 – 14 Mar 1973: *Patrick Joseph Lalor* (b. Dublin 21 Jul 1926)
Transport and Power	2 Jul 1969 – 29 Dec 1972: *Brian Joseph Lenihan* (see Lemass II)
	29 Dec 1972 – 14 Mar 1973: *Michael O'Kennedy* (b. Nenagh, County Tipperary 21 Feb 1936)
Posts and Telegraphs	2 Jul 1969 – 8 May 1970: *Patrick Joseph Lalor* (see above)
	8 May 1970 – 14 Mar 1973: *James Gerard Collins* (b. County Limerick 16 Oct 1938)
Agriculture and Fisheries	2 Jul 1969 – 6 May 1970: *Neil T. Blaney* (see De Valera IX)
	8 May 1970 – 14 Mar 1973: *James Gibbons* (see above)
Lands	*Sean M. Flanagan* (see Lemass III)
Irish-speaking Regions	*George J. Colley* (see Lemass III)
Education	*Pádraig Faulkner* (see Lynch I)
Local Government	2 Jul 1969 – 6 May 1970: *Kevin Boland* (see De Valera IX)
	8 May 1970 – 14 Mar 1973: *Robert Michael Molloy* (b. 6 Jul 1936)
Health	*Erskine H. Childers* (see Presidents)
Social Welfare	2 Jul 1969 – 6 May 1970: *Kevin Boland* (see De Valera IX)
	8 May 1970 – 14 Mar 1973: *Joseph Brennan* (see Lemass III)
Labour	*Joseph Brennan* (see Lemass III)

Without Portfolio	14 Dec 1972 – 14 Mar 1973: *Michael O'Kennedy* (see above)

from 14 Mar 1973: Liam Cosgrave (Coalition)

Prime Minister	*Liam Cosgrave* (Fine Gael) (see Costello II)
Deputy Prime Minister	*Brendan Corish* (Lab) (see Costello II)
Justice	*Patrick Mark Cooney* (Fine Gael) (b. 2 Mar 1931)
Defence	*Patrick Sarsfield Donegan* (Fine Gael) (b. Drogheda, County Louth, 29 Oct 1923)
Foreign Affairs	*Garret Michael Desmond Fitzgerald* (Fine Gael) (b. Dublin 9 Feb 1926)
Finance	*Richie Ryan* (Fine Gael) (b. Dublin 1929)
Industry and Commerce	*Justin Keating* (Lab) (b. Dublin 7 Jan 1930)
Transport and Power	*Peter Barry* (Fine Gael) (b. Cork 10 Aug 1928)
Posts and Telegraphs	*Conor Cruise O'Brien* (Lab) (b. 3 Nov 1917)
Agriculture and Fisheries	*Mark Clinton* (Fine Gael)
Local Government	*James Tully* (Lab) (b. Kells, County Meath, 18 Sep 1915)
Irish-speaking Regions	*Tomás Gearóid Ó Domhnall* (Fine Gael) (b. Limerick 30 Aug 1926)
Education	*Richard Burke* (Fine Gael) (b. New York 29 Mar 1932)
Lands	*Thomas Fitzpatrick* (Fine Gael) (b. County Cork 29 Jul 1928)
Health	*Brendan Corish* (Lab) (see Costello II)
Social Welfare	*Brendan Corish* (Lab) (see Costello II)
Labour	*Michael O'Leary* (Lab) (b. 8 May 1936)
Attorney-General	*Declan Costello* (Fine Gael)

Israel

State set up on termination of the British Mandate of Palestine (q.v.)

HEADS OF STATE

Presidents

15 May 1948 – 9 Nov 1952	*Chaim Weizmann* (b. Motyli 27 Nov 1874; d. Tel Aviv 9 Nov 1952)
8 Dec 1952 – 23 Apr 1963	*Isaac Ben Zvi* (b. Poltava 8 Dec 1884; d. Jerusalem 23 Apr 1963)
21 May 1963	*Zalman Schazar* (b. Mir 6 Oct 1889)
from 24 May 1973	*Ephraim Katzir*, formerly *Katchalski* (b. Kiev 1916)

MEMBERS OF GOVERNMENT

17 May 1948/9 Mar 1949 – 15 Oct 1950: Ben Gurion I

Prime Minister	*David Ben Gurion* (for 1st time) (b. Warsaw 16 Oct 1886; d. 1 Dec 1973)
Foreign Affairs	*Moses Sharett* (b. Kherson, Ukraine, Oct 1894; d. Jerusalem 7 Jul 1965)
Finance	*Elisha Kaplan* (b. Minsk 27 Jan 1891; d. Genoa 13 Jul 1952)

30 Oct 1950 – 14/21 Sep 1951: Ben Gurion II

Prime Minister	*David Ben Gurion* (for 2nd time) (see Ben Gurion I)
Foreign Affairs	*Moses Sharett* (see Ben Gurion I)
Finance	*Elisha Kaplan* (see Ben Gurion I)

7 Oct 1951 – 19 Dec 1952: Ben Gurion III

Prime Minister	*David Ben Gurion* (for 3rd time) (see Ben Gurion I)
Foreign Affairs	*Moses Sharett* (see Ben Gurion I)
Finance	7 Oct 1951 – 21 May 1952: *Elisha Kaplan* (see Ben Gurion I)
	25 Jun – 19 Dec 1952: *Levi Eshkol* (b. Oratova 10 Oct 1895; d. Jerusalem 26 Feb 1969)

22 Dec 1952 – 7 Dec 1953: Ben Gurion IV

Prime Minister	*David Ben Gurion* (for 4th time) (see Ben Gurion I)
Foreign Affairs	*Moses Sharett* (see Ben Gurion I)
Finance	*Levi Eshkol* (see Ben Gurion III)

7 Dec 1953 /26 Jan 1954 – 29 Jun 1955: Sharett I

Prime Minister and Foreign Affairs	*Moses Sharett* (Mapai) (for 1st time) (see Ben Gurion I)
Home Affairs	*Israel Rokach* (Zionist)
Finance	*Levi Eshkol* (Mapai) (see Ben Gurion III)
Education	*Benzion Dinur* (Mapai) (b. Poltava 2 Jan 1894; d. 7 Jul 1973)
Defence	24 Jan 1954 – 19 Feb 1955: *Pinechas Lavon* (Mapai) (b. Poland 1904; d. 24 Jan 1976)
	19 Feb – 29 Jun 1955: *David Ben Gurion* (Mapai) (see Ben Gurion I)

30 Jun – 15 Aug 1955: Sharett II

Prime Minister and Foreign Affairs	*Moses Sharett* (Mapai) (for 2nd time) (see Ben Gurion I)
Home Affairs	*Chaim Moses Shapiro* (Nat Rel) (b. Gródno 26 Mar 1902; d. Jerusalem night of 16/17 Jul 1970)
Finance	*Levi Eshkol* (Mapai) (see Ben Gurion III)
Education	*Benzion Dinur* (Mapai) (see Sharett I)
Defence	*David Ben Gurion* (Mapai) (see Ben Gurion I)

2 Nov 1955/1 Jan 1956 – 31 Dec 1957 and 7 Jan 1958 – 5 Jul 1959: Ben Gurion V

Prime Minister	*David Ben Gurion* (Mapai) (for 5th time) (see Ben Gurion I)
Foreign Affairs	1 Jan – 18 Jun 1956: *Moses Sharett* (Mapai) (see Ben Gurion I)
	18 Jun 1956 – 5 Jul 1959: *Golda Meïr* (Mapai) (b. Kiev 3 May 1898)
Home Affairs	*Israel Bar-Judah* (Achduth Avoda) (b. Ukraine 15 Nov 1895)
Finance	*Levi Eshkol* (Mapai) (see Ben Gurion III)
Education	*Zalman Aranne* (Mapai) (b. Ukraine 1899; d. 7 Sep 1970)
Defence	*David Ben Gurion* (Mapai) (see Ben Gurion I)

16 Dec 1959 – 31 Jan/1 Nov 1961: Ben Gurion VI

Prime Minister	*David Ben Gurion* (Mapai) (for 6th time) (see Ben Gurion I)
Foreign Affairs	*Golda Meïr* (Mapai) (see Ben Gurion V)

ISRAEL

Home Affairs	*Chaim Moses Shapiro* (Nat Rel) (see Sharett II)
Finance	*Levi Eshkol* (Mapai) (see Ben Gurion III)
Education	16 Dec 1959 – 24 Apr 1960: *Zalman Aranne* (Mapai) (see Ben Gurion V)
	24 Apr – 28 Jul 1960 (acting:) *David Ben Gurion* (Mapai) (see Ben Gurion I)
	28 Jul 1960 – 31 Jan/1 Nov 1961: *Abba Eban* (b. Capetown 2 Feb 1915)
Defence	*David Ben Gurion* (Mapai) (see Ben Gurion I)

1/2 Nov 1961 – 16 Jun 1963: Ben Gurion VII

Prime Minister	*David Ben Gurion* (Mapai) (for 7th time) (see Ben Gurion I)
Foreign Affairs	*Golda Meïr* (Mapai) (see Ben Gurion V)
Home Affairs	*Chaim Moses Shapiro* (Nat Rel) (see Sharett II)
Finance	*Levi Eshkol* (Mapai) (see Ben Gurion III)
Education	*Abba Eban* (Mapai) (see Ben Gurion VI)
Defence	*David Ben Gurion* (Mapai) (see Ben Gurion I)

24 Jun 1963 – 14 Dec 1964: Eshkol I

Prime Minister	*Levi Eshkol* (Mapai) (for 1st time) (see Ben Gurion III)
Deputy Premier	*Abba Eban* (Mapai) (see Ben Gurion VI)
Foreign Affairs	*Golda Meïr* (Mapai) (see Ben Gurion V)
Home Affairs and Health	*Chaim Moses Shapiro* (Nat Rel) (see Sharett II)
Finance	*Pinchas Sapir* (Mapai) (b. Suwatki 1909; d. 12 Aug 1975)
Education	*Zalman Aranne* (Mapai) (see Ben Gurion V)
Defence	*Levi Eshkol* (Mapai) (see Ben Gurion III)

23 Dec 1964 – 12 Jan 1966: Eshkol II

Prime Minister	*Levi Eshkol* (Mapai) (for 2nd time) (see Ben Gurion III)
Deputy Premier	*Abba Eban* (Mapai) (see Ben Gurion IV)
Foreign Affairs	*Golda Meïr* (Mapai) (see Ben Gurion V)
Home Affairs and Health	*Chaim Moses Shapiro* (Nat Rel) (see Sharett II)
Finance	*Pinchas Sapir* (Mapai) (see Eshkol I)
Education	*Zalman Aranne* (Mapai) (see Ben Gurion V)

Defence	*Levi Eshkol* (see Ben Gurion III)
Tourism (new post)	*Akiva Govrin* (Mapai) (b. Russia 12 Aug 1902)

12 Jan 1966 – 26 Feb 1969: Eshkol III

Prime Minister	*Levi Eshkol* (Mapai) (for 3rd time) (see Ben Gurion III)
Deputy Premier	*Ygal Allon* (Achduth Avoda) (b. Kfar Tabor 10 Oct 1918)
Foreign Affairs	*Abba Eban* (Mapai) (see Ben Gurion IV)
Home Affairs	*Chaim Moses Shapiro* (Nat Rel) (see Sharett II)
Health	*Israel Barzilai* (Mapai) (b. Poland 1 Oct 1913; d. 12 Jun 1970)
Finance	*Pinchas Sapir* (Mapai) (see Eshkol I)
Education	*Zalman Aranne* (Mapai) (see Ben Gurion V)
Defence	12 Jan 1966 – 2 Jun 1967: *Levi Eshkol* (Mapai) (see Ben Gurion III)
	2 Jun 1967 – 26 Feb 1969: *Moshe Dayan* (Mapai) (b. Degania 20 May 1915)
Tourism	*Moses Kol* (Ind Lib) (b. Pinsk 28 May 1911)

26 Feb – 14 Mar 1969: Allon (Transitional Government)

Prime Minister	(acting:) *Ygal Allon* (Achduth Avoda) (see Eshkol III) Other ministers continued in same offices as in previous cabinet

14 Mar – 13 Dec 1969: Meïr I (Coalition)

Prime Minister	*Golda Meïr* (Mapai) (for 1st time) (see Ben Gurion V) Other ministers continued in same offices as in previous cabinet

13 Dec 1969 – 6 Mar 1974: Meïr II (Coalition)

Prime Minister	*Golda Meïr* (Mapai) (for 2nd time) (see Ben Gurion V)
Deputy Prime Minister	*Ygal Allon* (Achduth Avoda (see Eshkol III)
Foreign Affairs	*Abba Eban* (Mapai) (see Ben Gurion IV)
Home Affairs	13 Dec 1969 – 16 Jul 1970: *Chaim Moses Shapiro* (Nat Rel) (see Sharett II)
	Jul 1970 – 6 Mar 1974: *Salomon Joseph Burg* (Nat Rel) (b. Dresden 31 Jan 1909)

Finance	*Pinchas Sapir* (Mapai) (see Eshkol I)
Education	*Ygal Allon* (Achduth Avoda) (see Eshkol III)
Defence	*Moshe Dayan* (Mapai) (see Eshkol III)
Tourism	*Moses Kol* (Ind Lib) (see Eshkol III)

6 Mar – 28 May 1974: Meïr III (Coalition)

Prime Minister	*Golda Meïr* (Lab, Mapai) (for 3rd time) (see Ben Gurion V)
Deputy Prime Minister	*Ygal Allon* (Lab, Mapai) (see Eshkol III)
Foreign Affairs	*Abba Eban* (Lab, Mapai) (see Ben Gurion IV)
Home Affairs	*Salomon Joseph Burg* (Nat Rel) (see Meïr II)
Finance	*Pinchas Sapir* (Lab, Mapai) (see Eshkol I)
Education	*Ygal Allon* (Lab, Mapai) (see Eshkol III)
Defence	*Moshe Dayan* (Lab, Mapai) (see Eshkol III)
Tourism	*Moses Kol* (Ind Lib) (see Eshkol III)
Commerce, Industry and Development	*Haim Bar-Lev* (Lab, Mapai) (b. Vienna 16 Nov 1911)
Agriculture	*Chaim Gvati* (Lab, Mapai) (b. Pinsk 29 Jan 1901)
Police	*Shlomo Hillel* (Lab, Mapai) (b. Baghdad 23 Apr 1923)
Transport	*Aharon Yariv* (Lab, Mapai) (b. Latvia 1920)
Information	*Shimon Peres* (Lab, Mapai) (b. 1923)
Justice	*Haim Joseph Zadok* (Lab, Mapai) (b. Poland 2 Oct 1913)
Labour	*Itzhak Rabin* (Lab, Mapai) (b. Jerusalem 1922)
Housing	*Yehoshua Rabinowitz* (Lab, Mapai) (b. Poland 13 Nov 1911)
Communications	*Aharon Uzan* (Lab, Mapai) (b. Tunisia)
Health	*Victor Shemtov* (Lab, Mapam)
Integration of Immigrants	*Shlomo Rosen* (Lab, Mapam) (b. Moravská Ostrava 21 Jun 1905)
Religious Affairs	*Itzhak Raphael* (Nat Rel)
Social Welfare	*Michael Hazani* (Nat Rel) (d. 2 Jul 1975)
Without Portfolio	*Israel Galili* (Lab, Mapai) (b. 1911)
	Gideon Hausner (Ind Lib) (b. Poland 26 Sep 1915)

from 28 May 1974: Rabin (Coalition)

Prime Minister	*Itzhak Rabin* (Lab) (see Meïr III)
Deputy Prime Minister	*Ygal Allon* (Lab) (see Eshkol III)

Foreign Affairs	*Ygal Allon* (Lab) (see Eshkol III)
Home Affairs	28 May – 29 Oct 1974: *Shlomo Hillel* (Lab) (see Meïr III)
	from 29 Oct 1974: *Salomon Joseph Burg* (Nat Rel) (see Meïr II)
Finance	*Yehoshua Rabinowitz* (Lab) (see Meïr III)
Education	*Aharon Yadlin* (Lab) (b. Ben-Shemen, Israel, 17 Apr 1926)
Defence	*Shimon Peres* (Lab) (see Meïr III)
Tourism	*Moses Kol* (Ind Lib) (see Eshkol III)
Commerce and Industry	*Haim Bar-Lev* (Lab) (see Meïr III)
Agriculture	*Aharon Uzan* (Lab) (see Meïr III)
Police	*Shlomo Hillel* (Lab) (see Meïr III)
Transport	*Gad Yaakobi* (Lab) (b. Kfar Witkin 18 Jan 1935)
Information	28 May 1974 – 29 Jan 1975: *Aharon Yariv* (Lab) (see Meïr III)
	29 Jan – 9 Mar 1975 (acting:) *Itzhak Rabin* (Lab) (see Meïr III)
	9 Mar 1975: ministry incorporated in Education and Culture (see above)
Justice	*Haim Joseph Zadok* (Lab) (see Meïr III)
Labour	*Moshe Baram* (Lab) (b. Zdolvinov, Ukraine, 1911)
Housing	*Avraham Ofer* (Lab) (b. Poland 1922)
Communications	28 May 1974 – 9 Mar 1975 (acting:) *Itzhak Rabin* (Lab) (see Meïr III)
	9 Mar 1975: ministry incorporated in Agriculture (see above)
Health	*Victor Shemtov* (Mapam) (see Meïr III)
Integration of Immigrants	*Shlomo Rosen* (Mapam) (see Meïr III)
Religious Affairs	28 May – 29 Oct 1974: *Haim Joseph Zadok* (Lab) (see Meïr III)
	from 29 Oct 1974: *Itzhak Raphael* (Nat Rel) (see Meïr III)
Social Welfare	29 Oct 1974 – 2 Jul 1975: *Michael Hazani* (Nat Rel) (see Meïr III)
	2 Jul – 4 Nov 1975 (acting:) *Salomon Joseph Burg* (Nat Rel) (see Meïr II)
	from 4 Nov 1975: *Zevulun Hammer* (Nat Rel)
Without Portfolio	*Israel Galili* (Lab) (see Meïr III)
	Gideon Hausner (Ind Lib) (see Meïr III)
	Shulamit Aloni (Civil Rights) (b. Israel 1932)

Italy

HEADS OF STATE

Kings

29 Jul 1900 – 9 May 1946	*Victor Emmanuel III*, son of Humbert I (b. 11 Nov 1869; d. 28 Dec 1947)
9 May – 12 Jun 1946	*Humbert II*, son (b. Racconigi 15 Sep 1904) from 9 Jun 1944 'Governor General of the Kingdom'; from 9 May 1946 King; 13 Jun 1946 abdicated and moved to Portugal
Jun 1946	Republic

Presidents

28 Jun 1946 – 10 May 1948	*Enrico de Nicola* (b. Naples 9 Nov 1877; d. 1 Oct 1959)
11 May 1948	*Luigi Einaudi* (b. Carru 24 Mar 1874; d. Rome 30 Oct 1961)
11 May 1955	*Giovanni Gronchi* (b. Pisa 10 Sep 1887)
11 May 1962 – 6 Dec 1964	*Antonio Segni* (b. Sassari, Sardinia, 2 Feb 1891; d. 1 Dec 1972)
29 Dec 1964	*Giuseppi Saragat* (b. Turin 12 Sep 1898)
from 29 Dec 1971	*Giovanni Leone* (b. Naples 3 Nov 1908)

MEMBERS OF GOVERNMENT

30 Oct 1922 – 25 Jul 1943: Mussolini I*

Prime Minister	*Benito Mussolini* (for 1st time) (b. Predappio 29 Jul 1883; d. Villa Belmonte, Lake Como, 28 Apr 1945)
Foreign Affairs	12 Sep 1929 – 20 Jul 1932: *Dino* (from 1937: *Count*) *Grandi di Mordano* (b. Mordano 4 Jun 1895)
	20 Jul 1932 – 9 Jun 1936: *Benito Mussolini* (see above)
	9 Jun 1936 – 5 Feb 1943: *Galeazzo, Count Ciano di Cortellazzo* (b. Livorno 18 Mar 1903; d. Verona 11 Jan 1944)
	5 Feb – 25 Jul 1943: *Benito Mussolini* (see above)

*For ministers no longer in office in 1930 see vol. 2

Home Affairs	5/6 Nov 1926 – 25 Jul 1943: *Benito Mussolini* (see above)
Justice	5 Jan 1925 – 20 Jul 1932: *Alfredo Rocca* (b. Naples 1875; d. Rome 28 Aug 1935)
	20 Jul 1932 – 24 Jan 1935: *Pietro de Francisci* (b. Rome 18 Dec 1883)
	24 Jan 1935 – 12 Jul 1939: *Arrigo Solmi* (b. Finale Emilia 27 Jan 1873; d. Rome 5 Mar 1941)
	12 Jul 1939 – 5 Feb 1943: *Dino, Count Grandi di Mordano* (see above)
	5 Feb – 25 Jul 1943: *Alfredo de Marsico* (b. Sala Consilina 29 May 1888)
Finance	8 Jul 1928 – 20 Jul 1932: *Antonio Mosconi* (b. Vicenza 9 Sep 1866)
	20 Jul 1932 – 24 Jan 1935: *Guido Jung* (b. Palermo 1 Feb 1876; d. 26 Dec 1949)
	24 Jan 1935 – 5 Feb 1943: *Paolo Ignazio Maria, Count Thaon di Revel* (b. Toulon 2 May 1888)
	5 Feb – 25 Jul 1943: *Giacomo Acerbo* (b. Loreto Aprutino 25 Jul 1888)
Education	12 Sep 1929 – 20 Jul 1932: *Giuliano Balbino* (b. Forsano 1879)
	20 Jul 1932 – 24 Jan 1935: *Francesco Ercole* (b. La Spezia 1 May 1884; d. Gardone Riviera 18 May 1945)
	24 Jan 1935 – 11 Nov 1936: *Cesare Maria* (from 1936(?): *Count*) *Vecchi di Valcismon* (b. Casale Monferrato 14 Nov 1884; d. Rome 23 Jun 1959)
	11 Nov 1936 – 31 Oct 1939: *Giuseppe Bottai* (b. Rome 3 Sep 1895; d. 9 Jan 1959)
	31 Oct 1939 – 5 Feb 1943: *Alessandro Pavolini* (b. Florence 27 Sep 1903; d. Lake Como 28 Apr 1945)
	5 Feb – 25 Jul 1943: *Carlo Alberto Biggini* (b. Sarzana 9 Dec 1902; d. Padua 19 Nov 1945)
War	12 Sep 1929 – 22 Jul 1933: *Pietro Gazzera* (b. Bene Vagienna 11 Dec 1879; d. Turin 30 Jun 1953)
	22 Jul 1933 – 25 Jul 1943: *Benito Mussolini* (see above)
	Paolo, Count Thaon di Revel, Duca del Mare (b. Turin 10 Jun 1859; d. Rome 24 Mar 1948)
Navy	10 May 1925 – 6 Nov 1933: *Giuseppe Sirianni* (b. Genoa 18 Apr 1874; d. Pieve Ligure 16 Aug 1955)
	6 Nov 1933 – 25 Jul 1943: *Benito Mussolini* (see above)

327

Aviation	12 Sep 1929 – 6 Nov 1933: *Italo Balbo* (b. Quartesana 5 Jun 1896; d. Tobruk 28 Jun 1940) 6 Nov 1933 – 25 Jul 1945: *Benito Mussolini* (see above)

27 Jul – 30 Sep 1943: Badoglio I

Prime Minister	*Pietro Badoglio* (1936 – 1943: *Duke of Addis Ababa*) (for 1st time) (b. Grazzano 28 Sep 1871; d. 31 Oct 1956)
Foreign Affairs	*Raffaele Guariglia* (b. Naples 19 Feb 1889; d. Rome 27(?) Apr 1970)
Home Affairs	27 Jul – 11 Aug 1943: *Bruno Fornaciari* (b. Sonders 17 Oct 1881) 11 Aug – 30 Sep 1943: *Umberto Ricci* (b. Bari Province 13 Nov 1878)
Justice	*Gaetano Azzariti* (b. Naples 26 Mar 1881; d. Rome 5 Jan 1961)
Finance	*Domenico Bartolini* (b. Rome 26 Aug 1880; d. 5 Apr 1960)
Education	*Leonardo Severi* (b. Fano 31 Dec 1882)
War	*Antonio Sorice* (b. Nola 3 Nov 1897)
Navy	*Raffaele de Courten* (b. Milan 23 Sep 1888)
Aviation	*Renato Sandalli* (b. Genoa 1897; d. 24 Oct 1968)

15 Sep 1943 – 28 Apr 1945: Mussolini II (Republican Fascist Opposition Government at Salò on Lake Garda)

Prime Minister and Foreign Affairs	*Benito Mussolini* (for 2nd time) (see Mussolini I)
Home Affairs	15 Sep 1943 – 22 Feb 1945: *Guido Buffarini-Guidi* (b. Pisa 17 Aug 1895; d. Milan 10 Jul 1945) 22 Feb – 28 Apr 1945: *Paolo Zerbino* (d. Lake Como 28 Apr 1945)
Justice	*Antonio Tringall-Casanova* (b. Cecina 11 Apr 1888)
Finance	—— *Pellegrini*
Education	*Carlo Alberto Biggini* (see Mussolini I)
War	*Rodolfo Graziani* (from 1936: *Marquess of Neghelli*) (b. Filettino 11 Aug 1882; d. Rome 11 Jan 1955)

30 Sep – 25 Dec 1943: Badoglio II (Interim Military Administration)

Prime Minister	*Pietro Badoglio* (for 2nd time) (see Badoglio I)

Chief of General Staff	*Vittorio Ambrosio* (b. Turin 28 Jul 1879; d. Alassio 19 Nov 1958)
Army Chief of Staff	*Mario Roatta* (b. Modena 2 Jan 1887)
Navy	*Raffaele de Courten* (see Badoglio I)
Aviation	*Renato Sandalli* (see Badoglio I)
Lord Chamberlain	*Pietro, Count Aquarone* (b. Genoa 9 Apr 1890)

25 Dec 1943/11 Feb – 17 Apr 1944: Badoglio III (Cabinet of Experts)

Prime Minister and Foreign Affairs	*Pietro Badoglio* (for 3rd time) (see Badoglio I)
Home Affairs	*Vito Reale*
Justice	*Ettore Casati*
Finance	*Guido Jung* (see Mussolini I)
Education	*Giovanni Cuomo*
War	*Taddeo Orlando* (b. Gaeta 23 Jun 1885)
Navy	*Raffaele de Courten* (see Badoglio I)
Aviation	*Renato Sandalli* (see Badoglio I)

22 Apr – 6/10 Jun 1944: Badoglio IV

Prime Minister and Foreign Affairs	*Pietro Badoglio* (for 4th time) (see Badoglio I)
Home Affairs	*Salvatore Aldisio* (b. Gela, Sicily, 29 Dec 1890)
Justice	*Vincenzo Arangio-Ruiz* (b. Naples 7 May 1884; d. Rome 2 Feb 1964)
Finance	*Quinto Quintieri* (b. Sorrento 12 Aug 1894)
Education	*Adolfo Omodeo*
War	*Taddeo Orlando* (see Badoglio III)
Navy	*Raffaele de Courten* (see Badoglio I)
Aviation	*Renato Sandalli* (see Badoglio I)
Without Portfolio	*Palmiro Togliatti* (Comm) (b. Genoa 25 Mar 1893; d. Yalta 21 Aug 1964)
	Carlo, Count Sforza (b. Montignoso 23 Sep 1872; d. Rome 4 Sep 1952)*
	Benedetto Croce (b. Pescasseroli 25 Feb 1866; d. Rome 20 Nov 1952)*

*For earlier career see vol. 2

9 Jun – 25 Nov 1944: Bonomi II

Prime Minister, Foreign and Home Affairs	*Ivanoe Bonomi* (for 2nd time) (b. Mantua 18 Oct 1873; d. Rome 20 Apr 1951)*
Justice	*Umberto Tupini* (Chr Dem) (b. Rome 27 May 1889)
Finance	*Stefano Siglienti* (b. Sassari, Sardinia, 17 Jan 1898)
War	*Alessandro, Count Casati* (Lib) (b. Milan 5 Mar 1881; d. Arcore 4 Jun 1953)*
Air Force	*Pietro Piacentini*
Navy	*Raffaele de Courten* (see Badoglio I)

12 Dec 1944 – 8 Jun 1945: Bonomi III

Prime Minister	*Ivanoe Bonomi* (for 3rd time) (see Bonomi II)
Deputy Prime Ministers	*Palmiro Togliatti* (Comm) (see Badoglio IV)
	Ugo Rodino (Chr Dem)
Foreign Affairs	*Alcide de Gasperi* (Chr Dem) (b. Pieve di Tesine 3 Apr 1881; d. Sella di Valsugana 19 Aug 1954)
Home Affairs	*Ivanoe Bonomi* (see Bonomi II)
Justice	*Umberto Tupini* (Chr Dem) (see Bonomi II)
Finance	*Antonio Mario Pesenti* (Comm) (b. Verona 25 Oct 1910)
Education	*Vincenzo Arangio-Ruiz* (Lib) (see Badoglio IV)
War	*Alessandro, Count Casati* (Lib) (see Bonomi II)
Navy	*Raffaele de Courten* (see Badoglio I)
Aviation	10 Dec 1944 – 14 Jan 1945: *Antonio Scialoja* (Dem Lab) (b. Rome 19 Nov 1879(?))
	14 Jan – 8 Jun 1945: *Luigi Gasparotto* (b. Sacile 31 May 1873; d. Roccolo di Cantello 29 Jun 1954)*

19/25 Jun – 26 Nov 1945: Parri

Prime Minister	*Feruccio Parri* (Soc) (b. Pinerolo 19 Jun 1890)
Deputy Prime Ministers	*Pietro Nenni* (Soc) (b. Faenza 9 Feb 1891)
	Manlio Giovanni Brosio (Lib) (b. Turin 10 Jul 1897)
Foreign Affairs	*Alcide de Gasperi* (Chr Dem) (see Bonomi III)
Home Affairs	*Feruccio Parri* (Soc) (see above)
Justice	*Palmiro Togliatti* (Comm) (see Badoglio IV)
Finance	25 Jun – 21 Jul 1945: *Mauro Scoccimarro* (Comm) (b. Udine 1895; d. Rome night of 1/2 Jan 1972)

*For earlier career see vol. 2

	21 Jul – 21 Nov 1945: *Federico Ricci* (b. Genoa 20 Dec 1876)
Education	*Vincenzo Arangio-Ruiz* (Lib) (see Badoglio IV)
War	*Stefano, Count Jacini* (Chr Dem) (b. Milan 3 Nov 1886; d. 31 May 1952)
Navy	*Raffaele de Courten* (see Badoglio I)
Aviation	*Mario Cevalotto* (Dem Lab) (b. Treviso 1 Apr 1887)

4/10 Dec 1945 – 28 Jun 1946: De Gasperi I

Prime Minister	*Alcide de Gasperi* (Chr Dem) (for 1st time) (see Bonomi III)
Deputy Prime Minister	*Pietro Nenni* (Soc) (see Parri)
Foreign Affairs	*Alcide de Gasperi* (Chr Dem) (see Bonomi III)
Home Affairs	*Giuseppe Romita* (Soc) (b. Tortona 7 Jan 1887; d. Rome 14 Mar 1958)
Justice	*Palmiro Togliatti* (Comm) (see Badoglio IV)
Finance	*Mauro Scoccimarro* (Comm) (see Parri)
Education	*Enrico Mole* (Dem Lab) (b. Catanzaro 7 Nov 1889)
War	*Manlio Giovanni Brosio* (Lib) (see Parri)
Navy	*Raffaele de Courten* (see Badoglio I)
Aviation	*Mario Cevalotto* (Dem Lab) (see Parri)

16 Jul 1946 – 20 Jan 1947: De Gasperi II

Prime Minister	*Alcide de Gasperi* (Chr Dem) (for 2nd time) (see Bonomi III)
Foreign Affairs	16 Jul – 18 Oct 1946 (acting:) *Alcide de Gasperi* (Chr Dem) (see Bonomi III)
	18 Oct 1946 – 17 Jan 1947: *Pietro Nenni* (Soc) (see Parri)
Home Affairs	*Alcide de Gasperi* (Chr Dem) (see Bonomi III)
Justice	*Fausto Gullo* (Comm) (b. Catanzaro 16 Jun 1887)
Treasury	16 Jul – 5 Sep 1946: *Epicarmo Corbino* (b. Augusta, Syracuse, 18 Jul 1890)
	18 Sep 1946 – 17 Jan 1947: *Giovanni Battista Bertone* (b. Mondovì 17 Dec 1874; d. Mondovì 15 Sep 1969)*
Finance	*Mauro Scoccimarro* (Comm) (see Parri)
Education	*Guido Gonella* (Chr Dem) (b. Verona 18 Sep 1905)
War	*Cipriano Facchinetti* (b. Campobasso 13 Jan 1889; d.

*For earlier career see vol. 2

Rome 17/18 Feb 1952)
Mercantile Marine   *Salvatore Aldisio* (Chr Dem) (see Badoglio IV)

3 Feb - 13 May 1947: De Gasperi III

Prime Minister	*Alcide de Gasperi* (Chr Dem) (for 3rd time) (see Bonomi III)
Foreign Affairs	*Carlo, Count Sforza* (see Badoglio IV)
Home Affairs	*Mario Scelba* (Chr Dem) (b. Caltagirone, Sicily, 5 Sep 1905)
Justice	*Fausto Gullo* (Comm) (see De Gasperi II)
Finance and Treasury	*Pietro Campilli* (Chr Dem) (b. Frascati 30 Nov 1891; d. 8 Jul 1974)
Education	*Guido Gonella* (Chr Dem) (see De Gasperi II)
Defence	*Luigi Gasparotto* (Ind) (see Bonomi III)
Mercantile Marine	*Salvatore Aldisio* (Chr Dem) (see Badoglio IV)

31 May - 15 Dec 1947: De Gasperi IV

Prime Minister	*Alcide de Gasperi* (Chr Dem) (for 4th time) (see Bonomi III)
Deputy Prime Minister and Budget	*Luigi Einaudi* (Lib) (see Presidents)
Foreign Affairs	*Carlo, Count Sforza* (Lib) (see Badoglio IV)
Home Affairs	*Mario Scelba* (Chr Dem) (see De Gasperi III)
Justice	*Giuseppe Grassi* (Ind Lib) (b. Manduria 8 May 1883; d. Rome 25 Jan 1950)
Finance	*Giuseppe Pella* (Chr Dem) (b. Valdengo 18 Apr 1902)
Education	*Guido Gonella* (Chr Dem) (see De Gasperi II)
War	*Mario Cingolani* (b. Rome 2 Aug 1883)
Commerce and Industry	*Giuseppe Togni* (b. Pisa 5 Dec 1903)

15 Dec 1947 - 4 May 1948: De Gasperi V

Prime Minister	*Alcide de Gasperi* (Chr Dem) (for 5th time) (see Bonomi III)
Deputy Prime Minister (Co-ordinator of Economic Affairs)	*Luigi Einaudi* (see Presidents)

Deputy Prime Minister (Chairman of Committee for Social Affairs)	*Giuseppe Saragat* (Right Soc) (see Presidents)
Deputy Prime Minister (Chairman of Committee for Public Order)	*Randolfo Pacciardi* (Rep) (b. Giuncarico 1 Jan 1899)
Foreign Affairs	*Carlo, Count Sforza* (Lib) (see Badoglio IV)
Home Affairs	*Mario Scelba* (Chr Dem) (see De Gasperi III)
Justice	*Giuseppe Grassi* (Ind Lib) (see De Gasperi IV)
Finance	*Giuseppe Pella* (Chr Dem) (see De Gasperi IV)
Education	*Guido Gonella* (Chr Dem) (see De Gasperi II)
War	*Cipriano Facchinetti* (see De Gasperi II)
Commerce and Industry	*Roberto Tremelloni* (Soc Dem) (b. Milan 10 Oct 1900)

23 May 1948 – 11 Jan 1950: De Gasperi VI

Prime Minister	*Alcide de Gasperi* (Chr Dem) (for 6th time) (see Bonomi III)
Deputy Prime Ministers	23 May 1948 – 31 Oct 1949: *Giuseppe Saragat* (Right Soc) (see Presidents)
	Attilio Piccioni (Chr Dem) (b. Poggio 14 Jun 1892)
	Giovanni Porzio (Ind Lib) (b. Portici 6 Oct 1873)
Foreign Affairs	*Carlo, Count Sforza* (Ind Lib) (see Badoglio IV)
Home Affairs	*Mario Scelba* (Chr Dem) (see De Gasperi III)
Justice	*Giuseppe Grassi* (Ind Lib) (see De Gasperi IV)
Finance	*Ezio Vanoni* (Chr Dem) (b. Morbegno 6 Aug 1903; d. Rome 16 Feb 1956)
Education	*Guido Gonella* (Chr Dem) (see De Gasperi II)
War	*Randolfo Pacciardi* (Rep) (see De Gasperi V)
Foreign Trade	23 May 1948 – 13 Mar 1949: *Cesare Merzagora* (Ind) (b. Milan 9 Nov 1898)
	3 Apr 1949 – 11 Jan 1950: *Giovanni Battista Bertone* (Chr Dem) (see De Gasperi II)

26 Jan 1950 – 16 Jul 1951: De Gasperi VII

Prime Minister	*Alcide de Gasperi* (Chr Dem) (for 7th time) (see Bonomi III)

Foreign Affairs	*Carlo, Count Sforza* (Ind Lib) (see Badoglio IV)
Home Affairs	*Mario Scelba* (Chr Dem) (see De Gasperi III)
Justice	*Attilio Piccioni* (Chr Dem) (see De Gasperi VI)
Finance	*Ezio Vanoni* (Chr Dem) (see De Gasperi VI)
Education	*Guido Gonella* (Chr Dem) (see De Gasperi II)
Defence	*Randolfo Pacciardi* (Rep) (see De Gasperi V)
Foreign Trade	26 Jan 1950 – 4 Apr 1951: *Ivan Matteo Lombardo* (Right Soc) (b. Milan 22 May 1902)
	5 Apr – 16 Jul 1951: *Ugo La Malfa* (Rep) (b. Palermo 16 May 1903)

24 Jul 1951 – 29 Jun 1953: De Gasperi VIII

Prime Minister and Foreign Affairs	*Alcide de Gasperi* (Chr Dem) (for 8th time) (see Bonomi III)
Home Affairs	*Mario Scelba* (Chr Dem) (see De Gasperi III)
Justice	*Adone Zoli* (Chr Dem) (b. Cesena 16 Dec 1887; d. Rome 20 Feb 1960)
Finance	*Ezio Vanoni* (Chr Dem) (see De Gasperi VI)
Education	*Antonio Segni* (Chr Dem) (see Presidents)
Defence	*Randolfo Pacciardi* (Rep) (see De Gasperi V)
Foreign Trade	*Ugo La Malfa* (Rep) (see De Gasperi VII)
Without Portfolio (European Council)	24 Jul 1951 – 4 Sep 1952: *Carlo, Count Sforza* (Ind Lib) (see Badoglio IV)

16 – 28 Jul 1953: De Gasperi IX

Prime Minister	*Alcide de Gasperi* (Chr Dem) (for 9th time) (see Bonomi III)
Deputy Premier	*Attilio Piccioni* (Chr Dem) (see Gasperi VI)
Foreign Affairs	*Alcide de Gasperi* (Chr Dem) (see Bonomi III)
Home Affairs	*Amintore Fanfani* (Chr Dem) (b. Pieve 6 Feb 1908)
Justice	*Guido Gonella* (Chr Dem) (see De Gasperi II)
Finance	*Ezio Vanoni* (Chr Dem) (see De Gasperi VI)
Education	*Giuseppe Bettiol* (Chr Dem) (b. Cervignano 26 Sep 1907)
Defence	*Giuseppe Codacci-Pisanelli* (Chr Dem) (b. Rome 28 Mar 1913)
Foreign Trade	*Paolo Emilio Taviani* (Chr Dem) (b. Genoa 6 Nov 1912)

15 Aug 1953 - 6 Jan 1954: Pella (Chr Dem)

Prime Minister and Foreign Affairs	*Giuseppe Pella* (see De Gasperi IV)
Home Affairs	*Amintore Fanfani* (see De Gasperi IX)
Justice	*Antonio Azara* (b. Tempio, Sardinia, 18 Jan 1883)
Finance	*Ezio Vanoni* (see De Gasperi VI)
Education	*Antonio Segni* (see Presidents)
Defence	*Paolo Emilio Taviani* (see De Gasperi IX)

18 - 31 Jan 1954: Fanfani I

Prime Minister	*Amintore Fanfani* (Chr Dem) (for 1st time) (see De Gasperi IX)
Deputy Premier	*Giulio Andreotti* (Chr Dem) (b. Rome 14 Jan 1919)
Foreign Affairs	*Attilio Piccioni* (Chr Dem) (see De Gasperi VI)
Home Affairs	*Giulio Andreotti* (Chr Dem) (see above)
Justice	*Michele de Pietro* (Chr Dem) (b. Cursi 26 Feb 1884)
Finance	*Adone Zoli* (Chr Dem) (see De Gasperi VIII)
Education	*Egidio Tosatti* (b. Parma 7 Apr 1913)
Defence	*Paolo Emilio Taviani* (Chr Dem) (see De Gasperi IX)
Foreign Trade	*Giordano dell'Amore*

9 Feb 1954 - 22 Jun 1955: Scelba (Chr Dem, Soc Dem and Lib Coalition)

Prime Minister	*Mario Scelba* (Chr Dem) (see De Gasperi III)
Foreign Affairs	9 Feb - 17 Sep 1954: *Attilio Piccioni* (Chr Dem) (see De Gasperi VI)
	18 Sep 1954 - 22 Jun 1955: *Gaetano Martino* (Lib) (b. Messina 25 Nov 1900; d. Rome 21 Jul 1967)
Home Affairs	*Mario Scelba* (Chr Dem) (see De Gasperi III)
Justice	*Michele de Pietro* (Chr Dem) (see Fanfani I)
Finance	*Roberto Tremelloni* (Soc Dem) (see De Gasperi V)
Education	9 Feb - 18 Sep 1954: *Gaetano Martino* (Lib) (see above)
	18 Sep 1954 - 22 Jun 1955: *Giuseppe Ermini* (Chr Dem) (b. Rome 20 Jul 1900)
Defence	*Paolo Emilio Taviani* (Chr Dem) (see De Gasperi IX)
Foreign Trade	*Mario Martinelli* (Chr Dem) (b. Como 12 May 1906)

6 Jul 1955 - 6 May 1957: Segni I (Chr Dem, Soc Dem and Lib Coalition)

Prime Minister	*Antonio Segni* (Chr Dem) (for 1st time) (see Presidents)

335

Deputy Prime Minister	*Giuseppe Saragat* (Soc Dem) (see Presidents)
Foreign Affairs	*Gaetano Martino* (Lib) (see Scelba)
Home Affairs	*Fernando Tambroni* (Chr Dem) (b. Ascoli Piceno 25 Nov 1901; d. Rome 18 Feb 1963)
Justice	*Aldo Moro* (Chr Dem) (b. Maglie 23 Sep 1916)
Finance	*Giulio Andreotti* (Chr Dem) (see Fanfani I)
Education	*Paolo Rossi* (Soc Dem) (b. Bordighera 15 Sep 1900)
Defence	*Paolo Emilio Taviani* (Chr Dem) (see De Gasperi IX)
Foreign Trade	*Bernardo Mattarella* (Chr Dem) (b. Castellamare del Golfo 15 Sep 1905; d. 1 Mar 1971)

19 May 1957 – 19 Jun 1958: Zoli (Chr Dem)

Prime Minister	*Adone Zoli* (see De Gasperi VIII)
Deputy Prime Minister and Foreign Affairs	*Giuseppe Pella* (see De Gasperi IV)
Home Affairs	*Fernando Tambroni* (see Segni I)
Justice	*Guido Gonella* (see De Gasperi II)
Finance	*Giulio Andreotti* (see Fanfani I)
Education	*Aldo Moro* (see Segni I)
Defence	*Paolo Emilio Taviani* (see De Gasperi IX)
Foreign Trade	*Guido Carli* (non-party expert) (b. Brescia 28 Mar 1914)

2 Jul 1958 – 26 Jan/5 Feb 1959: Fanfani II (Chr Dem and Soc Dem Coalition)

Prime Minister	*Amintore Fanfani* (Chr Dem) (for 2nd time) (see De Gasperi IX)
Deputy Prime Minister	*Antonio Segni* (Chr Dem) (see Presidents)
Foreign Affairs	*Amintore Fanfani* (Chr Dem) (see De Gasperi IX)
Home Affairs	*Fernando Tambroni* (Chr Dem) (see Segni I)
Justice	*Guido Gonella* (Chr Dem) (see De Gasperi II)
Finance	*Luigi Preti* (Soc Dem) (b. Ferrara 23 Oct 1914)
Education	*Aldo Moro* (Chr Dem) (see Segni I)
Defence	*Antonio Segni* (Chr Dem) (see Presidents)
Foreign Trade	*Emilio Colombo* (b. Potenza 11 Apr 1920)

15 Feb 1959 – 24 Feb 1960: Segni II (Chr Dem)

Prime Minister	*Antonio Segni* (for 2nd time) (see Presidents)
Foreign Affairs	*Giuseppe Pella* (see De Gasperi IV)
Home Affairs	*Antonio Segni* (see Presidents)
Justice	*Guido Gonella* (see De Gasperi II)
Finance	*Paolo Emilio Taviani* (see De Gasperi IX)
Education	*Giuseppe Medici* (b. Sassuolo 24 Apr 1907)
Defence	*Giulio Andreotti* (see Fanfani I)
Foreign Trade	*Rinaldo del Bo* (b. Milan 19 Nov 1916)

25 Mar – 19 Jul 1960: Tambroni (Chr Dem)

Prime Minister	*Fernando Tambroni* (see Segni I)
Foreign Affairs	*Antonio Segni* (see Presidents)
Home Affairs	*Giuseppe Spataro* (b. Vasto 26 Jun 1897)
Justice	*Guido Gonella* (see De Gasperi II)
Finance	*Giuseppe Trabucchi* (b. Verona 29 Jun 1904)
Education	*Giuseppe Medici* (see Segni II)
Defence	*Giulio Andreotti* (see Fanfani I)
Foreign Trade	*Mario Martinelli* (see Scelba)

26 Jul 1960 – 2 Feb 1962: Fanfani III (Chr Dem)

Prime Minister	*Amintore Fanfani* (for 3rd time) (see De Gasperi IX)
Deputy Prime Minister	*Attilio Piccioni* (see De Gasperi VI)
Foreign Affairs	*Antonio Segni* (see Presidents)
Home Affairs	*Mario Scelba* (see De Gasperi III)
Justice	*Guido Gonella* (see De Gasperi II)
Finance	*Giuseppe Trabucchi* (see Tambroni)
Education	*Giacinto Bosco* (b. Capua 25 Jan 1905)
Defence	*Giulio Andreotti* (see Fanfani I)
Foreign Trade	*Mario Martinelli* (see Scelba)

21 Feb/3 Mar 1962 – 16 May 1963: Fanfani IV (Chr Dem and Soc Dem Coalition)

Prime Minister	*Amintore Fanfani* (for 4th time) (Chr Dem) (see De Gasperi IX)
Deputy Prime Minister	*Attilio Piccioni* (Chr Dem) (see De Gasperi VI)

ITALY

Foreign Affairs	3 Mar – 11 May 1962: *Antonio Segni* (Chr Dem) (see Presidents)
	31 May 1962 – 16 May 1963: *Attilio Piccioni* (Chr Dem) (see De Gasperi VI)
Home Affairs	*Paolo Emilio Taviani* (Chr Dem) (see De Gasperi IX)
Justice	*Giacinto Bosco* (Chr Dem) (see Fanfani III)
Finance	*Giuseppe Trabucchi* (Chr Dem) (see Tambroni)
Education	*Luigi Gui* (Chr Dem) (b. Padua 26 Sep 1914)
Defence	*Giulio Andreotti* (Chr Dem) (see Fanfani I)
Foreign Trade	*Luigi Preti* (Soc Dem) (see Fanfani II)

21 Jun – 5 Nov 1963: Leone I (Chr Dem Minority Government)

Prime Minister	*Giovanni Leone* (for 1st time) (see Presidents)
Foreign Affairs	*Attilio Piccioni* (see De Gasperi VI)
Home Affairs	*Mariano Rumor* (b. Vicenza 16 Jun 1915)
Justice	*Giacinto Bosco* (see Fanfani III)
Finance	*Mario Martinelli* (see Scelba)
Education	*Luigi Gui* (see Fanfani IV)
Defence	*Giulio Andreotti* (see Fanfani I)
Foreign Trade	*Giuseppe Trabucchi* (see Tambroni)

5 Dec 1963 – 25 Jun 1964: Moro I (Centre-Left Coalition)

Prime Minister	*Aldo Moro* (Chr Dem) (for 1st time) (see Segni I)
Deputy Prime Minister	*Pietro Nenni* (Soc) (see Parri)
Foreign Affairs	*Giuseppe Saragat* (Soc Dem) (see Presidents)
Home Affairs	*Paolo Emilio Taviani* (Chr Dem) (see De Gasperi IX)
Justice	*Oronzo Reale* (Rep) (b. Lecce 24 Oct 1902)
Finance	*Roberto Tremelloni* (Soc Dem) (see De Gasperi V)
Education	*Luigi Gui* (Chr Dem) (see Fanfani IV)
Defence	*Giulio Andreotti* (Chr Dem) (see Fanfani I)
Foreign Trade	*Bernardo Mattarella* (Chr Dem) (see Segni I)

23 Jul 1964 – 21 Jan 1966: Moro II (Centre-Left Coalition)

Prime Minister	*Aldo Moro* (Chr Dem) (for 2nd time) (see Segni I)
Deputy Prime Minister	*Pietro Nenni* (Soc) (see Parri)
Foreign Affairs	23 Jul – 29 Dec 1964: *Giuseppe Saragat* (Soc Dem) (see Presidents)

29 Dec 1964 – 5 Mar 1965 (deputy:) *Aldo Moro* (Chr Dem) (see Segni I)
5 Mar – 29 Dec 1965: *Amintore Fanfani* (Chr Dem) (see De Gasperi IX)
29 Dec 1965 – 21 Jan 1966 (deputy:) *Aldo Moro* (Chr Dem) (see Segni I)

Home Affairs	*Paolo Emilio Taviani* (Chr Dem) (see De Gasperi IX)
Justice	*Oronzo Reale* (Rep) (see Moro I)
Finance	*Roberto Tremelloni* (Soc Dem) (see De Gasperi V)
Education	*Luigi Gui* (Chr Dem) (see Fanfani IV)
Defence	*Giulio Andreotti* (Chr Dem) (see Fanfani I)
Foreign Trade	*Bernardo Mattarella* (Chr Dem) (see Segni I)

23 Feb 1966 – 5 Jun 1968: Moro III (Centre-Left Coalition)

Prime Minister	*Aldo Moro* (Chr Dem) (for 3rd time) (see Segni I)
Deputy Prime Minister	*Pietro Nenni* (Soc, from Oct 1966 Ind Soc) (see Parri)
Foreign Affairs	*Amintore Fanfani* (Chr Dem) (see De Gasperi IX)
Home Affairs	*Paolo Emilio Taviani* (Chr Dem) (see De Gasperi IX)
Justice	*Oronzo Reale* (Rep) (see Moro I)
Finance	*Luigi Preti* (Soc Dem, from Oct 1966 Ind Soc) (see Fanfani II)
Education	*Luigi Gui* (Chr Dem) (see Fanfani IV)
Defence	*Roberto Tremelloni* (Soc Dem, from Oct 1966 Ind Soc) (see De Gasperi V)
Foreign Trade	*Giusto Tolloy* (b. Trieste 3 Nov 1907)

25 Jun – 19 Nov 1968: Leone II (Chr Dem)

Prime Minister	*Giovanni Leone* (for 2nd time) (see Presidents)
Foreign Affairs	*Giuseppe Medici* (see Segni II)
Home Affairs	*Franco Restivo* (b. Palermo 25 May 1911; d. 17 Apr 1976)
Justice	*Guido Gonella* (see De Gasperi II)
Finance	*Mario Ferrari Aggradi* (b. 13 Mar 1916)
Education	*Giovanni Battista Scaglia* (b. 20 Sep 1910)
Defence	*Luigi Gui* (see Fanfani IV)
Foreign Trade	*Carlo Russo* (b. 19 Mar 1920)

13 Dec 1968 – 5 Jul 1969: Rumor I (Centre-Left Coalition)

Prime Minister	*Mariano Rumor* (Chr Dem) (for 1st time) (see Leone I)

339

Deputy Prime Minister	*Francesco de Martino* (Ind Soc) (b. Naples 31 May 1907)
Foreign Affairs	*Pietro Nenni* (Ind Soc) (see Parri)
Home Affairs	*Franco Restivo* (Chr Dem) (see Leone II)
Justice	*Silvio Gava* (Chr Dem) (b. Treviso 25 Apr 1901)
Finance	*Oronzo Reale* (Rep) (see Moro I)
Education	*Fiorentino Sullo* (Chr Dem) (b. 29 Mar 1921)
Defence	*Luigi Gui* (Chr Dem) (see Fanfani IV)
Foreign Trade	*Vittorino Colombo* (Chr Dem) (b. Abbiategrasso 3 Apr 1925)

5 Aug 1969 – 7 Feb 1970: Rumor II (Chr Dem)

Prime Minister	*Mariano Rumor* (for 2nd time) (see Leone I)
Foreign Affairs	*Aldo Moro* (see Segni I)
Home Affairs	*Franco Restivo* (see Leone II)
Justice	*Silvio Gava* (see Rumor I)
Finance	*Giacinto Bosco* (see Fanfani III)
Budget and Economic Planning	*Giuseppe Caron* (b. Treviso 24 Feb 1904)
Treasury	*Emilio Colombo* (see Fanfani II)
Defence	*Luigi Gui* (see Fanfani IV)
Education	*Mario Ferrari Aggradi* (see Leone II)
Public Works	*Lorenzo Natali* (b. Florence 2 Oct 1922)
Agriculture and Forestry	*Giacomo Sedati* (b. Lanciano 25 Aug 1921)
Transport and Civil Aviation	*Remo Gaspari* (b. Gissi 10 Jul 1921)
Posts and Tele-communications	*Athos Valsecchi* (b. Gravedona 26 Nov 1919)
Industry, Commerce, and Arts and Crafts	*Domenico Magri* (b. Catania 10 Oct 1903)
Labour and Social Security	*Carlo Donat Cattin* (b. Finale Ligure 2 Jun 1919)
Foreign Trade	*Riccardo Misasi* (b. Cosenza 14 Jul 1932)
Merchant Marine	*Vittorino Colombo* (b. Albiate 3 Apr 1925)
State Investments	*Franco Maria Malfatti* (b. Rome 13 Jun 1927)
Health	*Camillo Ripamonti* (b. Gorgonzola 25 May 1919)
Tourism and Enter-tainments	*Giovanni Battista Scaglia* (see Leone II)
Without Portfolio	*Paolo Emilio Taviani* (see De Gasperi IX)
	Giorgio Bo (b. Sestri Levante 4 Feb 1905)

Carlo Russo (see Leone II)
Eugenio Gatto (b. Venice 22 Oct 1911)

27 Mar – 6 Jul 1970: Rumor III (Centre-Left Coalition)

Prime Minister	Mariano Rumor (Chr Dem) (for 3rd time) (see Leone I)
Deputy Prime Minister	Francesco de Martino (Soc) (see Rumor I)
Foreign Affairs	Aldo Moro (Chr Dem) (see Segni I)
Home Affairs	Franco Restivo (Chr Dem) (see Leone II)
Justice	Oronzo Reale (Rep) (see Moro I)
Finance	Luigi Preti (Soc) (see Fanfani II)
Budget and Economic Planning	Antonio Giolitti (b. Rome 12 Feb 1915)
Treasury	Emilio Colombo (Chr Dem) (see Fanfani II)
Defence	Mario Tanassi (Soc) (b. Ururi 17 Mar 1916)
Education	Riccardo Misasi (Chr Dem) (see Rumor II)
Public Works	Salvatore Lauricella (b. Ravanusa 18 May 1922)
Agriculture and Forests	Lorenzo Natali (Chr Dem) (see Rumor II)
Transport and Civil Aviation	Italo Viglianesi (b Caltagirone 1 Jan 1916)
Posts and Tele-communications	27 Mar – 29 May 1970: Franco Maria Malfatti (Chr Dem) (see Rumor II) 29 May – 6 Jul 1970: Giacinto Bosco (Chr Dem) (see Fanfani III)
Industry, Commerce, and Arts and Crafts	Silvio Gava (Chr Dem) (see Rumor I)
Labour and Social Security	Carlo Donat Cattin (Chr Dem) (see Rumor II)
Foreign Trade	Mario Zagari (Soc) (b. Milan 14 Sep 1913)
Merchant Marine	Salvatore Mannironi (b. Nuoro 10 Dec 1901; d. 7 Apr 1971)
State Investments	Flaminio Piccoli (b. Kirchbichi Concentration Camp, Austria, 28 Dec 1915)
Health	Luigi Mariotti (b. Florence 23 Dec 1912)
Tourism and Entertainments	Giuseppe Lupis (b. Ragusa 28 Mar 1896)
Without Portfolio	Paolo Emilio Taviani (Chr Dem) (see Leone II) Remo Gaspari (Chr Dem) (see Rumor II) Camillo Ripamonti (Chr Dem) (see Rumor II)

Mario Ferrari Aggradi (Chr Dem) (see Leone II)
27 Mar – 29 May 1970: *Giacinto Bosco* (Chr Dem) (see Fanfani III)
Eugenio Gatto (Chr Dem) (see Rumor II)
29 May – 6 Jul 1970: *Carlo Russo* (Chr Dem) (see Leone II)

6 Aug 1970 – 15 Jan 1972: Colombo (Centre-Left Coalition)

Prime Minister	*Emilio Colombo* (Chr Dem) (see Fanfani II)
Deputy Prime Minister	*Francesco de Martino* (Soc) (see Rumor I)
Foreign Affairs	*Aldo Moro* (Chr Dem) (see Segni I)
Home Affairs	*Franco Restivo* (Chr Dem) (see Leone II)
Justice	6 Aug 1970 – 27 Feb 1971: *Oronzo Reale* (Rep) (see Moro I)
	6 Mar 1971 – 15 Jan 1972: *Emilio Colombo* (Chr Dem) (see Fanfani II)
Finance	*Luigi Preti* (Soc) (see Fanfani II)
Budget and Economic Planning	*Antonio Giolitti* (see Rumor III)
Treasury	*Mario Ferrari Aggradi* (Chr Dem) (see Leone II)
Defence	*Mario Tanassi* (Soc) (see Rumor III)
Education	*Riccardo Misasi* (Chr Dem) (see Rumor II)
Public Works	*Salvatore Lauricella* (see Rumor III)
Agriculture and Forests	*Lorenzo Natali* (Chr Dem) (see Rumor II)
Transport and Civil Aviation	*Italo Viglianesi* (see Rumor III)
Posts and Tele-communications	*Giacinto Bosco* (Chr Dem) (see Fanfani III)
Industry, Commerce, and Arts and Crafts	*Silvio Gava* (Chr Dem) (see Rumor I)
Labour and Social Security	*Carlo Donat Cattin* (Chr Dem) (see Rumor II)
Foreign Trade	*Mario Zagari* (Soc) (see Rumor III)
Merchant Marine	6 Aug 1970 – 7 Apr 1971: *Salvatore Mannironi* (see Rumor III)
	10 Apr 1971 – 15 Jan 1972: *Gioacchino Attaguile* (b. Grammichele 26 Oct 1915)
State Investments	*Flaminio Piccoli* (see Rumor III)
Health	*Luigi Mariotti* (see Rumor III)

Tourism and Entertainments	*Matteo Matteotti* (Unitarian Soc) (b. Rome 17 Feb 1921)
Without Portfolio	*Paolo Emilio Taviani* (Chr Dem) (see Leone II)
	Remo Gaspari (Chr Dem) (see Rumor II)
	Camillo Ripamonti (Chr Dem) (see Rumor II)
	Eugenio Gatto (Chr Dem) (see Rumor II)
	Carlo Russo (Chr Dem) (see Leone II)
	Giuseppe Lupis (see Rumor III)

18 – 28 Feb 1972: Andreotti I (Chr Dem)

Prime Minister	*Giulio Andreotti* (for 1st time) (see Fanfani I)
Foreign Affairs	*Aldo Moro* (see Segni I)
Home Affairs	*Mariano Rumor* (see Leone I)
Justice	*Guido Gonella* (see De Gasperi II)
Budget and Economic Planning	*Paolo Emilio Taviani* (see Leone II)
Finance	*Giuseppe Pella* (see De Gasperi IV)
Treasury	*Emilio Colombo* (see Fanfani II)
Defence	*Franco Restivo* (see Leone II)
Education	*Riccardo Misasi* (see Rumor II)
Public Works	*Mario Ferrari Aggradi* (see Leone II)
Agriculture and Forests	*Lorenzo Natali* (see Rumor II)
Transport and Civil Aviation	*Oscar Luigi Scalfaro* (b. Novara 9 Sep 1918)
Posts and Telecommunications	*Giacinto Bosco* (see Fanfani III)
Industry and Commerce	*Silvio Gava* (see Rumor I)
Labour and Social Security	*Carlo Donat Cattin* (see Rumor II)
Foreign Trade	*Camillo Ripamonti* (see Rumor II)
Merchant Marine	*Gennaro Cassiani* (b. Spezzano Albanese 19 Sep 1903)
State Investments	*Flaminio Piccoli* (see Rumor III)
Health	*Athos Valsecchi* (see Rumor II)
Tourism and Entertainments	*Giovanni Battista Scaglia* (see Leone II)
Without Portfolio	*Carlo Russo* (see Leone II)
	Eugenio Gatto (see Rumor II)
	Italo Giulio Caiati (b. Bitonto 12 Jan 1916)
	Remo Gaspari (see Rumor II)
	Fiorentino Sullo (b. Paternopoli 29 Mar 1921)

26 Jun 1972 – 12 Jun 1973: Andreotti II (Centre Coalition)

Prime Minister	*Giulio Andreotti* (DC) (for 2nd time) (see Fanfani I)
Foreign Affairs	*Giuseppe Medici* (DC) (see Segni II)
Home Affairs	*Mariano Rumor* (DC) (see Leone I)
Defence	*Mario Tanassi* (PSDI) (see Rumor III)
Justice	*Guido Gonella* (DC) (see De Gasperi II)
Budget and Economic Planning	*Paolo Emilio Taviani* (DC) (see Leone II)
Finance	*Athos Valsecchi* (DC) (see Rumor II)
Treasury	*Giovanni Malagodi* (PLI) (b. London 12 Oct 1904)
Education	*Oscar Luigi Scalfaro* (DC) (see Andreotti I)
Public Works	*Antonino Gullotti* (DC) (b. Ucria 14 Jan 1922)
Agriculture	*Lorenzo Natali* (DC) (see Rumor II)
Transport and Civil Aviation	*Aldo Bozzi* (PLI) (b. Rome 22 Feb 1909)
Posts and Telecommunications	*Giovanni Gioia* (DC) (b. Palermo 16 Jan 1925)
Industry	*Mauro Ferri* (PSDI) (b. Rome 15 Mar 1920)
Labour and Social Security	*Dionigi Coppo* (DC) (b. Brescia 15 Dec 1921)
Foreign Trade	*Matteo Matteotti* (PSDI) (see Colombo)
Merchant Marine	*Giuseppe Lupis* (PSDI) (see Rumor III)
State Investments	*Mario Ferrari Aggradi* (DC) (see Leone II)
Health	*Remo Gaspari* (DC) (see Rumor II)
Tourism and Entertainments	*Vittorio Badini Confalonieri* (PLI) (b. Turin 14 Mar 1914)
Without Portfolio	*Emilio Colombo* (DC) (see Fanfani II)
	Silvio Gava (DC) (see Rumor I)
	Fiorentino Sullo (DC) (see Andreotti I)
	Italo Giulio Caiati (DC) (see Andreotti I)
	Pier Luigi Romita (PSDI) (b. Turin 27 Jul 1924)
	Giorgio Bergamasco (PLI) (b. Milan 30 Jan 1904)

8 Jul 1973 – 15 Mar 1974: Rumor IV (Centre-Left Coalition)

Prime Minister	*Mariano Rumor* (DC) (for 4th time) (see Leone I)
Foreign Affairs	*Aldo Moro* (DC) (see Segni I)
Home Affairs	*Paolo Emilio Taviani* (DC) (see Leone II)
Defence	*Mario Tanassi* (PSDI) (see Rumor III)
Justice	*Mario Zagari* (PSI) (see Rumor III)
Budget	*Antonio Giolitti* (PSI) (see Rumor III)

Finance	*Emilio Colombo* (DC) (see Fanfani II)
Treasury	*Ugo La Malfa* (PRI) (see De Gasperi VII)
Education	*Franco Maria Malfatti* (DC) (see Rumor II)
Public Works	*Salvatore Lauricella* (PSI) (see Rumor III)
Agriculture	*Mario Ferrari Aggradi* (DC) (see Leone II)
Transport and Civil Aviation	*Luigi Preti* (PSDI) (see Fanfani II)
Posts and Tele-communications	*Giuseppe Togni* (DC) (see De Gasperi IV)
Industry, Commerce, and Arts and Crafts	*Luigi Ciriaco de Mita* (DC) (b. Nusco 2 Feb 1928)
Labour and Social Security	*Luigi Bertoldi* (PSI) (b. S. Candido 31 Jan 1920)
Foreign Trade	*Matteo Matteotti* (PSDI) (see Colombo)
Merchant Marine	*Giovanni Pieraccini* (PSI) (b. Viareggio 25 Nov 1918)
State Participation	*Antonino Gullotti* (DC) (see Andreotti II)
Health	*Luigi Gui* (DC) (see Fanfani IV)
Tourism and Enter-tainments	*Nicola Signorella* (DC) (b. St Nicola da Crissa 18 Jun 1926)
Without Portfolio	*Silvio Gava* (DC) (see Rumor I)
	Achille Corona (PSI) (b. Rome 30 Jul 1914)
	Camillo Ripamonti (DC) (see Rumor II)
	Giuseppe Lupis (PSDI) (see Rumor III)
	Carlo Donat Cattin (DC) (see Rumor II)
	Giovanni Gioia (DC) (see Andreotti II)
	Dionigi Coppo (DC) (see Andreotti II)
	Mario Toros (DC) (b. Pagnacco 9 Dec 1922)
	Pietro Bucalossi (PRI) (b. San Miniato 9 Aug 1905)

15 Mar – 23 Nov 1974: Rumor V (Coalition)

Prime Minister	*Mariano Rumor* (DC) (for 5th time) (see Leone I)
Foreign Affairs	*Aldo Moro* (DC) (see Segni I)
Home Affairs	*Paolo Emilio Taviani* (DC) (see Leone II)
Defence	*Giulio Andreotti* (DC) (see Fanfani I)
Budget and Planning	*Antonio Giolitti* (PSI) (see Rumor III)
Finance	*Mario Tanassi* (PSDI) (see Rumor III)
Treasury	*Emilio Colombo* (DC) (see Fanfani II)
Justice	*Mario Zagari* (PSI) (see Rumor III)
Education	*Franco Maria Malfatti* (DC) (see Rumor II)
Public Works	*Salvatore Lauricella* (PSI) (see Rumor III)
Agriculture	*Antonio Bisaglia* (DC) (b. Rovigo 31 Mar 1929)

Transport and Civil Aviation	*Luigi Preti* (PSDI) (see Fanfani II)
Posts and Tele-communications	*Giuseppe Togni* (DC) (see De Gasperi IV)
Industry and Commerce	*Luigi Ciriaco de Mita* (DC) (see Rumor IV)
Labour	*Luigi Bertoldi* (PSI) (see Rumor IV)
Foreign Trade	*Matteo Matteotti* (PSDI) (see Colombo)
Merchant Marine	*Dionigi Coppo* (DC) (see Andreotti II)
State Participation	*Antonino Gullotti* (DC) (see Andreotti II)
Health	*Vittorino Colombo* (DC) (see Rumor I)
Tourism and Entertainments	*Camillo Ripamonti* (DC) (see Rumor II)
Without Portfolio	*Luigi Gui* (DC) (see Fanfani IV)
	Giovanni Pieraccini (PSI) (see Rumor IV)
	Giacomo Mancini (PSI) (b. Cosenza 21 Apr 1916)
	Giuseppe Lupis (PSDI) (see Rumor III)
	Giovanni Gioia (DC) (see Andreotti II)
	Mario Toros (DC) (see Rumor IV)

from 23 Nov 1974: Moro IV (DC and PRI Coalition)

Prime Minister	*Aldo Moro* (DC) (for 4th time) (see Segni I)
Deputy Prime Minister	*Ugo La Malfa* (PRI) (see De Gasperi VII)
Foreign Affairs	*Mariano Rumor* (DC) (see Leone I)
Home Affairs	*Luigi Gui* (DC) (see Fanfani IV)
Justice	*Oronzo Reale* (PRI) (see Moro I)
Economic Planning and the South	*Giulio Andreotti* (DC) (see Fanfani I)
Finance	*Bruno Visentini* (PRI) (b. Treviso 1 Aug 1914)
Treasury	*Emilio Colombo* (DC) (see Fanfani II)
Defence	*Arnaldo Forlani* (DC) (b. Pesaro 8 Dec 1925)
Education	*Franco Maria Malfatti* (DC) (see Rumor II)
Public Works	*Pietro Bucalossi* (PRI) (see Rumor IV)
Agriculture	*Giovanni Marcora* (DC) (b. Inveruno 28 Dec 1922)
Transport	*Mario Martinelli* (DC) (see Scelba)
Posts	*Giulio Orlando* (DC) (b. Martina Franca 25 May 1926)
Industry	*Carlo Donat Cattin* (DC) (see Rumor II)
Labour	*Mario Toros* (DC) (see Rumor IV)
Foreign Trade	*Luigi Ciriaco de Mita* (DC) (see Rumor IV)
Merchant Navy	*Giovanni Gioia* (DC) (see Andreotti II)

State Participation   *Antonio Bisaglia* (DC) (see Rumor V)
Health   *Antonino Gullotti* (DC) (see Andreotti II)
Tourism   *Adolfo Sarti* (DC) (b. Saluzzo 13 Sep 1897)
Cultural Treasures   from 16 Dec 1974: *Giovanni Spadolini* (PRI) (see
  and Environment   above)
Without Portfolio   *Francesco Cossiga* (DC) (b. Sassari 26 Jul 1928)
                        Tommaso Morlino (DC) (b. Irsina 26 Aug 1925)
                        Mario Pedini (DC) (b. Montichari 27 Dec 1918)
                        Giovanni Spadolini (PRI) (b. Florence 21 Jun 1925)

Ivory Coast

4 Dec 1958   Member of French Community
7 Aug 1960   Left French Community

HEAD OF STATE

President (also Head of Government)

from 27 Nov 1960   *Félix Houphouet-Boigny* (b. Yamoussoukro 18 Oct
                    1905)

MEMBER OF GOVERNMENT

Prime Minister

2 May 1959 – 27   *Félix Houphouet-Boigny* (see President)
  Nov 1960

Jamaica

6 Aug 1962   Independence within British Commonwealth

HEADS OF STATE

Governors-General

19 Oct 1962	*Sir Clifford (Clarence) Campbell* (b. 28 Jun 1892)
from 1973	*Florizel Augustus Glasspole* (b. Kingston 25 Sep 1909)

MEMBERS OF GOVERNMENT

Prime Ministers

6 Aug 1962	*Sir (William) Alexander Bustamante* (until c. 1899: *Clarke*) (b. Blenheim 24 Feb 1884; d. Kingston 6 Aug 1977)
22 Feb 1967	*Sir Donald Burns Sangster* (b. Kingston 26 Oct 1911; d. Montreal 11 Apr 1967) from 1965 acting Prime Minister
11 Apr 1967 – 1 Mar 1972	*Hugh Lawson Shearer* (b. Martha Brae 18 May 1923)
from 2 Mar 1972	*Michael Norman Manley* (b. Kingston 10 Dec 1923)

Japan

HEAD OF STATE

Emperor

from 24 Dec 1926	*Hirohito (Showa)*, son of the Emperor Yoshihito (b. 29 Apr 1901) Regent from 25 Nov 1921

MEMBERS OF GOVERNMENT

Prime Ministers

3 Jul 1929 – 9 Apr 1931	*Osachi Hamaguchi* (b. Apr 1870; d. 25 Aug 1931)

14 Jun – 11 Dec 1931	*Baron Reijiro Wakatsuki* (for 2nd time) (b. 1866; d. Ito 21 Nov 1949)*
14 Dec 1931	*Ki Inukai* (b. 1855; d. 16 May 1932)
16 May 1932	*Count Korekiyo Takahashi* (for 2nd time) (b. Jul 1854; d. 26 Feb 1936)*
26 May 1932 – 2 Jul 1934	*Count Makato Saito* (b. Oct 1858; d. 26 Feb 1936)
8 Jul 1934	*Keisuke Okada* (for 1st time) (b. 1862; d. 1952)
26 Feb 1936	*Count Fumio Goto* (b. 1884) Deputy
29 Feb 1936	*Keisuke Okada* (for 2nd time)
9 Mar 1936 – 23 Jan 1937	*Koki Hirota* (b. 1878; d. 24 Dec 1948)
2 Feb – 31 May 1937	*Senjuro Hayashi* (b. Feb 1870; d. 4 Feb 1943)
4 Jun 1937	*Prince Fumimaro Konoye* (for 1st time) (b. Oct 1891; d. 15/16 Dec 1945)
5 Jan – 27 Aug 1939	*Baron Kiichiro Hiranuma* (b. Sep 1867; d. Tokyo 20 Aug 1952)
30 Aug 1939 – 12 Jan 1940	*Nobuyuki Abe* (b. Ishikawa Nov 1875; d. Tokyo 7 Sep 1953)
16 Jan – 16 Jul 1940	*Mitsumasa Yonai* (b. 1880; d. 20 Apr 1948)
21 Jul 1940 – 16 Jul 1941	*Prince Fumimaro Konoye* (for 2nd time)
18 Jul – 16 Oct 1941	*Prince Fumimaro Konoye* (for 3rd time)
18 Oct 1941 – 20 Jul 1944	*Hideki Tojo* (d. 24 Dec 1948)
22 Jul 1944 – 5 Apr 1945	*Kunaiki Koiso* (b. 1879; d. 3 Nov 1950)
7 Apr – 14 Aug 1945	*Baron Kantaro Susuki* (b. 1867; d. 17 Apr 1948)
17 Aug 1945	*Prince Naruhiko Higashikuni* (b. 1887)
6 Oct 1945 – 22 Apr 1946	*Baron Kijuro Shidehara* (b. Osaka 11 Aug 1872; d. 10 Mar 1951)*
22 May 1946 – 29 Jan 1947	*Shigeru Yoshida* (for 1st time) (b. 22 Sep 1878; d. Oiso 20 Oct 1967)
6 Feb – 20 May 1947	*Shigeru Yoshida* (for 2nd time)
24 May 1947 – 9 Feb 1948	*Tetsu Katayama* (b. 1887)
23 Feb – 7 Oct 1948	*Hitoshi Ashida* (b. Kyoto 15 Nov 1887; d. Tokyo 20 Jun 1959)
14 Oct 1948 – 10 Feb 1949	*Shigeru Yoshida* (for 3rd time)
13 Feb 1949	*Shigeru Yoshida* (for 4th time)

*For earlier career see vol. 2

27 Jun 1950	*Shigeru Yoshida* (for 5th time)
4 Jul 1951	*Shigeru Yoshida* (for 6th time)
24/29 Oct 1952 – 14 Mar 1953	*Shigeru Yoshida* (for 7th time)
19/21 May 1953 – 7 Nov 1954	*Shigeru Yoshida* (for 8th time)
9 Dec 1954	*Ichiro Hatoyama* (for 1st time) (b. Tokyo 1 Jan 1883; d. 7 Mar 1959)
19 Mar 1955	*Ichiro Hatoyama* (for 2nd time)
22 Nov 1955	*Ichiro Hatoyama* (for 3rd time)
20 Dec 1956 – 22 Feb 1957	*Tanzan Ishibashi* (b. 25 Sep 1884; d. 24 Apr 1973)
24 Feb 1957	*Nobosuke Kishi* (for 1st time) (b. Yamaguchi Province 23 Nov 1896)
12 Jun 1958 – 15 Jul 1960	*Nobosuke Kishi* (for 2nd time)
18 Jul – 5 Dec 1960	*Hayato Ikeda* (for 1st time) (b. Yoshina 3 Dec 1899; d. Tokyo 13 Aug 1965)
8 Dec 1960	*Hayato Ikeda* (for 2nd time)
17 Jul 1963	*Hayato Ikeda* (for 3rd time)
9 Dec 1963 – 25 Oct 1964	*Hayato Ikeda* (for 4th time)
9 Nov 1964	*Eisaku Sato* (for 1st time) (b. Yamaguchi 27 Mar 1901; d. Tokyo 2 Jun 1975)
2 Jun 1965	*Eisaku Sato* (for 2nd time)
14 Jan 1970	*Eisaku Sato* (for 3rd time)
6 Jul 1972	*Kakuei Tanaka* (b. Niigata Prefecture 4 May 1918)
from 9 Dec 1974	*Takeo Miki* (b. Tokushima Prefecture 17 Mar 1907)

Foreign Ministers

3 Jul 1929 – 11 Dec 1931	*Baron Kijuro Shidehara* (for 2nd time) (see Prime Ministers)
16 Dec 1931 – 16 May 1932	*Kenkichi Yoshizawa* (b. Nigata 25 Jan 1874; d. Tokyo 5 Jan 1965)
25 May 1932	*Count Makoto Saito* (see Prime Ministers)
14 Jun 1932	*Count Yasuya Uchida* (for 2nd time) (b. Kumamoto 1865; d. 1936)*
13 Sep 1933	*Koki Hirota* (for 1st time) (see Prime Ministers)
1 Apr 1936 – 23 Jan 1937	*Hachiro Arita* (for 1st time) (b. 1884; d. 4 Mar 1965)

*For earlier career see vol. 2

2 Feb 1937	*Senjuro Hayashi* (see Prime Ministers)
8 Mar – 31 May 1937	*Naotake Sato* (b. Osaka 30 Oct 1882)
4 Jun 1937	*Koki Hirota* (for 2nd time)
27 May – 29 Sep 1938	*Kazushige Ugaki* (b. 1868; d. Tokyo 30 Apr 1956)
29 Oct 1938 – 28 Aug 1939	*Hachiro Arita* (for 2nd time)
1 Sep 1939	*Nobuyuki Abe* (see Prime Ministers)
24 Sep 1939 – 14 Jan 1940	*Kichisaburo Nomura* (b. 1877)
17 Jan – 16 Jul 1940	*Hachiro Arita* (for 3rd time)
21 Jul 1940 – 16 Jul 1941	*Yosuke Matsuoka* (b. Yamaguchi Province Mar 1880; d. Tokyo Jun 1946)
18 Jul – 16 Oct 1941	*Teijiro Toyoda* (b. Wakayama 1885; d. Tokyo 21 Nov 1961)
18 Oct 1941 – 1 Sep 1942	*Shigenori Togo* (for 1st time) (b. Kagoshima Province 1882; d. Tokyo 23 Jul 1950)
17 Sep 1942	*Masayuki Tani* (b. Kumamoto 1889; d. Tokyo 26 Oct 1962)
20 Apr 1943 – 5 Apr 1945	*Mamoru Shigemitsu* (for 1st time) (b. Oita 29 Jul 1887; d. Tokyo 25 Jan 1957)
9 Apr – 14 Aug 1945	*Shigenori Togo* (for 2nd time)
17 Aug 1945	*Mamoru Shigemitsu* (for 2nd time)
17 Sep 1945 – May 1947	*Shigeru Yoshida* (for 1st time) (see Prime Ministers)
1 Jun 1947 – 6 Oct 1948	*Hitoshi Ashida* (see Prime Ministers)
19 Oct 1948†	*Shigeru Yoshida* (for 2nd time)
10 Dec 1954 – 20 Dec 1956	*Mamoru Shigemitsu* (for 3rd time)
23 Dec 1956	*Nobosuke Kishi* (see Prime Ministers)
9 Jul 1957 – 15 Jul 1960	*Aiichiro Fujiyama* (b. Saga 22 May 1897)
18 Jul 1960	*Zentaro Kosaka* (b. Nagano 23 Jan 1912)
18 Jul 1962	*Masayoshi Ohira* (for 1st time) (b. 12 Mar 1910)
17 Jul 1964	*Etsusaburo Shiina* (b. 1898)
3 Dec 1966 – 29 Oct 1968	*Takeo Miki* (see Prime Ministers)
30 Nov 1968 – 5 Jul 1971	*Kiichi Aichi* (b. Tokyo (or Miyagi District, North Eastern Japan?) 10 Oct 1907; d. 17 Aug 1973)

† Minister without Portfolio, special responsibility for relations with the USA: 25 Dec 1951 – 7 Dec 1954: *Katsuo Okazaki* (b. Kanagawa district 1897; d. 10 Oct 1965)

351

5 Jul 1971	*Takeo Fukuda* (b. 14 Jan 1905)
7 Jul 1972	*Masayoshi Ohira* (for 2nd time)
12 Jul 1974	*Toshio Kimura* (b. 1909)
from 9 Dec 1974	*Kiichi Miyazawa* (b. 8 Oct 1919)

Jordan

| 1919/1920 – 1946 | Mandated to Great Britain by League of Nations |
| 1920 – Apr 1949 | Kingdom of Transjordan; after acquisition of the Palestine area took its present name |

HEADS OF STATE

Kings

21 Mar 1921	*Emir Abd Allah*, son of Sharif Husain of Hejaz (b. 1882)
20 Jul 1951	*Talal I*, son (b. 1911) abdicated. Declared mentally unfit and spent rest of life in sanatorium in Turkey (d. 9 Jul 1972)
from 11 Aug 1952	*Hussein II*, son (b. 2 May 1935) until 2 May 1953 under the guidance of a Regency Council: *Ibrahim Hashim* (b. Nablus 1888; d. Baghdad 14 Jul 1958) *Suleiman Tukan* *Abd ar-Rahman Rusheida*

MEMBERS OF GOVERNMENT

Prime Ministers

1924 – 1933	*Rida ar-Riqabi* (for 2nd time)*
1933 – 1938	*Ibrahim Hashim* (for 1st time) (see Kings)
6 Aug 1939 – 1945	*Taufiq Abu'l-Huda* (for 1st time) (b. 1864(?); d. Amman 1 Jul 1956)

*For earlier career see vol. 2

Aug 1945 – 1948	*Ibrahim Hashim* (for 2nd time)
Mar 1948	*Taufiq Abu'l-Huda* (for 2nd time)
13 Apr – 11 Oct 1950	*Said al-Mufti* (for 1st time) (b. East Jordan 1898)
14 Oct 1950	*Said al-Mufti* (for 2nd time)
4 Dec 1950	*Samir ar-Rifai* (for 1st time) (b. Safad 30 Jan 1901; d. Amman 12 Oct 1965)
26 Jul 1951	*Taufiq Abu'l-Huda* (for 3rd time)
7 Sep 1951 – 28 Sep 1952	*Taufiq Abu'l-Huda* (for 4th time)
30 Sep 1952	*Taufiq Abu'l-Huda* (for 5th time)
5 May 1953 – 2 May 1954	*Fauzi al-Mulqi* (b. Arbela 1910; d. 10 Jan 1962)
4 May – 21 Oct 1954	*Taufiq Abu'l-Huda* (for 6th time)
24 Oct 1954 – 28 May 1955	*Taufiq Abu'l-Huda* (for 7th time)
30 May 1955	*Said al-Mufti* (for 3rd time)
15 Dec 1955	*Hazza al-Majali* (for 1st time) (b. Transjordan 1917; d. Amman 29 Aug 1960)
21 Dec 1955 – 7 Jan 1956	*Ibrahim Hashim* (for 3rd time)
9 Jan – 20 May 1956	*Samir ar-Rifai* (for 2nd time)
22 May 1956	*Said al-Mufti* (for 4th time)
1 Jul – 22 Oct 1956	*Ibrahim Hashim* (for 4th time)
29 Oct 1956 – 10 Apr 1957	*Suleiman Nabulsi* (b. Palestine 1910; d. 14 Oct 1976)
15 Apr 1957	*Husain Fakhri al-Khalidi* (b. Jerusalem 1894/95; d. Amman night of 6/7 Feb 1962)
25 Apr 1957	*Ibrahim Hashim* (for 5th time)
19 May 1958	*Nuri Pasha Al Said* (b. 1888; d. Baghdad 15 Jul 1958) Joint Ministry formed within the framework of the Arabian Federation between Jordan and Iraq, which ceased with the Iraqi revolution of 14 Jul 1958
20 May 1958 – 5 May 1959	*Samir ar-Rifai* (for 3rd time) Head of Jordanian provincial cabinet
6 May 1959	*Hazza al-Majali* (for 2nd time)
29 Aug 1960	*Bahjat Talhuni* (for 1st time) (b. Maan 1913)
29 Jun 1961 – 25 Jan 1962	*Bahjat Talhuni* (for 2nd time)
27 Jan 1962	*Wasfi (Mustafa) at-Tall* (for 1st time) (b. Irbid 1920/21; d. Cairo 28 Nov 1971)
28 Mar 1963	*Samir ar-Rifai* (for 4th time)
21 Apr 1963	*Sharif Husain bin Nasir* (for 1st time)
10 Jul – 31 Oct 1963	*Sharif Husain bin Nasir* (for 2nd time)

353

4 Nov 1963	*Sharif Husain bin Nasir* (for 3rd time)
7 Jul 1964	*Bahjat Talhuni* (for 3rd time)
13 Feb 1965	*Wasfi (Mustafa) at-Tall* (for 2nd time)
23 Dec 1966	*Wasfi (Mustafa) at-Tall* (for 3rd time)
5 Mar 1967	*Sharif Husain bin Nasir* (for 4th time)
24 Apr – 15 Jul 1967	*Saad Jumaa* (for 1st time) (b. 1916)
3 Aug 1967	*Saad Jumaa* (for 2nd time)
7 Oct 1967	*Bahjat Talhuni* (for 4th time)
24 Mar 1969	*Abdul Munem Rifai* (for 1st time) (b. Tyre 1917)
12 Aug 1969	*Bahjat Talhuni* (for 5th time)
27 Jun 1970	*Abdul Munem Rifai* (for 2nd time)
16 – 24 Sep 1970	*General Mohammed Daud* (d. Amman 19 Jan 1972) Head of military administration
26 Sep 1970	*Mohammed Ahmed Tukan* (b. 15 Aug 1903)
28 Oct 1970 – 28 Nov 1971	*Wasfi (Mustafa) at-Tall* (for 4th time)
29 Nov 1971	*Ahmad Lozi*
from 26 May 1973	*Zaid Rifai* (b. 27 Nov 1936)

Kanem-Bornu

For the Sheikhdom of Bornu and Dikwa see vol. 1.

Kenya

1 Jun 1963	Internal self-government
12 Dec 1963	Independence from Great Britain

HEADS OF STATE

Governor-General

12 Dec 1963 – 11 Dec 1964	*Malcolm John Macdonald* (b. Lossiemouth, Scotland, 1901)

President

from 11 Dec 1964   *Jomo Kenyatta* (b. Gatundu, Kenya, 20 Oct 1891)

MEMBER OF GOVERNMENT

Prime Minister

from 1 Jun 1963   *Jomo Kenyatta* (see President)

Korea

29 Aug 1910   Became Japanese province of Chosen

HEADS OF STATE

Japanese Residents-General

Aug 1929 – 1931	*Count Makoto Saito* (for 2nd time) (b. Oct 1858; d. 26 Feb 1936)*
Jun 1931 – 1936	*Kazushige Ugaki* (b. 1868; d. Tokyo 30 Apr 1956)
1936 – 1942	*Jiro Minami* (b. Oita district 1874; d. 1957)
1942 – 8 Sep 1945	*Nobuyuki Abe* (b. Ishikawa Nov 1875; d. Tokyo 7 Sep 1953)
Aug/Sep 1945	Korea partitioned into two zones of occupation: North of the 38th parallel (Soviet) and South of the 38th parallel (American)
25 Jun 1950	Outbreak of Korean War
27 Jul 1953	Cease-fire agreement at Panmunjong

*For earlier career see vol. 2

Korea, Democratic People's Republic of (North)

HEADS OF STATE

Presidents

1948 – 1958	*Kim Doo-bong (Kim Tu-bong)* (b. 1889)
Sep 1957	*Choi Yong Kun (Ch'oe Yŏng-gŏn)* (b. Sossok 21 Jun 1900)
from 26 Dec 1972	*Kim Il-sung** (b. Pyongyang 1912/ 1915(?))

Vice-President

from 3 Aug 1953	*Nam Il*

MEMBERS OF GOVERNMENT

Prime Ministers

9 Sep 1948	*Kim Il-sung* (for 1st time) (see Presidents)
19 Sep 1957	*Kim Il-sung* (for 2nd time)
from 26 Dec 1972	*Kim Il*

Foreign Ministers

Aug 1948	*Pak Hun Yang (Pak Hŏn-yŏng)* (b. 1900; d. (sentenced to death) 15 Dec 1955)
Dec 1952	*Nam Il* (see Vice President)
25 Oct 1959	*Pak Sung Chul (Pak Sŏng-ch'ŏl)* †
from 11 Jul 1970	*Ho Dam (Hŏ Tam)*

*Russian transcription Kim Ir Sen
† Russian transcription Pak Sen Cher

Korea, Republic of (South)

HEADS OF STATE

Presidents

12 Aug 1948	*Syngman Rhee (Yi Sŏng-man)* (b. North Korea 26 Apr 1875; d. Honolulu, Hawaii, 19 Jul 1965)
27 Apr 1960	*Huh Chung (Hŏ Chŏng)*
12 Aug 1960	*Yun Bo Sun (Yun Po-Sŏn)* (for 1st time) (b. Namdo 1898(?))
19 May 1961	*Chang Do Yung (Chang To-yŏng)*
20 May 1961 – 22 Mar 1962	*Yun Bo Sun* (for 2nd time)
from 24 Mar 1962	*Park Chung-hee (Pak Chŏng-hi)* (b. Sangmo-ri 30 Sep 1917) Leader of Military Junta, confirmed as President from 15 Oct 1963

MEMBERS OF GOVERNMENT

Prime Ministers

Aug 1948	*Yi Bom Sok*
Apr 1950	*Shin Sung Mo (Shin Sŏng-mo)*
Nov 1951 – Apr 1952	*John Myun Chang (Chang Myŏn)* (for 1st time) (b. 1899(?); d. Seoul 4 Jun 1966)
May – 30 Sep 1952	*Chang Taik Sang (Chang T'aek-sang)*
Oct 1952 – 24 Apr 1953	No appointment made
24 Apr 1953 – 18 Jun 1954	*Paik Too Chin (Paek Tu-jin)* (for 1st time) (b. 1909)
Jun – 2 Jul 1954	*Pyun Yung Tai (Pyŏn Yŏng-t'ae)* (for 1st time) (b. Seoul; d. Seoul 10 Mar 1969)
1954 – 20 May 1956	*Syngman Rhee* (for 1st time) (see Presidents)
May – 14 Aug 1956	*Syngman Rhee* (for 2nd time)
(?) – 21 Apr 1960	*Pyun Yung Tai* (for 2nd time)
16 Aug 1960 – 16 May 1961	*John Myun Chang* (for 2nd time)
18 May 1961	*General Chang Do Yung (Chang To-yŏng)* (see Presidents) Leader of military cabinet

357

3 Jul 1961 – 16 Jun 1962	*Song Yo-Chan*
18 Jun 1962	(acting:) *Park Chung-hee* (see Presidents)
10 Jul 1962	*Kim Hyun Chul (Kim Hyŏn-ch'ŏl)*
12 Dec 1963	*Choi Doo-sun (Ch'oe Tu-sŏn)* (b. 1904)
10 May 1964	*Chung Il Kwon (Chŏng Il-kwon)* (for 1st time) (b. 1917)
21 Oct 1969 – 9 Dec 1970	*Chung Il Kwon* (for 2nd time)
21 Dec 1970	*Paik Too Chin* (for 2nd time)
3 Jun 1971	*Kim Jong-pil* (b. Puyo 7 Jan 1926)
from 19 Dec 1975	*Choi Kyu-hah* (b. Wonju 16 Jun 1919)

Kuwait

HEADS OF STATE

Emirs

1921 – 1950	*Sheikh Ahmad*, nephew of Sheikh Salim
25 Feb 1950 – 24 Nov 1965	*Sheikh Abdullah as-Salim as-Sabbah* (b. Kuwait 1899)
from 24 Nov 1965	*Sabbah as-Salim as-Sabbah*, brother (b. 1913)

Heads of Government

17 Jan 1962	*Jabir al-Ahmad al-Jabir as-Sabbah* (for 1st time) (b. 1928) Finance Minister, from 31 May 1966 Crown Prince
2 Feb 1963 – 24 Nov 1965	*Sabbah as-Salim as-Sabbah* (see Emirs) Prime Minister
4 Dec 1965 – 28 Jan 1967	*Jabir al-Ahmad al-Jabir as-Sabbah* (for 2nd time)
from 4 Feb 1967	*Jabir al-Ahmad al-Jabir as-Sabbah* (for 3rd time)

Laos

19 Jul 1949	Independent kingdom within French Union
22 Oct 1953	Fully sovereign state

HEADS OF STATE

Kings

24 Mar 1904 – 21 Aug 1959	*Sisavang Vong* (b. 14 Jul 1885; d. Luang Prabang 30 Oct 1959) Viceroy: 1941 – 1945: *Prince Petsarath* (b. 1891; d. Luang Prabang 14 Oct 1959)
21 Aug/4 Nov 1959 – 1 Dec 1975	*Savang Vatthana* (b. Luang Prabang 13 Nov 1907) abdicated

President

from 2 Dec 1975	*Prince Souphanouvong* (b. 1902)

MEMBERS OF GOVERNMENT

Prime Ministers

(?) – 15 Sep 1945	*Prince Petsarath* (see Kings)
20 Oct 1945 – 29 Apr 1946	*Prince Khammao* (b. Luang Prabang 23 Sep 1911)
1946 – (?)	*Prince Savang Vatthana* (see Kings)
1951 – 1954	*Prince Souvanna Phouma* (for 1st time) (b. Luang Prabang 7 Oct 1901)
1954 – 29 Dec 1955	*Katay Don Sasorith* (b. 1904; d. Vientiane 29 Dec 1955)
21 Mar 1956 – Nov 1957	*Prince Souvanna Phouma* (for 2nd time)
19 Nov 1957 – 22 Jul 1958	*Prince Souvanna Phouma* (for 3rd time)
15 Aug 1958	*Phoui Sananikone* (for 1st time) (b. 1903)
24 Jan 1959	*Phoui Sananikone* (for 2nd time)

359

31 Dec 1959	*General Sunthone Patthamavong*
7 Jan 1960	*Kou Abhay* (b. 1892)
31 May 1960	*Prince (Tiame) Somsanith*
15 Aug 1960	*Prince Souvanna Phouma* (for 4th time)
10 Dec 1960	*General Sunthone Patthamavong* (for 2nd time)
11 – 13/16 Dec 1960	*Quinim Pholsena* (b. 1915(?); d. Vientiane 2 Apr 1963)
13 Dec 1960	*Prince Boun Oum na Champassac* (b. 12 Dec 1912)
24 Jun 1962	*Prince Souvanna Phouma* (for 5th time)
6 Sep 1965	*Prince Souvanna Phouma* (for 6th time)
from 2 Dec 1975	*Kaysone Phomvihan*

Latvia

HEADS OF STATE

Presidents

8 Apr 1927	*Gustavs Zemgals* (b. 12 Aug 1871; d. 7 Jan 1939)
9 Apr 1930	*Albert Kviesis* (b. 2/3 Dec 1881; d. 1944)
9 Apr 1936 – Jun 1940	*Kārlis Ulmanis* (for 2nd time) (b. 4 Sep 1877; d. 1942)
Aug 1940	Incorporated in Union of Soviet Socialist Republics
1941 – 1944	German occupation

MEMBERS OF GOVERNMENT

Prime Ministers

1 Dec 1928 – 3 Mar 1931	*Hugo Celmiņš* (for 2nd time) (b. 1877) deported in 1941*

*For earlier career see vol. 2

24 Mar – 4 Nov 1931	*Kārlis Ulmanis* (for 4th time) (see Presidents)
4 Dec 1931 – 3 Feb 1933	*Marǵers Skujenieks* (for 2nd time) (b. 23 Jun 1886; d. 1941(?))
23 Mar 1933 – 2 Mar 1934	*Adolfs Bļodnieks* (b. 1889(?); d. New York 21 Mar 1962)
16 Mar 1934	*Kārlis Ulmanis* (for 5th time)
18 May 1934	*Kārlis Ulmanis* (for 6th time)
22 Jun 1940 – Jul 1941	*Augusts Kirhenšteins* (b. Mazsakica 18 Sep 1872; d. Riga 9 Nov 1963) under Soviet occupation
1941 – Oct 1944	—— *Danker,* Director-General of Internal Administration, under German occupation

Lebanon

HEADS OF STATE

Presidents

26 May 1926	*Charles Dabbas* (b. Beirut 1885; d. Paris 23 Aug 1935)
28 Jan 1934	*Habib Bacha as-Saad* (d. Beirut 6 May 1942)*
20 Jan 1936 – 5 Apr 1941	*Emile Eddé* (b. Beirut 1886; d. 28 Sep 1949)
10 Apr 1941	*Alfred Naccache* (b. 1887?)
20 Mar 1943	(acting:) *Ayoub Tabet*
26 Jul – 20 Sep 1943	*Pétro Trad* (d. Beirut(?) 5 Apr 1948)
27 Sep 1943	*Béchara al-Khoury* (b. 1890(?); d. 11 Jan 1964)*
18 Sep 1952	(acting:) *Fouad Chehab* (for 1st time) (b. Ghazir 9 Mar 1902; d. 25 Apr 1973)
23 Sep 1952	*Camille Chamoun* (b. Deir al-Kamar 1900)
23 Sep 1958	*Fouad Chehab* (for 2nd time)
23 Sep 1964	*Charles Helou (Hulw)* (b. Beirut 24 Sep 1912)
from 23 Sep 1970	*Suleiman Frangié* (b. Zegharta, Northern Lebanon, 14 Jun 1910)

*For earlier career see vol. 2

LEBANON

MEMBERS OF GOVERNMENT

Prime Ministers

11 Oct 1929 – 20 Mar 1930	*Emile Eddé* (see Presidents)
25 Mar 1930	*Auguste Pasha Adib* (for 2nd time) (b. Constantinople 1860; d. Paris 12 Jul 1936)*
9 Mar 1932	*Charles Dabbas* (see Presidents)
29 Jan 1934	*Abd Abdullah Baihum* (for 1st time)
30 Jan 1936	*Ayoub Tabet* (for 1st time) (see Presidents)
6 Jan 1937 – 18 Mar 1938	*Khair ad-Din Ahdab*
21 Mar – 24 Oct 1938	*Khaled Chehab* (for 1st time) (b. Hasbaya 1892)
1 Nov 1938 – 20 Jan 1939	*Abdullah Yafi* (for 1st time) (b. Beirut 1901)
22 Jan 1939	*Abdullah Yafi* (for 2nd time)
21 Sep 1939 – 4 Apr 1941	*Abd Abdullah Baihum* (for 2nd time)
10 Apr 1941	*Alfred Naccache* (see Presidents)
1 Dec 1941 – 24 Jul 1942	*Ahmad Daouk* (for 1st time) (b. Beirut 1892)
29 Jul 1942	*Sami Solh* (for 1st time) (b. Akkon 1888; d. Beirut 6 Nov 1968)
19 Mar 1943	*Ayoub Tabet* (for 2nd time)
22 Jul 1943	*Pétro Trad* (see Presidents) Leader of Triumvirate
25 Sep 1943	*Riad Solh* (for 1st time) (b. 1894)
14 Nov 1943 – 1 Jul 1944	*Henry Pharaon*
3 Jul 1944	*Riad Solh* (for 2nd time)
10 Jan – 20 Aug 1945	*Abdul Hamid Karame*
22 Aug 1945 – 18 May 1946	*Sami Solh* (for 2nd time)
22 May 1946	*Saadi Munla*
14 Dec 1946 – 26 Jul 1948	*Riad Solh* (for 3rd time)
28 Jul 1948 – 21 Sep 1949	*Riad Solh* (for 4th time)
1 Oct 1949 – 13 Feb 1951	*Riad Solh* (for 5th time)

*For earlier career see vol. 2

362

14 Feb 1951	*Hussein Oweini* (for 1st time) (b. Beirut 1900; d. Beirut 11 Jan 1971)
7 Apr 1951 – 9 Feb 1952	*Abdullah Yafi* (for 3rd time)
11 Feb – 9 Sep 1952	*Sami Solh* (for 3rd time)
12 – 14 Sep 1952	*Nazem Accari* (b. Beirut 1902)
15 – 17 Sep 1952	*Saeb Salam* (for 1st time) (b. 1905)
18 – 25 Sep 1952	*Fouad Chehab* (see Presidents)
30 Sep 1952 – 28 Apr 1953	*Khaled Chehab* (for 2nd time)
30 Apr – 10 Aug 1953	*Saeb Salam* (for 2nd time)
16 Aug 1953 – 16 Feb 1954	*Abdullah Yafi* (for 4th time)
1 Mar – 9 Sep 1954	*Abdullah Yafi* (for 5th time)
16 Sep 1954 – 6 Jul 1955	*Abdullah Yafi* (for 6th time)
9 Jul – 13 Sep 1955	*Sami Solh* (for 4th time)
19 Sep 1955	*Rashid Karami* (for 1st time) (b. Miriata 1921)
15 Jan – 15 Mar 1956	*Rashid Karami* (for 2nd time)
20 Mar – 6 Jun 1956	*Abdullah Yafi* (for 7th time)
8 Jun – 16 Nov 1956	*Abdullah Yafi* (for 8th time)
18 Nov 1956 – 14 Aug 1957	*Sami Solh* (for 5th time)
18 Aug 1957 – 12 Mar 1958	*Sami Solh* (for 6th time)
14 Mar – 20 Sep 1958	*Sami Solh* (for 7th time)
24 Sep – 8 Oct 1958	*Rashid Karami* (for 3rd time)
14 Oct 1958	*Rashid Karami* (for 4th time)
8 Oct 1959	*Rashid Karami* (for 5th time)
14 May – 20 Jul 1960	*Ahmad Daouk* (for 2nd time)
2 Aug 1960 – 16 May 1961	*Saeb Salam* (for 3rd time)
17/20 May – 23 Oct 1961	*Saeb Salam* (for 4th time)
31 Oct 1961 – 19 Feb 1964	*Rashid Karami* (for 6th time)
20 Feb – 13 Nov 1964	*Hussein Oweini* (for 2nd time)
18 Nov 1964 – 20 Jul 1965	*Hussein Oweini* (for 3rd time)
26 Jul 1965 – 30 Mar 1966	*Rashid Karami* (for 7th time)
10 Apr – 2 Dec 1966	*Abdullah Yafi* (for 9th time)

6 Dec 1966 – 5 Feb 1968	*Rashid Karami* (for 8th time)
8 Feb – 10 Oct 1968	*Abdullah Yafi* (for 10th time)
20 Oct 1968 – 8 Jan 1969	*Abdullah Yafi* (for 11th time)
16 Jan – 24 Apr 1969	*Rashid Karami* (for 9th time)
25 Apr – 22 Oct 1969	*Rashid Karami* (for 10th time)
25 Nov 1969 – 30 Sep 1970	*Rashid Karami* (for 11th time)
13 Oct 1970	*Saeb Salam* (for 5th time)
25 Apr 1973	*Amin al-Hafez* (b. 1911)
8 Jul 1973	*Takieddin Solh* (b. 1909)
from 31 Oct 1974	*Rashid Solh* (b. Beirut 1926)

Lesotho

Formerly Basutoland.

4 Oct 1966	Independence from Great Britain

HEADS OF STATE

Kings

14 Oct 1966	*Moshoeshoe II* (for 1st time) (b. Thabang, Mokhotlong district, 2 May 1938) 31 Mar – 4 Dec 1970 exiled to the Netherlands
2 Apr 1970	*Queen Mamaohato*, Regent
from 5 Dec 1970	*Moshoeshoe II* (for 2nd time)

MEMBER OF GOVERNMENT

Prime Minister

from 4 Oct 1966	*(Joseph) Leabua Jonathan*, cousin of King Moshoeshoe II (b. Leribe 30 Oct 1914)

Liberia

HEADS OF STATE

Presidents

1920 – 1930	*Charles Dunbar Burgess King* (b. between 1872 and 1878; d. Monrovia 4 Sep 1961)
1930 – 1943	*Edwin J. Barclay* (b. 1882(?); d. 6 Nov 1955)
7 May 1943/ 1 Jan 1944	*William Tubman* (b. Harper, Liberia, 29 Nov 1895; d. London 23 Jul 1971)
from 23 Jul 1971	(acting until 3 Jan 1972:) *William Richard Tolbert* (b. Bensonville 13 May 1913)

Libya

Until 1945	Part of Italy
1945 – 1951	Administered by France and the UK
24 Dec 1951	Declared independent by the United Nations
1 Sep 1969	Formation of Republic

HEADS OF STATE

King

3 Dec 1950/ 24 Dec 1951 – 1 Sep 1969	*Idris as-Sanusi* (b. Yaghbub Oasis 12 Mar 1890) went into exile in Egypt

President

from 1/ 13 Sep 1969	*Muammar al-Gadhafi (Qadhafi)* (b. Misurata 1942) Chairman of Revolutionary Council

MEMBERS OF GOVERNMENT

Prime Ministers

30 Mar 1951 – 15 Feb 1954	(acting until 25 Dec 1951:) *Mahmud al-Muntasir* (for 1st time) (b. 1903)
18 Feb – 8 Apr 1954	*Muhammad Saqizli*
12 Apr 1954	*Mustafa ben Halim* (for 1st time) (b. 1921)
26 Apr 1955	*Mustafa ben Halim* (for 2nd time)
25 Mar 1956	*Mustafa ben Halim* (for 3rd time)
26 May 1957	*Abdul Majid Kubar* (for 1st time) (b. 1909)
11 Oct 1958 – Oct 1960	*Abdul Majid Kubar* (for 2nd time)
17 Oct 1960	*Muhammad Uthman as-Said* (b. Fez 1910/22?)
19 Mar 1963	*Mohieddin Fekini*
22 Jan 1964	*Mahmud al-Muntasir* (for 2nd time)
20 Mar 1965	*Husain (Yusuf ibn) Maziq* (b. 1910)
1 Jul 1967	*Abdel Kadir al-Badri*
Oct 1967	*Abdel Hamid Bakkouche*
4 Sep 1968	*Wanis al-Geddafi (Qadhafi)* (b. Benghazi 22 Nov 1922)
8 Sep 1969	*Mahmud Sulaiman al-Maghrabi* (b. Syria 1934)
16 Jan 1970 – 16 Jul 1972	President also Prime Minister
from 16 Jul 1972	*Abdel Salam Ahmed Jalloud* (b. Mizda 15 Dec 1944)

Liechtenstein

HEADS OF STATE

Princes

Franz Dynasty

11 Feb 1929	*Franz von Paula*, brother of Johann II (b. 28 Aug 1853; d. 25 Jul 1938)
from 30 Mar 1938	*Franz Josef II*, great-grandson of Johann I (b. 16 Aug 1906)

MEMBERS OF GOVERNMENT

Prime Ministers

Aug 1928 – 20 Jul 1945	*Franz Josef Hoop* (b. Essen 14 Dec 1895; d. 19 Oct 1959)
2 Sep 1945	*Alexander Frick* (b. 18 Feb 1910)
16 Jul 1962	*Gérard Batliner* (b. 9 Dec 1928)
18 Mar 1970	*Alfred J. Hilbe* (b. Gmunden, Austria, 22 Jul 1928)
from 27 Mar 1974	*Walter Kieber*

Lithuania

HEADS OF STATE

Presidents

17 Dec 1926 – Jun 1940	*Antanas Smetona* (for 2nd time) (b. Uželenis 10 Aug 1874; d. Cleveland, Ohio, 9 Jan 1944)*
Aug 1940	Incorporated in Union of Soviet Socialist Republics
1940 – 1944	*Stansys Lozoraitis* (b. Kaunas 5 Sep 1898) in exile from 1944

MEMBERS OF GOVERNMENT

Prime Ministers

23 Sep 1929 – 8 Jun 1934	*Juozas Tubelis* (for 1st time) (b. Ilgalankiai 18 Apr 1882; d. Kaunas 30 Sep 1939)
12 Jun 1934	*Juozas Tubelis* (for 2nd time)
25 Mar 1938	*Vladas Mironas* (for 1st time) (b. Kuodiškiai 22 Jun 1880; d. Vladimir prison 1954)
5 Dec 1938	*Vladas Mironas* (for 2nd time)
28 Mar 1939	*Jonas Černius* (b. Kupiškis 6 Jan 1898) emigrated to USA 1948

*For earlier career see vol. 2

21 Nov 1939   *Antanas Merkys* (b. Bajorai 1 Feb 1887; d. USSR Mar 1955)

Luxembourg

HEADS OF STATE

Grand Dukes

14 Jan 1919	*Charlotte* (b. Colmar-Berg 23 Jan 1896) abdicated
from 12 Nov 1964	*Jean*, son (b. Colmar-Berg 5 Jan 1921)

MEMBERS OF GOVERNMENT

Prime Ministers

16 Jul 1926 – mid Apr 1932	*Joseph Bech* (for 1st time) (b. 17 Feb 1887; d. 8 Mar 1975)
mid Apr 1932 – 10 Jun (19 Oct) 1937	*Joseph Bech* (for 2nd time)
5/6 Nov 1937 – Nov 1945	*Pierre Dupong* (for 1st time) (b. Luxembourg 1 Nov 1885; d. night of 22/23 Dec 1953) 10 May 1940 – Sep 1944 in exile
20 Nov 1945 – 13 Feb 1947	*Pierre Dupong* (for 2nd time)
1 Mar 1947 – 6 Jun 1951	*Pierre Dupong* (for 3rd time)
18 Jul 1951 – 22 Dec 1953	*Pierre Dupong* (for 4th time)
28 Dec 1953 – 26 Mar 1958	*Joseph Bech* (for 3rd time)
11 Apr – 10 Dec 1958	*Pierre Frieden* (b. Mertert 28 Oct 1892; d. Arosa 23 Feb 1959)
26 Feb 1959 – 14 Jun 1964	*Christian Pierre Werner* (for 1st time) (b. St. André 29 Dec 1913)
21 Jul 1964 – 24 Nov 1966	*Christian Pierre Werner* (for 2nd time)

23 Dec 1966 – 29 Oct 1968	*Christian Pierre Werner* (for 3rd time)
31 Jan 1969	*Christian Pierre Werner* (for 4th time)
from 15 Jun 1974	*Gaston Thorn* (b. Luxembourg 3 Sep 1928)

Foreign Ministers

Sep 1918 – 19 Oct 1937	Prime Minister discharged office
5 Nov 1937 – 10 Dec 1958	*Joseph Bech* (see Prime Ministers)
26 Feb 1959 – 14 Jun 1964	*Eugene Schaus* (b. Gondingen 12 May 1901)
21 Jul 1964 – 24 Nov 1966	*Christian Pierre Werner* (see Prime Ministers)
4 Jan 1967 – 29 Oct 1968/30 Jan 1969	*Pierre Grégoire* (b. 9 Nov 1907)
30 Jan 1969	*Gaston Thorn* (for 1st time) (see Prime Ministers)
from 15 Jun 1974	*Gaston Thorn* (for 2nd time)

Malagasy Republic

| 14 Oct 1958 | Member of French Community |
| 30 Jul 1960 | Left French Community |

HEADS OF STATE

Presidents

25 Jun/30 Jul 1960	*Philibert Tsiranana* (b. Anahidrano 18 Oct 1912)
11 Oct 1972	*Gabriel Ramanantsoa* (b. Tananarive 13 Apr 1906)
5 Feb 1975	*Richard Ratsimandrava* (b. Tananarive 21 Mar 1931; d. (assassinated) 11 Feb 1975)
12 Feb 1975	*Gilles Andriamahazo* (b. Fort Dauphin 5 May 1919) Head of National Military Directorate
from 15 Jun 1975	*Didier Ratsiraka* (b. Vatomandry 4 Nov 1936)

369

Malawi

Called Nyasaland until 6 Jul 1964.

6 Jul 1964 Independence from Great Britain

HEAD OF STATE

President and Prime Minister

from 6 Jul 1964 *Hastings Kamuzu Banda* (b. Ksungu 14 May 1906)

Malaya, Federation of

31 Aug 1957 Independence from Great Britain

HEADS OF STATE

Kings

31 Aug 1957	*Tuanku Abdul Rahman*, Yang di Pertuan Besar of Negri Sembilan (b. 24 Aug 1895; d. Kuala Lumpur 1 Apr 1960)
1 Apr – 1 Sep 1960	*Hishamuddin Alam Shah*, Sultan of Selangor (b. 13 May 1898; d. Kuala Lumpur 1 Sep 1960)
21 Sep 1960 – 16 Sep 1963	*Tuanku Syed Putra ibni al-Marhum Syed Hassan Jamalullah*, Rajah of Perlis (b. 1921)

MEMBERS OF GOVERNMENT

Prime Ministers

31 Aug 1957 *Tuanku Abdul Rahman Putra bin Abdul Hamid*

	Halim Shah (for 1st time) (b. Alor Star, Kedah, 8 Feb 1902)
15 Apr 1959	*Tuan Haji Abdul Razak bin Datuk Hussein* (b. 1922; d. London 14 Jan 1976)
22 Aug 1959	*Tuanku Abdul Rahman Putra bin Abdul Hamid Halim Shah* (for 2nd time)
16 Sep 1963	Formation of Malaysia (q.v.), comprising the Federation of Malaya, Singapore, Sarawak and Sabah (formerly British North Borneo)

Malaysia

16 Sep 1963	Formed by the union of the Federation of Malaya, Singapore, Sarawak and Sabah (formerly British North Borneo)

HEADS OF STATE

Yang di-Pertuan Agong (Supreme Head of State)

16 Sep 1963	*Tuanku Syed Putra ibni al-Marhum Syed Hassan Jamalullah*, Rajah of Perlis (b. 1921)
21 Sep 1965	*Sultan Ismail Nasiruddin Shah ibni al-Marhum Sultan Zainal Abidin*, Sultan of Trengganu (b. 24 Jan 1907)
from 21 Sep 1970	*Sultan Tuanku Abdul Halim Muadzam Shah ibni al-Marhum Sultan Badlishah*, Sultan of Kedah

MEMBERS OF GOVERNMENT

Prime Ministers

16 Sep 1963	*Tuanku Abdul Rahman Putra bin Abdul Hamid Halim Shah* (b. Alor Star, Kedah, 8 Feb 1902)
from 21 Sep 1970	*Tuan Haji Abdul Razak bin Datuk Hussein* (b. 1922; d. London 14 Jan 1976)

371

Maldives

26 Jul 1965	Independence and abolition of British protectorate
11 Nov 1968	Proclamation of Republic

HEADS OF STATE

Sultan

4 Mar 1954 – 11 Nov 1968	*Al-Amir Mohammed Farid Didi*

President

from 11 Nov 1968	*Amir Ibrahim Nasir* (b. Male 2 Sep 1926)

MEMBERS OF GOVERNMENT

Prime Ministers

26 Jul 1965	*Amir Ibrahim Nasir* (for 1st time) (see President)
11 Nov 1968 – (?)	President also Prime Minister
(?) – 6 Mar 1975	*Ahmed Zaki* (b. 1932?)
from 6 Mar 1975	*Amir Ibrahim Nasir* (for 2nd time)

Mali

24 Nov 1958	Member of French Community (called Sudanese Republic, previously French Sudan)
4 Apr 1959	Associated with Senegal in the Mali Federation (see p. 373)
22 Sep 1960	Adopted name of Republic of Mali

HEADS OF STATE

Presidents

23 Sep 1960	*Modibo Keita* (b. Bamako 4 Jun 1915; d. Bamako 17 May 1977)
from 19 Nov 1968	*Moussa Traoré* (b. Kayes 25 Sep 1936)

MEMBERS OF GOVERNMENT

Prime Ministers

23 Sep 1960 – 19 Nov 1968	President also Prime Minister
23 Nov 1968 – 1970	(acting until 19 Sep 1969:) *Yoro Diakité* (b. Bangassi-Arbala 17 Oct 1932; d. 1973)
from 26 Nov 1970	President also Prime Minister

Mali Federation

4 Apr 1959	Formed between Senegal and Sudanese Republic
20 Jun 1960	Left French Community
22 Aug 1960	Secession of Senegal

Prime Minister

4 Apr 1959 – 22 Aug 1960	*Modibo Keita* (b. Bamako 4 Jun 1915; d. Bamako 17 May 1977)

President of the Federal Assembly

4 Apr 1959 – 22 Aug 1960	*Léopold-Sédar Senghor* (b. Joal-la-Portugaise 9 Oct 1906)

Malta

21 Sep 1964	Independence from Great Britain
13 Dec 1974	Republic

HEADS OF STATE

Governors

9 Jul 1946	*Sir Francis Douglas* (from 1950: *1st Baron Douglas of Barloch*) (b. Manitoba 21 Oct 1889)
30 Jun 1949	*Sir Gerald Hallen Creasy* (b. 1 Nov 1897)
3 Aug 1954	*Sir Robert Edward Laycock* (b. 18 Apr 1907; d. Wiseton 10(?) Mar 1968)
Jun 1959	*Sir Guy Grantham* (b. 1900)
Jun/2 Jul 1962 – 20 Sep 1964	*Sir Maurice Dorman* (b. Stafford 7 Aug 1912)

Governors-General

21 Sep 1964 – 20 Jun 1971	*Sir Maurice Dorman* (previously Governor)
from 21 Jun 1971	(acting until 5 Jul 1971:) *Sir Anthony Joseph Mamo* (b. Birkirhara 9 Jun 1909)

President

from 13 Dec 1974	*Sir Anthony Joseph Mamo* (see Governors-General)

MEMBERS OF GOVERNMENT

Prime Ministers

4 Nov 1947	*Paul Boffa* (from 1956: *Sir*) (Lab, from Oct 1949 Ind Lab) (b. 1890(?); d. 6 Jul 1962)
17 Sep 1950	*Enrico Mizzi* (Nat) (d. Malta 20 Dec 1950)
20 Dec 1950	*Borg Olivier* (Nat) (for 1st time) (b. Valetta 5 Jul 1911)

374

9 Jan 1954	*Borg Olivier* (Nat) (for 2nd time)
11 Mar 1955 – 21	*Dom(inic) Mintoff* (Lab) (for 1st time) (b. Cospicua
Apr 1958	6 Aug 1916)
26 Apr 1958	Administration by Governor-General
3 Mar 1962	*Borg Olivier* (Nat) (for 3rd time)
from 21 Jun 1971	*Dom(inic) Mintoff* (Lab) (for 2nd time)

Manchukuo

18 Feb 1932	Declaration of independence of Manchuria, from China, as Manchukuo
15 Sep 1932	Under Japanese protection

HEAD OF STATE

Regent

9 Mar/ 15 Sep 1932	*Engk'e Erdemtü*, earlier *P'u-i*, Emperor of China 14 Nov 1908 – 1912 (b. 11 Feb 1906; d. Peking 17 Oct 1967) captured by the Russians and interned at Fushan 1945

Emperor

1 Mar 1934 – Aug 1945	*Engk'e Erdemtü* (see above)
1945	Dissolution of state, territory subsequently incorporated in China

MEMBER OF GOVERNMENT

Prime Minister

21 May 1935 – Aug 1945	*Chang Ching-hui*

375

Mauritania

28 Nov 1958   Member of French Community
28 Nov 1960   Left French Community

HEAD OF STATE

President (also Head of Government)

from 20 Aug 1961   *Mokhtar Ould Daddah* (b. Boutilimit 25 Dec 1924)

MEMBER OF GOVERNMENT

Prime Minister

28 Nov 1958 – 20   *Mokhtar Ould Daddah* (see President)
   Aug 1961

Mauritius

1961   Internal self-government
12 Mar 1968   Independence from Great Britain

HEADS OF STATE

Governors-General

12 Mar 1968   *Sir Arthur Leonard Williams* (b. 22 Jan 1904; d. 27
                     Dec 1972)
from Dec 1972   *Sir (Abdool) Raman (Mahomed) Osman* (b. 29 Aug
                     1902)

MEMBER OF GOVERNMENT

Prime Minister

from 1964   *Sir Seewoosagur Ramgoolam* (b. Belle Rive 18 Sep
                 1900) Chief Minister 1961 – 1964

Memel Territory

1924 – 1939   Autonomous state under Lithuania
22 Mar 1939   Absorbed into Germany

HEADS OF STATE

Lithuanian Governors

7 Sep 1927   *Antonas Merkys* (b. Bajoriai 1 Feb 1887; d. USSR
                  Mar 1955)
7 Mar 1932   *Vytautas Gylys* (b. 1886; d. Toronto 14 Jun 1959)
16 Sep 1933   *Dr Navakas* (b. 1896)
4 Apr 1935   *Vladas Kurkauskas* (b. Tashkent 1895)
15 Oct 1936   —— *Kubilius*
12 Dec 1938 – 22 *Viktoras Gailius* (b. Berštinkai 27 Aug 1893; d.
  Mar 1939   Pfullingen 7 Jul 1956)*

MEMBERS OF GOVERNMENT

2 Dec 1927 – 28 May 1930: Kadgiehn

Prime Minister   —— *Kadgiehn*
Ministers   —— *Vorbeck*
                      —— *Sziegaud* (b. Trakeningken 31 May 1886)
                      Martynas Reisgys (b. Venckai 11 Dec 1886; d.
                      Mauthausen 2 Apr 1942)*

*For earlier career see vol. 2

377

16 Aug - 29 Oct 1930: Reisgys I

Prime Minister   *Martynas Reisgys* (for 1st time) (see Kadgiehn)
Ministers   14 Aug - 9 Oct 1930: —— *Dugnus*
                 14 Aug - 9 Oct 1930: —— *Czeskleba**
                 9 - 29 Oct 1930: —— *Šulcas*
                 9 - 29 Oct 1930: —— *Sziegaud* (see Kadgiehn)

12 Jan 1931 - 23 Feb 1932: Böttcher

Prime Minister   *Otto Böttcher* (b. Memel 14 Sep 1872; d. Königsberg
                 16 Jun 1932)
Ministers   —— *Sziegaud* (see Kadgiehn)
                 —— *Podszus*

27 Feb - 26 May 1932: Simmat

Prime Minister   *Eduard Simmat*
Ministers   14 Mar 1932: —— *Toleikis*, refused nomination*
                 14 Mar 1932: —— *Vongehr*, refused nomination
                 14 Mar - 26 May 1932: —— *Tolischus*
                 14 Mar - 26 May 1932: *Martynas Reisgys* (see
                 Kadgiehn)
                 14 Mar - 26 May 1932: —— *Kadgiehn* (see Kadgiehn)

6 Jun 1932 - 19 Mar 1934: Schreiber

Prime Minister   *Ottomar Schreiber* (b. Marienburg 1 May 1889; d.
                 Munich night of 5/6 Feb 1955)
Ministers   —— *Sziegaud* (see Kadgiehn)
                 Fritz Walgahn (b. Memel 22 Aug 1891)

Mar - 1 Dec 1934: Reisgys II

Prime Minister   *Martynas Reisgys* (for 2nd time) (see Kadgiehn)

4 Dec 1934 - 5 Nov 1935: Bruvelaitis

Prime Minister   *Georg Bruvelaitis*
Ministers   *Ludwig Buttgereit*
                 Martin Anysas
                 Martin Grigat

*For earlier career see vol. 2

378

28 Nov 1935 - 7 Jan 1939: Baldschus

Prime Minister	*August Baldschus**
Ministers	—— *Sziegaud* (see Kadgiehn)
	Willy Betke
	Ernst Surau

26 Jan - 22 Mar 1939: Bertuleit

Prime Minister	*Wilhelm Bertuleit*
Ministers	—— *Sziegaud* (see Kadgiehn)
	Herbert Böttcher
	—— *Monien*

Mexico

HEADS OF STATE

Presidents

1 Dec 1928	*Emilio Portes Gil* (b. 30 Oct 1891)
5 Feb 1930	*Pascual Ortiz Rubio* (b. 1877; d. Mexico City 4 Nov 1963)
4 Sep 1932	*Abelardo Rodríguez* (b. 1889; d. La Jolla, California, 13 Feb 1967)
1 Dec 1934	*Lázaro Cárdenas* (b. Jiquilpán 21 May 1895; d. Mexico City 19 Oct 1970)
1 Dec 1940	*Miguel Ávila Camacho* (b. 24 Apr 1897; d. 13 Oct 1955)
1 Dec 1946	*Miguel Alemán Váldez* (b. 27 Sep 1903)
1 Dec 1952	*Adolfo Ruiz Cortines* (b. 30 Dec 1891; d. 3 Dec 1973)
1 Dec 1958	*Alfonso López Mateos* (b. 26 May 1910; d. Mexico City 22 Sep 1969)
1 Dec 1964	*Gustavo Díaz Ordaz* (b. Ciudad Serda 12 Mar 1911)
from 1 Dec 1970	*Luis Echeverría Alvárez* (b. Mexico City 17 Jan 1922)

*For earlier career see vol. 2

MEMBERS OF GOVERNMENT

Foreign Ministers

1 Dec 1964 – 30 Nov 1970	*Antonio Carrillo Flores* (b. 1909)
1 Dec 1970	*Emilio Óscar Rabasa* (b. Mexico City 23 Jan 1925)
from 29 Dec 1975	*Alfonso García Robles* (b. 29 Mar 1911)

Monaco

HEADS OF STATE

Princes

House of Grimaldi

26 Jun 1922 – 9 May 1949	*Louis II*, son of Albert (b. 12 Jul 1870)

House of Polignac

from 9 May 1949	*Rainier III*, grandson (b. 31 May 1923)

Mongolia

HEADS OF STATE

Chairmen of the Presidium

1948 – 23 Sep 1953	*Gonchighiin Bumatsende* (d. 29 Sep 1953)
Jul 1954	*Jamsarangiin Sambu(u)* (d. 20 May 1972)

20 May 1972   (acting:) *Sonomyn Luvsan*
from 10 Jun 1974   *Yumsjhagiin Tsedenbal* (b. 17 Sep 1916) †

MEMBERS OF GOVERNMENT

Prime Ministers

1928	*Amor* (for 1st time) (b. 1886; d. 1939)
1932	*Gendun* (d. 22 Aug 1937)
1936 – 1938	*Amor* (for 2nd time)
1939	*Khorloghiin Choibalsan* (b. 8 Feb 1895; d. Moscow 26 Jan 1952) Commander-in-Chief 1924 – 1952
Feb/ 28 May 1952	*Yumsjhagiin Tsedenbal* (for 1st time) (see Chairmen of the Presidium)
7 Jul 1952	*Yumsjhagiin Tsedenbal* (for 2nd time)
from 10 Jun 1974	*Jambyn Batmunkh*

Foreign Ministers

1926	*Dorlikjab*
1930	*Khorloghiin Choibalsan* (see Prime Ministers)
1932 – 1952	Prime Minister also Foreign Minister
1954	*Bayaryn Jargalsaikhan*
1955	*Sandavyn Ravdan*
1956 – 1957	*Dashyn Adilbish*
Summer 1958 / 20 Jan 1959	*Puntsagiin Shagdarsuren*, initially acting
29 Mar 1963	*Mangalyn Dugersuren*
Jul 1968 – 29 Jul 1970	*Luvsandagchiin Toiv* (b. 1915; d. Ulan Bator 29 Jul 1970)
from 1970	*Lodongiin Rinchin* (b. 25 Jul 1929)

Morocco

2 Mar 1956   Independence from France

† First Secretary of Mongolian People's Revolutionary Party

MOROCCO

HEADS OF STATE

Sultans (from 14 Aug 1957 Kings)

House of Sad (Filali branch)

17 Nov 1927 – 20 Aug 1953	*(Sidi) Muhammad V* (for 1st time) (b. Fez 10 Aug 1909; d. Rabat 26 Feb 1961)
20 Aug 1953 – 1/29 Oct 1955	*Muhammad VI, ben Arafa*, uncle (b. 1890; d. Nice 18 Jul 1976)
12 Nov 1955	*(Sidi) Muhammad V* (for 2nd time)
from 26 Feb 1961	*Hassan II*, son (b. Rabat 9 Jul 1929)

French Residents

Jan 1929	*Lucien Saint* (b. Evreux 1867; d. 1938)
Aug 1933 – Mar 1936	*Henri Ponsot* (b. Bologna 2 Mar 1877)
21 Mar – Sep 1936	*Marcel Peyrouton* (b. Paris 2 Jul 1887)
16 Sep 1936 – 14 Nov 1942/14 Jun 1943	*Auguste Noguès* (b. Mauléon-Magnoac 13 Aug 1876; d. Paris 20 Apr 1971)
5 Jun 1943 – 15 Mar 1946	*Gabriel Puaux* (b. Paris 19 May 1883)
5/16 Mar 1946	*Eirik Labonne* (b. Paris 4 Oct 1888)
14 May 1947	*Alphonse Juin* (b. Bône, Algeria, 16 Dec 1888; d. Paris 27 Jan 1967)
Oct 1951 – Jun 1954	*Augustin Guillaume* (b. Guillestre 30 Jul 1895)
20 May/14 Jun 1954 – Jun 1955	*Francis Lacoste* (b. Paris 27 Nov 1905)
20 Jun 1955	*Gilbert Grandval* (b. Paris 12 Feb 1904)
31 Aug – 9 Nov 1955	*Pierre, Comte Boyer de la Tour du Moulin* (b. Maisons-Laffitte 18 Jun 1896)
9 Nov 1955 – 1956	*André Dubois* (b. Bône, Algeria, 8 Mar 1903)

MEMBERS OF GOVERNMENT

Grand Vizier

29 Aug 1917 – 1955	*Muhammad al-Muqri* (b. Fez 1854; d. Rabat 10 Sep 1957)

Prime Ministers

25 Oct – 22 Nov 1955	*Ibn Sulaiman*

7 Dec 1955 – 26 Oct 1956	*Si Muhammad Bekkai* (for 1st time) (b. 1907; d. Rabat 13 Apr 1961)
27 Oct 1956 – 16 Apr 1958	*Si Muhammad Bekkai* (for 2nd time)
8 May – 3 Dec 1958	*Ahmad Balafrej* (b. Rabat 1908)
23 Dec 1958 – 20 May 1960	*Abd Allah Ibrahim* (b. Marrakesh 1918)
23/25 May 1960	*(Sidi) Muhammad V* (see Kings) assumed duties of Prime Minister with Crown-Prince Hassan, later King Hassan II, as deputy
2 Jun 1961	*Hassan* (see Kings) Leader of Government with *Ahmad Balafrej* (see above) as personal representative
13 Nov 1963	*Ahmad Bahnini* (b. 1909)
8 Jun 1965	*Hassan* (see Kings) assumed personal charge of Government
7 Jul 1967	*Mohammed Ben Hima* (b. Safi 25 Jun 1924)
6 Oct 1969 – 4 Aug 1971	*Moulay Ahmed Laraki* (b. Casablanca 15 Oct 1931)
6 Aug 1971	*Mohammed Karim Lamrani* (b. 1919?)
from 19 Nov 1972	*Ahmed Osman* (b. Oujda 3 Jan 1930)

Mossi/Dagomba States

For the Kingdom of Wagadugu see vol. 1.

Mozambique

25 Jun 1975	Independence from Portugal

HEAD OF STATE

President (also head of government)

from 25 Jun 1975	*Samora Moises Machel* (b. Gaza Province Oct 1933)

Nauru

1919	Administered by Australia under trusteeship agreements with League of Nations and United Nations
31 Jan 1968	Independence

HEAD OF STATE

Chairman of the National Assembly

31 Jan – 17 May 1968	*Hammer de Roburt* (b. Nauru 25 Sep 1922)

President and Head of the Government

from 18 May 1968	*Hammer de Roburt* (see above)

Nepal

HEADS OF STATE

Kings

11 Dec 1911	*Tribhuvan Bir Bikram Shah* (for 1st time) (b. 30 Jun 1906; d. 13 Mar 1955)
7 Nov 1950 – 1952	*Bir Bikram*, grandson (b. 1947)
1952 – 13 Mar 1955	*Tribhuvan Bir Bikram Shah* (for 2nd time)

2 May 1956	*Mahendra Bir Bikram Shah* (b. 11 Jun 1920)
from 31 Jan 1972	*Birendra Bir Bikram Shah Dev* (b. Katmandu 28 Dec 1945)

MEMBERS OF GOVERNMENT

Prime Ministers (until 1951 hereditary Major-Domos from the Rana family)

1929 – 1931	*Maharajah Bhim Sham Sher Rana*, brother of Chandra, Prime Minister 1901 – 1929 (b. 1869; d. 1931)
1931 – 1945	*Maharajah Juddha Sham Sher Rana*, brother
Nov 1945	*Maharajah Padma Sham Sher Jang Bahadur Rana*, son of Bhim (b. 1882)
Apr 1948	*Maharajah Mohan Sham Sher Jang Bahadur Rana*, son of Chandra, Prime Minister 1901 – 1929 (for 1st time) (b. 23 Dec 1885)
May 1951	*Maharajah Mohan Sham Sher Jang Bahadur Rana* (for 2nd time)
Nov 1951	*Matrika Prasad Koirala* (for 1st time) (b. 1 Jan 1912)
10 Aug 1952	*Tribhuvan Bir Bikram Shah* (see Kings)
15 Jun 1953 – Jan 1955	*Matrika Prasad Koirala* (for 2nd time)
Feb 1955 – Jan 1956	*Crown Prince Mahendra Bir Bikram Shah* (see Kings)
Jan 1956 – 8 Jul 1957	*Tanka Prasad Acharya*
14 Nov 1957	King also Prime Minister
27 May 1959 – 15 Dec 1960	*Sri Bishawa Prasad Koirala*, brother of Matrika Prasad Koirala
15 Dec 1960	Abolition of Parliamentary government by King
5 Apr 1963	*Tulsi Giri* (for 1st time) (b. Sep 1926) also Foreign Minister; Deputy Prime Minister since 2 Jul 1962
26 Jan 1965 – May 1967	*Surya Bahadur Thapa* (for 1st time) (b. Muga 20 Mar 1928)
30 May 1967 – 2 Apr 1969	*Surya Bahadur Thapa* (for 2nd time)
7 Apr 1969	*Kirti Nidhi Bista* (for 1st time) (b. 1927)
13 Apr 1970	King functioned as Prime Minister, his Chief Minister being the Foreign Minister, *Gahendra Bahadur Rajbhandari*
14 Apr 1971	*Kirti Nidhi Bista* (for 2nd time)
16 Jul 1973	*Nagendra Prasad Rijal*
from 1 Dec 1975	*Tulsi Giri* (for 2nd time)

Netherlands

HEADS OF STATE

Queens

23 Nov 1890	*Wilhelmina* (b. 31 Aug 1880; d. Apeldoorn 28 Nov 1962) abdicated
from 2 Sep 1948	*Juliana*, daughter (b. The Hague 30 Apr 1909)

MEMBERS OF GOVERNMENT

10 Aug 1929 – 25 Apr 1933: Ruys III

Prime Minister †	*Charles Joseph Maria Ruys de Beerenbrouck* (Cath) (for 3rd time) (b. Roermond 1 Dec 1873; d. Utrecht 17 Apr 1936)*
Foreign Affairs	10 Aug 1929 – 20 Apr 1933: *Frans Beelaerts van Blokland* (b. The Hague 21 Jan 1872; d. The Hague 27 Mar 1956)*
	20 – 25 Apr 1933 (acting: *Charles Joseph Maria Ruys de Beerenbrouck* (Cath) (see above)
Home Affairs	*Charles Joseph Maria Ruys de Beerenbrouck* (Cath) (see above)
Justice	*Jan Donner* (Anti-rev) (b. Assen 3 Feb 1891)*
Finance	*Dirk Jan de Geer* (b. Groningen 14 Dec 1870; d. Soest 27 Nov 1960)*
Waterways and Waterworks	*Paul Johan Reymer* (Cath)
Education	*Jan Terpstra* (Anti-rev) (b. Scheemda 8 Jun 1888; d. The Hague 14 Dec 1952)
Labour (from 1 May 1932: Economic Affairs)	*Timotheus Josephus Verschuur* (Cath) (b. Utrecht 18 Mar 1886; d. Messenthin 1 May 1945)
Defence	*Laurentius Nicolaas Deckers* (Cath) (b. Heeze 14 Feb 1883)

† Up to 1945–1946 there was strictly speaking no office of Prime Minister. The task of forming a cabinet was assigned to one or other of the departmental ministers
*For earlier career see vol. 2

Colonies   *Simon de Graaff* (b. Lisse 24 Aug 1861; d. Oegstgeest, Leiden, 2 Oct 1948)*

26 May 1933 – 25 Jul 1935: Colijn II

Prime Minister	*Hendrikus Colijn* (Anti-rev) (for 2nd time) (b. Haarlemmermeer 22 Jun 1869; d. Ilmenau, Thuringia, 18 Sep 1944)*
Foreign Affairs	*Andries Cornelis Dirk de Graeff* (b. The Hague 7 Aug 1872; d. 24 Apr 1957)
Home Affairs	*Jacob Adriaan de Wilde* (Anti-rev) (b. Goes 7 Jan 1879; d. The Hague 10 Jan 1956)
Justice	*Josephus Robertus Hendrikus van Schaik* (Cath) (b. Breda 31 Jan 1882; d. The Hague 23 Mar 1962)
Finance	*Pieter Jacobus Oud* (Lib) (b. Purmerend 5 Dec 1886)
Water Affairs	26 May 1933 – 13 Jan 1935: *Jacob Adriaan Kalff* (Lib) (b. Zwolle 27 Apr 1869; d. Wassenaar 13 Jan 1935)
	14 Jan – 15 Mar 1935 (acting:) *Hendrikus Colijn* (Anti-rev) (see above)
	15 Mar – 25 Jul 1935: *Otto Cornelis Adriaan van Lidth de Jeude* (Lib) (b. Tiel 7 Jul 1881; d. The Hague 1 Feb 1952)
Education	26 May 1933 – 18 May 1935: *Hendrik Pieter Marchant* (Lib) (b. Deventer 12 Feb 1869; d. The Hague 12 May 1956)
	18 May – 25 Jul 1935 (acting:) *Joseph Rudolf Slotemaker de Bruïne* (b. Sliedrecht 6 May 1869; d. Wassenaar 1 May 1941)*
Economic Affairs	26 May 1933 – 17 Apr 1934: *Timotheus Josephus Verschuur* (Cath) (see Ruys III)
	17 Apr – 25 Jun 1934 (acting:) *Hendrikus Colijn* (Anti-rev) (see above)
	25 Jun 1934 – 6 Jun 1935: *Maximilien Paul Léon van Steenberghe* (Cath) (b. Leiden 2 May 1889; d. Goirle 22 Jan 1972)
	6 Jun – 25 Jul 1935: *Henri Caspar Joseph Hubert Gelissen* (Cath) (b. Venlo 15 May 1895)
Social Affairs	*Joseph Rudolf Slotemaker de Bruïne* (see above)
Defence	*Laurentius Nicolaas Deckers* (Cath) (see Ruys III)
Colonies	*Hendrikus Colijn* (Anti-rev) (see above)

*For earlier career see vol. 2

31 Jul 1935 - 25 May 1937: Colijn III

Prime Minister	*Hendrikus Colijn* (Anti-rev) (for 3rd time) (see Colijn II)
Foreign Affairs	*Andries Cornelis Dirk de Graeff* (see Colijn II)
Home Affairs	*Jacob Adriaan de Wilde* (Anti-rev) (see Colijn II)
Justice	*Josephus Robertus Hendrikus van Schaik* (Cath) (see Colijn II)
Finance	*Pieter Jacobus Oud* (Lib) (see Colijn II)
Water Affairs	*Otto Cornelis Adriaan van Lidth de Jeude* (Lib) (see Colijn II)
Education	*Joseph Rudolf Slotemaker de Bruïne* (see Colijn II)
Commerce, Industry and Shipping	*Henri Caspar Joseph Hubert Gelissen* (Cath) (see Colijn II)
Agriculture and Fisheries	2 Sep 1935 - 25 May 1937: *Laurentius Nicolaas Deckers* (Cath) (see Ruys III)
Social Affairs	*Marcus Slingenberg* (Lib) (b. Beerta 21 Oct 1881; d. Haarlem 9 May 1941)
Defence	31 Jul - 2 Sep 1935: *Laurentius Nicolaas Deckers* (Cath) (see Ruys III)
	2 Sep 1935 - 25 May 1937 (acting:) *Hendrikus Colijn* (Anti-rev) (see Colijn II)
Colonies	*Hendrikus Colijn* (Anti-rev) (see Colijn II)

24 Jun 1937 - 29 Jun 1939: Colijn IV

Prime Minister	*Hendrikus Colijn* (Anti-rev) (for 4th time) (see Colijn II)
General Affairs (Co-ordination and Information)	8 Jul 1937 - 29 Jun 1939: *Hendrikus Colijn* (Anti-rev) (see Colijn II)
Foreign Affairs	24 Jun - 1 Oct 1937 (acting:) *Hendrikus Colijn* (Anti-rev) (see Colijn II)
	1 Oct 1937 - 29 Jun 1939: *Jacob Adriaan Nicolaas Patijn* (b. Rotterdam 9 Dec 1873; d. The Hague 13 Jul 1961)
Home Affairs	*Hendrik van Boeyen* (b. Putten 23 May 1889; d. Soesterberg 30 Mar 1947)
Justice	*Carvens Maria Johannes Franciscus Goseling* (Cath) (b. Amsterdam 10 Jun 1891; d. Buchenwald Concentration Camp 14 Apr 1941)

Finance	24 Jun 1937 – 19 May 1939: *Jacob Adriaan de Wilde* (Anti-rev) (see Colijn II)
	19 May – 29 Jun 1939 (acting:) *Hendrikus Colijn* (Anti-rev) (see Colijn II)
Water Affairs	*Johannes Antonius Marie van Buuren* (b. Schiedam 8 Aug 1884)
Education	*Joseph Rudolf Slotemaker de Bruïne* (see Colijn II)
Economic Affairs	*Maximilien Paul Léon van Steenberghe* (Cath) (see Colijn II)
Agriculture and Fisheries	24 Jun 1937 – 15 Jul 1937 (acting:) *Maximilien Paul Léon van Steenberghe* (Cath) (see Colijn II)
	15 Jul 1937: post abolished
Social Affairs	*Carl Paul Maria Romme* (Cath) (b. Oirschot 21 Dec 1896)
Defence	*Jannes Johannes Cornelis van Dijk* (Anti-rev) (b. Leeuwarden 11 Dec 1871; d. The Hague 1953)*
Colonies	*Charles Joseph Ignace Marie Welter* (Cath) (b. The Hague 6 Apr 1880)*

25 – 27 Jul 1939: Colijn V

Prime Minister	*Hendrikus Colijn* (Anti-rev) (for 5th time) (see Colijn II)
General Affairs	*Hendrikus Colijn* (Anti-rev) (see Colijn II)
Foreign Affairs	*Jacob Adriaan Nicolaas Patijn* (see Colijn IV)
Home Affairs	*Hendrik van Boeyen* (see Colijn IV)
Justice	*Johannes Anthonie de Visser* (b. Leusden 28 Apr 1883; d. 28 Aug 1950)
Finance	*Christiaan Wilhelm Bodenhausen* (Lib) (b. Leeuwarden 24 Jun 1869)
Water Affairs	*Otto Cornelis Adriaan van Lidth de Jeude* (Lib) (see Colijn II)
Education	*Bertram Johannes Otto Schrieke* (b. Zandvoort 18 Sep 1890; d. London 14 Sep 1945)
Economic Affairs	(acting:) *Hendrikus Colijn* (Anti-rev) (see Colijn II)
Social Affairs	*Marinus Hendrikus Damme* (b. Breda 10 Nov 1876)
Defence	*Jannes Johannes Cornelis van Dijk* (Anti-rev) (see Colijn IV)
Colonies	*Cornelis van den Bussche* (b. Bergen op Zoom 2 Mar 1884; d. Arnhem 23 Sep 1941)

*For earlier career see vol. 2

10 Aug 1939 – 3 Sep 1940 (from May 1940 in exile in London): De Geer II

Prime Minister	*Dirk Jan de Geer* (for 2nd time) (see Ruys III)
General Affairs	(acting:) *Dirk Jan de Geer* (see Ruys III)
Foreign Affairs	*Eelco Nicolaas van Kleffens* (b. Heerenveen 17 Nov 1894)
Home Affairs	*Hendrik van Boeyen* (see Colijn IV)
Justice	*Pieter Sjoerd Gerbrandy* (Anti-rev) (b. Goengamieden 13 Apr 1885; d. The Hague 7 Sep 1961)
Finance	*Dirk Jan de Geer* (see Ruys III)
Water Affairs	*Johan Willem Albarda* (Soc) (b. Leeuwarden 5 Jun 1877; d. The Hague 19 Apr 1957)
Education	*Gerrit Bolkestein* (Lib) (b. Amsterdam 9 Oct 1871; d. The Hague 8 Sep 1956)
Economic Affairs	*Maximilien Paul Léon van Steenberghe* (Cath) (see Colijn II)
Agriculture and Fisheries	9 May – 3 Sep 1940: *Arie Adriaan van Rhijn* (Soc) (b. Groningen 23 Oct 1892)
Social Affairs	*Jan van den Tempel* (Soc) (b. Willemstad, Curaçao, 1 Aug 1877; d. Amsterdam 27 Jun 1955)
Defence	*Adriaan Quirinus Hendrik Dyxhoorn* (b. Rotterdam 10 Sep 1889; d. The Hague 22 Jan 1952)
Colonies	*Charles Joseph Ignace Marie Welter* (Cath) (see Colijn IV)

3 Sep 1940 – 8 Feb 1945: Gerbrandy I (in exile in London)

Prime Minister	*Pieter Sjoerd Gerbrandy* (Anti-rev) (for 1st time) (see De Geer II)
General Affairs	*Hendrik van Boeyen* (see Colijn IV)
Foreign Affairs	*Eelco Nicolaas van Kleffens* (see De Geer II)
Home Affairs	3 Sep 1940 – 31 May 1944: *Hendrik van Boeyen* (see Colijn IV)
	31 May 1944 – 27 Jan 1945: *Jacob Albertus Wilhelmus Burger* (Soc) (b. Willemstad, Curaçao, 20 Aug 1904)
	27 Jan – 8 Feb 1945 (acting:) *Hendrik van Boeyen* (see Colijn IV)
Justice	3 Sep 1940 – 21 Feb 1942: *Pieter Sjoerd Gerbrandy* (Anti-rev) (see De Geer II)
	21 Feb 1942 – 11 Jul 1944: *Johannes Regnerus Marie van Angeren* (Cath) (b. Utrecht 9 May 1894; d. The Hague 19 Mar 1959)

	11 Jul 1944 – 8 Feb 1945: *Gerrit Jan van Heuven Goedhart* (b. Bussum 19 Mar 1901; d. Genf 8 Jul 1956)
Finance	3 Sep 1940 – 27 Jul 1941 (acting:) *Charles Joseph Ignace Marie Welter* (Cath) (see Colijn IV)
	27 Jul – 17 Nov 1941 (acting:) *Maximilien Paul Léon van Steenberghe* (Cath) (see Colijn II)
	20 Nov 1941 – 9 Dec 1942 (acting:) *Johan Willem Albarda* (Soc) (see De Geer II)
	9 Dec 1942 – 8 Feb 1945: *Johannes van den Broek* (b. Haarlem 26 Oct 1882; d. The Hague 22 Oct 1946)
Water Affairs	*Johan Willem Albarda* (Soc) (see De Geer II)
Education	*Gerrit Bolkestein* (Lib) (see De Geer II)
Commerce, Industry and Shipping	3 Sep 1940 – 17 Nov 1941: *Maximilien Paul Léon van Steenberghe* (Cath) (see Colijn II)
	17 Nov 1941 – 8 Jan 1942 (acting:) *Jan van den Tempel* (Soc) (see De Geer II)
	8 Jan 1942 – 31 May 1944: *Pieter Adriaan Kerstens* (Cath) (b. Ginneken 23 Aug 1896)
	31 May 1944 – 8 Feb 1945 (acting:) *Johannes van den Broek* (see above)
Agriculture and Fisheries	3 Sep 1940 – 1 May 1941: *Arie Adriaan van Rhijn* (Soc) (see De Geer II)
	1 May 1941: functions taken over by Commerce, Industry and Shipping (see above)
Shipping and Fisheries	2 Jun 1944 – 8 Feb 1945: *James Marnix de Booy* (Cath) (b. Kralingen 24 Jul 1885)
Social Welfare	*Jan van den Tempel* (Soc) (see De Geer II)
War Effort	21 May 1942 – 8 Feb 1945: *Pieter Sjoerd Gerbrandy* (Anti-rev) (see De Geer II)
Defence (from 27 Jul 1941: War)	3 Sep 1940 – 12 Jun 1941: *Adriaan Quirinus Hendrik Dyxhoorn* (see De Geer II)
	12 Jun 1941 – 15 Sep 1942 (acting until 27 Jul 1941:) *Hendrik van Boeyen* (see Colijn IV)
	15 Sep 1942 – 8 Feb 1945: *Otto Cornelis Adriaan van Lidth de Jeude* (Lib) (see Colijn II)
Navy	27 Jul 1941 – 8 Feb 1945: *Johannes Theodorus Fürstner* (b. Amsterdam 16 Jan 1887)
Colonies	3 Sep 1940 – 17 Nov 1941: *Charles Joseph Ignace Marie Welter* (Cath) (see Colijn IV)
	17 Nov 1941 – 25 May 1942: *Pieter Sjoerd Gerbrandy* (Anti-rev) (see De Geer II)
	25 May 1942 – 8 Feb 1945: *Hubertus Johannes van Mook* (b. Semarang, Java, 30 May 1894; d. L'Isle-sur-

	la-Sorgue 10 May 1965)
Without Portfolio	1 Jan 1942 – 8 Feb 1945: *Edgar Frederik Marie Justin Michiels van Verduynen* (b. The Hague 2 Dec 1885; d. London 13 May 1952) 9 Jun 1942 – 5 Jan 1943: *Raden Adipati Ario Soejono* (b. Tulungagung 31 Mar 1886; d. London 5 Jan 1943) 11 Aug 1943 – 31 May 1944: *Jacob Albertus Wilhelmus Burger* (Soc) (see above)

23 Feb – 16 May 1945: Gerbrandy II (in exile in London)

Prime Minister	*Pieter Sjoerd Gerbrandy* (Anti-rev) (for 2nd time) (see De Geer II)
Foreign Affairs	*Eelco Nicolaas van Kleffens* (see De Geer II)
Home Affairs	*Louis Joseph Maria Beel* (Cath) (b. Roermond 12 Apr 1902; d. Utrecht 11 Feb 1977)
Justice	(acting:) *Pieter Sjoerd Gerbrandy* (Anti-rev) (see De Geer II)
Finance	*Gerardus Wilhelmus Maria Huysmans* (Cath) (b. Eindhoven 29 Apr 1902; d. The Hague 18 Mar 1948)
Water Affairs	23 Feb – 4 Apr 1945 (acting:) *Franciscus Cornelis Marie Wijffels* (Cath) (b. Stratum 10 Apr 1899) 4 Apr – 16 May 1945: *Theodoor Philibert Tromp* (Cath) (b. Voorburg 9 Jun 1903)
Education	*Gerrit Bolkestein* (Lib) (see De Geer II)
Commerce, Industry and Agriculture	*Johannes Hendrik Gispen* (b. Baarn 11 Aug 1905)
Shipping and Transport	*James Marnix de Booy* (Cath) (see Gerbrandy I)
Social Affairs	*Franciscus Cornelis Marie Wijffels* (Cath) (see above)
War Effort	*Pieter Sjoerd Gerbrandy* (Anti-rev) (see De Geer II)
War	23 Feb – 4 Apr 1945 (acting:) *James Marnix de Booy* (Cath) (see Gerbrandy I) 4 Apr – 16 May 1945: *Jan Eduard de Quay* (Cath) (b. 's Hertogenbosch 26 Aug 1901)
Navy	*James Marnix de Booy* (Cath) (see Gerbrandy I)
Overseas Territories	*Josef Ignax Julius Maria Schmutzer* (b. Vienna 11 Nov 1882; d. Utrecht 26 Sep 1946)
Without Portfolio	*Edgar Frederik Marie Justin Michiels van Verduynen* (see Gerbrandy I)

24 Jun 1945 – 17 May 1946: Schermerhorn

Prime Minister	*Willem Schermerhorn* (Soc) (b. Akersloot 17 Dec 1894)

Foreign Affairs	24 Jun 1945 – 1 Mar 1946: *Eelco Nicolaas van Kleffens* (see De Geer II) 1 Mar – 17 May 1946: *Jan Herman van Royen* (b. Constantinople 10 Apr 1905)
Home Affairs	*Louis Joseph Maria Beel* (Cath) (see Gerbrandy II)
Justice	*Henri Anthony Melchior Tieleman van Kolfschoten* (Cath) (b. Arnhem 17 Aug 1903)
Finance	*Pieter Lieftinck* (Soc) (b. Muiden 30 Sep 1902)
Education	*Gerardus van der Leeuw* (Soc) (b. The Hague 18 Mar 1890; d. Utrecht 18 Nov 1950)
Commerce and Industry	*H. Vos* (Soc) (b. Tijne 5 Jul 1903)
Shipping	*James Marnix de Booy* (Cath) (see Gerbrandy I)
Transport and Energy	*Theodorus Stephanus Gerardus Johannes Marie van Schaik* (Cath) (b. Maastricht 8 Dec 1888)
Food, Agriculture and Fisheries	*Sicco Leendert Mansholt* (Soc) (b. Ulrum 13 Sep 1908)
Public Works	*Johannes Aleidis Ringers* (b. Alkmaar 2 Jan 1885)
Social Affairs	*Willem Drees* (Soc) (b. Amsterdam 5 Jul 1886)
War Effort	*Willem Schermerhorn* (Soc) (see above)
War	*Johannes Meynen* (Anti-rev) (b. Winsum 13 Apr 1901)
Navy	*James Marnix de Booy* (Cath) (see Gerbrandy I)
Overseas Territories	*Johann Heinrich Adolf Logemann* (Soc) (b. Rotterdam 19 Jan 1892)
Without Portfolio	24 Jun 1945 – 1 Mar 1946: *Jan Herman van Royen* (see above) 1 Mar – 17 May 1946: *Eelco Nicolaas van Kleffens* (see De Geer II)

3 Jul 1946 – 7 Jul 1948: Beel I

Prime Minister	*Louis Joseph Maria Beel* (Cath) (for 1st time) (see Gerbrandy II)
General Affairs	11 Oct 1947 – 7 Jul 1948: *Louis Joseph Maria Beel* (Cath) (see Gerbrandy II)
Foreign Affairs	*Carel Godfried Willem Hendrik, Baron van Boetzelaer van Oosterhout* (b. Amersfoort 17 Nov 1892)
Home Affairs	3 Jul – 15 Sep 1947: *Louis Joseph Maria Beel* (Cath) (see Gerbrandy II) 15 Sep 1947 – 7 Jul 1948: *Petrus Johannes Witteman* (Cath) (b. Nieuwendam 26 Feb 1892)
Justice	*Johannes Hendrikus van Maarseveen* (Cath) (b. Utrecht 3 Aug 1894; d. 18 Nov 1951)

393

Finance	*Pieter Lieftinck* (Soc) (see Schermerhorn)
Education	*Josephus Johannes Gielen* (Cath) (b. Rucphen 26 Sep 1898)
Economic Affairs	3 Jul 1946 – 14 Jan 1948: *Gerardus Wilhelmus Maria Huysmans* (Cath) (see Gerbrandy II) 14 – 21 Jan 1948 (acting:) *Sicco Leendert Mansholt* (Soc) (see Schermerhorn) 21 Jan – 7 Jul 1948: *Johannes Roelof Marie van den Brink* (Cath) (b. Laren 12 Mar 1915)
Transport	*H. Vos* (Soc) (see Schermerhorn)
Food, Agriculture and Fisheries	*Sicco Leendert Mansholt* (Soc) (see Schermerhorn)
Public Works (from 28 Feb 1947: Reconstruction and Housing)	3 Jul – 15 Nov 1946: *Johannes Aleidis Ringers* (see Schermerhorn) 15 Nov 1946 – 28 Feb 1947 (acting:) *H. Vos* (Soc) (see Schermerhorn) 28 Feb 1947 – 1 Mar 1948: *Lambertus Neher* (Soc) (b. Amsterdam 13 Sep 1889) 1 Mar – 7 Jul 1948: *Joris in 't Veld* (Soc) (b. Dubbeldam 5 Jul 1895)
Social Affairs	*Willem Drees* (Soc) (see Schermerhorn)
War	*Alexander Helenus Johannes Leopoldus Fiévez* (Cath) (b. Zutphen 22 Jun 1902; d. The Hague 30 Apr 1949)
Navy	3 Jul – 7 Aug 1946 (acting:) *Alexander Helenus Johannes Leopoldus Fiévez* (Cath) (see above) 7 Aug 1946 – 25 Nov 1947: *Jules Jacob Adriaan Schagen van Leeuwen* (b. Pretoria 28 Aug 1896) 25 Nov 1947 – 7 Jul 1948 (acting:) *Alexander Helenus Johannes Leopoldus Fiévez* (Cath) (see above)
Overseas Territories	*Jan Anne Jonkman* (b. Utrecht 13 Sep 1891)
Without Portfolio	3 Jul 1946 – 1 Jul 1947: *Eelco Nicolaas van Kleffens* (see De Geer II) 10 Nov 1947 – 7 Jul 1948: *Lubertus Götzen* (b. Amsterdam 10 Oct 1894)

7 Aug 1948 – 24 Jan 1951: Drees I

Prime Minister	*Willem Drees* (Soc) (for 1st time) (see Schermerhorn)
General Affairs	*Willem Drees* (Soc) (see Schermerhorn)
Foreign Affairs	*Dirk Ulco Stikker* (Lib) (b. Winschoten 5 Feb 1897)
Home Affairs	7 Aug 1948 – 15 Jun 1949: *Johannes Hendrikus van Maarseveen* (Cath) (see Beel I) 15 – 20 Sep 1949 (acting:) *Josephus Robertus*

	Hendrikus van Schaik (Cath) (see Colijn II)
	20 Sep 1949 – 24 Jan 1951: *Franciscus Gerardus Cornelis Josephus Maria Teulings* (Cath) (b. 's Hertogenbosch 15 Nov 1891)
Justice	7 Aug 1948 – 15 May 1950: *Theodorus Renerus Josephus Wijers* (Cath) (b. Roermond 27 Jan 1891)
	15 May – 10 Jul 1950 (acting:) *Johannes Hendrikus van Maarseveen* (Cath) (see Beel I)
	10 Jul 1950 – 24 Jan 1951: *Anton Arnold Marie Struycken* (Cath) (b. Breda 27 Dec 1906)
Finance	*Pieter Lieftinck* (Soc) (see Schermerhorn)
Education	*Frans Josef Theo Rutten* (Cath) (b. Schinnen 15 Sep 1899)
Economic Affairs	*Johannes Roelof Marie van den Brink* (Cath) (see Beel I)
Transport and	7 Aug – 1 Nov 1948 (acting:) *Josephus Robertus Hendrikus van Schaik* (Cath) (see Colijn II)
Water Affairs	1 Nov 1948 – 24 Jan 1951: *Dirk Gerard Willem Spitzen* (b. Wageningen 18 Mar 1896; d. The Hague 26 Jan 1957)
Food	*Sicco Leendert Mansholt* (Soc) (see Schermerhorn)
Reconstruction and Housing	*Joris in 't Veld* (Soc) (see Beel I)
Social Affairs	*Adolf Marcus Joekes* (Soc) (b. Boea 5 May 1885; d. The Hague 1 Jun 1962)
War	7 Aug 1948 – 16 Oct 1950: *Willem Frederik Schokking* (b. Amsterdam 14 Aug 1900; d. Amsterdam 5 Jul 1960)
	16 Oct 1950 – 24 Jan 1951: *Hendrik Laurentius s' Jacob* (b. Driebergen 5 Apr 1906; d. Voorburg(?) 29 Sep 1967)
Navy	7 Aug 1948 – 16 Oct 1950: *Willem Frederik Schokking* (see above)
	16 Oct 1950 – 24 Jan 1951: *Hendrik Laurentius s' Jacob* (see above)
Overseas Territories	7 Aug 1948 – 14 Feb 1949: *Emmanuel Marie Joseph Antony Sassen* (Cath) (b. 's Hertogenbosch 8 Sep 1911)
	14 Feb 1949 – 24 Jan 1951: *Johannes Hendrikus van Maarseveen* (Cath) (see Beel I)
Without Portfolio	*Lubertus Götzen* (see Beel I)
	Josephus Robertus Hendrikus van Schaik (Cath) (see Colijn II)

15 Mar 1951 - 25 Jun/2 Sep 1952: Drees II

Prime Minister	*Willem Drees* (Soc) (for 2nd time) (see Schermerhorn)
Deputy Prime Minister	*Franciscus Gerardus Cornelis Josephus Maria Teulings* (Cath) (see Drees I)
General Affairs	*Willem Drees* (Soc) (see Schermerhorn)
Foreign Affairs	*Dirk Ulco Stikker* (Lib) (see Drees I)
Home Affairs	15 Mar - 18 Nov 1951: *Johannes Hendrikus van Maarseveen* (Cath) (see Beel I)
	18 Nov - 6 Dec 1951 (acting:) *Franciscus Gerardus Cornelis Josephus Maria Teulings* (Cath) (see Drees I)
	6 Dec 1951 - 25 Jun 1952: *Louis Joseph Maria Beel* (Cath) (see Gerbrandy II)
Justice	*Hendrik Mulderije* (b. Zutphen 4 Jan 1896)
Finance	15 Mar 1951 - 1 Jul 1952: *Pieter Lieftinck* (Soc) (see Schermerhorn)
	1 Jul - 2 Sep 1952: administered by Cabinet under *Willem Drees* (Soc) (see Schermerhorn)
Education	*Frans Josef Theo Rutten* (Cath) (see Drees I)
Economic Affairs	*Johannes Roelof Marie van den Brink* (Cath) (see Beel I)
Transport and Water Affairs	*Hendrik Hermanus Wemmers* (b. Rotterdam 1 Oct 1897)
Agriculture	*Sicco Leendert Mansholt* (Soc) (see Schermerhorn)
Reconstruction and Housing	*Joris in 't Veld* (Soc) (see Beel I)
Social Affairs	*Adolf Marcus Joekes* (Soc) (see Drees I)
War	*Cornelis Staf* (b. Ede 23 Apr 1905; d. 1973)
Navy	*Cornelis Staf* (see above)
Overseas Territories	15 - 30 Mar 1951 (acting:) *Willem Drees* (Soc) (see Schermerhorn)
	30 Mar 1951 - 25 Jun 1952: *Leonard Antoon Hubert Peters* (Cath) (b. Well 8 Jul 1900)
Without Portfolio	*Franciscus Gerardus Cornelis Josephus Maria Teulings* (Cath) (see Drees I)
	Augustinus Hendrikus Martinus Albregts (Cath) (b. Vught 22 Nov 1900)

2 Sep 1952 - 25 Jun/13 Oct 1956: Drees III

Prime Minister	*Willem Drees* (Soc) (for 3rd time) (see Schermerhorn)
Deputy Prime Minister	*Louis Joseph Maria Beel* (Cath) (see Gerbrandy II)

General Affairs	*Willem Drees* (Soc) (see Schermerhorn)
Foreign Affairs	*Johan Willem Beyen* (b. Utrecht 2 May 1897; d. 29 Apr 1976)
Home Affairs	2 Sep 1952 – 7 Jul 1956: *Louis Joseph Maria Beel* (Cath) (see Gerbrandy II) 7 Jul – 13 Oct 1956 (acting:) *Julius Christiaan van Oven* (Soc) (b. Dordrecht 17 Nov 1881; d. Leiden 16 Mar 1963)
Justice	2 Sep 1952 – 4 Feb 1956: *Leendert Antonie Donker* (Soc) (b. Almkerk 7 Sep 1899; d. Rotterdam 4 Feb 1956) 4 – 15 Feb 1956 (acting:) *Louis Joseph Maria Beel* (Cath) (see Gerbrandy II) 15 Feb – 25 Jun 1956: *Julius Christiaan van Oven* (Soc) (see above)
Finance	*Johan van de Kieft* (Soc) (b. Amsterdam 21 May 1884)
Education	*Joseph Maria Laurens Theo Cals* (Cath) (b. Roermond 18 Jul 1914)
Economic Affairs	*Jelle Zijlstra* (Anti-rev) (b. Oosterbierum 27 Aug 1918)
Transport and Water Affairs	*Jacob Algera* (Anti-rev) (b. Leeuweradeel 28 Mar 1902)
Agriculture	*Sicco Leendert Mansholt* (Soc) (see Schermerhorn)
Public Works	*Adrianus Cornelis de Bruijn* (Cath) (b. Utrecht 5 Nov 1887)
Social Affairs	*Jacobus Gerardus Suurhoff* (Soc) (b. Amsterdam 23 Jul 1905; d. night of 13/14 Mar 1967)
Social Work (new post split off from Social Affairs)	9 Sep 1952 – 25 Jun 1956: *Frans Joseph Fritz Marie van Thiel* (Cath) (b. Helmond 19 Dec 1906)
Reconstruction and Housing	*Herman Bernard Jan Witte* (Cath) (b. Harlingen 18 Aug 1909)
War	*Cornelis Staf* (see Drees II)
Navy	*Cornelis Staf* (see Drees II)
Overseas Territories	2 Sep 1952 – 18 Jul 1956: *Willem Jan Arend Kernkamp* (b. Edam 18 Jul 1899; d. Utrecht 18 Jul 1956) 18 Jul – 13 Oct 1956 (acting:) *Cornelis Staf* (see Drees II)
Without Portfolio	*Joseph Maria Antoine Hubert Luns* (Cath) (b. Rotterdam 28 Aug 1911)

397

13 Oct 1956 - 12 Dec 1958: Drees IV

Prime Minister	*Willem Drees* (Soc) (for 4th time) (see Schermerhorn)
Deputy Prime Minister	29 Oct 1956 - 12 Dec 1958: *Anton Arnold Marie Struycken* (Cath) (see Drees I)
General Affairs	*Willem Drees* (Soc) (see Schermerhorn)
Foreign Affairs	*Joseph Maria Antoine Hubert Luns* (Cath) (see Drees III)
Home Affairs	13 - 29 Oct 1956 (acting:) *Jacobus Gerardus Suurhoff* (Soc) (see Drees III) 29 Oct 1956 - 12 Dec 1958: *Anton Arnold Marie Struycken* (Cath) (see Drees I)
Justice	*Ivo Samkalden* (Soc) (b. Rotterdam 10 Aug 1912)
Finance	*Hendrik Jan Hofstra* (Soc) (b. Amsterdam 28 Sep 1904)
Education	*Joseph Maria Laurens Theo Cals* (Cath) (see Drees III)
Economic Affairs	*Jelle Zijlstra* (Anti-rev) (see Drees III)
Transport and Water Affairs	13 Oct 1956 - 10 Oct 1958: *Jacob Algera* (Anti-rev) (see Drees III) 10 Oct - 1 Nov 1958 (acting:) *Herman Bernard Jan Witte* (Cath) (see Drees III) 1 Nov - 12 Dec 1958: *Johannes van Aartsen* (Anti-rev) (b. Amsterdam 15 Sep 1909)
Agriculture	13 Oct 1956 - 1 Jan 1958: *Sicco Leendert Mansholt* (Soc) (see Schermerhorn) 1 - 11 Jan 1958 (acting:) *Cornelis Staf* (see Drees II) 11 Jan - 12 Dec 1958: *Anne Vondeling* (Soc) (b. Appelscha 2 Mar 1916)
Social Affairs	*Jacobus Gerardus Suurhoff* (Soc) (see Drees III)
Social Work	*Margaretha Albertina Maria Klompé* (Cath) (b. Arnhem 16 Aug 1912)
Reconstruction and Housing	*Herman Bernard Jan Witte* (Cath) (see Drees III)
War	*Cornelis Staf* (see Drees II)
Navy	*Cornelis Staf* (see Drees II)
Overseas Territories	13 Oct 1956 - 16 Feb 1957 (acting:) *Cornelis Staf* (see Drees II) 16 Feb 1957 - 12 Dec 1958: *Gerardus Philippus Helders* (b. Rotterdam 9 Mar 1905)

22 Dec 1958 - 12 Mar 1959: Beel II

Prime Minister	*Louis Joseph Maria Beel* (Cath) (for 2nd time) (see Gerbrandy II)
Deputy Prime Minister	*Anton Arnold Marie Struycken* (Cath) (see Drees I)
General Affairs	*Louis Joseph Maria Beel* (Cath) (see Gerbrandy II)
Foreign Affairs	*Joseph Maria Antoine Hubert Luns* (Cath) (see Drees III)
Home Affairs	*Anton Arnold Marie Struycken* (Cath) (see Drees I)
Justice	(acting:) *Anton Arnold Marie Struycken* (Cath) (see Drees I)
Finance	(acting:) *Jelle Zijlstra* (Anti-rev) (see Drees III)
Education	*Joseph Maria Laurens Theo Cals* (Cath) (see Drees III)
Economic Affairs	*Jelle Zijlstra* (Anti-rev) (see Drees III)
Transport and Water Affairs	*Johannes van Aartsen* (Anti-rev) (see Drees IV)
Agriculture	(acting:) *Cornelis Staf* (see Drees II)
Social Affairs	(acting:) *Louis Joseph Maria Beel* (Cath) (see Gerbrandy II)
Social Work	*Margaretha Albertina Maria Klompé* (Cath) (see Drees IV)
Reconstruction and Housing	*Herman Bernard Jan Witte* (Cath) (see Drees III)
War and Navy	*Cornelis Staf* (see Drees II)
Overseas Territories	*Gerardus Philippus Helders* (see Drees IV)

19 May 1959 - 23 Dec 1960: Quay I

Prime Minister	*Jan Eduard de Quay* (Cath) (for 1st time) (see Gerbrandy II)
Deputy Prime Minister	*Hendrik Albertus Korthals* (Lib) (b. Dordrecht 3 Jul 1911)
General Affairs	*Jan Eduard de Quay* (Cath) (see Gerbrandy II)
Foreign Affairs	*Joseph Maria Antoine Hubert Luns* (Cath) (see Drees III)
Home Affairs	*Edzo Hendrik Toxopeus* (Lib) (b. Amersfoort 19 Feb 1918)
Justice	*Albert Christiaan Willem Beerman* (b. Amsterdam 29 Jan 1901)
Finance	*Jelle Zijlstra* (Anti-rev) (see Drees III)

Education	*Joseph Maria Laurens Theo Cals* (Cath) (see Drees III)
Economic Affairs	*Jan Willem de Pous* (b. Aalsmeer 23 Jan 1920)
Transport and Water Affairs	*Hendrik Albertus Korthals* (Lib) (see above)
Agriculture and Fisheries	*Victor Gérard Marie Marijnen* (Cath) (b. Arnhem 21 Feb 1917; d. 5 Apr 1975)
Social Affairs	*Charles Joan Marie Adriaan van Rooy* (Cath) (b. Rotterdam 23 Jan 1912)
Social Work	*Margaretha Albertina Maria Klompé* (Cath) (see Drees IV)
Housing	*Johannes van Aartsen* (Anti-rev) (see Drees IV)
Defence	19 May – 31 Jul 1959: *Sidney James van den Bergh* (Lib) (b. Rotterdam 25 Oct 1898)
	31 Jul – 4 Sep 1959 (acting:) *Jan Eduard de Quay* (Cath) (see Gerbrandy II)
	4 Sep 1959 – 23 Dec 1960: *Simon Hendrik Visser* (Lib) (b. Texel 3 Jan 1908)
Overseas Territories	19 May – 1 Sep 1959 (acting:) *Hendrik Albertus Korthals* (Lib) (see above)
	1 Sep 1959: post abolished

2 Jan 1961 – 15 May 1963: Quay II

Prime Minister	*Jan Eduard de Quay* (Cath) (for 2nd time) (see Gerbrandy II)
Social Affairs	2 Jan – 3 Jul 1961: *Charles Joan Marie Adriaan van Rooy* (Cath) (see Quay I)
	3 – 17 Jul 1961 (acting:) *Victor Gérard Marie Marijnen* (Cath) (see Quay I)
	17 Jul 1961 – 14 May 1963: *Gerardus Matheus Johannes Veldkamp* (Cath) (b. Breda 27 Jun 1921)
	Other ministers continued in same offices as previous cabinet

24 Jul 1963 – 26 Feb 1965: Marijnen

Prime Minister	*Victor Gérard Marie Marijnen* (Cath) (see Quay I)
Deputy Prime Minister	*Barend Willem Biesheuvel* (Anti-rev) (b. 5 Apr 1920)
General Affairs	*Victor Gérard Marie Marijnen* (Cath) (see Quay I)
Foreign Affairs	*Joseph Maria Antoine Hubert Luns* (Cath) (see Drees III)
Home Affairs	*Edzo Hendrik Toxopeus* (Lib) (see Quay I)

Justice	*Yvo Scholten* (b. 1 Feb 1918)
Finance	*Hendrikus Johannes Witteveen* (Lib) (b. Zeist 12 Jun 1921)
Education	*Theodorus Hendrikus Bot* (Cath) (b. Dordrecht 20 Jul 1911)
Economic Affairs	*Jacobus Eye Andriessen* (b. 25 Jul 1928)
Transport and Water Affairs	*Johannes van Aartsen* (Anti-rev) (see Drees IV)
Agriculture and Fisheries	*Barend Willem Biesheuvel* (Anti-rev) (see above)
Social Affairs	*Gerardus Matheus Johannes Veldkamp* (Cath) (see Quay II)
Social Work	*Johanna Frederika Schouwenaar* (Lib) (b. Rotterdam 3 May 1909)
Housing	*Pieter Clemens Wilhelmus Maria Bogaers* (Cath) (b. Cuyck 2 Jul 1924)
Defence	*Petrus Josef Sietse de Jong* (Cath) (b. Apeldoorn 3 Apr 1915)

27 Apr 1965 – 14 Oct 1966: Cals

Prime Minister	*Joseph Maria Laurens Theo Cals* (Cath) (see Drees III)
Deputy Prime Ministers	*Anne Vondeling* (Soc) (see Drees IV)
	Barend Willem Biesheuvel (Anti-rev) (see Marijnen)
General Affairs	*Joseph Maria Laurens Theo Cals* (Cath) (see Drees III)
Foreign Affairs	*Joseph Maria Antoine Hubert Luns* (Cath) (see Drees III)
Home Affairs	27 Apr 1965 – 29 Aug 1966: *Jan Smallenbroek* (Anti-rev) (b. Assen 21 Feb 1909)
	29 Aug 1966 – 14 Oct 1966: *Pieter Jacobus Verdam* (b. Amsterdam 15 Jan 1915)
Justice	*Ivo Samkalden* (Soc) (see Drees IV)
Finance	*Anne Vondeling* (Soc) (see Drees IV)
Education	*Isaac (Arend) Diepenhorst* (Cath) (b. Rotterdam 18 Jul 1916)
Cultural Affairs	*Maarten Vrolijk* (b. Scheveningen 14 May 1919)
Economic Affairs	*Joop M. den Uyl* (b. Hilversum 9 Aug 1919)
Transport	*Jacobus Gerardus Suurhoff* (Soc) (see Drees)
Agriculture	*Barend Willem Biesheuvel* (Anti-rev) (see Marijnen)
Social Affairs	*Gerardus Matheus Johannes Veldkamp* (Cath) (see Quay I)

401

NETHERLANDS

Housing	*Pieter Clemens Wilhelmus Maria Bogaers* (Cath) (see Marijnen)
Defence	*Petrus Josef Sietse de Jong* (Cath) (see Marijnen)
Without Portfolio (Aid to Under-developed Territories)	*Theodorus Hendrikus Bot* (Cath) (see Marijnen)

22 Nov 1966 - 15 Feb/3 Apr 1967: Zijlstra

Prime Minister	*Jelle Zijlstra* (Anti-rev) (see Drees III)
Deputy Prime Minister	*Jan Eduard de Quay* (Cath) (see Gerbrandy II)
Foreign Affairs	*Joseph Maria Antoine Hubert Luns* (Cath) (see Drees III)
Home Affairs	*Pieter Jacobus Verdam* (Anti-rev) (see Cals)
Justice	*Anton Arnold Marie Struycken* (Cath) (see Drees I)
Finance	*Jelle Zijlstra* (Anti-rev) (see Drees III)
Education and Science	*Isaac (Arend) Diepenhorst* (Anti-rev) (see Cals)
Cultural Affairs	*Margaretha Albertina Maria Klompé* (Cath) (see Drees IV)
Economic Affairs	*Johannes A. Bakker* (Anti-rev) (b. Bolsward 27 May 1921)
Transport and Water Affairs	*Jan Eduard de Quay* (Cath) (see Gerbrandy II)
Agriculture and Food	*Barend Willem Biesheuvel* (Anti-rev) (see Marijnen)
Social Affairs and Health	*Gerardus Matheus Johannes Veldkamp* (Cath) (see Quay II)
Housing	*Herman Bernard Jan Witte* (Cath) (see Drees III)
Development Aid	*Theodorus Hendrikus Bot* (Cath) (see Marijnen)
Defence	*Petrus Josef Sietse de Jong* (Cath) (see Marijnen)

3 Apr 1967 - 29 Apr/1 Jul 1971: Jong

Prime Minister	*Petrus Josef Sietse de Jong* (Cath) (see Marijnen)
First Deputy Prime Minister	*Hendrikus Johannes Witteveen* (Lib) (see Marijnen)
Second Deputy Prime Minister	*Johannes A. Bakker* (Anti-rev) (see Zijlstra)
Foreign Affairs	*Joseph Maria Antoine Hubert Luns* (Cath) (see Drees III)

402

Home Affairs	*Hendrik Karel Jan Beernink* (b. Maarssen 2 Feb 1910)
Justice	*Carel Hendrik Frederik Polak* (Lib) (b. Rotterdam 2 Sep 1909)
Finance	*Hendrikus Johannes Witteveen* (Lib) (see Marijnen)
Education and Science	*Gerard H. Veringa* (Cath) (b. Groningen 13 Apr 1924)
Cultural Affairs	*Margaretha Albertina Maria Klompé* (Cath) (see Drees IV)
Economic Affairs	3 Apr 1967 – 5 Jan 1970: *Leo de Block* (Cath) (b. The Hague 14 Aug 1904)
	14 Jan 1970 – 1 Jul 1971: *Roelof J. Nelissen* (Cath) (b. Hoofdplaat 4 Apr 1931)
Transport and Water Affairs	*Johannes A. Bakker* (Anti-rev) (see Zijlstra)
Agriculture and Fisheries	*Pierre Joseph Lardinois* (Cath) (b. Noorbeek 13 Aug 1924)
Social Affairs	*Bouke Roolvink* (Anti-rev) (b. Wijtaard 31 Jan 1912)
Housing	*Willem Fredrik Schut* (Anti-rev) (b. Amsterdam 21 Aug 1920)
Defence	*Willem den Toom* (Lib) (b. Rotterdam 11 Jul 1911)
Without Portfolio (Development Aid)	*Berend Jan Udink* (CHU) (b. Deventer 12 Feb 1926)

6 Jul 1971 – 29 Nov 1972/11 May 1973: Biesheuvel

Prime Minister	*Barend Willem Biesheuvel* (Anti-rev) (see Marijnen)
First Deputy Prime Minister	*Roelof J. Nelissen* (Cath) (see Jong)
Second Deputy Prime Minister	*Willem Jacob Geertsema* (Lib) (b. Utrecht 18 Oct 1918)
Foreign Affairs	*Wilhelmus Klaes Nobert Schmelzer* (Cath) (b. Rotterdam 22 Mar 1921)
Home Affairs	*Willem Jacob Geertsema* (Lib) (see above)
Justice	*Andreas A. M. van Agt* (Cath) (b. Geldrop 2 Feb 1931)
Finance	*Roelof J. Nelissen* (Cath) (see Jong)
Education and Science	*Christian van Veen* (CHU) (b. Barneveld 19 Dec 1922)
Culture, Recreation and Welfare	*P. J. Engels* (Cath)
Economic Affairs	*Hargert Langman* (Lib) (b. 1931)

403

Transport and Water Affairs	6 Jul 1971 – 21 Jul 1972: *Willem Drees* (DS-70) (see Schermerhorn) 9 Aug 1972 – 11 May 1973: *Berend Jan Udink* (CHU) (see Jong)
Agriculture and Fisheries	6 Jul 1971 – 1 Jan 1973: *Pierre Joseph Lardinois* (Cath) (see Jong) 1 Jan – 11 May 1973: *J. Boersma* (Anti-rev)
Social Affairs	*J. Boersma* (Anti-rev) (see above)
Housing and Town Planning	*Berend Jan Udink* (CHU) (see Jong)
Defence	*Henri Johan de Koster* (Lib) (b. Leiden 11 May 1914)
Public Health and Environment	*L. B. J. Stuyt* (Cath) (b. Amsterdam 16 Jun 1914)
Without Portfolio (Development Aid)	*C. Boertien* (Anti-rev)
Without Portfolio (Scientific Research)	6 Jul 1971 – 21 Jul 1972: *Jonkheer M. L. de Brauw* (DS-70) (b. The Hague 14 Sep 1925) 9 Aug 1972 – 11 May 1973: *Christian van Veen* (CHU) (see above)

from 11 May 1973: Den Uyl

Prime Minister	*Joop M. den Uyl* (PvdA) (see Cals)
Deputy Prime Minister	*Andreas A. M. van Agt* (KVP) (see Biesheuvel)
Foreign Affairs	*Max van der Stoel* (PvdA) (b. Voorschoten 3 Aug 1924)
Home Affairs	*William Friedrich de Gaay Fortman* (ARP) (b. Amsterdam 8 May 1911)
General Affairs	*Joop den Uyl* (PvdA) (see above)
Justice	*Andreas A. M. van Agt* (KVP) (see Biesheuvel)
Finance	*Willem Frederick Duisenberg* (PvdA) (b. Heerenveen 9 Jul 1935)
Education and Science	*Josephus Antonius van Kemenade* (PvdA) (b. Amsterdam 6 Mar 1937)
Culture, Recreation and Social Work	*Henri Willem van Doorn* (PPR) (b. The Hague 6 Oct 1915)
Economic Affairs	*Rudolph Frans Marie Lubbers* (KVP) (b. Rotterdam 7 May 1939)
Transport and Water Affairs	*Theodorus Engelbertus (Tjerk) Westerterp* (KVP) (b. Rotterdam 2 Dec 1930)
Agriculture and Fisheries	11 May – 1 Nov 1973: *T. Brouwer* (KVP) from 1 Nov 1973: *Alfons Petrus Johannes Mathildus*

Maria van der Stee (b. Terheyden 30 Jul 1928)

Social Affairs	Jacob Boersma (ARP) (see Biesheuvel)
Housing and Town Planning	Johannes Petrus Adrianus Gruijters (D-66) (b. Helmond 30 June 1931)
Defence	Henk Vredeling (PvdA) (b. 20 Nov 1924)
Public Health and Environment	Irene Vorrink (PvdA) (b. The Hague 7 Jan 1918)
Without Portfolio (Development Aid)	Johannes Pieter Pronk (PvdA) (b. The Hague 16 Mar 1940)
Without Portfolio (Scientific Research)	Fokele Hendrik Pieter Trip (PPR) (b. Amersfoot 10 Oct 1921)

New Zealand

HEADS OF STATE

Governors-General

1 Dec 1929	Charles Bathurst Bledisloe (from 1935: 1st Viscount Bledisloe) (b. Lydney House, Gloucestershire, 21 Sep 1867; d. 3 Jul 1958)
12 Apr 1935	George Vere Arundell Monckton-Arundell, 8th Viscount Galway (b. 24 May 1882; d. 27 Mar 1943)
5 Oct 1940/22 Feb 1941	Sir Cyril (Louis Norton) Newall (from 1946: 1st Baron Newall) (b. 15 Feb 1886; d. 30 Nov 1963)
22 Feb/9 Sep 1946	Sir Bernard Cyril Freyberg (from 1951: 1st Baron Freyberg) (b. London 1889; d. Windsor 4 Jul 1963)
2 Dec 1952 – 1957	Sir Willoughby Norrie (from 1957: Baron Norrie) (b. 26 Sep 1893; d. 25 May 1977)
1957	Charles John Lyttelton, 10th Viscount Cobham (b. 8 Aug 1900)
9 Nov 1962 – 1967	Sir Bernard Fergusson (b. London 6 May 1911)
Sep 1967 – 1972	Sir Arthur Porritt (b. Wanganui, New Zealand, 10 Aug 1900)
from Sep 1972	Sir (Edward) Denis Blundell (b. Wellington 29 May 1907)

MEMBERS OF GOVERNMENT

Prime Ministers

7 Dec 1928 – 15 May 1930	*Sir Joseph Ward* (for 2nd time) (b. Emerald Hill, Melbourne, 26 Apr 1856; d. Christchurch 8 Jul 1930)*
May 1930	*George William Forbes* (b. Lyttelton, New Zealand, 12 Mar 1869; d. Wellington 18 May 1947)
27 Nov 1935 – 26 Mar 1940	*Michael Joseph Savage* (b. Benalla, Victoria, 7 Mar 1872; d. 26 Mar 1940)
1 Apr 1940	*Peter Fraser* (for 1st time) (b. Fearn, Scotland, 1884; d. Wellington 12 Dec 1950)
22 Feb 1944	*Peter Fraser* (for 2nd time)
9 Jun 1947	*Peter Fraser* (for 3rd time)
8 Dec 1949	*Sydney George Holland* (b. Canterbury, New Zealand, 18 Oct 1893; d. 4 Aug 1961)
20 Sep 1957	*Walter Nash* (b. Kidderminster 12 Dec 1822; d. Wellington 4 Jun 1968)
12 Dec 1960	*Keith Jacka Holyoake* (b. Pahiatua 11 Feb 1904)
7 Feb 1972	*Sir John Ross Marshall* (b. Wellington 5 Mar 1912)
8 Dec 1972 – 31 Aug 1974	*Norman E. Kirk* (b. 1933; d. 31 Aug 1974)
6 Sep 1974	*Wallace Edward Rowling* (b. Motheha 15 Nov 1927)
from 12 Dec 1975	*Robert David Muldoon* (b. Auckland 21 Sep 1921)

Nicaragua

HEADS OF STATE

Presidents

1 Jan 1929 – 31 Dec 1932	*José María Moncada* (b. 1867; d. 1945)
1 Jan 1933	*Juan Bautista Sacasa* (for 2nd time) (b. 21 Dec 1874; d. 1946)*

*For earlier career see vol. 2

6 Jun – 18 Dec 1936	*Carlos Brenes Jarquin*
1 Jan 1937	*Anastasio Somoza García* (for 1st time) (b. 1 Feb 1896; d. 29 Sep 1956) from 1944 Dictator
1 – 26 May 1947	*Leonardo Arguello* (b. 1875; d. Mexico City 15 Dec 1947)
28 May 1947	*Benjamín Lascayo Sacasa* (b. 1884(?); d. 4 May 1959)
15 Aug 1947 – 6 May 1950	*Victor Manuel Román y Reyes* (b. 1873; d. 6 May 1950)
21 May 1950	*Anastasio Somoza García* (for 2nd time)
29 Sep 1956	*Luis Somoza Debayle*, son (for 1st time) (b. 18 Nov 1922; d. Managua 13 Apr 1967)
1 May 1957	*Luis Somoza Debayle* (for 2nd time)
1 May 1963	*René Schick Gutiérrez* (b. Managua 1910; d. 3 Aug 1966)
3 Aug 1966	*Lorenzo Guerrero Gutiérrez* (b. Granada 13 Nov 1900)
1 May 1967	*Anastasio Somoza Debayle*, son of Anastasio Somoza García (for 1st time) (b. Leon 5 Dec 1925)
1 May 1972	Triumvirate: *Roberto Martínez Laclayo* *Alfonso Lobo Cordero* *Fernando Aguero Rocha* (b. Managua 11 Jun 1917)
from 1 Dec 1974	*Anastasio Somoza Debayle* (for 2nd time)

Niger

18 Dec 1958	Member of French Community
3 Aug 1960	Left French Community

HEADS OF STATE

Presidents and Prime Ministers

10 Nov 1960	*Hamani (Alhaji) Diori* (b. Soudoure 6 Jun 1916) Prime Minister from 3 Nov 1960
from 15 Apr 1974	*Seyni Kountché* (b. Fandou 1931)

Nigeria

1 Oct 1960	Independence from Great Britain
1 Oct 1963	Republic

HEADS OF STATE

Governor-General

1 Oct 1960 – 1 Oct 1963	*Benjamin Nnamdi Azikiwe* (b. Zungeru 16 Nov 1904)

Presidents

1 Oct 1963	*Benjamin Nnamdi Azikiwe* (see Governor-General)
17 Jan 1966	*Johnson Aguiyi-Ironsi* (b. 3 Mar 1924; d. Iwo 3(?) Aug 1966) Military Dictator
1 Aug 1966	*Yakubu Gowon* (b. Lur Pankshin Division, Benue Plateau State, 19 Oct 1934) Military Dictator
from 29 Jul 1975	*Murtala Ramat Mohammed* (b. Jun 1937; d. Lagos (assassinated) 13 Feb 1976)

MEMBERS OF GOVERNMENT

Prime Ministers

1 Oct 1960 – Jan 1965	*Al-haji Sir Abu Bakar Tafawa Balewa* (for 1st time) (b. Bauchi Dec 1912; d. 15 Jan 1966)
7 Jan 1965	*Al-haji Sir Abu Bakar Tafawa Balewa* (for 2nd time)
16 Jan 1966	*Johnson Aguiyi-Ironsi* (see Presidents)
from 1 Aug 1966	President also Prime Minister

Northern Ireland

HEADS OF STATE

Governors

11 Dec 1922	*James Albert Edward Hamilton, 3rd Duke of Abercorn* (b. London 30 Nov 1869; d. 12 Sep 1953)
7 Sep 1945	*William Spencer Leveson-Gower, 4th Earl Granville* (b. 11 Jul 1880; d. 25 Jun 1953)
1 Dec 1952	*John de Vere Loder Wakehurst* (b. London 5 Feb 1895; d. London 30 Oct 1970)
1 Dec 1964	*John Maxwell Erskine, 1st Baron Erskine of Rerrick* (b. 14 Dec 1893)
2 Dec 1968 – 19 Jul 1973	*Ralph Francis Alnwick Grey, Baron Grey of Naunton* (b. 15 Apr 1910)
19 Jul 1973	Office abolished

MEMBERS OF GOVERNMENT

Prime Ministers

Jun 1921 – 24 Nov 1940	*Sir James Craig, bart* (from 1927: *1st Viscount Craigavon*) (b. Sydenham, Belfast, 8 Jan 1871; d. Glencraig, County Down, 24 Nov 1940)
27 Nov 1940	*John Miller Andrews* (b. 17 Jul 1871; d. Cumber 5 Aug 1956)
Apr 1943	*Sir Basil Stanlake Brooke* (from 1952: *1st Viscount Brookeborough*) (b. 9 Jun 1888; d. 18 Aug 1973)
26 Mar 1963 – 30 Apr 1969	*Terence Marne O'Neill* (from 1970: *Baron O'Neill of the Maine*) (b. 10 Sep 1914)
3 May 1969 – 20 Mar 1971	*James Dawson Chichester-Clark* (from Jun 1971: *Baron Moyola*) (b. Castledawson 12 Feb 1923)
23 Mar 1971 – 30 Mar 1972	*(Arthur) Brian (Deane) Faulkner* (from 9 Feb 1977: *Baron Faulkner of Downpatrick*) (for 1st time) (b. 18 Feb 1921; d. Saintfield 3 Mar 1977)
30 Mar 1972 – 31 Dec 1973	Direct rule by the United Kingdom
1 Jan – May 1974	*(Arthur) Brian (Deane) Faulkner* (for 2nd time) Chief Executive
May 1974	Direct rule resumed

409

Norway

HEADS OF STATE

Kings

House of Oldenburg

7 Nov 1905	*Haakon VII*, brother of King Christian X of Denmark (b. 3 Aug 1872)
from 21 Sep 1957	*Olaf V*, son (b. Sandringham, England, 2 Jul 1903)

MEMBERS OF GOVERNMENT

Prime Ministers

15 Feb 1928 – 9 May 1931	*Johan Ludwig Mowinckel* (for 2nd time) (b. Bergen 22 Oct 1870; d. New York 30 Sep 1943)*
11 May 1931 – 5 Mar 1932	*Peter Ludwig Kolstad* (b. 28 Nov 1878; d. 5 Mar 1932)
14 Mar 1932 – 25 Feb 1933	*Jens Hundseid* (b. 6 May 1883)
2 Mar 1933 – 16 Mar 1935	*Johan Ludwig Mowinckel* (for 3rd time)
19 Mar 1935 – 9 Apr 1940	*Johann Nygaardsvold* (b. 6 Sep 1879; d. 13 Mar 1952)
15/24 Apr 1940 – 9 May 1945	*Vidkun Quisling* (b. 18 Jul 1887; d. 24 Oct 1945) Head of Administrative Council, then of National Government
24 Apr 1940 – 30 Apr 1945	*Josef Terboven* (b. Essen 23 May 1898; d. Oslo 11 May 1945 (Reich Commissioner)
9 May 1945	*Einar Gerhardsen* (Soc) (for 1st time) (b. 10 May 1897)
8/26 Jun 1945 – 13 Nov 1951	*Einar Gerhardsen* (Soc) (for 2nd time)
13/17 Nov 1951 – 14 Jan 1955	*Oscar Torp* (b. 8 Jan 1893; d. 1 May 1958)
22 Jan 1955 – 23 Aug 1963	*Einar Gerhardsen* (Soc) (for 3rd time)

*For earlier career see vol. 2

410

27 Aug 1963	*John Lyng* (Cons) (b. Drontheim 22 Aug 1905)
25 Sep 1963	*Einar Gerhardsen* (Soc) (for 4th time)
12 Oct 1965	*Per Borten* (Centre) (b. Fla, Gaudal, 1913)
16 Mar 1971	*Trygve Martin Bratteli* (for 1st time) (b. Nøtterøy 11 Jan 1910)
17 Oct 1972	*Lars Korvald* (b. Nedre Eiker 29 Apr 1916)
from 15 Oct 1973	*Trygve Martin Bratteli* (for 2nd time)

Foreign Ministers

15 Feb 1928 – 8 May 1931	*Johan Ludwig Mowinckel* (for 3rd time) (see Prime Ministers)*
12 May 1931 – 24 Feb 1933	*Birger Braadland* (b. Idd 1879)
3 Mar 1933 – 16 Mar 1935	*Johan Ludwig Mowinckel* (for 4th time)
20 Mar 1935	*Halvdan Koht* (b. Tromsø 7 Jul 1873; d. Oslo 12 Dec 1965) from May/Jun 1940 in exile in London
22 Feb 1941	*Trygve Lie* (b. Grogud 16 Jul 1896; d. Geilo 30 Dec 1968) until May 1945 in exile in London
1 Feb 1946 – 23 Aug 1963	*Halvard Lange* (Soc) (for 1st time) (b. Oslo 16 Sep 1902; d. Oslo 19 May 1970)
27 Aug 1963	*Erling Wikborg* (Cons) (b. Drammen 1894)
25 Sep 1963	*Halvard Lange* (Soc) (for 2nd time)
12 Oct 1965	*John Lyng* (Cons) (see Prime Ministers)
22 May 1970	*Svenn Stray* (Cons) (b. 11 Feb 1922)
16 Mar 1971	*Andreas Cappelen* (b. Vang 31 Jan 1915)
18 Oct 1972	*Dagsinn Vårvik* (b. Leinstrand 8 Jun 1924)
from 15 Oct 1973	*Knut Frydenlund* (b. Drammen 31 Mar 1927)

Oyo

See vol. 1.

*For earlier career see vol. 2

Pakistan

HEADS OF STATE

Governors-General

15 Aug 1947	*Mohammad Ali Jinnah* (b. Karachi 1876; d. Karachi 11 Sep 1948)
11 Sep 1948	*Khawaja Nazimuddin* (b. Dacca 19 Jul 1894; d. Dacca 22 Oct 1964)
17 Oct 1951 – 6 Aug 1955	*Ghulam Mohammad* (b. 1895(?); d. Karachi 29 Aug 1956)
7 Aug 1955 – 5 Mar 1956	(acting:) *Iskander Mirza* (b. Murchidabad 13 Nov 1899; d. London 13 Nov 1969)

Presidents

4/23 Mar 1956	*Iskander Mirza* (see Governors-General)
27 Oct 1958 – 25 Mar 1969	*Mohammad Ayub Khan* (b. Abbotabad 14 May 1907; d. 20 Apr 1974)
31 Mar 1969	*Agha Muhammad Yahya Khan* (b. Peshawar 4 Feb 1917)
20 Dec 1971	*Zulfikar Ali Bhutto* (b. Larkhana, Sind, 5 Jan 1928)
from 14 Aug 1973	*Fazal Elahi Chaudhry* (b. Punjab 1 Jan 1904)

MEMBERS OF GOVERNMENT

Prime Ministers

15 Aug 1947 – 16 Oct 1951	*Liaqat Ali Khan* (b. Karnal, East Punjab, 1 Oct 1895; d. Rawalpindi 16 Oct 1951)
17 Oct 1951	*Khawaja Nazimuddin* (see Governors-General)
18 Apr 1953 – 24 Oct 1954	*Mohammad Ali* (for 1st time) (b. Bogra, East Bengal, 19 Oct 1909; d. 23 Jan 1963)
27 Oct 1954 – 7 Aug 1955	*Mohammad Ali* (for 2nd time)
11 Aug 1955 – 8 Sep 1956	*Chaudry Mohammad Ali* (b. 1905)
12 Sep 1956 – 11 Oct 1957	*Husain Shahid Suhrawardi* (b. Midnapur, Bengal, 1893; e. Beirut 5 Eec 1563)

17 Oct – 11 Dec 1957	*Ismail Chundrigar* (b. 1897; d. London 25 Sep 1960)
16 Dec 1957 – 8 Oct 1958	*Malik Feroz Khan Nton* (b. 7 May 1893; d. Lahore 9 Dec 1970)
26 – 29 Oct 1958	*Mohammad Ayub Khan* (see Presidents)
29 Oct 1958 – 7 Dec 1971	Post of Prime Minister abolished and Presidential system introduced
7 Dec 1971	*Nurul Amin* (b. 1894)
from 24 Dec 1971	*Zulfikar Ali Bhutto* (see Presidents)

Foreign Ministers

19 Jul/ 14 Aug 1947	*Liaqat Ali Khan* (see Prime Ministers)
28 Dec 1947 – 24 Oct 1954	*Sir Chaudhury Muhammad Zafrullah Khan* (b. Sialkot 6 Feb 1893)
27 Oct 1954 – 7 Aug 1955	*Mohammad Ali* (for 1st time) (see Prime Ministers)
11 Aug 1955 – 8 Sep 1956	*Chaudry Mohammad Ali* (see Prime Ministers)
12 Sep 1956 – Oct 1958	*Malik Feroz Khan Noon* (see Prime Ministers)
28 Oct 1958 – 7 Jun 1962	*Manzoor Qadir*
8 Jun 1962 – 23 Jan 1963	*Mohahmad Ali* (for 2 d time)
24 Jan 1963 – 20 Jul 1966	*Zulfikar Ali Bhutto* (see Presidents)
20 Jul 1966 – 3 Jan 1968	*Shaif ud-Din Pirzada* (b. Burhanpur 12 Jun 1923)
3 Jan 1968	(acting:) *Mohammad Ayub Khan* (see Presidents)
24 Apr 1968	*Arshad Mijan A. Husain*
25 Mar 1969	(acting) *Sheikh Mohammad Yousuf*
4 Aug 1969	*Agha Muhammad Yahya Khan* (see Presidents)
22 Feb 1971	*Sultan Mohammad Khan*
from 7 Dec 1971	*Zulfikar Ali Bhutto* (see Presidents)

Palestine

1920 – 1948	Under British Mandate

HEADS OF STATE

Commissioners

1928	*Sir John Robert Chancellor* (b. Edinburgh 20 Oct 1870; d. Shieldhill, Lanarkshire 31 Jul 1952)
1 Nov 1931 – 1938	*Sir Arthur Grenfell Wauchope* (b. 1 Mar 1874; d. London 14 Sep 1947)
1938 – Jul 1944	*Sir Harold (Alfred) MacMichael* (b. Cambridge 15 Oct 1882; d. Folkestone 21(?) Sep 1969)
20 Jul 1944 – 1945	*John Standish Surtees Prendergast Vereker, 6th Viscount Gort* (b. Jul 1886; d. London 31 Mar 1946)
1945 – 15 May 1948	*Sir Alan Gordon Cunningham* (b. 1 May 1887)
15 May 1948	Mandate terminated and state of Israel set up

Panama

HEADS OF STATE

Presidents

1 Oct 1928	*Florencio Harmodio Arosemena* (b. 17 Sep 1872; d. 1945)
3 Jan 1931	*Harmodio Arias* (for 1st time) (b. 3 Jul 1886; d. Miami, Florida, 23 Dec 1962)
16 Jan 1931	*Ricardo Alfaro* (b. 20 Aug 1882; d. Ciudad de Panamá 28 Feb 1971)
5 Jun 1932	*Harmodio Arias* (for 2nd time)
8 Jun 1936 – 16 Dec 1939	*Juan Demóstenes Arosemena* (b. 1879; d. 16 Dec 1939)
18 Dec 1939	*Augusto (Samuel) Boyd* (b. 1879; d. 17 Jun 1957)
1940	*Arnulfo Arias Madrid* (for 1st time) (b. Penonomé 15 Aug 1901)
8 Oct 1941	*Ricardo Adolfo de la Guardia* (b. 14 Mar 1899; d. Ciudad de Panamá 29 Dec 1969)
15 Jun 1945	*Enrique Adolfo Jiménez* (b. 1887)
7 Aug 1948	*Domingo Díaz Arosemena* (b. 25 Jun 1875; d. 23 Aug 1949)

3 Aug 1949	*Daniel Chanis Pinzón* (b. 1892)
0 Nov 1949	*Roberto Francisco Chiari Junior* (for 1st time) (b. 2 Mar 1905)
4 Nov 1949	*Arnulfo Arias Madrid* (for 2nd time)
May 1951	*Alcibiades Arosemena* (b. 1882(?); d. 8 Apr 1958)
Oct 1952 – 2 Jan 1955	*José Antonio Ramón Cantero* (b. 1 Jul 1908; d. 2 Jan 1955)
Jan 1955	*José Ramón Guizado* (b. 1899?; d. Miami Beach, USA, 3(?) Nov 1964)
5 Jan 1955	(acting:) *Ricardo M. Arias Espinosa*
Oct 1955	*Ernesto de la Guardia Junior* (b. 13 May 1904)
Oct 1960	*Roberto Francisco Chiari Junior* (for 2nd time)
Oct 1964 – 1 Oct 1968	*Marcos Aurelio Robles Méndez* (b. Aguadulce 8 Nov 1905 (1906?))
25 Mar – 1 Oct 1968	*Max Delvalle*, rival President
– 11 Oct 1968	*Arnulfo Arias Madrid* (for 3rd time)
3 Oct 1968	*José María Pinilla Fábrega* (b. Ciudad de Panamá 28 Mar 1919) Head of Junta as Co-President with *Bolívar Urrutía*, Deputy
9 Dec 1969	*Demetrio Basilio Lakas Bahas* (for 1st time) (b. Colón 29 Aug 1925) Head of Junta as Co-President with *Arturo Sucre Pereira*, Deputy
from 18 Sep 1972	*Demetrio Basilio Lakas Bahas* (for 2nd time)

Chief of Government

from 13 Sep 1972	*Omar Torrijos* (b. Santiago, Panama, 13 Feb 1929) from 12 Oct 1965 de facto Military Dictator†

Papacy

POPES

6 Feb 1922 – 10 Feb 1939	*Pius XI* (Ratti) (b. Desio 31 May 1857)

†The President has purely ceremonial powers

2 Mar 1939 – 9 Oct 1958	*Pius XII* (Pacelli) (b. Rome 2 Mar 1876; d. Castelgandolfo)
28 Oct 1958 – 3 Jun 1963	*John XXIII* (Roncalli) (b. Bergamo 25 Nov 1881)
from 21 Jun 1963	*Paul VI* (Montini) (b. Concesio 26 Sep 1897)

CARDINAL SECRETARIES OF STATE

Oct 1914 – 7 Feb 1930	*Pietro Gasparri* (b. Ussita 5 May 1852; d. Rome 18 Nov 1934)
9 Feb 1930 – 10 Feb 1939	*Eugenio Pacelli*, later Pius XII (see Popes)
10 Mar 1939 – 22 Aug 1944	*Luigi Maglione* (b. Naples 2 Mar 1877; d. Rome 22 Aug 1944)
22 Aug 1944 – 29 Nov 1952	No new Cardinal Secretary of State appointed
29 Nov 1952 – 9 Oct 1958	(acting:) *Domenico Tardini* (b. Rome 29 Feb 1888; d. Vatican 30 Jul 1961)
29 Nov 1952 – 3 Nov 1954	(acting:) *Giovanni Battista Montini*, later Paul VI (see Popes)
17 Nov 1958 – 30 Jul 1961	*Domenico Tardini* (see above)
14 Aug 1961 – 3 Jun 1963	*Amleto Cicognani* (for 1st time) (b. Brisighella 24 Feb 1883; d. 17 Dec 1973)
21 Jun 1963	*Amleto Cicognani* (for 2nd time)
from 2 May 1969	*Jean-Marie Villot* (b. Saint-Amant-Tallende 11 Oct 1905)

Papua New Guinea

Formed from Territory of Papua (part of Australia from Sep 1906) and Trust Territory of New Guinea (administered by Australia under Trusteeship Agreements with League of Nations and United Nations from 1920). Papua and New Guinea administered as one territory from 1949

1 Dec 1973	Internal self-government
16 Sep 1975	Independence (member of Commonwealth)

HEADS OF STATE

Australian High Commissioners

1 Dec 1973	*Leslie Wilson Johnson* (b. Tambellup, Western Australia, 2 Apr 1916)
29 Mar 1974	*Thomas Kingston Critchley* (b. Melbourne 27 Jan 1916)

British Governor-General

from 16 Sep 1975	*Sir John Guise* (b. Papua 29 Aug 1914)

MEMBER OF GOVERNMENT

Prime Minister

from 1 Dec 1973	*Michael Thomas Somare* (b. 9 Apr 1936) (Chief Minister until 16 Sep 1975)

Paraguay

HEADS OF STATE

Presidents

15 Aug 1928	*José Particio Guggiari* (for 1st time) (b. Lugano 17 Mar 1884; d. Buenos Aires 29 Oct 1957)
26 Oct 1931	*Emiliano González Navero* (for 3rd time) (b. Caraguatay 1861; d. 18 Oct 1934)*
28 Jan 1932	*José Particio Guggiari* (for 2nd time)
15 Aug 1932	*Eusebio Ayala* (for 2nd time) (b. 13/14 Aug 1875; d. 4 Jun 1942)*
19 Feb 1936	*Rafael Franco*
16 Aug 1937	*Félix Paiva* (for 2nd time)*

*For earlier career see vol. 2

PARAGUAY

15 Aug 1939 – 5 5 Sep 1940	*José Félix Estigarribia* (b. 21 Feb 1888; d. 5 Sep 1940)
8 Sep 1940	*Higino Moríñigo* (b. 11 Jan 1897)
3 Jun 1948	*Juan Manuel Frutos*
15 Aug 1948	*Juan Natalicio González* (b. 1897; d. Mexico City 6 Dec 1966)
30 Jan 1949	*Raimundo Rolón* (b. 1903)
26 Feb 1949	*Felipe Molas López* (b. 1901; d. 2 Mar 1954)
10 Sep 1949	*Federico Chaves* (b. 1878)
4 May 1954	(acting:) *Tomás Romero Pareira*
from 11 Jul 1954	*Alfredo Stroessner* (b. Encarnación 3 Nov 1912) until 1963 Dictator

Peru

HEADS OF STATE

Presidents

20 Jul 1919	*Augusto Bernardino Leguía* (for 2nd time) (b. 19 Feb 1864; d. 6 Feb 1932)*
25 Aug 1930	*Pedro Pablo Martínez Ledesma* (b. 29 Jun 1875)
28 Aug 1930	*Luis Sánchez Cerro* (for 1st time) (b. 1894; d. 30 Apr 1933)
2 Mar 1931	*Ricardo Leoncio Elias*
6 Mar 1931	*Gustavo Jiménez*
9 Mar 1931	*David Samánez Ocampo* (b. 1861; d. 1937)
8 Dec 1931	*Luis Sánchez Cerro* (for 2nd time)
30 Apr 1933	*Oscar Raimundo Benavides* (for 2nd time) (b. 18 May 1876; d. 2 Jul 1946)*
8 Dec 1939	*Manuel Prado y Ugarteche* (for 1st time) (b. Lima 21 Apr 1889; d. Paris 14 Aug 1967)
28 Jul 1945 – 30 Oct 1948	*José Luis Bustamente y Rivero* (b. 1894)
2 Nov 1948	*Manuel A. Odría Amoretti* (for 1st time) (b. 26 Nov 1897; d. 18 Feb 1974) Leader of Military Junta

*For earlier career see vol. 2

1 Jun 1950	*Zenon Noriega* Chairman of Military Junta pending elections
28 Jul 1950	*Manuel A. Odría Amoretti* (for 2nd time)
28 Jul 1956	*Manuel Prado y Ugarteche* (for 2nd time)
18 Jul 1962	*Ricardo Pérez Godoy* (b. 1903?) Leader of Military Junta, nominated President 24 Jul 1962
3 Mar 1963	*Nicolás Lindley López*, Leader of Military Junta
28 Jul 1963	*Fernando Belaúnde Terry* (b. Lima 7 Oct 1912)
3 Oct 1968	*Juan Velasco Alvarado* (b. Piura 16 Jun 1910 (1909?)) Leader of Military Junta
from 30 Aug 1975	*Francisco Morales Bermúdez* (b. 1922?)

MEMBERS OF GOVERNMENT

Prime Ministers

13 Sep 1965	*Daniel Becerra de la Flor*
7 Sep 1967	*Edgardo Seoane Corrales*
16 Nov 1967 – 29 May 1968	*Raúl Ferrero Rebagliati* (b. Lima 1911)
31 May 1968	*Osvaldo Hercelles*
1 Oct 1968	*Miguel Mujica Gallo*
3 Oct 1968	*Ernesto Montagne Sánchez* (b. Barranco 18 Aug 1916)
1973 – Feb 1975	*Luis Edgardo Mercado Jarrín* (b. Barranco 19 Sep 1919)
Feb – Aug 1975	*Francisco Morales Bermúdez* (see Presidents)
from 1 Sep 1975	*Oscar Vargas Prieto*

Philippines

HEADS OF STATE

American Governors-General

1929 – 1932	*Dwight Filley Davis* (b. St. Louis, Montana, 5 Jul 1879; d. Washington 28 Nov 1945)

PHILIPPINES

| 1932 – 1933 | *Theodore Roosevelt* (b. Oyster Bay, New York, 13 Sep 1887; d. Normandy 12 Jul 1944) |
| 1933 – 13 Nov 1935 | *Frank Murphy* (b. Harbor Beach, Michigan, 13 Apr 1890; d. Detroit 19 Jul 1949) |

American High Commissioners

15 Nov 1935 – 1937	*Frank Murphy* (see American Governors-General)
1937 – 1939	*Paul Vories McNutt* (for 1st time) (b. Franklin, Indiana, 19 Jul 1891; d. Springfield, Illinois, 24 Oct 1957)
1939 – 24 Dec 1941	*Francis Bowes Sayre* (b. South Bethlehem, Pennsylvania, 30 Sep 1885; d. 29 Mar 1972)
Dec 1941 – Feb 1945	Japanese occupation
7 Sep 1942 – 4 Jul 1946	*Paul Vories McNutt* (for 2nd time) remained until 1948 as Ambassador to the Philippines

Presidents

17 Sep 1935 – Dec 1941	*Manuel Luis Quesón y Molina* (b. 9 Sep 1878; d. 1 Aug 1944)
14 Oct 1943 – Apr 1945	*José Paciano Laurel* (b. 1891; d. 6 Nov 1959)
Apr(Sep) 1945 – May 1946	*Sergio Osmeña* (b. Cebu 9 Sep 1878; d. Manila 19 Oct 1961) in exile since 1 Aug 1944
27 May 1946	*Manuel Roxas* (b. 1892(?); d. 16 Apr 1948)
16 Apr 1948	*Elpidio Quirino* (b. 16 Nov 1880; d. Novaliches 29 Feb 1956)
12 Nov 1953	*Ramón Magsaysay* (b. Subic Bay 31 Aug 1907; d. (in air crash) Bago Mountain, Cebu, 17 Mar 1957)
17 Mar 1957	*Carlos P. García* (b. Prov. Bohol 4 Nov 1896; d. Manila 14 Jun 1971)
30 Dec 1961	*Diosdado Macapagal* (b. Lubao 28 Sep 1910)
30 Dec 1965	*Ferdinand Edralin Marcos* (b. Sarrat 11 Sep 1917)

MEMBER OF GOVERNMENT

Foreign Minister

| from 1968 | *Carlos P. Rómulo* (b. 14 Jan 1899) |

420

Poland

HEADS OF STATE

Presidents (of the Council)

1 Jun 1926 – 18 Sep 1939	*Ignacy Mościcki* (b. Mierzanów 1 Dec 1867; d. Versoix 1 Oct 1946)
18 Sep 1939	Polish government fled to Romania
Sep 1939 – 6 Jun 1947	*Władysław Raczkiewicz* (b. Minsk 16 Jan 1885; d. Ruthin Castle, Wales, 6 Jun 1947) in exile*
Jan 1945	*Bolesław Bierut* (b. Lublin 18 Apr 1892; d. Moscow 12 Mar 1956)
20 Nov 1956 – 7 Aug 1964	*Aleksander Zawadzki* (b. Dąbrowa Górnicza 16 Dec 1899; d. Warsaw 7 Aug 1964)
12 Aug 1964 – 9 Apr 1968	*Edward Ochab* (b. Kraków 16 Apr 1906)
11 Apr 1968	*Marian Spychalski* (b. Łódź 6 Dec 1906)
23 Dec 1970	*Józef Cyrankiewicz* (b. Tarnów 21 Jul 1911)
from 28 Mar 1972	*Henryk Jabłoński* (b. Waliszewo 27 Dec 1909)

MEMBERS OF GOVERNMENT

29 Dec 1929 - 15 Mar 1930: Bartel IV

Prime Minister	*Kazimierz Bartel* (for 4th time) (b. Lvov 3 Mar 1882; d. Lvov 26 Jul 1941)*
Foreign Affairs	*August Zaleski* (b. Warsaw 13 Sep 1883)*
Home Affairs	*Henryk Józewski* (b. Kiev 6 Aug 1892)
Justice	*Feliks Dutkiewicz* (b. Lublin 1872; d. Warsaw 27 May 1932)
Finance	*Ignacy Matuszewski* (b. Warsaw 10 Sep 1891; d. New York 3 Aug 1946)*
Religious Affairs and Education	*Sławomir Czerwiński* (b. Sompolno 24 Oct 1885; d. Warsaw 4 Aug 1931)*
Agriculture	29 Dec 1929 – 16 Jan 1930: *Wiktor Leśniewski* 16 Jan – 15 Mar 1930: *Leon Janta Połczyński*

*For earlier career see vol. 2

421

POLAND

Industry and Commerce	*Eugeniusz Felicjan Kwiatkowski* (b. Kraków 30 Dec 1888)*
Transport	*Alfons Walenty Kühn* (b. Przejmy 14 Feb 1879; d. Warsaw 27 Jan 1944)*
Public Works	*Maksymilian Matakiewicz* (b. Niepołomice 27 Jun 1875; d. Lvov 3 Feb 1940)
Labour and Social Welfare	*Aleksander Prystor* (b. Vilnius 2 Jan 1874; d. Soviet Union 1941)
Agrarian Reform	*Witold Staniewicz* (b. Vilnius 16 Sep 1888; d. Poznań 14 Jul 1966)
Posts and Telegraphs	*Ignacy Boerner* (b. Zduńska Wola 11 Aug 1875; d. Warsaw 12 Apr 1933)*
War	*Józef Pilsudski* (b. Żułów 4 Jul 1867; d. Warsaw 12 May 1935)*

29 Mar – 23 Aug 1930: Sławek I

Prime Minister	*Walery Sławek* (for 1st time) (b. 2 Nov 1879; d. Warsaw 3 Apr 1939)
Foreign Affairs	*August Zaleski* (see Bartel IV)
Home Affairs	29 Mar – 3 Jun 1930: *Henryk Józewski* (see Bartel IV) 3 Jun – 23 Aug 1930: *Felicjan Sławoj-Składkowski* (b. Gąbin 9 Jun 1885; d. London 31 Aug 1962)*
Justice	*Stanisław Car* (b. Warsaw 26 Apr 1882; d. Warsaw 18 Jun 1938)*
Finance	*Ignacy Matuszewski* (see Bartel IV)
Education	*Sławomir Czerwiński* (see Bartel IV)
Agriculture	*Leon Janta Połczyński* (see Bartel IV)
Industry and Commerce	*Eugeniusz Felicjan Kwiatkowski* (see Bartel IV)
Transport	*Alfons Walenty Kühn* (see Bartel IV)
Public Works	*Maksymilian Matakiewicz* (see Bartel IV)
Labour and Social Welfare	*Aleksander Prystor* (see Bartel IV)
Agrarian Reform	*Witold Staniewicz* (see Bartel IV)
Posts and Telegraphs	*Ignacy Boerner* (see Bartel IV)
War	*Józef Pilsudski* (see Bartel IV)

25 Aug – 28 Nov 1930: Piłsudski II

Prime Minister	*Józef Piłsudski* (for 2nd time) (see Bartel IV)

*For earlier career see vol. 2

Foreign Affairs	*August Zaleski* (see Bartel IV)
Home Affairs	*Felicjan Sławoj-Składkowski* (see Sławek I)
Justice	*Czesław Michałowski* (b. 1885)
Finance	*Ignacy Matuszewski* (see Bartel IV)
Education	*Sławomir Czerwiński* (see Bartel IV)
Agriculture	*Leon Janta Połczyński* (see Bartel IV)
Industry and	*Aleksander Prystor* (see Bartel IV)
Commerce	
Transport	*.Alfons Walenty Kühn* (see Bartel IV)
Public Works	*Mieczysław Norwid Neugebauer*
Labour and Social	*Stefan Hubicki*
Welfare	
Agrarian Reform	*Leon Kozłowski* (b. Rębieszyce 1892; d. Berlin Nov 1944)
Posts and Telegraphs	*Ignacy Boerner* (see Bartel IV)
War	*Józef Piłsudski* (see Bartel IV)
Without Portfolio	*Józef Beck* (b. Warsaw 4 Oct 1894; d. Bucharest 5 Jun 1944)

5 Dec 1930 - 26 May 1931: Sławek II

Prime Minister	*Walery Sławek* (for 2nd time) (see Sławek I)
Foreign Affairs	*August Zaleski* (see Bartel IV)
Home Affairs	*Felicjan Sławoj-Składkowski* (see Sławek I)
Justice	*Czesław Michałowski* (see Piłsudski II)
Finance	*Ignacy Matuszewski* (see Bartel IV)
Education	*Sławomir Czerwiński* (see Bartel IV)
Agriculture	*Leon Janta Połczyński* (see Bartel IV)
Industry and	*Aleksander Prystor* (see Bartel IV)
Commerce	
Transport	*Alfons Walenty Kühn* (see Bartel IV)
Public Works	*Mieczysław Norwid Neugebauer* (see Piłsudski II)
Labour and Social	*Stefan Hubicki* (see Piłsudski II)
Welfare	
Agrarian Reform	*Leon Kozłowski* (see Piłsudski II)
Posts and Telegraphs	*Ignacy Boerner* (see Bartel IV)
War	*Józef Piłsudski* (see Bartel IV)
Without Portfolio	*Bronisław Pieracki* (b. 1895; d. Kraków 14 Jun 1934)

27 May 1931 - 9 May 1933: Prystor

Prime Minister	*Aleksander Prystor* (see Bartel IV)
Foreign Affairs	27 May 1931 – 2 Nov 1932: *August Zaleski* (see Bartel IV)

423

	2 Nov 1932 – 9 May 1933: *Józef Beck* (see Piłsudski II)
Home Affairs	27 May – 17 Jun 1931: *Felicjan Sławoj-Składkowski* (see Sławek I)
	17 Jun 1931 – 9 May 1933: *Bronisław Pieracki* (see Sławek II)
Justice	*Czesław Michałowski* (see Piłsudski II)
Finance	27 May 1931 – 15 Sep 1932: *Jan Piłsudski* (b. Vilnius 15 Jan 1876)
	15 Sep 1932 – 9 May 1933: *Władysław Marian Zawadzki* (b. Vilnius 8 Sep 1885; d. 8 Mar 1939)
Education	27 May – 4 Aug 1931: *Sławomir Czerwinski* (see Bartel IV)
	13 Aug 1931 – 9 May 1933: *Janusz Jędrzejewicz* (b. Spiczyńce 21 Jun 1885; d. 1951)
Agriculture (from 20 Mar 1932: Agriculture and Agrarian Reform)	27 May 1931 – 20 Mar 1932: *Leon Janta Połczyński* (see Bartel IV)
	20 Mar 1932 – 9 May 1933: *Seweryn Ludkiewicz*
Industry and Commerce	*Ferdynand Zarzycki*
Transport (from 1 Jul 1932: Transport and Public Works)	27 May 1931 – 5 Sep 1932: *Alfons Walenty Kühn* (see Bartel IV)
	5 Sep 1932 – 9 May 1933 (acting:) *Michał Butkiewicz*
Public Works	27 May 1931 – 20 Mar 1932: *Mieczysław Norwid Neugebauer* (see Piłsudski II)
	20 Mar – 1 Jul 1932 (acting:) *Alfons Walenty Kühn* (see Bartel IV)
	1 Jul 1932: merged with Transport (see above)
Social Welfare	*Stefan Hubicki* (see Piłsudski II)
Agrarian Reform	27 May 1931 – 20 Mar 1932: *Leon Kozłowski* (see Piłsudski II)
	20 Mar 1932: merged with Agriculture (see above)
Posts and Telegraphs	27 May 1931 – 12 Apr 1933: *Ignacy Boerner* (see Bartel IV)
	15 Apr – 9 May 1933: *Emil Kaliński* (b. Łódź 17 Oct 1890)
War	*Józef Piłsudski* (see Bartel IV)
Without Portfolio	27 May – 22 Jun 1931: *Bronisław Pieracki* (see Sławek II)
	20 Apr – 5 Sep 1932: *Władysław Marian Zawadzki* (see above)

10 May 1933 - 13 May 1934: Jędrzejewicz

Prime Minister	*Janusz Jędrzejewicz* (see Prystor)
Foreign Affairs	*Józef Beck* (see Piłsudski II)
Home Affairs	*Bronisław Pieracki* (see Sławek II)
Justice	*Czesław Michałowski* (see Piłsudski II)
Finance	*Władysław Marian Zawadzki* (see Prystor)
Education	10 May 1933 - 24 Feb 1934: *Janusz Jędrzejewicz* (see Prystor) 24 Feb - 13 May 1934: *Wacław Jędrzejewicz* (b. Spiczyńce 21 Jan 1893)
Agriculture and Agrarian Reform	*Bronisław Nakoniczników-Kłukowski* (b. Warsaw 9 Oct 1888)
Industry and Commerce	*Ferdynand Zarzycki* (see Prystor)
Transport	*Michał Butkiewicz* (see Prystor)
Social Welfare	*Stefan Hubicki* (see Piłsudski II)
Posts and Telegraphs	*Emil Kaliński* (see Prystor)
War	*Józef Piłsudski* (see Bartel IV)

13 May 1934 - 28 Mar 1935: Kozłowski

Prime Minister	*Leon Kozłowski* (see Piłsudski II)
Foreign Affairs	*Józef Beck* (see Piłsudski II)
Home Affairs	13 May - 14 Jun 1934: *Bronisław Pieracki* (see Sławek II) 16 - 28 Jun 1934: *Leon Kozłowski* (see Piłsudski II) 28 Jun 1934 - 28 Mar 1935: *Marian Zyndram-Kościałkowski* (b. Ponedele 16 Mar 1892; d. 1946)
Justice	*Czesław Michałowski* (see Piłsudski II)
Finance	*Władysław Marian Zawadzki* (see Prystor)
Religious Affairs and Education	*Wacław Jędrzejewicz* (see Jędrzejewicz)
Agriculture and Agrarian Reform	13 May - 28 Jun 1934: *Bronisław Nakoniczników-Kłukowski* (see Jędrzejewicz) 28 Jun 1934 - 28 Mar 1935: *Juliusz Poniatowski* (b. St. Petersburg 17 Jan 1886)
Industry and Commerce	*Henryk Floyar-Rajchman* (b. Warsaw 7 Dec 1893; d. New York 22 Mar 1951)
Transport	*Michał Butkiewicz* (see Prystor)
Social Welfare	*Jerzy Paciorkowski*
Posts and Telegraphs	*Emil Kaliński* (see Prystor)
War	*Józef Piłsudski* (see Bartel IV)

POLAND

28 Mar – 12 Oct 1935: Sławek III

Prime Minister	*Walery Sławek* (for 3rd time) (see Sławek I)
War	29 Mar – 12 May 1935: *Józef Piłsudski* (see Bartel IV)
	13 May – 12 Oct 1935: *Tadeusz Kasprzycki* (b.
	Warsaw 16 Jan 1891)
	Other ministers continued in same offices as in
	previous cabinet

13 Oct 1935 – 15 May 1936: Zyndram-Kościałkowski

Prime Minister	*Marian Zyndram-Kościałkowski* (see Kozłowski)
Foreign Affairs	*Józef Beck* (see Piłsudski II)
Home Affairs	*Władysław Raczkiewicz* (see Presidents)
Justice	*Czesław Michałowski* (see Piłsudski II)
Finance	*Eugeniusz Felicjan Kwiatkowski* (see Bartel IV)
Religious Affairs and	13 Oct – 19 Dec 1935: *Konstantin Chyliński* (b.
Education	Shmerinka 1881)
	19 Dec 1935 – 15 May 1936: *Wojciech Alojzy*
	Świętosławski (b. Kuryjówka 1881; d. Warsaw 29 Apr
	1968)
Agriculture and	*Juliusz Poniatowski* (see Kozłowski)
Agrarian Reform	
Industry and	*Roman Górecki* (b. Stara Sola 27 Aug 1889; d.
Commerce	Whitchurch, Shropshire, 9 Aug 1946)
Transport	*Juliusz Ulrych* (b. Kalisz 9 Apr 1883; d. London 4 Nov
	1959)
Social Welfare	*Władysław Jaszczołt*
Posts and Telegraphs	*Emil Kaliński* (see Prystor)
War	*Tadeusz Kasprzycki* (see Sławek III)

15 May 1936 – 17 Sep 1939: Sławoj-Składkowski

Prime Minister	*Felicjan Sławoj-Składkowski* (see Sławek I)
Foreign Affairs	*Józef Beck* (see Piłsudski II)
Home Affairs	*Felicjan Sławoj-Składkowski* (see Sławek I)
Justice	*Witold Grabowski* (b. in the Caucasus 19 Mar 1898)
Finance	*Eugeniusz Felicjan Kwiatkowski* (see Bartel IV)
Religious Affairs and	*Wojciech Alojzy Świętosławski* (see Zyndram-
Education	Kościałkowski)
Agriculture	*Juliusz Poniatowski* (see Kozłowski)
Industry and	*Antoni Mikołai Roman* (b. Warsaw 10 Sep 1892; d.
Commerce	Warsaw 28 Apr 1951)

Transport	*Juliusz Ulrych* (see Zyndram-Kościałkowski)
Social Welfare	*Marian Zyndram-Kościałkowski* (see Kozłowski)
Posts and Telegraphs	*Emil Kaliński* (see Prystor)
War	*Tadeusz Kasprzycki* (see Sławek III)

Sep 1939 – 3 Jul 1943: Sikorski II (in exile in London)

Prime Minister	*Władysław Sikorski* (for 2nd time) (b. Tuszów Narodowy 20 May 1881; d. near Gibraltar 3 Jul 1943)*
Deputy Prime Minister and Home Affairs	1940 – 3 Jul 1943: *Stanisław Mikołajczyk* (Farmers) (b. Holsterhausen 18 Jul 1901; d. Chevy Chase, Maryland, 13 Dec 1966)
Foreign Affairs	Sep 1939 – 30 Jul 1941: *August Zaleski* (see Bartel IV) 30 Jul 1941 – 3 Jul 1943: *Tadeusz, Count Romer* (b. Antonosz 6 Dec 1894)
Justice	1942 – 3 Jul 1943: *Wacław Komarnicki* (b. Warsaw 29 Jul 1891; d. London 23(?) Mar 1954)
Finance	*Adam J. Koc* (b. 1889(?); d. New York 3 Feb 1969)
Education	Sep 1939 – May 1943: *Józef Haller de Hallenburg* (b. Jurczyce 13 Aug 1873; d. London 4 Jun 1960)

13 Jul 1943 – 24 Nov 1944: Mikołajczyk (in exile in London)

Prime Minister	*Stanisław Mikołajczyk* (Farmers) (see Sikorski II)
Foreign Affairs	*Tadeusz, Count Romer* (see Sikorski II)
Defence	*Marian Kukiel* (b. Dąbrów 15 May 1885; d. 15 Aug 1973)
Liaison with Near East	*Henryk Leo Strasburger* (b. 28 May 1887; d. London 2 May 1951)
Justice	*Wacław Komarnicki* (see Sikorski II)

1 Dec 1944 – 28 Jun 1945: Arciszewski (in London)

Prime Minister	*Tomasz Arciszewski* (b. Sierzchow 4 Nov 1877; d. London 20 Nov 1955)

1 Jan – 28 Jun 1945: Osóbka-Morawski I (initially in Lublin, from 18 Jan 1945 in Warsaw)

Prime Minister and Foreign Affairs	*Edward Osóbka-Morawski* (for 1st time) (b. Bliżyn 5 Oct 1909)

*For earlier career see vol. 2

Home Affairs	*Józef Maślanka*
Public Security	*Stanisław Radkiewicz* (Comm/Pol Lab) (b. 19 Jan 1903)
Justice	*Edmund Zalewski*
Finance	*Konstantin Dąbrowski*
War	*Michał Żymierski* (b. Kraków 4 Sep 1890)
Labour and Public Works	*Wiktor Trojanowski*
Agriculture	*Edward Bertold*
Information	*Stefan Matuszewski*

28 Jun 1945 – 4 Feb 1947: Osóbka-Morawski II

Prime Minister	*Edward Osóbka-Morawski* (for 2nd time) (see Osóbka-Morawski I)
Deputy Prime Minister	*Stanisław Mikołajczyk* (Farmers/Pol Peoples) (see Sikorski II)
	Władysław Gomułka (Comm/Pol Lab) (b. Krosno 6 Feb 1905)
Foreign Affairs	*Wincenty Rzymowski* (b. Mława 19 Jul 1883; d. Warsaw 30 Apr 1950)
Interior	*Władysław Kiernik* (Farmers/Pol Peoples) (b. Bochnia 27 Jul 1879)*
Security	*Stanisław Radkiewicz* (Comm/Pol Lab) (see Osóbka-Morawski I)
Finance	*Kostantin Dąbrowski* (see Osóbka-Morawski I)
Education	*Władysław Kowalski* (b. Paprotnia 26 Aug 1894; d. Warsaw 14 Dec 1958)
Post	*Stanisław Thugutt*
War	*Michał Żymierski* (see Osóbka-Morawski I)
Agriculture	*Stanisław Mikołajczyk* (Farmers/Pol Peoples) (see Sikorski II)
Commerce and Trade	*Hilary Minc* (Comm/Pol Lab) (b. Kazimierz Dolny 24 Aug 1905)
Labour	*Jan Stańczyk* (Soc) (b. Galicia 23 Dec 1886)

7 Feb 1947 – 20 Nov 1952: Cyrankiewicz I

| Prime Minister | *Józef Cyrankiewicz* (Soc, then Pol Utd Lab) (for 1st time) (see Presidents) |

*For earlier career see vol. 2

Deputy Prime Ministers	7 Feb 1947 – 21 Jan 1949: *Władysław Gomułka* (Comm/Pol Lab) (see Osóbka-Morawski II) 21 Jan 1949 – 20 Nov 1952: *Aleksander Zawadzki* (see Presidents) *Antoni Korzycki* (Farmers/Utd Peoples) (b. Podkonice Duże 7 Nov 1904) *Hilary Minc* (Comm, then Pol Utd Lab) (see Osóbka-Morawski II) *Stefan Jędrychowski* (Pol Utd Lab) (b. Warsaw 19 May 1910) *Hilary Chełchowski* (b. Mosaki 10 Jan 1908) 2 Jul – 20 Nov 1952: *Tadeusz Gede*
Foreign Affairs	7 Feb 1947 – 17 Mar 1951: *Zygmunt Modzelewski* (Comm, then Pol Utd Lab) (b. Częstochowa 15 Apr 1900; d. Warsaw 18 Jun 1954) 17 Mar 1951 – 20 Nov 1952: *Stanisław Skrzeszewski* (Comm, then Pol Utd Lab) (b. Nowy Sącz 27 Apr 1901)
Home Affairs (from 21 Jan 1949: Interior)	7 Feb 1947 – Jun 1950: *Stanisław Wolski* 15 Nov 1950: office abolished
Justice	*Henryk Świątkowski* (Soc, then Pol Utd Lab)
Finance	*Konstantin Dąbrowski* (see Osóbka-Morawski I)
Public Administration	7 Feb 1947 – 21 Jan 1949: *Edward Osóbka-Morawski* (Soc, then Pol Utd Lab) (see Osóbka-Morawski I)
Security	*Stanisław Radkiewicz* (Comm, then Pol Utd Lab) (see Osóbka-Morawski I)
Occupied Territories	7 Feb 1947 – 30 Dec 1948: *Władysław Gomułka* (Comm/Pol Lab) (see Osóbka-Morawski II) 30 Dec 1948: office abolished
Commerce and Food	7 Feb 1947 – 23 Oct 1948: *Włodzimierz Lechowicz* (Dem) 23 Oct 1948: office abolished
Agriculture	*Jan Dąb-Kocioł* (Farmers/Utd Peoples) (b. 1878)
Education	7 Feb – Sep 1947: *Czesław Wycech* (b. Wilczogęby 20 Jul 1899) Sep 1947 – 8 Jul 1950: *Stanisław Skrzeszewski* (Comm, then Pol Utd Lab) (see above) 8 Jul 1950 – 20 Nov 1952: *Witold Jarosiński* (b. Warsaw 18 Sep 1909)
War	7 Feb 1947 – 7 Nov 1949: *Michał Żymierski* (see Osóbka-Morawski I) 7 Nov 1949 – 20 Nov 1952: *Konstantin Rokossovsky* (b. 1896; d. Moscow 3 Aug 1968) Soviet Marshal

429

POLAND

21 Nov 1952 – 19 Mar 1954: Bierut

Prime Minister	*Bolesław Bierut* (Pol Utd Lab) (see Presidents)
Deputy Prime Ministers	*Józef Cyrankiewicz* (Pol Utd Lab) (see Presidents) *Władysław Dworakowski* *Stefan Jędrychowski* (Pol Utd Lab) (see Cyrankiewicz I) *Zenon Nowak* (b. Pabianice 27 Jan 1905) *Tadeusz Gede* (see Cyrankiewicz I) *Piotr Jaroszewicz* (b. Nyesvizh 8 Oct 1909) *Hilary Minc* (Pol Utd Lab) (see Osóbka-Morawski II) *Konstantin Rokossovsky* (see Cyrankiewicz I)
Foreign Affairs	*Stanisław Skrzeszewski* (Pol Utd Lab) (see Cyrankiewicz I)
State Security	21 Nov 1952 – 12 Mar 1954: *Stanisław Radkiewicz* (Pol Utd Lab) (see Osóbka-Morawski I)
Audit †	*Franciszek Jóźwiak* (b. Huta Baranowska 20 Oct 1895)
Justice	*Henryk Światkowski* (Pol Utd Lab) (see Cyrankiewicz I)
Finance	*Tadeusz Dietrich* (d. Warsaw 28 Jul 1960)
Education	*Witold Jarosiński* (see Cyrankiewicz I)
Agriculture	*Jan Dąb-Kocioł* (Farmers/Utd Peoples) (see Cyrankiewicz I)
Food Industry	*Mesko Hoffman*
War	*Konstantin Rokossovsky* (see Cyrankiewicz I)

19 Mar 1954 – 20 Feb 1957: Cyrankiewicz II

Prime Minister	*Józef Cyrankiewicz* (Pol Utd Lab) (for 2nd time) (see Presidents)
First Deputy Prime Ministers	19 Mar 1954 – 9 Oct 1956: *Hilary Minc* (Pol Utd Lab) (see Osóbka-Morawski II) 19 Mar 1954 – 23 Oct 1956: *Zenon Nowak* (see Bierut)
Deputy Prime Ministers	*Piotr Jaroszewicz* (see Bierut) 19 Mar 1954 – 5 May 1956: *Jakub Berman* (Pol Utd Lab) (b. Warsaw 24 Dec 1901; d. 25 Nov 1958) 19 Mar 1954 – 13 Nov 1956: *Konstantin Rokossovsky* (see Cyrankiewicz I) 15 May 1954 – 23 Oct 1956: *Stanisław Lapot*

†Previously an organ of the Council of State, not a ministry

430

	19 Mar 1954 - 23 Oct 1956: *Tadeusz Gede* (see Cyrankiewicz I)

19 Mar 1954 - 23 Oct 1956: *Tadeusz Gede* (see
Cyrankiewicz I)
19 Mar 1954 - 23 Oct 1956: *Stefan Jędrychowski* (Pol
Utd Lab) (see Cyrankiewicz I)
(?) - 23 Oct 1956: *Eugen Stawiński*
17 Apr 1955 - 23 Oct 1956: *Franciszek Jóźwiak* (see
Bierut)
23 Oct 1956 - 20 Feb 1957: *Zenon Nowak* (see Bierut)
23 Oct 1956 - 20 Feb 1957: *Stefan Ignar* (Utd
Farmers/ Utd Peoples) (b. Bałdrzychowa 17 Feb 1908)

Foreign Affairs 19 Mar 1954 - 28 Apr 1956: *Stanisław Skrzeszewski*
(Pol Utd Lab) (see Cyrankiewicz I)
28 Apr 1956 - 20 Feb 1957: *Adam Rapacki* (Pol Utd
Lab) (b. Lublin 24 Dec 1909; d. Warsaw 10 Oct 1970)

State Security (from 19 Mar - 7 Dec 1954: *Stanisław Radkiewicz* (Pol Utd
7 Dec 1954: Lab) (see Osóbka-Morawski I)
Home Affairs) 7 Dec 1954 - 20 Feb 1957: *Władysław Wicha* (b. 1904)

Audit 19 Mar 1954 - 17 Apr 1955: *Franciszek Jóźwiak* (see
Bierut)
17 Apr 1955 - 23 Oct 1956: *Roman Ząbrowski*
23 Oct 1956: functions transferred to a chamber
directly responsible to Parliament

Justice 19 Mar 1954 - 23 Apr 1956: *Henryk Świątkowski* (Pol
Utd Lab) (see Cyrankiewicz I)
28 Apr 1956 - 20 Feb 1957: *Zofia Wasilkowska* (Pol
Utd Lab)

Finance *Tadeusz Dietrich* (see Bierut)

Higher Education 19 Mar 1954 - 29 Apr 1956: *Adam Rapacki* (see
above)
28 Apr 1956 - 20 Feb 1957: *Stefan Żółkiewski* (b.
1911)

Education 19 Mar 1954 - 29 Apr 1956(?): *Witold Jarosiński* (see
Cyrankiewicz I)
29 Apr(?) - 13 Nov 1956: *Feliks Baranowski*
13 Nov 1950 - 20 Feb 1957: *Władysław Bieńkowski*
(Pol Utd Lab) (b. Łódź 17 Mar 1906)

Agriculture 19 Mar 1954 - 31 Mar 1956: *Edmund Czunkowski*
31 Mar 1956 - 9 Jan 1957: *Anton Kuligowski*
9 Jan - 20 Feb 1957: *Edward Ochab* (Pol Utd Lab) (see
Presidents)

Food Industry *Mesko Hoffman* (see Bierut)

Defence 19 Mar 1954 - 29 Oct 1956: *Konstantin Rokossovsky*
(see Cyrankiewicz I)

431

13 Nov 1956 – 20 Feb 1957: *Marian Spychalski* (see Presidents)

20/26 Feb 1957 – 16 May 1961: Cyrankiewicz III

Prime Minister	*Józef Cyrankiewicz* (Pol Utd Lab) (for 3rd time) (see Cyrankiewicz I)
Deputy Prime	*Zenon Nowak* (see Bierut)
Ministers	*Piotr Jaroszewicz* (see Bierut)
	Stefan Ignar (Utd Farmers/Utd Peoples) (see Cyrankiewicz II)
	27 Oct 1959 – 16 May 1961: *Eugeniusz Szyr* (b. Łodygowice 16 Apr 1915)
	27 Oct 1959 – 16 May 1961: *Julian Tokarski* (b. Stanisławów 29 Mar 1883; d. Kraków 17 Oct 1961)
Chairman of State Planning Commission	*Stefan Jędrychowski* (Pol Utd Lab) (see Cyrankiewicz I)
Foreign Affairs	*Adam Rapacki* (see Cyrankiewicz II)
Home Affairs	*Władysław Wicha* (see Cyrankiewicz II)
Justice	*Marian Rybicki* (b. Warsaw 1915)
Finance	26 Feb 1957 – 28 Jul 1960: *Tadeusz Dietrich* (see Bierut)
	16 Nov 1960 – 16 May 1961: *Jerzy Albrecht* (b. Łódź 7 Oct 1914)
Education	26 Feb 1957 – 27 Oct 1959: *Władysław Bieńkowski* (see Cyrankiewicz II)
	27 Oct 1959 – 16 May 1961: *Wacław Tułodziecki*
Higher Education	26 Feb 1957 – 18 Jun 1959: *Stefan Żółkiewski* (see Cyrankiewicz II)
	18 Jun 1959 – 16 May 1961: *Henryk Gołański* (b. Łódź 1 Jan 1908)
Agriculture	26 Feb 1957 – 27 Oct 1959: *Edward Ochab* (see Presidents)
	27 Oct 1959 – 16 May 1961: *Mesko Jagielski* (Pol Utd Lab) (b. Kolomea 21 Jan 1924)
Food Industry	*Feliks Pisula* (Utd Farmers/Utd Peoples)
Defence	*Marian Spychalski* (see Presidents)

18 May 1961 – 28 May 1969: Cyrankiewicz IV

Prime Minister	*Józef Cyrankiewicz* (Pol Utd Lab) (for 4th time) (see Cyrankiewicz I)

Deputy Prime Ministers	18 May 1961 – 20 Dec 1968: *Zenon Nowak* (Pol Utd Lab) (see Bierut) *Piotr Jaroszewicz* (Pol Utd Lab) (see Bierut) *Stefan Ignar* (Pol Utd Lab) (see Cyrankiewicz II) *Eugeniusz Szyr* (Pol Utd Lab) (see Cyrankiewicz III) 18 May 1961 – 15 Dec 1965: *Julian Tokarski* (see Cyrankiewicz III) 18 May 1961 – 20 Dec 1968: *Franciszek Waniółka* (b. Teschen 1912(?); d. Warsaw 14 Apr 1971)
Chairman of State Planning Commission	18 May 1961 – 20 Dec 1968: *Stefan Jędrychowski* (Pol Utd Lab) (see Cyrankiewicz I) 20 Dec 1968 – 28 May 1969: *Józef Kulesza* (b. Warsaw 1919)
Foreign Affairs	18 May 1961 – 20 Dec 1968: *Adam Rapacki* (Pol Utd Lab) (see Cyrankiewicz II) 20 Dec 1968 – 28 May 1969: *Stefan Jędrychowski* (Pol Utd Lab) (see Cyrankiewicz I)
Home Affairs	18 May 1961 – 12 Dec 1964: *Władysław Wicha* (see Cyrankiewicz II) 12 Dec 1964 – 15 Jul 1968: *Mieczysław Moczar* (Pol Utd Lab) (b. Łódź 25 Dec 1913) 15 Jul 1968 – 28 May 1969: *Kazimierz Świtala* (b. Rakvice 21 Apr 1921)
Justice	18 May 1961 – 25 Jun 1965: *Marian Rybicki* (see Cyrankiewicz III) 25 Jun 1965 – 28 May 1969: *Stanisław Wałczak* (Pol Utd Lab) (b. Wadowice 9 Apr 1913)
Finance	18 May 1961 – 15 Jul 1968: *Jerzy Albrecht* (Pol Utd Lab) (see Cyrankiewicz III) 15 Jul 1968 – 28 May 1969: *Stanisław Majewski* (b. Chelyabinsk, Siberia, 1915)
Education	*Wacław Tułodziecki* (see Cyrankiewicz III)
Higher Education	18 May 1961 – 15 Dec 1965: *Henryk Gołański* (see Cyrankiewicz III) 15 Dec 1965 – 28 May 1969: *Henryk Jabłoński* (Pol Utd Lab) (see Presidents)
Culture and Art	18 May 1961 – 1 Sep 1965: *Tadeusz Galiński* 1 Sep 1965 – 28 May 1969: *Lucjan Motyka*
Health and Social Welfare	*Jerzy Sztachelski*
Construction and Construction Materials Industry	*Marian Olewiński* (b. Warsaw 15 Sep 1912)

Local Economy	*Stanisław Sroka*
Mining and Energy	*Jan Mitręga* (b. Michałkowice 21 Apr 1917)
Internal Trade	18 May 1961 – 1966: *Mieczysław Lesz*
	1966 – 28 May 1969: *Edward Sznajder*
Foreign Trade	*Witold Trąmpczyński* (b. Podlesie 22 Oct 1909)
Transport	18 May 1961 – Nov 1963: *Józef Popielas*
	Nov 1963 – 28 May 1969: *Piotr Lewiński*
Forestry and Timber Industry	*Roman Gesing*
Telecommunications	*Żygmunt Moskwa* (b. Warsaw 26 Apr 1908)
Chemical Industry	18 May 1961 – 1 Sep 1965: *Antoni Radliński*
	1 Sep 1965 – 28 May 1969: *Janusz Hrynkiewicz*
Heavy Industry	*Zygmunt Ostrowski*
Light Industry	*Eugeniusz Stawiński*
Food Industry and Procurement	*Feliks Pisula* (Utd Farmers/Utd Peoples) (see Cyrankiewicz III)
Shipping	18 May 1961 – 1 Sep 1965: *Stanisław Darski*
	1 Sep 1965 – 28 May 1969: *Janusz Burakiewicz*
Agriculture	*Mesko Jagielski* (Pol Utd Lab) (see Cyrankiewicz III)
Defence	18 May 1961 – 11 Apr 1968: *Marian Spychalski* (see Presidents)
	11 Apr 1968 – 28 May 1969: *Wojciech Jaruzelski* (Pol Utd Lab) (b. Lublin 6 Jul 1923)
Committee on Construction, Town Planning and Architecture	1965 – 28 May 1969: *Stefan Pietruszewicz*
Committee on Labour and Wages	*Aleksander Burski*
Committee on Small Business	*Włodzimierz Lechowicz* (b. Szczecin 16 Jan 1911)
Committee for Questions of Technology	28 May 1961 – 1962: *Dionizy Smoleński* (b. Łódź 6 Dec 1902)
Committee on Science and Technology	Dec 1962 – 28 May 1969: *Eugeniusz Szyr* (Pol Utd Lab) (see Cyrankiewicz III)

28 May 1969 – 28 Mar 1972: Cyrankiewicz V/Jaroszewicz I

Prime Minister	28 May 1969 – 23 Dec 1970: *Józef Cyrankiewicz* (Pol Utd Lab) (for 5th time) (see Cyrankiewicz I)
	from 23 Dec 1970: *Piotr Jaroszewicz* (Pol Utd Lab) (for 1st time) (see Bierut)

Deputy Prime Ministers	28 May 1969 – 23 Dec 1970: *Piotr Jaroszewicz* (Pol Utd Lab) (see Bierut) *Eugeniusz Szyr* (Pol Utd Lab) (see Cyrankiewicz III) *Zdzisław Tomal* (Utd Farmers) (b. Rogów 19 Mar 1921) 28 Jun 1969 – 13 Feb 1971: *Stanisław Majewski* (see Cyrankiewicz IV) 28 Jun 1969 – 1 Jul 1970: *Marian Olewiński* (see Cyrankiewicz IV) 1 Jul – 23 Dec 1970: *Stanisław Kociołek* (Pol Utd Lab) (b. Warsaw 3 May 1933) 1 Jul 1970 – 28 Mar 1972: *Mesko Jagielski* (Pol Utd Lab) (see Cyrankiewicz III) 23 Dec 1970 – 28 Mar 1972: *Jan Mitręga* (see Cyrankiewicz IV) 23 Dec 1970 – 28 Mar 1972: *Franciszek Kaim* (b. Wola Drwińska 13 Feb 1919) 13 Feb 1971 – 28 Mar 1972: *Wincenty Krasko*
Chairman of State Planning Commission	28 May 1969 – 13 Feb 1971: *Józef Kulesza* (see Cyrankiewicz IV) 13 Feb – 26 Oct 1971 (acting:) *Witold Trąmpczyński* (see Cyrankiewicz IV) 26 Oct 1971 – 28 Mar 1972: *Mesko Jagielski* (Pol Utd Lab) (see Cyrankiewicz III)
Foreign Affairs	28 May 1969 – 22 Dec 1971: *Stefan Jędrychowski* (Pol Utd Lab) (see Cyrankiewicz I) 22 Dec 1971 – 28 Mar 1972: *Stefan Olszowski*
Home Affairs	28 May 1969 – 13 Feb 1971: *Kazimierz Świtala* (see Cyrankiewicz IV) 13 Feb – 22 Dec 1971: *Franciszek Szlachcic* 22 Dec 1971 – 28 Mar 1972: *Wiesław Ociepka* (d. 28 Feb 1973)
Justice	28 May 1969 – 26 Oct 1971: *Stanisław Wałczak* (Pol Utd Lab) (see Cyrankiewicz IV) 26 Oct 1961 – 28 Mar 1972: *Włodzimierz Berutowicz*
Finance	28 May 1969 – 22 Dec 1971: *Józef Trendota* (b. Tarnów 1921) 22 Dec 1971 – 28 Mar 1972: *Stefan Jędrychowski* (Pol Utd Lab) (see Cyrankiewicz I)
Education	*Henryk Jabłoński* (Pol Utd Lab) (see Presidents)
Agriculture	28 May 1969 – 1 Jul 1970: *Mesko Jagielski* (Pol Utd Lab) (see Cyrankiewicz III) from 1 Jul 1970: *Józef Okuniewski*

435

Defence	*Wojciech Jaruzelski* (Pol Utd Lab) (see Cyrankiewicz IV)
Culture and Art	28 May 1969 – 26 Oct 1971: *Lucjan Motyka* (see Cyrankiewicz IV)
	22 Dec 1971 – 28 Mar 1972: *Stanisław Wronski*
Health and Social Welfare	*Jerzy Sztachelski* (see Cyrankiewicz IV)
Construction and Construction Materials Industry (Building)	28 May 1969 – 22 Dec 1971: *Marian Olewiński* (see Cyrankiewicz IV)
	22 Dec 1971 – 28 Mar 1972: *Alojzy Karkoszka*
Local Economy	*Stanisław Sroka* (see Cyrankiewicz IV)
Mining and Energy	*Jan Mitręga* (see Cyrankiewicz IV)
Internal Trade	*Edward Sznajder* (see Cyrankiewicz IV)
Foreign Trade	28 May 1969 – 13 Feb 1971: *Witold Trąmpczyński* (see Cyrankiewicz IV)
	13 Feb 1971 – 28 Mar 1972: *Kazimierz Olszewski*
Transport	*Piotr Lewiński* (see Cyrankiewicz IV)
Forestry and Timber Industry	*Roman Gesing* (see Cyrankiewicz IV)
Telecommunications	*Zygmunt Moskwa* (see Cyrankiewicz IV)
Chemical Industry	28 May 1969 – 26 Oct 1971: *Janusz Hrynkiewicz* (see Cyrankiewicz IV)
	26 Oct 1971 – 28 Mar 1972: *Jerzy Olszewski*
Heavy Industry	*Włodzimierz Lechowicz* (see Cyrankiewicz IV)
Light Industry	*Eugeniusz Stawiński* (see Cyrankiewicz IV)
Engineering	*Tadeusz Wrzaszczyk*
Food Industry and Procurement	28 May 1969 – 13 Feb 1971: *Feliks Pisula* (Utd Farmers/ Utd Peoples) (see Cyrankiewicz III)
	13 Feb 1971 – 28 Mar 1972: *Emil Kolodziej*
Shipping	*Janusz Burakiewicz* (see Cyrankiewicz IV)
Committee on Construction, Town Planning and Architecture	*Stefan Pietruszewicz* (see Cyrankiewicz IV)
Committee on Labour and Wages	*Aleksander Burski* (see Cyrankiewicz IV)
Committee on Small Businesses	*Włodzimierz Lechowicz* (see Cyrankiewicz IV)
Vice-Chairman of Committee for Science and Technology	*Janusz Hrynkiewicz* (see Cyrankiewicz IV)

from 28 Mar 1972: Jaroszewicz II

Prime Minister	*Piotr Jaroszewicz* (Pol Utd Lab) (for 2nd time) (see Bierut)
Deputy Prime Ministers	28 Mar 1972 – 22 Feb 1975: *Jan Mitręga* (see Cyrankiewicz IV)
	Mesko Jagielski (Pol Utd Lab) (see Cyrankiewicz III)
	Franciszek Kaim (see Cyrankiewicz V/Jaroszewicz I)
	Zdzisław Tomal (Utd Farmers) (see Cyrankiewicz V/Jaroszewicz I)
	Kazimierz Olszewski (see Cyrankiewicz V/Jaroszewicz I)
	Józef Tejchma
	from 12 May 1975: *Alojzy Karkoszka* (see Cyrankiewicz V/Jaroszewicz I)
	from 23 Oct 1975: *Tadeusz Wrzaszczyk* (see Cyrankiewicz V/Jaroszewicz I)
	from 23 Oct 1975: *Tadeusz Pyka*
Chairman of State Planning Commission	28 Mar 1972 – 23 Oct 1975: *Mesko Jagielski* (Pol Utd Lab) (see Cyrankiewicz III)
	from 23 Oct 1975: *Tadeusz Wrzaszczyk* (see Cyrankiewicz V/Jaroszewicz I)
Foreign Affairs	*Stefan Olszowski* (see Cyrankiewicz V/Jaroszewicz I)
Home Affairs	28 Mar 1972 – 28 Feb 1973: *Wiesław Ociepka* (see Cyrankiewicz V/Jaroszewicz I)
	from 23 Mar 1973: *Stanisław Kowalczyk*
Justice	*Włodzimierz Berutowicz* (see Cyrankiewicz V/Jaroszewicz I)
Finance	28 Mar 1972 – 21 Nov 1974: *Stefan Jędrychowski* (Pol Utd Lab) (see Cyrankiewicz I)
	from 21 Nov 1974: *Henryk Kisiel*
Education	*Jerzy Kuberski*
Agriculture	28 Mar 1972 – 16 Feb 1974: *Józef Okuniewski* (see Cyrankiewicz V/Jaroszewicz I)
	from 16 Feb 1974: *Kazimierz Barcikowski*
Defence	*Wojciech Jaruzelski* (Pol Utd Lab) (see Cyrankiewicz IV)
Culture and Art	28 Mar 1972 – 16 Feb 1974: *Stanisław Wronski* (see Cyrankiewicz V/Jaroszewicz I)
	from 16 Feb 1974: *Józef Tejchma* (see above)
Health and Social Welfare	*Marian Sliwinski*

Building and Building Materials Industry	28 Mar 1972 – 12 May 1975: *Alojzy Karkoszka* (see Cyrankiewicz V/Jaroszewicz I) from 12 May 1975: *Adam Glazur*
Local Economy and Environment	28 Mar 1972 – 12 May 1975: *Jerzy Kusiak* from 12 May 1975: *Tadeusz Bejm*
Mining and Energy	28 Mar 1972 – 24 Sep 1974: *Jan Mitręga* (see Cyrankiewicz IV) from 24 Sep 1972: *Jan Kulpinski*
Internal Trade and Services	28 Mar 1972 – 12 May 1975: *Edward Sznajder* (see Cyrankiewicz IV) from 12 May 1975: *Jerzy Gawrysiak*
Foreign Trade (from 10 Apr 1974: and Mercantile Marine)	28 Mar 1972 – 10 Apr 1974: *Tadeusz Olechowski* 10 Apr – 21 Nov 1974: *Kazimierz Olszewski* (see Cyrankiewicz V/Jaroszewicz I) from 21 Nov 1974: *Jerzy Olszewski*
Transport	*Mieczysław Zajfryd*
Forestry and Timber Industry	28 Mar 1972 – 22 Nov 1973: *Jerzy Popko* from 22 Nov 1973: *Tadeusz Skwirzynski*
Telecommunications	*Edward Kowalczyk*
Chemical Industry	28 Mar 1972 – 21 Nov 1974: *Jerzy Olszewski* (see above) from 21 Nov 1974: *Maciej Wirowski*
Heavy Industry	*Włodzimierz Lechowicz* (see Cyrankiewicz IV)
Light Industry	*Tadeusz Kunicki*
Engineering	28 Mar 1972 – 23 Oct 1975: *Tadeusz Wrzaszczyk* (see Cyrankiewicz V/Jaroszewicz I) from 23 Oct 1975: *Alexander Kopec*
Food Industry and Procurement	*Emil Kolodziej*
Shipping	28 Mar 1972 – 22 Nov 1973: *Jerzy Szopa* 22 Nov 1973 – 10 Apr 1974: *Kazimierz Olszewski* (see Cyrankiewicz V/Jaroszewicz I) 10 Apr 1974: amalgamated with Foreign Trade (see above)
Wages, Labour and Social Security	28 Mar 1972 – 21 Nov 1974: *Wicenty Kawalec* from 21 Nov 1974: *Tadeusz Rudolf*
Science, Higher Education and Technology	*Jan Kaczmarek*
Without Portfolio	from 16 Feb 1974: *Stanisław Wronksi* (see Cyrankiewicz V/Jaroszewicz I)

Portugal

HEADS OF STATE

Presidents

9 Aug 1926 – 18 Apr 1951	*António Óscar Fragoso Carmona* (b. 24 Nov 1869; d. 18 Apr 1951)*
9 Aug 1951	*Francisco Higino Craveiro Lopes* (b. 12 Apr 1894; d. 3. Sep 1964)
9 Aug 1958 – 25 Apr 1974	*Américo (Deus Rodriguez) Tomás* (b. Lisbon 19 Nov 1894)
15 May 1974	*Antônio Sebastião Ribeiro de Spínola* (b. Estremoz 11 Apr 1910)
from 30 Sep 1974	*Francisco da Costa Gomes* (b. Chaves 30 Jun 1914)

MEMBERS OF GOVERNMENT

Prime Ministers

9 Jul 1929 – 10 Jan 1930	*Arturo Ivens Ferraz* (b. 1 Dec 1870; d. 16 Jan 1933)
21 Jan 1930 – 25 Jun 1932	*Domingos de Costa Oliveira* (b. 30 Jun 1873; d. 24 Dec 1957)
5 Jul 1932	*António de Oliveira Salazar* (for 1st time) (b. Vimeiro 28 Apr 1889; d. Lisbon 27 Jul 1970)
11 Apr 1933	*António de Oliveira Salazar* (for 2nd time)
23 Oct 1934	*António de Oliveira Salazar* (for 3rd time)
18 Jan 1936	*António de Oliveira Salazar* (for 4th time)
26 Sep 1968 – 25 Apr 1974	*Marcelo Caetano* (b. Lisbon 17 Aug 1906)
16 May – 9 Jul 1974	*Adelino da Palma Carlos* (b. 1905?)
12 Jul 1974	*Vasco dos Santos Gonçalves* (b. Lisbon 3 May 1921)
from 29 Aug 1975	*José Baptista Pinheiro de Azevedo* (b. Angola 1917)

Foreign Ministers

9 Sep 1929 – 10 Jan 1930	*J. Fonseca Monteira*

*For earlier career see vol. 2

21 Jan 1930	*Fernando Augusto Branco* (b. 24 Jun 1890)
5 Jul 1932 – 11 Apr 1933	*César de Sousa Mendes do Amaral e Abranches* (b. 18 Jul 1885)
13 Apr 1933	*José Caeiro de Mata* (for 1st time) (b. Vimieiro 1883; d. 3 Jan 1963)
27 Mar 1935	(acting:) *Aníbal Mesquita Guimarães* (b. Oporto 5 Nov 1882; d. Lisbon 22 May 1952)
4 Jan 1936	*Armindo Monteiro* (b. Villa Velha de Ródão 16 Dec 1896; d. Loures 15 Oct 1955)
24 Nov 1936	*António de Oliveira Salazar* (see Prime Ministers)
3 Feb 1947	*José Caeiro de Mata* (for 2nd time)
1 Aug 1950	*Paulo Cunha* (b. Sep 1908)
13 Aug 1958	*Marcello Mathias* (b. 15 Aug 1903)
3 May 1961	*Alberto Franco Nogueira* (b. Lisbon 17 Sep 1918)
5 Oct 1969	*Marcelo Caetano* (see Prime Ministers)
14 Jan 1970	*Rui Manuel de Medeiros d'Espiney Patricio* (b. 17 Aug 1932)
16 May 1974	*Mário Alberto Nobre Lopes Soares* (b. Lisbon 7 Dec 1924)
25 Mar 1975	*Eduardo Augusto de Melo Antunes* (for 1st time) (b. 1933)
8 Aug 1975	*Mario Ruivo* (b. 1927?)
from 19 Sep 1975	*Eduardo Augusto de Melo Antunes* (for 2nd time)

Qatar

1916	British protectorate
1 Sep 1971	Independent

HEADS OF STATE

Amirs

4 Sep 1970	*Sheikh Ahmad bin Ali bin Abdullah al-Thani* (b. 1917) from Oct 1960: ruler of Qatar; deposed 22 Feb 1972
from 22 Feb 1972	*Sheikh Khalifa bin Hamad al-Thani*, cousin (b. 1934)

MEMBER OF GOVERNMENT

Prime Minister

from 29 May 1970   *Sheikh Khalifa bin Hamad al-Thani* (see Amirs)

Rhodesia

Formerly Southern Rhodesia.

HEADS OF STATE [†]

Governors

1 Oct 1923	*Sir John Robert Chancellor* (b. Edinburgh 20 Oct 1870; d. Shieldhill, Lanarkshire, 31 Jul 1952)
24 Nov 1928	*Sir Cecil Hunter Rodwell* (b. 29 Dec 1874; d. 23 Feb 1953)
8 Jan 1935	*Sir Herbert James Stanley* (b. Manchester 25 Jul 1872; d. Cape Town 5 Jun 1955)
10 Dec 1942	*Sir Evelyn Baring* (from 1960: *1st Baron Howick of Glendale*) (b. 29 Sep 1903; d. 10 Mar 1973)
20 Feb 1945 – 17 Jul 1946	*Sir (William Eric) Campbell Tait* (b. Morice Town, Devonport, 12 Aug 1886; d. Salisbury, Rhodesia, 17 Jul 1946)
14 Jan 1947	*Sir John Noble Kennedy* (b. 31 Aug 1893; d. 15 Jun 1970)
16 Sep 1954	*Sir Peveril (Barton Reibey Wallop) William-Powlett* (b. 5 Mar 1898)
28 Dec 1959 – 24 Jun 1969	*Sir Humphrey Vicary Gibbs* (b. 22 Nov 1902) from 16 Nov 1965 under house arrest, resigned in 1969
17 Nov 1965 – 14 Apr 1970	*Clifford (Walter) Dupont* (b. London 6 Dec 1905) Rhodesian appointment to administer government, acting President from 24 Jun 1969
2 Mar 1970	Unilateral Declaration of Independence from United Kingdom and proclamation of Republic

[†] Information 1923-1930 included because it did not appear in vol. 2

President

from 14/16 Apr 1970   *Clifford (Walter) Dupont* (see Governors)

MEMBERS OF GOVERNMENT †

Prime Ministers

1 Oct 1923	*Sir Charles Patrick John Coghlan* (b. King William's Town 24 Jun 1863; d. Salisbury, Rhodesia, 28 Aug 1927)
2 Sep 1927	*Howard Unwin Moffat* (b. 13 Jan 1869; d. 19 Jan 1951)
5 Jul 1933	*George Mitchell* (b. 1 Apr 1867; d. 4 Jul 1937)
12 Sep 1933	*Sir Godfrey Huggins* (from 1955: *1st Viscount Malvern*) (b. Bexley 6 Jul 1883; d. Salisbury, Rhodesia, 8 May 1971)
7 Sep 1953	*Sir Reginald Steven Garfield Todd* (b. Invercargill, New Zealand, 13 Jul 1908)
17 Feb 1958	*Sir Edgar (Cuthbert Fremantle) Whitehead* (b. Berlin 8 Feb 1905; d. Newbury night of 22/23 Sep 1971)
17 Dec 1962	*Winston (Joseph) Field* (b. Bromsgrove 6 Jun 1904; d. Salisbury, Rhodesia, 17 Mar 1969)
from 13 Apr 1964	*Ian (Douglas) Smith* (b. Selukwe 8 Apr 1919)

Romania

HEADS OF STATE

Kings

20 Jul 1927	*Michael*, son of Carol II, see below (for 1st time) (b. 25 Oct 1921)
8 Jun 1930	*Carol II*, son of King Ferdinand I (b. 15 Oct 1893; d. Lisbon 4 Apr 1953) abdicated 1940 in favour of his son Michael

† Information 1923–1930 included because it did not appear in vol. 2

6 Oct 1940 – 30 Dec 1947	*Michael* (for 2nd time)
30 Dec 1947	Republic

Presidents (Chairmen of the Presidium)

30 Dec 1947	*Mihai Sadoveanu* (b. Pascani, Moldau, 5 Nov 1880; d. Bucharest(?) 19 Oct 1961) Leader of five-man acting Presidium
2 Apr 1948	*Constantin I. Parhon* (b. Cîmpolung-Mușcel 27 Oct 1874)
3 Jun 1952 – 7 Jan 1958	*Petru Groza* (b. 6 Dec 1884; d. Bucharest 7 Jan 1958)
11 Jan 1958	*Ion Gheorghe Maurer* (b. Bucharest 23 Sep 1902)
21 Mar 1961 – 19 Mar 1965	*Gheorghe Gheorghiu-Dej* (b. Moldau 8 Nov 1901; d. Bucharest 19 Mar 1965) Chairman of State Assembly
25 Mar 1965	*Chivu Stoica* (b. 8 Aug 1908; d. 18 Feb 1975)
from 9 Dec 1967	*Nicolae Ceaușescu* (b. Scornicești 26 Jan 1918)

MEMBERS OF GOVERNMENT

Prime Ministers

10 Nov 1928	*Juliu Maniu* (for 1st time) (b. 8 Jan 1873; d. Feb(?) 1948)
7 – 8 Jun 1930	*Gheorghe C. Mironescu* (for 1st time) (b. 28 Jan 1874)
13 Jun – 6 Oct 1930	*Juliu Maniu* (for 2nd time)
10 Oct 1930 – 4 Apr 1931	*Gheorghe C. Mironescu* (for 2nd time)
18 Apr 1931 – 31 May 1932	*Nicolae Iorga* (b. 17 Jun 1871; d. 27/28 Nov 1940)
6 Jun 1932	*Alexandru Vaida-Voievod* (for 2nd time) (b. 27 Feb 1873)*
11 Aug 1932	*Alexandru Vaida-Voievod* (for 3rd time)
19 Oct 1932 – 12 Jan 1933	*Juliu Maniu* (for 3rd time)
16 Jan – 12 Nov 1933	*Alexandru Vaida-Voievod* (for 4th time)
14 Nov 1933 – 29 Dec 1933	*Ion G. Duca* (b. 20 Dec 1879; d. 29 Dec 1933)
30 Dec 1933	*Constantin Angelescu* (b. 1870(?); d. 14 Sep 1948)

*For earlier career see vol. 2

443

3 Jan 1934	*Gheorghe Tătărescu* (for 1st time) (b. 1892; d. 28 Mar 1957)
2 Oct 1934	*Gheorghe Tătărescu* (for 2nd time)
29 Aug 1936 – 14 Nov 1937	*Gheorghe Tătărescu* (for 3rd time)
18 Nov 1937	*Gheorghe Tătărescu* (for 4th time)
28 Dec 1937	*Octavian Goga* (b. 1 Apr 1880; d. 7 May 1938)
11 Feb 1938	*Miron Cristea* (for 1st time) (b. 18 Jul 1868; d. 6 Mar 1939) Patriarch
31 Mar 1938	*Miron Cristea* (for 2nd time)
2 Feb 1939	*Miron Cristea* (for 3rd time)
6 Mar 1939	*Armand Călineşcu* (b. 1893; d. 21 Sep 1939)
21 Sep 1939	*Gheorghe Argeşanu*
28 Sep – 23 Nov 1939	*Constantine Argetoianu* (b. 1871?)
25 Nov 1939	*Gheorghe Tătărescu* (for 5th time)
11 May – 18 Jun 1940	*Gheorghe Tătărescu* (for 6th time)
27 Jun 1940	*Gheorghe Tătărescu* (for 7th time)
4 Jul 1940	*Ion Gigurtu* (b. 1886)
5 Sep 1940	*Ion Antonescu* (for 1st time) (b. 14 Jun 1882; d. 1 Jun 1946)
27 Jan 1941	*Ion Antonescu* (for 2nd time)
23 Aug 1944 †	*Constantin Sănătescu* (for 1st time) (b. 1884(?); d. 9 Nov 1947)
2 Nov – 2 Dec 1944	*Constantin Sănătescu* (for 2nd time)
6 Dec 1944 – 28 Feb 1945	*Nicolae Rădescu* (b. Bucharest 30 Jun 1874; d. New York 16 May 1953)
6 Mar 1945	*Petru Groza* (for 1st time) (see Presidents)
2 Dec 1946	*Petru Groza* (for 2nd time)
1 Jan 1948	*Petru Groza* (for 3rd time)
2 Jun 1952	*Gheorghe Gheorghiu-Dej* (for 1st time) (see Presidents)
24 Jan 1953	*Gheorghe Gheorghiu-Dej* (for 2nd time)
3 Oct 1955	*Chivu Stoica* (see Presidents)
21 Mar 1961	*Ion Gheorghe Maurer* (see Presidents)
from 29 Mar 1974	*Manea Mănescu* (b. Braila 9 Aug 1916)

Foreign Ministers

10 Nov 1928	*Gheorghe C. Mironescu* (see Prime Ministers)

†National Government in Germany:

24 Aug 1944	*Horia Sima* (for 1st time) 'Führer of the Iron Guards'
13 Dec 1944 – May 1945	*Horia Sima* (for 2nd time)

18 Apr 1931	(acting:) *Constantin Argetoianu* (for 1st time) (see Prime Ministers)
27 Apr 1931 – 6 Jun 1932	*Demetrie I. Ghica* (b. Constantinople 21 Jan 1875)
10 Jun – 18 Jul 1932	*Grigore Gafencu* (for 1st time) (b. Bucharest 30 Jan 1892; d. Paris 30 Jan 1957)
11 Aug 1932	*Alexandru Vaida-Voievod* (for 2nd time) (see Prime Ministers)
20 Oct 1932	*Nicolae Titulescu* (for 2nd time) (b. Craiova 4 Oct 1883; d. Cannes 17 Mar 1941)*
30 Aug 1936	*Victor Antonescu*
28 Dec 1937	*Istrate Micescu* (b. Ploieşti 22 May 1881)
10 Feb 1938	(acting:) *Gheorghe Tătărescu* (for 1st time) (see Prime Ministers)
30 Mar 1938	*Nicolae Petrescu-Comnen* (b. Bucharest 24 Aug 1881)
21 Dec 1938	*Grigore Gafencu* (for 2nd time)
1 Jun 1940	*Ion Gigurtu* (see Prime Ministers)
28 Jun 1940	*Constantin Argetoianu* (for 2nd time)
4 Jul – 4 Sep 1940	*Mihai Manoilescu* (b. 1891; d. 1950)
15 Sep – 19 Dec 1940	*Mihai Sturdza* (for 1st time)
21 Dec 1940	(until 27 Jan 1941 acting:) *Ion Antonescu* (see Prime Ministers)
3 Jul 1941	*Mihai A. Antonescu* (b. 1899; d. Bucharest 1 Jun 1946)
24 Aug 1944 †	*Grigore Niculescu-Buzeşti*
5 Nov 1944	*Constantin Vişoianu* (b. 4 Dec 1897)
6 Mar 1945	*Gheorghe Tătărescu* (for 2nd time)
6 Nov 1947	*Ana Pauker* (b. Herţa 1894; d. Bucharest 8(?) Jun 1960)
5 Jul 1952	*Simion Bughici*
4 Oct 1955	*Grigore Preoteasa* (b. 25 Aug 1915; d. Moscow 4 Nov 1957)
14 Jul 1957	*Ion Gheorghe Maurer* (see Presidents)
11 Jan 1958	*Avram Bunaciu*
21 Mar 1961	*Corneliu Mănescu*
from 19 Oct 1972	*Gheorghe Macovescu*

† National Government in Germany:

24 Aug 1944 – May 1945	*Mihai Sturdza* (for 2nd time)

Rwanda

Formerly part of Ruanda-Urundi.
For the Kingdom of Rwanda, see also vol. 1.

1 Jul 1962   End of Belgian trusteeship

HEADS OF STATE

Presidents and Prime Ministers

1 Jul 1962   *Grégoire Kayibanda* (b. Nyakibanda 1 May 1924)
from 5 Jul 1973   *Juvenal Habyarimana* (b. Rambura 3 Aug 1937)

São Tomé e Principe

12 Jul 1975   Independence from Portugal

HEAD OF STATE

President

from 12 Jul 1975   *Manuel Pinto da Costa*

MEMBER OF GOVERNMENT

Prime Minister

from 12 Jul 1975   *Miguel Trovoada*

Sarawak

HEADS OF STATE

Rajahs

17/24 May 1917 – 1 Jul 1946	*Sir Charles Vyner de Windt Brooke* (b. London 26 Sep 1874; d. 9 May 1963)
Apr 1942 – 15 Apr 1946	Invaded by Japanese; Sarawak Commission convened in London under chairmanship of *Bertram Brooke*, brother of the Rajah
1 Jul 1946	Became a British Crown Colony
16 Sep 1963	Joined the Federation of Malaysia (q.v.)

Saudi Arabia

18 Sep 1932	Kingdom of Saudi Arabia formed from Hejaz and Nejd

HEADS OF STATE

Kings

Wahhabite Dynasty

8 May 1926	*Abdul Aziz III (ibn Saud)* (b. Riyadh 21 Oct 1882) King of Hejaz 8 Jan 1926, King of Nejd 1927, King of Asir 1930
9 Nov 1953	*Saud*, son (b. Kuwait 15 Jan 1902; d. Athens 23 Feb 1969)
2 Nov 1964	*Faisal*, brother (for 1st time) (b. 1906; d. (assassinated) 25 Mar 1975) Crown Prince, Regent and Viceroy

447

| 2 Nov 1964 | *Faisal* (for 2nd time) |
| from 25 Mar 1975 | *Khaled ibn Abdul Aziz*, brother (b. 1913) |

MEMBERS OF GOVERNMENT

Prime Ministers

11 Oct – 9 Nov 1953	*Saud* (for 1st time) (see Kings) Crown Prince
17 Mar 1954	*Faisal* (for 1st time) (see Kings) Crown Prince
21 Dec 1960	*Saud* (for 2nd time) Chairman of Ministers
15 Mar – 17 Oct 1962	*Saud* (for 3rd time)
31 Oct 1962	*Faisal* (for 2nd time) Crown Prince
from 2 Nov 1964	King also Prime Minister

Senegal

| 25 Nov 1958 | Member of French Community |
| 4 Apr 1959 – 22 Aug 1960 | Part of Mali Federation (see p. 373) |

HEAD OF STATE

President

| from 5 Sep 1960 | *Léopold-Sédar Senghor* (b. Joal-la-Portugaise 9 Oct 1906) |

MEMBERS OF GOVERNMENT

Prime Ministers

25 Nov 1958	*Mamadou Dia* (b. Khombole 18 Jul 1910)
18 Dec 1962	President also Prime Minister
from 26 Feb 1970	*Abdou Diouf* (b. Louga 7 Sep 1935)

Sierra Leone

27 Apr 1961	Independence from Great Britain
19 Apr 1971	Republic

HEADS OF STATE

Governors-General

27 Apr 1961 – May(?) 1962	*Sir Maurice Dorman* (b. Stafford 7 Aug 1912)
Jul 1962	*Sir Henry Lightfoot Boston* (b. 19 Aug 1898; d. 11 Jan 1969)
26 Mar 1967 – 19 Apr 1968	Prime Minister also Governor-General
22 Apr 1968	*Sir Banja Tejan-Sie* (b. Moyamba 7 Aug 1917)
31 Mar – 19 Apr 1971	(acting:) *Christopher Okero Cole*

Presidents

19 Apr 1971	*Christopher Okero Cole* (see Governors-General)
from 21 Apr 1971	*Siaka (Probyn) Stevens* (b. Moyamba 24 Aug 1903)

MEMBERS OF GOVERNMENT

Prime Ministers

27 Apr 1961 – 28 Apr 1964	*Sir Milton Margai* (b. Gbangbatoke 7 Dec 1895; d. Freetown 28 Apr 1964)
30 Apr 1964 – 17 Mar 1967	*Sir Albert Michael Margai*, brother (b. Gbangbatoke 10 Oct 1910)
21 Mar 1967	*Siaka (Probyn) Stevens* (for 1st time) (see Presidents)
21 Mar 1967	*David Lansana*
24 Mar 1967	*Ambrose Genda* (b. Gerihun 20 Apr 1927) Head of National Reformation Council
27 Mar 1967	*Andrew Juxon-Smith* (b. Freetown 1933) Creole, Head of National Reformation Council
20 Apr 1968	*John Bangura*

449

SIERRA LEONE

26 Apr 1968	*Siaka (Probyn) Stevens* (for 2nd time)
19 Apr 1971	*Sorie Ibrahim Koroma* (b. Port Luko 30 Jan 1930)
from Jul 1975	*Christian Alusine Kamara Taylor* (b. Ka-Hanta 3 Jun 1917)

Singapore

3 Jan 1959	Self-governing within the British Commonwealth
1 Sep 1963	Independence from Great Britain
16 Sep 1963 – 9 Aug 1965	Member of Malaysian Federation (see p. 370)

HEADS OF STATE

Yang di-Pertuan Negara

3 Jan 1959	*Sir William (Allmond Codrington) Goode* (b. 9 Sep 1905) previously Governor
3 Dec 1959 – 8 Aug 1965	*Yusof Bin Ishaq* (b. Padang Gajah, Perak, 12 Aug 1910; d. Singapore 23 Nov 1970)

Presidents

9 Aug 1965 – 23 Nov 1970	*Yusof Bin Ishaq* (see Yang di-Pertuan Negara)
from 30 Dec 1970	*Benjamin Henry Sheares* (b. Singapore 1907)

MEMBERS OF GOVERNMENT

Prime Ministers

Jun 1956	*Lim Yew Hock* (b. Singapore 15 Oct 1914) Chief Minister
from 6 May 1959	*Lee Kuan Yew* (b. 1923)

450

Slovakia

See also Czechoslovakia.

7/8 Oct 1938	Autonomous state within Czechoslovakia
14 Mar 1939	Independent state
5 Apr 1945	Re-integrated as part of Czechoslovakia

HEAD OF STATE

President

26 Oct 1939 – 5 Apr 1945   *Jozef Tiso* (b. Velká Bytča 13 Oct 1887; d. Bratislava 18 Apr 1947)

MEMBERS OF GOVERNMENT

7/8 Oct – 29 Nov 1938: Tiso I

Prime Minister	*Jozef Tiso* (Slov Pop) (for 1st time) (see President)
Home Affairs	*Jozef Tiso* (Slov Pop) (see President)
Finance, Public Works and Agriculture	*Pavo Teplaiský* (Slov Farmers) (b. Trvna 22 Apr 1896)
Justice, Health and Social Welfare	*Ferdinand D'určanský* (Slov Pop) (b. Rajec 18 Dec 1906) lives in exile
Transport	*Ján Lichner* (Slov Farmers)
Education	*Matúš Černák* (Slov Pop) (b. 23 Aug 1903; d. Munich 5 Jul 1955)

1 Dec 1938 – 20 Jan 1939: Tiso II

Prime Minister	*Jozef Tiso* (Slov Pop) (for 2nd time) (see President)
Home Affairs	*Jozef Tiso* (Slov Pop) (see President)
Economic Affairs (Commerce, Industry and Finance)	*Pavol Teplanský* (Slov Farmers) (see Tiso I)
Justice	*Miloš Vančo*
Education	*Matúš Černák* (Slov Pop) (see Tiso I)

451

Railways, Post and   *Ferdinand D'určanský* (Slov Pop) (see Tiso I)
Telegraph, and
Public Works
(and from 11 Dec
1938: Transport)

20 Jan – 10 Mar 1939: Tiso III

Prime Minister	*Jozef Tiso* (Slov Pop) (for 3rd time) (see President)
Deputy Prime Minister	2 – 10 Mar 1939: *Jozef Sivák* (Slov Pop) (b. Bobrovec 14 Jan 1896)
Home Affairs	*Jozef Tiso* (see President)
Commerce	*Mikuláč Pruzinský* (b. Sv. Mikuláš Liptovský 13 Dec 1886)
Finance	*Pavol Teplanský* (Slov Farmers) (see Tiso I)
Justice	*Miloš Vančo* (see Tiso II)
Education	*Jozef Sivák* (Slov Pop) (see above)
Transport	*Ferdinand D'určanský* (Slov Pop) (see Tiso I)

14 Mar – 26 Oct 1939: Tiso IV

Prime Minister	*Jozef Tiso* (for 4th time) (see President)
Deputy Prime Minister	*Vojtěch Tuka* (b. Piary 4 Jul 1880; d. Bratislava 20 Aug 1946)
Foreign Affairs	*Ferdinand D'určanský* (see Tiso I)
Home Affairs	14 – 15 Mar 1939: *Karol Sidor* (b. Ružomberok 16 Jul 1901; d. Montreal Oct 1953)
	15 Mar – 26 Oct 1939: *Vojtěch Tuka* (see above)
Finance	*Mikuláč Pruzinský* (see Tiso III)
Justice	*Gejza Fritz* (b. Solivar 19 Sep 1880)
Defence	*Ferdinand Čatloš* (b. Sv. Petr Liptovský 17 Oct 1895; d. (shot) probably in 1944/45)
Education	*Jozef Sivák* (see Tiso III)
Economic Affairs	*Gejza Medrický* (b. Radwan an der Glan 12 Nov 1901)
Transport	*Julius Stano* (b. Ružomberok 22 Feb 1900)
Propaganda	*Šaňo Mach* (b. Modern 11 Oct 1902)

29 Oct 1939 – 5 Sep 1944: Tuka

Prime Minister	*Vojtěch Tuka* (see Tiso IV)
Deputy Prime Minister	*Ferdinand D'určanský* (see Tiso I)

Foreign Affairs	29 Oct 1939 – 29 Jul 1940: *Ferdinand D'určanský* (see Tiso I)
	29 Jul 1940 – 5 Sep 1944: *Vojtěch Tuka* (see Tiso IV)
Home Affairs	29 Oct 1939 – 29 Jul 1940: *Ferdinand D'určanský* (see Tiso I)
	29 Jul 1940 – 5 Sep 1944: *Šaňo Mach* (see Tiso IV)
Finance	*Mikuláč Pruzinský* (see Tiso III)
Justice	*Gejza Fritz* (see Tiso IV)
Defence	*Ferdinand Čatloš* (see Tiso IV)
Education	*Jozef Sivák* (see Tiso III)
Economic Affairs	*Gejza Medrický* (see Tiso IV)
Transport	*Julius Stano* (see Tiso IV)
Propaganda	29 Oct 1939 – 29 Jul 1940: *Šaňo Mach* (see Tiso IV)
	29 Jul 1940 – (?): *Karol Murgaš* (b. Budapest 12 Sep 1899)
	(?) – 5 Sep 1944: *Tido Gašpar* (b. Starin)

5 Sep 1944 – 5 Apr 1945: Štefan Tiso

Prime Minister	*Štefan Tiso*
Foreign Affairs	*Štefan Tiso* (see above)
Home Affairs	*Šaňo Mach* (see Tiso IV)
Finance	*Mikuláč Pruzinský* (see Tiso IIi)
Justice	*Štefan Tiso* (see above)
Defence	*Štefan Haššik* (b. Duhopol 25 Nov 1898) lives in exile
Education	*Aladár Kočiš* (b. Trencin 8 Apr 1907)
Commerce	*Gejza Medrický* (see Tiso IV)
Transport	*František Lednár*
Propaganda Chief	*Tido Gašpar* (see Tuka)
Propaganda Deputy	*Štefan Polakovič* (b. Chtelnica 22 Sep 1912)

Somali Democratic Republic

1 Jul 1960	Somali Republic formed from British Somaliland Protectorate and Italian Trust Territory of Somaliland

453

HEADS OF STATE

Presidents

1 Jul 1960 – 30 Jun 1967	(until 6 Jul 1960 acting:) *Aden Abdullah Othman Daar* (b. Belet Uen 1908)
1 Jul 1967 – 15 Oct 1969	*Abdi Rashid Ali Shirmarke* (b. Harardera 16 Oct 1919; d.(assassinated) Las Anod 15 Oct 1969)
from 21 Oct 1969	*General Siad Barre* (b. Lugh district 1919) President of Revolutionary Council

MEMBERS OF GOVERNMENT

Prime Ministers

12/22 Jul 1960 – Jun 1964	*Abdi Rashid Ali Shirmarke* (see Presidents)
15 Jun – 14 Jul 1964	*Abdi Razik Haji Hussein* (for 1st time) (b. 1924)
1(?) Sep 1964 – Jul 1967	*Abdi Razik Haji Hussein* (for 2nd time)
Jul 1967 – Mar 1969	*Mohamed Haji Ibrahim Egal* (for 1st time) (b. 15 Aug 1928)
Mar – 21 Oct 1969	*Mohamed Haji Ibrahim Egal* (for 2nd time)
30(?) Oct 1969 – end of Apr 1970	*General Jama Ali Khorshel*, Head of Administration as Secretary for Home Affairs
from end of Apr(?) 1970	*Husain Kulmye*, Secretary for Home Affairs

South Africa, Republic of

from 31 May 1910	Known as Union of South Africa (member of the Commonwealth)
31 May 1961	Republic established; left the Commonwealth

HEADS OF STATE

Governors-General

1924	*Alexander Cambridge, 1st Earl of Athlone* (b. London 14 Apr 1874; d. London 16 Jan 1957)
1931	*George Herbert Hyde Villiers, 6th Earl of Clarendon* (b. 7 Jun 1877; d. London 13 Dec 1955)
1937	*Sir Patrick Duncan* (b. Fortrie, Banffshire, 21 Dec 1870; d. Pretoria 17 Jul 1943)*
1943	*Nicolaas Jacobus de Wet* (b. Aliwal North 11 Sep 1873; d. Pretoria 16 Mar 1960) Administrator*
1945	*Gideon Brand van Zyl* (b. Sea Point 3 Jun 1873; d. 1 Nov 1956)
Jan 1951 – 25 Nov 1959	*Ernest George Jansen* (b. Strathearn 7 Aug 1881; d. Pretoria 25 Nov 1959)
26 Nov 1959	*Lucas Cornelius Steyn* (b. Gerluksdam 21 Dec 1903) Administrator
7 Dec 1959 – 31 May 1961	*Charles Robberts Swart* (d. Winberg 5 Dec 1894)

Presidents

31 May 1961	*Charles Robberts Swart* (see Governors-General)
Jun – 6 Dec 1967	*Theophilus Ebenhaezer Dönges* (b. Klerksdorp 8 Mar 1898; d. Cape Town 10 Jan 1968)
Jun 1967 – 10 Apr 1968	(acting:) *Jozua François (Tom) Naudé* (b. Middelburg 15 Apr 1889; d. Cape Town 31 May 1969)
10 Apr 1968	*Jacobus Johannes Fouché* (b. Wepener 6 Jun 1898)
from 21 Feb 1975	*Nicolaas Diederichs* (b. Ladybrand 17 Nov 1903)

MEMBERS OF GOVERNMENT

Nov 1928 – 30 Mar 1933: Hertzog II †

Prime Minister and External Affairs	*James Barry Munnik Hertzog* (for 2nd time) (b. Wellington 3 Apr 1866; d. Pretoria 21 Nov 1942)*

For earlier career see vol. 2

† For ministers no longer in office in 1930 see vol. 2

Interior	*Daniel François Malan* (b. Riebeck West 22 May 1874; d. Cape Town 7 Feb 1959)*
Agriculture	*Jan Christoffel Greyling Kemp* (b. 10 Jun 1872; d. Piet Retief 31 Dec 1946)*
Defence	*Frederic Hugh Page Creswell* (b. Gibraltar 13 Nov 1866; d. Kuilsrivier 25 Aug 1948)*
Education	*Daniel François Malan* (see above)
Finance	*Nicolaas Christiaan Havenga* (b. Blesbok 1 May 1882; d. Cape Town 13 Mar 1957)*
Irrigation	*Ernest George Jansen* (see Governors-General)
Justice	19 Jun 1929 – 30 Mar 1933: *Oswald Pirow* (b. Aberdeen, Cape Province, 14 Aug 1890; d. Pretoria 11 Oct 1959)
Labour	19 Jun 1929 – 30 Mar 1933: *Frederic Hugh Page Creswell* (see above)
Lands	*Pieter Gert Wessel Grobler* (b. Rustenburg district 1 Feb 1873; d. Pretoria 22 Aug 1942)*
Mines and Industries	30 Aug 1929 – 30 Mar 1933: *Adriaan Paulus Johannes Fourie* (b. Klein Disselfontein 11 Aug 1882; d. Leydsdorp 6 Jul 1941)
Native Affairs	19 Jun 1929 – 30 Mar 1933: *Ernest George Jansen* (see Governors-General)
Posts and Telegraphs	*Henry William Sampson* (b. London 12 May 1872; d. Sea Point 6 Aug 1938)
Public Health	*Daniel François Malan* (see above)
Public Works	*Henry William Sampson* (see above)
Railways and Harbours	6 Nov 1928 – 6 Feb 1933: *Charles Wynand Marais Malan* (b. Leeuwenjacht 9 Aug 1883; d. Cape Town 6 Feb 1933)*

30 Mar 1933 – 5 Sep 1939: Hertzog III

Prime Minister and External Affairs	*James Barry Munnik Hertzog* (for 3rd time) (see Hertzog II)
Interior	31 Mar 1933 – 8 Dec 1936: *Jan Frederik Hendrik Hofmeyr* (b. Cape Town 20 Mar 1894; d. Pretoria 3 Dec 1948)
	9 Dec 1936 – 5 Sep 1939: *Richard Stuttaford* (b. Cape Town 13 Jun 1870; d. Stellenbosch 19 Oct 1945)
Agriculture (from 31 Oct 1934: and Forestry)	30 Mar 1933 – 7 Jan 1935: *Jan Christoffel Greyling Kemp* (see Hertzog II)
	8 Jan 1935 – 7 Nov 1938: *Deneys Reitz* (b.

*For earlier career see vol. 2

456

	Bloemfontein 2 Aug 1882; d. London 19 Oct 1944)* 8 Nov 1938 – 5 Sep 1939: *William Richard Collins* (b. Lydenburg district 31 Dec 1876; d. 1944)
Commerce and Industries	23 May 1933 – 11 Jul 1938 and 10 Sep – 29 Dec 1938: *Adriaan Paulus Johannes Fourie* (see Hertzog II)† 30 Dec 1938 – 5 Sep 1939: *Oswald Pirow* (see Hertzog II)
Defence	*Oswald Pirow* (see Hertzog II)
Education	31 Mar 1933 – 9 Sep 1938: *Jan Frederik Hendrik Hofmeyr* (see above) 7 Oct 1938 – 5 Sep 1939: *Henry Allan Fagan* (b. Tulbagh 4 Apr 1889; d. Claremont 6 Dec 1963)
Finance	*Nicolaas Christiaan Havenga* (see Hertzog II)
Justice	*Jan Christiaan Smuts* (b. Bovenplaats 24 May 1870; d. Doornkloof 11 Sep 1950)*
Labour (8 Jan 1935 – 30 Sep 1937: and Social Welfare)	31 Mar 1933 – 30 Nov 1936: *Adriaan Paulus Johannes Fourie* (see Hertzog II) 1 Dec 1936 – 19 Jul 1938: *Jan Frederik Hendrik Hofmeyr* (see above) 20 Jul 1938 – 5 Sep 1939: *Harry Gordon Lawrence* (b. Rondebosch 17 Oct 1901)
Lands	30 Mar 1933 – 7 Jan 1935: *Deneys Reitz* (see above) 8 Jan 1935 – 5 Sep 1939: *Jan Christoffel Greyling Kemp* (see Hertzog II)
Mines	30 Mar 1933 – 30 Nov 1936: *Patrick Duncan* (see Governors-General) 1 Dec 1936 – 9 Sep 1938: *Jan Frederik Hendrik Hofmeyr* (see above) 7 Oct – 7 Nov 1938: *Jan Christiaan Smuts* (see above) 8 Nov 1938 – 5 Sep 1939: *Deneys Reitz* (see above)
Native Affairs	30 Mar 1933 – 2 Jun 1938: *Pieter Gert Wessel Grobler* (see Hertzog II) 3 Jun 1938 – 5 Sep 1939: *Henry Allan Fagan* (see above)
Posts and Telegraphs	*Charles Francis Clarkson* (b. Durban 1 Nov 1881; d. 27 Nov 1959)
Public Health	31 Mar 1933 – 8 Dec 1936: *Jan Frederik Hendrik Hofmeyr* (see above) 9 Dec 1936 – 5 Sep 1939: *Richard Stuttaford* (see above)

*For earlier career see vol. 2

†Ceased to be a minister three months after losing his seat and was not replaced. Nominated as senator 8 Sep 1938.

Public Works	*Charles Francis Clarkson* (see above)
Railways and Harbours	30 Mar 1933 – 7 Nov 1938: *Oswald Pirow* (see Hertzog II)
	8 Nov 1938 – 5 Sep 1939: *Adriaan Paulus Johannes Fourie* (see Hertzog II)
Social Welfare	8 Jan 1935 – 30 Sep 1937: merged with Justice (see above)
	1 Oct 1937 – 9 Sep 1938: *Jan Frederik Hendrik Hofmeyr* (see above)
	7 Oct 1938 – 5 Sep 1939: *Henry Allan Fagan* (see above)
Without Portfolio	31 Mar 1933 – 30 Nov 1936: *Richard Stuttaford* (see above)
	1 Dec 1936 – 9 Sep 1938: *Frederick Claud Sturrock* (b. Newport, Scotland, 25 May 1882; d. Aug 1958)
	8 Nov 1938 – 5 Sep 1939: *Robert Hugh Henderson* (b. Kildarton(?), Northern Ireland)

6 Sep 1939 – 3 Jun 1948: Smuts II

Prime Minister and External Affairs	*Jan Christiaan Smuts* (for 2nd time) (see Hertzog III)
Interior	6 Sep 1939 – 15 Aug 1943: *Harry Gordon Lawrence* (see Hertzog III)
	16 Aug 1943 – 15 Jan 1948: *Charles Francis Clarkson* (see Hertzog III)
	16 Jan – 3 Jun 1948: *Harry Gordon Lawrence* (see Hertzog III)
Agriculture and Forestry	6 Sep 1939 – 28 Feb 1944: *William Richard Collins* (see Hertzog III)
	6 Mar 1944 – 3 Jun 1948: *Jacobus Gideon Nel Strauss* (b. Calvinia 17 Dec 1900)
Commerce and Industries (from 11 Apr 1944: Economic Development	6 Sep 1939 – 9 Jan 1943: *Richard Stuttaford* (see Hertzog III)
	28 Jan 1943 – 15 Jan 1948: *Sidney Frank Waterson* (b. 4 Jun 1896)
	16 Jan – 3 Jun 1948: *James Wellwood Mushet* (b. Kilmarnock 1882)
Defence	*Jan Christiaan Smuts* (see Hertzog III)
Education	*Jan Frederik Hendrik Hofmeyr* (see Hertzog III)
Finance	6 Sep 1939 – 15 Jan 1948: *Jan Frederik Hendrik Hofmeyr* (see Hertzog III)

16 Jan – 3 Jun 1948: *Frederick Claud Sturrock* (see Hertzog III)

Justice 6 Sep 1939 – 8 Nov 1945: *Colin Fraser Steyn* (b. Bloemfontein 27 Nov 1887; d. Bloemfontein 23 Apr 1959)

9 Nov 1945 – 3 Jun 1948: *Harry Gordon Lawrence* (see Hertzog III)

Labour 6 Sep 1939 – 31 Oct 1945: *Walter Bayley Madeley* (b. Woolwich 28 Jul 1873; d. Boksburg 1 Mar 1947)*

9 Nov 1945 – 3 Jun 1948: *Colin Fraser Steyn* (see above)

Lands *Andrew Meintjes Conroy* (b. Hanover, Cape Province, 27 Oct 1877; d. Koffiefontein 7 Dec 1951)

Mines 6 Sep 1939 – 4 Dec 1945: *Charles Frampton Stallard* (b. London 4 Jun 1871; d. Hope Woolith 13 Jun 1971)

5 Dec 1945 – 15 Jan 1948: *Sidney Frank Waterson* (see above)

16 Jan – 3 Jun 1948: *Jan Frederik Hendrik Hofmeyr* (see Hertzog III)

Native Affairs 6 Sep 1939 – 10 Jan 1943: *Deneys Reitz* (see Hertzog III)

11 Jan 1943 – 3 Jun 1948: *Pieter Voltelyn Graham van der Byl* (b. Caledon 21 Feb 1899)

Posts and Telegraphs 6 Sep 1939 – 4 Dec 1945: *Charles Francis Clarkson* (see Hertzog III)

5 Dec 1945 – 15 Jan 1948: *James Wellwood Mushet* (see above)

16 Jan – 3 Jun 1948: *Charles Francis Clarkson* (see Hertzog III)

Public Health (reconstituted 9 Nov 1945 as Health) 6 Sep 1939 – 10 Apr 1944: *Harry Gordon Lawrence* (see Hertzog III)

11 Apr 1944 – 8 Nov 1945: incorporated in Welfare and Demobilisation (see below)

9 Nov 1945 – 3 Jun 1948: *Henry Gluckman* (b. 12 Jun 1893)

Public Works 6 Sep 1939 – 4 Dec 1945: *Charles Francis Clarkson* (see Hertzog III)

5 Dec 1945 – 15 Jan 1948: *James Wellwood Mushet* (see above)

16 Jan – 3 Jun 1948: *Charles Francis Clarkson* (see Hertzog III)

*For earlier career see vol. 2

Railways and Harbours (from 11 Apr 1944: Transport)	6 Sep 1939 – 15 Jan 1948: *Frederick Claud Sturrock* (see Hertzog III) 16 Jan – 3 Jun 1948: *Sidney Frank Waterson* (see above)
Social Welfare (11 Apr 1944 – 8 Nov 1945: Welfare and Demobilisation; 9 Nov 1945 – 15 Jan 1948: Social Welfare and Demobilisation)	6 Sep 1939 – 15 Aug 1943: *Walter Bayley Madeley* (see above) 16 Aug 1943 – 15 Jan 1948: *Harry Gordon Lawrence* (see Hertzog III) 16 Jan – 3 Jun 1948: *Colin Fraser Steyn* (see above)
Without Portfolio	6 Sep 1939 – 10 Jan 1943: *Pieter Voltelyn Graham van der Byl* (see above)

4 Jun 1948 – 30 Nov/2 Dec 1954: Malan †

Prime Minister and External Affairs	*Daniel François Malan* (see Hertzog II)
Interior	*Theophilus Ebenhaezer Dönges* (see Presidents)
Agriculture (until 13 Sep 1949: and Forestry)	*Stephanus Petrus le Roux*
Defence	*François Christiaan Erasmus* (b. Merweville 19 Jan 1896; d. De Mond 7 Jan 1967)
Economic Development (from 27 Aug 1948: Economic Affairs)	*Erik Hendrik Louw* (b. Jacobsdal 21 Nov 1890; d. Cape Town 24 Jun 1968)
Education (from 30 Aug 1949: Education, Arts and Science)	4 Jun 1948 – 29 Aug 1949: *Albert Jacobus Stals* (b. Oude Kloof 24 Aug 1880; d. Cape Town 5 Feb 1951) 30 Aug 1949 – 18 Oct 1950: *Charles Robberts Swart* (see Governors-General) 19 Oct 1950 – 2 Dec 1954: *Johannes Hendrikus Viljoen* (d. 5 Dec 1957)
Finance	4 Jun 1948 – 30 Nov 1954: *Nicolaas Christiaan Havenga* (see Hertzog II)

†The Prime Minister retired on 30 Nov 1954. Unless otherwise stated ministers remained in office until 2 Dec 1954.

Forestry	13 Sep 1949: separated from Agriculture (see above) 13 Sep 1949 – 18 Oct 1950: *Johannes Gerardus Strijdom* (b. Willowmore 14 Jul 1893; d. Cape Town 24 Aug 1958) 19 Oct 1950 – 2 Dec 1954: *Barend Jacobus Schoeman* (b. 19 Jan 1905)
Health	4 Jun 1948 – 5 Feb 1951: *Albert Jacobus Stals* (see above) 13 Feb 1951 – 18 Jul 1953: *Karl Bremer* (b. Hopefield 27 Apr 1885; d. Cape Town 18 Jul 1953) 8 Sep 1953 – 2 Dec 1954: *Albertus Johannes Roux van Rhijn* (b. Van Rhynsdorp 7 Jul 1890)
Justice	*Charles Robberts Swart* (see Governors-General)
Labour	*Barend Jacobus Schoeman* (see above)
Lands (from 13 Sep 1949: and Irrigation)	*Johannes Gerardus Strijdom* (see above)
Mines	4 Jun 1948 – 26 Aug 1949: *Erik Hendrik Louw* (see above) 27 Aug 1949 – 18 Oct 1950: *Theophilus Ebenhaezer Dönges* (see Presidents) 19 Oct 1950 – 7 Sep 1953: *Johannes Hendrikus Viljoen* (see above) 8 Sep 1953 – 2 Dec 1954: *Albertus Johannes Roux van Rhijn* (see above)
Native Affairs	4 Jun 1948 – 30 Sep 1950: *Ernest George Jansen* (see Governors-General) 19 Oct 1950 – 2 Dec 1954: *Hendrik Frensch Verwoerd* (b. Amsterdam 8 Sep 1901; d. Cape Town 6 Sep 1966)
Posts and Telegraphs	4 Jun 1948 – 26 Aug 1949: *Theophilus Ebenhaezer Dönges* (see Presidents) 27 Aug 1949 – 8 Nov 1950: *François Christiaan Erasmus* (see above) 9 Nov 1950 – 2 Dec 1954: *Jozua François (Tom) Naudé* (see Presidents)
Public Works	*Barend Jacobus Schoeman* (see above)
Social Welfare	4 Jun 1948 – 5 Feb 1951: *Albert Jacobus Stals* (see above) 13 Feb 1951 – 18 Jul 1953: *Karl Bremer* (see above) 13 Aug 1953 – 2 Dec 1954: *Johannes Hendrikus Viljoen* (see above)
Transport	*Paul Oliver Sauer* (b. Wynberg 1898)

461

SOUTH AFRICA, REPUBLIC OF

3 Dec 1954 – 24 Aug/2 Sep 1958: Strijdom†

Prime Minister	*Johannes Gerardus Strijdom* (see Malan)
External Affairs	3 Dec 1954 – 9 Jan 1955: *Johannes Gerardus Strijdom* (see Malan)
	10 Jan 1955 – 2 Sep 1958: *Erik Hendrik Louw* (see Malan)
Interior	*Theophilus Ebenhaezer Dönges* (see Presidents)
Agriculture	3 Dec 1954 – 30 Apr 1958: *Stephanus Petrus le Roux* (see Malan)
	1 May – 2 Sep 1958: *Petrus Mattheus Kruger le Roux* (b. De Rust 11 Nov 1904)
Defence	*François Christiaan Erasmus* (see Malan)
Economic Affairs	*Albertus Johannes Roux van Rhijn* (see Malan)
Education, Arts and Science	3 Dec 1954 – 5 Dec 1957: *Johannes Hendrikus Viljoen* (see Malan)
	1 May – 2 Sep 1958: *Michiel Daniël Christiaan de Wet Nel*
Finance	3 Dec 1954 – 5 Aug 1956: *Erik Hendrik Louw* (see Malan)
	6 Aug 1956 – 2 Sep 1958: *Jozua François (Tom) Naudé* (see Presidents)
Forestry	3 Dec 1954 – 5 Aug 1956: *Johannes Hendrikus Viljoen* (see Malan)
	6 Aug 1956 – 2 Sep 1958: *François Christiaan Erasmus* (see Malan)
Health	3 Dec 1954 – 5 Aug 1956: *Jozua François (Tom) Naudé* (see Presidents)
	6 Aug 1956 – 5 Dec 1957: *Johannes Hendrikus Viljoen* (see Malan)
	1 May – 2 Sep 1958: *Michiel Daniël Christiaan de Wet Nel·* (see above)
Irrigation (from 17 Jul 1956: Water Affairs)	*Paul Oliver Sauer* (see Malan)
Justice	*Charles Robberts Swart* (see Governors-General)
Labour	*Johannes de Klerk* (b. Burghersdorp 22 Jul 1903)
Lands	*Paul Oliver Sauer* (see Malan)
Mines	*Albertus Johannes Roux van Rhijn* (see Malan)
Native Affairs	*Hendrik Frensch Verwoerd* (see Malan)
Posts and Telegraphs	*Jan Jonathan Serfontein* (b. Reitz 3 Feb 1898; d. 17 Oct 1967)

†The Prime Minister died on 24 Aug 1958. Ministers remained in office until 2 Sep 1958.

462

Public Works	*Johannes de Klerk* (see above)
Social Welfare	*Jan Jonathan Serfontein* (see above)
Transport	*Barend Jacobus Schoeman* (see Malan)

3 Sep 1958 – 6/13 Sep 1966: Verwoerd†

Prime Minister	*Hendrik Frensch Verwoerd* (see Malan)
External Affairs	3 Sep 1958 – 1 Jan 1964: *Erik Hendrik Louw* (see
(from 31 May	Malan)
1961: Foreign	9 Jan 1964 – 13 Sep 1966: *Hilgard Muller* (b.
Affairs)	Potchefstroom 4 May 1914)
Interior	3 Sep – 22 Oct 1958: *Theophilus Ebenhaezer Dönges* (see Presidents)
	23 Oct 1958 – 20 Jan 1961: *Jozua François (Tom) Naudé* (see Presidents)
	21 Jan 1961 – 4 Apr 1966: *Johannes de Klerk* (see Strijdom)
	5 Apr – 13 Sep 1966: *Petrus Mattheus Kruger le Roux* (see Strijdom)
Agricultural	5 Apr – 13 Sep 1966: *Dirk Cornelius Hermannus*
Credit and	*Uys* (b. Bredasdorp district 15 May 1909)
Land Tenure	
Agriculture	3 Sep – 22 Oct 1958: *Petrus Mattheus Kruger le Roux* (see Strijdom)
	23 Oct 1958: ministry divided into Agricultural Economics and Marketing and Agricultural Technical Services (see below)
Agricultural	23 Oct 1958 – 13 Sep 1966: *Dirk Cornelius Hermannus*
Economics and	*Uys* (see above)
Marketing	
Agricultural	23 Oct 1958 – 4 Apr 1966: *Petrus Mattheus Kruger*
Technical	*le Roux* (see Strijdom)
Services	5 Apr – 13 Sep 1966: *Jacobus Johannes Fouché* (see Presidents)
Bantu Administration	23 Oct 1958 – 4 Apr 1966: *Michiel Daniël Christiaan de*
and Development	*Wet Nel* (see Strijdom)
	5 Apr – 13 Sep 1966: *Michiel Coenraad Botha* (b. Lindley 14 Dec 1912)
Bantu Education	23 Oct 1958 – 4 Apr 1966: *Willem Adriaan Maree* (b. Brandfort 7 Aug 1920)
	5 Apr – 13 Sep 1966: *Michiel Coenraad Botha* (see above)

† The Prime Minister died on 6 Sep 1966. Ministers remained in office until 13 Sep 1966.

Coloured Affairs	3 Aug 1961 – 4 Apr 1966: *Pieter Willem Botha* (b. Paul Roux) 5 Apr – 13 Sep 1966: *Marais Viljoen* (b. Robertson 2 Dec 1915)
Community Development	3 Aug 1961 – 4 Apr 1966: *Pieter Willem Botha* (see above) 5 Apr – 13 Sep 1966: *Willem Adriaan Maree* (see above)
Defence	3 Sep – 13 Dec 1958: *François Christiaan Erasmus* (see Malan) 14 Dec 1958 – 4 Apr 1966: *Jacobus Johannes Fouché* (see Presidents) 5 Apr – 13 Sep 1966: *Pieter Willem Botha* (see above)
Economic Affairs	3 Sep – 30 Nov 1958: *Albertus Johannes Roux van Rhijn* (see Malan) 1 Dec 1958 – 13 Sep 1966: *Nicolaas Diederichs* (see Presidents)
Education, Arts and Science	3 Sep – 22 Oct 1958: *Michiel Daniël Christiaan de Wet Nel* (see Strijdom) 23 Oct 1958 – 2 Aug 1961: *Jan Jonathan Serfontein* (see Strijdom) 3 Aug 1961 – 13 Sep 1966: *Johannes de Klerk* (see Strijdom)
Finance	3 Sep – 22 Oct 1958: *Jozua François (Tom) Naudé* (see Presidents) 23 Oct 1958 – 13 Sep 1966: *Theophilus Ebenhaezer Dönges* (see Presidents)
Forestry	3 Sep – 22 Oct 1958: *François Christiaan Erasmus* (see Malan) 23 Oct 1958 – 4 Apr 1966: *Paul Oliver Sauer* (see Malan) 5 Apr – 13 Sep 1966: *Frank Walter Waring* (b. Kenilworth, Cape Province, 7 Nov 1908)
Health	3 Sep – 22 Oct 1958: *Michiel Daniël Christiaan de Wet Nel* (see Strijdom) 23 Oct 1958 – 13 Sep 1966: *(Johannes) Albertus (Munnik) Hertzog* (b. Bloemfontein 4 Jul 1899)
Immigration	3 Aug 1961 – 13 Sep 1966: *Alfred Ernest Trollip* (b. Johannesburg 16 Jul 1895; d. 12 Mar 1972)
Indian Affairs	3 Aug 1961 – 4 Apr 1966: *Willem Adriaan Maree* (see above) 5 Apr – 13 Sep 1966: *Alfred Ernest Trollip* (see above)

Information	3 Aug 1961 – 4 Apr 1966: *Frank Walter Waring* (see above)
	5 Apr – 13 Sep 1966: *Johannes de Klerk* (see Strijdom)
Justice (from 5 Apr 1966: Justice, Police and Prisons)	3 Sep 1958 – 6 Dec 1959: *Charles Robberts Swart* (see Governors-General)
	7 Dec 1959 – 2 Aug 1961: *François Christiaan Erasmus* (see Malan)
	3 Aug 1961 – 13 Sep 1966: *Balthasar Johannes Vorster* (b. Jamestown 13 Dec 1915)
Labour	3 Sep 1958 – 2 Aug 1961: *Johannes de Klerk* (see Strijdom)
	3 Aug 1961 – 4 Apr 1966: *Alfred Ernest Trollip* (see above)
	5 Apr – 13 Sep 1966: *Marais Viljoen* (see above)
Lands	3 Sep 1958 – 4 Apr 1966: *Paul Oliver Sauer* (see Malan)
	5 Apr 1966: superseded by Agricultural Credit and Land Tenure (see above)
Mines	3 Sep – 22 Oct 1958: *Albertus Johannes Roux van Rhijn* (see Malan)
	23 Oct 1958 – 2 Aug 1961: *Johannes de Klerk* (see Strijdom)
	3 Aug 1961 – 4 Aug 1964: *Nicolaas Diederichs* (see Presidents)
	5 Aug 1964 – 13 Sep 1966: *Jan Friedrich Wilhelm Haak* (b. Prince Albert 20 Apr 1917)
Native Affairs	3 Sep – 22 Oct 1958: *Hendrik Frensch Verwoerd* (see Malan)
	23 Oct 1958: ministry divided into Bantu Administration and Development and Bantu Education (see above)
Planning	5 Aug 1964 – 13 Sep 1966: *Jan Friedrich Wilhelm Haak* (see above)
Posts and Telegraphs	3 Sep – 22 Oct 1958: *Jan Jonathan Serfontein* (see Strijdom)
	23 Oct 1958 – 13 Sep 1966: *(Johannes) Albertus (Munnik) Hertzog* (see above)
Public Works	3 Sep – 22 Oct 1958: *Johannes de Klerk* (see Strijdom)
	23 Oct 1958 – 1 Aug 1964: *Paul Oliver Sauer* (see Malan)
	5 Apr 1966 – 13 Sep 1966: *Willem Adriaan Maree* (see above)

Social Welfare (from 23 Oct 1958: and Pensions)	3 Sep 1958 – 4 Apr 1966: *Jan Jonathan Serfontein* (see Strijdom) 5 Apr – 13 Sep 1966: *Willem Adriaan Maree* (see above)
Tourism	5 Apr – 13 Sep 1966: *Frank Walter Waring* (see above)
Transport	*Barend Jacobus Schoeman* (see Malan)
Water Affairs	3 Sep – 22 Oct 1958: *Paul Oliver Sauer* (see Malan) 23 Oct 1958 – 4 Apr 1966: *Petrus Mattheus Kruger le Roux* (see Strijdom) 5 Apr – 13 Sep 1966: *Jacobus Johannes Fouché* (see Presidents)

from 14 Sep 1966: Vorster

Prime Minister	*Balthasar Johannes Vorster* (see Verwoerd)
Foreign Affairs	*Hilgard Muller* (see Verwoerd)
Interior	14 Sep 1966 – 11 Aug 1968: *Petrus Mattheus Kruger le Roux* (see Strijdom) 12 Aug 1968 – 11 May 1970: *Stefanus Laurens Muller* (b. Beaufort West 27 Sep 1917) 12 May – 19 Nov 1970: *Marais Viljoen* (see Verwoerd) 19 Nov 1970 – 30 Jul 1972: *Theodor J. A. Gerdener* (b. Cape Town 19 Mar 1916) from 31 Jul 1972: *Cornelius Petrus Mulder* (b. Warmbaths 27 Sep 1917)
Agriculture	12 Aug 1968 – 22 Aug 1972: *Dirk Cornelius Hermannus Uys* (see Verwoerd) from 23 Aug 1972: *Hendrik Schoeman* (b. 19 Jan 1905)
Agricultural Credit and Land Tenure	14 Sep 1966 – 11 Aug 1968: *Dirk Cornelius Hermannus Uys* (see Verwoerd) 12 Aug 1968: ministry incorporated in Agriculture (see above)
Agricultural Economics and Marketing	14 Sep 1966 – 11 Aug 1968: *Dirk Cornelius Hermannus Uys* (see Verwoerd) 12 Aug 1968: ministry incorporated in Agriculture (see above)
Agricultural Technical Services	14 Sep 1966 – 11 Aug 1968: *Jacobus Johannes Fouché* (see Presidents) 12 Aug 1968: ministry incorporated in Agriculture (see above)

Bantu Administration and Development	*Michiel Coenraad Botha* (see Verwoerd)
Bantu Education	*Michiel Coenraad Botha* (see Verwoerd)
Coloured Affairs (from 23 Aug 1972: Coloured Relations and Rehoboth Affairs)	14 Sep 1966 – 11 May 1970: *Marais Viljoen* (see Verwoerd) 12 May 1970 – 22 Aug 1972: *Jan Jurie Loots* (b. Prieska) from 23 Aug 1972: *Schalk Willem van der Merwe* (b. Citrusdal 18 Sep 1922)
Community Development	14 Sep 1966 – 11 Aug 1968: *Willem Adriaan Maree* (see Verwoerd) 12 Aug 1968 – 22 Aug 1972: *Barzillai Coetzee* (b. Hopetown 14 May 1914) 23 Aug 1972 – 16 Nov 1975: *Abraham Hermannus du Plessis* (b. Prieska district 28 Aug 1914) from 17 Nov 1975 (acting:) *Jan Jurie Loots* (see above)
Defence	*Pieter Willem Botha* (see Verwoerd)
Economic Affairs	14 Sep 1966 – 22 Jun 1967: *Nicolaas Diederichs* (see Presidents) 23 Jun 1967 – 11 May 1970: *Jan Friedrich Wilhelm Haak* (see Verwoerd) 12 May 1970 – 28 Apr 1974: *Stefanus Laurens Muller* (see above) 29 Apr 1974 – 4 Feb 1975: *Owen Pieter Fourie Horwood* (b. Somerset West 6 Dec 1916) from 5 Feb 1975: *Jan Christiaan Heunis* (b. Uniondale 20 Apr 1927)
Education, Arts and Science (12 Aug 1968 – 11 May 1970: National Education and Cultural Affairs; from 12 May 1970: National Education)	14 Sep 1966 – 3 Aug 1969: *Johannes de Klerk* (see Strijdom) from 4 Aug 1969: *Johannes Petrus van der Spuy* (b. Reitz 24 Nov 1912)
Finance	14 Sep 1966 – 22 Jun 1967: *Theophilus Ebenhaezer Dönges* (see Presidents) 23 Jun 1967 – 5 Feb 1975: *Nicolaas Diederichs* (see Presidents) from 6 Feb 1975: *Owen Pieter Fourie Horwood* (see above)

467

Forestry	14 Sep 1966 – 11 Aug 1968: *Frank Walter Waring* (see Verwoerd) from 12 Aug 1968: *Stephanus Petrus Botha* (b. Lusaka)
Health	14 Sep 1966 – 11 Aug 1968: *(Johannes) Albertus (Munnik) Hertzog* (see Verwoerd) 12 Aug 1968 – 22 Aug 1972: *Carel de Wet* (b. Memel, Orange Free State, 25 May 1924) from 23 Aug 1972: *Schalk Willem van der Merwe* (see above)
Immigration	14 Sep 1966 – 11 Aug 1968: *Alfred Ernest Trollip* (see Verwoerd) 12 Aug 1968 – 22 Aug 1972: *Cornelius Petrus Mulder* (see above) from 23 Aug 1972: *Pieter Gerhardus Jacobus Koornhof* (b. Leeudoornstad 2 Aug 1925)
Indian Affairs	14 Sep 1966 – 11 Aug 1968: *Alfred Ernest Trollip* (see Verwoerd) 12 Aug 1968 – 22 Aug 1972: *Frank Walter Waring* (see Verwoerd) 23 Aug 1972 – 30 Aug 1974: *Owen Pieter Fourie Horwood* (see above) 31 Aug 1974 – 4 Feb 1975: *Jan Christiaan Heunis* (see above) from 5 Feb 1975: *S. J. Marais Steyn* (b. Dordrecht, Cape Province, 25 Dec 1914)
Information	14 Sep 1966 – 11 Aug 1968: *Johannes de Klerk* (see Malan) from 12 Aug 1968: *Cornelius Petrus Mulder* (see above)
Justice and Prisons (from 31 Aug 1974: non-Cabinet post)	14 Sep 1966 – 30 Aug 1974: *Petrus Cornelius Pelser* (b. Orange Free State 28 Feb 1907)
Labour	*Marais Viljoen* (see Verwoerd)
Mines	14 Sep 1966 – 14 Feb 1967: *Jan Friedrich Wilhelm Haak* (see Verwoerd) 15 Feb 1967 – 22 Aug 1972: *Carel de Wet* (see above) from 23 Aug 1972: *Pieter Gerhardus Jacobus Koornhof* (see above)
Planning (from 23 Aug 1972: Planning, Environment and Statistics)	14 Sep 1966 – 14 Feb 1967: *Jan Friedrich Wilhelm Haak* (see Verwoerd) 15 Feb 1967 – 11 May 1970: *Carel de Wet* (see above) from 12 May 1970: *Jan Jurie Loots* (see above)

Police	12 Aug 1968 – 28 Apr 1974: *Stefanus Laurens Muller* (see above) from 29 Apr 1974: *James Thomas Kruger* (b. Bethlehem, Orange Free State, 20 Dec 1917)
Posts and Telegraphs	14 Sep 1966 – 11 Aug 1968: *(Johannes) Albertus (Munnik) Hertzog* (see Verwoerd) 12 Aug 1968 – 19 Nov 1970: *Matthys Cornelius Grové Janse van Rensburg* (b. Lindley 12 Dec 1919) from 19 Nov 1970: *Marais Viljoen* (see Verwoerd)
Public Works	14 Sep 1966 – 11 Aug 1968: *Willem Adriaan Maree* (see Verwoerd) 12 Aug 1968 – 22 Aug 1972: *Barzillai Coetzee* (see above) 23 Aug 1972 – 16 Nov 1975: *Abraham Hermannus du Plessis* (see above) from 17 Nov 1975 (acting:) *Jan Jurie Loots* (see above)
Social Welfare and Pensions	14 Sep 1966 – 11 Aug 1968: *Willem Adriaan Maree* (see Verwoerd) 12 Aug 1968 – 30 Aug 1974: *Cornelius Petrus Mulder* (see above) from 31 Aug 1974: *Johannes Petrus van der Spuy* (see above)
Sport and Recreation	12 Aug 1968 – 22 Aug 1972: *Frank Walter Waring* (see Verwoerd) from 23 Aug 1972: *Pieter Gerhardus Jacobus Koornhof* (see above)
Tourism	14 Sep 1966 – 22 Aug 1972: *Frank Walter Waring* (see Verwoerd) 23 Aug 1972 – 30 Aug 1974: *Owen Pieter Fourie Horwood* (see above) 31 Aug 1974 – 4 Feb 1975: *Jan Christiaan Heunis* (see above) from 5 Feb 1975: *S. J. Marais Steyn* (see above)
Transport	14 Sep 1966 – 24 Apr 1974: *Barend Jacobus Schoeman* (see Malan) from 29 Apr 1974: *Stefanus Laurens Muller* (see above)
Water Affairs	14 Sep 1966 – 11 Aug 1968: *Jacobus Johannes Fouché* (see Presidents) from 12 Aug 1968: *Stephanus Petrus Botha* (see above)

469

Spain

HEADS OF STATE

King †

17 May 1886 – 14 Apr 1931	*Alfonso XIII*, son of Alfonso XII (b. 17 May 1886; d. 28 Feb 1941)
14 Apr 1931	Republic

Presidents

14 Apr 1931	(until 10 Dec 1931 acting:) *Niceto Alcalá Zamora y Torres* (b. Priego 6 Jun 1877; d. Buenos Aires 18 Feb 1949)
7 Apr 1936	(acting:) *Diego Martínez Barrio* (b. Seville 25 Nov 1883; d. Paris 1 Jan 1962)
10 May 1936 – 5 Feb 1939	*Manuel Azaña y Díez* (b. Alcalá de Henares 10 Jan 1880; d. Montauban 4 Nov 1940)
24 Jul – 1 Oct 1936	*Miguel Cabanellas Ferrer* (b. Cartagena 1 Jan 1862; d. Malaga 14 May 1938)
1 Oct 1936 – 20 Nov 1975	*Francisco Franco Bahamonde* (b. El Ferrol 4 Dec 1892; d. Madrid 20 Nov 1975)

King

from 22 Nov 1975	*Juan Carlos*, son of Pretender Juan (see footnote) (b. Rome, 5 Jan 1938)

MEMBERS OF GOVERNMENT

Prime Ministers

13 Sep 1923 – 28 Jan 1930	*Miguel Primo de Riveray Oraneja, Marquess of Estella* (from 1925: *Duke of Agadir)* (b. Jérez de la Frontera 8 Jan 1870; d. Paris 16 Mar 1930)
30 Jan 1930 – 14 Feb 1931	*Dámaso Berenguer y Fusté, Count of Xauen* (b. 4 Aug 1873; d. Madrid 19 May 1953)

† From 28 Feb 1941 there was a Pretender, *Juan,* third son of Alfonso XIII (b. 20 Jun 1913)

18 Feb 1931	*Juan Bautista Aznar-Cabañas* (b. 5 Sep 1860; d. 19 May 1953)
14 Apr 1931	*Niceto Alcalá Zamora y Torres* (see Presidents)
14 Oct – 12 Dec 1931	*Manuel Azaña y Díez* (for 1st time) (see Presidents)
16 Dec 1931 – 8 Jun 1933	*Manuel Azaña y Díez* (for 2nd time)
13 Jun – 8 Sep 1933	*Manuel Azaña y Díez* (for 3rd time)
12 Sep – 3 Oct 1933	*Alejandro Lerroux y García* (for 1st time) (b. 28 Feb 1866; d. Madrid 27 Jun 1949)
9 Oct 1933	*Diego Martínez Barrio* (for 1st time) (see Presidents)
16 Dec 1933 – 1 Mar 1934	*Alejandro Lerroux y García* (for 2nd time)
3 Mar – 25 Apr 1934	*Alejandro Lerroux y García* (for 3rd time)
28 Apr – 1 Oct 1934	*Ricardo Samper Ibáñez* (b. 25 Aug 1881; d. 1938)
4 Oct 1934 – 29 Mar 1935	*Alejandro Lerroux y García* (for 4th time)
3 Apr – 3 May 1935	*Alejandro Lerroux y García* (for 5th time)
7 May – 20 Oct 1935	*Alejandro Lerroux y García* (for 6th time)
25 Oct – 9 Dec 1935	*Joaquín Chapaprieta y Terragosa* (b. 26 Oct 1871; d. Madrid 15 Oct 1951)
31 Dec 1935	*Manuel Portela Valladares* (b. 1867; d. 1952)
19 Feb – 11 May 1936	*Manuel Azaña y Díez* (for 4th time)
13 May 1936	*Santiago Casares Quiroga* (b. La Coruña 1884; d. Paris 1950)
19 Jul 1936	*Diego Martínez Barrio* (for 2nd time)
19 Jul 1936	*José Giral y Pereyra* (b. Santiago de Cuba 22 Oct 1879; d. Mexico City 23 Dec 1962)
4 Sep 1936	*Francisco Largo Caballero* (for 1st time) (b. Madrid 15 Oct 1869; d. Paris 25 Mar 1946)
2 Nov 1936 – 15 May 1937	*Francisco Largo Caballero* (for 2nd time)
18 May 1937	*Juan Negrín* (for 1st time) (b. Las Palmas 1887; d. Paris 13 Nov 1956)
5 Apr – 15 Aug 1938	*Juan Negrín* (for 2nd time)
Aug 1938 – 5 Feb 1939	*Juan Negrín* (for 3rd time) moved to France
12 Feb – 5 Mar 1939	*Juan Negrín* (for 4th time) returned to Madrid
1 Apr 1939 – 9 Jun 1973	*Francisco Franco Bahamonde* (see Presidents) Chairman of the Council of Ministers
10 Jul 1962	Creation of the post of Deputy Prime Minister to conduct cabinet business:
10 Jul 1962 – 28 Jul 1967	*Agustín Muñoz Grandes* (b. Garabanchel Bajo/ Prov. Madrid 27 Jan 1896; d. Madrid 11 Jul 1970) also Deputy Head of State

21 Sep 1967	*Luis Carrero Blanco* (b. Santoña 4 Mar 1903; d. Madrid 20 Dec 1973) also Deputy Head of State
20 Dec 1973	(acting:) *Torcuato Fernández Miranda y Hevía* (b. Gijón 10 Nov 1915)
from 29 Dec 1973	*Carlos Arias Navarro* (b. Madrid 11 Dec 1908)

Foreign Ministers

27 Feb 1927	*Miguel Primo de Rivera y Oraneja, Duke of Agadir* (see Prime Ministers)
30 Jan 1930	*Jacobo Fitz-James Stuart Falcó Portocarrero y Osorio, 17th Duke of Alba* (b. Madrid 17 Oct 1878; d. Lausanne 1953)
18 Feb 1931	*Álvaro Figueroa y Torres, Count Romanones* (b. Madrid 1 Aug 1863; d. Madrid 11 Sep 1950)*
14 Apr 1931	*Alejandro Lerroux y García* (for 1st time) (see Prime Ministers)
16 Dec 1931 – 8 Jun 1933	*Luis de Zulueta* (b. Barcelona 1878; d. New York 2 Aug 1964)
13 Jun – 8 Sep 1933	*Fernando de los Rios Urruti* (b. Ronda 1879; d. New York Jun 1949)
12 Sep 1933	*Claudio Sánchez Albornoz* (b. Madrid 7 Apr 1893)
16 Dec 1933 – 1 Oct 1934	*Leónida Pita Romero*
4 Oct 1934	*Ricardo Samper Ibáñez* (see Prime Ministers)
18 Nov 1934 – 20 Sep 1935	*Juan José Rocha*
25 Sep 1935	*Alejandro Lerroux y García* (for 2nd time)
31 Oct 1935	*José Martínez de Velasco* (b. Madrid 1875; d. Madrid 22 Aug 1936)
31 Dec 1935 – Feb 1936	*Joaquín Ursaiz*
19 Feb – 19 Jul 1936	*Augusto Barcia y Trelles* (b. Vegadeo 1881)

Republican Administration

19 Jul – 4 Sep 1936	*Faustino Azcárate*
7 Sep 1936 – 15 May 1937	*Julio Alvárez del Vayo* (for 1st time) (b. Villaviciosa de Odón 1891)
18 May 1937	*José Giral y Pereyra* (see Prime Ministers)
5 Apr 1938 – 28 Mar 1939	*Julio Alvárez del Vayo* (for 2nd time)

*For earlier career see vol. 2

National Administration

31 Jan 1938	*Francisco Gómez, Count Jordana y Souza* (for 1st time) (b. Castile 1876; d. San Sebastian 3 Aug 1944)
10 Aug 1939	*Juan Beigbeder y Atienza* (b. 1888; d. Madrid 6 Jun 1957)
17 Oct 1940	*Ramón Serrano Súñer* (b. Cartagena 12 Dec 1901)
3 Sep 1942 – 3 Aug 1944	*Francisco Gómez, Count Jordana y Souza* (for 2nd time)
11 Aug 1944	*José Félix de Lequerica y Erquicia* (b. Bilbao 1891; d. Bilbao 11 Jun 1963)
20 Jul 1945	*Alberto Martín Artajo* (b. Madrid 2 Oct 1905)
23 Feb 1957	*Fernando María Castiella y Maiz* (b. Bilbao 9 Oct 1907; d. 25 Nov 1976)
11 Jun 1973	*Laureano López Rodó* (b. Barcelona 18 Nov 1920)
3 Jan 1974	*Pedro Cortina Mauri*
from 11 Dec 1975	*José María de Areilza y Martínez Rodas, Count of Motrico* (b. Bilbao 3 Aug 1909)

Sri Lanka

4 Feb 1948	Self-governing dominion (called Ceylon) in British Commonwealth
22 May 1972	Became Republic of Sri Lanka

HEADS OF STATE

Governors-General

15 Feb 1948 – 1949	*Sir Henry Monck-Mason Moore* (b. 1887; d. 26 Mar 1964)
6 Jul 1949 – Jul 1954	*Herwald Ramsbotham, 1st Baron* (from 1954: *1st Viscount) Soulbury* (b. 6 Mar 1887; d. 30 Jan 1971)
17 Jul 1954 – 27 Feb 1962	*Sir Oliver (Ernest) Goonetilleke* (b. 20 Sep 1892)
2 Mar 1962 – 22 May 1972	*William Gopallawa* (b. 16 Sep 1897)

President

from 22 May 1972	*William Gopallawa* (see Governors-General)

MEMBERS OF GOVERNMENT

Prime Ministers

15 Aug 1947/4 Feb 1948 – 22 Mar 1952	*Don Stephen Senanayake* (b. 20 Oct 1884; d. Colombo 22 Mar 1952)
26 Mar 1952 – 7 Oct 1953	*Dudley (Shelton) Senanayake* (for 1st time) (b. Colombo 19 Jun 1911; d. 13 Apr 1973)
12 Oct 1953	*Sir John (Lionel) Kotelawala* (b. 1897; d. 1958)
12 Apr 1956	*Solomon West Ridgway Dias Bandaranaike* (b. Colombo 8 Jan 1899; d. 26 Sep 1959)
26 Sep 1959	*Wijayananda Dahanayake*
21 Mar – 23 Apr/ 21 Jul 1960	*Dudley (Shelton) Senanayake* (for 2nd time)
21 Jul 1960	*Sirimavo Bandaranaike*, widow of Solomon Bandaranaike (for 1st time) (b. Kandy 17 Apr 1916)
25 Mar 1965 – 28 May 1970	*Dudley (Shelton) Senanayake* (for 3rd time)
from 31 May 1970	*Sirimavo Bandaranaike* (for 2nd time)

Sudan

1899 – 1955	Administered by a Governor-General on the joint behalf of Egypt and the UK
1 Jan 1956	Independence, governed by Council of State

HEADS OF STATE

17 Nov 1958	*General Ibrahim Abboud* (b. Mohammad-Gol on the Red Sea 26 Oct 1900)
15 Nov 1964	Five-man Council of Sovereignty under rotating chairmanship
8 Jul 1965	*Ismail el-Azhari* (b. Omdurman 1902; d. Khartoum 26 Aug 1969) Chairman
from 25 May 1969	*Jaafir an-Numery* (b. Omdurman 1 Jan 1930) Head of Revolutionary Council

MEMBERS OF GOVERNMENT

Prime Ministers

1951 – Nov 1953	*Said Sir Abdur Rahman*, son of the Mahdi (b. Khartoum 1885; d. 24 Mar 1959)
9 Jan 1954 – 10 Nov 1955	*Ismail el-Azhari* (for 1st time) (see Heads of State)
1 Jan – 4 Jul 1956	*Ismail el-Azhari* (for 2nd time)
5 Jul 1956 – 20 Mar 1958	*Abdullah Khalil* (for 1st time) (b. Egypt 1891; d. Khartoum 23 Jul 1970)
20/27 Mar – 17 Nov 1958	*Abdullah Khalil* (for 2nd time)
18 Nov 1958 – (?) 1964	*General Ibrahim Abboud* (see Heads of State) also Chairman of the Committee of the Armed Forces
30 Oct 1964	*Ser al-Khatm Khalifa* (for 1st time) (b. 1917)
18 Feb – 4 Jun 1965	*Ser al-Khatm Khalifa* (for 2nd time)
11 Jun 1965 – 25 Jul 1966	*Mohammed Ahmed Mahgoub* (for 1st time) (b. Buam, Blue Nile Province, 1907 or 1908)
26 Jul 1966 – 15 May 1967	*Sadik el-Mahdi* (b. Sep 1935(1936?))
18 May 1967 – 28 May 1968	*Mohammed Ahmed Mahgoub* (for 2nd time)
2 Jun 1968 – 23 Apr 1969	*Mohammed Ahmed Mahgoub* (for 3rd time)
25 May – 27 Oct 1969	*Babiker Awadalla* (b. El Citaina, Blue Nile Province, 1917)
from 28 Oct 1969	Head of Revolutionary Council also Prime Minister

Swaziland

25 Apr 1967	Internal self-government (Protectorate)
6 Sep 1968	Independence (member of the Commonwealth)

SWAZILAND
HEAD OF STATE

King

from 25 Apr 1967   *Sobhuza II* (b. Jul 1899) Chief since 1921

MEMBER OF GOVERNMENT

Prime Minister

from 25 Apr 1967/6   *Prince Makhosini Dlamini*, son of King Sobhuza (b.
Sep 1968   Enhletsheni 1914)

Sweden

HEADS OF STATE

Kings

House of Bernadotte
8 Dec 1907   *Gustaf V*, son of Oscar II (b. 16 Jun 1858)
29 Oct 1950   *Gustaf VI, Adolf*, son (b. 11 Nov 1882)
from 15 Sep 1973   *Carl XVI, Gustaf*, grandson (b. 30 Apr 1946)

MEMBERS OF GOVERNMENT

Prime Ministers

1 Oct 1928 – 2   *Arvid Lindman* (for 2nd time) (b. 19 Sep 1862; d. 8
Jun 1930   Dec 1936)*

*For earlier career see vol. 2

476

6 Jun 1930	*Karl Gustav Ekman* (for 2nd time) (b. 5 Oct 1872; d. 15 Jun 1945)*
6 Aug – 19 Sep 1932	*Felix Theodor Hamrin* (b. 14 Jan 1875; d. 27 Nov 1937)
24 Sep 1932 – 15 Jun 1936	*Per Albin Hansson* (for 1st time) (b. 28 Oct 1885; d. 6 Oct 1946)
19 Jun – 23 Sep 1936	*Axel Pehrsson-Bramstorp* (b. 19 Aug 1883; d. Trelleborg 19 Feb 1954)
28 Sep 1936	*Per Albin Hansson* (for 2nd time)
13 Dec 1939	*Per Albin Hansson* (for 3rd time)
31 Jul 1945 – 6 Oct 1946	*Per Albin Hansson* (for 4th time)
10 Oct 1946 – 24 Oct 1957	*Tage Fritiof Erlander* (for 1st time) (b. Ransäter 16 Jun 1901)
30 Oct 1957 – 9 Oct 1969	*Tage Fritiof Erlander* (for 2nd time)
from 14 Oct 1969	*(Sven) Olof Palme* (Soc) (b. Stockholm 30 Jan 1927)

Foreign Ministers

1 Oct 1928 – 2 Jun 1930	*Ernst Trygger* (b. 20 Oct 1857; d. 24 Sep 1943)*
7 Jun 1930 – 19 Sep 1932	*(Sten Gustav) Fredrik, Baron von Ramel* (b. Malmö 9 Dec 1872; d. 30 Oct 1947)
24 Sep 1932	*Richard Sandler* (b. 29 Jan 1884; d. Stockholm 12 Nov 1964)*
13 Dec 1939	*Christian Günther* (b. Stockholm 5 Dec 1886; d. Stockholm 6 Mar 1966)
12 Aug 1945 – 15 Sep 1962	*Bo Östen Undén* (for 2nd time) (b. Karlstad 25 Aug 1886; d. 15 Jan 1974)*
19 Sep 1962 – 30 Jun 1971	*Torsten Nilsson* (Soc) (b. Nevishög 1 Apr 1905)
1 Jul 1971	*Krister Wickmann* (b. Stockholm Apr 1924)
from early Nov 1973	*Sven Olaf Morgan Andersson* (b. Gothenburg 5 Apr 1910)

*For earlier career see vol. 2

Switzerland

HEADS OF STATE

Presidents

1930	*Jean-Marie Musy* (for 2nd time) (b. Albeuve 10 Apr 1876)*
1931	*Heinrich Häberlin* (for 2nd time) (b. Weinfelden 6 Sep 1868; d. Thurgau 26 Feb 1947)*
1932	*Giuseppe Motta* (for 4th time) (b. Airolo 17 Dec 1871; d. Berne 23 Jan 1940)*
1933	*Edmund Schulthess* (for 4th time) (b. Villnachern 2 Mar 1868; d. Berne 22 Apr 1944)*
1934	*Marcel Pilet-Golaz* (for 1st time) (b. Cossonay 31 Dec 1889; d. Paris 11 Apr 1958)
1935	*Rudolf Minger* (b. Berne 13 Nov 1881; d. Schüpfen 23 Aug 1955)
1936	*Albert Meyer* (b. Fällanden 13 Mar 1870; d. Zurich 22 Oct 1953)
1937	*Giuseppe Motta* (for 5th time)
1938	*Johannes Baumann* (b. Herisau 27 Nov 1874)
1939	*Philipp Etter* (for 1st time) (b. Menzingen 21 Dec 1891)
1940	*Marcel Pilet-Golaz* (for 2nd time)
1941	*Ernst Wetter* (b. Winterthur 27 Aug 1877)
1942	*Philipp Etter* (for 2nd time)
1943	*Enrico Celio* (for 1st time) (b. Ambri 19 Jun 1889)
1944	*Walter Stampfli* (b. Büren 3 Dec 1884; d. Zurich 11 Oct 1965)
1945	*Eduard von Steiger* (for 1st time) (b. Langnau 2 Jul 1881; d. Berne 10 Feb 1962)
1946	*Karl Kobelt* (for 1st time) (b. St. Gall 1 Aug 1891; d. Berne 5 Jan 1968)
1947	*Philipp Etter* (for 3rd time)
1948	*Enrico Celio* (for 2nd time)
1949	*Ernst Nobs* (b. Seedorf 14 Jul 1886; d. Zurich 13 Mar 1957)
1950	*Max Petitpierre* (for 1st time) (b. Neuenburg 26 Feb 1899)

*For earlier career see vol. 2

951	*Eduard von Steiger* (for 2nd time)
952	*Karl Kobelt* (for 2nd time)
953	*Philipp Etter* (for 4th time)
954	*Rodolphe Rubattel* (b. 4 Sep 1896; d. Lausanne 18 Oct 1961)
955	*Max Petitpierre* (for 2nd time)
956	*Markus Feldmann* (b. Thun 21 May 1897; d. Berne 3 Oct 1958)
957	*Hans Streuli* (b. Zurich 13 Jul 1892; d. Aarau 23 May 1970)
958	*Thomas Holenstein* (b. St. Gall 7 Feb 1896; d. Locarno 31 Oct 1962)
959	*Paul Chaudet* (for 1st time) (b. Rivaz 17 Nov 1901)
960	*Max Petitpierre* (for 3rd time)
961	*Friedrich (Traugott) Wahlen* (b. Gmeiss 10 Apr 1899)
962	*Paul Chaudet* (for 2nd time)
963	*Willy Spühler* (for 1st time) (b. Zurich 31 Jan 1902)
964	*Ludwig von Moos* (for 1st time) (b. Sachseln 31 Jan 1910)
965	*Hans-Peter Tschudi* (for 1st time) (b. Basle 22 Oct 1913)
966	*Hans Schaffner* (b. Gränichen 16 Dec 1908)
967	*Roger Bonvin* (for 1st time) (b. Icogne 12 Sep 1907)
968	*Willy Spühler* (for 2nd time)
969	*Ludwig von Moos* (for 2nd time)
970	*Hans-Peter Tschudi* (for 2nd time)
971	*Rudolf Gnägi* (for 1st time) (b. Schwadernau 3 Aug 1917)
972	*Nello Celio* (b. Luino 12 Feb 1914)
973	*Roger Bonvin* (for 2nd time)
974	*Pierre Graber* (b. La Chaux-de-Fonds 6 Dec 1908)
975	*Rudolf Gnägi* (for 2nd time)

Syria

25 Apr 1920 – 27 Sep 1941	Under French mandate from the League of Nations

479

HEADS OF STATE

High Commissioners (from 1943 Delegates-General for Syria and Lebanon)

12 Oct 1926	*Henri Ponsot* (b. Bologna 2 Mar 1877)
12 Oct 1931 – Oct 1938	*Damien, Comte de Martel* (b. 1878)
5 Jan 1939	*Gabriel Puaux* (b. Paris 19 May 1883)
24 – 27 Nov 1940	*Jean Chiappe* (b. Ajaccio 1878; d. 27 Nov 1940)
9 Dec 1940 – 14 Jul 1941	*Henri Dentz* (b. Reims 1872(?); d. Paris 13 Dec 1945)
21 Jun 1941 – 1943	*Georges (Albert Julien) Catroux* (b. Limoges 29 Jan 1877; d. Paris 21 Dec 1969) Free French Delegate-General
7 Jun 1943	*Jean Helleu*
23 Nov 1943 – Feb 1944	*Yves Chataigneau* (b. Vouillé 22 Sep 1891; d. 5 Mar 1969)
1944 – 6 Jul 1946	*General Beynet*
1946	Independent republic on evacuation of English and French forces

Presidents

11 Jun 1932	*Muhammad Ali Abid* (b. 1870(?); d. 22 Oct 1939)
21 Dec 1936	*Hashim al-Atasi* (for 1st time) (b. Hims 1864; d. 6 Dec 1960)*
7 Jul 1939	Direct rule by French Commissioners
18 Sep 1941 – 18 Jan 1943	*Taj ad-Din al-Hasani* (d. Damascus 18 Jan 1943)*
21 Jan 1943	*Jamil al-Ulshi*, Deputy President
25 Mar – Jul 1943	*Ata al-Aiyubi* (b. Damascus) Deputy President
17 Jul 1943 – 30 Mar 1949	*Shukri al-Quwwatli* (for 1st time) (b. Damascus 1891; d. Beirut 30 Jun 1967)
25 Jun – 13 Aug 1949	*Husni az-Zaim* (d. 13 Aug 1949)
14 Dec 1949	*Hashim al-Atasi* (for 2nd time)
2 Dec 1951	*Adib Shishaqli* (b. Hama 1909; d. (murdered) Goiás state, Brazil, 27 Sep 1964) Military Dictator, from 10 Jul 1953 President
25 Feb 1954	*Hashim al-Atasi* (for 3rd time)
6 Sep 1955	*Shukri al-Quwwatli* (for 2nd time)
22 Feb 1958 – 26/28 Sep 1961	Syria part of United Arab Republic (see p. 550)

*For earlier career see vol. 2

14 Dec 1961 – 28 Mar 1962	*Nazim Kudsi* (for 1st time) (b. 1905)
13 Apr 1962 – 8 Mar 1963	*Nazim Kudsi* (for 2nd time)
24 Mar 1963	*Luai al-Atassi*, Chairman of Revolutionary Council
27 Jul 1963	*Amin Hafez* (b. Aleppo 1911(?) or 1923(?)) Chairman of Revolutionary Council
27 Feb 1966 – 18 Oct/ 16 Nov 1970	*Nureddin Atassi* (b. Hims 1929)
18 Nov 1970	*Ahmad Khatib* (b. Al Suwaidaa 1933)
from 22 Feb 1971	(acting until 14 Mar 1971:) *Hafez al Assad* (b. 1928)

MEMBERS OF GOVERNMENT

Prime Ministers

15 Feb 1928 – 19 Nov 1931	*Taj ad-Din al-Hasani* (for 2nd time) (see Presidents)
19 Nov 1931 – 15 Jun 1932	Direct rule by French Commissioners
15 Jun 1932	*Haqqi al-Azm* (for 1st time)
5 May 1933	*Haqqi al-Azm* (for 2nd time)
17 Mar 1934	*Taj ad-Din al-Hasani* (for 3rd time)
24 Feb 1936	*Ata al-Aiyubi* (for 1st time) (see Presidents)
21 Dec 1936 – 18 Feb 1939	*Jamil Mardam Bey* (for 1st time) (b. Damascus 1895; d. Cairo 28 Mar 1960)
23 Feb – 13 Mar 1939	*Lutfi Haffar*
6 Apr – 14 May 1939	*Nasuhi al-Bukhari*
9 Jul 1939	*Bahij al-Khatib*, Leader of Directorate
3 Apr – Sep 1941	*Khalid al-Azm* (for 1st time) (b. Damascus 1903; d. Beirut 18 Feb 1965)
20 Sep 1941	*Hasan al-Hakim* (for 1st time)
18 Apr 1942	*Husni 'l-Barazi* (b. Hama 1893)
10 Jan 1943	*Jamil al-Ulshi* (see Presidents)
25 Mar – Aug 1943	*Ata al-Aiyubi* (for 2nd time)
22 Aug 1943	*Sa'd Allah Jabiri* (for 1st time) (b. Aleppo 1892)
14 Oct 1944 – 5 Apr 1945	*Faris al-Khuri* (for 1st time) (d. Damascus 3 Jan 1962)
8 Apr 1945	*Faris al-Khuri* (for 2nd time)
23 Aug 1945	*Faris al-Khuri* (for 3rd time)
1 Oct 1945 – 21 Dec 1946	*Sa'd Allah Jabiri* (for 2nd time)
29 Dec 1946 – 2 Dec 1948	*Jamil Mardam Bey* (for 2nd time)

17 Dec 1948 – 30 Mar 1949	*Khalid al-Azm* (for 2nd time)
20 Apr 1949	*Husni az-Zaim* (see Presidents)
27 Jun – 13 Aug 1949	*Muhsin al-Barazi* (d. 13 Aug 1949)
15 Aug – 14 Dec 1949	*Hashim al-Atasi* (for 2nd time) (see Presidents)
24 – 25 Dec 1949	*Nazim Kudsi* (for 1st time) (see Presidents)
28 Dec 1949 – 29 May 1950	*Khalid al-Azm* (for 3rd time)
4 Jun – 5 Sep 1950	*Nazim Kudsi* (for 2nd time)
9 Sep 1950 – 10 Mar 1951	*Nazim Kudsi* (for 3rd time)
27 Mar – 30 Jul 1951	*Khalid al-Azm* (for 4th time)
10 Aug – 9 Nov 1951	*Hasan al-Hakim* (for 2nd time)
29 Nov – 1 Dec 1951	*Maruf ad-Dawalibi* (for 1st time) (b. 1907)
3 Dec 1951	*Fauzi as-Salu* (for 1st time)
9 Jun 1952	*Fauzi as-Salu* (for 2nd time)
17 Jul 1953	*Adib Shishaqli* (see Presidents)
26 Feb 1954	*Shewket Shukair*
1 Mar – 12 Jun 1954	*Sabri al-Asali* (for 1st time) (b. Damascus 1903)
19 Jun – 14 Oct 1954	*Said al-Ghazzi* (for 1st time)
28 Oct 1954 – 6 Feb 1955	*Faris al-Khuri* (for 4th time)
13 Feb – 7 Sep 1955	*Sabri al-Asali* (for 2nd time)
13 Sep 1955 – 2 Jun 1956	*Said al-Ghazzi* (for 2nd time)
14 Jun – 22 Dec 1956	*Sabri al-Asali* (for 3rd time)
1 Jan 1957 – 22 Feb 1958	*Sabri al-Asali* (for 4th time)
22 Feb 1958 – 26/28 Sep 1961	Syria part of United Arab Republic and ruled by Council of Ministers
17 Aug – 26 Sep 1961	*Abd al-Hamid Sarraj* (b. Hama 1923?) Head of Syrian provincial government of United Arab Republic
29 Sep 1961	*Mamun Kuzbari* (b. Damascus 1914(?) or 1917(?))
21 Nov – 14 Dec 1961	*Izzet an-Nuss*
26 Dec 1961 – 28 Mar 1962	*Maruf ad-Dawalibi* (for 2nd time)
17 Apr 1962	*Bashir Azmah* (for 1st time) (b. 1910)
20 Jun 1962	*Bashir Azmah* (for 2nd time)
14 Sep 1962	*Khalid al-Azm* (for 5th time)
9 Mar 1963	*Salah ad-Din Bitar* (for 1st time) (b. Damascus 1912)
12/13 May 1963	*Sami al-Jundi*
13 May 1963	*Salah ad-Din Bitar* (for 2nd time)
5 Aug 1963	*Salah ad-Din Bitar* (for 3rd time)

3 Nov 1963	*Amin Hafez* (for 1st time) (see Presidents)
4 May 1964	*Salah ad-Din Bitar* (for 4th time)
Oct 1964	*Amin Hafez* (for 2nd time)
23 Sep – 21 Dec 1965	*Yussif Zeayen* (for 1st time) (b. 1931)
3 Jan – 23 Feb 1966	*Salah ad-Din Bitar* (for 5th time)
27 Feb 1966	*Yussif Zeayen* (for 2nd time)
28 Oct 1968 – 18 Oct 1970	(acting:) *Nureddin Atassi* (see Presidents)
3 Nov 1970	*Hafez al Assad* (see Presidents)
Apr 1971 – 21 Dec 1972	*Abdel Rahman Khleifawi* (b. 1930)
from 24 Dec 1972	*Mahmoud Ben Saleh al-Ayoubi* (b. 1932)

Tanzania

1919 – 1961	Tanganyika administered by UK under Trusteeship agreements with League of Nations and United Nations
9 Dec 1961	Independence of Tanganyika (member of Commonwealth)
9 Dec 1962	Republic
26 Apr 1964	Union with Zanzibar to form United Republic of Tanganyika and Zanzibar
29 Oct 1964	Renamed United Republic of Tanzania

HEADS OF STATE

Governor-General

9 Dec 1961	*Sir Richard (Gordon) Turnbull* (b. 7 Jul 1909)

President

from 9 Dec 1962	*Julius Kambarage Nyerere* (b. Butiama 1923)

483

MEMBERS OF GOVERNMENT

Prime Ministers

9 Dec 1961	*Julius Kambarage Nyerere* (see President)
22 Jan 1962	*Rashidi Mfaume Kawawa* (for 1st time) (b. 1928)
9 Dec 1962	President also Prime Minister
from 26 Apr 1964	*Rashidi Mfaume Kawawa* (for 2nd time)

Thailand

HEADS OF STATE

Kings

Ramadhibadi Dynasty

26 Nov 1925 – 2 Mar 1935	*Rama VII (Prajadhipok)*, brother of Rama VI (b. 8 Nov 1893; d. 30 May 1941)
2 Mar 1935	*Rama VIII (Ananda Mahidol)*, nephew (b. 20 Sep 1925; d. 9 Jun 1946)
c. 1939 – 1946	*Nai Pridi Phanomyong*, Regent
from 9 Jun 1946	*Rama IX (Phumiphon Adundet)*, brother of Rama VIII (b. Cambridge, Massachusetts, 5 Dec 1927)
9 Jun 1946 – 5 May 1950	*Prince Rangsit of Chainat* (b. 12 Nov 1885; d. 8 Mar 1951) Regent

MEMBERS OF GOVERNMENT

Prime Ministers

1932 – 1933	*Phraya Manopakorn*
Nov 1933 – 1938	*Phraya Phahon Phonphahuyasena*
26 Dec 1938 – 24 Jul 1944	*Luang Phibun Songgram* (for 1st time) (b. Nondaburi 14 Jul 1897; d. Tokyo 11 Jun 1964)
Aug 1944 – Aug 1945	*Nai Khuang Aphaiwong* (for 1st time)
Aug – Sep 1945	*Thawi Bunyaket*

Sep 1945 – Jan 1946	*Mom Rachawongse Seni Pramoj* (b. Nakhon Sawan Province 26 May 1905)
31 Jan – Mar 1946	*Nai Khuang Aphaiwong* (for 2nd time)
Mar – 8 Aug 1946	*Nai Pridi Phanomyong* (see Kings)
Aug 1946 – 8 Sep 1947	*Luang Thamrong Nawasawat*
Sep 1947 – Apr 1948	*Nai Khuang Aphaiwong* (for 3rd time)
15 Apr 1948	*Luang Phibun Songgram* (for 2nd time)
29 Mar 1957	*Luang Phibun Songgram* (for 3rd time)
17 Sep 1957	*Sarit Thanarat* (for 1st time) (b. Bangkok 1908; d. 8 Dec 1963)
21 Sep 1957	*Nai Pote Sarasin* (b. 1905?)
24 Dec 1957/1 Jan 1958	*Thanom Kittikatchorn* (for 1st time) (b. Tak 11 Aug 1911)
20 Oct 1958	(acting:) *Sarit Thanarat* (for 2nd time)
10 Feb 1959	*Sarit Thanarat* (for 3rd time)
9 Dec 1963	*Thanom Kittikatchorn* (for 2nd time)
14 Oct 1973	*Sanya Dharmasakti (Thammasak)* (for 1st time) (b. 1907)
23 May 1974	*Sanya Dharmasakti (Thammasak)* (for 2nd time)
from 17 Mar 1975	*Mom Rachawongse Kukrit Pramoj* (b. 20 Apr 1911)

Tibet

HEADS OF STATE

Dalai Lamas

1876 – Dec 1933	*Thupten Gyatso* (b. 1875)
from 1935/1950	*Tenzin Gyatso* (b. Amdo, Tsinghai Province, 7 Jun 1935) enthroned 22 Feb 1940; assumed full powers 17 Nov 1950; from 30 Mar 1959 in exile in India

Regents

1933 – 1941	*Reting Hutuktu II*, resigned (d. 8 May 1947)
1941 – 17 Nov 1950	*Taktra Rimpoche*

485

TIBET

Panchen Lamas

1888 – Dec 1937	*Chökyi Nyima*, fled to China in 1923
from 1938	*Chökyi Gyaltsen* (b. Tsinghai Province), proclaimed 1944 by exiled staff of Chökyi Nyima but never recognized by court in Lhasa
1959	Chinese military administration
from 1965	Administered as an autonomous region of the People's Republic of China

Togo

until 27 Apr 1960   French trusteeship under United Nations

HEADS OF STATE

Presidents

9 Apr 1961 – 12 Jan 1963	*Sylvanus Olympio* (b. Lomé 6 Sep 1902; d. 12 Jan 1963) Head of State as Prime Minister until Apr 1961
16 Jan/5 May 1963	*Nicolas Grunitzky* (b. Atakpamé 5 Apr 1913; d. Paris 27 Sep 1969)
13 Jan 1967	*Étienne Eyadema* (for 1st time) (b. Pya, Lama-Kara district, 1935/39) Leader of Military Administration
from 18 Apr 1967	*Étienne Eyadema* (for 2nd time)

MEMBERS OF GOVERNMENT

Prime Ministers

27 Apr 1960 – Apr 1961	*Sylvanus Olympio* (see Presidents)
Apr 1961 – 13 Jan 1967	President also Prime Minister
13 Jan 1967	*Kléber Dadjo* (b. 1914?) Chairman of Committee of National Revival
from 18 Apr 1967	President also Prime Minister

486

Tonga

8 May 1900   British protectorate
Jun 1970   Fully independent

HEAD OF STATE

Kings

Apr 1918   (Queen) *Salote* (b. 13 Mar 1900)
from 16 Dec 1965   *Taufa'ahau Tupou IV*, son (b. 4 Jul 1918)

MEMBER OF GOVERNMENT

Prime Minister

from 4 Jun 1970   *Prince Fatafehi Tu'ipelehake*, brother of Taufa'ahau
                   Tupou IV

Transkei

Bantu Homeland within Republic of South Africa

HEAD OF GOVERNMENT

from 6 Dec 1963   *Kaizer Matanzima* (b. Quamata, Saint Mark's
                   District, 1915)

Trieste

1947 – 1954	Free territory under the United Nations

MILITARY GOVERNORS

Zone A: British and American occupation

16 Sep 1947 – 1951	*Major-General Sir Terence Sydney Airey* (b. 9 Jul 1900) British
1951 – 5 Oct 1954	*General Sir (Thomas) John Willoughby Winterton* (b. 13 Apr 1898) British

Zone B: Yugoslav occupation

1947 – 1954	*Colonel Stomatović*, Yugoslav
5 Oct 1954	Majority of Zone A ceded to Italy; the remainder and Zone B to Yugoslavia

Trinidad and Tobago

HEADS OF STATE

Governors-General

31 Aug 1962	*Sir Solomon Hochoy* (b. 20 Apr 1905)
from 1 Jan 1973	*Sir Ellis Emmanuel Innocent Clarke* (b. Port of Spain 28 Dec 1917)

MEMBER OF GOVERNMENT

Prime Minister

from 31 Aug 1962	*Eric Eustace Williams* (b. Port of Spain 25 Sep 1911)

Tunisia

12 May 1881 – 1 Sep 1955	French protectorate
1 Sep 1955	Independence from France

HEADS OF STATE

Beys

11 Feb 1929	*Ahmad II*
19 Jul 1942	*Muhammad VII, al-Munsif* (d. 1 Sep 1948)
14 May 1943 – 25 Jul 1957	*Muhammad VIII, al-Amin* (b. 4 Sep 1881; d. Tunis 1 Oct 1962)

French Governors

Jan 1929	*François Manceron* (b. 1872; d. 1937)
Jul 1933	*Marcel Peyrouton* (for 1st time) (b. Paris 2 Jul 1887)
Mar 1936	*Armand Guillon* (b. 1880)
Nov 1938	*Eirik Labonne* (b. Paris 4 Oct 1888)
3 Jun – 23 Jul 1940	*Marcel Peyrouton* (for 2nd time)
26 Jul 1940 – May 1943	*Jean Estéva* (b. 14 Sep 1880; d. Reims 12 Jan 1951)
22 Feb/10 May 1943	*Emmanuel Mast* (b. Paris 7 Jan 1889)
21 Feb 1947	*Jean Mons* (b. Argentrat 25 Feb 1906)
Jun 1950	*Louis Périllier* (b. Nîmes 1 Apr 1900)
Dec 1951	*Jean, Count Hautecloque* (b. 11 Feb 1893; d. Paris 27 Sep 1957)
2 Sep 1953 – 30 Jul 1954	*Pierre Voizard* (b. Toul 22 Aug 1896)
30 Jul/5 Nov 1954 – 31 Aug 1955	*Pierre, Count Boyer de la Tour du Moulin* (b. Maisons-Laffitte 18 Jun 1896)

President

from 25 Jul 1957	*Habib Bourguiba (Abu Ruqayba)* (b. Monastir, Tunisia, 3 Aug 1903)

TUNISIA

MEMBERS OF GOVERNMENT

Prime Ministers

1943 – 1947	*Salah ed-Din Baccouche* (for 1st time) (b. 1885; d. Tunis 25 Dec 1959)
17 Aug 1950 – 26 Mar 1952	*Muhammad Chenik*
28 Mar 1952	*Salah ed-Din Baccouche* (for 2nd time)
2 Mar 1954	*Salah ed-Din Mzali*
2 Aug 1954 – 9 Apr 1956	*Tahhar Ben Ammar*
10/15 Apr 1956 – 26 Jul 1957	*Habib Bourguiba* (see President)
30 Jul 1957	President also Head of Government
8 Nov 1969	*Bahi Ladgham* (for 1st time) (b. Tunis 10 Jan 1913)
9 Jun 1970	*Bahi Ladgham* (for 2nd time)
from 2 Nov 1970	*Hedi Nouira* (b. Monastir, Tunisia, 6 Apr 1911)

Turkey

HEADS OF STATE

Presidents

30 Oct 1923 – 10 Nov 1938	*Mustafa Kemal Pasha* (from 26 Nov 1934: *Kemal Atatürk*) (b. Salonica 1881; d. Istanbul 10 Nov 1938)*
11 Nov 1938	*İsmet İnönü* (to 1934: *Mustafa İsmet Pasha*) (b. Smyrna 25 Sep 1884; d. 26 Dec 1973)*
22 May 1950	*Celâl Bayar* (b. Umurbey 15 May 1883?)
27 May 1960	*Cemal Gürsel* (b. Erzerum 1895; d. Ankara 14 Sep 1966) Head of Military Government
28 Mar 1966 – 28 Mar 1973	*Cevdet Sunay* (b. Trebizond 10 Feb 1900)
from 6 Apr 1973	*Fahri Korutürk* (b. Istanbul 1903)

*For earlier career see vol. 2

MEMBERS OF GOVERNMENT

3 Nov 1927 - 25 Sep 1930: İsmet IV (Peoples)**

Prime Minister	*Mustafa İsmet Pasha* (from 1934: *İsmet İnönü*) (for 4th time) (see Presidents)
Foreign Affairs	*Tevfik Rüştü Bey* (from 1934: *Tevfik Rüştü Araş*) (b. Çanakkale 1883; d. Istanbul 6 Jan 1972)*
Home Affairs	*Şükrü Kaya Bey* (from 1934: *Şükrü Kaya*) (b. İstanköy 1884; d. Istanbul 1959)*
Justice	3 Nov 1927 - 22 Sep 1930: *Mahmut Esat Bey* (from 1934: *Bozkurt*) (b. Karaferria 1874; d. 21 Dec 1943)*
Defence	*Mustafa Abdülhalik Bey* (from 1934: *Abdülhalik Renda*) (b. Yanya 1881; d. Istanbul 30 Sep 1957)*
Finance	*Saracoğlu Şükrü Bey* (from 1934: *Şükrü Saracoğlu*) (b. Ödemiş 1887; d. Istanbul 27 Dec 1953)*
Education	10 Apr 1929 - 2 Sep 1930: *Cemal Hüsnü Bey* 16 - 25 Sep 1930: *Mahmut Esat Bey* (see above)
Public Works	11 Oct 1928 - 22 Sep 1930: *Recep Bey* (from 1934: *Recep Peker*) (b. Istanbul 1888; d. Istanbul 2 Apr 1950)*
Commerce	29 May 1929 - 25 Sep 1930: *Şakir Bey* (from 1934: *Şakir Kesebir*) (b. Veles 1889)
Health	*Refik Bey* (from 1934: *Refik Saydam*) (b. Istanbul 1881; d. Istanbul 8 Jul 1942)*

27 Sep 1930 - 25 Oct 1937: İsmet V (Peoples)

Prime Minister	27 Sep 1930 - 20 Sep 1937: *İsmet İnönü* (for 5th time) (see Presidents) 23 Sep - 25 Oct 1937 (acting:) *Celâl Bayar* (see Presidents)
Foreign Affairs	*Tevfik Rüştü Araş* (see İsmet IV)
Home Affairs	*Sükrü Kaya* (see Ismet IV)
Justice	27 Sep 1930 - 22 May 1933: *Yusuf Kemal Bey* (from 1934: *Yusuf Tengirşenk*) (b. Bayabat 1878) 23 May 1933 - 23 Sep 1937: *Şükrü Saracoğlu* (see Ismet IV)
Defence	27 Sep - 26 Dec 1930: *Mustafa Abdülhalik Bey* (see Ismet IV)

**For ministers no longer in office in 1930 see vol. 2
*For earlier career see vol. 2

TURKEY

	26 Dec 1930 – 1 Mar 1935: *Zekâi Bey* (from 1934: *Zekâi Apaydın*)*
	1 Mar 1935 – 23 Sep 1937: *Kâzim Pasha* (from 1934: *Kâzim Özalp*) (b. Veles 1880)
Finance	27 Sep – 22 Dec 1930: *Saracoglu Şükrü Bey* (see İsmet IV)
	23 Dec 1930 – 26 Oct 1933: *Mustafa Abdülhalik Bey* (see İsmet IV)
	26 Oct 1933 – 23 Sep 1937: *Fuat Agralı* (to 1934: *Fuat Bey*) (d. 25 Nov 1964)
Education	27 Sep 1930 – 19 Sep 1932: *Mahmut Esat Bey* (see İsmet IV)
	19 Sep 1932 – 12 Aug 1933: *Reşit Galip Bey* (d. Ankara 5 Mar 1934)
	27 Oct 1933 – 9 Jul 1934: *Yusuf Hikmet Bey*
	9 Jul 1934 – 10 Jun 1935: *Zeynül-Abidin Özmen*
	10 Jun 1935 – 23 Sep 1937: *Saffet Arıkan* (b. Erzerum 1888; d. 26 Nov 1947)
Public Works	27 Sep – 27 Dec 1930: *Zekâi Bey* (see above)
	27 Dec 1930 – 26 Oct 1933: *Hilmi Bey* (from 1934: *Hilmi Uran*) (b. Bodrum 1889; d. 21 Oct 1957)
	26 Oct 1933 – 14 Feb 1934: *Fuat Bey* (from 1934: *Fuat Ağralı*) (see above)
	14 Feb 1934 – 23 Sep 1937: *Ali Çetinkaya* (b. Afyon Karahisar 1873; d. 21 Feb 1949)
Commerce	27 Sep 1930 – 9 Sep 1932: *Mustafa Şeref Özkan* (b. Burdur 1884; d. Ankara 10 Sep 1938)
	9 Sep 1932 – 23 Sep 1937: *Celâl Bayar* (see Presidents)
Health	*Refik Saydam* (see İsmet IV)
Agriculture (new post)	30 Dec 1931 – 10 Jun 1937: *Muhlis* (from 1934: *Muhlis Erkmen*) (b. Brussa 1891)
	10 Jun – 23 Sep 1937: *Şakir Kesebir* (see İsmet IV)
Customs and Monopolies (new post)	30 Dec 1931 – 23 Sep 1937: *Ali Râna Tarhan* (b. 1882)

25 Oct 1937 – 11 Nov 1938: Bayar I (Peoples)

Prime Minister	*Celâl Bayar* (for 1st time) (see Presidents)
Foreign Affairs	*Tevfik Rüştü Araş* (see İsmet IV)
Home Affairs	*Şükrü Kaya* (see İsmet IV)
Justice	*Şükrü Saracoğlu* (see İsmet IV)

*For earlier career see vol. 2

492

Defence	Kazim Özalp (see İsmet V)
Finance	Fuat Ağralı (see İsmet V)
Education	Saffet Arıkan (see İsmet V)
Public Works	Ali Çetinkaya (see İsmet V)
Commerce	Şakir Kesebir (see İsmet IV)
Agriculture	25 Oct 1937 – 12 Apr 1938: Şakir Kesebir (see İsmet IV)
	12 Apr – 11 Nov 1938: Faik Kurdoğlu (b. 1894)
Customs and Monopolies	Ali Râna Tarhan (see İsmet V)
Health and Social Welfare	Hulûsi Alataş

11 Nov 1938 – 25 Jan 1939: Bayar II (Peoples)

Prime Minister	Celâl Bayar (for 2nd time) (see Presidents)
Foreign Affairs	Şükrü Saracoğlu (see İsmet IV)
Home Affairs	Refik Saydam (see İsmet IV)
Justice	11 Nov 1938 – 3 Jan 1939: Hilmi Uran (see İsmet V)
	3 – 25 Jan 1939: Tevfik Fikret Sılay
Defence	11 Nov 1938 – 17 Jan 1939: Kazim Özalp (see İsmet V)
	17 – 25 Jan 1939: Naci Tınaz (d. 25 Nov 1964)
Finance	Fuat Ağralı (see İsmet V)
Education	11 Nov – 28 Dec 1938: Saffet Arıkan (see İsmet V)
	28 Dec 1938 – 25 Jan 1939: Hasan-Âli Yücel (b. Istanbul 1897; d. Istanbul 26 Feb 1961)
Public Works	Ali Çetinkaya (see İsmet V)
Commerce	11 Nov – 28 Dec 1938: Şakir Kesebir (see İsmet IV)
	28 Dec 1938 – 25 Jan 1939: Hüsnü Çakır (b. Hopa 1892)
Agriculture	Faik Kurdoğlu (see Bayar I)
Customs and Monopolies	Ali Râna Tarhan (see İsmet V)
Health and Social Welfare	Hulûsi Alataş (see Bayar I)

25 Jan – 3 Apr 1939: Saydam I (Peoples)

Prime Minister	Refik Saydam (for 1st time) (see İsmet IV)
Foreign Affairs	Şükrü Saracoğlu (see İsmet IV)
Home Affairs	Fayık Öztrak (b. Malkara 1882; d. Ankara 30 May 1951)
Justice	Tevfik Fikret Sılay (see Bayar II)

493

Defence	*Naci Tınaz* (see Bayar II)
Finance	*Fuat Ağralı* (see İsmet V)
Education	*Hasan-Âli Yücel* (see Bayar II)
Public Works	*Ali Çetinkaya* (see İsmet V)
Commerce	*Hüsnü Cakır* (see Bayar II)
Agriculture	*Muhlis Erkmen* (see İsmet V)
Customs and Mono-	*Ali Râna Tarhan* (see İsmet V)
polies	
Health and Social	*Hulûsi Alataş* (see Bayar I)
Welfare	

3 Apr 1939 - 8 Jul 1942: Saydam II (Peoples)

Prime Minister	*Refik Saydam* (for 2nd time) (see İsmet IV)
Foreign Affairs	*Şükrü Saracoğlu* (see İsmet IV)
Home Affairs	3 Apr 1939 - 6 May 1942: *Fayık Öztrak* (see Saydam I)
	6 May - 8 Jul 1942: *A. Fikri Tuzer* (d. Ankara 16 Aug 1942)
Justice	3 Apr - 26 May 1939: *Tevfik Fikret Sılay* (see Bayar II)
	26 May 1939 - 12 Mar 1941: *Fethi Okyar* (to 1934: *Ali Fethi Bey*) (b. Prilep, Macedonia, 1880; d. Istanbul 7 May 1943)*
	12 Mar 1941 - 8 Jul 1942: *Hasan Menemencioğlu*
Defence	3 Apr 1939 - 4 Apr 1940: *Naci Tınaz* (see Bayar II)
	4 Apr 1940 - 12 Nov 1941: *Saffet Arıkan* (see İsmet V)
	12 Nov 1941 - 8 Jul 1942: *Ali Rıza Artunkal*
Finance	*Fuat Ağralı* (see İsmet V)
Education	*Hasan-Âli Yücel* (see Bayar II)
Public Works	*Ali Fuat Cebesoy* (b. Istanbul 1882)
Commerce	3 Apr 1939 - 1 Aug 1941: *Hüsnü Çakır* (see Bayar II)
	1 Aug 1941 - 8 Jul 1942: *Sırrı Day*
Transport (new post)	3 Apr 1939 - 20 Nov 1940: *Ali Çetinkaya* (see Ismet V)
	21 Nov 1940 - 12 Nov 1941: *Cevdet Kerim Incedayı* (b. Sinope 1895)
	12 Nov 1941 - 8 Jul 1942: *Fahri Engin*
Trade (new post)	3 Apr - 31 Oct 1939: *Cezmi Erçin*
	31 Oct 1939 - 26 Nov 1940: *Nazmi Topçuoğlu*
	26 Nov 1940 - 8 Jul 1942: *Mümtaz Ökmen*
Agriculture	*Muhlis Erkmen* (see İsmet V)

*For earlier career see vol. 2

Customs and Mono- polies	3 Apr – 26 May 1939: *Ali Râna Tarhan* (see İsmet V) 26 May 1939 – 8 Jul 1942: *Raif Karadeniz* (b. Vakfıkebir 1897)
Health and Social Welfare	*Hulûsi Alataş* (see Bayar I)

9 Jul 1942 – 9 Mar 1943: Saracoğlu I (Peoples)

Prime Minister	*Şükrü Saracoğlu* (for 1st time) (see İsmet IV)
Foreign Affairs	10 Jul – 13 Aug 1942 (acting:) *Şükrü Saracoğlu* (see Ismet IV) 13 Aug 1942 – 9 Mar 1943: *Numan Menemencioğlu* (b. Baghdad 1892; d. Ankara 15 Feb 1958)
Home Affairs	10 Jul – 16 Aug 1942: *A. Fikri Tuzer* (see Saydam II) 17 Aug 1942 – 9 Mar 1943: *Recep Peker* (see İsmet IV)
Justice	*Hasan Menemencioğlu* (see Saydam II)
Defence	*Ali Rıza Artunkal* (see Saydam II)
Finance	*Fuat Ağralı* (see İsmet V)
Education	*Hasan-Âli Yücel* (see Bayar II)
Public Works	*Ali Fuat Cebesoy* (see Saydam II)
Commerce	*Sırrı Day* (see Saydam II)
Transport	*Fahri Engin* (see Saydam II)
Trade	*Behçet Uz* (b. 1893)
Agriculture	*Şefket Rasit Hatipoğlu* (b. Menemen 1898)
Customs and Mono- polies	*Raif Karadeniz* (see Saydam II)
Health and Social Welfare	*Hulûsi Alataş* (see Bayar I)

9 Mar 1943 – 5 Aug 1946: Saracoğlu II (Peoples)

Prime Minister	*Şükrü Saracoğlu* (for 2nd time) (see İsmet IV)
Foreign Affairs	9 Mar 1943 – 15 Jun 1944: *Numan Menemencioğlu* (see Saracoğlu I) 15 Jun – 13 Sep 1944 (acting:) *Şükrü Saracoğlu* (see Ismet IV) 13 Sep 1944 – 5 Aug 1946: *Hasan Saka* (to 1934: *Hasan Hüsnü Bey*) (b. Trebizond 1886; d. Istanbul 29 Jul 1960)*
Home Affairs	9 Mar – 20 May 1943: *Recep Peker* (see Ismet IV) 20 May 1943 – 5 Aug 1946: *Hilmi Uran* (see İsmet V)

*For earlier career see vol. 2

Justice	9 Mar 1943 – 6 Apr 1946: *Ali Rıza Türel* (b. Salonica 1899)
Defence	*Ali Rıza Artunkal* (see Saydam II)
Finance	9 Mar 1943 – 13 Sep 1944: *Fuat Ağralı* (see İsmet V) 13 Sep 1944 – 5 Aug 1946: *Nurullah Esat Sumer* (b. Smyrna 1899)
Education	*Hasan-Âli Yücel* (see Bayar II)
Labour (new post)	7 Jun 1945 – 5 Aug 1946: *Sadı Irmak* (b. Seydişehir 1904)
Public Works	*Sırrı Day* (see Saydam II)
Commerce	*Ali Fuat Sirmen* (b. Istanbul 1899)
Transport	*Ali Fuat Cebesoy* (see Saydam II)
Trade	9 Mar 1943 – 31 May 1945: *Celâl Sait Siren* (b. Adana 1905) 31 May 1945 – 5 Aug 1946: *Raif Karadeniz* (see Saydam II)
Agriculture	*Şefket Raşit Hatipoğlu* (see Saracoğlu I)
Customs and Monopolies	9 Mar 1943 – 19 Feb 1946: *Suat Hayri Ürgüplü* (b. Damascus 1903) 19 Feb – 5 Aug 1946: *Tahsin Coşkan*
Health and Social Welfare	9 Mar 1943 – 18 Jan 1945: *Hulûsi Alataş* (see Bayar I) 18 Jan 1945 – 5 Aug 1946: *Sadi Konuk*

5 Aug 1946 – 9 Sep 1947: Peker (Peoples)

Prime Minister	*Recep Peker* (see İsmet IV)
Deputy Prime Minister	20 Sep 1946 – 9 Sep 1947: *Mümtaz Ökmen* (see Saydam II)
Foreign Affairs	*Hasan Saka* (see Saracoğlu II)
Home Affairs	*Şükrü Sökmensüer*
Justice	5 Aug – 20 Sep 1946: *Mümtaz Ökmen* (see Saydam II) 20 Sep 1946 – 9 Sep 1947: *Şinasi Devrin*
Defence	5 Aug 1946 – 5 Sep 1947: *Cemil Toydemir* (b. 1883) 5 – 9 Sep 1947: *Münir Bilsel*
Finance	*Halit Nazmi Keşmir* (d. 23 Mar 1948)
Education	*Reşat Şemsettin Sirer* (b. 1903; d. 2 Oct 1953)
Labour	*Sadi Irmak* (see Saracoğlu II)
Public Works	*Cevdet Kerim Incedayı* (see Saydam II)
Commerce	5 Aug 1946 – 5 Sep 1947: *Tahsin Bekir Balta* 5 – 9 Sep 1947: *Cavit Ekin* (b. 1896)
Trade	5 Aug 1946 – 5 Sep 1947: *Atif Inan* 5 – 9 Sep 1947: *Halit Nazmi Keşmir* (see above)
Transport	*Şükrü Koçak* (d. 16 Sep 1961)

Agriculture	5 Aug 1946 – 5 Sep 1947: *Faik Kurdoğlu* (see Bayar I)
	5 – 9 Sep 1947: *Şevket Adalan* (b. Smyrna 1901)
Customs and Mono-	*Tahsin Coşkan* (see Saracoğlu II)
polies	
Health	*Behçet Uz* (see Saracoğlu I)
Minister of State	20 Sep 1946 – 5 Sep 1947: *Abdülhalik Renda* (see İsmet IV)

9 Sep 1947 - 8 Jun 1948: Saka I (Peoples)

Prime Minister	*Hasan Saka* (for 1st time) (see Saracoğlu II)
Deputy Prime Minister	*Faik Ahmet Barutçu*
Foreign Affairs	*Necmettin Sadak* (b. Isparta 1890; d. New York 21 Sep 1953)
Home Affairs	*Münir Göle*
Justice	*Şinasi Devrin* (see Peker)
Defence	*Münir Bilsel* (see Peker)
Finance	10 Sep 1947 – 23 Mar 1948: *Halit Nazmi Keşmir* (see Peker)
	27 Mar – 8 Jun 1948: *Şevket Adalan* (see Peker)
Education	*Reşat Şemsettin Sirer* (see Peker)
Labour	*Tahsin Bekir Balta* (see Peker)
Public Works	*Kasım Gülek* (b. Adana 1906)
Commerce	*Cavit Ekin* (see Peker)
Trade	*Mehmet Nedim Gündüzalp* (b. Tutrakan, Danube, 1892)
Transport	*Şükrü Koçak* (see Peker)
Agriculture	*Tahsin Coşkan* (see Saracoğlu II)
Customs and Mono-	*Şevket Adalan* (see Peker)
polies	
Minister of State	10 Sep 1947 – 20 Feb 1948: *Abdülhalik Renda* (see İsmet IV)

10 Jun 1948 - 14 Jan 1949: Saka II

Prime Minister	*Hasan Saka* (for 2nd time) (see Saracoğlu II)
Deputy Prime Minister	*Faik Ahmet Barutçu* (see Saka I)
Foreign Affairs	*Necmettin Sadak* (see Saka I)
Home Affairs	*Münir Göle* (see Saka I)
Justice	*Ali Fuat Sirmen* (see Saracoğlu II)

497

Defence	*Hüsnü Çakır* (see Bayar II)
Finance	*Şevket Adalan* (see Peker)
Education	*Hasan Tahsin Banguoğlu* (b. Drama 1904)
Labour	*Tahsin Bekir Balta* (see Peker)
Public Works	*Nihat Erim* (b. 1912)
Commerce	*Cavit Ekin* (see Peker)
Transport	*Kasım Gülek* (see Saka I)
Trade	*Cemil Sait Barlas* (b. 1905)
Agriculture	*Cavit Oral* (b. Adana 1902/04?)
Customs and Mono- polies	*Emin Erişirgil* (b. Istanbul 1901)
Health	*Kemalî Bayazıt* (b. 1903)
Minister of State	*Şemsettin Günaltay* (b. Kemaliye 1883; d. Istanbul 19 Oct 1961)

16 Jan 1949 – 22 May 1950: Günaltay

Prime Minister	*Şemsettin Günaltay* (see Saka II)
Deputy Prime Minister	*Nihat Erim* (see Saka II)
Foreign Affairs	*Necmettin Sadak* (see Saka I)
Home Affairs	*Emin Erişirgil* (see Saka II)
Justice	*Ali Fuat Sirmen* (see Saracoğlu II)
Defence	*Hüsnü Çakır* (see Bayar II)
Finance	*İsmail Rüştü Aksal* (b. Pamukova 1911)
Education	*Hasan Tahsin Banguoğlu* (see Saka II)
Labour	*Reşat Şemsettin Sirer* (see Peker)
Public Works	*Şevket Adalan* (see Peker)
Co-ordination and Marshall Plan Affairs	16 Jan – 7 Jun 1949: *Nurullah Esat Sumer* (see Saracoğlu II) 7 Jun 1949 – 22 May 1950: *Cemil Sait Barlas* (see Saka II)
Commerce and Trade	16 Jan – 7 Jun 1949: *Cemil Sait Barlas* (see Saka II) 7 Jun 1949 – 22 May 1950: *Vedat Dicleli* (b. Diyarbakır 1912)
Transport and Public Utilities	16 Jan – 7 Jun 1949: *Kemal Satır* (b. Adana 1911) 7 Jun 1949 – 22 May 1950: *Münir Bilsel* (see Peker)
Agriculture	*Cavit Oral* (see Saka II)
Customs and Mono- polies	*Fazıl Şerefeddin Bürge*
Health	*Kemalî Bayazıt* (see Saka II)
Minister of State	*Ali Rıza Erten*

22 May 1950 – 1 Mar 1951: Menderes I (Dem)

Prime Minister	*Adnan Menderes* (for 1st time) (b. Aydın 1899; d. Imralı Island Prison 17 Sep 1961)
Deputy Prime Minister	6 Jun 1950 – 1 Mar 1951: *Samet Ağaoğlu* (b. Karadağ 1909)
Foreign Affairs	*Mehmet Fuat Köprülü* (b. Istanbul 5 Dec 1890; d. Istanbul 28 Jun 1966)
Home Affairs	*Rüknettin Nasuhioğlu* (b. 1894)
Justice	*Halil Özyörük*
Defence	*Refik Şevket İnce* (b. Mytilene 1885; d. Istanbul 24 Apr 1955)
Finance	22 May – 14 Dec 1950: *Halil Ayan* (b. Bursa 1904) 14 Dec 1950 – 1 Mar 1951: *Hasan Polatkan* (b. 1915; d. İmralı Island Prison 16 Sep 1961)
Education	22 May – 11 Aug 1950: *Avni Başman* (b. Istanbul 1887) 11 Aug 1950 – 1 Mar 1951: *Tevfik İleri* (b. Gumno 1910; d. Ankara night of 31 Dec 1961/1 Jan 1962)
Labour	22 May – 14 Dec 1950: *Hasan Polatkan* (see above) 22 Dec 1950 – 1 Mar 1951: *Hulûsi Köymen* (b. 1891)
Public Works	22 May – 28 Oct 1950: *K. G. Fahri Belen* (b. 1892) 28 Oct – 22 Dec 1950 (acting:) *Hasan Polatkan* (see above) 22 Dec 1950 – 1 Mar 1951: *Kemal Zeytinoğlu* (b. 1911; d. Gatwick Airport 17 Feb 1959)
Public Utilities	*Muhlis Ete* (b. 1904)
Commerce and Trade	*Zühtü Velibeşe*
Transport	22 May – 11 Aug 1950: *Tevfik İleri* (see above) 11 Aug 1950 – 1 Mar 1951: *Seyfi Kurtbek* (b. Gallipoli 1906)
Agriculture	*Nihat Eğriboz* (b. Salonica 1891/92)
Customs and Monopolies	*Nuri Özsan* (b. 1905)
Health	22 May – 19 Sep 1950: *Nihat Reşat Belger* (b. Istanbul 1881) 19 Sep 1950 – 1 Mar 1951: *Ekrem Hayri Üstündağ* (b. 1886)
Minister of State	10 Jul 1950 – 1 Mar 1951: *Fevzi Lûtfi Karaosmanoğlu* (b. Manisa 1900)

499

9 Mar 1951 – 17 May 1954: Menderes II (Dem)

Prime Minister	*Adnan Menderes* (for 2nd time) (see Menderes I)
Deputy Prime Minister	9 Mar 1951 – Oct 1952: *Samet Ağaoğlu* (see Menderes I)
Foreign Affairs	*Mehmet Fuat Köprülü* (see Menderes I)
Home Affairs	9 Mar – 20 Oct 1951: *Halil Özyörük* (see Menderes I)
	20 Oct 1951 – 7 Apr 1952: *Fevzi Lûtfi Karaosmanoğlu* (see Menderes I)
	7 Apr – 1 Aug 1952 (acting:) *Adnan Menderes* (see Menderes I)
	1 Aug 1952 – 17 May 1954: *Ethem Menderes* (b. Smyrna 1899)
Justice	9 Mar 1951 – 7 Nov 1952: *Rüknettin Nasuhioğlu* (see Menderes I)
	17 Nov 1952 – 17 May 1954: *Osman Şevki Çiçekdağ*
Defence	9 Mar 1951 – 4 Nov 1952: *Hulûsi Köymen* (see Menderes I)
	4 Nov 1952 – 28 Jul 1953: *Seyfi Kurtbek* (see Menderes I)
	28 Jul 1953 – 17 May 1954: *Kenan Yılmaz* (b. Erzerum 1900)
Finance	*Hasan Polatkan* (see Menderes I)
Education	9 Mar 1951 – 6 Apr 1953: *Tevfik İleri* (see Menderes I)
	8 Apr 1953 – 17 May 1954: *Rıfkı Salim Burçak* (b. Erzerum 1913)
Labour	9 Mar 1951 – 5 Nov 1952: *Nuri Özsan* (see Menderes I)
	5 Nov 1952 – 8 Apr 1953: *Samet Ağaoğlu* (see Menderes I)
	8 Apr 1953 – 17 May 1954: *Hayrettin Erkmen* (b. Tirebolu 1915)
Public Works	*Kemal Zeytinoğlu* (see Menderes I)
Public Utilities	9 Mar – 12 Dec 1951: *Hakkı Gedik*
	12 Dec 1951 – 17 May 1954: *Nuri Özsan* (see Menderes I)
Commerce and Trade	9 Mar 1951 – 23 Jun 1952: *Muhlis Ete* (see Menderes I)
	23 Jun 1952 – 26 May 1953: *Enver Güreli* (b. Burhaniye 1914)
	26 May 1953 – 17 May 1954 (acting:) *Hayrettin Erkmen* (see above)
Transport	9 Mar 1951 – 5 Nov 1952: *Seyfi Kurtbek* (see Menderes I)
	5 Nov 1952 – 17 May 1954: *Yümnü Üresin* (b. Elâzığ 1898)

Agriculture	*Nedim Ökmen* (b. Kilis 1908)
Customs and Mono-	9 Mar 1951 – 26 Oct 1951: *Rıfkı Salim Burçak* (see
polies	above)
	26 Oct – 2 Dec 1951: *Nuri Özsan* (see Menderes I)
	2 Dec 1951 – 8 Apr 1953: *Sıtkı Yırcalı*
	8 Apr 1953 – 17 May 1954: *Emin Kalafat* (b. Salonica 1902)
Health	*Ekrem Hayri Üstündağ* (see Menderes I)
Ministers of State	9 – 30 Mar 1951: *Refik Şevket İnce* (see Menderes I)
	18 Jun 1951 – 7 Apr 1952: *Fevzi Lûtfi Karaosmanoğlu* (see Menderes I)
	23 Jun 1952 – 8 Apr 1953: *Muammer Alakant*
	8 Apr 1953 – 17 May 1954: *Celâl Yardımcı* (b. Doğu Beyazit 1911)
	8 Apr 1953 – 17 May 1954: *Fethi Çelikbaş* (b. Burdur 1912)

17 May 1954 – 30 Nov 1955: Menderes III (Dem)

Prime Minister	*Adnan Menderes* (for 3rd time) (see Menderes I)
Deputy Prime	17 May 1954 – 26 May 1955: *Fatin Rüştü Zorlu* (b.
Minister	1910; d. İmralı Island Prison 16 Sep 1961)
	26 May – 30 Nov 1955: *Mehmet Fuat Köprülü* (see Menderes I)
Ministers of State	17 May 1954 – 15 Apr 1955: *Osman Kapanî*
	17 May 1954 – 12 Oct 1955: *Mükerrem Sarol*
	26 May – 9 Jul 1955: *Mehmet Fuat Köprülü* (see Menderes I)
	30 Sep – 30 Nov 1955: *Fahrettin Ulaş* (b. Istanbul 1911)
Foreign Affairs	17 May 1954 – 15 May 1955: *Mehmet Fuat Köprülü* (see Menderes I)
	15 May – 26 Jul 1955 (acting:) *Adnan Menderes* (see Menderes I)
	26 Jul – 30 Nov 1955 (acting:) *Fatin Rüştü Zorlu* (see above)
Home Affairs	17 May 1954 – 10 Sep 1955: *Namık Gedik* (b. Istanbul 1911; d. 29 May 1960)
	10/30 Sep – 30 Nov 1955: *Ethem Menderes* (see Menderes II)
Justice	*Osman Şevki Çiçekdağ* (see Menderes II)
Defence	17 May 1954 – 15 Sep 1955: *Ethem Menderes* (see Menderes II)

501

	15 Sep – 30 Nov 1955: *Mehmet Fuat Köprülü* (see Menderes I)
Finance	*Hasan Polatkan* (see Menderes I)
Education	*Celâl Yardımcı* (see Menderes II)
Labour	*Hayrettin Erkmen* (see Menderes II)
Public Works	*Kemal Zeytinoğlu* (see Menderes I)
Nationalised Industries	17 May – 6 Dec 1954: *Fethi Çelikbaş* (see Menderes II)
	6 Dec 1954 – 30 Nov 1955: *Samet Ağaoğlu* (see Menderes I)
Commerce and Trade	*Sıtkı Yırcalı* (see Menderes II)
Transport	*Muammer Çavuşoğlu* (b. Kuşadası 1903)
Agriculture	*Nedim Ökmen* (see Menderes II)
Customs and Monopolies	*Emin Kalafat* (see Menderes II)
Health	*Behçet Uz* (see Saracoğlu I)

9 Dec 1955 – 25 Nov 1957: Menderes IV (Dem)

Prime Minister	*Adnan Menderes* (for 4th time) (see Menderes I)
Ministers of State	*Cemil Bengü* (b. Mesudiye 1914; d. 15 Apr 1958)
	9 Dec 1955 – 28 Jul 1957: *Şem'i Ergin* (b. Gebze 1913)
	28 Jul – 25 Nov 1957: *Fatin Rüştü Zorlu* (see Menderes III)
	Emin Kalafat (see Menderes II)
	Celâl Yardımcı (see Menderes II)
Foreign Affairs	9 Dec 1955 – 20 Jun 1956: *Mehmet Fuat Köprülü* (see Menderes I)
	20 Jun 1956 – 25 Nov 1957: *Ethem Menderes* (see Menderes II)
Home Affairs	9 Dec 1955 – 12 Oct 1956: *Ethem Menderes* (see Menderes II)
	12 Oct –.22 Dec 1956 (acting:) *Huseyin Avni Göktürk* (b. Niğde 1901)
	22 Dec 1956 – 25 Nov 1957: *Namık Gedik* (see Menderes III)
Justice	*Huseyin Avni Göktürk* (see above)
Defence	9 Dec 1955 – 28 Jul 1957 (acting:) *Adnan Menderes* (see Menderes I)
	28 Jul – 25 Nov 1957: *Şem'i Ergin* (see above)
Finance	9 Dec 1955 – 23 Aug 1956: *Nedim Ökmen* (see Menderes II)

	23 Aug – 1 Dec 1956 (acting:) *Adnan Menderes* (see Menderes I)
	1 Dec 1956 – 25 Nov 1957: *Hasan Polatkan* (see Menderes I)
Education	9 Dec 1955 – 12 Apr 1957: *Ahmet Özel* (b. Sivas 1910)
	12 Apr – 25 Nov 1957: *Tevfik İleri* (see Menderes I)
Labour	*Mümtaz Tarhan* (b. Istanbul 1907)
Public Works	9 Dec 1955 – 12 Oct 1956: *Muammer Çavuşoğlu* (see Menderes III)
	12 Oct 1956 – 25 Nov 1957: *Ethem Menderes* (see Menderes II)
Nationalised Industries	*Samet Ağaoğlu* (see Menderes I)
Commerce and Trade	9 Dec 1955 – 7 May 1956: *Fahrettin Ulaş* (see Menderes III)
	7 May 1956 – 25 Nov 1957: *Zeyyat Mandalinci*
Transport	*Arif Demiret* (b. Afyon 1909)
Agriculture	*Esat Budakoğlu* (b. Balıkesir 1911)
Customs and Mono-polies	*Hadi Hüsman* (b. Komotini 1904)
Health	*Nafiz Körez* (b. Kula 1909)

25 Nov 1957 – 27 May 1960: Menderes V (Dem)

Prime Minister	*Adnan Menderes* (for 5th time) (see Menderes I)
Deputy Prime Minister	25 Nov 1957 – 11 Dec 1959: *Tevfik İleri* (see Menderes I)
	11 Dec 1959 – 27 May 1960: *Medenî Berk* (b. 1913)
Ministers of State	*Emin Kalafat* (see Menderes II)
	Muzaffer Kurbanoğlu (b. Manisa 1913)
	4 Sep 1958 – 27 May 1960 (acting:) *Halûk Şaman* (b. Istanbul 1911)
	4 Sep 1958 – 27 May 1960: *Abdullah Aker* (b. 1905)
Foreign Affairs	*Fatin Rüştü Zorlu* (see Menderes III)
Home Affairs	*Namık Gedik* (see Menderes III)
Justice	*Esat Budakoglu* (see Menderes IV)
Defence	25 Nov 1957 – 19 Jan 1958: *Şem'i Ergin* (see Menderes IV)
	19 Jan 1958 – 27 May 1960: *Ethem Menderes* (see Menderes II)
Finance	*Hasan Polatkan* (see Menderes I)
Education	25 Nov 1957 – 23 May 1959: *Celâl Yardımcı* (see Menderes II)

503

	23 May – 7 Dec 1959 (acting:) *Tevfik İleri* (see Menderes I)
	7 Dec 1959 – 27 May 1960: *Atıf Benderlioğlu*
Labour	25 Nov 1957 – 4 Sep 1958: *Hayrettin Erkmen* (see Menderes II)
	4 Sep 1958 – 27 May 1960: *Halûk Şaman* (see above)
Public Works	25 Nov 1957 – 19 Jan 1958: *Ethem Menderes* (see Menderes II)
	19 Jan 1958 – 27 May 1960: *Tevfik İleri* (see Menderes I)
Industry	25 Nov 1957 – 8 Feb 1958: *Samet Ağaoğlu* (see Menderes I)
	8 Feb – 10 May 1958 (acting:) *Abdullah Aker* (see above)
	10 May – 1 Sep 1958: *Sıtkı Yırcalı* (see Menderes II)
	1 Sep – 3 Oct 1958 (acting:) *Hasan Polatkan* (see Menderes I)
	3 Oct 1958 – 27 May 1960: *Sebati Ataman* (b. Yanya 1908)
Buildings and Housing (new post)	25 Nov 1957 – 11 Dec 1959: *Medenî Berk* (see above)
	11 Dec 1959 – 27 May 1960 (acting:) *Hayrettin Erkmen* (see Menderes II)
Trade	25 Nov 1957 – 4 Sep 1958: *Abdullah Aker* (see above)
	4 Sep 1958 – 27 May 1960: *Hayrettin Erkmen* (see Menderes II)
Transport	25 Nov 1957 – 18 Sep 1958: *Fevzi Uçaner* (b. Erzerum 1900)
	18 Sep 1958 – 7 Dec 1959: *Muzaffer Kurbanoğlu* (see above)
	7 Dec 1959 – 27 May 1960: *Şem'i Ergin* (see Menderes IV)
Press and Tourism (new post)	25 Nov 1957 – 10 Jul 1958: *Sıtkı Yırcalı* (see Menderes II)
	10 Jul 1958 – 17 Feb 1959: *Server Somuncuoğlu* (d. Gatwick Airport 17 Feb 1959)
	18 Feb – 14 Nov 1959 (acting:) *Abdullah Aker* (see above)
	14 Nov 1959 – 27 May 1960 (acting:) *Halûk Şaman* (see above)
Co-ordination (new post)	10 Jul 1958 – 11 Dec 1959: *Sebati Ataman* (see above)
	11 Dec 1959 – 27 May 1960: *Abdullah Aker* (see above)
Agriculture	*Nedim Ökmen* (see Menderes II)

Customs and Mono- polies	*Hadi Hüsman* (see Menderes IV)
Health	*Lûtfi Kırdar* (b. 1889; d. Yassı ada Island Prison 17 Feb 1961)

28 May 1960 - 4 Jan 1961: Gürsel I (Chairman of Committee of National Unity)

Prime Minister	*Cemal Gürsel* (for 1st time) (see Presidents)
Assistant to Prime Minister	20 Oct 1960 - 4 Jan 1961: *Fahri Özdilek*
Ministers of State	28 May - 25 Aug 1960: *Âmil Artus* (b. Istanbul 1912) 28 May - 25 Aug 1960: *Şefik İnan* (b. Simav 1910) 25 Aug/3 Sep 1960 - 4 Jan 1961: *Hayri Mumcuoğlu* (b. Istanbul 1914) 25 Aug/3 Sep 1960 - 4 Jan 1961: *Nasir Zeytinoğlu*
Foreign Affairs	*Selim Sarper* (b. Istanbul 1897/99; d. Ankara 12 Oct 1968)
Home Affairs	*Muharrem İhsan Kızıloğlu* (b. Sebinkarahisar)
Justice	28 May - 25 Aug 1960: *Abdullah Gözübüyük* (b. Kayseri 1949) 25 Aug 1960 - 4 Jan 1961: *Âmil Artus* (see above)
Defence	28 May - 4 Jun 1960: *Cemal Gürsel* (see Presidents) 4 Jun 1960 - 4 Jan 1961: *Fahri Özdilek* (see above)
Finance	28 May - 24 Dec 1960: *Ekrem Alican* (b. Adapazarı 1916) 24 Dec 1960 - 4 Jan 1961: *Kemal Kurdaş*
Education	28 May - 8 Sep 1960: *Fehmi Yavuz* (b. Isparta 1912) 10 Sep 1960 - 4 Jan 1961: *Bedrettin Tunçel*
Labour	28 May - 25 Aug 1960: *Cahit Talaş* (b. Trebizond 1917) 3 Sep 1960 - 4 Jan 1961: *Mehmet Raşit Beşerler*
Public Works	28 May - 25 Aug 1960: *Danıs Koper* (b. Diyadin 1906) 10 Sep 1960 - 4 Jan 1961: *Mukbil Gökdoğan* (b. Istanbul 1909)
Industry	28 May - 25 Aug 1960: *Muhtar Uluer* (b. Konya 1908) 3 Sep 1960 - 4 Jan 1961: *Şahap Kocatopçuoğlu*
Buildings and Housing	28 May - 25 Aug 1960: *Orhan Kubat* (b. Istanbul 1904) 25 Aug/10 Sep 1960 - 4 Jan 1961: *Fehmi Yavuz* (see above)
Commerce and Trade	28 May - 25 Aug 1960: *Cahit İren* (b. Istanbul 1916) 3 Sep 1960 - 4 Jan 1961: *Mehmet Baydur* (b. 1919)
Transport	*Sıtkı Ulay*

505

Press, Radio and Tourism	28 May – 25 Aug 1960: *Zühtü Tarhan* (b. Istanbul 1913)
Agriculture	28 May – 25 Aug 1960: *Feridun Üstün* (b. Istanbul 1916)
	10 Sep 1960 – 4 Jan 1961: *Osman Tosun* (b. Adagüme 1913)
Customs and Monopolies	*Fethi Aşkin* (b. Kandıra 1916)
Health and Social Affairs	28 May – 25 Aug 1960: *Nusret Karasu* (b. Erzerum 1902)
	10 Sep 1960 – 4 Jan 1961: *Ragıp Üner*

5 Jan – 28 Oct 1961: Gürsel II

Prime Minister	*Cemal Gürsel* (for 2nd time) (see Presidents)
Deputy Prime Minister	5 Jan – 4 Feb 1961: *Fahri Özdilek* (see Gürsel I)
	4 Feb – 2 Mar 1961: *Muharrem İhsan Kızıloğlu* (see Gürsel I)
	2 Mar – 28 Oct 1961: *Fahri Özdilek* (see Gürsel I)
Ministers of State	5 Jan – 3 Feb 1961: *Hayri Mumcuoğlu* (see Gürsel I)
	5 Jan – 4 Feb 1961: *Nasir Zeytinoğlu* (see Gürsel I)
	2 Mar – 28 Oct 1961: *Sıtkı Ulay* (see Gürsel I)
	25 Aug – 28 Oct 1961: *Adnan Erzi*
Foreign Affairs	*Selim Sarper* (see Gürsel I)
Home Affairs	5 Jan – 4 Feb 1961: *Muharrem İhsan Kızıloğlu* (see Gürsel I)
	4 Feb – 28 Oct 1961: *Nasir Zeytinoğlu* (see Gürsel I)
Justice	5 Jan – 16 Aug 1961: *Ekrem Tüzemen* (b. Tunçeli 1915)
	16 Aug – 28 Oct 1961: *Kemal Türkoğlu* (b. Mardin 1911)
Defence	5 Jan – 28 Jun 1961: *Muzaffer Alankuş* (b. Erzerum 1897)
	28 Jun – 28 Oct 1961: *Fahri Özdilek* (see Gürsel I)
Finance	*Kemal Kurdaş* (see Gürsel I)
Education	5 Jan – 7 Feb 1961: *Turhan Feyzioğlu* (b. Kayseri 1922)
	7 Feb – 28 Oct 1961: *Ahmet Tahtakılıç* (b. Uşak 1909)
Labour	5 Jan – 2 Mar 1961: *Ahmet Tahtakılıç* (see above)
	2 Mar – 28 Oct 1961: *Cahit Talas* (see Gürsel I)
Public Works	5 Jan – 21 Aug 1961: *Mukbil Gökdoğan* (see Gürsel I)
	21 Aug – 28 Oct 1961 (acting:) *Sıtkı Ulay* (see Gürsel I)
Industry	5 Jan – 14 Apr 1961: *Şahap Kocatopçuoğlu* (see Gürsel I)

	29 Apr – 28 Oct 1961: *Ihsan Soyak* (b. Skopje 1909)
Buildings and	5 Jan – 3 Feb 1961: *Fehmi Yavuz* (see Gürsel I)
Housing	6 Feb – 20 Nov 1961: *Rüştü Özal*
Trade	*Mehmet Baydur* (see Gürsel I)
Transport	*Orhan Mersinli*
Press, Radio and	5 Jan – 29 Aug 1961: *Cihat Baban* (b. Istanbul 1911)
Tourism	2 Sep – 28 Oct 1961: *Sahir Kurutluoğlu* (b. Kırşehir 1910)
Agriculture	*Osman Tosun* (see Gürsel I)
Customs and	*Fethi Aşkin* (see Gürsel I)
Monopolies	
Health and Social	*Ragıp Üner* (see Gürsel I)
Affairs	

20 Nov 1961 – 30 May 1962: İsmet VI (Peoples and Justice Coalition)

Prime Minister	*İsmet İnönü* (Peoples) (for 6th time) (see İsmet IV)
Deputy Prime Minister	*Akif İyidoğan* (Just) (b. Istanbul 1893/4)
Ministers of State	*Turhan Feyzioğlu* (Peoples) (see Gürsel II)
	20 Nov 1961 – 23 May 1962: *Avni Doğan* (Peoples) (b. Yozgat 1892)
	Nazmi Ökten (b. Istanbul 1905/06)
	Nihat Su (Just) (b. Antalya 1918)
Foreign Affairs	20 Nov 1961 – 15 Mar 1962: *Selim Sarper* (see Gürsel I)
	24 Mar – 30 May 1962: *Feridun Cemal Erkin* (no party)
Home Affairs	*Ahmet Topaloğlu* (Just) (b. Kadirli 1914)
Justice	*Sahir Kurutluoğlu* (Peoples) (see Gürsel II)
Defence	*İlhami Sancar* (Peoples) (b. Gördes 1909)
Finance	*Şefik İnan* (Peoples) (see Gürsel I)
Education	*Hilmi Incesulu* (b. Sungurlu 1917)
Labour	*Bülent Ecevit* (Peoples) (b. Istanbul 1925)
Buildings and Housing	*Muhittin Güven* (Just) (b. 1917)
Public Works	*Emin Paksüt* (Peoples) (b. Istanbul 1914)
Industry	*Fethi Çelikbaş* (Peoples) (see Menderes II)
Trade	*İhsan Gürsan* (b. Istanbul 1885/86)
Transport	*Cahit Akyar* (b. Kuşadasi 1908)
Press and Tourism	*Kâmuran Evliyaoğlu* (Just) (b. Malatya 1926)
Agriculture	*Cavit Oral* (Just) (see Saka II)
Customs and Monopolies	*Şevket Budakoğlu* (Just) (b. Trebizond 1911)

Health and Social Aid   *Suat Seren* (Just) (b. Isparta 1910)

25 Jun 1962 – 2 Dec 1963: İsmet VII (Peoples, NTP and CNP Coalition)

Prime Minister	*İsmet İnönü* (Peoples) (for 7th time) (see İsmet IV)
Deputy Prime	*Turhan Feyzioğlu* (Peoples) (see Gürsel II)
Ministers	*Hasan Dinçer* (CNP) (b. Sandıklı 1910)
	Ekrem Alican (NTP) (see Gürsel I)
Ministers of State	25 Jun 1962 – 17 Oct 1963: *Hıfzı Oğuz Bekata* (Peoples) (b. Ankara 1911)
	Nazmi Ökten (see İsmet VI)
	Raif Aybar (NTP) (b. Karacabey 1915)
	27 Oct 1962 – 15 Jun 1963: *Ali Şakir Ağanoğlu* (Peoples) (b. Akçaabat 1910)
Minister of State	15 Jun – 2 Dec 1963: *Vefik Pirinççioğlu* (Peoples) (b.
(for Tourism	Diyarbakır 1909)
and Information)	
Foreign Affairs	*Feridun Cemal Erkin* (no party) (see İsmet VI)
Home Affairs	*Sahir Kurutluoğlu* (Peoples) (see Gürsel II)
Justice	*Abdülhak Kemal Yörük* (CNP) (b. Istanbul 1897)
Defence	*İlhami Sancar* (Peoples) (see İsmet VI)
Finance	*Ferit Melen* (Peoples) (b. Van 1906)
Education	25 Jun 1962 – 8 Jun 1963: *Şefket Raşit Hatipoğlu* (Peoples) (see Saracoğlu I)
	10 Jun – 2 Dec 1963: *İbrahim Öktem* (Peoples) (b. Karaman 1904)
Labour	*Bülent Ecevit* (Peoples) (see İsmet VI)
Buildings and	25 Jun 1962 – 5 Nov 1963: *Fahrettin Kerim Gökay*
Housing	(NTP) (b. Eskişehir 1900)
	5 Nov – 2 Dec 1963: *Hayri Mumcuoğlu* (see Gürsel I)
Public Works	25 Jun 1962 – 18 Oct 1963: *İlyas Seçkin* (Peoples) (b. Ayas 1918)
	18 Oct – 2 Dec 1963: *Arif Hikmet Onat* (Peoples) (b. Ordu 1908)
Industry	*Fethi Çelikbaş* (Peoples) (see Menderes II)
Trade	25 Jun 1962 – 15 Jun 1963: *Muhlis Ete* (CNP) (see Menderes I)
	15 Jun – 2 Dec 1963: *Ahmet Oğuz* (b. Eskişehir 1912)
Transport	25 Jun 1962 – 7 Jun 1963: *Rifat Öçten* (NTP) (b. Sivas 1913)
	11 Jun – 2 Dec 1963: *Ihsan Şeref Dura* (NTP) (b. Bursa 1901)

Press and Tourism	25 Jun 1962 – 15 Jun 1963: *Celâl Tevfik Karasapan* (CNP) (b. Medina 1899)
	15 Jun – 2 Dec 1963: *Nurettin Ardiçoğlu* (CNP) (b. Elâziğ 1914)
Agriculture	*Mehmet İzmen* (NTP) (b. Giresun 1909)
Customs and Monopolies	*Orhan Öztrak* (Peoples) (b. Malkara 1914)
Health and Social Aid	25 Jun 1962 – 25 Oct 1963: *Yusuf Azizoğlu* (NTP) (b. Silvan 1917)
	5 Nov – 2 Dec 1963: *Fahrettin Kerim Gökay* (NTP) (see above)

25 Dec 1963 – 13 Feb 1965: İsmet VIII†

Prime Minister	*İsmet İnönü* (for 8th time) (see İsmet IV)
Minister of State and Deputy Prime Minister	*Kemal Satır* (see Günaltay)
Ministers of State	*İbrahim Saffet Omay* (b. Rize 1909)
	Malik Yolaç (no party)
Minister of State (and Ecclesiastical Affairs)	25 Dec 1963 – 12 Mar 1964: *Vefik Pirinççioğlu* (see İsmet VII)
Foreign Affairs	*Feridun Cemal Erkin* (no party) (see İsmet VI)
Home Affairs	*Orhan Öztrak* (see İsmet VII)
Justice	*Sedat Çumralı* (b. Konya 1904)
Defence	*İlhami Sancar* (see İsmet VI)
Finance	*Ferit Melen* (see İsmet VII)
Education	*İbrahim Öktem* (see İsmet VII)
Labour	*Bülent Ecevit* (see İsmet VI)
Buildings and Housing	25 Dec 1963 – 10 Dec 1964: *Celâlettin Uzer* (b. Van 1914)
Public Works	*Arif Hikmet Onat* (see İsmet VII)
Industry	*Muammer Erten* (b. Atabey 1923)
Fuel and Fuel Wells (new post)	*Hüdai Oral* (b. Buldan 1925)
Trade	*Fehmi İslimyeli*
Transport	*Ferit Alpiskender* (no party) (b. Diyarbakır 1908)
Press and Tourism	*Ali İhsan Göğüş* (b. Gaziantep 1924)
Agriculture	*Turan Şahin*
Rural Development (new post)	*Lebit Yurdoğlu*

† Ministers were all members of the Peoples' party unless otherwise indicated

509

Customs and Monopolies	Mehmet Yüceler (no party)
Health and Social Aid	Kemal Demir (b. Sürmene 1921)

20 Feb – 22 Oct 1965: Ürgüplü (Coalition)

Prime Minister	Suat Hayri Ürgüplü (Ind) (see Saracoğlu II)
Deputy Prime Minister	Süleyman Demirel (Just) (b. İslâmköy 6 Oct 1924)
Ministers of State	Şekip İnal (NTP) (b. Antioch 1908)
	Hüseyin Ataman (Peoples) (b. 1901)
	Mehmet Altınsoy (CNP) (b. Niğde 1924)
Foreign Affairs	Hasan Esat Işık (b. Istanbul 1916)
Home Affairs	İsmail Hakkı Akdoğan (Peoples) (b. Yozgat 1910)
Justice	Irfan Baran (CNP until 5 Aug 1965) (b. Karaman 1927)
Defence	20 Feb – 5 Aug 1965: Hasan Dinçer (CNP until 5 Aug 1965, then Just) (see İsmet VII)
	7 Aug – 22 Oct 1965: Hazım Dağlı (CNP)
Finance	İhsan Gürsan (Just) (see İsmet VI)
Education	Cihat Bilgehan (Just) (b. Keskin 1923)
Labour	İhsan Sabri Cağlayangil (Just) (b. Istanbul 1908)
Buildings and Housing	Turan Kapanlı (NTP) (b. Istanbul 1916)
Public Works	Orhan Alp (Peoples) (b. Isparta 1913)
Industry	Ali Naili Erdem (Just) (b. Kemalpaşa 1927)
Mining and Fuel	Mehmet Turgut (b. Killis 1920)
Trade	Macit Zeren (Just) (b. Amasya 1921)
Transport	Mithan San (NTP) (b. Nizip 1904)
Press and Tourism	Zekai Dörmen (Peoples) (b. Istanbul 1903)
Agriculture	Recai Iskenderoğlu (NTP) (b. Diyarbakır 1926)
Rural Development	20 Feb – 5 Aug 1965: Seyfi Öztürk (CNP until 5 Aug 1965, then Just) (b. Eskişehir 1927)
	7 Aug – 22 Oct 1965: Mustafa Kepir (CNP)
Customs and Monopolies	Ahmet Topaloğlu (Just) (see İsmet VI)
Health	Faruk Sükan (Just) (b. Karaman 1921)

27 Oct 1965 – 23 Oct 1969: Demirel I (Just)

Prime Minister	Süleyman Demirel (for 1st time) (see Ürgüplü)

Ministers of State	27 Oct 1965 – 1 Apr 1967: *Cihat Bilgehan* (see Ürgüplü) 27 Oct 1965 – 1 Apr 1967: *Ali Fuat Alişan* (b. Çarsamba 1930) 27 Oct 1965 – 1 Apr 1967: *Refat Sezgin* (b. Bitlis 1925) 1 Apr 1967 – 23 Oct 1969: *Hüsamettin Atabeyli* 1 Apr 1967 – 23 Oct 1969: *Seyfi Öztürk* (see Ürgüplü) 1 Apr 1967 – 23 Oct 1969: *Sadık Tekin Müftüoğlu* (b. Caycuma 1927) *Kamil Ocak* (b. Gaziantep 1914)
Foreign Affairs	*Ihsan Sabri Çağlayangil* (see Ürgüplü)
Home Affairs	27 Oct 1965 – 30 Jul 1969: *Faruk Sükan* (see Ürgüplü) 30 Jul – 23 Oct 1969 (acting:) *Ragıp Üner*
Justice	27 Oct 1965 – 30 Jul 1969: *Hasan Dinçer* (see İsmet VII) 30 Jul – 23 Oct 1969: *Hidayet Aydıner*
Defence	*Ahmet Topaloğlu* (see İsmet VI)
Finance	27 Oct 1965 – 1 Apr 1967: *İhsan Gürsan* (see İsmet VI) 1 Apr 1967 – 23 Oct 1969: *Cihat Bilgehan* (see Ürgüplü)
Education	27 Oct 1965 – 1 Apr 1967: *Orhan Dengiz* (b. Uşak 1918) 1 Apr 1967 – 23 Oct 1969: *İlhami Ertem* (b. Adrianople 1918)
Labour	*Ali Naili Erdem* (see Ürgüplü)
Buildings	*Haldun Menteşeoğlu* (b. Köyceğiz 1916)
Public Works	27 Oct 1965 – 1 Apr 1967: *Ethem Erdinç* (b. Kütahya 1913) 1 Apr 1967 – 23 Oct 1969: *Orhan Alp* (see Ürgüplü)
Industry	*Mehmet Turgut* (see Ürgüplü)
Energy and Natural Resources	27 Oct 1965 – 1 Apr 1967: *İbrahim Deriner* (b. Smyrna 1908) 1 Apr 1967 – 23 Oct 1969: *Refat Sezgin* (see above)
Trade	27 Oct 1965 – 24 Aug 1966: *Macit Zeren* (see Ürgüplü) early Sep 1966 – 1 Apr 1967: *Sadık Tekin Müftüoğlu* (see above) 1 Apr 1967 – 23 Oct 1969: *Ahmet Müntekim Türkel* (b. Inegül 1922)
Transport	27 Oct 1965 – 1 Apr 1967: *Seyfi Öztürk* (see Ürgüplü) 1 Apr 1967 – 30 Jul 1969: *Sadettin Bilgiç* 30 Jul – 23 Oct 1969: *Mehmet İzmen* (see İsmet VIII)
Press and Tourism	*Nihat Kürşat* (b. Kandiya 1918)
Agriculture	*Bahri Dağdaş* (b. Zarsat 1919)

511

Rural Development	27 Oct 1965 – 1 Apr 1967: *Sabit Osman Avcı* (b. Artvin 1921)
	1 Apr 1967 – 16 Dec 1968: *Turgut Toker*
	16 Dec 1968 – 23 Oct 1969: *Salahattin Kılıç*
Customs and Monopolies	*İbrahim Tekin* (b. Adana 1923)
Health	27 Oct 1965 – 1 Apr 1967: *Edip Somunoğlu* (b. Erzerum 1904)
	1 Apr 1967 – 23 Oct 1969: *Vedat Ali Özkan*

2 Nov 1969 – 14 Feb 1970: Demirel II (Just)

Prime Minister	*Süleyman Demirel* (for 2nd time) (see Ürgüplü)
Ministers of State	*Refat Sezgin* (see Demirel I)
	Hüsamettin Atabeyli (see Demirel I)
	Gürhan Titrek
	Turhan Bilgin
Foreign Affairs	*Ihsan Sabri Cağlayangil* (see Ürgüplü)
Home Affairs	*Haldun Menteseoğlu* (see Demirel I)
Justice	*Yusuf Ziya Önder*
Defence	*Ahmet Topaloğlu* (see İsmet VI)
Finance	*Mesut Erez* (b. Kütahya 1922)
Education	*Orhan Oğuz*
Labour	*Seyfi Öztürk* (see Ürgüplü)
Buildings and Housing	*Hayrettin Nakiboğlu*
Public Works	*Turgut Gülez*
Industry	*Selahattin Kılıç* (see Demirel I)
Energy and Natural Resources	*Sabit Osman Avcı* (see Demirel I)
Trade	*Gürhan Titrek* (see above)
Transport	*Nahit Menteşe*
Tourism	*Necmettin Cevheri*
Agriculture	*İlhami Ertem* (see Demirel I)
Forestry	*Hüseyin Özalp*
Rural Affairs	*Turhan Kapanlı*
Customs and Monopolies	*Ahmet İhsan Birincioğlu*
Health and Social Welfare	*Vedat Ali Özkan* (see Demirel I)
Youth and Sport	*İsmet Sezgin*

6/15 Mar 1970 – 12 Mar 1971: Demirel III (Just)

Prime Minister	*Süleyman Demirel* (for 3rd time) (see Ürgüplü)

Ministers of State	*Refat Sezgin* (see Demirel I)
	Hüsamettin Atabeyli (see Demirel I)
	Turhan Bilgin (see Demirel II)
Foreign Affairs	*İhsan Sabri Çağlayangil* (see Ürgüplü)
Home Affairs	*Haldun Menteşeoğlu* (see Demirel I)
Justice	*Yusuf Ziya Önder* (see Demirel II)
Defence	*Ahmet Topaloğlu* (see İsmet VI)
Finance	*Mesut Erez* (see Demirel II)
Education	*Orhan Oğuz* (see Demirel II)
Labour	*Seyfi Öztürk* (see Ürgüplü)
Buildings and Housing	*Hayrettin Nakiboğlu* (see Demirel II)
Public Works	*Turgut Gülez* (see Demirel II)
Industry	*Salahattin Kılıç* (see Demirel I)
Energy and Natural Resources	*Sabit Osman Avcı* (see Demirel I)
Trade	*Gürhan Titrek* (see Demirel II)
Transport	*Nahit Menteşe* (see Demirel II)
Tourism	*Necmettin Cevheri* (see Demirel II)
Agriculture	*İlhami Ertem* (see Demirel I)
Forestry	*Hüseyin Özalp* (see Demirel II)
Rural Affairs	*Turhan Kapanlı* (see Demirel II)
Customs and Monopolies	*Ahmet İhsan Birincioğlu* (see Demirel II)
Health and Social Welfare	*Vedat Ali Özkan* (see Demirel I)
Youth and Sport	*İsmet Sezgin* (see Demirel II)

26 Mar – 3 Dec 1971: Erim I (Coalition)

Prime Minister	*Nihat Erim* (Ind) (for 1st time) (see Saka II)
Minister of State and Deputy Prime Minister (Political and Administrative Affairs)	*Sadi Koças* (RPP)
Minister of State and Deputy Prime Minister (Economic Affairs)	*Attilâ Karaosmanoğlu*

513

Minister of State (Religious and Land Regis- tration Affairs)	*Mehmet Özgüneş*
Minister of State (Personnel and Information)	*Dogan Kitaplı* (JP)
Foreign Affairs	*Osman Olcay* (b. Istanbul 17 Jan 1924)
Home Affairs	*Hamdi Ömeroğlu*
Justice	*İsmail Arar*
National Defence	*Ferit Melen* (NRP) (see İsmet VII)
Finance	*Said Naci Ergin*
Education	*Sinasi Orel*
Labour	*Atilâ Sau*
Reconstruction and Housing	*Selâhattin Babüroğlu*
Public Works	26 Mar – 9 Nov 1971: *Cahit Karalcas* (JP) 9 Nov – 3 Dec 1971: *Mukadder Öztekin* (b. Bor, Niğde Province, 1919)
Industry and Commerce	*Ayhan Çilingiroğlu*
Power and Natural Resources	*Ihsan Topaloğlu* (RPP)
Communications	*Haûk Arik*
Tourism	*Erol Yilmaz Akçal* (JP)
Agriculture	*Orhan Dikmen*
Forestry	*Selâhattin Inal*
Rural Affairs	*Cevdet Aykan*
Customs and Monopolies	*Haydar Özalp* (JP)
Health and Social Welfare	*Türkân Akyol*
Youth and Sport	*Sezai Ergun* (JP)
External Economic Relations (new post)	*Ozer Derbil*
Culture (new post)	13 Jul – 3 Dec 1971: *Talât Sait Halman*

11 Dec 1971 – 17 Apr 1972: Erim II (Coalition)

Prime Minister	*Nihat Erim* (Ind) (for 2nd time) (see Saka II)
Ministers of State	*Dogan Kitaplı* (JP) (see Erim I) *Ali İhsan Göğüş* (RPP) (see İsmet VIII)

	İlyas Karaöz (JP)
	İlhan Öztrak (b. Ankara 1925)
Foreign Affairs	Ümit Halûk Bayülken (b. Istanbul 7 Jul 1921)
Home Affairs	Ferit Kubat (b. Diyarbekir 1917
Justice	Suat Bilge (b. Istanbul 1921)
National Defence	Ferit Melen (NRP) (see İsmet VII)
Finance	Said Naci Ergin (see Erim I)
Education	Ismail Arar (RRP) (see Erim I)
Public Works	Mukadder Öztekin (RPP) (see Erim I)
Commerce	Naim Talû (b. Istanbul 1919)
Health and Social Welfare	Cevdet Aykan (see Erim I)
Customs and Monopolies	Haydar Özalp (JP) (see Erim I)
Agriculture	Orhan Dikmen (see Erim I)
Communications	Rıfkı Danışman (JP)
Labour	Ali Rıza Uzuner (RPP)
Industry and Technology	Mesut Erez (JP) (see Demirel II)
Power and Natural Resources	Nezih Devres
Tourism and Information	Erol Yilmaz Akçal (JP) (see Erim I)
Housing and Reconstruction	Serbülent Bingöl
Rural Affairs	Necmi Sönmez
Forestry	Selâhattin Inal (see Erim I)
Youth and Sports	Adnan Karaküçük (JP)

22 May 1972 – 10 Apr 1973: Melen (Coalition)

Prime Minister	Ferit Melen (NRP) (see İsmet VII)
Ministers of State	Dogan Kitaplı (JP) (see Erim I)
	İsmail Arar (RPP) (see Erim I)
	Zeyyat Baykara
	İlhan Öztrak (see Erim II)
Foreign Affairs	Ümit Halûk Bayülken (see Erim II)
Home Affairs	Ferit Kubat (see Erim II)
Justice	Fehmi Alparslan (NRP)
National Defence	Mehmet İzmen (see İsmet VIII)
Finance	Ziya Müezzinoğlu
Education	Sabahattin Özbek (Ind) (b. Erzincan 1915)
Public Works	Mukadder Öztekin (RPP) (see Erim I)

515

TURKEY

Commerce	*Naim Talû* (see Erim II)
Health and Social Welfare	*Kemal Demir* (RPP) (see Ismet VIII)
Customs and Monopolies	*Haydar Özalp* (JP) (see Erim I)
Agriculture	*İlyas Karaöz* (JP) (see Erim II)
Communications	*Rıfkı Danışman* (JP) (see Erim II)
Labour	*Ali Rıza Uzuner* (RPP) (see Erim II)
Industry and Technology	*Mesut Erez* (JP) (see Demirel II)
Power and Natural Resources	*Nuri Kodamanoğlu* (RPP)
Tourism and Information	*Erol Yilmaz Akçal* (JP) (see Erim I)
Housing and Reconstruction	*Turgut Toker* (JP)
Rural Affairs	*Necmi Sönmez* (see Erim II)
Forestry	*Selâhattin Inal* (see Erim I)
Youth and Sports	*Adnan Karaküçük* (JP) (see Erim II)

15 Apr 1973 - 25 Jan 1974: Talû (Coalition)

Prime Minister	*Naim Talû* (see Erim II)
Deputy Prime Ministers and Ministers of State	*Nizamettin Erkmen* (JP) (b. Giresun 1919)
	Kemal Satır (RRP) (see Günaltay)
Ministers of State	*İsmail Hakkı Tekinel* (JP) (b. Babaeski, Edirne, 1925)
	İlhan Öztrak (see Erim II)
Foreign Affairs	*Ümit Halûk Bayülken* (see Erim II)
Home Affairs	*Mukadder Öztekin* (see Erim I)
Justice	*Hayri Mumcuoğlu* (see Gürsel I)
National Defence	*İlhami Sancar* (RRP) (see İsmet VI)
Finance	*Sadık Tekin Müftüoğlü* (JP) (see Demirel I)
Education	*Orhan Dengiz* (JP) (see Demirel I)
Public Works	*Nurettin Ok* (JP) (b. Çankırı 1928)
Commerce	*Ahmet Müntekim Türkel* (JP) (see Demirel I)
Health and Social Welfare	*Vefa Tanır* (RRP) (b. Konya 1927)
Customs and Monopolies	*Fethi Çelikbaş* (see Menderes II)
Agriculture	*Ahmet Nusret Tuna* (JP) (b. Kirşehir)
Communications	*Sabahattin Özbek* (Ind) (see Melen)
Labour	*Ali Naili Erdem* (JP) (see Ürgüplü)

516

Industry and Technology	*Nuri Bayar* (JP) (b. Adapazarı 1927)
Energy and Natural Resources	*Kemal Demir* (RRP) (see Ismet VIII)
Tourism and Information	*Ahmet Ihsan Kırımlı* (JP) (b. Balıkesir 1920)
Housing and Recon- struction	*Mehmet Nebil Oktay* (RRP) (b. Siirt 1930)
Rural Affairs	*Orhan Kürümoglu* (JP) (b. Adılcevaz 1927)
Forestry	*İsa Bingöl* (JP) (b. Muş 1919)
Youth and Sports	*Celâlettin Coskun* (JP) (b. Nazilli 1916)

25 Jan - 18 Sep 1974: Ecevit (Coalition)

Prime Minister	*Bülent Ecevit* (RRP) (see Ismet VI)
Minister of State and Deputy Prime Minister	*Necmettin Erbakan* (NSP) (b. Smyma 28 Jan 1915)
Ministers of State	*Orhan Eyüboğlu* (RPP)
	İsmail Hakkı Birler (RPP)
	Süleyman Arif Emre
Foreign Affairs	*Turan Günes* (RPP)
Home Affairs	*Oguzhan Asiltürk* (NSP)
Justice	*Sevket Kazan* (NSP)
National Defence	*Hasan Esat Işık* (RPP) (b. Istanbul 1916)
Finance	*Deniz Baykal* (RPP)
Education	*Mustafa Üstündag* (RPP)
Public Works	*Erol Cevikçe* (RPP)
Commerce	*Fehim Adak* (NSP)
Health and Social Welfare	*Selâhattin Cizrelioglu* (RPP)
Customs and Monopolies	*Mahmut Türkmenoglu* (RPP)
Food, Agriculture and Animal Husbandry	*Korkut Özal* (NSP)
Communications	*Ferda Güley* (RPP)
Labour	*Önder Sav* (RPP)
Industry and Technology	*Abdülkerim Dogru* (NSP)
Energy and Natural Resources	*Cahit Kayra* (RPP)

517

TURKEY

Tourism and Information	*Orhan Birgit* (RPP)
Housing and Recon-struction	*Ali Topuz* (RPP)
Rural Affairs and Co-operatives	*Mustafa Ok* (RPP)
Forestry	*Ahmet Şener* (RPP)
Youth and Sport	*Muslihittin Yilmaz Mete* (RPP)

17 Nov 1974 – 31 Mar 1975: Irmak (Coalition)

Prime Minister	*Sadı Irmak* (see Saracoğlu II)
Minister of State and Deputy Prime Minister	*Zeyyat Baykara* (see Melen)
Ministers of State	*Mehmet Özgüneş* (see Erim I) *Muslih Fer* *Salih Yıldız*
Foreign Affairs	*Melih Esenbel* (b. Istanbul 15 Mar 1915)
Home Affairs	*Mukadder Öztekin* (RRP) (see Erim I)
Justice	*Hayri Mumcuoğlu* (see Gürsel I)
National Defence	*İlhami Sancar* (RRP) (see İsmet VI)
Finance	*Bedri Gürsoy*
Education	*Safa Reisoğlu*
Public Works	*Vefa Tanır* (see Talû)
Commerce	*Haluk Cillov*
Health and Social Welfare	*Kemal Demir* (RRP) (see İsmet VIII)
Customs and Monopolies	*Baran Tuncer*
Food, Agriculture and Animal Husbandry	*Resat Atıkan*
Communications	*Sabahattin Özbek* (see Melen)
Labour	*Turhan Esener*
Industry and Technology	*Mehmet Golhan*
Energy and Natural Resources	*Erhan Işıl*
Tourism and Information	*İlhan Evliyaoğlu*
Housing and Recon-struction	*Selâhhatin Babüroğlu* (see Erim I)

518

Rural Affairs and Co-operatives	*İsmail Hakkı Aydınoğlu*
Forestry	*Fikret Saatçıoğlu*
Youth and Sport	*Zekai Baloğlu* (RRP)
Culture	*Nermin Neftçi* (RRP)
Social Security	*Sadık Sıde*

From 31 Mar 1975: Demirel IV (Coalition)

Prime Minister	*Süleyman Demirel* (JP) (for 4th time) (see Ürgüplü)
Deputy Prime Ministers	*Necmettin Erbakan* (NSP) (see Ecevit)
	Turhan Feyzioglu (RRP) (see Gürsel II)
	Alparslan Türkes (NAP)
Ministers of State	*Seyfi Öztürk* (JP) (see Ürgüplü)
	Hasan Aksay (NSP)
	Mustafa Kemal Erkovan (NAP)
	Giyasettin Karaca (JP)
Foreign Affairs	*İhsan Sabri Çağlayangil* (JP) (see Ürgüplü)
Home Affairs	*Oğuzhan Asiltürk* (NSP) (see Ecevit)
Justice	*İsmail Müftüoğlü* (NSP) (b. Adapazarı 1 Jan 1939)
National Defence	*Ferit Melen* (RRP) (see İsmet VII)
Finance	*Yılmaz Ergenekon* (JP)
Education	*Ali Naili Erdem* (JP) (see Ürgüplü)
Public Works	*Fehim Adak* (NSP) (see Ecevit)
Commerce	*Halil Başol* (JP)
Health and Social Welfare	*Kemal Demir* (RRP) (see İsmet VIII)
Customs and Monopolies	*Orhan Öztrak* (RRP) (see İsmet VII)
Food, Agriculture and Animal Husbandry	*Korkut Özal* (NSP)
Communications	*Nahit Mentese* (JP) (see Demirel II)
Labour	*Ahmet Tevfik Paksu* (NSP)
Industry and Technology	*Abdülkerim Doğru* (NSP) (see Ecevit)
Energy and National Resources	*Selâhattin Kılıç* (JP) (see Demirel I)
Tourism and Information	*Lütfü Tokoğlu* (JP)
Housing and Reconstruction	*Nurettin Ok* (JP) (see Talû)

Rural Affairs and Co-operatives	*Vefa Poyraz* (JP)
Forestry	*Turhan Kapanlı* (JP) (see Demirel II)
Youth and Sport	*Alı Şevki Erek* (JP)
Culture	*Rıfkı Danışman* (JP) (see Erim II)
Social Security	*Ahmet Mahir Ablum* (JP)

Uganda

9 Oct 1962	Independence from United Kingdom
10 Oct 1963	Republic

HEADS OF STATE

Governor-General

9 Oct 1962 – 9 Oct 1963	*Sir Walter Coutts* (b. Aberdeen 30 Nov 1912)

Presidents

9 Oct 1963	*Sir Edward William Frederick David Walugembe Luwangula Mutebi (Mutesa II, Kabaka of Buganda)* (b. Makindye, Kampala, 19 Nov 1924; d. London 22 Nov 1969)
2 Mar 1966 – 25 Jan 1971	*Milton Obote* (b. Ankoro 1925)
from 25 Jan 1971	*Idi Amin Dada* (b. West Nile 1925)

MEMBERS OF GOVERNMENT

Prime Ministers

9 Oct 1962	*Milton Obote* (see Presidents)
from 15 Apr 1966	President also Prime Minister

Union of Soviet Socialist Republics

HEADS OF STATE

Presidents (Chairmen of the Presidium of the Supreme Soviet)

Dec 1922	*Mikhail Ivanovich Kalinin* (b. Verkhnaya Troitsa (now in Kalinin Oblast) 7 Nov 1875; d. Moscow 3 Jun 1946) (until Jan 1938: Chairman of the Central Executive Committee of the USSR)
19 Mar 1946	*Nikolai Mikhailovich Shvernik* (b. St. Petersburg (now Leningrad) 19 May 1888; d. Moscow 24 Dec 1971)
6 Mar 1953	*Kliment Efremovich Voroshilov* (b. Verkhneye 4 Feb 1881; d. Moscow 3 Dec 1969)*
7 May 1960	*Leonid Ilyich Brezhnev* (b. Kamenskoye (now Dneprodzerzhinsk) 19 Dec 1906)
15 Jul 1964	*Anastas Ivanovich Mikoyan* (b. Sanain 25 Nov 1895; d. 9 Dec 1970)
from 9 Dec 1965	*Nikolai Viktorovich Podgorny* (b. Karlovka, near Poltava, 18 Feb 1903)

MEMBERS OF GOVERNMENT

Chairmen of the Council of People's Commissars (from 1946 Prime Ministers)

2 Feb 1924	*Aleksei Ivanovich Rykov* (b. Saratov 13 Feb 1881; d. Moscow night of 14/15 Mar 1938)
19 Dec 1930	*Vyacheslav Mikhailovich Molotov*, original name *Skryabin* (b. Kukarka (now Sovetsk) 9 Mar 1890)
7 May 1941 – 5 Mar 1953	*Iosif Vissarionovich Stalin*, original name *Djugashvili* (b. Gori, Georgia, 21 Dec 1879; d. Moscow 5 Mar 1953)*

*For earlier career see vol. 2

521

UNION OF SOVIET SOCIALIST REPUBLICS

Commissars and Ministers for Foreign Affairs

1918–5 Feb 1930	*Georgy Vasilyevich Chicherin* (b. Kagaul 24 Nov 1872; d. Moscow 2 Jul 1936)
21 Jul 1930	*Maksim Maksimovich Litvinov* (original name *Meir Wallach*) (b. Belostok (now Białystok) 17 Jul 1876; d. Moscow 31 Dec 1951)
4 May 1939	*Vyacheslav Mikhailovich Molotov* (see Chairmen of the Council of People's Commissars)
5 Mar 1949 – 6 Mar 1953	*Andrei Yanuaryevich Vyshinsky* (b. Odessa 10 Dec 1883; d. New York 22 Nov 1954)

Commissars and Ministers for Home Affairs (and State Security)

27 Jul 1926	*Vyacheslav Rudolfovich Menzhinsky* (b. 1880; d. (assassinated) Moscow 10 May 1934) Head of the Unified State Political Department (OGPU)
10 Jul 1934	*Genrikh Georgievich Yagoda* (b. Nizhni Novgorod (now Gorki) 1891; d. (executed) Moscow night of 14/15 Mar 1938)
26 Sep 1936	*Nikolai Ivanovich Ezhov* (b. St. Petersburg (now Leningrad) 1895; d. (executed) Mar 1939)
8 Dec 1938 – 20 Jul 1941	*Lavrenty Pavlovich Beriya* (b. Merkheuli 29 Mar 1899; d. (executed) Moscow 23 Dec 1953)
3 Feb 1941	*Vsevolod Nikolaevich Merkulov* (b. 1895(?); d. (executed) Moscow 23 Dec 1953) responsible for separated State Security
20 Jul 1941 – Apr 1943	*Lavrenty Pavlovich Beriya* (see above) responsible for Home Affairs and State Security, united once again
Apr 1943 – 14 Jan 1946	*Lavrenty Pavlovich Beriya* (see above) Home Affairs
Apr 1943 – Mar 1946	*Vsevolod Nikolaevich Merkulov* (see above) State Security
14 Jan 1946 – 6 Mar 1953	*Sergei Nikiforovich Kruglov* (b. 1905) Home Affairs
Mar 1946 – Oct or Nov 1951	*V. S. Abakumov* (d. Moscow 25(?) Dec 1954) State Security
autumn 1951 – 15 Mar 1953	*Semyon D. Ignatyev* (b. 1903) State Security

Commissars and Ministers for Naval and Military Affairs †

7 Nov 1925	*Kliment Efremovich Voroshilov* (see Presidents)
8 May 1940	*Semyon Konstantinovich Timoshenko* (b. Furmanovka 18 Feb 1895; d. Moscow 31 Mar 1970)
20 Jul 1941 – 3 Feb 1947	*Iosif Vissarionovich Stalin* (see Chairmen of the Council of People's Commissars)
5 Feb 1947	*Nikolai Aleksandrovich Bulganin* (b. Nizhni Novgorod (now Gorki) 11 Jun 1895; d. 24 Feb 1975)
25 Mar 1949 – 6 Mar 1953	*Aleksandr Mikhailovich Vasilyevsky* (b. Povopokrovsk 30 Sep 1895)

Commissars for the Navy (from 25 Feb 1946 to 25 Feb 1950 a Department of the Ministry for the Armed Forces)

30 Dec 1937	Ministry established
30 Dec 1937 – Jul(?) 1938	*Pyotr A. Smirnov* (b. 1899)
7 Nov 1938	*Mikhail P. Frinovsky*
28 Apr 1939 – 25 Feb 1946	*Nikolai Gerasimovich Kuznetsov* (for 1st time) (b. Medvedyevka 1902; d. 8 Dec 1974)
25 Feb 1950	*Ivan Stepanovich Yumashev* (b. 1895)
21 Jul 1951 – 6 Mar 1953	*Nikolai Gerasimovich Kuznetsov* (for 2nd time)
6 Mar 1953	Absorbed by the Ministry of Defence

Commissars and Ministers of Finance

Early 1930 – 17 Aug 1937	*Grigory Fyodorovich Grinko* (b. 1890; d. Moscow night of 14/15 Mar 1938)
23 Aug 1937	*Vlas Yakovlevich Chubar* (b. Ukraine 1891; d. 1939)
19 Jan 1938	*Arseny Grigoryevich Zverev* (for 1st time) (b. Tikhomirovo 1900; d. Moscow 27 Jul 1969)
17(?) Feb 1948	*Aleksei Nikolaevich Kosygin* (b. St. Petersburg (now Leningrad) 21 Feb 1904)
28 Dec 1948 – 6 Mar 1953	*Arseny Grigoryevich Zverev* (for 2nd time)

† 1934: People's Commissariat for Defence; 1937: Separate Navy Ministry formed; 1946: Ministry for Armed Forces (including Navy); 1950: Ministry of War (with separate Navy Ministry).

Commissars and Ministers of Justice

20 Jul 1936	*Nikolai M. Rychkov*
29 Jan 1948 – 6 Mar 1953	*Konstantin Petrovich Gorshenin* (b. 1907)

Ministers of Higher Education

10 Apr 1946	*Sergei Vasilyevich Kaftanov* (b. 1905)
13 Feb 1951 – 6 Mar 1953	*Vsevolod Nikolaevich Stolyetov* (b. 1906)

Commissars and Ministers for Internal and Foreign Trade

18 Nov 1925	*Anastas Ivanovich Mikoyan* (for 1st time) (see Presidents) Internal and Foreign Trade
22 Nov 1930 – 14 Jun 1937	*Aaron Pavlovich Rozengolts* † (b. 1889; d. Moscow night of 14/15 Mar 1938) Foreign Trade
29 Jul 1934 – (?)	*Israel Yakovlevich Veitser*, Internal Trade
15 Oct 1937 – (?)	*M. P. Smirnov*, Internal Trade
19 Jan 1938	*Sergei D. Shvyalev*, Foreign Trade
19 Nov 1938 – 4 Mar 1949	*Anastas Ivanovich Mikoyan* (for 2nd time) Foreign Trade
May 1939	*Aleksandr V. Lyubimov*, Internal Trade
1 Mar 1948 – 6 Mar 1953	*Vasily Gavrilovich Zhavoronkov* (b. 1906) Internal Trade
4 Mar 1949	*Mikhail Alekseevich Menshikov* (b. 1902) Foreign Trade
10 Nov 1951 – 6 Mar 1953	*Pavel Nikolaevich Kumykin* (b. 1901) Foreign Trade

Commissars and Ministers for Railways

2 Feb 1924 – 1930	*Yan Ernestovich Rudzutak* (b. Courland 3 Aug 1887; d. 1938)
1930 – 2 Oct 1931	*Moisei Lvovich Rukhimovich* (b. 1889; d. 1938)
3 Oct 1931 – 1 Mar 1935	*Andrei Andreevich Andreev* (b. Smolensk 30 Oct 1895; d. Moscow 5 Dec 1971)
1 Mar 1935 – 22 Aug 1937	*Lazar Moiseevich Kaganovich* (for 1st time) (b. Kiev 1893)
22 Aug 1937 – 4 Apr 1938	*Aleksei V. Bakulin*

† Appears in vol. 2 as Rosenholz, his German name.

11 Apr 1938	*Lazar Moiseevich Kaganovich* (for 2nd time)
6 Apr 1942 – 1943	(acting:) *Andrei Vasilyevich Khrulyov* (b. Bolshaya Aleksandrovka 10 (30?) Sep 1892; d. 9 Jun 1962)
Dec 1944 – 5 Jun 1948	*Ivan Kovalyov*
5 Jun 1948 – 5 Mar 1953	*Boris Pavlovich Beshchev* (b. 1903)

Commissars for Posts and Telegraphs (from 17 Jan 1932: Commissars and Ministers for Communications)

1928	*Nikolai Kirillovich Antipov* (b. 1894; d. in prison 1941)
30 Mar 1931 – 26 Sep 1936	*Aleksei Ivanovich Rykov* (see Chairmen of the Council of People's Commissars)
27 Sep 1936 – 5 Apr 1937	*Genrikh Georgievich Yagoda* (see Commissars and Ministers for Home Affairs)
6 Apr – 17 Aug 1937	*Innokenty Andreevich Khalepsky* (b. Minusinsk 1893; d. in prison 1938)
21 Aug 1937 – Dec 1938	*Matvei Davidovich Berman*
10 Jun 1939 – 1941	*Ivan Terentyevich Peresypkin* (b. 1904)
Mar 1946	*Konstantin Yakovlevich Sergeichuk* (b. 1906)
1948 – 5 Mar 1953	*Nikolai Demyanovich Psurtsev* (b. Kiev 4 Feb 1900)

Commissars for Heavy Industry

5 Jan 1932 – 18 Feb 1937	*Grigory Konstantinovich Ordzhonikidze* (b. Goresha 28 Nov 1886; d. Moscow 18 Feb 1937)
26 Feb 1937	*Valery Ivanovich Mezhlauk* (b. Kharkov 7 Feb 1893; d. in prison 29 Jul 1938)
23 Aug 1937	*Lazar Moiseevich Kaganovich* (see Commissars for Railways)
26 Jan 1939	Broken up into six new Commissariats

Chairmen of State Planning Commission (Gosplan)

22 Feb 1921	*Gleb Maksimilianovich Krzhyzhanovsky* (b. Samara (now Kuibyshev) 24 Jan 1872; d. Moscow 31 Mar 1959)
6 Nov 1930 – Feb 1934	*Valerian Vladimirovich Kuibyshev* (b. Omsk 25 May 1888; d. Moscow 25 Jan 1935)
Apr 1934	*Valery Ivanovich Mezhlauk* (for 1st time) (see Commissars for Heavy Industry)

525

26 Feb – 19 Oct 1937	*Gennady Ivanovich Smirnov* (b. 1903; d. 1937)
29 Oct 1937	*Valery Ivanovich Mezhlauk* (for 2nd time)
19 Jan 1938	*Nikolai Aleksandrovich Vosnesensky* (b. Tyoploe 30 Nov 1903; d. (executed) 30 Sep 1950)
5 Mar 1949 – 5 Mar 1953	*Maksim Zakharovich Saburov* (b. 19 Feb 1900)

Commissars for Workers' and Peasants' Inspection (Audit)

3 Nov 1926	*Grigory Konstantinovich Ordzhonikidze* (see Commissars for Heavy Industry)
6 Nov 1930	*Andrei Andreevich Andreev* (see Commissars and Ministers for Railways)
9 Oct 1931 – 1934	*Yan Ernestovich Rudzutak* (see Commissars and Ministers for Railways)
11 Feb 1934	Post abolished
27 Feb 1934	Post re-established as Chairman of Commission for Soviet Control
27 Feb 1934 – 25 Jan 1935	*Valerian Vladimirovich Kuibyshev* (see Chairmen of State Planning Commission)
Apr 1935	*Nikolai Kirillovich Antipov* (see Commissars for Posts and Telegraphs)
19 Jan – Apr 1938	*Stanislav Vikentyevich Kosior* (or *Kossior*) (b. Vengerov 18 Nov 1889; d. in prison 26 Feb 1939)
Feb 1939 (?)	*Rozaliya Samoilovna Zemlyachka* (b. Kiev 1 Apr 1876; d. 21 Jan 1947)
6 Sep 1940	Post renamed Commissar for State Control
6 Nov 1940	*Lev Zakharovich Mekhlis* (b. Jan 1889; d. Moscow 13 Feb 1953)
27 Oct 1950 – 6 Mar 1953	*Vsevolod Nikolaevich Merkulov* (see Commissars and Ministers for Home Affairs)

6/15 Mar 1953 – 8 Feb 1955: Malenkov

Prime Minister	*Georgy Maksimilianovich Malenkov* (b. Orenburg 8 Jan 1902)
First Deputy Prime Ministers	6 Mar – 9 Jul 1953: *Lavrenty Pavlovich Beriya* (see Commissars and Ministers for Home Affairs)
	Nikolai Aleksandrovich Bulganin (see Commissars and Ministers for Military and Naval Affairs)
	Lazar Moiseevich Kaganovich (see Commissars for Railways)

	Vyacheslav Mikhailovich Molotov (see Chairmen of the Council of People's Commissars)
Deputy Prime Ministers	*Anastas Ivanovich Mikoyan* (see Presidents) 21 Dec 1953 – 21 Apr 1955:
	Aleksei Nikolaevich Kosygin (see Commissars and Ministers of Finance)
	Vyacheslav Aleksandrovich Malyshev (b. Ust-Sysolsk 16 Feb 1902; d. Moscow 20 Feb 1957)
	Mikhail Georgievich Pervukhin (b. Yuryuzan, Chelyabinsk Oblast, 1904)
	Maksim Zakharovich Saburov (see Chairmen of State Planning Commission)
	Ivan Fyodorovich Tevosyan (b. Shusha 1903; d. Tokyo 30 Mar 1958)
Foreign Affairs	*Vyacheslav Mikhailovich Molotov* (see Chairmen of the Council of People's Commissars)
Home Affairs*	6 Mar – 9 Jul 1953: *Lavrenty Pavlovich Beriya* (see Commissars and Ministers for Home Affairs)
	9 Jul 1953 – 8 Feb 1955: *Sergei Nikiforovich Kruglov* (see Commissars and Ministers for Home Affairs)
Defence	*Nikolai Aleksandrovich Bulganin* (see Commissars and Ministers for Military and Naval Affairs)
Internal and Foreign Trade	6 Mar – 15 Sep 1953: *Anastas Ivanovich Mikoyan* (see Presidents)
	15 Sep 1953: divided into two separate ministries
Internal Trade	15 Sep 1953 – 24 Jan 1955: *Anastas Ivanovich Mikoyan* (see Presidents)
	24 Jan – 8 Feb 1955: *Dmitry Vasilyevich Pavlov* (b. 1905)
Foreign Trade	15 Sep 1953 – 8 Feb 1955: *Ivan Grigoryevich Kabanov* (b. 1898)
Chairman of State Planning Commission	6 Mar – 29 Jun 1953: *Grigori Petrovich Kosyachenko*
	29 Jun 1953 – 8 Feb 1955: *Maksim Zakharovich Saburov* (see Chairmen of State Planning Commission)
Finance	9 Jul 1953 – 8 Feb 1955: *Arseny Grigoryevich Zverev* (see Commissars and Ministers for Finance)
Justice	*Konstantin Petrovich Gorshenin* (see Commissars and Ministers of Justice)
Culture	6 Mar 1953 – 16 Mar 1954: *Panteleimon Kondratyevich Ponomarenko* (b. Kuban 1902)

*A State Security Committee was set up on 13 Feb 1954, see p. 531.

16 Mar 1954 – 8 Feb 1955: *Georgy Fyodorovich Aleksandrov* (b. St. Petersburg (now Leningrad) 7 Apr 1908; d. Moscow 21 Jul 1961)

Higher Education (new post)
9 Mar 1954 – 8 Feb 1955: *Vyacheslav Petrovich Elyutin* (b. Saratov 1907)

Railways
Boris Pavlovich Beshchev (see Commissars for Railways)

Communications
Nikolai Demyanovich Psurtsev (see Commissars for Posts and Telegraphs)

State Control (Audit)
6/15 Mar – (before?) 7 Dec 1953: *Vsevolod Nikolaevich Merkulov* (see Commissars and Ministers for Home Affairs)
7 Dec 1953 – 8 Feb 1955: *Vasily Gavrilovich Zhavoronkov* (see Commissars and Ministers for Internal and Foreign Trade)

Health
15 Mar 1953 – 1(?) Mar 1954: *Andrei Fyodorovich Tretyakov* (b. 1905)
1(?) Mar 1954 – 8 Feb 1955: *Maria Dmitrievna Kovrigina* (b. Troitskoe (now in Kurgan Oblast) 1910)

Agriculture
6 Mar – 15 Sep 1953: *Aleksei Ivanovich Kozlov* (b. 1911)
15 Sep 1953 – 8 Feb 1955: *Ivan Aleksandrovich Benediktov* (b. Novaya Vichuga, Ivanovo Oblast, 1902)

State Farms (new post)
15 Sep 1953 – 8 Feb 1955: *Aleksei Ivanovich Kozlov* (see above)

Timber Industry (new post)
27 Apr 1954 – 8 Feb 1955: *Georgy Mikhailovich Orlov* (b. Lubyanki (now in Orel Oblast) 1903)

Fisheries (new post)
11(?) Apr 1954 – 8 Feb 1955: *Aleksandr Akimovich Ishkov* (b. Stavropol 1905)

Paper and Timber Products Industry (new post)
Fyodor Dimitrievich Varaksin

State Purchases
27 Apr 1954 – 8 Feb 1955: *Leonid Romanovich Korniets* (b. Bobrinets (now in Kirovograd Oblast) 8 Aug 1901; d. Moscow 29 May 1969)

Meat and Dairy Industry (new post)
27 Apr 1954 – 8 Feb 1955: *Sergei Fyodorovich Antonov* (b. 1911)

Shipping and Inland Navigation
6 Mar 1953 – 25 Aug 1954: *Zosima Alekseevich Shashkov* (b. Nowinki 1905)
25 Aug 1954: divided into two ministries

Shipping	25 Aug 1954 – 8 Feb 1955: *Victor Georgievich Bakaev* (b. Berdyansk 1902)
Inland Navigation	25 Aug 1954 – 8 Feb 1955: *Zosima Alekseevich Shashkov* (see above)
Motor Transport and Highways (new post)	16 Sep 1953 – 8 Feb 1955: *Ivan Alekseevich Likhachov* (b. Ozerenty 15 Jun 1896; d. Moscow 24 Jun 1956)
Coal	*Aleksandr Fyodorovich Zasyadko* (b. 1910; d. Moscow 6 Apr 1963)
Petroleum	*Nikolai Konstantinovich Baibakov* (b. Sabunchi 1911)
Power Stations and Electrical Engineering	15 Mar 1953 – 19 Apr 1954: *Mikhail Georgievich Pervukhin* (see above) 19/27 Apr 1954: ministry reorganized
Power Stations (new post)	27 Apr 1954 – 8 Feb 1955: *Aleksei Sergeevich Pavlenko* (b. 1904)
Engineering	15 Mar – 9 Aug 1953: *Maksim Zakharovich Saburov* 9 Aug 1953 – 19 Apr 1954: *Stepan Akopovich Akopov* (b. Tiflis 1899; d. 9 Aug 1958) 19/27 Apr 1954: engineering ministries reorganized
Electrical Engineering (new post)	27 Apr 1954 – 8 Feb 1955: *Ivan Timofeevich Skidanenko*
Instrument Engineering (new post)	27 Apr 1954 – 8 Feb 1955: *Pyotr Ivanovich Parshin*
Machine-tool Manufacture and Toolmaking (new post)	27 Apr 1954 – 8 Feb 1955: *Anatoly Ivanovich Kostousov* (b. Nofrinskoe (now in Yaroslavl Oblast) 6 Oct 1906)
Motor Vehicles, Tractors and Agricultural Machinery (new post)	27 Apr 1954 – 8 Feb 1955: *Stepan Akopovich Akopov* (see above)
Construction and Roadmaking Equipment (new post)	27 Apr 1954 – 8 Feb 1955: *Efim Stepanovich Novosyolov* (b. Kramatorsk, Ukraine, 1906)
Construction of Plant for the Metal-Manufacture and Chemicals Industries (new post)	27 Apr 1954 – 8 Feb 1955: *David Yakovlevich Raizer* (b. Kherson 1904; d. 26 Dec 1962)

Transport and Heavy Engineering	15 Mar – 14 Jul 1953: *Vyacheslav Aleksandrovich Malyshev* (see above) 14 Jul 1953 – 19 Apr 1954: *Ivan Isidorovich Nosenko* (b. 1902; d. Moscow 2 Aug 1956) 19/27 Apr 1954: divided into two ministries
Heavy Engineering	27 Apr 1954 – 8 Feb 1955 *Nikolai Stepanovich Kazakov* (b. 27 Jun 1900)
Transport Engineering	27 Apr 1954 – 8 Feb 1955 *Sergei Aleksandrovich Stepanov* (b. 1903)
Nuclear Engineering* (new post)	17 Jul 1953 – 8 Feb 1955: *Vyacheslav Aleksandrovich Malyshev* (see above)
Metal Manufacture	6/15 Mar 1953 – 8 Feb 1954: *Ivan Fyodorovich Tevosyan* (see above) 8 Feb 1954: divided into ministries for Ferrous and for Non-ferrous Metal Manufacture
Ferrous Metal Manufacture	8 Feb – 29 Oct 1954: *Anatoly Nikolaevich Kuzmin* (d. Moscow 29 Oct 1954) 15 Nov 1954 – 8 Feb 1955: *Aleksandr Grigoryevich Sheremetyev*
Non-ferrous Metal Manufacture	8 Feb 1954 – 8 Feb 1955 *Pyotr Faddeevich Lomako* (b. Temryuk 1904)
Light Industry and Food Industry	6 Mar 1953 – 23 Feb 1954: *Aleksei Nikolaevich Kosygin* (see Commissars and Ministers of Finance) 15 Sep 1953: divided into Ministry for Industrial Consumer Goods and Ministry for Food Industry
Industrial Consumer Goods	15 Sep 1953 – 23 Feb 1954: *Aleksei Nikolaevich Kosygin* 23 Feb 1954 – 8 Feb 1955: *Nikita Semyonovich Ryzhov* (b. 1907)
Food Industry	15 Sep 1953 – 8 Feb 1955: *Vasily Petrovich Zotov* (b. Mamonovo 1899; d. 8 Feb 1977)
Chemicals Industry	*Sergei Mikhailovich Tikhomirov* (b. Moscow 1905)
Shipbuilding (new post)	27 Apr 1954 – 8 Feb 1955: *Ivan Isidorovich Nosenko* (see above)
Aircraft Manufacture (new post)	24 Aug 1953 – 8 Feb 1955: *Pyotr Vasilyevich Dementyev* (b. Ubei 1907)
Defence Industry	*Dmitry Fyodorovich Ustinov* (b. Samara (now Kuibyshev) 1908)
Radio Industry (new post)	27 Apr 1954 – 8 Feb 1955: *Valery Dmitrievich Kalmykov* (b. Rostov-on-Don 1908; d. 22 Mar 1974)
Light Industry (new post)	27 Apr 1954 – 8 Feb 1955: *Nikolai Nikolaevich Mirotvortsev*

*Given the camouflage title 'Medium Engineering'.

Chairman of State Committee for Construction	6/15 Mar 1953 – 19 Apr 1954: *Konstantin Mikhailovich Sokolov* 19/27 Apr 1954: committee abolished
Construction	*Nikolai Aleksandrovich Dygai* (b. Pokrovshoye 1908; d. Moscow 6 Mar 1963)
Building Materials	*Pavel Aleksandrovich Yudin* (b. 1902; d. 10 Apr 1956) *Leonid Romanovich Korniets* (b. Bobrinets (now in Kirovograd Oblast) 1901; d. 29 May 1969)
Geology (new post)	16 Sep 1953 – 8 Feb 1955: *Pyotr Yakovlevich Antropov* (b. Kulmesh 1905)
Chairman of State Security Committee (KGB)	13 Feb 1954 – 8 Feb 1955: *Ivan Aleksandrovich Serov* (b. Sokol 1905)

8 Feb 1955 – 27 Mar 1958: Bulganin

Prime Minister	*Nikolai Aleksandrovich Bulganin* (see Commissars and Ministers for Naval and Military Affairs)
First Deputy Prime Ministers	8 Feb 1955 – 4 Jul 1957: *Vyacheslav Mikhailovich Molotov* (see Chairmen of the Council of People's Commissars) 8 Feb 1955 – 4 Jul 1957: *Lazar Moiseevich Kaganovich* (see Commissars for Railways) 28 Feb 1955 – 27 Mar 1958: *Anastas Ivanovich Mikoyan* (see Presidents) 28 Feb 1955 – 5 Jul 1957: *Maksim Zakharovich Saburov* (see Chairmen of State Planning Commission) 28 Feb 1955 – 5 Jul 1957: *Mikhail Georgievich Pervukhin* (see Malenkov I) 3 May 1957 – 27 Mar 1958: *Iosif Iosifovich Kuzmin* (b. Astrakhan 1910)
Deputy Prime Ministers	8 Feb 1955 – 25 Dec 1956: *Vyacheslav Aleksandrovich Malyshev* (see Malenkov I) 8 Feb 1955 – 25 Dec 1956: *Aleksei Nikolaevich Kosygin* (see Commissars and Ministers of Finance) 9 Feb 1955 – 4 Jul 1957: *Georgy Maksimilianovich Malenkov* (see Malenkov I) 8 Feb 1955 – 30 Dec 1956: *Ivan Fyodorovich Tevosyan* (see Malenkov I) 28 Feb 1955 – 31 Dec 1956: *Avraam Pavlovich Zavenyagin* (b. Uzlovaya 14 Apr 1901; d. Moscow 31 Dec 1956)

	28 Feb 1955 – 25 Dec 1956: *Vladimir Alekseevich Kucherenko* (b. Lozovaya, Kharkov Oblast, 18 Jul 1909; d. 26 Nov 1963)
	28 Feb 1955 – 9 Apr 1956: *Pavel Pavlovich Lobanov* (b. Staro 1902)
	28 Feb 1955 – 25 Dec 1956: *Mikhail Vasilyevich Khrunichev* (b. Shubin 1901; d. Moscow 2 Jun 1961)
	9 Apr 1956 – 25 Dec 1956(?): *Vladimir Vladimirovich Matskevich* (b. Privolnoe 1909)
	14 Dec 1956 – 28 Mar 1957: *Dmitry Fyodorovich Ustinov* (see Malenkov I)
Foreign Affairs*	8 Feb 1955 – 1 Jun 1956: *Vyacheslav Mikhailovich Molotov* (see Chairmen of the Council of People's Commissars)
	1 Jun 1956 – 15 Feb 1957: *Dmitry Trofimovich Shepilov* (b. Ekatrinodar (now Krasnodar) 4 Nov 1905)
	15 Feb 1957 – 27 Mar 1958: *Andrei Andreevich Gromyko* (b. Minsk 6 Jul 1909)
Home Affairs*	8 Feb 1955 – 1 Feb 1956: *Sergei Nikiforovich Kruglov* (see Commissars and Ministers for Home Affairs)
	1 Feb 1956 – 27 Mar 1958: *Nikolai Pavlovich Dudorov* (b. 1906)
Defence*	9 Feb 1955 – 26 Oct 1957: *Georgy Konstantinovich Zhukov* (b. Strelkova 2 Dec 1896; d. 18 Jun 1974)
	26 Oct 1957 – 27 Mar 1958: *Rodion Yakovlevich Malinovsky* (b. Odessa 23 Nov 1898; d. Moscow 31 Mar 1967)
Internal Trade*	*Dmitry Vasilyevich Pavlov* (see Malenkov)
Foreign Trade**	*Ivan Grigoryevich Kabanov* (see Malenkov)
Chairman of State Planning Commission (Gosplan)	8 Feb – 25 May 1955: *Maksim Zakharovich Saburov* (see Chairmen of State Planning Commission)
	25 May 1955 – 3 May 1957: *Nikolai Konstantinovich Baibakov* (see Malenkov)
	3 May 1957 – 27 Mar 1958: *Iosif Iosifovich Kuzmin* (see above)

*Became a Union-Republican Ministry following reorganization announced on 10 May 1957. Union-Republican Ministries coordinate work of government departments in the constituent republics.

**Became an All-Union Ministry following reorganization announced on 10 May 1957. All-Union Ministries are directly responsible for their areas of activity throughout the USSR.

Other Gosplan Officials of Ministerial Rank from 25 May 1957 to 25 Mar 1958	First Vice-Chairman: *Aleksei Nikolaevich Kosygin* (see Commissars and Ministers of Finance) Vice-Chairmen: *Mikhail Vasilyevich Khrunichev* (see above), *Nikolai Ivanovich Strokin* (b. Moscow 1906), *Vasily Petrovich Zotov* (see Malenkov) Department Heads: *Grigory Sergeevich Khlamov* (b. Nizhni Novgorod (now Gorki) 1903), *Efim Stepanovich Novosyolov* (see Malenkov), *Aleksandr Fyodorovich Zasyadko* (see Malenkov)
Chairman of State Economic Commission (new post)	25 May 1955 – 25 Dec 1956: *Maksim Zakharovich Saburov* (see Chairmen of State Planning Commission) 25 Dec 1956 – 30 Apr 1957: *Mikhail Georgievich Pervukhin* (see Malenkov) 30 Apr 1957: Commission abolished
Other Officials of State Economic Commission of Ministerial Rank from 25 Dec 1956 to 30 Apr 1957	First Vice-Chairmen: *Aleksei Nikolaevich Kosygin* (see Commissars and Ministers of Finance), *Vyacheslav Aleksandrovich Malyshev* (see Malenkov) Vice-Chairmen: *Mikhail Vasilyevich Khrunichev* (see above), *Vladimir Alekseevich Kucherenko* (see above)
Finance*	*Arseny Grigoryevich Zverev* (see Commissars and Ministers of Finance)
Justice	*Konstantin Petrovich Gorshenin* (see Commissars and Ministers of Justice) 31 May 1956: duties taken over by ministries in each of the constituent republics
Culture*	8 Feb – 22 Mar 1955: *Georgy Fyodorovich Aleksandrov* (see Malenkov) 22 Mar 1955 – 27 Mar 1958: *Nikolai Aleksandrovich Mikhailov* (b. Moscow 1906)
Higher Education*	*Vyacheslav Petrovich Elyutin* (see Malenkov)
Railways**	*Boris Pavlovich Beshchev* (see Commissars for Railways)

*Became a Union-Republican Ministry following reorganization announced on 10 May 1957. Union-Republican Ministries coordinate work of government departments in the constituent republics.

**Became an All-Union Ministry following reorganization announced on 10 May 1957. All-Union Ministries are directly responsible for their areas of activity throughout the USSR.

Communications*	*Nikolai Demyanovich Psurtsev* (see Commissars for Posts and Telegraphs)
State Control (Audit)	8 Feb 1955 – 21 Nov 1956: *Vasily Gavrilovich Zhavoronkov* (see Commissars and Ministers for Internal and Foreign Trade) 21 Nov 1956 – 4 Jul 1957: *Vyacheslav Mikhailovich Molotov* (see Chairmen of the Council of People's Commissars) 23 Aug 1957: ministry abolished and replaced by Commission for Soviet Control
Health*	*Maria Dmitrievna Kovrigina* (see Malenkov)
Agriculture*	8 Feb – 2 Mar 1955: *Ivan Aleksandrovich Benediktov* (see Malenkov) 2 Mar – 17 Oct 1955 (acting): *Pavel Pavlovich Lobanov* (see above) 17 Oct 1955 – 27 Mar 1958: *Vladimir Vladimirovich Matskevich* (see above)
State Farms*	8 – 18 Feb/2 Mar 1955: *Aleksei Ivanovich Kozlov* (see Malenkov) 2 Mar 1955 – 1957: *Ivan Aleksandrovich Benediktov* (see Malenkov)
Timber Industry§	*Georgy Mikhailovich Orlov* (see Malenkov)
Paper and Timber Products Industry§	*Fyodor Dmitrievich Varaksin* (see Malenkov)
Grain Products	*Leonid Romanovich Korniets* (see Malenkov)
Fisheries§	*Aleksandr Akimovich Ishkov* (see Malenkov)
Meat and Dairy Industry§	*Sergei Fyodorovich Antonov* (see Malenkov)
Shipping**	*Viktor Georgievich Bakaev* (see Malenkov)
Inland Navigation	8 Feb 1955 – 30 May 1956: *Zosima Alekseevich Shashkov* (see Malenkov) 30 May 1956: post abolished
Motor Transport and Highways	8 Feb 1955 – 24 Jun 1956: *Ivan Alekseevich Likhachov* (see Malenkov)

*Became a Union-Republican Ministry following reorganization announced on 10 May 1957. Union-Republican Ministries coordinate work of government departments in the constituent republics.

**Became an All-Union Ministry following reorganization announced on 10 May 1957. All-Union Ministries are directly responsible for their areas of activity throughout the USSR.

§Ministry abolished following reorganization announced on 10 May 1957.

Coal§	*8 Feb – 2 Mar, 1955: Aleksandr Fyodorovich Zasyadko* (see Malenkov) *2 Mar 1955 – 10 May 1957: Aleksandr Nikolaevich Zademidko*
Petroleum§	*8 Feb – 25 May 1955: Nikolai Konstantinovich Baibakov* (see Malenkov) *26 May 1955 – 10 May 1957: Mikhail Adrianovich Evseenko* (b. 1908)
Power Stations**	*9 Feb 1955 – 4 Jul 1957: Georgy Maksimilianovich Malenkov* (see Malenkov) *4 Jul 1957 – 27 Mar 1958: Aleksei Sergeevich Pavlenko* (see Malenkov)
Electrical Engineering§	*8 Feb 1955 – 10 May 1957: Ivan Timoffevich Skidanenko* (see Malenkov)
Instrument Engineering§	*8 Feb 1955 – 10 May 1957: Pyotr Ivanovich Parshin* (see Malenkov)
Transport Development** (new post)	*Evgeny Fyodorovich Kozhevnikov* (b. Tsaritsyn (now Volgograd) 1905)
Machine-tool Manufacture and Toolmaking§	*8 Feb 1955 – 10 May 1957: Anatoly Ivanovich Kostousov* (see Malenkov)
Motor Vehicles, Tractors and Agricultural Machinery	*8 Feb – 24 Jul 1955: Stepan Akopovich Akopov* 24 Jul 1955: divided into two ministries
Motor Vehicles§	*24 Jul 1955 – 10 May 1957: Nikolai Ivanovich Strokin* (see above)
Tractors and Agricultural Machinery§	*24 Jul 1955 – 10 May 1957: Grigory Sergeevich Khlamov* (see above)
Construction and Roadmaking Equipment§	*8 Feb 1955 – 10 May 1957: Efim Stepanovich Novosyolov* (see Malenkov)
Heavy Engineering§	*8 Feb – 30 Jul 1955: Nikolai Stepanovich Kazakov* (see Malenkov) *1 Aug 1955 – 10 May 1957: Konstantin Dmitrievich Petukhov* (b. 1914)

**Became an All-Union Ministry following reorganization announced on 10 May 1957. All-Union Ministries are directly responsible for their areas of activity throughout the USSR.

§Ministry abolished following reorganization announced on 10 May 1957.

Transport Engineering§	8 Feb 1955 – 10 May 1957: *Sergei Aleksandrovich Stepanov*
Nuclear Engineering**	8 – 28 Feb 1955: *Vyacheslav Aleksandrovich Malyshev* (see Malenkov)
	28 Feb 1955 – 1 Jan 1957: *Avraam Pavlovich Zavenyagin* (see above)
	3 May 1957 – 27 Mar 1958: *Mikhail Georgievich Pervukhin* (see Malenkov)
Shipbuilding	8 Feb 1955 – 2 Aug 1956: *Ivan Isidorovich Nosenko* (see Malenkov)
	15 Sep 1956 – 14 Dec 1957: *A. M. Redkin*
	14 Dec 1957: ministry replaced by State Committee for Shipbuilding (see p. 543)
Aircraft Manufacture	8 Feb 1955 – 14 Dec 1957: *Pyotr Vasilyevich Dementyev* (see Malenkov)
	14 Feb 1957: ministry replaced by State Committee for Aviation Engineering (see p. 543)
Defence Industry	8 Feb 1955 – 14 Dec 1957: *Dmitry Fyodorovich Ustinov* (see Malenkov)
	14 Dec 1957: ministry replaced State Committee for Defence Equipment (see p. 543)
Radio Industry	8 Feb 1955 – 14 Dec 1957: *Valery Dmitrievich Kalmykov* (see Malenkov)
	14 Dec 1957: ministry replaced by State Committee for Radio Engineering (see p. 543)
General Engineering (new post)	2 Apr 1955 – 10 May 1957: *Pyotr Nikolaevich Goremykin*
	10 May 1957: ministry merged with Ministry of Defence Equipment
Automation§ (new post)	22 Jan 1956 – 10 May 1957: *Mikhail Avksentyevich Lesechko* (b. 1909)
Ferrous Metal Manufacture§	8 Feb 1955 – 10 May 1957: *Aleksandr Grigoryevich Sheremetyev* (see Malenkov)
Non-ferrous Metal Manufacture§	8 Feb 1955 – 10 May 1957: *Pyotr Faddeevich Lomako* (see Malenkov)
Light Industry§	25 Sep 1955 – 10 May 1957: *Nikolai Nikolaevich Mirotvortsev* (see Malenkov)
Food Industry§	8 Feb 1955 – 10 May 1957: *Vasily Petrovich Zotov* (see Malenkov)

**Became an All-Union Ministry following reorganization announced on 10 May 1957. All-Union Ministries are directly responsible for their areas of activity throughout the USSR.

§Ministry abolished following reorganization announced on 10 May 1957.

Chemicals Industry**	*Sergei Mikhailovich Tikhomirov* (see Malenkov)
Construction	*Nikolai Aleksandrovich Dygai* (see Malenkov)
Building Materials§	8 Feb 1955 – 10 Apr 1956: *Pavel Aleksandrovich Yudin* (see Malenkov)
	4 Sep 1956 – 10 May 1957: *Lazar Moiseevich Kaganovich* (see Commissars for Railways)
Urban and Rural Construction§ (new post)	10 Feb 1955 – 10 May 1957: *Ivan Kornilovich Kozyula*
Construction of Plant for the Coal Industry§ (new post)	5 Apr 1955 – 10 May 1957: *Leonid Georgievich Melnikov* (b. 1906)
Construction of Plant for the Petroleum Industry§ (new post)	10 Feb – 26 May 1955: *Mikhail Adrianovich Evseenko* (see above) 26 May 1955 – 10 May 1957: *Aleksei Kirillovich Kortunov* (b. 1907)
Construction of Power Stations (new post)	10 Feb 1955 – 10 May 1957: *Fyodor Georgievich Loginov* (b. 19 Feb 1900; d. 2 Aug 1958) 10 May 1957: ministry merged with Ministry of Power Stations
Geology*	*Pyotr Yakovlevich Antropov* (see Malenkov)

Chairmen of State Committees

State Security (KGB)	*Ivan Aleksandrovich Serov* (see Malenkov)
Labour and Wages (new committee)	24 May 1955 – 8 Jun 1956: *Lazar Moiseevich Kaganovich* (see Commissars for Railways) 8 Jun 1956 – 27 Mar 1958: *Aleksandr Petrovich Volkov* (b. Vidogozh 1910)
Foreign Economic Relations (new committee)	24 Jul 1957 – 10 Jan 1958: *Mikhail Georgievich Pervukhin* (see Malenkov) 7 Feb – 27 Mar 1958: *Semyon Andreevich Skachkov* (b. Kharkov 1907)
Foreign Cultural Relations (new committee)	28 Dec 1957 – 27 Mar 1958: *Georgy Aleksandrovich Zhukov* (b. 1908)

*Became a Union-Republican Ministry following reorganization announced on 10 May 1957. Union-Republican Ministries coordinate work of government departments in the constituent republics.

**Became an All-Union Ministry following reorganization announced on 10 May 1957. All-Union Ministries are directly responsible for their areas of activity throughout the USSR.

§Ministry abolished following reorganization announced on 10 May 1957.

Soviet Control (Audit) (new commission)	18 Dec 1957 – 27 Mar 1958: *Georgy Vasilyevich Enyutin* (b. Mariupol (now Zhdanov) 4 Apr 1903; d. Moscow Mar 1969)

Prime Ministers of the Constituent Republics

Following the government reorganization announced on 10 May 1957, the prime ministers of the constituent republics became ex officio members of the USSR Council of Ministers. They are listed on p. 552.

27/31 Mar 1958 – 15 Oct 1964: Khrushchov

Prime Minister	*Nikita Sergeevich Khrushchov* (b. Kalinovka 17 Apr 1894; d. Moscow 11 Sep 1971)
First Deputy Prime Ministers	31 Mar 1958 – 15 Jul 1964: *Anastas Ivanovich Mikoyan* (see Presidents)
	31 Mar 1958 – 4 May 1960: *Frol Romanovich Kozlov* (b. Loshchinino 17 Aug 1908; d. Moscow 30 Jan 1965)
	4 May 1960 – 15 Oct 1964: *Aleksei Nikolaevich Kosygin* (see Commissars and Ministers of Finance)
	13 Mar 1963 – 15 Oct 1964: *Dmitry Fyodorovich Ustinov* (see Malenkov)
Deputy Prime Ministers	31 Mar 1958 – 4 May 1960: *Aleksei Nikolaevich Kosygin* (see Commissars and Ministers of Finance)
	31 Mar 1958 – 20 Mar 1959: *Iosif Iosifovich Kuzmin* (see Bulganin)
	31 Mar 1958 – 13 Mar 1963: *Dmitry Fyodorovich Ustinov* (see Malenkov)
	31 Mar 1958 – 9 Nov 1962: *Aleksandr Fyodorovich Zasyadko* (see Malenkov)
	4 May 1960 – 26 Dec 1962: *Nikolai Grigoryevich Ignatov* (b. Tishinskaya 15 May 1901; d. Moscow 14 Nov 1966)
	4 May 1960 – 24 Nov 1962: *Vladimir Nikolaevich Novikov* (b. 1907)
	1961 – 15 Oct 1964: *Konstantin Nikolaevich Rudnev* (b. Tula 1911)
	7 Jul 1962 – 15 Oct 1964: *Venyamin Emanuilovich Dymshits* (b. Feodosya, Crimea, 1910)
	9 Nov 1962 – 15 Oct 1964: *Pyotr Faddeevich Lomako* (see Malenkov)
	24 Nov 1962 – 15 Oct 1964: *Mikhail Avksentyevich Lesechko* (see Bulganin)
	24 Nov 1962 – 15 Oct 1964: *Ignaty Trofimovich*

Novikov (b. Ukraine 1909)
24 Nov 1962 – 15 Oct 1964: *Dmitry Stepanovich Polyansky* (b. Slavyanoserbsk, Ukraine, 1917)
24 Nov 1962 – 15 Oct 1964: *Aleksandr Nikolaevich Shelepin* (b. Voronezh 1918)

Chairmen of Committees of the Council of Ministers

State Planning Commission (Gosplan)	27 Mar 1958 – 20 Mar 1959: *Iosif Iosifovich Kuzmin* (see Bulganin)
	20 Mar 1959 – 4 May 1960: *Aleksei Nikolaevich Kosygin* (see Commissars and Ministers of Finance)
	4 May 1960 – 17 Jul 1962: *Vladimir Nikolaevich Novikov* (see above)
	17 Jul – 9 Nov 1962: *Venyamin Emanuilovich Dymshits* (see above)
	9 Nov 1962: Commission reorganized and renamed National Economic Council
National Economic Council	9 Nov 1962 – 15 Oct 1964: *Venyamin Emanuilovich Dymshits* (see above)
Supreme Council of the National Economy (new organization)	13 Mar 1963 – 15 Oct 1964: *Dmitry Fyodorovich Ustinov* (see Malenkov)
Scientific and Economic Council	20 Mar 1959 – end Apr 1960: *Iosif Iosifovich Kuzmin* (see Bulganin)
	end Apr 1960 – 9 Nov 1962: *Aleksandr Fyodorovich Zasyadko* (see Malenkov)
	9 Nov 1962: Council reorganized and renamed the State Planning Committee
State Planning Committee	9 Nov 1962 – 14 Oct 1964: *Pyotr Faddeevich Lomako* (see Malenkov)
Committee for State Security (KGB)	31 Mar – 25 Dec 1958: *Ivan Aleksandrovich Zerov* (see Malenkov)
	25 Dec 1958 – 13 Nov 1961: *Aleksandr Nikolaevich Shelepin* (b. Voronezh 1918)
	13 Nov 1961 – 14 Oct 1964: *Vladimir Efimovich Semichastny* (b. 1924)
Commission for Soviet Control (Audit)	31 Mar 1958 – 23 Nov 1962: *Georgy Vasilyevich Enyutin* (see Bulganin)
	24 Nov 1962: Commission replaced by the Committee for Party and State Control
Committee for Party and State Control (Audit)	24 Nov 1962 – 15 Oct 1964: *Aleksandr Nikolaevich Shelepin* (see above)

Committee for Co-ordination of Scientific Research	8 Apr – 2 Jun 1961: *Mikhail Vasilyevich Khrunichev* (see Bulganin) 10 Jun 1961 – 15 Oct 1964: *Konstantin Nikolaevich Rudnev* (see above)
Committee for Science and Technology (renamed Inventions and Discoveries in 1960 or 1961)	*Yury Evgenyevich Maksaryov* (b. Port Arthur (Lü-shun) 10 Aug 1903)
Committee for Farm Produce (new organization)	26 Feb 1961 – 26 Dec 1962: *Nikolai Grigoryevich Ignatov* (see above) 17 Jan 1963 – 15 Oct 1964: *Leonid Romanovich Korniets* (see Malenkov)
Organization for the Supply of Agricultural Equipment (Soyuzsel-khoztekhnika) (new organization)	20 Feb 1961 – 26 Dec 1962: *Pavel Sergeevich Kuchumov* (b. 1904) 26 Dec 1962 – 15 Oct 1964: *Aleksandr Aleksandrovich Ezhevsky* (b. Tulun 3 Nov 1915)
State Committee for Construction	(?) – 26 Jan 1961: *Vladimir Alekseevich Kucherenko* (see Bulganin) 26 Jan 1961 – 24 Nov 1962: *Ivan Aleksandrovich Grishmanov* (b. 1906) 24 Nov 1962 – 15 Oct 1964: *Ignaty Trofimovich Novikov* (see above)
Committee for Labour and Wages	*Aleksandr Petrovich Volkov* (see Bulganin)
Committee for Foreign Economic Relations	*Semyon Andreevich Skachkov* (see Bulganin)
Committee for Foreign Cultural Relations	27 Mar 1958 – 24 Apr 1962: *Georgy Aleksandrovich Zhukov* (see Bulganin) 25 Apr 1962 – 15 Oct 1964: *Sergei Kalistratovich Romanovsky*
Committee for the Press	10 Aug 1963 – 14 Oct 1964: *Pavel Konstantinovich Romanov* (b. 1913)
Committee for Radio and Television	Before 24 Apr 1962 – 15 Oct 1964: *Mikhail Averkievich Kharlamov*
Committee for Films	23 Mar 1963 – 15 Oct 1964: *Aleksei Vladimirovich Romanov* (b. 1908)

All-Union Ministers

Foreign Trade	31 Mar – 26 Aug 1958: *Ivan Grigoryevich Kabanov* (see Malenkov) 26 Aug 1958 – 15 Oct 1964: *Nikolai Semyonovich Patolichev* (b. Solino 1908)
Railways	*Boris Pavlovich Beshchev* (see Commissars for Railways)
Shipping	*Viktor Georgievich Bakaev* (see Malenkov)
Power Stations (from 3 Jan 1959: Construction of Power Stations)	31 Mar 1958 – 3 Jan 1959: *Aleksei Sergeevich Pavlenko* (see Malenkov) 3 Jan 1959 – 12 Oct 1962: *Ignaty Trofimovich Novikov* (b. Ukraine 1909) 12 Oct 1962: reorganized as Union-Republican Ministry of Power and Electrification
Transport Development	*Evgeny Fyodorovich Kozhevnikov* (see Bulganin)
Nuclear ('Medium') Engineering	*Efim Pavlovich Slavsky* (b. 1898)
Chemicals Industry	31 Mar – 9 Jun 1958: *Sergei Mikhailovich Tikhomirov* (see Malenkov) 9 Jun 1958: ministry replaced by State Committee for Chemistry

Union-Republican Ministers

Foreign Affairs	*Andrei Andreevich Gromyko* (see Bulganin)
Home Affairs	31 Mar 1958 – 14 Jan 1960: *Nikolai Pavlovich Dudorov* (see Malenkov) 14 Jan 1960: duties taken over by ministries in each of the constituent republics
Defence	*Rodion Yakovlevich Malinovsky* (see Bulganin)
Internal Trade	31 Mar – 27 Nov 1958: *Dmitry Vasilyevich Pavlov* (see Malenkov) 27 Nov 1958: duties taken over by ministries in each of the constituent republics
Finance	31 Mar 1958 – 16 May 1960: *Arseny Grigoryevich Zverev* (see Commissars and Ministers of Finance) 16 May 1960 – 15 Oct 1964: *Vasily Fyodorovich Garbuzov*
Culture	31 Mar 1958 – 24 Apr 1962: *Nikolai Aleksandrovich Mikhailov* (see Malenkov) 25 Apr 1962 – 15 Oct 1964: *Ekaterina Alekseevna Furtseva* (b. Vyshni Volochek 7 Dec 1910; d. 24 Oct 1974)

Communications	*Nikolai Demyanovich Psurtsev* (see Commissars for Posts and Telegraphs)
Health	31 Mar 1958 – 12 Jan 1959: *Maria Dmitrievna Kovrigina* (see Malenkov)
	12 Jan 1959 – 15 Oct 1964: *Sergei Vladimirovich Kurashov* (b. 1910; d. 27 Aug 1965)
Agriculture	31 Mar 1958 – 29 Dec 1960: *Vladimir Vladimirovich Matskevich* (see Bulganin)
	29 Dec 1960 – 24 Apr 1962: *Mikhail Alexandrovich Olshanski* (b. 1908)
	25 Apr 1962 – 8 Mar 1963: *Konstantin Georgievich Pysin* (b. 24 Dec 1910)
	8 Mar 1963 – 15 Oct 1964: *Ivan Platonovich Volovchenko* (b. Karsh 1917)
Grain Products	31 Mar – 26 Nov 1958: *Leonid Romanovich Korniets* (see Malenkov)
	26 Nov 1958: Ministry abolished
Geology and Mineral Resources	31 Mar 1958 – 24 Feb 1962: *Pyotr Yakovlevich Antropov* (see Malenkov)
	24 Feb 1962 – 15 Oct 1964: *Aleksandr Vasilyevich Sidorenko* (b. 1917)
Power and Electrification	12 Oct 1962 – 23 Nov 1963: *Ignaty Trofimovich Novikov* (see above)
	23 Nov 1963 – 15 Oct 1964: *Pyotr Neporozhny*
Civil Aviation (new post)	25 Aug – 15 Oct 1964: *Evgeny Fyodorovich Loginov* (b. Helsinki 23 Oct 1907; d. Moscow 7 Oct 1970)

Heads of Other Organizations who had Ministerial Status

State Bank	27 Mar – 15 Aug 1958: *Nikolai Aleksandrovich Bulganin* (see Commissars and Ministers for Military and Naval Affairs)
	16 Aug 1958 – 15 Oct 1964: *Aleksandr Konstantinovich Korovushkin* (b. 1909)
Capital Investments Bank	25 Apr 1962 – 24 Jan 1963: *Georgy Arkadyevich Karavaev* (b. 1913)
	24 Jan 1963 – 15 Oct 1964: *Semyon Zakharovich Ginsburg*
Central Statistical Board	25 Apr 1962 – 15 Oct 1964: *Vladimir Nikonovich Starovsky* (b. 1905; d. 20 Oct 1975)

Prime Ministers of the Constituent Republics
The prime ministers of the constituent republics were ex officio members of the USSR Council of Ministers. They are listed on p. 552.

Chairmen of State Committees for Industries
Following the abolition, in 1957, of centralized ministries for many industries, committees were set up, initially for four defence-related industries and eventually for many more. The chairmen of these committees usually had ministerial status. The committees were abolished in 1965 when ministries for the industries were re-established. The following list covers the whole period of their existence.

Aviation Engineering   14 Dec 1957 – 3 Mar 1965: *Pyotr Vasilyevich Dementyev* (see Malenkov)

Defence Equipment   14 Dec 1957 – 10 Jun 1961: *Konstantin Nikolaevich Rudnev* (see above)
10 Jun 1961 – 13 Mar 1963: *Leonid Vasilyevich Smirnov* (b. 1916)
13 Mar 1963 – 3 Mar 1965: *Sergei Alekseevich Zverev* (b. Sofronkovo 18 Oct 1912)

Radio Engineering   14 Dec 1957 – 3 Mar 1965: *Valery Dmitrievich Kalmykov* (see Malenkov)

Shipbuilding   14 Dec 1957 – 3 Mar 1965: *Boris Evstafyevich Butoma* (b. Makhachkale 1907; d. 11 Jul 1976)

Automation and Machine-building (new committee)   28 Feb 1959 – 2 Oct 1965: *Anatoly Ivanovich Kostousov* (see Malenkov)

Electronics Engineering (new committee)   17 Mar 1961 – 2 Oct 1965: *Aleksandr Ivanovich Shokin* (b. 1909)

Chemistry (from May 1963, Chemicals and Petroleum Industry)   (?) – 8 Mar 1963: *Viktor Stepanovich Fyodorov* (b. 1912)
8 Mar 1963 – 27 Jan 1964: *Nikolai Konstantinovich Baibakov* (see Malenkov)

Metal Manufacture (new committee)   2 Dec 1961 – 2 Oct 1965: *Vsevolod Efimovich Boiko* (b. 1914)

Fuel Industry (new committee)   1961 – 2 Oct 1965: *Nikolai Vasilyevich Melnikov* (b. 1909)

Atomic Energy   Feb 1962 – 2 Oct 1965: *Andronik Melkonovich Petrosyants*

Timber and Paper Industry and Forestry   before 24 Apr 1962 – 2 Oct 1965 *Georgy Mikhailovich Orlov* (see Malenkov)

Food Industry (new committee)   26 Dec 1962 – 2 Oct 1965: *Pyotr Vasilyevich Naumenko*

543

Light Industry (new committee)	26 Dec 1962 – 2 Oct 1965: *Nikolai Nikiforovich Tarasov* (b. 1911)
Trade (new committee)	26 Dec 1962 – 2 Oct 1965: *Aleksandr Ivanovich Struev* (b. 1906)
Motor Vehicles, Tractors and Agricultural Machinery (new committee)	8 Mar 1963 – 2 Oct 1965: *Nikolai Ivanovich Strokin* (see Bulganin)
Assembly and Special Construction Projects (new committee)	8 Mar 1963 – 2 Oct 1965: *Fuad Borisovich Yakubovsky* (b. 1908 or 1915; d. 27 Mar 1975)
Fisheries	before 24 Apr 1962 – 2 Oct 1965: *Aleksandr Akimovich Ishkov* (see Malenkov)
Electrical Engineering (new committee)	13 Mar 1963 – 2 Oct 1965: *Nikolai Aleksandrovich Obolensky* (b. 1908)
Petroleum Extraction (new committee)	27 Jan 1964 – 2 Oct 1965: *Nikolai Konstantinovich Baibakov* (see Malenkov)
Farm Produce (new committee)	17 Jan 1963 – 2 Oct 1965: *Leonid Romanovich Korniets* (see Malenkov)
Structural and Civil Engineering Equipment (new committee)	26 Apr 1963 – 2 Oct 1965: *Efim Stepanovich Novosyolov* (see Malenkov)
Automation and Control Systems (new committee)	26 Apr 1963 – 2 Oct 1965: *Mikail Evgenyevich Rakovsky*
Construction of Plant for the Chemicals and Petroleum Industries (new committee)	28 Jan 1964 – 2 Oct 1965: *Konstantin Ivanovich Brekhov* (b. Slavyansk 6 Mar 1907)
Heavy, Power and Transport Engineering (new committee)	*Aleksei Vasilevich Topchiev*
Building Materials (new committee)	22 Jan 1963 – 2 Oct 1965: *Ivan Aleksandrovich Grishmanov* (see above)

Irrigation and Water Supply (new committee)	20 Nov 1963 – 2 Oct 1965: *Evgeny Evgenyevich Alekseevsky* (b. Bobrov 20 Mar 1906)
Oil-refining and Petrochemical Industries (new committee)	28 Jan 1964 – 2 Oct 1965: *Viktor Stepanovich Fyodorov* (see above)
Chemicals Industry	27 Jan 1964 – 2 Oct 1965: *Leonid Arkadyevich Kostandov* (b. Kerki 27 Nov 1915)
Housing Construction and Architecture	21 Jan 1963 – 2 Oct 1965: *Mikhail Vasilyevich Posokhin*

from 15 Oct 1964: Kosygin

Prime Minister	*Aleksei Nikolaevich Kosygin* (see Commissars and Ministers of Finance)
First Deputy Prime Ministers	15 Oct 1964 – 26 Mar 1965: *Dmitry Fyodorovich Ustinov* (see Malenkov)
	from 26 Mar 1965: *Kirill Trofimovich Mazurov* (b. Rudnya-Pribytovskaya 7 Apr 1914)
	2 Oct 1965 – 2 Feb 1972: *Dmitry Stepanovich Polyansky* (see Khrushchov)
Deputy Prime Ministers	15 Oct 1964 – 9 Dec 1965: *Aleksandr Nikolaevich Shelepin* (see Khrushchov)
	15 Oct 1964 – 2 Oct 1965: *Pyotr Faddeevich Lomako* (see Malenkov II)
	15 Oct 1964 – 2 Oct 1965: *Dmitry Stepanovich Polyansky* (see Khrushchov)
	15 Oct 1964 – 2 Oct 1965: *Konstantin Nikolaevich Rudnev* (see Khrushchov)
	Venyamin Emanuilovich Dymshits (see Khrushchov)
	Mikhail Avksentyevich Lesechko (see Bulganin)
	Ignaty Trofimovich Novikov (see Khrushchov)
	Leonid Vasilyevich Smirnov (see Khrushchov)
	from 26 Mar 1965: *Vladimir Nikolaevich Novikov* (see Khrushchov)
	from 2 Oct 1965: *Nikolai Konstantinovich Baibakov* (see Malenkov)
	from 2 Oct 1965: *Vladimir Alekseevich Kirillin* (b. Moscow 7 Jan 1913)
	from 2 Oct 1965: *Nikolai Aleksandrovich Tikhonov* (b. 1906)

13 Nov 1965 – Oct 1971: *Mikhail Timofeevich Efremov* (b. Nikolaevka 22 May 1911)
19 May 1972 – 27 Apr 1973: *Petro Shelest* (b. 1908)
from (?): *Ivan V. Arkhipov*

Chairmen of Committees

Supreme Council of the National Economy	15 Oct 1964 – 26 Mar 1965: *Dmitry Fyodorovich Ustinov* (see Malenkov) 26 Mar – 2 Oct 1965: *Vladimir Nikolaevich Novikov* (see Khrushchov) 2 Oct 1965: Council abolished
National Economic Council	15 Oct 1964 – 2 Oct 1965: *Venyamin Emanuilovich Dymshits* (see Khrushchov) 2 Oct 1965: Council abolished
State Committee for Material and Technical Supplies (new organization)	from 2 Oct 1965: *Venyamin Emanuilovich Dymshits* (see Khrushchov)
State Planning Committee	15 Oct 1964 – 2 Oct 1965: *Pyotr Faddeevich Lomako* (see Malenkov) from 2 Oct 1965: *Nikolai Konstantinovich Baibakov* (see Malenkov)
State Committee for Construction	*Ignaty Trofimovich Novikov* (see Khrushchov)
State Committee for Farm Produce	15 Oct 1964 – 29 May 1969: *Leonid Romanovich Korniets* (see Malenkov) Jun 1969 – 1973: *Ziya Nuriev* (b. Verkhnelakhentau 21 Mar 1915) from 1973: *Grigory Sergeevich Zolotukhin* (b. 1911)
Organization for the Supply of Agricultural Equipment (Soyuzselkhoztekhnika)	*Aleksandr Aleksandrovich Ezhevsky* (see Khrushchov)
Committee for State Security (KGB)	15 Oct 1964 – before 19 May 1967: *Vladimir Efimovich Semichastny* (see Khrushchov) from before 19 May 1967: *Yury Vladimirovich Andropov* (b. Nagutskaya 15 Jun 1914)
Committee for Party and State Control (from 9 Dec 1965: People's Control)	15 Oct 1964 – 9 Dec 1965: *Aleksandr Nikolaevich Shelepin* (see Khrushchov) 9 Dec 1965 – 23 Jul 1971: *Pavel Vasilyevich Kovanov* (b. 1907)

23 Jul 1971 – 27 Apr 1973: *Gennady Ivanovich Voronov* (b. Rameshiki (now in Kalinin Oblast) 31 Aug 1910)

from 26 Jul 1974: *Aleksei Mikhailovich Shkolnikov* (b. 1914)

Central Statistical Organization

15 Oct 1964 – 20 Oct 1975: *Vladimir Nikonovich Starovsky* (see Khrushchov)

Coordination of Scientific Research (from 2 Oct 1965: Science and Technology)

15 Oct 1964 – 1 Oct 1965: *Konstantin Nikolaevich Rudnev* (see Khrushchov I)

from 2 Oct 1965: *Vladimir Alekseevich Kirillin* (see above)

Films

15 Oct 1964 – 9 Dec 1965[†]: *Aleksei Vladimirovich Romanov* (see Khrushchov)

Foreign Cultural Relations

15 Oct 1964 – 9 Dec 1965[†]: *Sergei Kalistratovich Romanovsky* (see Khrushchov)

Foreign Economic Relations

Semyon Andreevich Skachkov (see Khrushchov)

Forestry

11 Mar 1966 – 6 Jun 1968: *Vasily Ivanovich Rubtsov* (b. 1913)

6 Jun 1968 – 24 Apr 1970: *I. E. Voronov*

from 24 Apr 1970: *Georgy Ivanovich Vorobyov* (b. 1914)

Inventions and Discoveries

Yury Evgenyevich Maksaryov (see Khrushchov)

Labour and Wages

15 Oct 1964 – 25 Jul 1974: *Aleksandr Petrovich Volkov* (b. Vidogozh 1910)

from 26 Jul 1974: vacant

Press

15 Oct 1964 – 9 Dec 1965[†]: *Pavel Konstantinovich Romanov* (see Khrushchov)

Prices (new post)

Jan 1970 – 25 Jul 1974: *Vladimir Ksenofontovich Sitnin* (b. 1908?)

from 26 Jul 1974: vacant

Publishing, Printing and the Book Trade

from 24 Jul 1970: *Boris Ivanovich Stukalin*

Sport (new post)

9 Jun 1968 – 26 Jul 1974: *Sergei Pavlovich Pavlov* (b. Rzhev 19 Jan 1929)

Standards

from 2 Oct 1965: *Vasily V. Boitsov*

[†] The chairman of this committee ceased to be a member of the Council of Ministers on 9 Dec 1965.

State Bank   14 Aug 1963 – Sep 1969: *Aleksei Andreevich Poskonov* (b. 1929)
from Sep 1969: *Mefody Naumovich Sveshnikov* (b. 1911)

Television and Broadcasting   30 Oct 1964 – Apr 1970[†]: *Nikolai Nikolaevich Mesyatsev* from 25 Apr 1970: *Sergei Georgievich Lapin* (b. 1912)

Vocational and Technical Education   from 16 Oct 1965: *Aleksandr Aleksandrovich Bulgakov* (b. Kharkov 19 Mar 1907)

All-Union Ministers

Aircraft Industry   from 3 Mar 1965: *Pyotr Vasilyevich Dementyev* (see Malenkov)

Automation and Control Systems   from 2 Oct 1965: *Konstantin Nikolaevich Rudnev* (see Khrushchov)

Automobile Industry   2 Oct 1965 – 28 Jun 1975: *Aleksandr Mikhailovich Tarasov*
from 28 Jun 1975: *Viktor Nikolaevich Polyakov*

Chemical and Petroleum Engineering   from 2 Oct 1965: *Konstantin Ivanovich Brekhov* (see Khrushchov)

Chemicals Industry   from 2 Oct 1965: *Leonid Arkadyevich Kostandov* (see Khrushchov)

Civil Aviation   15 Aug 1964 – May 1970: *Evgeny Fyodorovich Loginov* (see Khrushchov)
from May 1970: *Boris Pavlovich Bugaev* (b. 1923)

Communications Equipment   from 12 Apr 1974: *Erlen K. Pervyshin*

Construction and Roadmaking Equipment, and Municipal Engineering   from 2 Oct 1965: *Efim Stepanovich Novosyolov* (see Malenkov)

Construction of Plant for the Petroleum and Gas Industries   Sep 1972 – Jul 1970/1974: *Aleksei Kirillovich Kortunov* (see Bulganin)
from Jul 1970/1974: *Boris Evdokimovich Shcherbina* (b. 1919)

Construction of Power Stations (new post)   from 30 May 1975: *Viktor Vasilyevich Krotov* (b. 1912)

[†]The chairman of this committee ceased to be a member of the Council of Ministers on 9 Dec 1965.

Defence Industry	from 3 Mar 1965: *Sergei Alekseevich Zverev* (see Khrushchov)
Electrical Engineering	from 2 Oct 1965: *Aleksei Konstantinovich Antonov* (b. Grodno 8 Jun 1912)
Electronics Industry	from 3 Mar 1965: *Aleksandr Ivanovich Shokin* (see Khrushchov)
Engineering (new post created 6 Feb 1968)	from 26 Jun 1968: *Vyacheslav V. Bakhirev*
Engineering for the Light and Food Industries and Household Appliances	from 2 Oct 1965: *Vasily Nikolaevich Doenin* (b. Yalta 24 Sep 1909; d. Feb 1977)
Equipment for Animal Husbandry and Fodder Production	from (?): *Konstantin Nikitovich Belyak* (b. 1916)
Foreign Trade	*Nikolai Semyonovich Patolichev* (see Khrushchov)
Gas Industry	2 Oct 1965 – Sep 1972: *Aleksei Kirillovich Kortunov* (b. 1907) from Sep 1972: *Sabit A. Orudzhev*
General Engineering (new post)	from 3 Mar 1965: *Sergei Alekseevich Afanasyev* (see Khrushchov)
Heavy, Power and Transport Engineering	2 Oct 1965 – 29 May 1970: *Vladimir Fyodorovich Zhigalin* (b. Petrograd 3 Mar 1907) 29 May 1970: divided into separate ministries for Heavy and Transport Engineering and Construction of Power Stations (q.v.)
Heavy and Transport Engineering	from 30 May 1970: *Vladimir Fyodorovich Zhigalin* (see above)
Machine-tool Manufacture and Toolmaking	from 2 Oct 1965: *Anatoly Ivanovich Kostousov* (see Malenkov)
Medical Industry (new post)	25 Apr 1967 – 28 Jan 1975: *Pyotr Vasilyevich Gusenkov* (b. 1905; d. 28 Jan 1975)
Nuclear ('Medium') Engineering	from 3 Mar 1965: *Efim Pavlovich Slavsky* (see Khrushchov)
Petroleum Extraction Industry	from 2 Oct 1965: *Valentin Dmitrievich Shashin* (b. 1916; d. Mar 1977)
Pulp and Paper Industry (new post)	from 11 Jun 1968: *Konstantin Ivanovich Galanshin* (b. 1912)
Radio Industry	3 Mar 1965 – 22 Mar 1974: *Valery Dmitrievich*

	Kalmykov (see Malenkov)
	from 26 Jul 1974: *Pyotr S. Pleshakov*
Railways	*Boris Pavlovich Beshchev* (see Commissars for Railways)
Shipbuilding	from 3 Mar 1965: *Boris Evstafyevich Butoma* (see Bulganin)
Shipping	15 Oct 1964 – Jan 1970(?): *Viktor Georgievich Bakaev* (see Bulganin) from 15 Jan 1970: *Timofei Borisovich Guzhenko* (b. Tatarinovo 15 Feb 1918)
Tractors and Agricultural Machinery	from 2 Oct 1965: *Ivan Flegontovich Sinitsyn* (b. 1911)
Transport Development	from 2 Oct 1965: *Evgeny Fyodorovich Kozhevnikov*

Union-Republican Ministers

Foreign Affairs	*Andrei Andreevich Gromyko* (see Bulganin)
Public Order (new post created 28 Jul 1966) (from 28 Nov 1968: Home Affairs)	from 17 Sep 1966: *Nikolai Anisimovich Shcholokov* (b. 1910)
Agricultural Construction (post re-established)	from 21 Feb 1967: *Stepan Dmitrievich Khitrov* (b. 1910)
Agriculture	15 Oct 1964 – 18 Feb 1965: *Ivan Platonovich Volovchenko* (see Khrushchov) 18 Feb 1965 – 2 Feb 1972: *Vladimir Vladimirovich Matskevich* (see Bulganin) from 3 Feb 1972: *Dmitry Stepanovich Polyansky* (see Khrushchov)
Assembly and Special Construction Work	2 Oct 1965 – 27 Mar 1975: *Fuad Borisovich Yakubovsky* (see Khrushchov)
Building Materials Industry	from 2 Oct 1965: *Ivan Aleksandrovich Grishmanov* (see Khrushchov)
Coal Industry	from 2 Oct 1965: *Boris Fyodorovich Bratchenko* (b. Armavir 9 Oct 1912)
Communications	15 Oct 1964 – 12 Sep 1975: *Nikolai Demyanovich Psurtsev* (see Commissars for Posts and Telegraphs) from 13 Sep 1975: *Nikolai Talyzin*
Construction (post re-established)	from 21 Feb 1967: *Georgy Arkadyevich Karavaev* (b. 1913)

Construction of Heavy Engineering Works (post re-established)	from 21 Feb 1967: *Nikolai Vasilyevich Goldin* (b. Grishino 20 Mar 1910)
Culture	15 Oct 1964 – 24 Oct 1974: *Ekaterina Alekseevna Furtseva* (see Khrushchov) from 14 Nov 1974: *Pyotr Nikolaevich Demichev* (b. Posochnaya 3 Jan 1918)
Defence	15 Oct 1964 – 31 Mar 1967: *Rodion Yakovlevich Malinovsky* (see Bulganin) from 12 Apr 1967: *Andrei Antonovich Grechko* (b. Golodaevka 17 Oct 1903; d. 26 Apr 1976)
Education (new post)	from Dec 1966: *Mikhail Alekseevich Prokofyev* (b. Voskresenskoe 18 Nov 1910)
Ferrous Metal Manufacture	from 2 Oct 1965: *Ivan Pavlovich Kazanets* (b. 1918)
Finance	*Vasily Fyodorovich Garbuzov* (see Khrushchov I)
Fisheries	from 2 Oct 1965: *Aleksandr Akimovich Ishkov* (see Malenkov)
Food Industry	2 Oct 1965 – 16 Jan 1970: *Vasily Petrovich Zotov* (see Malenkov) from 16 Jan 1970: *Voldemar Lein* (b. Bugrysh 7 Jul 1920)
Geology	15 Oct 1964 – before 29 Dec 1975: *Aleksandr Vasilyevich Sidorenko* (see Khrushchov) from before 27 Dec 1975: *Evgeny Kozlovsky*
Health	15 Oct 1964 – 27 Aug 1965: *Sergei Vladimirovich Kurashov* (see Khrushchov) from 9 Sep 1965: *Boris Vasilyevich Petrovsky* (b. Essentuki 27 Jun 1908)
Higher and Secondary Specialized Education	*Vyacheslav Petrovich Elyutin* (see Malenkov)
Industrial Construction (post re-established)	from 21 Feb 1967: *Aleksandr Maksimovich Tokaryov* (b. 1921)
Irrigation and Water Conservation	from 2 Oct 1965: *Evgeny Evgenyevich Alekseevsky* (see Khrushchov)
Light Industry	from 2 Oct 1965: *Nikolai Nikiforovich Tarasov* (see Khrushchov)
Justice (post re-established)	from 1 Sep 1970: *Vladimir I. Terebilov* (b. 1916?)

Meat and Dairy Industry	from 2 Oct 1965: *Sergei Fyodorovich Antonov* (see Malenkov)
Non-ferrous Metal Manufacture	from 2 Oct 1965: *Pyotr Faddeevich Lomako* (see Malenkov)
Petroleum Refining and Petrochemical Industry	from 2 Oct 1965: *Viktor Stepanovich Fyodorov* (see Khrushchov)
Timber, Pulp and Paper, and Timber Products	2 Oct 1965 – 11 Jun 1968: *Nikolai Vladimirovich Timofeev* (b. 1913)
	11 Jun 1968: divided into separate ministries for Pulp and Paper Industry, and Timber and Timber Products Industry (see below)
Timber and Timber Products Industry (new post)	from 11 Jun 1968: *Nikolai Vladimirovich Timofeev* (see above)
Trade (Internal)	from 2 Oct 1965: *Aleksandr Ivanovich Struev* (see Khrushchov)

Prime Ministers of the Constituent Republics

Armenia	Nov 1952 – Feb 1966: *Anton Kochinyan* (b. Vaagin 25 Oct 1913)
	Feb 1966 – 1972: *Badal Muradyan* (b. 1915)
	from 1972: *Grigory Arzumanyan*
Azerbaijan	2 Mar 1954 – 1958: *Sadykh Gadzhiyaralievich Ragimov* (b. Balakhany (now Lenin Rayon, Baku) 1914)
	1958 – Dec 1961: *M. E. Iskenderov*
	Dec 1961 – Apr 1970: *Enver Ali Khan* (b. Baku 1917)
	from Apr 1970: *Ali Ismailovich Ibragimov* (b. Ust-Kara 1 Oct 1913)
Byelorussia	1956 – 9 Apr 1959: *Nikolai Efremovich Avkhimovich* (b. Borisov, Byelorussia, 1907)
	from 9 Apr 1959: *Tikhon Yakovlevich Kiselyov* (b. Ogorodnya (now in Gomel Oblast) 12 Aug 1917)
Estonia	29 Mar 1951 – 12 Oct 1961: *Alexei A. Müürisepp* (b. Revel (now Tallinn) 1902)
	from 12 Oct 1961: *Walter I. Klauson* (b. Tolmachovo 2 Jan 1914)
Georgia	1953 – 17 Dec 1975: *Givi Dzhavakhshvili* (b. Tiflis 18 Sep 1912)
	from 17 Dec 1975: *Zurab A. Pataridze*

Kazakhstan	1955 – 20 Jan 1960: *Dinmukhamed Akhmedovich Kunaev* (for 1st time) (b. Verny (now Alma-Ata) 1912) 20 Jan 1960 – 5 Jan 1961: *Zhumabek Akhmetovich Tashenev* (b. Tanagul, Kazakhstan, 1915) 24 Jan 1961 – 13 Sep 1962: *Salken Daulenov* 13 Sep – 26 Dec 1962: *Masymkhan B. Beisebaev* (for 1st time) 26 Dec 1962 – 1964: *Dinmukhamed Akhmedovich Kunaev* (for 2nd time) 1964 – (?): *Masymkhan B. Beisebaev* (for 2nd time) from (?): *Baiken A. Ashimov*
Kirgizia	before Apr 1958 – 10 May 1961: *Kazy Dikambaev* 10 May 1961 – 1968: *Bolot Mambetov* (b. 1907) from 1968: *Akhmatbek Suyumbaev* (b. 1920)
Latvia	4 May 1955 – 27 Nov 1959: *Vilis T. Lācis* (b. Rinuzki, near Riga, 1904) 27 Nov 1959 – 25 Apr 1962: *Jan Peive* (b. Semenzevo, near Velikiye Luki, 1906) 25 Apr 1962 – 15 Jul 1970: *Vitalis Rubenis* (b. Moscow 26 Feb 1914) from 15 Jul 1970: *Jurijs Vitalis* (b. 1925)
Lithuania	15 Jan 1956 – 17 Apr 1967: *Motejus Šumauskas* (b. Kaunas 15 Nov 1905) from 17 Apr 1967: *Juozas Maniušis* (b. 1910)
Moldavia	Jan 1958 – Apr 1970: *Alexander Diordita* (b. Gandrabudy (now in Odessa Oblast) 1911) from 1970: *Petru Pascar* (b. 1929)
RSFSR	24 Jan 1956 – 19 Dec 1957: *Mikhail Alekseevich Yasnov* (b. Gori (now in Moscow Oblast) 1906) 19 Dec 1957 – 31 Mar 1958: *Frol Romanovich Kozlov* (see Khrushchov) 31 Mar 1958 – Nov 1962: *Dmitry Stepanovich Polyansky* (see Khrushchov) Nov 1962 – 23 Jul 1971: *Gennady Ivanovich Voronov* (b. Rameshki (now in Kalinin Oblast) 31 Aug 1910) from 28 Jul 1971: *Mikhail Sergeevich Solomontsev* (b. 1913)
Tadzhikistan	before Apr 1958 – 12 Apr 1961: *Nazarsho Dodkhudoev* 12 Apr 1961 – Jul 1973: *Abdulakhad Kakharovich Kakharov* (b. Kanibadam 17 Apr 1913) from Jul 1973: *Rakhman Nabiev* (b. 1930)

Turkmenistan	before Apr 1958 – before Oct 1959: *Djuma Karaev*
	before Oct 1959 – (?): *B. O. Ovezov*
	Mar 1963 – Dec 1969: *Mukhamednazar Gapurov* (b. 15 Feb 1922)
	Dec 1969 – 19 Dec 1975: *Oraz Orazmukhamedov* (b. Karndamak 15 May 1928)
	from 19 Dec 1975: *Bally Yazkuliev*
Ukraine	1954 – 28 Feb 1961: *Nikifor Timofeevich Kalchenko* (b. Koshmanovka (now in Poltava Oblast) 1906)
	28 Feb 1961 – 1963: *Volodymyr Shcherbitsky* (for 1st time) (b. Ukraine 1918)
	1963 – 1965: (?)
	4 Oct 1965 – 25 May 1972: *Volodymyr Shcherbitsky* (for 2nd time)
	from 9 Jun 1972: *Aleksandr Lyashko* (b. 30 Dec 1915)
Uzbekistan	Dec 1955 – 28 Dec 1957: *Sabir Kamalovich Kamalov* (b. Tashkent 1910)
	28 Dec 1957 – 15 Mar 1959: *Mansur Mirza-Akhmedov*
	16 Mar 1959 – 27 Sep 1961: *Arif Alimov*
	27 Sep 1961 – 26 Feb 1971: *Rakhmankul Kurbanov* (b. 1912)
	from Feb 1971: *Narmakhonmadi Dzhuraevich Khudaiberdiev* (b. 1928)

United Arab Emirates

Dec 1971	Formed after the withdrawal of British forces from the Gulf of Oman by the union of Abu Dhabi, Dubai, Sharjah, Ajman, Umm al-Qaiwain, Ras al-Khaimah (acceded Feb 1972) and Fujairah

HEAD OF STATE

President

from 2 Dec 1971	*Zayed bin Sultan al Nahayan* (b. 1918)

United Arab Republic

See also Egypt and Syria.

1/21 Feb 1958	Formed by the union of Egypt and Syria
28 Sep 1961	Union terminated

HEAD OF STATE

President

21 Feb 1958 – 28 Sep 1961	*Gamal Abdul Nasser* (b. Beni Mor 15 Jan 1918; d. Heliopolis 28 Sep 1970)

United Kingdom

HEADS OF STATE

Kings and Queens

6 May 1910	*George V*, son of Edward VII (b. 3 Jun 1865)
20 Jan 1936	*Edward VIII* (*Edward Albert Christian George Andrew Patrick David Windsor;* from 8 Mar 1937: *Duke of Windsor*), son (b. 23 Jun 1894; d. Paris 28 May 1972) 10 Dec 1936 renounced throne and thereafter lived abroad
10 Dec 1936	*George VI*, brother (b. 14 Dec 1895)
from 6 Feb 1952	*Elizabeth II*, daughter (b. 21 Apr 1926)

MEMBERS OF GOVERNMENT

8 Jun 1929 – 24 Aug 1931: Macdonald II (Lab)

Prime Minister	*James Ramsay Macdonald* (for 2nd time) (b. Lossiemouth 12 Oct 1866; d. on journey from England to South America 9 Nov 1937)*
Foreign Affairs	*Arthur Henderson* (b. Glasgow 1 Aug 1863; d. London 20 Oct 1935)*

*For earlier career see vol. 2

555

Home Affairs	*John Robert Clynes* (b. Oldham 27 Mar 1869; d. London 23 Oct 1949)*
Chancellor of the Exchequer	*Philip Snowden* (from 1931: *Viscount Snowden*) (b. Cowling, Yorkshire, 18 Jul 1864; d. Frensham, Surrey, 15 May 1937)*
War	*Thomas Shaw* (b. Colne, Lancashire, 9 Apr 1872; d. London 26 Sep 1938)*
First Lord of the Admiralty	*Albert Victor Alexander* (from 1950: *Viscount;* from 1963: *Earl Alexander of Hillsborough;* from 1964: *Sir*) (b. Weston-super-Mare 1 May 1885; d. 11 Jan 1965)
Air	8 Jun 1929 – 5 Oct 1930: *Christopher Birdwood Thomson, 1st Baron Thomson* (b. Nasik, India, 13 Apr 1875; d. in Airship R101 disaster 5 Oct 1930)* 15 Oct 1930 – 24 Aug 1931: *William Warrender Mackenzie, Baron Amulree* (b. Scone, Perthshire, 19 Aug 1860; d. Winterbourne Stoke 5 May 1942)
Colonies	*Sidney James Webb, Baron Passfield* (b. London 13 Jul 1859; d. Liphook 13 Oct 1947)*
Dominions	8 Jun 1929 – 6 Jun 1930: *Sidney James Webb, Baron Passfield* (see above) 6 Jun 1930 – 24 Aug 1931: *James Henry Thomas* (b. Newport 3 Oct 1874; d. London 21 Jan 1949)*
India	*William Wedgwood Benn* (from 1942: *Viscount Stansgate*) (b. 10 May 1877; d. London 17 Nov 1960)
Lord President	*Charles Alfred Cripps, Baron Parmoor* (b. West Ilshey, Berkshire, 3 Oct 1852; d. Henley-on-Thames 30 Jun 1941)*
Lord Privy Seal (Unemployment)	8 Jun 1929 – 6 Jun 1930: *James Henry Thomas* (see above) 6 Jun 1930 – 13 Mar 1931: *Vernon Hartshorn* (b. Monmouthshire 16 Mar 1872; d. Maesteg 13 Mar 1931)*
Lord Chancellor	*John Sankey, Baron* (from 1932: *Viscount*) *Sankey* (b. Moreton-in-Marsh 26 Oct 1866; d. London 6 Feb 1948)
Education	8 Jun 1929 – 2 Mar 1931: *Sir Charles Philips Trevelyan, bart* (b. London 28 Oct 1870; d. London 24 Jan 1958)* 2 Mar – 24 Aug 1931: *Hastings Bertrand Lees-Smith* (b. India 1878; d. 18 Dec 1941)

*For earlier career see vol. 2

Health	*Arthur Greenwood* (b. Hunslet, Leeds, 8 Feb 1880; d. London 9 Jun 1954)
Trade	*William Graham* (b. Peebles 29 Jul 1887; d. London 8 Jan 1932)
Agriculture	8 Jun 1929 – 6 Jun 1930: *Noel Edward Buxton* (from 1930: *N. E. Noel-Buxton, 1st Baron Noel-Buxton*) (b. London 9 Jan 1869; d. London 12 Sep 1948)*
	6 Jun 1930 – 24 Aug 1931: *Christopher Addison* (from 1937: *1st Baron*; from 1945: *1st Viscount Addison*) (b. Hogsthorpe 19 Jun 1869; d. West Wycombe 11 Dec 1951)*
Secretary of State for Scotland	*William Adamson* (b. 2 Apr 1863; d. 26 Feb 1936)*
Labour	*Margaret Grace Bondfield* (b. Chard 17 Mar 1873; d. Sanderstead, Surrey, 16 Jun 1953)
Public Works	*George Lansbury* (b. Lowestoft 21 Feb 1859; d. London 7 May 1940)
Postmaster General	8 Jun 1929 – 2 Mar 1931: *Hastings Bertrand Lees-Smith* (see above)
	2 Mar – 24 Aug 1931: *Clement Richard Attlee* (from 1955: *Earl Attlee*) (b. London 3 Jan 1883; d. London 8 Oct 1967)
Chancellor of the Duchy of Lancaster	8 Jun 1929 – 20 May 1930: *Sir Oswald Ernald Mosley, bart* (b. London 16 Nov 1896)
	20 May 1930 – 2 Mar 1931: *Clement Richard Attlee* (see above)
	14 Mar – 24 Aug 1931: *Arthur Augustus William Harry Ponsonby, Baron Ponsonby of Shulbrede* (b. Windsor Castle 16 Feb 1871; d. Hindhead, Surrey, 24 Mar 1946)

25 Aug – 5 Nov 1931: Macdonald III (National Government)

Prime Minister	*James Ramsay Macdonald* (Lab) (for 3rd time) (see Macdonald II)
Foreign Affairs	*Sir Rufus Daniel Isaacs, Marquess of Reading* (Lib) (b. London 10 Oct 1860; d. London 30 Dec 1935)*
Home Affairs	*Sir Herbert Louis Samuel* (from 1937: *1st Viscount Samuel*) (Lib) (b. Liverpool 6 Nov 1870; d. 5 Feb 1963)*
Chancellor of the Exchequer	*Philip Snowden, Viscount Snowden* (Lab) (see Macdonald II)

*For earlier career see vol. 2

557

Colonies and Dominions	*James Henry Thomas* (Lab) (see Macdonald II)
Lord Chancellor	*John Sankey, Baron Sankey* (Lab) (see Macdonald II)
Lord President	*Stanley Baldwin* (from 1937: *Earl Baldwin of Bewdley*) (Cons) (b. Bewdley 3 Aug 1867; d. Stourport-on-Severn 14 Dec 1947)*
India	*Sir Samuel John Gurney Hoare* (from 1944: *1st Viscount Templewood*) (Cons) (b. Cromer 24 Feb 1880; d. London 7 May 1959)*
Trade	*Sir Philip Cunliffe-Lister* (from 1935: *1st Viscount*; from 1955: *1st Earl Swinton*) (Cons) (b. 1 May 1884; d. 27 Jul 1972)*
Health	*Neville Chamberlain* (Cons) (b. Birmingham 18 Mar 1869; d. Heckfield 9 Nov 1940)*

5 Nov 1931 – 7 Jun 1935: Macdonald IV (National Government)

Prime Minister	*James Ramsay Macdonald* (Nat Lab) (for 4th time) (see Macdonald II)
Foreign Affairs	*Sir John Allsebrook Simon* (from 1940: *1st Viscount Simon*) (Nat Lib) (b. Manchester 28 Feb 1873; d. London 11 Jan 1954)*
Home Affairs	5 Nov 1931 – 28 Sep 1932: *Sir Herbert Louis Samuel* (Nat Lib) (see Macdonald III)
	28 Sep 1932 – 7 Jun 1935: *Sir John Gilmour, bart* (Cons) (b. Fife 27 May 1876; d. London 30 Mar 1940)*
Chancellor of the Exchequer	*Neville Chamberlain* (Cons) (see Macdonald III)
War	*Sir Douglas McGarel Hogg, 1st Viscount Hailsham* (Cons) (b. London 28 Feb 1872; d. Carter's Place, Sussex, 16 Aug 1950)*
Colonies	*Sir Philip Cunliffe-Lister* (Cons) (see Macdonald III)
Dominions	*James Henry Thomas* (Nat Lab) (see Macdonald II)
Lord Chancellor	*John Sankey, Baron* (from 1932: *Viscount*) *Sankey* (Nat Lab) (see Macdonald II)
Lord President	*Stanley Baldwin* (Cons) (see Macdonald III)
Lord Privy Seal	5 Nov 1931 – 28 Sep 1932: *Philip Snowden, Viscount Snowden* (Nat Lab) (see Macdonald II)
	29 Sep 1932 – 1 Jan 1934: *Stanley Baldwin* (Cons) (see Macdonald III)

*For earlier career see vol. 2

First Lord of the Admiralty	*Sir Bolton Meredith Eyres-Monsell* (from 1935: *1st Viscount Monsell*) (Cons) (b. 22 Feb 1881; d. 21 Mar 1969)
Trade	*Walter Runciman* (from 1937: *1st Viscount Runciman*) (Nat Lib) (b. South Shields 19 Nov 1870; d. Doxford 14 Nov 1949)*
India	*Sir Samuel John Gurney Hoare* (Cons) (see Macdonald III)
Education	5 Nov 1931 – 15 Jun 1932: *Sir Donald Maclean* (Nat Lib) (b. Farnworth, Lancashire, 9 Jan 1864; d. London 15 Jun 1932)
	16 Jul 1932 – 7 Jun 1935: *Edward Frederick Lindley Wood, 1st Baron Irwin* (from 1934: *3rd Viscount*; from 1944: *1st Earl of Halifax*) (Cons) (b. Powderham Castle 16 Apr 1881; d. Garrowby Hall 23 Dec 1959)*
Seretary of State for Scotland	5 Nov 1931 – 8 Sep 1932: *Sir Archibald Sinclair* (from 1952: *1st Viscount Thurso*) (Lib) (b. Thurso 22 Oct 1890; d. London 15 Jun 1970)
	28 Sep 1932 – 5 Jun 1935: *Sir Godfrey P. Collins* (Nat Lib) (b. 26 Jun 1875; d. Zurich 13 Oct 1936)
Public Works	*William George Ormsby-Gore* (from 1938: *4th Baron Harlech*) (Cons) (b. 11 Apr 1885; d. 14 Feb 1964)
Agriculture and Fisheries	5 Nov 1931 – 28 Sep 1932: *Sir John Gilmour, bart* (Cons) (see above)
	28 Sep 1932 – 7 Jun 1935: *Walter Elliot Elliot* (Cons) (b. 1888; d. Hawick, Scotland, 8 Jan 1958)
Labour	5 Nov 1931 – 29 Jun 1934: *Sir Henry Bucknall Betterton, bart* (from 1935: *Baron Rushcliffe*) (Cons) (b. 1872; d. 18 Nov 1949)
	29 Jun 1934 – 7 Jun 1935: *Oliver Stanley* (Cons) (b. London 4 May 1896; d. London 11 Dec 1950)
Health	*Sir Edward Hilton|Young|* (from 1935: *Baron Kennet*) (b. 20 Mar 1879; d. London 11 Jul 1960)
Air	*Sir Charles Stewart Henry Vane-Tempest-Stewart, 7th Marquess of Londonderry* (b. London 13 May 1876; d. Newtownards, Ulster, 11 Feb 1949)

7 Jun 1935 – 28 May 1937: Baldwin III (National Government)

Prime Minister	*Stanley Baldwin* (Cons) (for 3rd time) (see Macdonald III)
Foreign Affairs	7 Jun – 18 Dec 1935; *Sir Samuel John Gurney Hoare* (Cons) (see Macdonald III)

*For earlier career see vol. 2

	22 Dec 1935 – 28 May 1937: *Anthony Eden* (from 1954: *Sir;* from 1961: *Earl of Avon*) (Cons) (b. Windleston 12 Jun 1897; d. 14 Jan 1977)
Home Affairs	*Sir John Allsebrook Simon* (Nat Lib) (see Macdonald IV)
Chancellor of the Exchequer	*Neville Chamberlain* (Cons) (see Macdonald III)
War	7 Jun – 22 Nov 1935: *Edward Frederick Lindley Wood, 3rd Viscount Halifax* (Cons) (see Macdonald IV)
	22 Nov 1935 – 28 May 1937: *Alfred Duff Cooper* (from 1952: *Viscount Norwich*) (Cons) (b. London 22 Feb 1890; d. en route for Vigo, Spain, 1 Jan 1954)
Colonies	7 Jun – 22 Nov 1935: *Malcolm John Macdonald* (Nat Lab) (b. Lossiemouth 1901)
	22 Nov 1935 – 22 May 1936: *James Henry Thomas* (Nat Lab) (see Macdonald II)
	28 May 1936 – 28 May 1937: *William George Ormsby-Gore* (Cons) (see Macdonald IV)
Dominions	7 Jun – 22 Nov 1935: *James Henry Thomas* (Nat Lab) (see Macdonald II)
	22 Nov 1935 – 28 May 1937: *Malcolm John Macdonald* (Nat Lab) (see above)
Lord Chancellor	*Sir Douglas McGarel Hogg, 1st Viscount Hailsham* (Cons) (see Macdonald IV)
Lord President	*James Ramsay Macdonald* (Nat Lab) (see Macdonald II)
Lord Privy Seal	7 Jun – 22 Nov 1935: *Sir Charles Stewart Henry Vane-Tempest-Stewart, 7th Marquess of Londonderry* (see Macdonald IV)
	22 Nov 1935 – 28 May 1937: *Edward Frederick Lindley Wood, 3rd Viscount Halifax* (Cons) (see Macdonald IV)
First Lord of the Admiralty	7 Jun 1935 – 6 Jun 1936: *Sir Bolton Meredith Eyres-Monsell, 1st Viscount Monsell* (Cons) (see Macdonald IV)
	6 Jun 1936 – 28 May 1937: *Sir Samuel John Gurney Hoare* (Cons) (see Macdonald III)
Trade	*Walter Runciman* (Nat Lib) (see Macdonald IV)
India	*Lawrence John Lumley Dundas, 2nd Marquess of Zetland* (Cons) (b. 11 Jun 1876; d. Richmond, Yorkshire, 6 Feb 1961)

*For earlier career see vol. 2

Education	*Oliver Stanley* (Cons) (see Macdonald IV)
Secretary of State for Scotland	7 Jun 1935 – 13 Oct 1936: *Sir Godfrey P. Collins* (Nat Lib) (see Macdonald IV)
	29 Oct 1936 – 28 May 1937: *Walter Elliot Elliot* (Cons) (see Macdonald IV)
Public Works	7 Jun 1935 – 28 May 1936: *William George Ormsby-Gore* (Cons) (see Macdonald IV)
	17 Jun 1936 – 28 May 1937: *James Richard Stanhope, 7th Earl Stanhope* (from 1952: *13th Earl of Chesterfield)* (b. 11 Nov 1880; d. Kent 15 Aug 1967)
Agriculture	7 Jun 1935 – 29 Oct 1936: *Walter Elliot Elliot* (Cons) (see Macdonald IV)
	29 Oct 1936 – 28 May 1937: *William Shepherd Morrison* (from 1959: *Viscount Dunrossil)* (Cons) (b. 10 Aug 1893; d. 3 Feb 1961)
Labour	*Ernest Brown* (Nat Lib) (b. Torquay 27 Aug 1881; d. 16 Feb 1962)
Health	*Sir Kingsley Wood* (Cons) (b. Hull 19 Aug 1881; d. London 21 Sep 1943)
Transport	(in cabinet from Oct 1936:) *Leslie Hore-Belisha* (from 1954: *1st Baron Hore-Belisha)* (Nat Lib) (b. London 7 Sep 1895; d. Reims 16 Feb 1957)
Air	*Sir Philip Cunliffe-Lister, 1st Viscount Swinton* (Cons) (see Macdonald III)
Defence (new post)	13 Mar 1936 – 28 May 1937: *Sir Thomas Inskip* (from 1939: *Viscount Caldecote)* (b. Bristol 5 Mar 1876; d. Surrey 11 Oct 1947)
Without Portfolio (League of Nations)	7 Jun – 22 Dec 1935: *Anthony Eden* (Cons) (see Baldwin III)
Without Portfolio	8 Jun 1935 – 28 May 1936: *Lord Eustace (Sutherland Campbell) Percy* (from 1953: *1st Baron Percy of Newcastle)* (Cons) (b. 21 Mar 1887; d. London 3 Apr 1958)*

28 May 1937 – 3 Sep 1939: Chamberlain I (National Government)

Prime Minister	*Neville Chamberlain* (Cons) (for 1st time) (see Macdonald III)
Foreign Affairs	28 May 1937 – 21 Feb 1938: *Anthony Eden* (Cons) (see Baldwin III)
	25 Feb 1938 – 3 Sep 1939: *Edward Frederick Lindley*

*For earlier career see vol. 2

	Wood, 3rd Viscount Halifax (Cons) (see Macdonald IV)
Home Affairs	*Sir Samuel John Gurney Hoare* (Cons) (see Macdonald III)
Chancellor of the Exchequer	*Sir John Allsebrook Simon* (Nat Lib) (see Macdonald IV)
War	*Leslie Hore-Belisha* (Nat Lib) (see Baldwin III)
Colonies	28 May 1937 – 16 May 1938: *William George Ormsby-Gore* (Cons) (see Macdonald IV)
	16 May 1938 – 3 Sep 1939: *Malcolm John Macdonald* (Nat Lab) (see Baldwin III)
Dominions	28 May 1937 – 16 May 1938: *Malcolm John Macdonald* (Nat Lab) (see Baldwin III)
	16 May – 15 Oct 1938: *Edward Montague Cavendish Stanley, Lord Stanley* (b. 9 Jul 1894; d. London night of 15/16 Oct 1938)
	31 Oct 1938 – 28 Jan 1939: *Malcolm John Macdonald* (Nat Lab) (see Baldwin III)
	28 Jan – 3 Sep 1939: *Sir Thomas Inskip* (Cons) (see Baldwin III)
Lord Chancellor	28 May 1937 – 10 Mar 1938: *Sir Douglas McGarel Hogg, 1st Viscount Hailsham* (Cons) (see Macdonald IV)
	10 Mar 1938 – 3 Sep 1939: *Frederick Herbert Maugham, Baron* (from 1939: *1st Viscount*) *Maugham* (b. 1866; d. London 23 Mar 1958)
Lord President	28 May 1937 – 25 Feb 1938: *Edward Frederick Lindley Wood, 3rd Viscount Halifax* (Cons) (see Macdonald IV)
	10 Mar – 31 Oct 1938: *Sir Douglas McGarel Hogg, 1st Viscount Hailsham* (Cons) (see Macdonald IV)
	31 Oct 1938 – 3 Sep 1939: *Walter Runciman, 1st Viscount Runciman* (Nat Lib) (see Macdonald IV)
Lord Privy Seal	28 May 1937 – 31 Oct 1938: *Herbrand Edward Dundonald Brassey Sackville, 9th Earl De La Warr* (b. 20 Jun 1900; d. London 28 Jan 1976)
	31 Oct 1938 – 3 Sep 1939: *Sir John Anderson* (from 1952: *Viscount Waverley*) (b. Midlothian 8 Jul 1882; d. London 4 Jan 1955)
First Lord of the Admiralty	28 May 1937 – 1 Oct 1938: *Alfred Duff Cooper* (Cons) (see Baldwin III)
	27 Oct 1938 – 3 Sep 1939: *James Richard Stanhope, 7th Earl Stanhope* (see Baldwin III)

Trade	*Oliver Stanley* (Cons) (see Macdonald IV)
India and Burma	*Lawrence John Lumley Dundas, 2nd Marquess of Zetland* (Cons) (see Baldwin III)
Chancellor of the Duchy of Lancaster	28 May 1937 (in cabinet from 10 Mar 1938) – 28 Jan 1939: *Edward Turnour, 6th Earl Winterton* (b. 4 Apr 1883; d. 26 Aug 1962)
	28 Jan – 3 Sep 1939: *William Shepherd Morrison* (Cons) (see Baldwin III)
Education	28 May 1937 – 27 Oct 1938: *James Richard Stanhope, 7th Earl Stanhope* (see Baldwin III)
	27 Oct 1938 – 3 Sep 1939: *Herbrand Edward Dundonald Brassey Sackville, 9th Earl De La Warr* (see above)
Secretary of State for Scotland	28 May 1937 – 16 May 1938: *Walter Elliot Elliot* (Cons) (see Macdonald IV)
	16 May 1938 – 3 Sep 1939: *David John Colville* (from 1948: *Baron Clydesmuir*) (b. Motherwell House 13 Feb 1894; d. Braidwood 31 Oct 1954)
Agriculture	28 May 1937 – 28 Jan 1939: *William Shepherd Morrison* (Cons) (see Baldwin III)
	28 Jan – 3 Sep 1939: *Sir Reginald Hugh Dorman-Smith* (b. 1899; d. 20 Mar 1977)
Labour	*Ernest Brown* (Nat Lib) (see Baldwin III)
Health	28 May 1937 – 16 May 1938: *Sir Kingsley Wood* (Cons) (see Baldwin III)
	16 May 1938 – 3 Sep 1939: *Walter Elliot Elliot* (Cons) (see Macdonald IV)
Transport	28 May 1937 – 21 Apr 1939: *Edward Leslie Burgin* (Lib) (b. 13 Jul 1887; d. 16 Aug 1945)
	21 Apr – 3 Sep 1939: *David Euan Wallace* (b. 1892; d. 9 Feb 1941)
Air	28 May 1937 – 12 May 1938: *Sir Philip Cunliffe-Lister, 1st Viscount Swinton* (see Macdonald III)
	16 May 1938 – 3 Sep 1939: *Sir Kingsley Wood* (Cons) (see Baldwin III)
Defence	28 May 1937 – 28 Jan 1939: *Sir Thomas Inskip* (Cons) (see Baldwin III)
	28 Jan – 3 Sep 1939: *Alfred Ernle Montacute Chatfield, Baron Chatfield* (b. 27 Sep 1873; d. London 15 Nov 1967)
Supply	Jul – Sep 1939: *Edward Leslie Burgin* (see above)
Without Portfolio	21 Apr – Jul 1939: *Edward Leslie Burgin* (see above)

3 Sep 1939 – 10 May 1940: Chamberlain II (War Cabinet)

Prime Minister	*Neville Chamberlain* (Cons) (for 2nd time) (see Macdonald III)
Foreign Affairs	*Edward Frederick Lindley Wood, 3rd Viscount Halifax* (see Macdonald IV)
Home Affairs	*Sir John Anderson* (see Chamberlain I)
Chancellor of the Exchequer	*Sir John Allsebrook Simon* (Nat Lib) (see Macdonald IV)
War	3 Sep 1939 – 6 Jan 1940: *Leslie Hore-Belisha* (Nat Lib) (see Baldwin III)
	6 Jan – 10 May 1940: *Oliver Stanley* (Cons) (see Macdonald IV)
Lord Privy Seal	3 Sep 1939 – 3 Apr 1940: *Sir Samuel John Gurney Hoare* (Cons) (see Macdonald III)
	3 Apr – 10 May 1940: *Sir Kingsley Wood* (Cons) (see Baldwin III)
First Lord of the Admiralty	*Winston (Leonard Spencer) Churchill* (from 1953: *Sir*) (Cons) (b. Blenheim Palace 30 Nov 1874; d. London 24 Jan 1965)*
Air	3 Sep 1939 – 3 Apr 1940: *Sir Kingsley Wood* (Cons) (see Baldwin III)
	3 Apr – 10 May 1940: *Sir Samuel John Gurney Hoare* (Cons) (see Macdonald III)
Defence	3 Sep 1939 – 3 Apr 1940: *Alfred Ernle Montacute Chatfield, Baron Chatfield* (see Chamberlain I)
Without Portfolio	*Maurice Pascal Alers Hankey, 1st Baron Hankey* (b. 1 Apr 1877; d. 26 Jan 1963)

10 May 1940 – 23 May 1945: Churchill I (War Cabinet)

Prime Minister	*Winston (Leonard Spencer) Churchill* (Cons) (for 1st time) (see Chamberlain II)
Deputy Prime Minister	20 Feb 1942 – 23 May 1945: *Clement Richard Attlee* (Lab) (see Macdonald II)
Foreign Affairs	10 May – 23 Dec 1940: *Edward Frederick Lindley Wood, 3rd Viscount Halifax* (Cons) (see Macdonald IV)
	23 Dec 1940 – 23 May 1945: *Anthony Eden* (Cons) (see Baldwin III)
Home Affairs	3 Oct 1940 (in cabinet from Oct 1942) – 23 May 1945:

*For earlier career see vol. 2

564

	Herbert Stanley Morrison (from 1959: Baron Morrison of Lambeth) (Lab) (b. 3 Jan 1888; d. 6 Mar 1965)
Chancellor of the Exchequer	10 May 1940 – 21 Sep 1943 (in cabinet 3 Oct 1940 – 19 Feb 1942): Sir Kingsley Wood (Cons) (see Baldwin III)
	24 Sep 1943 – 23 May 1945: Sir John Anderson (see Chamberlain I)
Colonies	22 Feb – 22 Nov 1942: Robert Arthur James Gascoyne-Cecil, Viscount Cranborne (from 1947: 5th Marquess of Salisbury) (b. Hatfield House, Hertfordshire, 27 Aug 1893; d. 23 Feb 1972)
	22 Nov 1942 – 23 May 1945: Oliver Stanley (Cons) (see Macdonald IV)
Dominions	20 Feb 1942 – 24 Sep 1943: Clement Richard Attlee (Lab) (see Macdonald II)
Lord President	10 May – 3 Oct 1940: Neville Chamberlain (Cons) (see Macdonald III)
	3 Oct 1940 – 24 Sep 1943: Sir John Anderson (see Chamberlain I)
	24 Sep 1943 – 23 May 1945: Clement Richard Attlee (Lab) (see Macdonald II)
Lord Privy Seal	10 May 1940 – 20 Feb 1942: Clement Richard Attlee (Lab) (see Macdonald II)
	20 Feb – 22 Nov 1942: Sir (Richard) Stafford Cripps (Lab) (b. London 24 Apr 1889; d. Zurich 1952)
India and Burma	Leopold Charles Maurice Stennett Amery (Cons) (b. Gorachpur, India, 22 Nov 1873; d. London 16 Sep 1955)*
Labour and National Service	13 May 1940 (in cabinet from 3 Oct 1940) – 23 May 1945: Ernest L. Bevin (Lab) (b. Winsford, Somerset, 9 Mar 1881; d. London 14 Apr 1951)
Supply	29 Jun 1941 – 4 Feb 1942: Sir William Maxwell Aitken, 1st Baron Beaverbrook (b. Newcastle, New Brunswick, 25 May 1879; d. London 9 Jun 1964)
Defence	Winston (Leonard Spencer) Churchill (Cons) (see Chamberlain II)
Aircraft Production	17 May 1940 – 1 May 1941: Sir William Maxwell Aitken, 1st Baron Beaverbrook (see above) from 1 May to 29 Jun 1941 Minister of State, remaining in the cabinet

*For earlier career see vol. 2

War Production (new post)	4 – 19 Feb 1942: *Sir William Maxwell Aitken, 1st Baron Beaverbrook* (see above)
Reconstruction	11 Nov 1943 – 22 May 1945: *Frederick James Marquis, 1st Baron* (from 1955: *1st Earl*) *Woolton* (b. 24 Aug 1883; d. 14 Dec 1964)
Minister Resident in the Middle East (new post)	1941 – 12 Mar 1942: *Oliver Lyttelton* (from 1954: *Viscount Chandos*) (b. 1893; d. 21 Jan 1972) 19 Mar 1942 – 29 Jan 1944: *Richard Gardiner Casey* (from 1960: *Baron Casey*) (b. Brisbane, Australia, 29 Aug 1890; d. Melbourne 18 Jun 1976) 29 Jan – 6 Nov 1944: *Walter Edward Guinness, 1st Baron Moyne* (b. Dublin 29 Mar 1880; d. Cairo 6 Nov 1944) 21 Nov 1944 – 23 May 1945: *Edward Grigg* (from 1945: *1st Viscount Altrincham*) (b. 8 Sep 1879; d. 1 Dec 1955)
Without Portfolio	11 May 1940 – 22 Feb 1942: *Arthur Greenwood* (Lab) (see Macdonald II)
Ambassador to the United States	23 Dec 1940 – May 1946: *Edward Frederick Lindley Wood, 3rd Viscount* (from 1944: *1st Earl of*) *Halifax* (Cons) (see Macdonald IV)

23 May – 27 Jul 1945: Churchill II (Cons)

Prime Minister	*Winston (Leonard Spencer) Churchill* (for 2nd time) (see Chamberlain II)
Foreign Affairs	*Anthony Eden* (see Baldwin III)
Home Affairs	*Sir Donald Bradley Somervell* (from 1954: *Baron Somervell of Harrow*) (b. 24 Aug 1889; d. London 18 Nov 1960)
Chancellor of the Exchequer	*Sir John Anderson* (see Chamberlain I)
War	*Sir James Grigg* (b. Exmouth 16 Dec 1890; d. London 5 May 1964)
Colonies	*Oliver Stanley* (see Macdonald IV)
Dominions	*Robert Arthur James Gascoyne-Cecil, Viscount Cranborne* (see Churchill I)
Lord President	*Frederick James Marquis, 1st Baron Woolton* (see Churchill I)
Lord Privy Seal	*Sir William Maxwell Aitken, 1st Baron Beaverbrook* (see Churchill I)
First Lord of the Admiralty	*Brendan Bracken* (from 1951: *1st Viscount Bracken*) (b. 1901; d. London 8 Aug 1958)
Trade	*Oliver Lyttelton* (see Churchill I)

India and Burma	*Leopold Charles Maurice Stennett Amery* (see Churchill I)
Secretary of State for Scotland	*Albert Edward Harry Meyer Archibald Primrose, 6th Earl of Rosebery* (b. 8 Jan 1882; d. 31 May 1974)
Agriculture and Fisheries	*Robert Spear Hudson* (from 1952: *1st Viscount Hudson* (b. 15 Dec 1886; d. Rhodesia 2 Feb 1957)
Labour and National Service	*Richard Austen Butler* (from 1965: *Baron Butler of Saffron Walden*) (b. India 9 Dec 1902)
Air	*Harold Macmillan* (b. London 10 Feb 1894)
Defence	*Winston (Leonard Spencer) Churchill* (see Chamberlain II)
Production	*Oliver Lyttelton* (see Churchill I)

27 Jul 1945 – 28 Feb 1950: Attlee I (Lab)

Prime Minister	*Clement Richard Attlee* (for 1st time) (see Macdonald II)
Foreign Minister	*Ernest L. Bevin* (see Churchill I)
Home Affairs	*James Chuter Ede* (from 1964: *J. C. Chuter-Ede, Baron Chuter-Ede*) (b. Epsom 1882; d. 11 Nov 1965)
Chancellor of the Exchequer	27 Jul 1945 – 13 Nov 1947: *Hugh Dalton* (from 1960: *Baron Dalton*) (b. Neath 1887; d. London 13 Feb 1962)
	13 Nov 1947 – 28 Feb 1950: *Sir (Richard) Stafford Cripps* (see Churchill I)
War	27 Jul 1945 – 4 Oct 1946: *John James Lawson* (from 1950: *1st Baron Lawson*) (b. Whitehaven 16 Oct 1881; d. 3 Aug 1965)
Colonies	27 Jul 1945 – 4 Oct 1946: *George Henry Hall* (from 1946: *1st Viscount Hall*) (b. Penrhiwceiber, Glamorgan, Dec 1881; d. 8 Nov 1965)
	4 Oct 1946 – 28 Feb 1950: *Arthur Creech Jones* (b. 1891; d. 23 Oct 1964)
Dominions (from 7 Jul 1947: Commonwealth Relations)	3 Aug 1945 – 7 Oct 1947: *Christopher Addison, 1st Viscount Addison* (see Macdonald II)
	7 Oct 1947 – 28 Feb 1950: *Philip John Noel-Baker* (from 1977: *Baron Noel-Baker*) (b. Nov 1889)
Lord Chancellor	*Sir William Allen Jowitt, 1st Baron* (from 1947: *1st Viscount) Jowitt* (b. Stevenage 15 Apr 1885; d. Suffolk 15 Aug 1957)
Lord President of the Council	*Herbert Stanley Morrison* (see Churchill I)
Lord Privy Seal	27 Jul 1945 – 17 Apr 1947: *Arthur Greenwood* (see Macdonald II)

	17 Apr – 7 Oct 1947: *Philip Albert Inman, 1st Baron Inman* (b. 12 Jun 1892)
	7 Oct 1947 – 28 Feb 1950: *Christopher Addison, 1st Viscount Addison* (see Macdonald II)
First Lord of the Admiralty	27 Jul 1945 – 4 Oct 1946: *Albert Victor Alexander* (see Macdonald II)
Board of Trade	27 Jul 1945 – 29 Sep 1947: *Sir (Richard) Stafford Cripps* (see Churchill I)
	29 Sep 1947 – 28 Feb 1950: *(James) Harold Wilson* (from 1976: *Sir*) (b. Huddersfield 11 Mar 1916)
India and Burma	27 Jul 1945 – 17 Apr 1947: *Frederick William Pethick-Lawrence* (from 1945: *1st Baron Pethick-Lawrence*) (b. 28 Dec 1871; d. 10 Sep 1961)
	17 Apr – 4 Jan 1948: *William Francis Hare, 5th Earl of Listowel* (b. 28 Sep 1906)
	4 Jan 1948: ministry abolished
Duchy of Lancaster	31 May 1948 – 28 Feb 1950: *Hugh Dalton* (see above)
Paymaster General	9 Jul 1946 – 5 Mar 1947: *Arthur Greenwood* (see Macdonald II)
	2 Jul 1948 – 1 Apr 1949: *Christopher Addison, 1st Viscount Addison* (see Macdonald II)
Education	3 Aug 1945 – 6 Feb 1947: *Ellen Wilkinson* (b. Manchester 8 Oct 1891; d. London 6 Feb 1947)
	10 Feb 1947 – 28 Feb 1950: *George Tomlinson* (b. Rishton, Lancashire, 21 Mar 1890; d. 23 Sep 1952)
Secretary of State for Scotland	3 Aug 1945 – 7 Oct 1947: *Joseph Westwood* (b. 11 Feb 1884; d. 17 Jul 1948)
	7 Oct 1947 – 28 Feb 1950: *Arthur Woodburn* (b. Edinburgh 25 Oct 1890)
Agriculture and Fisheries	*Tom Williams* (from 1961: *Baron Williams of Banburgh*) (b. 18 Mar 1888; d. 29/30 Mar 1967)
Labour and National Service	*George Alfred Isaacs* (b. London 1883)
Health	*Aneurin Bevan* (b. Tredegar 15 Nov 1897; d. London 6 Jul 1960)
Air	27 Jul 1945 – 4 Oct 1946: *William Wedgwood Benn, Viscount Stansgate* (see Macdonald II)
Defence	27 Jul 1945 – 20 Dec 1946: *Clement Richard Attlee* (see Macdonald II)
	20 Dec 1946 – 28 Feb 1950: *Albert Victor Alexander* (see Macdonald II)
Economic Affairs (new post)	29 Sep 1947 – 28 Feb 1950: *Sir (Richard) Stafford Cripps* (see Churchill I)

Civil Aviation	31 May 1948 – 28 Feb 1950: *Francis Aungier Pakenham, 1st Baron Pakenham* (from 1961: *7th Earl of Longford*) (b. 5 Dec 1905)
Fuel and Power	3 Aug 1945 – 7 Oct 1947: *Emanuel Shinwell* (from 1970: *Baron Shinwell*) (b. London 18 Oct 1884)
Without Portfolio	4 Oct – 20 Dec 1946: *Albert Victor Alexander* (see Macdonald II)

28 Feb 1950 – 26 Oct 1951: Attlee II (Lab)

Prime Minister	*Clement Richard Attlee* (for 2nd time) (see Macdonald II)
Foreign Affairs	28 Feb 1950 – 9 Mar 1951: *Ernest L. Bevin* (see Churchill I)
	9 Mar – 26 Oct 1951: *Herbert Stanley Morrison* (see Churchill I)
Home Affairs	*James Chuter-Ede* (see Attlee I)
Chancellor of the Exchequer	28 Feb – 19 Oct 1950: *Sir (Richard) Stafford Cripps* (see Churchill I)
	19 Oct 1950 – 26 Oct 1951: *Hugh Gaitskell* (b. London 9 Apr 1906; d. 18 Jan 1963)
Colonies	*James Griffiths* (b. Ammanford 19 Sep 1890; d. 7 Aug 1975)
Commonwealth Relations	*Patrick (Chrestien) Gordon Walker* (from 1974: *Baron Gordon-Walker*) (b. 7 Apr 1907)
Lord Chancellor	*Sir William Allen Jowitt, 1st Viscount Jowitt* (see Attlee I)
Lord President of the Council	28 Feb 1950 – 9 Mar 1951: *Herbert Stanley Morrison* (see Churchill I)
	9 Mar – 26 Oct 1951: *Christopher Addison, 1st Viscount Addison* (see Macdonald II)
Lord Privy Seal	28 Feb 1950 – 9 Mar 1951: *Christopher Addison, 1st Viscount Addison* (see Macdonald II)
	9 Mar – 14 Apr 1951: *Ernest L. Bevin* (see Churchill I)
	26 Apr – 26 Oct 1951: *Richard Stokes* (b. 27 Jan 1897; d. London 3 Aug 1957)
Board of Trade	28 Feb 1950 – 23 Apr 1951: *(James) Harold Wilson* (see Attlee I)
	24 Apr – 26 Oct 1951: *Sir Hartley Shawcross* (from 1959: *Baron Shawcross*) (b. 4 Feb 1902)
Chancellor of the Duchy of Lancaster	*Albert Victor Alexander* (from 1950: *Viscount Alexander of Hillsborough*) (see Macdonald II)

Education	*George Tomlinson* (see Attlee I)
Secretary of State for Scotland	*Hector MacNeil* (b. 10 Mar 1910; d. New York 11 Oct 1955)
Agriculture and Fisheries	*Tom Williams* (see Attlee I)
Labour and national Service	28 Feb 1950 – 17 Jan 1951: *George Alfred Isaacs* (see Attlee I) 17 Jan – 24 Apr 1951: *Aneurin Bevan* (see Attlee I) 24 Apr – 26 Oct 1951: *Alfred Robens* (from 1961: *Baron Robens of Woldingham*) (b. 18 Dec 1910)
Health	28 Feb 1950 – 17 Jan 1951: *Aneurin Bevan* (see Attlee I)
Defence	*Emanuel Shinwell* (see Attlee I)
Town and Country Planning (from 31 Jan 1951: Local Government and Planning)	*Hugh Dalton* (see Attlee I)

26/27 Oct 1951 – 9 Jan 1957: Churchill III/Eden (Cons)

Prime Minister	26 Oct 1951 – 5 Apr 1955: *Winston (Leonard Spencer) Churchill* (from 1953: *Sir*) (for 3rd time) (see Chamberlain II) 6 Apr 1955 – 9 Jan 1957: *Sir Anthony Eden* (see Baldwin III)
Foreign Affairs	26 Oct 1951 – 7 Apr 1955: *Anthony Eden* (from 1954: *Sir*) (see Baldwin III) 7 Apr – 20 Dec 1955: *Harold Macmillan* (see Churchill II) 20 Dec 1955 – 9 Jan 1957: *(John) Selwyn (Brooke) Lloyd* (from 1976: *J. S. B. Selwyn-Lloyd, Baron Selwyn-Lloyd*) (b. Liverpool 28 Jul 1904)
Home and Welsh Affairs	27 Oct 1951 – 18 Oct 1954: *Sir David Maxwell-Fyfe* (from 1954: *1st Viscount Kilmuir*) (b. 29 May 1900; d. Withyham 27 Jan 1967) 18 Oct 1954 – 9 Jan 1957: *Gwilym Lloyd George* (from 1957: *1st Viscount Tenby*) (b. Criccieth 4 Dec 1894; d. London 14 Feb 1967)
Chancellor of the Exchequer	27 Oct 1951 – 20 Dec 1955: *Richard Austen Butler* (see Churchill II) 20 Dec 1955 – 7 Jan 1957: *Harold Macmillan* (see Churchill II)

Colonies	27 Oct 1951 – 28 Jul 1954: *Oliver Lyttelton* (see Churchill I) 28 Jul 1954 – 9 Jan 1957: *Alan (Tindal) Lennox-Boyd* (from 1960: *1st Viscount Boyd of Merton*) (b. 18 Nov 1904)
Commonwealth Relations	27 Oct 1951 – 12 Mar 1952: *Hastings Lionel Ismay, 1st Baron Ismay* (b. Uttar Pradesh 21 Jun 1887; d. Broadway, Worcestershire, 17 Dec 1965) 12 Mar – 24 Nov 1952: *Robert Arthur James Gascoyne-Cecil, 5th Marquess of Salisbury* (see Churchill I) 24 Nov 1952 – 5 Apr 1955: *Sir Philip Cunliffe-Lister, 1st Viscount Swinton* (see Macdonald III) 5 Apr 1955 – 9 Jan 1957: *Alexander Frederick Douglas-Home* (until 23 Oct 1963: *14th Earl of Home*) (from 1962: *Sir*; from 19 Dec 1974: *Baron Home of the Hirsel*) (b. London 2 Jul 1903)
Lord Chancellor	27 Oct 1951 – 18 Oct 1954: *Gavin Turnbull Simonds, 1st Baron Simonds* (b. 28 Nov 1881; d. London 28 Jun 1971) 18 Oct 1954 – 9 Jan 1957: *Sir David Maxwell-Fyfe, 1st Viscount Kilmuir* (see above)
Lord President of the Council	27 Oct 1951 – 24 Nov 1952: *Frederick James Marquis, 1st Baron Woolton* (see Churchill I) 24 Nov 1952 – 9 Jan 1957: *Robert Arthur James Gascoyne-Cecil, 5th Marquess of Salisbury* (see Churchill I)
Lord Privy Seal	27 Oct 1951 – 7 May 1952: *Robert Arthur James Gascoyne-Cecil, 5th Marquess of Salisbury* (see Churchill I) 7 May 1952 – 20 Dec 1955: *Henry Frederick Comfort Crookshank* (b. 27 May 1893) 20 Dec 1955 – 7 Jan 1957: *Richard Austen Butler* (see Churchill II)
Board of Trade	*Peter Thorneycroft* (from 1967: *Baron Thorneycroft*) (b. 26 Jul 1909)
Chancellor of the Duchy of Lancaster	24 Nov 1952 – 20 Dec 1955: *Frederick James Marquis, 1st Baron Woolton* (see Churchill I) 20 Dec 1955 – 9 Jan 1957: *George Nigel Douglas-Hamilton, 10th Earl of Selkirk* (b. Wimborne 4 Jan 1906)
Paymaster General	27 Oct 1951 – 30 Oct 1953: *Frederick Alexander Lindemann, 1st Baron* (from 1956: *1st Viscount*)

	Cherwell (b. Berlin 1886; d. Oxford 3 Jul 1957)
	18 Oct 1956 – 7 Jan 1957: *Sir Walter Monckton* (from 1957: *1st Viscount Monckton of Brenchley*) (b. Plaxtol 17 Jan 1891; d. 9 Jan 1965)
Education	31 Oct 1951 (in cabinet from 3 Sep 1953) – 18 Oct 1954: *Florence Horsbrugh* (from 1959: *Baroness Horsbrugh*) (b. 1889; d. Edinburgh Dec 1969)
	18 Oct 1954 – 9 Jan 1957: *Sir David Eccles* (from 1962: *1st Baron Eccles*; from 1964: *1st Viscount Eccles*) (b. 18 Sep 1904)
Secretary of State for Scotland	30 Oct 1951 – 9 Jan 1957: *James Stuart* (from 1959: *1st Viscount Stuart of Findhorn*) (b. 9 Feb 1897; d. 1971)
Public Works	20 Dec 1955 – 7 Jan 1957: *Patrick George Thomas Buchan-Hepburn* (from 1957: *1st Baron Hailes*) (b. 2 Apr 1901; d. 5 Nov 1974)
Agriculture and Fisheries	27 Oct 1951 (in cabinet from 3 Sep 1953) 20 Jul 1954: *Sir Thomas Dugdale, bart* (from 1959: *1st Baron Crathorne*) (b. 20 Jul 1897; d. 26 Mar 1977)
	28 Jul 1954 – 9 Jan 1957: *Derick Heathcoat Amory* (from 1960: *1st Viscount Amory*) (b. 26 Dec 1899)
Food	31 Oct 1951 (in cabinet from 3 Sep 1953) – 18 Oct 1954: *Gwilym Lloyd George* (see above)
	18 Oct 1954: combined with Agriculture and Fisheries (see above)
Labour and National Service	27 Oct 1951 – 20 Dec 1955: *Sir Walter Monckton* (see above)
	20 Dec 1955 – 7 Jan 1957: *Iain (Norman) Macleod* (b. Skipton 11 Nov 1913; d. 20 Jul 1970)
Health	30 Oct 1951 – 7 May 1952: *Henry Frederick Comfort Crookshank* (see above)
Defence	27 Oct 1951 – 1 Mar 1952: *Winston (Leonard Spencer) Churchill* (see Chamberlain II)
	1 Mar 1952 – 18 Oct 1954: *Harold (Rupert Leofric George) Alexander, 1st Earl Alexander of Tunis* (b. Ireland 10 Dec 1891; d. London 16 Jun 1969)
	18 Oct 1954 – 7 Apr 1955: *Harold Macmillan* (see Churchill II)
	7 Apr – 20 Dec 1955: *(John) Selwyn (Brooke) Lloyd* (see above)
	20 Dec 1955 – 18 Oct 1956: *Sir Walter Monckton* (see above)
	18 Oct 1956 – 7 Jan 1957: *Anthony Henry Head* (from 1960: *1st Viscount Head*) (b. 19 Dec 1906)

Housing and Local Government	30 Oct 1951 – 18 Oct 1954: *Harold Macmillan* (see Churchill II)
	18 Oct 1954 – 9 Jan 1957: *Duncan Edwin Sandys* (from 1974: *D. E. Duncan-Sandys, Baron Duncan-Sandys*) (b. 24 Jan 1908)
Pensions and National Insurance	3 Sep 1953 (in cabinet from 18 Oct 1954) – 20 Dec 1955: *Osbert Peake* (from 1955: *1st Viscount Ingleby*) (b. 30 Dec 1897; d. 11 Oct 1966)
Co-ordination of Transport, Fuel and Power	30 Oct 1951 – 3 Sep 1953: *Frederick James Leathers, 1st Baron Leathers* (b. London 21 Nov 1883; d. London 19 Mar 1965)
	3 Sep 1953: ministry abolished

10/13 Jan 1957 – 18 Oct 1963: Macmillan (Cons)

Prime Minister	*Harold Macmillan* (see Churchill II)
First Secretary of State (with special responsibility for Africa and the European Economic Community)	13 Jul 1962 – 18 Oct 1963: *Richard Austen Butler* (see Churchill II)
Foreign Affairs	13 Jan 1957 – 27 Jul 1960: *(John) Selwyn (Brooke) Lloyd* (see Churchill III/Eden)
	27 Jul 1960 – 18 Oct 1963: *Alexander Frederick Douglas-Home, 14th Earl of Home* (see Churchill III/Eden)
Home Affairs	13 Jan 1957 – 13 Jul 1962: *Richard Austen Butler* (see Churchill II)
	13 Jul 1962 – 18 Oct 1963: *Henry Brooke* (from 1966: *Baron Brooke of Cumnor*) (b. 9 Apr 1903)
Chancellor of the Exchequer	13 Jan 1957 – 6 Jan 1958: *Peter Thorneycroft* (see Churchill III/Eden)
	6 Jan 1958 – 27 Jul 1960: *Derick Heathcoat Amory* (see Churchill III/Eden)
	27 Jul 1960 – 13 Jul 1962: *(John) Selwyn (Brooke) Lloyd* (see Churchill III/Eden)
	13 Jul 1962 – 18 Oct 1963: *Reginald Maudling* (b. 7 Mar 1917)
Colonies	13 Jan 1957 – 14 Oct 1959: *Alan (Tindal) Lennox-Boyd* (see Churchill III/Eden)

573

14 Oct 1959 – 9 Oct 1961: *Iain (Norman) Macleod* (see Churchill III/ Eden)

9 Oct 1961 – 13 Jul 1962: *Reginald Maudling* (see above)

13 Jul 1962 – 18 Oct 1963: *Duncan Edwin Sandys* (see Churchill III/ Eden)

Commonwealth Relations

13 Jan 1957 – 27 Jul 1960: *Alexander Frederick Douglas-Home, 14th Earl of Home* (see Churchill III/ Eden)

27 Jul 1960 – 18 Oct 1963: *Duncan Edwin Sandys* (see Churchill III/ Eden)

Lord Chancellor

14 Jan 1957 – 13 Jul 1962: *Sir David Maxwell-Fyfe, 1st Viscount Kilmuir* (see Churchill III/ Eden)

13 Jul 1962 – 18 Oct 1963: *Sir Reginald Edward Manningham-Buller, bart, 1st Baron* (from 1964: *1st Viscount*) *Dilhorne* (b. 1 Aug 1905)

Lord President of the Council

13 Jan – 29 Mar 1957: *Robert Arthur James Gascoyne-Cecil, 5th Marquess of Salisbury* (see Churchill I)

29 Mar – 17 Sep 1957: *Alexander Frederick Douglas-Home, 14th Earl of Home* (see Churchill III/ Eden)

17 Sep 1957 – 14 Oct 1959: *Quintin McGarel Hogg* (until 20 Nov 1963: *2nd Viscount Hailsham*; from 1970: *Baron Hailsham of St Marylebone*) (b. London 9 Oct 1907)

14 Oct 1959 – 27 Jul 1960: *Alexander Frederick Douglas-Home, 14th Earl of Home* (see Churchill III/ Eden)

27 Jul 1960 – 18 Oct 1963: *Quintin McGarel Hogg, 2nd Viscount Hailsham* (see above)

Lord Privy Seal

13 Jan 1957 – Oct 1959: *Richard Austen Butler* (see Churchill II)

14 Oct 1959 – 27 Jul 1960: *Quintin McGarel Hogg, 2nd Viscount Hailsham* (see above)

27 Jul 1960 – 18 Oct 1963: *Edward (Richard George) Heath* (b. Broadstairs, Kent, 9 Jul 1916)

Board of Trade

13 Jan 1957 – 14 Oct 1959: *Sir David Eccles* (see Churchill III/ Eden)

14 Oct 1959 – 9 Oct 1961: *Reginald Maudling* (see above)

9 Oct 1961 – 18 Oct 1963: *Frederick James Erroll* (from 1964: *1st Baron Erroll of Hale*) (b. 27 May 1914)

Chancellor of the Duchy of Lancaster	13 Jan 1957 – 9 Oct 1961: *Charles Hill* (from 1963: *Baron Hill of Luton*) (b. 15 Jan 1904) 9 Oct 1961 – 18 Oct 1963: *Iain (Norman) Macleod* (see Churchill III/Eden)
Chief Secretary to the Treasury (from 9 Oct 1961: and Pay-master General)	16 Jan (in cabinet from 17 Sep) 1957 – 14 Oct 1959: *Reginald Maudling* (see above) 14 Oct 1959 – 9 Oct 1961: *Sir Percy Herbert Mills, 1st Baron* (from 1962: *1st Viscount*) *Mills* (b. 4 Jan 1890; d. London 10 Sep 1968) 9 Oct 1961 – 13 Jul 1962: *Henry Brooke* (see above) 13 Jul 1962 – 18 Oct 1963: *John Archibald Boyd-Carpenter* (from 1972: *Baron Boyd-Carpenter*) (b. 2 Jun 1908)
Education	13 Jan – 16 Sep 1957: *Quintin McGarel Hogg, 2nd Viscount Hailsham* (see above) 16 Sep 1957 – 14 Oct 1959: *Geoffrey William Lloyd* (from 1974: *Baron Geoffrey-Lloyd*) (b. 17 Jan 1902) 14 Oct 1959 – 13 Jul 1962: *Sir David Eccles* (see Churchill III/Eden) 13 Jul 1962 – 18 Oct 1963: *Sir Edward Boyle, bart* (from 1970: *Baron Boyle of Handsworth*) (b. 31 Aug 1923)
Secretary of State for Scotland	13 Jan 1957 – 13 Jul 1962: *John Scott Maclay* (from 1964: *1st Viscount Muirshiel*) (b. 26 Oct 1905) 13 Jul 1962 – 18 Oct 1963: *(Michael) Antony (Cristobal) Nobel* (from 1974: *Baron Glenkinglas*) (b. 19 Mar 1913)
Agriculture, Fisheries and Food	13 Jan 1957 – 6 Jan 1958: *Derick Heathcoat Amory* (see Churchill III/Eden) 6 Jan 1958 – 27 Jul 1960: *John Hare* (from Oct 1963: *1st Viscount Blakenham*) (b. London 22 Jan 1911) 27 Jul 1960 – 18 Oct 1963: *Christopher Soames* (from 1972: *Sir*) (b. 12 Oct 1920)
Labour and National Service (from 12 Jan 1959: Labour)	13 Jan 1957 – 14 Oct 1959: *Iain (Norman) Macleod* (see Churchill III/Eden) 14 Oct 1959 – 27 Jul 1960: *Edward (Richard George) Heath* (see above) 27 Jul 1960 – 18 Oct 1963: *John Hare* (see above)
Health	22 Jul 1960 (in cabinet from 13 Jul 1962) – 18 Oct 1963: *Enoch Powell* (b. 16 Jun 1912)

Transport and Civil Aviation	13 Jan 1957 – 14 Oct 1959: *Harold Arthur Watkinson* (from 1964: *1st Viscount Watkinson*) (b. 25 Jan 1910)
	14 Oct 1959: divided into two separate ministries, Aviation and Transport (see below)
Aviation	14 Oct 1959 – 27 Jul 1960: *Duncan Edwin Sandys* (see Churchill III/Eden)
	27 Jul 1960 – 13 Jul 1962: *Peter Thorneycroft* (see Churchill III/Eden)
	16 Jul 1962 – 18 Oct 1963: *Julian Amery* (b. 27 Mar 1919)
Transport	14 Oct 1959 – 18 Oct 1963: *Ernest Marples* (from 1974: *Baron Marples*) (b. 9 Dec 1907)
Defence	13 Jan 1957 – 14 Oct 1959: *Duncan Edwin Sandys* (see Churchill III/Eden)
	14 Oct 1959 – 13 Jul 1962: *Harold Arthur Watkinson* (see above)
	13 Jul 1962 – 18 Oct 1963: *Peter Thorneycroft* (see Churchill III/Eden)
Power (new post)	13 Jan 1957 – 22 Oct 1959: *Percy Herbert Mills, 1st Baron Mills* (see above)
Housing and Local Government and Welsh Affairs	13 Jan 1957 – 9 Oct 1961: *Henry Brooke* (see above)
	9 Oct 1961 – 13 Jul 1962: *Charles Hill* (see above)
	13 Jul 1962 – 18 Oct 1963: *Sir Keith (Sinjohn) Joseph, bart* (b. 17 Jan 1918)
Science	14 Oct 1959 – 18 Oct 1963: *Quintin McGarel Hogg, 2nd Viscount Hailsham* (see above)
Without Portfolio	9 Oct 1961 – 13 Jul 1962: *Percy Herbert Mills, 1st Baron Mills* (see above)
	13 Jul 1962 – 18 Oct 1963: *William Francis Deedes* (b. 1 Jun 1913)

18/20 Oct 1963 – 16 Oct 1964: Douglas-Home (Cons)

Prime Minister	*Sir Alexander Frederick Douglas-Home* (see Churchill III/Eden)
Foreign Affairs	*Richard Austen Butler* (see Churchill II)
Home Affairs	*Henry Brooke* (see Macmillan)
Housing and Local Government	*Sir Keith (Sinjohn) Joseph, bart* (see Macmillan)
Chancellor of the Exchequer	*Reginald Maudling* (see Macmillan)

Defence	*Peter Thorneycroft* (see Churchill III/Eden)
Civil Aviation	*Julian Amery* (see Macmillan)
Transport	*Ernest Marples* (see Macmillan)
Power	*Frederick James Erroll* (see Macmillan)
Industry, Trade and Regional Development (new post)	*Edward (Richard George) Heath* (see Macmillan)
Colonies	*Duncan Edwin Sandys* (see Churchill III/Eden)
Commonwealth Relations	*Duncan Edwin Sandys* (see Churchill III/Eden)
Lord President of the Council	*Quintin McGarel Hogg* (see Macmillan)
Lord Privy Seal	*(John) Selwyn (Brooke) Lloyd* (see Churchill III/Eden)
Lord Chancellor	*Sir Reginald Edward Manningham-Buller, 1st Baron Dilhorne* (see Macmillan)
Education (from 1 Apr 1964: and Science)	18/20 Oct 1963 – 1 Apr 1964: *Sir Edward Boyle, bart* (see Macmillan)
	1 Apr – 16 Oct 1964: *Quintin McGarel Hogg* (see Macmillan)
Health	*Anthony Perrinott Lysberg Barber* (from 1974: *Baron Barber*) (b. 4 Jul 1920)
Board of Trade	*Edward (Richard George) Heath* (see Macmillan)
Chief Secretary to the Treasury and Paymaster General	*John Archibald Boyd-Carpenter* (see Macmillan)
Labour and National Service	*Joseph Bradshaw Godber* (b. 17 Mar 1914; d. 10 Apr 1976)
Public Works	*(Aubrey) Geoffrey (Frederick) Rippon* (b. May 1924)
Agriculture, Fisheries and Food	*Christopher Soames* (see Macmillan)
Secretary of State for Scotland	*(Michael) Antony (Cristobal) Noble* (see Macmillan)
Chancellor of the Duchy of Lancaster	*John Hare, 1st Viscount Blakenham* (see Macmillan)
Without Portfolio	*William Francis Deedes* (see Macmillan)
	Peter Alexander Rupert Carrington, 6th Baron Carrington (b. 6 Jun 1919)

16/17 Oct 1964 – 19 Jun 1970: Wilson I (Lab)

Prime Minister	*(James) Harold Wilson* (for 1st time) (see Attlee I)
First Secretary of	17 Oct 1964 – 10 Aug 1966: *George Alfred Brown*
State (Deputy	(from Aug 1970: *G. A. George-Brown, Baron George-*
Prime Minister)	*Brown*) (b. London 2 Sep 1914)
	10 Aug 1966 – 18 Mar 1968: *Michael Stewart* (b. 6 Nov 1906)
	6 Apr 1968 – 19 Jun 1970: *Barbara Anne Castle* (b. Chesterfield 6 Oct 1911)
Foreign (from 17	17 Oct 1964 – 22 Jan 1965: *Patrick (Chrestien)*
Oct 1968: and	*Gordon Walker* (see Attlee II)
Commonwealth)	23 Jan 1965 – 11 Aug 1966: *Michael Stewart* (see
Affairs	above)
	11 Aug 1966 – 16 Mar 1968: *George Alfred Brown* (see above)
	16 Mar 1968 – 19 Jun 1970: *Michael Stewart* (see above)
Home Affairs	17 Oct 1964 – 23 Dec 1965: *Sir Frank Soskice* (from 1966: *Baron Stow Hill*) (b. 23 Jul 1912)
	23 Dec 1965 – 30 Nov 1967: *Roy Harris Jenkins* (b. 11 Nov 1920)
	30 Nov 1967 – 19 Jun 1970: *(Leonard) James Callaghan* (b. Portsmouth 27 Mar 1912)
Chancellor of the	17 Oct 1964 – 30 Nov 1967: *(Leonard) James*
Exchequer	*Callaghan* (see above)
	30 Nov 1967 – 19 Jun 1970: *Roy Harris Jenkins* (see above)
Colonies	18 Oct 1964 – 22 Dec 1965: *Anthony (Arthur) Greenwood* (from Aug 1970: *Baron Greenwood of Rossendale*) (b. Leeds 14 Sep 1911)
	23 Dec 1965 – 5 Apr 1966: *Francis Aungier Pakenham, 7th Earl of Longford* (see Attlee I)
	6 Apr 1966 – 6 Jan 1967: *Frederick Lee* (from 1974: *Baron Lee of Newton*) (b. 3 Aug 1906)
	1 Jul 1966 – 6 Jan 1967: ministry subordinate to Commonwealth Affairs
	7 Jan 1967: ministry amalgamated with Commonwealth Affairs (see below)
Commonwealth	17 Oct 1964 – 11 Aug 1966: *Arthur George*
Relations	*Bottomley* (b. Walthamstow 7 Feb 1907)
(from 1 Aug	11 Aug 1966 – 29 Aug 1967: *Herbert William Bowden*

1966: Com- monwealth Affairs)	(b. 20 Jan 1905) 29 Aug 1967 – 17 Oct 1968: *George Morgan Thomson* (from 25 Mar 1977: *Baron Thomson of Monifieth*) (b. 16 Jan 1921) 17 Oct 1968: ministry amalgamated with Foreign Affairs (see above)
Lord Chancellor	*Gerald Austin Gardiner, Baron Gardiner* (b. 30 May 1900)
Lord President of the Council	17 Oct 1964 – 5 Apr 1966: *Herbert William Bowden* (see above) 6 Apr 1966 – 1 Nov 1968: *Richard Howard Stafford Crossman* (b. London 15 Feb 1907; d. 5 Apr 1974) 1 Nov 1968 – 19 Jun 1970: *(Thomas) Frederick Peart* (from 1976: *Baron Peart*) (b. 30 Apr 1914)
Lord Privy Seal	18 Oct 1964 – 23 Dec 1965: *Francis Aungier Pakenham, 7th Earl of Longford* (see Attlee I) 23 Dec 1965 – 6 Apr 1966: *Sir Frank Soskice* (see above) 6 Apr 1966 – Jan 1968: *Francis Aungier Pakenham, 7th Earl of Longford* (see Attlee I) Jan – Apr 1968: *Edward Arthur Alexander Shackleton, Baron Shackleton* (b. 15 Jul 1911) Apr – 1 Nov 1968: *(Thomas) Frederick Peart* (see above) 1 Nov 1968 – 19 Jun 1970: *Edward Arthur Alexander Shackleton, Baron Shackleton* (see above)
Board of Trade	17 Oct 1964 – 29 Aug 1967: *Douglas Patrick Thomas Jay* (b. 23 Mar 1907) 29 Aug 1967 – 6 Oct 1969: *(Charles) Anthony Raven Crosland* (b. St Leonards-on-Sea 29 Aug 1918; d. 19 Feb 1977) 6 Oct 1969 – 19 Jun 1970: *Roy Mason* (b. Barnsley 18 Apr 1924)
Chancellor of the Duchy of Lancaster	17 Oct 1964 – 5 Apr 1966: *(Arthur Leslie Noel) Douglas Houghton* (from 1974: *Baron Houghton of Sowerby*) (b. 11 Aug 1898) 6 Oct 1969 – 19 Jun 1970: *George Morgan Thomson* (see above)
Paymaster General	6 Apr – 1 Nov 1968: *Edward Arthur Alexander Shackleton, Baron Shackleton* (see above) 1 Nov 1968 – 6 Oct 1969: *Constance Mary Judith Hart* (b. 1924)

579

	6 Oct 1969 – 19 Jun 1970: *Harold Lever* (b. Manchester 15 Jan 1914)
Education and Science	17 Oct 1964 – 23 Jan 1965: *Michael Stewart* (see above)
	23 Jan 1965 – 29 Aug 1967: *(Charles) Anthony Raven Crosland* (see above)
	29 Aug 1967 – 6 Apr 1968: *Patrick (Chrestien) Gordon Walker* (see Attlee II)
	6 Apr 1968 – 19 Jun 1970: *Edward Watson Short* (from 1977: *Baron Short*) (b. 17 Dec 1912)
Secretary of State for Scotland	*William Ross* (b. 7 Apr 1911)
Agriculture, Fisheries and Food	17 Oct 1964 – 6 Apr 1968: *(Thomas) Frederick Peart* (see above)
	6 Apr 1968 – 19 Jun 1970: *Cledwyn Hughes* (b. 14 Sep 1916)
Labour (from 6 Apr 1968: Employment and Productivity)	17 Oct 1964 – 6 Apr 1968: *Raymond Jones Gunter* (b. Abertillery 30 Aug 1909; d. Scilly Isles 12 Apr 1977)
	6 Apr 1968 – 19 Jun 1970: *Barbara Anne Castle* (see above)
Health and Social Security	1 Nov 1968 – 19 Jun 1970: *Richard Howard Stafford Crossman* (see above)
Transport	17 Oct 1964 – 23 Dec 1965: *Thomas Fraser* (b. 18 Feb 1911)
	23 Dec 1965 – 5 Apr 1968: *Barbara Anne Castle* (see above)
	6 Apr 1968 – 5 Oct 1969: *Richard William Marsh* (from 1976: *Sir*) (b. 14 Mar 1928)
Defence	*Denis Winston Healey* (b. Keighley 30 Aug 1917)
Economic Affairs	6 Apr – 10 Aug 1966: *George Alfred Brown* (see above)
	10 Aug 1966 – 29 Aug 1967: *Michael Stewart* (see above)
	29 Aug 1967 – 6 Oct 1969: *Peter David Shore* (b. 20 May 1924)
	6 Oct 1969: ministry abolished
Power	17 Oct 1964 – 5 Apr 1966: *Frederick Lee* (see above)
	6 Apr 1966 – 6 Apr 1968: *Richard William Marsh* (see above)
	6 Apr – 29 Jun 1968: *Raymond Jones Gunter* (see above)
	1 Jul 1968 – 6 Oct 1969: *Roy Mason* (see above)
Housing and Local	17 Oct 1964 – 11 Aug 1966: *Richard Howard Stafford*

Government	*Crossman* (see above) 11 Aug 1966 – 5 Oct 1969: *Anthony (Arthur) Green- wood* (see above) 6 Oct 1969: ministry divided into Housing (non- cabinet office) and Local Government and Regional Planning (see below)
Local Government and Regional Planning	6 Oct 1969 – 19 Jun 1970: *(Charles) Anthony Raven Crosland* (see above)
Overseas Development	17 Oct 1964 – 23 Dec 1965: *Barbara Anne Castle* (see above) 23 Dec 1965 – 10 Aug 1966: *Anthony (Arthur) Green- wood* (see above) 10 Aug 1966 – 29 Aug 1967 (from 6 Jan 1967 not in cabinet:) *Arthur George Bottomley* (see above)
Technology (new post)	17 Oct 1964 – 4 Jul 1966: *Frank Cousins* (b. Bulwell 8 Sep 1904) 4 Jul 1966 – 19 Jun 1970: *Anthony (Neil) Wedgwood Benn* (b. 3 Apr 1925)
Secretary of State for Wales (new post)	17 Oct 1964 – 5 Apr 1966: *James Griffiths* (see Attlee II) 6 Apr 1966 – 5 Apr 1968: *Cledwyn Hughes* (see above) 6 Apr 1968 – 19 Jun 1970: *(Thomas) George Thomas* (b. 1909)
Chief Secretary to the Treasury (new post)	from 1 Nov 1968 in cabinet: *John Diamond* (from 1970: *Baron Diamond*) (b. Leeds 30 Apr 1907)
Without Portfolio	6 Apr 1966 – 6 Jan 1967: *(Arthur Leslie Noel) Douglas Houghton* (see above) 6 Jan – 29 Aug 1967: *Patrick (Chrestien) Gordon Walker* (see above) 17 Oct 1968 – 5 Oct 1969: *George Morgan Thomson* (see above) 5 Oct 1969 – 19 Jun 1970: *Peter David Shore* (see above)

19 Jun 1970 – 4 Mar 1974: Heath (Cons)

Prime Minister	*Edward (Richard George) Heath* (see Macmillan)
Foreign and Com- monwealth Affairs	*Sir Alexander Frederick Douglas-Home* (see Churchill III/Eden)

Home Affairs	20 Jun 1970 – 17 Jul 1972: *Reginald Maudling* (see Macmillan) 18 Jul 1972 – 4 Mar 1974: *(Leonard) Robert Carr* (from 18 Dec 1975: *Baron Carr of Hadley*) (b. 11 Nov 1916)
Chancellor of the Exchequer	20 Jun – 20 Jul 1970: *Iain (Norman) Macleod* (see Churchill III/Eden) 25 Jul 1970 – 4 Mar 1974: *Anthony Perrinott Lysberg Barber* (see Douglas-Home)
Lord Chancellor	*Quintin McGarel Hogg, Baron Hailsham of St Marylebone* (see Macmillan)
Lord President of the Council	20 Jun 1970 – 29 Mar 1972: *William (Stephen Ian) Whitelaw* (b. 28 Jun 1918) 7 Apr – 4 Nov 1972: *(Leonard) Robert Carr* (see above) 5 Nov 1972 – 4 Mar 1974: *James Michael Leathes Prior* (b. 11 Oct 1927)
Lord Privy Seal	20 Jun 1970 – 4 Jun 1973: *George Patrick John Rushworth Jellicoe, 2nd Earl Jellicoe* (b. 4 Apr 1918) 5 Jun 1973 – 4 Mar 1974: *David James George Hennessy, 3rd Baron Windlesham* (b. 28 Jan 1932)
Board of Trade (from 15 Oct 1970: Trade and Industry)	20 Jun – 15 Oct 1970: *(Michael) Antony (Cristobal) Noble* (see Macmillan) 15 Oct 1970 – 4 Nov 1972: *John (Emerson Harding) Davies* (b. London 8 Jan 1916) 5 Nov 1972 – 4 Mar 1974: *Peter Edward Walker* (b. 25 Mar 1932)
Trade and Consumer Affairs	5 Nov 1972 – 4 Mar 1974: *Sir (Richard Edward) Geoffrey Howe* (b. 20 Dec 1926)
Chancellor of the Duchy of Lancaster	20 Jun – 27 Jul 1970: *Anthony Perrinott Lysberg Barber* (see Douglas-Home) 28 Jul 1970 – 4 Nov 1972: *(Aubrey) Geoffrey (Frederick) Rippon* (see Douglas-Home) 5 Nov 1972 – 4 Mar 1974: *John (Emerson Harding) Davies* (see above)
Paymaster General	2 Dec 1973 – 4 Mar 1974: *Maurice Victor Macmillan* (b. 27 Jan 1921)
Education	*Margaret (Hilda) Thatcher* (b. 13 Oct 1925)
Secretary of State for Scotland	*Graham Gordon Campbell* (from 1975: *Baron Campbell of Croy*) (b. 8 Jun 1921)
Agriculture, Fisheries and Food	20 Jun 1970 – 4 Nov 1972: *James Michael Leathes Prior* (see above)

	5 Nov 1972 – 4 Mar 1974: *Joseph Bradshaw Godber* (see Douglas-Home)
Employment and Productivity	20 Jun 1970 – 6 Apr 1972: *(Leonard) Robert Carr* (see above) 7 Apr – 1 Dec 1973: *Maurice Victor Macmillan* (see above) 2 Dec 1973 – 4 Mar 1974: *William (Stephen Ian) Whitelaw* (see above)
Health and Social Security	*Sir Keith (Sinjohn) Joseph, bart* (see Macmillan)
Defence	20 Jun 1970 – 7 Jan 1974: *Peter Alexander Rupert Carrington, 6th Baron Carrington* (see Douglas-Home) 8 Jan – 4 Mar 1974: *Ian (Hedworth John Little) Gilmour* (b. 8 Jul 1926)
Energy	8 Jan – 4 Mar 1974: *Peter Alexander Rupert Carrington, 6th Baron Carrington* (see Douglas-Home)
Housing and Local Government	20 Jun – 14 Oct 1970: *Peter Edward Walker* (see above) 15 Oct 1970: ministry absorbed in Department of the Environment (see below)
Technology	20 Jun – 29 Jul 1970: *(Aubrey) Geoffrey (Frederick) Rippon* (see Douglas-Home) 29 Jul – 15 Oct 1970: *John (Emerson Harding) Davies* (see above) 15 Oct 1970: ministry absorbed in Department of the Environment (see below)
Secretary of State for Wales	*Peter John Mitchell Thomas* (b. 31 Jul 1920)
Environment (Housing and Local Government, Transport, and Public Buildings and Works)	15 Oct 1970 – 4 Nov 1972: *Peter Edward Walker* (see above) 5 Nov 1972 – 4 Mar 1974: *(Aubrey) Geoffrey (Frederick) Rippon* (see Douglas-Home)
Secretary of State for Northern Ireland (new post)	24 Apr 1972 – 1 Dec 1973: *William (Stephen Ian) Whitelaw* (see above) 2 Dec 1973 – 4 Mar 1974: *Francis Leslie Pym* (b. 13 Feb 1922)

from 4 Mar 1974: Wilson II (Lab)

Prime Minister	*(James) Harold Wilson* (for 2nd time) (see Attlee I)
Foreign and Commonwealth Affairs	*(Leonard) James Callaghan* (see Wilson I)
Home Affairs	*Roy Harris Jenkins* (see Wilson I)
Chancellor of the Exchequer	*Denis Winston Healey* (see Wilson I)
Lord Chancellor	*Frederick Elwyn Elwyn-Jones, Baron Elwyn-Jones* (b. 24 Oct 1909)
Lord President of the Council	*Edward Watson Short* (see Wilson I)
Lord Privy Seal	*Malcolm Newton Shepherd, 2nd Baron Shepherd* (b. 27 Sep 1918)
Trade	*Peter David Shore* (see Wilson I)
Industry	5 Mar 1974 – 10 Jun 1975: *Anthony (Neil) Wedgwood Benn* (see Wilson I)
	from 10 Jun 1975: *Eric Graham Varley* (b. 11 Aug 1932)
Chancellor of the Duchy of Lancaster	*Harold Lever* (b. Manchester 15 Jan 1914)
Education and Science	5 Mar 1974 – 10 Jun 1975: *Reginald Ernest Prentice* (b. 16 Jul 1923)
	from 10 Jun 1975: *Frederick William Mulley* (b. 3 Jul 1918)
Secretary of State for Scotland	*William Ross* (b. 7 Apr 1911)
Agriculture, Fisheries and Food	*(Thomas) Frederick Peart* (see Wilson I)
Employment	*Michael Foot* (b. 23 Jul 1913)
Health and Social Security	*Barbara Anne Castle* (see Wilson I)
Defence	*Roy Mason* (see Wilson I)
Energy	5 Mar 1974 – 10 Jun 1975: *Eric Graham Varley* (see above)
	from 10 Jun 1975: *Anthony (Neil) Wedgwood Benn* (see Wilson I)
Planning and Local Government	from 18 Oct 1974: *John Ernest Silkin* (b. 18 Mar 1923)
Secretary of State for Wales	*John Morris* (b. Nov 1931)

Environment	*(Charles) Anthony Raven Crosland* (see Wilson I)
Secretary of State for Northern Ireland	*Merlyn Rees* (b. Cilfynedd 18 Dec 1920)
Prices and Consumer Protection	*Shirley Vivien Teresa Brittain Williams* (b. 27 Jul 1930)
Principal Secretary to the Treasury	from 26 Jul 1974: *Robert Joseph Mellish* (b. 1913)

United Nations

SECRETARIES-GENERAL

29 Jan 1946 – 1 Apr 1953	*Trygve Lie* (b. Grogud 16 Jul 1896; d. Geilo 30 Dec 1968)
7/10 Apr 1953 – 18 Sep 1961	*Dag Hammarskjöld* (b. Jönköping 29 Jul 1905; d. Rhodesia 18 Sep 1961)
3 Nov 1961 – 31 Dec 1971	(acting until 30 Nov 1962:) *Sithu U Thant* (b. Pantanaw 22 Jan 1909; d. 25 Nov 1974)
from 1 Jan 1972	*Kurt Waldheim* (b. St. Andrä 21 Dec 1918)

United States of America

HEADS OF STATE

Presidents (also Heads of Government)

4 Mar 1929	*Herbert Clark Hoover* (b. West Branch, Iowa, 10 Aug 1874; d. New York 20 Oct 1964)
4 Mar 1933	*Franklin Delano Roosevelt* (b. Hyde Park, New York 30 Jan 1882; d. Hyde Park, New York, 12 Apr 1945)
12 Apr 1945	*Harry S Truman* (b. Lamar, Missouri, 8 May 1884; d. 26 Dec 1972)

585

20 Jan 1953	*Dwight David Eisenhower* (b. Denison, Texas, 14 Oct 1890; d. Washington 28 Mar 1969)
20 Jan 1961	*John Fitzgerald Kennedy* (b. Brookline, Massachusetts, 29 May 1917; d. (assassinated) Dallas, Texas, 22 Nov 1963)
22 Nov 1963	*Lyndon Baines Johnson* (b. Stonewall, Texas, 27 Aug 1908; d. 22 Jan 1973)
20 Jan 1969	*Richard Milhous Nixon* (b. Yorba Linda, California, 9 Jan 1913)
from 9 Aug 1974	*Gerald Rudolph Ford* (b. Omaha, Nebraska, 14 Jul 1913)

MEMBERS OF GOVERNMENT

4 Mar 1929 – 3 Mar 1933: Hoover (Rep)

President	*Herbert Clark Hoover* (see Heads of State)
Vice-President	*Charles Curtis* (b. Topeka, Kansas, 25 Jan 1860; d. Washington 8 Feb 1936)
Secretary of State	*Henry Lewis Stimson* (b. New York 21 Sep 1867; d. 20 Oct 1950)*
Treasury	4 Mar 1929 – 3 Feb 1932: *Andrew William Mellon* (b. Pittsburgh, Pennsylvania, 24 Mar 1854; d. Southampton, New York, 26 Aug 1937)*
	4 Feb 1932 – 3 Mar 1933: *Ogden Livingston Mills* (b. Newport, Rhode Island, 23 Aug 1884; d. New York 11 Oct 1937)
War	4 Mar 1929 – 6 Dec 1929: *James William Good* (b. Cedar Rapids, Iowa, 24 Sep 1866; d. Washington 18 Nov 1929)
	7 Dec 1929 – 3 Mar 1933: *Patrick Jay Hurley* (b. Choctaw, Oklahoma, 8 Jan 1883)
Navy	*Charles Francis Adams* (b. Quincy, Massachusetts, 2 Aug 1866; d. Boston 10 Jun 1954)
Interior	*Ray Lyman Wilbur* (b. Boone, Iowa 13 Apr 1875; d. Stanford, California, 26 Jun 1949)
Attorney-General	*William DeWitt Mitchell* (b. Winona, Massachusetts, 9 Sep 1874; d. Syosset, New York, 24 Aug 1955)
Postmaster General	*Walter Folger Brown* (b. Massillon, Ohio, 31 May 1869; d. Toledo, Ohio, 26 Jan 1961)*

*For earlier career see vol. 2

586

Agriculture	*Arthur M. Hyde* (b. Princeton, Missouri, 12 Jul 1877; d. 17 Oct 1947)
Trade	4 Mar 1929 – 2 Aug 1932: *Robert Patterson Lamont* (b. Detroit, Michigan, 1 Dec 1867; d. 19 Feb 1948) 3 Aug 1932 – 3 Mar 1933: *Roy Dikeman Chapin* (b. Lansing, Michigan, 23 Feb 1880; d. 16 Feb 1936)
Labour	4 Mar 1929 – 28 Nov 1930: *James John Davis* (b. Tredegar, South Wales, 27 Oct 1873; d. Washington 22 Nov 1947)* 28 Nov 1930 – 3 Mar 1933: *William Nuckles Doak* (b. 12 Dec 1882; d. New York 23 Oct 1933)

4 Mar 1933 – 12 Apr 1945: Roosevelt (Dem)

President	*Franklin Delano Roosevelt* (see Heads of State)
Vice-President	4 Mar 1933 – 19 Jan 1941: *John Nance Garner* (b. Red River County, Texas, 22 Nov 1868; d. Uvalde, Florida, 7 Nov 1967) 20 Jan 1941 – 19 Jan 1945: *Henry Agard Wallace* (b. Adair County, Iowa, 7 Oct 1888; d. Danbury, Connecticut, 18 Nov 1965) 20 Jan – 12 Apr 1945: *Harry S Truman* (see Heads of State)
Secretary of State	4 Mar 1933 – 26 Nov 1944: *Cordell Hull* (b. Overton (later Pickett) County, Tennessee, 2 Oct 1871; d. Washington 23 Jul 1955) 27 Nov 1944 – 12 Apr 1945: *Edward Reilly Stettinius jr.* (b. 22 Oct 1900; d. Greenwich, New York, 31 Oct 1949)
Treasury	4 Mar – 14 Nov 1933: *William Hartman Woodin* (b. Berwick, Pennsylvania, 27 May 1868; d. New York 3 May 1934) 15 Nov 1933 (acting until 1 Jan 1934) – 12 Apr 1945: *Henry Morgenthau jr.* (b. New York 11 May 1891; d. Poughkeepsie, New York, 6 Feb 1967)
War	4 Mar 1933 – 24 Sep 1934: *George Henry Dern* (b. Dodge County, Nebraska, 8 Sep 1872; d. 27 Aug 1936) 25 Sep 1936 – 20 Jun 1940: *Henry Hines Woodring* (b. Elk County, Kansas, 31 May 1890) 21 Jun 1940 – 12 Apr 1945: *Henry Lewis Stimson* (Rep) (see Hoover)

*For earlier career see vol. 2

587

Navy	4 Mar 1933 – 7 Jul 1939: *Claud Augustus Swanson* (b. Swansonville, Virginia, 31 Mar 1862; d. Washington 7 Jul 1939)
	1939 – 21 Jun 1940: *Charles Edison* (b. Llewellyn Park, West Orange, New Jersey, 3 Aug 1890; d. 31 Jul 1969)
	21 Jun 1940 – 10 May 1944: *Frank Knox* (Rep) (b. Boston, Massachusetts, 1 Jan 1874; d. Washington 28 Apr 1944)
	11 May 1944 – 12 Apr 1945: *James Forrestal* (b. Beacon, New York, 15 Feb 1892; d. Maryland 22 May 1949)
Interior	*Harold Le Claire Ickes* (b. Frankstown Township, Pennsylvania, 15 Mar 1874; d. 3 Feb 1952)
Postmaster General	4 Mar 1933 – 2 Sep 1940: *James Aloysius Farley* (b. Grassy Point, New York, 30 May 1888)
	3 Sep 1940 – 12 Apr 1945: *Frank Comerford Walker* (b. Plymouth, Pennsylvania, 30 May 1886; d. New York 13 Sep 1959)
Attorney-General	4 Mar 1933 – 1 Jan 1939: *Homer Stille Cummings* (b. Chicago, Illinois, 30 Apr 1870; d. Washington 10 Sep 1956)
	2 Jan 1939 – 25 Aug 1941: *Robert Houghwout Jackson* (b. Spring Creek, Pennsylvania, 13 Feb 1892; d. Washington 9 Oct 1954)
	26 Aug 1941 – 12 Apr 1945: *Francis Biddle* (b. Paris 9 May 1886; d. Cape Cod, Massachusetts, 4 Oct 1968)
Agriculture	4 Mar 1933 – 19 Aug 1940: *Henry Agard Wallace* (see above)
	20 Aug 1940 – 12 Apr 1945: *Claude Raymond Wickard* (b. Carroll County, Indiana, 28 Feb 1893; d. Apr 1967)
Trade (from 8 Sep 1939: Public Welfare)	4 Mar 1933 – 22 Dec 1938: *Daniel Calhoun Roper* (b. Marlboro County, South Carolina, 1 Apr 1867; d. 11 Apr 1943)
	23 Dec 1938 – 25 Aug 1940: *Harry Lloyd Hopkins* (b. Sioux City, Iowa, 17 Aug 1890; d. New York 29 Jan 1946)
	26 Aug 1940 – 20 Jan 1945: *Jesse Holman Jones* (b. Robertson County, Tennessee, 5 Apr 1874; d. Houston, Texas, 1 Jun 1956)
	21 Jan – 12 Apr 1945: *Henry Agard Wallace* (see above)

Labour	*Frances Perkins* (b. Boston, Massachusetts, 10 Apr 1882; d. New York 14 May 1965)

12 Apr 1945 – 20 Jan 1953: Truman (Dem)

President	*Harry S Truman* (see Heads of State)
Vice-President	20 Jan 1949 –20 Jan 1953: *Alban William Barkley* (b. Grave County, Kentucky, 24 Nov 1877; d. Lexington, Kentucky, 30 Apr 1956)
Secretary of State	1 Jul 1945 – 9 Jan 1947: *James Francis Byrnes* (b. Charleston, South Carolina, 2 May 1879; d. 24 Jan 1972)
	10 Jan 1947 – 6 Jan 1949: *George Catlett Marshall* (b. Union Town, Pennsylvania, 31 Dec 1880; d. Washington 16 Oct 1959)
	7 Jan 1949 – 20 Jan 1953: *Dean Gooderham Acheson* (b. Middletown, Connecticut, 11 Apr 1893; d. Sandy Springs, Maryland, 12 Oct 1971)
Treasury	12 Apr – 5 Jul 1945: *Henry Morgenthau jr.* (see Roosevelt)
	6 Jul 1945 – 24 Jun 1946: *Fred Moore Vinson* (b. Louisa, Kentucky, 22 Jan 1890; d. Washington 8 Sep 1953)
	25 Jun 1946 – 20 Jan 1953: *John Wesley Snyder* (b. Jonesboro, Arkansas, 21 Jun 1895)
Defence (new post)	28 Jul 1947 – 31 Mar 1949: *James Forrestal* (see Roosevelt)
	1 Apr 1949 – 11 Sep 1950: *Louis Arthur Johnson* (b. Roanoke, Virginia, 10 Jan 1891; d. Washington 24 Apr 1966)
	12 Sep 1950 – 11 Sep 1951: *George Catlett Marshall* (see above)
	12 Sep 1951 – 20 Jan 1953: *Robert Abercrombie Lovett* (b. Huntsville, Texas, 14 Sep 1895)
War	18 Sep 1945 – 17 Jul 1947: *Robert Porter Patterson* (b. Glens Falls, New York, 21 Feb 1891; d. Elizabeth, New Jersey, 22 Jan 1952)
	18 Jul 1947 – 27 Apr 1949: *Kenneth Claiborne Royall* (b. Goldsboro, North Carolina, 24 Jul 1894; d. Durham, North Carolina, 26 May 1971)
	7 Jun 1949 – 20 Jan 1953: *Gordon Gray* (b. Baltimore, Maryland, 30 May 1909)
Navy	12 Apr 1945 – 27 Jul 1947: *James Forrestal* (see Roosevelt)

28 Jul 1947 – 26 Apr 1949: *John Lawrence Sullivan* (b. Manchester, New Hampshire, 16 Jun 1899)

16 May 1949 – 26 Jun 1951: *Francis Patrick Matthews* (b. Albion, Nebraska, 18 May 1887; d. Omaha, Nebraska, 18 Oct 1952)

27 Jun 1951 – 20 Jan 1953: *Dan A. Kimball* (b. St. Louis, Missouri, 1 Mar 1896; d. Washington 30 Jul 1970)

Air Force
William Stuart Symington (b. Amherst, Massachusetts, 26 Jun 1901)

Interior
12 Apr 1945 – 12 Feb 1946: *Harold Le Claire Ickes* (see Roosevelt)

13 Feb 1946 – 10 Nov 1949: *Julius Albert Krug* (b. Madison, Wisconsin, 23 Nov 1907; d. Knoxville, Tennessee, 26 Mar 1970)

1 Dec 1949 – 20 Jan 1953: *Oscar Littleton Chapman* (b. Omega, Virginia, 22 Oct 1896)

Postmaster General
27 Jun 1945 – 25 Nov 1947: *Robert Emmet Hannegan* (b. St. Louis, Missouri, 30 Jun 1903; d. St. Louis, Missouri, 6 Oct 1949)

26 Nov 1947 – 20 Jan 1953: *Jesse Monroe Donaldson* (b. Shelby County, Illinois, 17 Aug 1885; d. Kansas City, Missouri, 25 Mar 1970)

Attorney-General
27 Jun 1945 – 26 Jul 1949: *Thomas Campbell Clark* (b. Dallas, Texas, 23 Sep 1899)

27 Jul 1949 – 3 Apr 1952: *James Howard McGrath* (b. Woonsocket, Rhode Island, 28 Nov 1903; d. 2 Sep 1966)

4 Apr 1952 – 20 Jan 1953: *James Patrick McGranery* (b. Philadelphia, Pennsylvania, 8 Jul 1895; d. 23 Dec 1962)

Agriculture
22 May 1945 – 10 May 1948: *Clinton Presha Anderson* (b. Centerville, South Dakota, 23 Oct 1895; d. 11 Nov 1975)

24 May 1948 – 11 Apr 1945: *Charles Franklin Brannan* (b. Denver, Colorado, 23 Aug 1903)

Trade
12 Apr 1945 – 20 Sep 1946: *Henry Agard Wallace* (see Roosevelt)

23 Sep 1946 – 29 Jan 1947: *William Averell Harriman* (b. New York 15 Nov 1891)

5 May 1948 – 20 Jan 1953: *Charles Lawyer* (b. Cincinnati, Ohio, 10 Feb 1887)

Labour
27 Jun 1945 – 10 Jun 1948: *Lewis Baxter Schwellen-*

bach (b. Superior, Wisconsin, 20 Oct 1894; d. Washington 10 Jun 1948)

13 Aug 1948 – 20 Jan 1953: *Maurice Joseph Tobin* (b. Roxbury, Massachusetts, 22 May 1901; d. Scituate, Massachusetts, 19 Jul 1953)

European Aid   9 Apr 1948 – 30 Sep 1950: *Paul Gray Hoffman* (b. Chicago, Illinois, 26 Apr 1891; d. 8 Oct 1974)

1 Oct 1950 – 20 Jan 1953: *William Chapman Foster* (b. Westfield, New Jersey, 27 Apr 1897)

20 Jan 1953 – 20 Jan 1961: Eisenhower (Rep)

President	*Dwight David Eisenhower* (see Heads of State)
Vice-President	*Richard Milhous Nixon* (see Heads of State)
Secretary of State	21 Jan 1953 – 15 Apr 1959: *John Foster Dulles* (b. Washington 25 Feb 1888; d. Washington 24 May 1959)
	18 Apr 1959 – 20 Jan 1961: *Christian (Archibald) Herter* (b. Paris 2 Mar 1895; d. Washington 30 Dec 1966)
Treasury	21 Jan 1953 – 29 May 1957: *George Magoffin Humphrey* (b. Cheboygan, Michigan, 8 Mar 1890; d. Cleveland, Ohio, 20 Jan 1970)
	29 May/28 Jun 1957 – 20 Jan 1961: *Robert Bernard Anderson* (b. Burleson, Texas, 4 Jun 1910)
Defence	26 Jan 1953 – 15 Sep 1957: *Charles Erwin Wilson* (b. Minerva, Ohio, 18 Jul 1890; d. Norwood, Louisiana, 26 Sep 1961)
	15 Sep 1957 – 1 Dec 1959: *Neil H. McElroy* (b. Berea, Ohio, 30 Oct 1904; d. 30 Nov 1972)
	2 Dec 1959 – 20 Jan 1961: *Thomas Sovereign Gates* (b. Germantown, Pennsylvania, 10 Apr 1906)
War (Army)	29 Jan 1953 – 31 Jul 1955: *Robert TenBroek Stevens* (b. Fanwood, New Jersey, 31 Jul 1899)
	1 Aug 1955 – 20 Jan 1961: *Wilber Marion Brucker* (b. Saginaw, Michigan, 23 Jun 1894; d. 28 Oct 1968)
Navy	29 Jan 1953 – 1 May 1954: *Robert Bernard Anderson* (see above)
	1 May 1954 – 1 Apr 1957: *Charles Sparks Thomas* (b. Independence, Montana, 28 Sep 1897)
	1 Apr 1957 – 2 Dec 1959: *Thomas Sovereign Gates* (see above)
Air Force	4 Feb 1953 – 11 Aug 1955: *Harold Elstner Talbott* (b. Dayton, Ohio, 31 May 1888; d. Palm Beach, Florida,

591

	2 Mar 1957)
	11 Aug 1955 – 26 Mar 1957: *Donald Aubrey Quarles* (b. Van Buren, Arkansas, 30 Jul 1894; d. Washington 8 May 1959)
	26 Mar 1957 – 10 Dec 1959: *James Henderson Douglas* (b. Cedar Rapids, Iowa, 11 Mar 1899)
	10 Dec 1959 – 20 Jan 1961: *Dudley Crawford Sharp* (b. Houston, Maryland, 16 Mar 1905)
Interior	21 Jan 1953 – 15 Apr 1956: *Douglas MacKay* (b. Portland, Oregon, 24 Jun 1893; d. 22 Jul 1959)
	28 May 1956 – 20 Jan 1961: *Frederick Andrew Seaton* (b. Washington 11 Dec 1909; d. 16 Jan 1974)
Postmaster General	21 Jan 1953 – 20 Jan 1961: *Arthur Ellsworth Summerfield* (b. Pinconning, Michigan, 17 Mar 1899; d. 26 Apr 1972)
Attorney-General	21 Jan 1953 – 23 Oct 1957: *Herbert Brownell* (b. Peru, Nebraska, 20 Feb 1904)
	23 Oct 1957 – 20 Jan 1961: *William Pierce Rogers* (b. Norfolk, New York, 23 Jun 1913)
Agriculture	21 Jan 1953 – 20 Jan 1961: *Ezra Taft Benson* (b. Whitney, Idaho, 4 Aug 1899)
Trade	21 Jan 1953 – 10 Nov 1958: *Sinclair Weeks* (b. West Newton, Massachusetts, 15 Jul 1893)
	13 Nov 1958 – 19 Jun 1959: *Lewis Lichtenstein Strauss* (b. Charleston, West Virginia, 31 Jan 1896; d. 21 Jan 1974) confirmation refused by Senate
	19 Jul 1959 – 20 Jan 1961: *Frederick Henry Mueller* (b. Grand Rapids, Michigan, 22 Nov 1893; d. Sarasota, Florida, 31 Aug 1976)
Labour	21 Jan – 10 Sep 1953: *Martin Patrick Durkin* (Dem) (b. Chicago, Illinois, 18 Mar 1894; d. New York 14 Nov 1955)
	8 Oct 1953 – 20 Jan 1961: *James Paul Mitchell* (b. Elizabeth, New Jersey, 12 Nov 1900; d. New York 19 Oct 1964)
Health, Education and Welfare (new post)	11 Apr 1953 – 1 Aug 1955: *Oveta Culp Hobby* (b. Killeen, Texas, 19 Jan 1905)
	1 Aug 1955 – 7 May/1 Aug 1958: *Marion Bayard Folsom* (b. McRae, Georgia, 23 Nov 1893)
	1 Aug 1958 – 20 Jan 1961: *Arthur Sherwood Flemming* (b. Kingston, New York, 12 Jun 1905)
Disarmament	19 Mar 1955 – 14 Feb 1958: *Harold Edward Stassen* (b. West St. Paul, Minnesota, 13 Apr 1907)

20 Jan 1961 - 20 Jan 1969: Kennedy/Johnson (Dem)

President	20 Jan 1961 - 22 Nov 1963: *John Fitzgerald Kennedy* (see Heads of State)
	22 Nov 1963 - 20 Jan 1969: *Lyndon Baines Johnson* (see Heads of State)
Vice-President	20 Jan 1961 - 22 Nov 1963: *Lyndon Baines Johnson* (see Heads of State)
	20 Jan 1965 - 20 Jan 1969: *Hubert Horatio Humphrey* (b. Wallace, South Dakota, 27 May 1911)
Secretary of State	*Dean Rusk* (b. Cherokee County, Georgia, 9 Feb 1909)
Treasury	20 Jan 1961 - 31 Mar 1965: *Douglas Dillon* (Rep) (b. Geneva 21 Aug 1909)
	1 Apr 1965 - 23 Dec 1968: *Henry Hamill Fowler* (b. Roanoke, Virginia, 5 Sep 1908)
	23 Dec 1968 - 20 Jan 1969: *Joseph Barr* (b. Vincennes, Indiana, 17 Jan 1918)
Defence	20 Jan 1961 - 29 Feb 1968: *Robert Strange McNamara* (b. San Francisco, California, 9 Jun 1916)
	1 Mar 1968 - 20 Jan 1969: *Clark McAdams Clifford* (b. Fort Scott, near St. Louis, Kansas, 25 Dec 1906)
Army	20 Jan 1961 - 30 Jun 1962: *Elvis Jacob Stahr* (b. Hickman, Kentucky, 9 Mar 1916)
	1 Jul 1962 - 20 Jan 1964: *Cyrus Roberts Vance* (b. Clarksburg, West Virginia, 27 Mar 1917)
	20 Jan 1964 - 30 Jun 1965: *Steven Ailes* (b. Romney, West Virginia, 25 May 1912)
	1 Jul 1965 - 20 Jan 1969: *Stanley Rogers Resor* (b. New York 5 Dec 1917)
Navy	20 Jan - 9 Dec 1961: *John Bowden Connally* (b. Floresville, Texas, 28 Feb 1917)
	9 Dec 1961 - 14 Oct 1963: *Fred Korth* (b. Yorktown, Texas, 9 Sep 1909)
	1 Nov 1963 - 30 Jun 1967: *Paul Nitze* (b. Amherst, Massachusetts, 16 Jan 1907)
	30 Jun - 19 Jul 1967: *John T. MacNaughton* (d. Hendersonville, North Carolina, 19 Jul 1967)
	4 Aug 1967 - 20 Jan 1969: *Paul Roland Ignatius* (b. Los Angeles, California, 11 Nov 1920)
Air Force	20 Jan 1961 - 1 Oct 1965: *Eugene Zuckert* (b. New York 9 Nov 1911)
	1 Oct 1965 - 20 Jan 1969: *Harold Brown* (b. New York

	19 Sep 1927)
Interior	*Stewart Udall* (b. St. Johns, Arizona, 31 Jan 1920)
Postmaster General	20 Jan 1961 – 26 Aug 1963: *Edward Day* (b. Jacksonville, Springfield, Illinois, 11 Oct 1914)
	10 Sep 1963 – 29 Aug 1965: *John Austin Gronouski* (b. Dunbar, Wisconsin, 26 Aug 1919)
	29 Aug 1965 – 20 Jan 1969: *Lawrence Francis O'Brien* (b. Springfield, Massachusetts, 7 Jul 1917)
Attorney-General	20 Jan 1961 – 3 Sep 1964: *Robert Francis Kennedy* (b. Brookline, Massachusetts, 20 Nov 1925; d. (assassinated) Los Angeles, California, 6 Jun 1968) brother of John Fitzgerald Kennedy
	4 Sep 1964 (acting until 28 Jan 1965) – 30 Sep 1966: *Nicholaus de Belleville Katzenbach* (b. Philadelphia, Pennsylvania, 17 Jan 1922)
	28 Nov 1966 – 20 Jan 1969: *Ramsey Clark* (b. Dallas, Texas, 18 Dec 1927)
Agriculture	*Orville Lothrop Freeman* (b. Minneapolis, Minnesota, 9 May 1918)
Trade	20 Jan 1961 – 16 Dec 1964: *Luther Hartwell Hodges* (b. Pittsylvania County, Virginia, 9 Mar 1898; d. 6 Oct 1974)
	15 Jan 1965 – 18 Jan 1967: *John Thomas Connor* (b. Syracuse, New York, 3 Nov 1914)
	18 Jan 1967 (acting until 23 May 1967) – 20 Jan 1969: *Alexander Buel Trowbridge* (b. Englewood, New Jersey, 12 Dec 1929)
Labour	20 Jan 1961 – 30 Aug 1962: *Arthur Joseph Goldberg* (b. Chicago, Illinois, 8 Aug 1908)
	30 Aug 1962 – 20 Jan 1969: *Willard Wirtz* (b. De Kalb, Illinois, 14 Mar 1912)
Health, Education, and Welfare	20 Jan 1961 – 13 Jul 1962: *Abraham Alexander Ribicoff* (b. New Britain, Connecticut, 9 Apr 1910)
	13 Jul 1962 – 27 Aug 1965: *Anthony Giuseppe Celebrezze* (b. Anzio, Italy, 4 Sep 1910)
	27 Jul 1965 – 29 Feb 1968: *John William Gardner* (b. Los Angeles, California, 8 Oct 1912)
	1/22 Mar 1968 – 20 Jan 1969: *Wilbur Joseph Cohen* (b. Milwaukee, Wisconsin, 10 Jun 1913)
Housing and Town Planning (new post)	13 Jan 1966 – 20 Jan 1969: *Robert Clifton Weaver* (b. Brookland, Washington, 29 Dec 1907)
Transport (new post)	19 Oct 1966 – 20 Jan 1969: *William Haddon* (b.

	Orange, New Jersey, 24 May 1926)
Solicitor-General	*Archibald Cox* (b. Plainfield, New Jersey, 17 May 1912)
Ambassador to the United Nations	20 Jan 1961 – 14 Jul 1965: *Adlai Ewing Stevenson* (b. Los Angeles, California, 5 Feb 1900; d. London 14 Jul 1965)
	28 Jul 1965 – 25 Apr 1968: *Arthur Joseph Goldberg* (see above)

from 20 Jan 1969: Nixon/Ford (Rep)

President	20 Jan 1969 – 8 Aug 1974: *Richard Milhous Nixon* (see Heads of State)
	from 8 Aug 1974: *Gerald Rudolph Ford* (see Heads of State)
Vice-President	20 Jan 1969 – 10 Oct 1973: *Spiro Theodore Agnew* (b. Baltimore, Maryland, 9 Nov 1918)
	13 Oct 1973 – 8 Aug 1974: *Gerald Rudolph Ford* (see Heads of State)
	from 20 Aug 1974: *Nelson Aldrich Rockefeller* (b. Bar Harbour, Maine, 8 Jul 1908)
Secretary of State	20 Jan 1969 – 22 Aug 1973: *William Pierce Rogers* (see Eisenhower)
	from 3/21 Sep 1973: *Henry Alfred Kissinger* (b. Fürth, Germany, 27 May 1923)
Treasury	20 Jan 1969 – 14 Dec 1970: *David Matthew Kennedy* (b. Randolph, Utah, 21 Jul 1905)
	14 Dec 1970 – 16 May 1972: *John Bowden Connally* (see Kennedy/Johnson)
	16 May 1972 – 17 Apr 1974: *George Pratt Shultz* (b. New York 13 Dec 1920)
	from 17 Apr 1974: *William Edward Simon* (b. Paterson, New Jersey, 1927)
Defence	20 Jan 1969 – 8 Dec 1972: *Melvin Robert Laird* (b. Omaha, Nebraska, 1 Sep 1922)
	8 Dec 1972 – 10 May 1973: *Elliot Lee Richardson* (b. Boston, Massachusetts, 20 Jul 1920)
	10 May 1973 – 3 Nov 1975: *James Rodney Schlesinger* (b. New York 15 Feb 1929)
	from 3/18 Nov 1975: *Donald Rumsfeld* (b. Chicago, Illinois, 9 Jul 1932)
Interior	20 Jan 1969 – 26 Nov 1970: *Walter Joseph Hickel* (b. Claflin, Kansas, 18 Aug 1919)

	26 Nov 1970 – 11 Jun 1975: *Rogers Clark Ballard Morton* (b. Louisville, Kentucky, 19 Sep 1914) 11 Jun – 17 Oct 1975: *Stanley K. Hathaway* (b. Osceola, Nebraska, 19 Jul 1924) from 17 Oct 1975: *Thomas S. Kleppe* (b. Kintyre, North Dakota, 1 Jul 1919)
Postmaster General	20 Jan 1969 – 1 Jul 1971: *Winton Malcolm Blount* (b. Union Springs, Alabama, 1 Feb 1921) 1 Jul 1971: no longer cabinet post
Attorney-General	20 Jan 1969 – 15 Feb 1972: *John Newton Mitchell* (b. Detroit, Michigan, 5 Sep 1913) 15 Feb 1972 – Apr 1973: *Richard Gordon Kleindienst* (b. Winslow, Arizona, Aug 1923) Apr 1973 – 20 Oct 1973: *Elliot Lee Richardson* (see above) 20 Oct – 17 Dec 1973 (acting:) *Robert Heron Bork* (b. Pittsburgh, Pennsylvania, 1 Mar 1927) 17 Dec 1973 – 14 Jan 1975: *William B. Saxbe* (b. Mechanicsburg, Ohio, 24 Jun 1916) from 14 Jan 1975: *Edward Hirsch Levi* (b. Chicago, Illinois, 26 Jun 1911)
Agriculture	20 Jan 1969 – 11 Nov 1971: *Clifford Hardin* (b. Knighttown, Indiana, 9 Oct 1915) from 11 Nov 1971: *Earl Lauer Butz* (b. Albion, Indiana, 3 Jul 1909)
Commerce (Trade)	20 Jan 1969 – 27 Jan 1972: *Maurice Hubert Stans* (b. Shakopee, Minnesota 22 Mar 1908) 27 Jan – 8 Dec 1972: *Peter G. Peterson* (b. Kearney, Nebraska, 5 Jun 1926) 8 Dec 1972 – 25 Apr 1975: *Frederick Baily Dent* (b. Cape May, New Jersey, 17 Aug 1922) 25 Apr – 3 Nov 1975: *Rogers Clark Ballard Morton* (see above) from 3 Nov 1975: *Elliot Lee Richardson* (see above)
Labour	20 Jan 1969 – 10 Jun 1970: *George Pratt Shultz* (see above) 10 Jun 1970 – 8 Dec 1972: *James Day Hodgson* (b. Dawson, Minnesota, 3 Dec 1915) 8 Dec 1972 – 6 Mar 1975: *Peter J. Brennan* (b. New York 24 May 1918) from 6 Mar 1975: *John Thomas Dunlop* (b. Placerville, California, 5 Jul 1914)

Health, Education and Welfare	20 Jan 1969 – 7 Jun 1970: *Robert Hutchinson Finch* (b. Tempe, Arizona, 9 Oct 1925) 7 Jun 1970 – 8 Dec 1972: *Elliot Lee Richardson* (see above) 8 Dec 1972 – 22 Jul 1975: *Caspar Willard Weinberger* (b. San Francisco, California, 18 Aug 1917) from 22 Jul 1975: *(Forrest) David Mathews* (b. Grove Hill, Alabama, 6 Dec 1935)
Housing and Urban Development	20 Jan 1969 – 8 Dec 1972: *George Wilcken Romney* (b. Chihuahua, Mexico, 8 Jul 1907) 8 Dec 1972 – 5 Mar 1975: *James T(homas) Lynn* (b. Cleveland, Ohio, 27 Feb 1927) from 5 Mar 1975: *Carla Anderson Hills* (b. Los Angeles, California, 3 Jan 1934)
Transportation	20 Jan 1969 – 8 Dec 1972: *John Anthony Volpe* (b. Wakefield, Massachusetts 8 Jul 1908) 8 Dec 1972 – 14 Jan 1975: *Claude Stout Brinegar* (b. Rockport, California, 16 Dec 1926) from 14 Jan 1975: *William Thaddeus Coleman* (b. Philadelphia, Pennsylvania, 7 Jul 1920)

Upper Volta

11 Dec 1958	Member of French Community
5 Aug 1960	Left French Community

HEADS OF STATE

Presidents

5 Aug 1960	*Maurice Yaméogo* (b. Koudougou 31 Dec 1921)
from 3 Jan 1966	*Sangoulé Lamizana* (b. Dianra, Tougan, 1916) Leader of Military Government

MEMBERS OF GOVERNMENT

Prime Ministers

21 Oct 1958 – 3 Jan 1966	*Maurice Yaméogo* (see Presidents)
from 3 Jan 1966	President also Prime Minister

Uruguay

HEADS OF STATE

Presidents

1 Mar 1927	*Juan Campisteguy* (b. 1859; d. Sep 1937)
1 Mar 1931 – Mar 1938	*Gabriel Terra* (b. 1 Aug 1873; d. 15 Sep 1942)
19 Jun 1938	*Alfredo Baldomir* (b. 27 Aug 1884; d. 25 Feb 1948)
1 Mar 1943	*Juan José de Amézaga* (b. 1881; d. 1956)
1 Mar 1947	*Tomás Berreta* (b. 1875; d. 2 Aug 1947)
2 Aug 1947	*Luis Batlle y Berres* (for 1st time) (b. 26 Nov 1897; d. Montevideo 16(?) Jul 1964)
1 Mar 1951	*Andrés Martínez Trueba* (for 1st time) (b. 1884; d. 19 Dec 1959)
1 Mar 1952 †	*Andrés Martínez Trueba* (for 2nd time)
1 Mar 1953	*Luis Batlle y Berres* (for 2nd time)
1 Mar 1954	*Luis Batlle y Berres* (for 3rd time)
1 Mar 1955	*Alberto Zubiria* (for 1st time)
1 Mar 1956	*Alberto Zubiria* (for 2nd time)
1 Mar 1957	*Arturo Lezama*
1 Mar 1958	*Carlos A. Fischer*
2 Mar 1959	*Martín Etchegoyen*
1 Mar 1960	*Benito Nardone* (b. Montevideo 1906; d. Montevideo 25 Mar 1964)
1 Mar 1961	*Eduardo Victor Haedo* (b. 1901?)
1 Mar 1962	*Faustino Harrison* (b. 1900(?); d. 20 Aug 1963)
1 Mar 1963	*Daniel Fernández Crespo* (b. 1900)
2 Mar 1964 – 7 Feb 1965	*Luis Giannattasio* (b. Montevideo 1894; d. Montevideo 7 Feb 1965)
Feb 1965	*Washington Beltrán* (b. Montevideo 6 Apr 1914)
1 Mar 1966	*Alberto Héber Usher* (b. 1 May 1916)
1 Mar 1967	*Oscar Gestido* (b. Montevideo 28 Nov 1901; d. Montevideo 6 Dec 1967)
6 Dec 1967 – 29 Feb 1972	*Jorge Pacheco Areco* (b. Montevideo 19 Apr 1920)
from Mar 1972	*Juan María Bordaberry Arocena* (b. Montevideo 1928)

† From 1 Mar 1952 to 1 Mar 1967 the Chairman of the National Assembly changed annually

Venezuela

HEADS OF STATE

Presidents

30 May 1929	*Juan Bautista Pérez* (b. 21 Dec 1869; d. 1952)
13 Jul 1931 – 18 Dec 1935	*Juan Vicente Gómez* (for 2nd time) (b. 24 Jul 1857; d. 18 Dec 1935)*
31 Dec 1935	(acting:) *Eleazar López Contreras* (for 1st time) (b. 1883)
19 Apr 1936	(acting:) *Arminio Borjas*
25 Apr 1936 – Apr 1941	*Eleazar López Contreras* (for 2nd time)
6 May 1941 – Oct 1945	*Isaías Medina Angarita* (b. 6 Jul 1897; d. 15 Sep 1953)
20 Oct 1945	*Rómulo Betancourt* (for 1st time) (b. 22 Feb 1908)
15 Feb – 23 Nov 1948	*Rómulo Gallegos* (b. 1884; d. Caracas 4 Apr 1969)
25 Nov 1948 – 13 Nov 1950	*Carlos Delgado Chaulbaud* (b. 1900; d. 13 Nov 1950)
27 Nov 1950 – 2 Dec 1952	*German Suárez Flammerich* (b. 1907)
2 Dec 1952/ 10 Jan 1953	*Marcos Pérez Jiménez* (b. 25 Apr 1914) Dictator
23 Jan – 14 Nov 1958	*Admiral Wolfgang Larrazábal* (b. 5 Mar 1911) Leader of Military Junta
12 Nov 1958	(acting:) *Edgar Sanabria* (b. 1911)
13 Feb 1959	*Rómulo Betancourt* (for 2nd time)
13 Feb 1964	*Raúl Leoni* (b. Upata, Bolívar, 26 Apr 1905; d. 5 Jul 1972)
11 Mar 1969	*Rafael Caldera Rodríguez* (b. San Felipe, Yaracuy, 24 Jan 1916)
from 11 Mar 1974	*Carlos Andres Pérez Rodríguez* (b. 1922)

*For earlier career see vol. 2

599

Vietnam

9 Mar 1945	Proclamation of end of French protectorate over Annam and Tonkin (central and northern Vietnam)

HEADS OF STATE

Emperor

1925 – 25 Aug 1945	*Bao Dai* (name adopted on accession; original name *Nguyen Vinh Thuy*) (b. Hue 22 Oct 1913) abdicated
2 Sep 1945	Establishment of Democratic Republic of Vietnam including French colony of Cochin-China (southern Vietnam) but French administration continued to operate in much of territory
14 Jun 1949	Establishment of State of Vietnam (member of French Union) rivalling Democratic Republic government for control of country
21 Jul 1954	Agreement at Geneva conference to establish North (Democratic Republic) and South (State of Vietnam) zones of administration; effective withdrawal of State of Vietnam from French Union

Presidents of Democratic Republic of Vietnam

2 Sep 1945 – 3 Sep 1969	*Ho Chi Minh* (name adopted in 1940; original name *Nguyen That Thanh*) (b. Hoang Tru 15 Jan 1894; d. Hanoi 3 Sep 1969)
from 24 Sep 1969	*Ton Duc Thang* (b. My Hoa Hung 20 Aug 1888)

Head of State (Quoc Trang) of State of Vietnam

14 Jun 1949 – 26 Oct 1955	*Bao Dai* (see above) deposed following referendum
26 Oct 1955	State of Vietnam renamed Republic of Vietnam

Presidents of Republic of Vietnam

26 Oct 1955	*Ngo Dinh Diem* (b. Kwang Binh or Hue Jan 1901; d. (assassinated) Saigon 2 Nov 1963)

2 Nov 1963	*Duong Van Minh* (for 1st time) (b. My Tho 19 Feb 1916)
17 Aug – 26 Oct 1964	*Nguyen Khanh* (b. 1927?)
4 Nov 1964 – 12 Jun 1965	*Phan Khac Suu*
19 Jun 1965	*Nguyen Van Thieu* (b. Ninh Truan, Phan Rang province, 5 Apr 1923)
21 Apr 1975	*Tran Van Huong* (b. 1 Dec 1903)
28 – 30 Apr 1975	*Duong Van Minh* (for 2nd time)
30 Apr 1975	Duong Van Minh surrendered to forces supporting Provisional Revolutionary Government of Republic of Vietnam set up in Jun 1969 to prepare for establishment of unified Vietnamese state *Huynh Tan Phat* (b. 1913) Chairman of Provisional Revolutionary Government (2 Jul 1976: reunification of country as Socialist Republic of Vietnam)

MEMBERS OF GOVERNMENT

Prime Minister of Democratic Republic

from 1955	*Pham Van Dong* (b. Quang Ngai province 1 Mar 1906)

Prime Ministers of State of Vietnam

14 Jun 1949	*Nguyen Van Xuan*
Jan 1950	*Nguyen Phan Long* (b. 1888(?); d. Saigon 16 Jul 1960)
27 Apr 1950	*Tran Van Huu*
8 Mar 1952	*Tran Van Huong* (b. Vinh Long 1 Dec 1903)
Jun 1952 – 17 Dec 1953	*Nguyen Van Tam*
Dec 1953	*Prince Buu Loc*, uncle of Bao Dai
19 Jun 1954	*Ngo Dinh Diem* (see Heads of State)

Prime Ministers of the Republic of Vietnam

19 Jun 1954 – 2 Nov 1963	President also head of government
4 Nov 1963	*Nguyen Ngoc Tho* (b. Long Xuyen province 26 May 1908)

601

30 Jan 1964	*Nguyen Khanh* (see Heads of State)
17 Aug – 26 Oct 1964	Direct rule by President
4 Nov 1964 – 27 Jan 1965	*Tran Van Huong* (for 1st time) (see Heads of State)
16 Feb – 12 Jun 1965	*Phan Huy Quat*
19 Jun 1965	*Nguyen Cao Ky* (b. Son Tay, Tonkin province, 9 Sep 1930)
31 Oct 1967 – 18 May 1968	*Nguyen Van Loc* (b. 24 Feb 1922)
25 May 1968	*Tran Van Huong* (for 2nd time)
23 Aug 1969	*Tran Thien Khiem* (b. Saigon 15 Dec 1925)
4 – 23 Apr 1975	*Nguyen Ba Can*
28 – 30 Apr 1975	*Vu Van Mau*

West Indies

3 Jan 1958	Established as federation of British colonies of Antigua; Barbados (q. v.); Dominica; Grenada (q. v.); Jamaica (q. v.); Montserrat; Saint Christopher, Nevis and Anguilla; Saint Lucia; Saint Vincent; and Trinidad and Tobago (q. v.)

HEAD OF STATE

Governor-General

3 Jan 1958 – 31 May 1962	*Patrick George Thomas Buchan-Hepburn, 1st Baron Hailes* (b. 2 Apr 1901; d. 5 Nov 1974)

MEMBER OF GOVERNMENT

Prime Minister

3 Jan 1958 – 31 May 1962	*Sir Grantley Herbert Adams* (b. Barbados 28 Apr 1898; d. 28 Nov 1971)
31 May 1962	Federation dissolved

Western Samoa

Until 1 Jan 1962	Administered by New Zealand under Trusteeship Agreement with United Nations

HEADS OF STATE

Presidents

1 Jan 1962	*Tupua Tamesehe Mea'ole* (d. 8 Apr 1963) and *Mallietoa Tanumafili II* (for 1st time) (b. 1913) Joint Presidents
from 8 Apr 1963	*Mallietoa Tanumafili II* (for 2nd time)

MEMBERS OF GOVERNMENT

Prime Ministers

1 Jan 1962 – Feb 1970	*Fiame Mata'afa Faumuina Mulinu'u II*
from Feb 1970	*Tupua Tamasese Leolofi IV*

Yemen, People's Democratic Republic of

30 Nov 1967	People's Republic of Southern Yemen formed from British-administered Federation of South Arabia and Eastern Aden Protectorate
30 Nov 1970	Name changed to People's Democratic Republic of Yemen

HEADS OF STATE

Presidents

30 Nov 1967 – 22 Jun 1969	*Qahtan Muhammad ash-Shaabi* (b. 1920)
from 24 Jun 1969	*Salim Ali Rubai*, Head of Presidential Council

MEMBERS OF GOVERNMENT

Prime Ministers

7 Apr – 22 Jun 1969	*Faisal Abd al-Latif ash-Shaabi*
23 Jun 1969	*Mohammed Ali Haithem* (b. 1940)
from 1 Aug 1971	*Ali Nasser Muhammed*

Yemen Arab Republic

HEADS OF STATE

Imams of Sana

1904 – 17 Feb 1948	*Yahya Muhammad ibn Muhammad*, grandson of Yahya Hamid ad-Din, from 1918 King
14 Mar 1948	*Ahmad an-Nasir li-din Allah*, son (b. Sana 1896) King
19 Sep 1962 – May 1970	*Muhammad Mansur bi'llah* (as Crown Prince: *Muhammad al-Badr*) son (b. 1927) left country Feb 1969, moved to England May 1970
27 Sep 1962	Civil war

Presidents

1 Oct 1962	*Abdullah as-Sallal* (b. 1917) in conflict with the Imam
5 Nov 1967 – 13 Jun 1974	*Abdur Rahman al-Iriani* (b. Iriane 1901)

Chairman of Military Command Council

from 13 Jun 1974	*Ibrahim al-Hamadi* (b. 1943?)

MEMBERS OF GOVERNMENT

Prime Ministers of the Imam

(?) – 11 Apr 1967	*Prince Ahmad al-Hasan ibn Yahya* (for 1st time)
11 Apr 1967 – (?)	*Prince Ahmad al-Hasan ibn Yahya* (for 2nd time)
(?) – 15 Jan 1969	*Abdur Rahman ibn Yahya*
15 Jan 1969 – May 1970	*Prince Ahmad al-Hasan ibn Yahya* (for 3rd time)

Republican Prime Ministers

28 Apr – 27 Dec 1964	*Hamud al-Jaifi* (b. 1918)
5 Jan – 21 Apr 1965	*Hassan al-Amri* (for 1st time)
24 Apr – 1 Jul 1965	*Ahmed Mohammed Numan* (for 1st time)
6 Jul 1965	*Abdullah as-Sallal* (see Presidents)

21 Jul 1965	*Hassan al-Amri* (for 2nd time)
18 Sep 1966 – 4 Nov 1967	President also Prime Minister
5 Nov 1967	*Muhsin al-Aini* (b. 1932) (for 1st time)
18 Dec 1967	*Hassan al-Amri* (for 3rd time)
4 Sep 1968 – 8 Jul 1969	*Hassan al-Amri* (for 4th time)
2 Sep 1969 – 1 Feb 1970	*Abd Allah Kurshumi* (b. Sana'a 1932)
5 Feb 1970 – 25 Feb 1971	*Muhsin al-Aini* (for 2nd time)
26 Feb 1971	(acting:) *Abdel Salam Sabra*, Deputy Prime Minister
3 May – 20 Jul 1971	*Ahmed Mohammed Numan* (for 2nd time)
24 Aug – 1 Sep 1971	*Hassan al-Amri* (for 5th time)
16 Sep 1971 – 28 Dec 1972	*Muhsin al-Aini* (for 3rd time)
30 Dec 1972	*Qadi Abdullah al-Hijri* (b. 1912 or 1913; d. (assassinated) London 10 Mar 1977)
11 Feb 1974	*Hassan Makki*
21 Jun 1974	*Muhsin al-Aini* (for 4th time)
16 Jan 1975	(acting:) *Abdel Latif Deifallah*
from 23 Jan 1975	*Abdel-Aziz Abdel-Ghani*

605

Yugoslavia

HEADS OF STATE

Kings

16 Aug 1921	*Alexander II*, son of Peter I (b. 16 Dec 1888; d. Marseilles 9 Oct 1934)
9 Oct 1934 – 29 Nov 1945	*Peter II*, son (b. 6 Sep 1923; d. Los Angeles 3 Nov 1970) in exile from Apr 1941

Regents

9 Oct 1934 – 27 Mar 1941	*Prince Paul*, cousin of King Alexander II (b. 28 Apr 1893; d. Paris 14 Sep 1976) *Radenko Stanković* (b. Sokolovac 1880; d. Belgrade 6 Dec 1960) *Ivo Perović*
1944 – 1945	*Ante Mandić* (b. 1881; d. Lovran 15 Nov 1959)
2 Mar – 29 Nov 1945	Regency Council: *Saša Budisavljević* (b. 1882(?); d. Zagreb 20(?) Feb 1968) *Ante Mandić* (see above) *Dušan Sernec* (b. Maribor 8 Jul 1882; d. Ljubljana 15 Feb 1952)
29 Nov 1945	Republic

Chairman of National Assembly

29 Dec 1945 – 14 Jan 1953	*Ivan Ribar* (b. Vukmanić 21 Jan 1884; d. Zagreb 2 Feb 1968)

President

14 Jan 1953	*Josip Tito Broz* (b. Kumrovec 25 May 1892)

MEMBERS OF GOVERNMENT

Prime Ministers

6 Jan 1929	*Petar Živković* (for 1st time) (b. 4 Feb 1879; d. Paris 3 Feb 1947)
5 Jan 1932	*Petar Živković* (for 2nd time)
4 Apr – 29 Jun 1932	*Vojislav Marinković* (b. 1 May 1876; d. 18 Sep 1935)*
2 Jul – 3 Nov 1932	*Milan Srškić* (for 1st time) (b. 1880)
15 Nov 1932 – 23 Jan 1934	*Milan Srškić* (for 2nd time)
27 Jan 1934	*Nikola Uzunović* (for 7th time) (b. Nish 1873; d. Belgrade(?) 20 Sep 1954)*
18 Apr – 20 Oct 1934	*Nikola Uzunović* (for 8th time)
23 Oct – 18 Dec 1934	*Nikola Uzunović* (for 9th time)
21 Dec 1934 – 20 Jun 1935	*Bogoljub Jevtić* (b. 24 Dec 1886; d. Paris 7 Jun 1960)
23 Jun 1935	*Milan Stojadinović* (for 1st time) (b. Čačak 23 Jul 1888; d. Buenos Aires 24 Oct 1961)
7 Mar 1936	*Milan Stojadinović* (for 2nd time)
5 Feb 1939	*Dragiša Cvetković* (for 1st time) (b. 15 Jan 1893; d. Paris 18 Feb 1969)
26 Aug 1939	*Dragiša Cvetković* (for 2nd time)
27 Mar – 18 Apr 1941	*Dušan Simović* (b. 28 Oct 1882; d. Belgrade 27 Aug 1962)
30 Aug 1941	*Milan Nedić* (for 1st time) (b. Grocka 20 Aug 1877; d. 4 Feb 1946) in occupied Serbia
7 Oct 1941 – 20 Oct 1944 †	*Milan Nedić* (for 2nd time) in occupied Serbia
29 Nov 1943	*Josip Tito Broz* (for 1st time) (see President)
27 Apr 1950	*Josip Tito Broz* (for 2nd time)

*For earlier career see vol. 2

†Government in exile

18 Apr 1941	*Dušan Simović* (see above)
13 Jan – 28 Dec 1942	*Slobodan Jovanović* (for 1st time) (b. 1869(?); d. London 12 Dec 1958)
3 Jan – 18 Jun 1943	*Slobodan Jovanović* (for 2nd time)
27 Jun 1943	*Miloš Trifunović* (b. 1876(?); d. Belgrade 21 Feb 1957)
11 Aug 1943 – 19 May 1944	*Božidar Purić* (b. 1891)
9 Jul 1944	*Ivan Subašić* (b. 1892; d. Agram 23 Mar 1955)
30 Jan – 5 Mar 1945	*Drago Marušić* (b. Opatje Selo 10 Dec 1884)

14 Jan 1953	*Josip Tito Broz* (for 3rd time)
30 Jun 1963	*Petar Stambolić* (b. Brezova 12 Jul 1912)
18 May 1967	*Mika Špiljak* (b. Odra 28 Nov 1916)
17 May 1969 – 29 Jul 1971	*Mitja Ribičič* (b. Trieste 1919)
from 30 Jul 1971	*Džemal Bijedić* (b. Mostar 1917; d. (aircraft crash) near Sarajevo 18 Jan 1977)

Foreign Ministers

17 Apr 1927 – 29 Jun 1932	*Vojislav Marinković* (for 2nd time)
2 Jul 1932 – 20 Jun 1935	*Bogoljub Jevtić* (see Prime Ministers)
24 Jun 1935	*Milan Stojadinović* (see Prime Ministers)
6 Feb 1939	*Aleksandar Cincar-Marković*
27 Mar – 18 Apr 1941	*Momčilo Ninčić* (for 3rd time) (b. Jagodina 10 Jun 1876; d. Lausanne 21 Dec 1949)*
30 Aug 1941 – Oct 1944 †	No Foreign Minister in occupied Serbia
5 Mar – 8 Oct 1945	*Ivan Subašić* (see Prime Ministers)
1 Feb 1946	*Stanoje Simić* (b. 1892(?); d. Belgrade 26 Feb 1970)
31 Aug 1948	*Edvard Kardelj* (b. Ljubljana 27 Jan 1910)
14 Jan 1953	*Koča Popović* (b. Belgrade 14 Mar 1908)
23 Apr 1965	*Marko Nikezić* (b. Belgrade 1921)
25 Dec 1968	(acting:) *Miso Pavičević* (b. 21 Apr 1915)
25 Apr 1969	*Mirko Tepavač* (b. 1922)
1 Nov 1972	(acting:) *Jaksa Petrić* (b. Postive 11 Jun 1922)
from 5 Dec 1972	*Miloš Minič* (b. Čačak 1914)

*For earlier career see vol. 2

† Foreign Ministers of Government in exile

3 Jan – 18 Jun 1943	(acting:) *Slobodan Jovanović* (see Prime Ministers)
27 Jun 1943	*Milan Grol* (b. Belgrade 31 Aug 1876; d. 3 Dec 1952)
11 Aug 1943 – 19 May 1944	*Božidar Purić* (see Prime Ministers)
9 Jul 1944	*Ivan Subašić* (see Prime Ministers)
30 Jan – 5 Mar 1945	*Drago Marušić* (see Prime Ministers)

Zaïre

Formerly the Belgian Congo.

30 Jun 1960	Independence from Belgium, as Republic of the Congo with capital at Léopoldville
11 Jul 1960 – Feb 1963	Secession of province of Katanga under Moïse Tshombe (see below)
10 Jul 1964	Renamed Democratic Republic of the Congo
2 May 1966	Léopoldville renamed Kinshasa
27 Oct 1971	Adopted name of Republic of Zaïre

HEADS OF STATE

Presidents

30 Jun 1960	*Joseph Kasavubu* (b. Majumbe 1917; d. 24 Mar 1969)
from 25 Nov 1965	*Mobuto Sese Seko*, formerly *Joseph Mobutu* (b. Lisala 14 Oct 1930)

MEMBERS OF GOVERNMENT

Prime Ministers

30 Jun 1960	*Patrice Lumumba* (b. Katoko-Kombe 2 Jul 1925; d. Kolwezi, Katanga, 17 Jan or 12 Feb 1961)
5 Sep 1960	*Joseph Ileo* (for 1st time) (b. 1922)
14 Sep 1960	Administration entrusted to a College of Commissioners after disputes between the Commander-in-Chief, General Joseph Mobutu (see above), and President Kasavubu (see above)
9 Feb – 27 Jul 1961	*Joseph Ileo* (for 2nd time)
3/15 Aug 1961	*Cyrille Adoula* (for 1st time) (b. Kinshasa Sep 1921 (1924?))
17 Apr 1963 – 30 Jun 1964	*Cyrille Adoula* (for 2nd time)
10 Jul 1964 – 13 Oct 1965	*Moïse Tshombe* (b. Musumba, Katanga, 10 Nov 1919; d. Algiers 29 Jun 1969)

ZAÏRE

18 Oct – 14 Nov 1965	*Evariste Kimba* (b. Katanga 16 Jul 1926; d. Kinshasa 2 Jun 1966)
25 Nov 1965	*Mulamba Nyunyu wa Kadima*, formerly *Léonard Mulamba*
from 26 Oct 1966	President also Prime Minister

Zambia

Called Northern Rhodesia until 24 Oct 1964.

22 Jan 1964	Internal self-government
24 Oct 1964	Independence from Great Britain

HEADS OF STATE

Governor

1959 – 1964	*Sir Evelyn Hone* (b. 13 Dec 1911)

President and Prime Minister

from 24 Oct 1964	*Kenneth Kaunda* (b. Lubwa 28 Apr 1924)

Zanzibar

Until 10 Dec 1963	Protectorate of the United Kingdom
27 Apr 1964	Union with Tanganyika

HEADS OF STATE

Sultans

9 Dec 1911 – 9 Oct 1960	*Khalifa II, ibn Harub*, cousin of Ali II (b. 26 Aug 1879; d. 9 Oct 1960 Dar-es-Salaam)
17 Oct 1960	*Said Abd Allah ibn Khalifa*, son (b. 12 Feb 1910)
1 Jul 1963 – 12 Jan 1964	*Said Shamshid ibn Abd Allah*, son (b. 1930?) lives in London

610

President

12 Jan 1964 – 7   *Abeid (Amani) Karume* (b. 1905; d. (assassinated) 7
   Apr 1972 †   Apr 1972)

MEMBERS OF GOVERNMENT

Prime Ministers

10 Dec 1963   *Muhammad Shamte Hamadi*
12 Jan – 27 Apr 1964   *Qasim Abd Allah Hanga*

†From 27 Apr 1964 also First Vice-President of United Republic of Tanganyika and Zanzibar (later Tanzania).

Index

This index includes everyone listed in volume 3 of *Rulers and Governments of the World*. It follows the principles set out in the *Anglo-American Cataloguing Rules*, British Text* (London: The Library Association, 1967) and the *ALA Rules for Filing Catalog Cards,* second edition (Chicago: American Library Association, 1968), slightly modified so that some of the work could be carried out by a computer.

In general, entries are made under surname, but hereditary monarchs and others (such as Burmese) who do not use surnames are entered under given name. In deciding which part of a person's name is to be regarded as the surname the conventions of that person's own country are followed. For example, a Dutch person whose surname is prefixed by 'van', 'van der' or 'van den' is entered under the surname without the prefix, whereas a Belgian or a South African with the same type of name is entered under Van.

Persons who have titles of nobility are entered under family name with a reference from the proper-name element of the title when it differs from the family name. Persons who have changed their surname are entered under the latest surname with a reference from an earlier one. (These two conventions differ from the Anglo-American Cataloguing Rules which require entry to be under the best known form of name.)

In the case of Chinese and Korean names the surname is followed by a comma to indicate that it alone is the entry-word. Such names (unless their owners have adopted a westernized form) are normally written with the surname first and in the body of the text they are set out in that way without commas.

Entries follow the order of the English alphabet. Accents and other modifications of letters are ignored, as are apostrophes. Dutch ij is regarded as two separate letters.

The entries are arranged word by word — that is, all entries beginning with the same word are grouped together and then arranged according to the alphabetical order of their second words (and so on).

Parts of a name joined by a hyphen are regarded as separate words.

*On all relevant points the North American Text is the same.

Parts of a name separated by an apostrophe, without a space or a hyphen, are regarded as forming one word.

Prefixes are regarded as separate words when so written or when joined to the next part of the name by a hyphen (this convention departs from the ALA filing rules which require some names with separately written prefixes to be regarded as single words).

When the same name occurs as both a surname and a given name then all the surname entries are listed before the given-name entries.

Entries for different people with the same surname are arranged in alphabetical order (word by word) of their given names (or initials of European-style given names).

When there are several entries for the same given name followed by numerals, those entries are arranged in numerical order (this convention departs from the ALA filing rules which require such entries to be arranged in alphabetical order of the titles of the persons indexed).

Honorifics, titles of nobility, military ranks, ranks of nobility, terms of address, and notes of alternative names or spellings of names, are set in italic. When such items occur before forenames they are ignored in determining the order of entries. (See also the note under 'al-' in the index.)

When the same person is mentioned more than once on the same page in the body of the text, the number of mentions is given in square brackets.

n indicates that the name concerned is mentioned in a footnote.

The following list of specimen entries, given in the order in which they occur in the index, illustrates some of these points:

Alexander, *Sir* A. V.

Alexander, H. (R. L. G.)   Alphabetical order of initials. The honorific Sir is ignored.

Alexander II   Alexander as a surname precedes Alexander as a given name.

Ó Moráin, M.   Ó is regarded as a separate word though it has the same meaning as O' in the entry after next.

Öçten, R.   The accent on Ö is ignored — in Turkish Öçten would be filed after all names beginning with unaccented O.

O'Kelly, S. T.   O'Kelly is regarded as a single word because there is no space after the apostrophe.

Van der Byl, P. V. G.

Van Rhijn, A. J. R.

Vandervelde, E.   Names beginning with the same separately written word are grouped together. Van der Byl is not regarded as a single word. Van Rhijn is not regarded as a single word (if it were it would come after Vandervelde).

INDEX

Dinsdale, W. G. 99, 100
Dinur, B. 321 [2]
Diomedes, A. 262
Diordita, A. 553
Diori, H. (A.) 407
Diouf, A. 448
Dixon, K. 311 [2], 312
Djugashvili, I. V.; see Stalin, I. V.
Dlamini, Prince Makhosini 476
Doak, W. N. 587
Dobi, I. 272, 276, 277, 278 [2], 279
Dobretsberger, J. 41
Dodkhudoev, N. 553
Doenin, V. N. 549
Doğan, A. 507
Dögei, I. 284
Doğru, A. 517, 519
Dohnanyi, K. von 256, 257
Dolanský, J. 136, 137 [2], 138 [2], 140 [2], 141
Dolinai, N. 113
Dollfuss, E. 37 [2], 38 [4], 39 [6], 40 [6]
Dollinger, W. 252, 253, 254, 255, 256
Donaldson, J. M. 590
Donda, A. 235
Donegan, P. S. 319
Dong, Pham Van; see Pham Van Dong
Dönges, T. E. 455, 460, 461 [2], 462, 463, 464, 467
Dönitz, K. 239, 245, 246 [2]
Donker, L. A. 397
Donner, J. 386
Doorn, H. W. van 404
Dorion, N. 100 [2]
Dorlikjab 381
Dorman, Sir M. 374 [2], 449
Dorman-Smith, Sir R. H. 81, 563
Dörmen, Z. 510
Dormoy, M. 177, 178, 180
Dorpmüller, J. 244, 247
Dórticos Torrado, O. 125
Dostálek, J. 127, 128 [2], 129 [2], 130, 131
Douglas, Sir F., 1st Baron Douglas of Barloch 374

Douglas, J. H. 592
Douglas-Hamilton, G. N., 10th Earl of Selkirk 571
Douglas-Home, Sir A. F., 14th Earl of Home, Baron Home of the Hirsel 571, 573, 574 [3], 576, 581
Douglas of Barloch, Sir F. Douglas, 1st Baron; see Douglas, Sir F.
Doumer, P. 165
Doumergue, G. 165, 174 [2]
Dovas, C. 263
Dragnov, P. 80
Dragoumis, Ph. 265
Drake-Brockman, T. C. 26, 28, 33
Drakeford, A. S. 16, 17
Draxler, L. 41, 42
Drees, W. 393, 394 [3], 396 [5], 397, 398 [2], 404
Drimmel, H. 47 [2], 48 [2], 49
Drtina, P. 135, 136
Druon, M. S. R. C. 218
Drury, C. M. 102 [2], 106, 107, 108 [2], 109, 110 [3]
Du Bus de Warnaffe, C. (P. M. L.), Vicomte 57, 58, 61, 64
Du Plessis, A. H. 467, 469
Dubček, A. 148
Dubé, J. E. 108, 110, 111
Dubois, A. 382
Duca, I. G. 443
Duchet, R. 198, 199 [2], 200, 203
Ducos, H. 172, 173, 174
Dudorov, N. P. 532, 541
Duesberg, J. 60
Dugan, Sir W., 1st Baron Dugan of Victoria 9 [2]
Dugan of Victoria, S. W. Dugan, 1st Baron; see Dugan, S. W.
Dugdale, Sir T., bart, 1st Baron Crathorne 572
Dugersuren, Mangalyn 381
Dugnus, —— 378
Duhalde Vázquez, A. 117
Duhamel, J. 216, 217, 218
Duisenberg, W. F. 404
Dulles, J. F. 591
Dumesnil, J. L. 167, 168, 169

INDEX

Kozhevnikov, E. F. 535, 541, 550
Kozlov, A. I. 528 [2], 534
Kozlov, F. R. 538, 553
Kozłovsky, E. 551
Kozlowski, L. 423 [2], 424, 425 [2]
Kozma, M. 273 [2]
Kozyula, I. K. 537
Krack, E. 234, 236, 238
Kraft, O. B. 150
Kraft, W. 250
Krag, J. O. 150 [6]
Krahulec, V. 145
Krajčír, F. 137, 139, 140, 141, 142
  [3], 143
Kramer, E. 227, 230, 232, 234, 236
Krasko, W. 435
Kratochvíl, J. 134
Krauland, P. 45, 46
Kraus, J. 45, 46 [2]
Krčmář, J. 128, 129 [2], 130
Kreisky, B. 35, 48 [2], 49 [2], 51
Krejčí, J. 133 [2], 134 [2], 143
Krishnamachari, T. T. 291 [2], 292
  [2]
Kristensen, K. 149
Krofta, K. 129, 130, 131
Krone, H. 252, 253, 254, 255
Krosnár, J. 142
Krotov, V. V. 548
Krug, J. A. 590
Krüger, H. 254
Kruger, J. T. 469
Kruglov, S. N. 522, 527, 532
Kruja, Mustafa Merlika- 3
Krutina, V. 143 [2]
Krzhyzhanovsky, G. M. 525
Kubar, Abdul Majid 366 [2]
Kubat, F. 515 [2]
Kubat, O. 505
Kuberski, J. 437
Kubilius, —— 377
Kubitschek de Oliveira, J. 76
Kučera, B. 145, 146, 147, 148
Kucherenko, V. A. 532, 533, 540
Küchük, F. 125
Kuchumov, P. S. 540
Kudrna, J. 144

Kudsi, Nazim 481 [2], 482 [3]
Kühn, A. W. 422 [2], 423 [2], 424 [2]
Kuhrig, H. 235, 238
Kuibyshev, V. V. 525, 526
Kukiel, M. 427
Kulesza, J. 433, 435
Kulichov, G. 80
Kuligowski, A. 431
Kulmye, Husain 454
Kulpinski, J. 438
Kumaramangalam, S. M. 296
Kumykin, P. N. 524
Kunaev, D. A. 553 [2]
K'ung, H. H.; see K'ung Hsiang-hsi
K'ung, Hsiang-hsi (H. H. K'ung) 118
Kunicki, T. 438
Kurashov, S. V. 542, 551
Kurbanoğlu, M. 503, 504
Kurbanov, R. 554
Kurdaş, K. 505, 506
Kurdoğlu, F. 493 [2], 497
Kurkauskas, V. 377
Kürşat, N. 511
Kurshumi, Abd Allah 605
Kurtawidjaja, Raden Haji
  Djuandra 299 [2]
Kurtbek, S. 499, 500 [2]
Kürümoğlu, O. 517
Kurutluoğlu, S. 507 [2], 508
Kusiak, J. 438
Kuuskoski, R. I. 162
Kuzbari, Mamun 482
Kuzmin, A. N. 530
Kuzmin, I. I. 531, 532, 538, 539 [2]
Kuznetsov, N. G. 523 [2]
Kviesis, A. 360
Kwiatkowski, E. F. 422 [2], 426 [2]
Ky, Nguyen Cao; see Nguyen Cao Ky
Kyoseivanov, G. 79 [3], 80
Kyselý, J. 137

'l-, see al-
La Chambre, G. 174, 179, 180, 181,
  203
La Malène, C. L. de 209, 214

650

Mathews
Matthews, F. P.   590
Matthews, R. C.   90
Matthöfer, H.   258
Mattila, O. J.   164 [2]
Matuszewski, I.   421, 422, 432 [2]
Matuszewski, S.   428
Maudling, R.   573, 574 [2], 575, 576, 582
Maugham, F. H., *1st Viscount and Baron Maugham*   562
Maupoil, H.   176
Maureaux, C.   65
Maurer, I. G.   443, 444, 445
Maurice-Bokanowski, M.   209, 210, 211
Maurin, L. F. T.   175 [2], 177
Mavromichalis, S.   263
Mavros, G.   265
Maximos, D.   262 [2], 264 [3]
Maxwell-Fyfe, *Sir* D., *1st Viscount Kilmuir*   570, 571, 574
Mayer, D.   190, 191, 192, 193 [2], 194
Mayer, R.   187, 192, 193, 195, 196 [2], 197, 200
Mayhew, R. W.   92, 96
Maziol, J.   210, 211
Maziq, Husain (Yusuf ibn)   366
Mazurov, K. T.   545
M'ba, L.   221 [3]
Mc, *names in which the prefix Mac is spelled Mc are filed as if spelled Mac*
Mea'ole, Tupua Tamesehe   603
Mecklinger, L.   237
Médici, E. G.   76
Medici, G.   337 [2], 339, 344
Medina Angarita, I.   599
Medrický, G.   452, 453 [2]
Meighen, A.   91
Meïr, G.   321 [2], 322 [3], 323 [2], 324
Meiser, H.   229
Meissner, A.   127 [2], 128
Meissner, O.   245
Mejía Colindres, V.   271
Mekhlis, L. Z.   526
Mekis, J.   280
Melas, G.   265

Melen, F.   508, 509, 514, 515 [2], 519
Melgar Castro, J. A.   271
Mellish, R. J.   585
Mellon, A. W.   586
Melnikov, L. G.   537, 543
Melo Franco, A. A. de   77 [2]
Melo Franco, A. de   77
Melsheimer, E.   227
Mende, E.   253, 254 [2], 255
Menderes, A.   499, 500 [2], 501 [2], 502 [2], 503 [2]
Menderes, E.   500, 501 [2], 502 [2], 503 [2], 504
Mendes, F.   268
Mendes do Amaral e Abranches, C. de S.   440
Mendès-France, P.   187, 201, 202, 204
Méndez Arancibia, G.   117
Méndez Montenegro, J. C.   267
Mendieta Montefur, C.   124
Mendoza Azurdia, O.   267
Menemencioğlu, H.   494, 495
Menemencioğlu, N.   495 [2]
Menéndez, A. I.   156
Menghin, O.   43
Menon, (V. K.) K.   291, 292
Menshikov, M. A.   524
Menteşe, N.   512, 513, 519
Menteşeoğlu, H.   511, 512, 513
Menthon, F. de   186, 189
Mentl, S.   131
Menzhinsky, V. R.   522
Menzies, *Sir* R. G.   11 [2], 12 [2], 13 [2], 14 [3], 15 [3], 18, 19 [2], 20 [2], 21
Mercado Jarrín, L. E.   419
Merchiers, L.   65
Merikoski, V.   164
Merkatz, H. J. von   250 [2], 251 [2], 252
Merkel, C.-H.   230
Merkulov, V. N.   522 [2], 526, 528
Merkys, A.   368, 377
Merlot, J.   59, 62
Merlot, J. J.   67 [2]
Mersinli, O.   507
Merzagora, C.   333

INDEX

WITHDRAWAL